WATERFALLS OF MICHIGAN

THE DEFINITIVE GUIDE TO THE WATERFALLS OF MICHIGAN

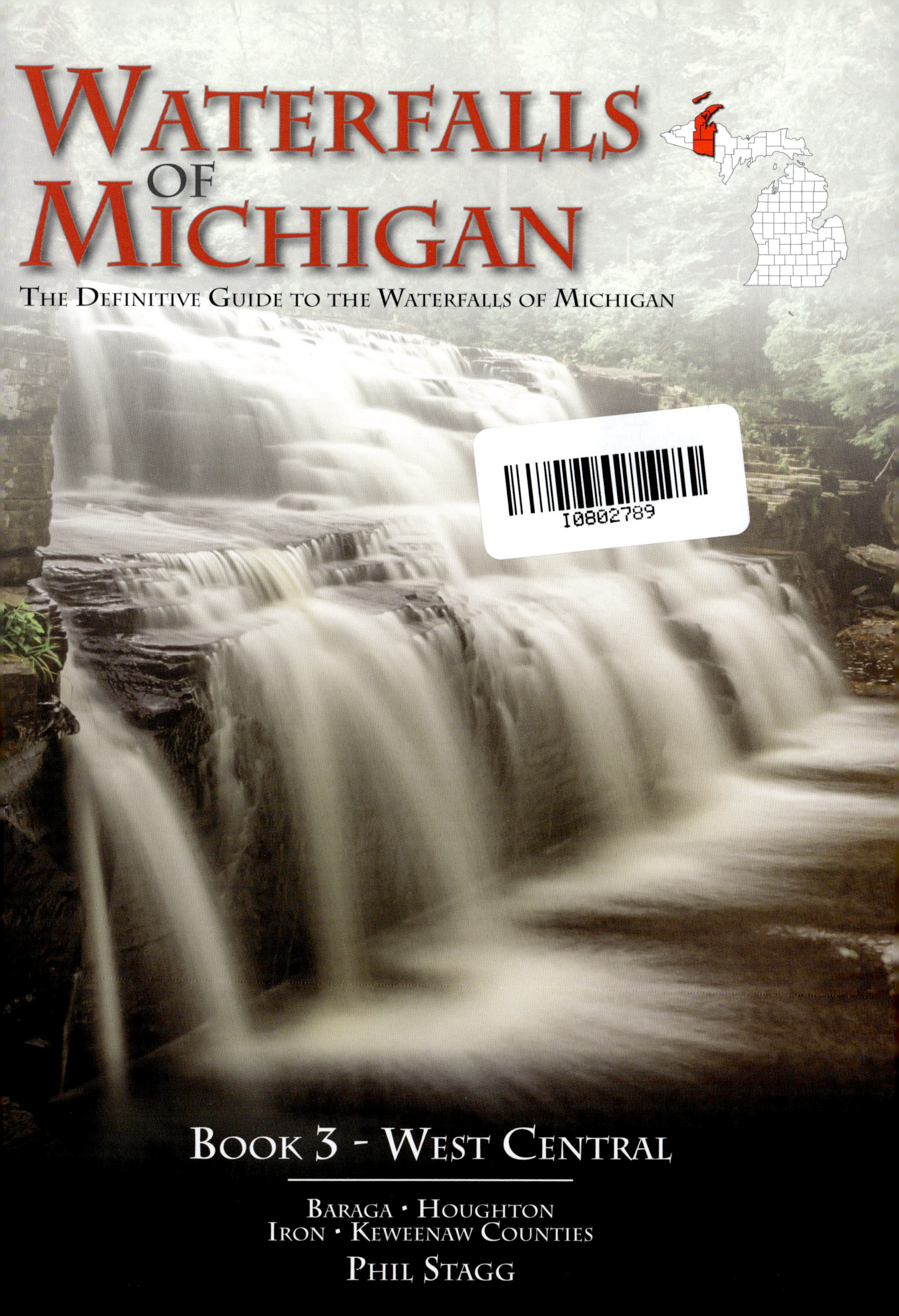

BOOK 3 - WEST CENTRAL

BARAGA • HOUGHTON
IRON • KEWEENAW COUNTIES

PHIL STAGG

Waterfalls of Michigan
Book 3 - West Central

Published by:

MI Falls Publishing
11765 West Cadillac Rd.
Cadillac, MI 49601
231•920•8416

www.mifalls.com

ISBN: 978-0-9971346-1-2
LCCN: 2016900613

Photography: Phil Stagg
Text: Phil Stagg
Design: Phil Stagg

Printed in the United States of America

First Printing: January 2017

WATERFALLS OF MICHIGAN

GUIDEBOOK SERIES

PHIL STAGG

Book 4 West	**Book 3** West Central	**Book 2** Central	**Book 1** East
Gogebic *Ontonagon* ** Porcupine Mtn.*	*Baraga* *Houghton* *Iron* *Keweenaw*	*Dickinson* *Marquette* *Menominee*	*Alger* *Chippewa* *Delta* *Luce* *Manistee* *Presque Isle*

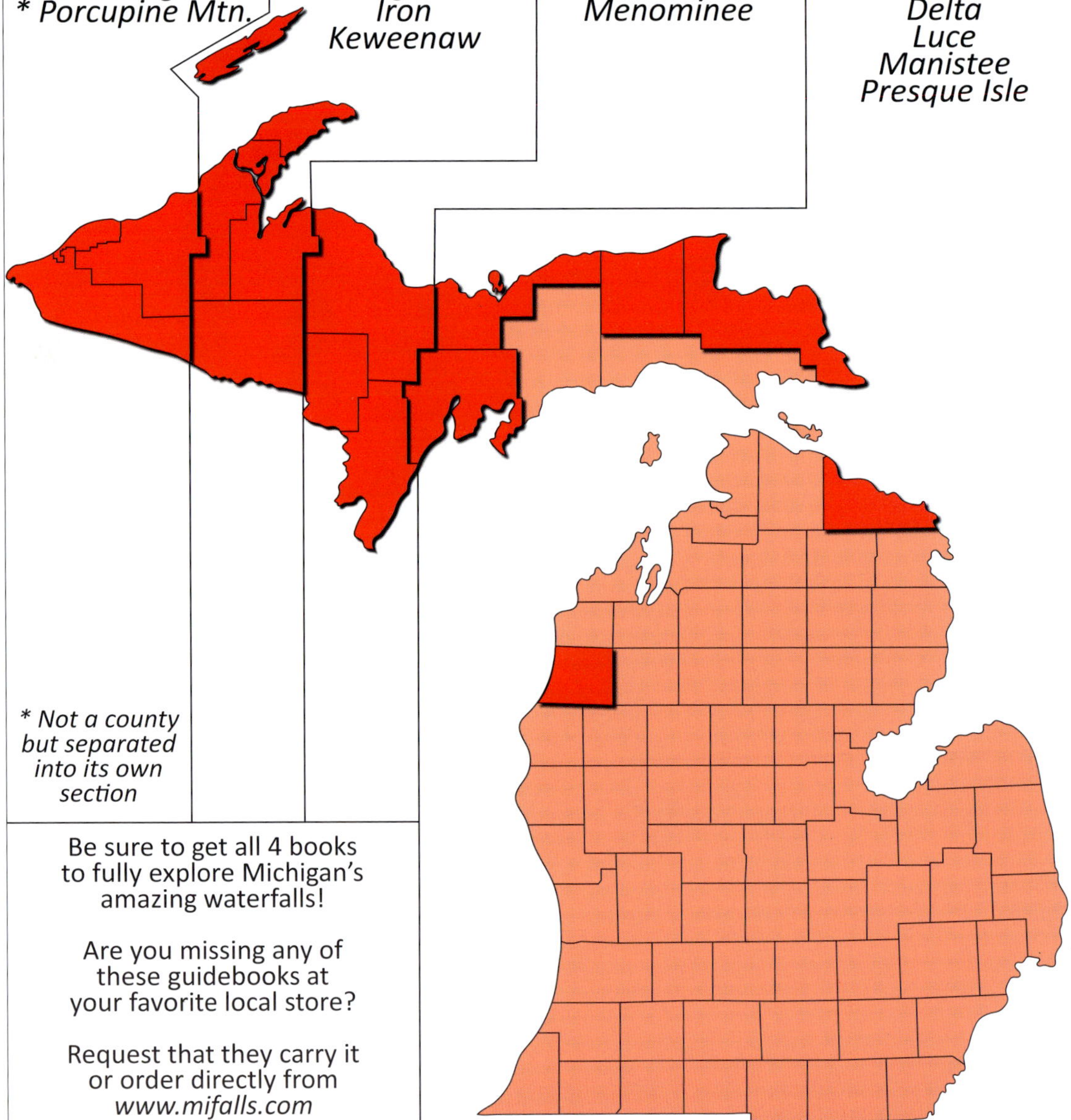

** Not a county but separated into its own section*

Be sure to get all 4 books to fully explore Michigan's amazing waterfalls!

Are you missing any of these guidebooks at your favorite local store?

Request that they carry it or order directly from *www.mifalls.com*

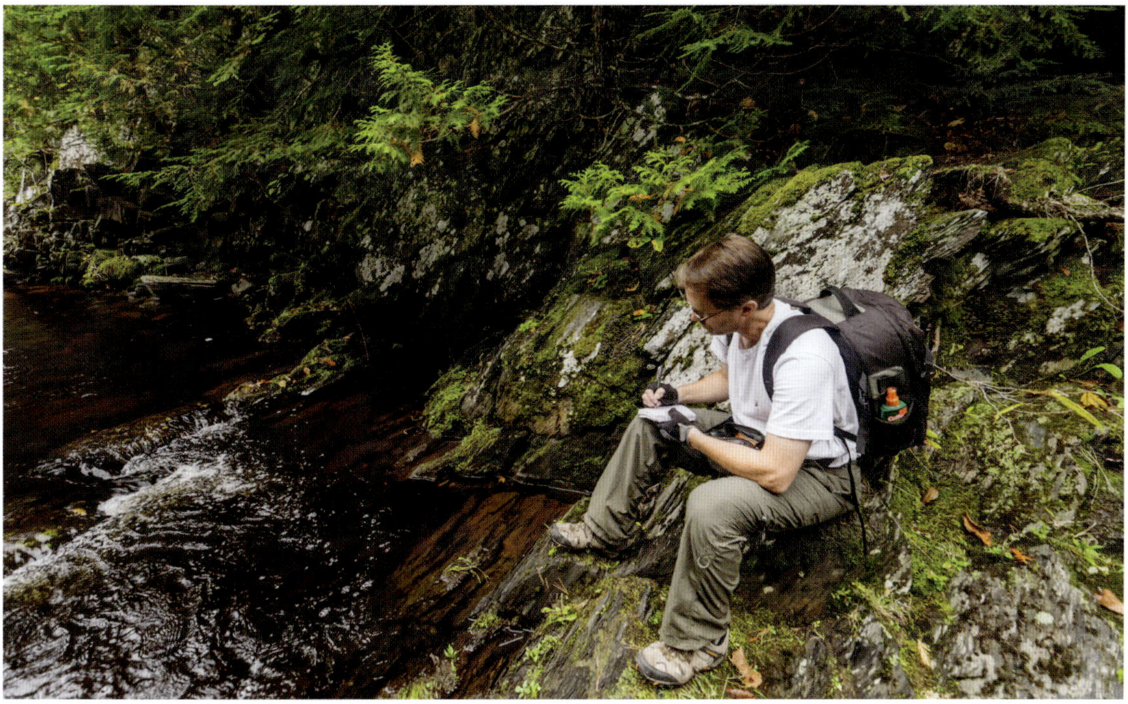

Phil Stagg

Michigan is a place that overflows with raw beauty. If you have been fortunate enough to enjoy dancing northern lights rippling like a curtain against a starry backdrop, you know what I mean. If you have begun your day before sunrise with a fiery sky reflecting blood-red on a serene Great Lake, you understand. And if you have traipsed down a faint forest trail, swishing through newly fallen golden leaves that exude an earthy autumn aroma, eager to reach a new-to-you waterfall, the sound of water on rock reaching your ears with the promise of a Michigan treasure soon to be seen, you know the thrill that countless other adventurers in this great state have felt.

The list of those that have helped me in some way in this quest to provide a helpful guide to Michigan's waterfalls is long. I take a second at the beginning of each of these books to recognize a few of them. Thanks to Bill and Corie Saarinen for information about waterfalls, creeks, and roads in the Huron Mountains. Barb and Dave Schumacher provided historical, mining, and waterfall information in the Eagle River area. Starlajane Thunder has helped me with obscure waterfall data about the U.P.'s western end. Thanks to all who have blessed me with their knowledge. It is a pleasure to meet so many helpful individuals in this great state!

Now it's YOUR turn to embrace more of Michigan's beauty. This book is packed with waterfalls, mostly in the Huron Mountains and the Keweenaw Peninsula. Enjoy the quest and the destination!

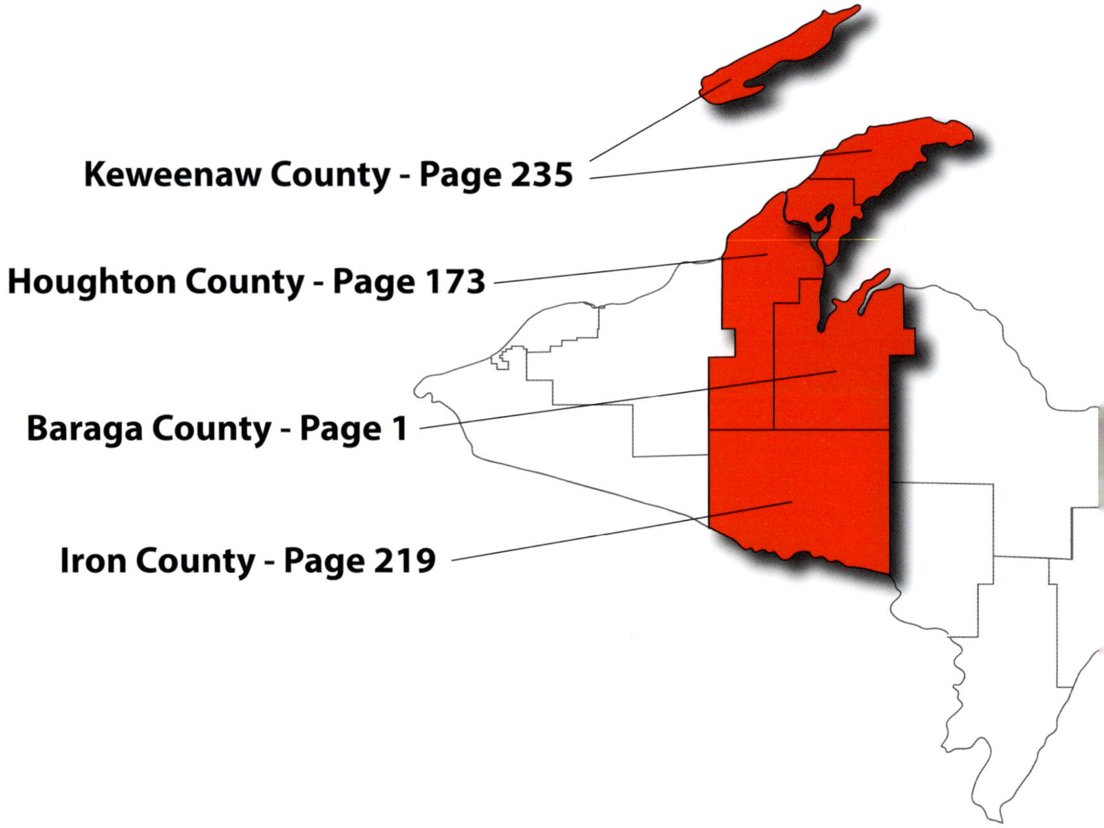

Keweenaw County - Page 235
Houghton County - Page 173
Baraga County - Page 1
Iron County - Page 219

TABLE OF CONTENTS

THE GUIDE TO THE GUIDE X

1 BARAGA COUNTY 1
2 HOUGHTON COUNTY 173
3 IRON COUNTY 219
4 KEWEENAW COUNTY 235

INDEX 284

Full Color **County Maps** *have Area Map Breakdowns.*

How to use the Maps and Data Clusters

(A) Pick a County Map
(B) Decide on an Area to check out
(C) Turn to the associated Area Map
(D) Find a waterfall to explore
(E) Review the Data Table for that waterfall

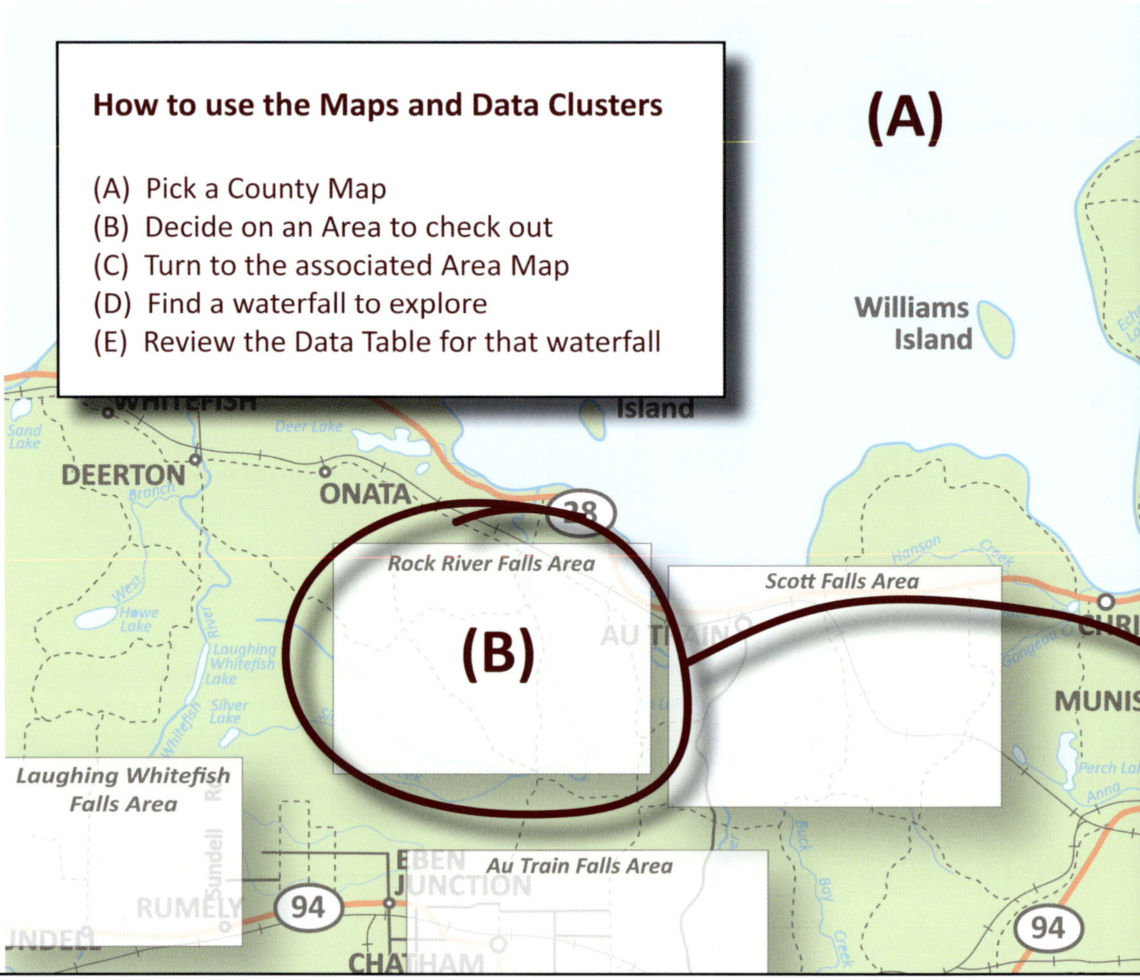

Data Table *is supplied for EVERY waterfall! Packed full of VITAL information.* **(E)**

(1) (2) ROCK RIVER FALLS (3) (Rock River) (12)

(4)

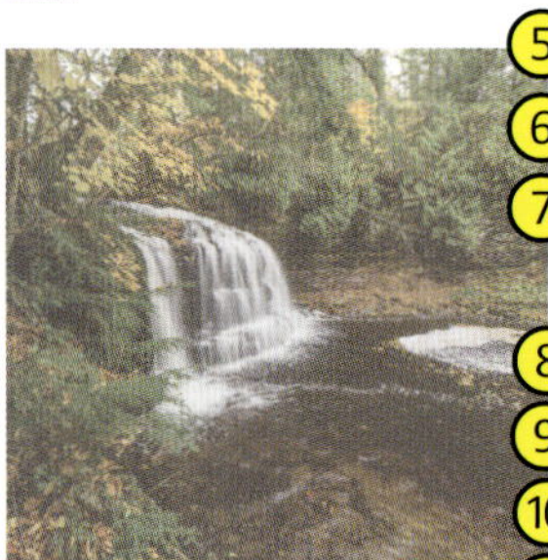

(5)	Must See:	9	(13) GPS:	N46 24.663 W86 58.583
(6)	Height:	18 feet		
(7)	Time:	60-90 minutes	**Hiking Information**	
			(14) Path:	Footpath
	Driving Information		(15) Length:	7/8 mile
(8)	Signs:	None	(16) Elev. Change:	Slight
(9)	Road:	Dirt Road	(17) GPS:	Helpful
(10)	Access:	Somewhat Difficu	(18) Danger:	Slight
(11)	4WD:	Helpful	(19) WP Boots:	Required

(20) There is a small parking area large enough for about 6 or 7 vehicles at the trail head. The trail is .86 miles long with the first 2/3 of the walk on a nice footpath. The last 1/4 mile is muddy and there are several places that the trail becomes a little difficult to follow.

Area Maps

Display roads and trails to ALL waterfalls - each waterfall has GPS coordinates!

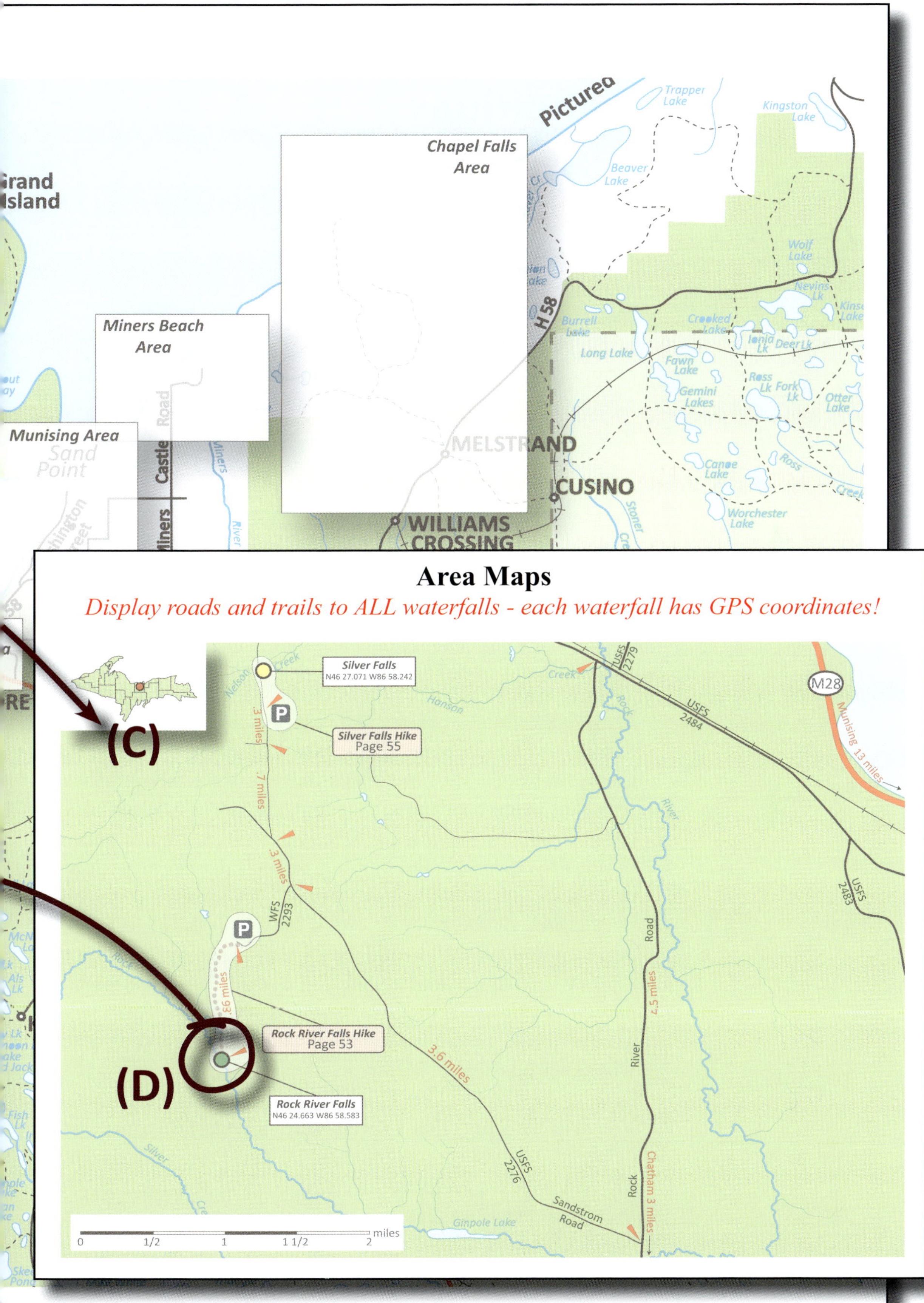

Data Table
Definitions

Must See Swatch ①

The colored square in the upper, left corner of the Waterfall Data Tables corresponds with the color in the Waterfall Area Map for each particular waterfall and is derived from the "Must See" rating. Those waterfalls with a "Must See" rating of 1-3 are "Red" waterfalls. "Yellow" waterfalls have ratings of 4-6, and "Green" waterfalls are rated 7-10. Think of the "Must See Colors" as you would a standard traffic light.

Green: GO!! You've got to check these out!
Yellow: SLOW DOWN!! These are OK waterfalls, perhaps it'll be nice to visit once or twice.
Red: STOP!! These are waterfalls, or at least considered waterfalls by some, but unless you are a die-hard waterfall fan, you probably won't enjoy them.

Waterfall Name ②

"Where did you get the names from?" Good question! Most waterfalls were named many years ago and those names were incorporated into the USGS maps which are the basis for most of the maps that we have today. These resultant maps bear those names which are now commonly recognized. In the cases where waterfalls were not named on the USGS maps, the naming of the falls becomes more interesting. I typically have named "unnamed" waterfalls by the area of the river or creek on which they are found. An example of this would be "Carp River Falls - Upper #3". Also, just because a waterfall doesn't have a published name doesn't mean that the residents of an area don't have a name for it. I have tried to use the locally accepted names whenever possible.

You will also find that I rarely start a waterfall name with "Upper", "Middle", or "Lower". For ease of indexing, the name of the fall typically comes first, followed by the locational modifier and/or number if applicable.

③ *Waterway Name*

Most of the waterways on which waterfalls are found have long established names. Just like waterfalls, there are some small creeks that have no published names, but do have locally accepted names. I have used these names whenever known.

④ *Waterfall Picture*

A small picture of each waterfall is attached. Some waterfalls are on posted, private land. If I wasn't able to receive permission to photograph the waterfall, there is obviously no picture.

⑤ *Must See Rating*

Each waterfall is rated on a 1-10 scale, with one being the least desirable and 10 being the most. The following is the guideline I use:

10. Gorgeous! Great eye appeal! Inspiring! One of the best waterfalls in Michigan.
9. Excellent waterfall! You will want to make many repeat visits.
8. Very nice waterfall! Very popular!
7. Nice waterfall. Worth coming back to see several times.
6. An above average waterfall. Might want to see it again.
5. A nice all-around waterfall. Perhaps worth a repeat visit.
4. An OK waterfall. Probably not worth coming back to.
3. Don't have your hopes too high - it's not that good.
2. Avid waterfall enthusiasts may want to check it out just to say that they did.
1. It's water. It's falling. Who cares?

The "Must See" rating is my attempt at describing only the visual desirability of each waterfall. It doesn't take into account the difficulty in getting to the waterfall. There are some very nice waterfalls that require a substantial hike over rough terrain. The difficulty in reaching the waterfall doesn't figure into "Must See" rating.

Everyone has their own taste in waterfalls. What I am looking for in a waterfall is a visually pleasing setting combined with water that is falling at angles and with rates in keeping with the overall genre of the waterfall. Consistency and lack of obvious flaws is also important.

There may be times when you disagree with my rating. Keep in mind that water level, season, temperature, weather conditions, sun position, and even frame of mind affect the visual desirability of any waterfall at any point in time.

I have included the "Must See" rating to offer you a standardized method of comparing waterfalls so that you have some idea of which waterfalls you may wish to view.

Waterfall Height (6) This is an estimate of the height of the waterfall in feet. This is a potentially poor piece of information. Let me explain. If a waterfall has a free drop of 20 feet, flattens out for 20 to 30 feet of river length and then it has small cascading drops of 4 to 6 inches per drop for another 20 feet of accumulated drop, there would be a total drop of 40 feet. When viewing the waterfall, some people may consider just the free drop as the waterfall height, while others may include the additional 20 feet of cascades downstream. I tried to include the "normal" waterfall portion of the falls in my height estimates. I think of most waterfalls as viewable from one location. If a portion of the waterfall is not photogenic, then I may not have included that part in the overall height of the waterfall.

Hike Time (7) How much time should you plan for a hike? I have included an estimated amount of minutes or hours to plan for a hike. I am assuming that a hike entails a leisurely walk to and from the waterfall and includes an "appropriate" amount of time for viewing the waterfall.

Is there a Sign? (8) Most waterfalls have no signs announcing their presence. The waterfalls that do, have signs that are made by the Federal Government, the State of Michigan, counties, and some by private individuals.

Worst Road Type (9) In the process of driving to a waterfall the roads typically go from good to worse. So the road that a waterfall is accessed from will tell you what to expect for the worst driving conditions on your waterfall quest.

Accessibility (10) There is a wide variety of difficulty when it comes to finding a particular waterfall. A waterfall on a main road with signs announcing its presence is very easy to find. The more turns that are required off of a main road, the more difficult or complicated it becomes to find.

Is a 4WD needed? (11) You will find it easier to drive to some waterfalls with a 4WD vehicle. High clearance vehicles are sometimes needed.

⑫ *Quick Reference*

Ghosted Symbols Private
Activated Symbols Private

The "activated symbols" are the ones (if any) that apply to this particular waterfall.

Private This waterfall is on private land and more often than not the land is posted and the waterfall is not accessible to the public. *Note that this information is to the best of my knowledge. There very well may be more waterfalls on private land, but since it was not posted I was unaware. Be respectful of property owners and follow their wishes.*

- The waterfall can be viewed from a vehicle.
- A particularly kid-friendly waterfall.
- Wheelchair accessible
- Bathroom facilities are available, normally at the beginning of the hike. There will be flush, composting, or vault toilets.

⑬ *GPS Coordinate*

The GPS coordinate for the waterfall is written in degrees and minutes.

⑭ *Type of Path*

There are a variety of hiking trails that you will encounter. Expect everything from graded and paved trails to narrow dirt footpaths to no paths at all! Note that sometimes there will be one type of path at the beginning of the hike and another one entirely by the end. The worst type of path to the waterfall is listed here.

⑮ *Hike Length*

This is the length of the hike to the falls. Remember to double the length for a round trip estimate. Some hikes have a number of waterfalls along the route. The length for any particular waterfall along that hike is the distance from the vehicle to that waterfall, typically including the previous waterfalls found along the way.

⑯ *Elevation Change*

Many waterfalls involve a change in elevation, either along the hike or climbing down into a ravine to the waterfall.

⑰ *GPS Needed?*

Do you need a handheld GPS to find this waterfall? If so, make sure that you are using a reliable GPS and are familiar with its functions and use. Don't forget to take spare batteries. Having a compass with you is a great backup as well.

Danger (18) Viewing waterfalls has some inherit danger. Walking along potentially wet or icy paths or boardwalks, hiking over uneven ground and climbing into and out of ravines and gorges, standing at the brink of a fifty foot waterfall, navigating moss covered rocks near swift moving waters. Yes, caution is always important. But some waterfalls are more difficult to view or get to, so I trust this "Danger" category will help you to decide which waterfalls are right for you to view.

Waterproof Boots? (19) I prefer to keep my feet dry on waterfall hikes. If there are muddy trails or rivers or creeks that need to be forded I recommend wearing waterproof boots. I wear calf high boots when needing something more than my waterproof hiking shoes that are only ankle high.

Description (20) Find out a little more about the waterfall or hike in this brief description.

Waterfall Etiquette

Proper waterfall etiquette begins with a proper attitude toward people and the environment. Many waterfalls in the Upper Peninsula are on private land. Fortunately for us, many of the land owners allow individuals to drive on their property, park on it, and hike across it.

1) NEVER trespass on posted property. Obey all signs. The private property rights of all land owners must be respected.

2) Don't invade someone's personal space. Just because there isn't a "No Trespassing" sign doesn't mean that you can drive up next to their house, park your vehicle, and walk across their back yard to a waterfall just behind their house. Use common sense. Have proper waterfall etiquette. Do unto others as you would want them to do unto you. This timeless principle always holds true.

There are some waterfalls that are "OK" to view, but they are also quite close to residences. Be quiet and considerate. Be courteous and respectful.

3) Clean up after yourself. I know of a land owner that doesn't allow waterfall enthusiasts onto his land because every year he removes several bags of garbage from around the waterfall on his property. We must do better. Don't leave anything behind on your hikes. In fact, help clean up after others. If we all would do our part, I believe that more land owners would allow us to view the beauty that resides within their estates.

Respecting land owners and the environment in which the wonderful waterfalls of Michigan reside must be our top priority. Forsaking these principles will result in the loss of access to more and more waterfall locations. We must not let that happen.

CHAPTER 1
BARAGA COUNTY

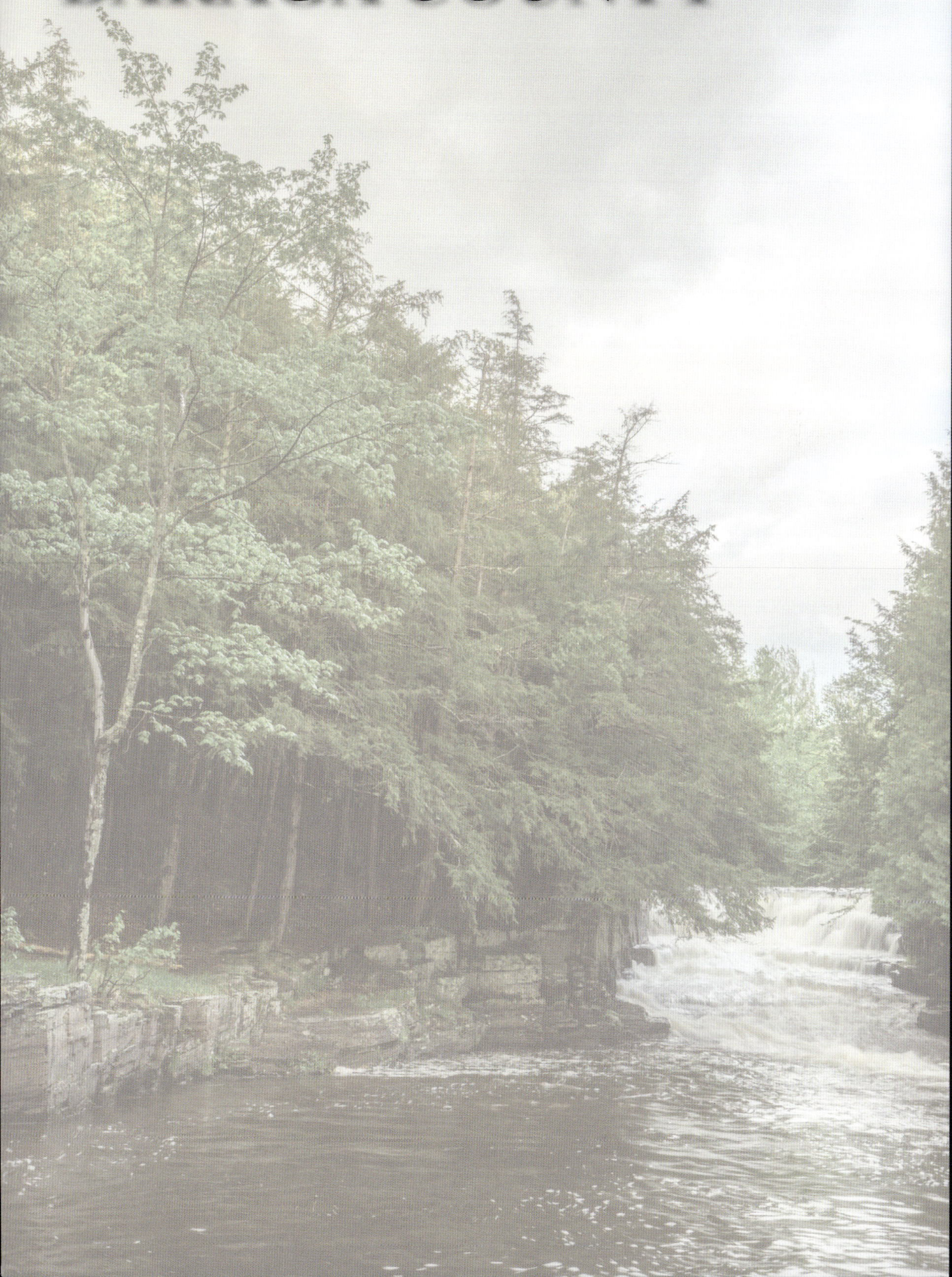

BARAGA COUNTY CONTENTS

BARAGA COUNTY MAP 8

CANYON FALLS AREA 9
CANYON FALLS HIKE 9
CANYON FALLS - UPPER (STURGEON RIVER) 10
CANYON FALLS (STURGEON RIVER) 11
CANYON FALLS - MIDDLE (STURGEON RIVER) 13
CANYON FALLS - LOWER (STURGEON RIVER) 14
OGEMAW FALLS (OGEMAW CREEK) 15
OGEMAW SLIDE (OGEMAW CREEK) 16
OGEMAW FALLS - LOWER (OGEMAW CREEK) 17
PLUMBAGO FALLS HIKE 18
PLUMBAGO FALLS (PLUMBAGO CREEK) 18
PLUMBAGO FALLS - LOWER (PLUMBAGO CREEK) 19
TAYLOR CREEK CANYON FALLS HIKE 20
TAYLOR CREEK CANYON FALLS #1 (TAYLOR CREEK) 20
TAYLOR CREEK CANYON FALLS #2 (TAYLOR CREEK) 21
TAYLOR CREEK CANYON FALLS #3 (TAYLOR CREEK) 22
TAYLOR CREEK CANYON FALLS #4 (TAYLOR CREEK) 23
TAYLOR CREEK CANYON FALLS #5 (TAYLOR CREEK) 24
TAYLOR CREEK CANYON FALLS #6 (TAYLOR CREEK) 25
TAYLOR CREEK CANYON FALLS #7 (TAYLOR CREEK) 26

FALLS RIVER AREA 27
DAULTS FALLS HIKE 28
DAULTS FALLS (DAULTS CREEK) 28
DAULTS FALLS - UPPER (DAULTS CREEK) 29
FALLS RIVER - LOWER HIKE 30
CASCADING FALLS (FALLS RIVER) 31
BARE HOLE FALLS (FALLS RIVER) 32
DAM HOLE FALLS (FALLS RIVER) 33
SUCKER HOLE (FALLS RIVER) 34
FALLS RIVER - MIDDLE HIKE 35
MITTEN HOLE FALLS (FALLS RIVER) 36
BIG HOLE FALLS (FALLS RIVER) 37
FALLS RIVER RAPIDS (FALLS RIVER) 38
SECRET HOLE FALLS (FALLS RIVER) 39
CHUTE FALLS (FALLS RIVER) 40
MARDALE FALLS (FALLS RIVER) 41
SAARINEN FALLS (FALLS RIVER) 42
FALLS RIVER - UPPER HIKE 43
POWER HOUSE FALLS (FALLS RIVER) 43
POWER DAM FALLS (FALLS RIVER) 45
POWER DAM FALLS - UPPER (FALLS RIVER) 46

HAYPRESS DAM FALLS AREA 47
HAYPRESS DAM FALLS HIKE 48
HAYPRESS DAM FALLS (PESHEKEE RIVER) 48
NELLIGAN CREEK FALLS HIKE 49
NELLIGAN CREEK FALLS (NELLIGAN CREEK) 49
NELLIGAN CREEK FALLS - LOWER #1 (NELLIGAN CREEK) 50
NELLIGAN CREEK FALLS - LOWER #2 (NELLIGAN CREEK) 51

MAPS...
HIKES...
WATERFALLS.........................

TABLE OF CONTENT KEY

HURON RIVER AREA **52**
BIG ERICK'S FALLS HIKE 53
BIG ERICK'S FALLS (HURON RIVER) 53
BIG ERICK'S FALLS #2 (HURON RIVER) 54
BIG ERICK'S FALLS #3 (HURON RIVER) 55
BIG FALLS HIKE 56
BIG FALLS (HURON RIVER - EAST BRANCH) 56
EAST BRANCH FALLS HIKE 57
EAST BRANCH FALLS (HURON RIVER - EAST BRANCH) 58
EAST BRANCH FALLS #2 (HURON RIVER - EAST BRANCH) 59
EAST BRANCH FALLS #3 (HURON RIVER - EAST BRANCH) 60
EAST BRANCH FALLS #4 (HURON RIVER - EAST BRANCH) 61
EAST BRANCH FALLS #5 (HURON RIVER - EAST BRANCH) 62
EAST BRANCH FALLS #6 (HURON RIVER - EAST BRANCH) 63
EAST BRANCH FALLS #7 (HURON RIVER - EAST BRANCH) 64
ERICK'S FALLS HIKE 65
ERICK'S FALLS (HURON RIVER - WEST BRANCH) 65
ERICK'S CASCADES (HURON RIVER - WEST BRANCH) 66
HURON GORGE HIKE 67
HURON GORGE CASCADES (HURON RIVER - EAST BRANCH) 67
LETHERBY FALLS HIKE 68
TRACEY'S FALLS (HURON RIVER - WEST BRANCH) 68
LETHERBY FALLS (HURON RIVER - WEST BRANCH) 69
LETHERBY CASCADES (HURON RIVER - WEST BRANCH) 70
LETHERBY - LOWER FALLS HIKE 71
LETHERBY FALLS - LOWER (HURON RIVER - WEST BRANCH) 71
LETHERBY - MIDDLE FALLS HIKE 72
LETHERBY FALLS - MIDDLE (HURON RIVER - WEST BRANCH) 72
LETHERBY - UPPER FALLS HIKE 73
LETHERBY FALLS - UPPER (HURON RIVER - WEST BRANCH) 73
RAVINE RIVER ROAD FALLS HIKE 74
RAVINE RIVER ROAD FALLS (UNNAMED TRIBUTARY) 74
RAVINE RIVER ROAD CASCADES (UNNAMED TRIBUTARY) 75
PEA CAN FALLS HIKE 76
PEA CAN FALLS - UPPER CASCADE (PEA CAN CREEK) 76
PEA CAN FALLS - UPPER SLIDE (PEA CAN CREEK) 77
PEA CAN FALLS - LOWER CASCADE (PEA CAN CREEK) 78
PEA CAN RUN (PEA CAN CREEK) 79
PEA CAN FALLS - LOWER SLIDE (PEA CAN CREEK) 80
TEA CUP FALLS HIKE 81
TEA CUP FALLS (UNNAMED CREEK) 81
WEST BRANCH FALLS HIKE 82
WEST BRANCH FALLS - LOWER (HURON RIVER - WEST BRANCH) 82
WEST BRANCH LEDGE (HURON RIVER - WEST BRANCH) 83
WEST BRANCH FALLS (HURON RIVER - WEST BRANCH) 84
WEST BRANCH FALLS - UPPER (HURON RIVER - WEST BRANCH) 85

SILVER RIVER - LOWER AREA **86**
ABUTMENT FALLS HIKE 86
ABUTMENT FALLS (SILVER RIVER) 87
SILVER RAPIDS HIKE 88
SILVER RAPIDS (SILVER RIVER) 88
SILVER FALLS HIKE 89
SILVER CANYON FALLS (SILVER RIVER) 89
SILVER FALLS - LOWER (SILVER RIVER) 90

MAPS..
HIKES..
WATERFALLS........................

TABLE OF CONTENT KEY

SILVER RIVER - MIDDLE AREA **91**
SILVER RIVER - MIDDLE HIKE #1 91
SILVER FALLS - MIDDLE #10 (SILVER RIVER) 92
SILVER FALLS - MIDDLE #9 (SILVER RIVER) 93
SILVER FALLS - MIDDLE #8 (SILVER RIVER) 94
SILVER FALLS - MIDDLE #7 (SILVER RIVER) 95
SILVER FALLS - MIDDLE #6 (SILVER RIVER) 96
GOMANCHE FALLS (GOMANCHE CREEK) 97
GOMANCHE FALLS - UPPER (GOMANCHE CREEK) 98
SILVER FALLS - MIDDLE #5 (SILVER RIVER) 99
SILVER FALLS - MIDDLE #4 (SILVER RIVER) 100
SILVER FALLS - MIDDLE #3 (SILVER RIVER) 101
SILVER RIVER - MIDDLE HIKE #2 102
SILVER FALLS - MIDDLE #1 (SILVER RIVER) 102
PAGE CREEK FALLS (PAGE CREEK) 103
SILVER FALLS - MIDDLE #2 (SILVER RIVER) 105
SILVER RIVER - MIDDLE HIKE #3 106
SILVER GORGE FALLS (SILVER RIVER) 106
SILVER GORGE FALLS - UPPER (SILVER RIVER) 107
DEAD MAN'S FALLS (SILVER RIVER) 108
THIMBLEBERRY FALLS - LOWER (SILVER RIVER) 109
THIMBLEBERRY FALLS (SILVER RIVER) 110
THIMBLEBERRY CASCADES (SILVER RIVER) 111

SILVER RIVER - UPPER AREA **112**
BARAGA FALLS HIKE 114
HERMAN CASCADES (SILVER RIVER) 115
HERMAN FALLS - UPPER (SILVER RIVER) 116
HERMAN FALLS (SILVER RIVER) 117
BARAGA FALLS - UPPER (SILVER RIVER) 118
BARAGA FALLS (SILVER RIVER) 119
HARLEY FALLS HIKE 120
HARLEY FALLS #1 (HARLEY CREEK) 120
HARLEY FALLS #2 (HARLEY CREEK) 121
HARLEY FALLS #3 (HARLEY CREEK) 122
HARLEY FALLS #4 (HARLEY CREEK) 123
HARLEY FALLS #5 (HARLEY CREEK) 124
HARLEY FALLS #6 (HARLEY CREEK) 125
HARLEY FALLS #7 (HARLEY CREEK) 126
HARLEY FALLS #8 (HARLEY CREEK) 127
HARLEY FALLS #9 (HARLEY CREEK) 128
HARLEY FALLS #10 (HARLEY CREEK) 129
HARLEY FALLS #11 (HARLEY CREEK) 130
SILVER FALLS - UPPER HIKE 131
SILVER FALLS - UPPER (SILVER RIVER) 131

SLATE RIVER - LOWER AREA **132**
BLACK SLATE FALLS HIKE 134
QUARTZITE FALLS (SLATE RIVER) 134
BLACK SLATE FALLS (SLATE RIVER) 135
BLACK SLATE FALLS - MIDDLE (SLATE RIVER) 136
BLACK SLATE FALLS - UPPER (SLATE RIVER) 137
GRAND STAIRCASE (SLATE RIVER) 138
ARROWHEAD FALLS (SLATE RIVER) 139
BABY STAIRCASE (SLATE RIVER) 140

MAPS..........
HIKES..........
WATERFALLS..........

TABLE OF CONTENT KEY

RAVINE RIVER FALLS HIKE 141
RAVINE RIVER FALLS (RAVINE RIVER) 141
RAVINE RIVER FALLS - LOWER #1 (RAVINE RIVER) 142
RAVINE RIVER FALLS - LOWER #2 (RAVINE RIVER) 143
RAVINE RIVER FALLS - LOWER #3 (RAVINE RIVER) 144
SLATE RIVER FALLS HIKE 145
SLATE RIVER FALLS (SLATE RIVER) 145
FELTMAN FALLS (SLATE RIVER) 146
SLATE CORNER FALLS (SLATE RIVER) 147
ECSTASY CASCADES (SLATE RIVER) 148
ECSTASY FALLS - LOWER (SLATE RIVER) 149
ECSTASY FALLS (SLATE RIVER) 150
ECSTASY FALLS - UPPER (SLATE RIVER) 151
SLATE SLIDE (SLATE RIVER) 152
KUCKUK'S FALLS (SLATE RIVER) 153

SLATE RIVER - UPPER AREA 154
BLACK BEAR FALLS HIKE 156
BLACK BEAR FALLS (SLATE RIVER) 156
BLACK BEAR CASCADES (SLATE RIVER) 157
HOBBIT RUN (SLATE RIVER) 158
QUARRY FALLS HIKE 159
QUARRY FALLS (SLATE RIVER) 159
SLATE FLUME FALLS HIKE 160
SLATE BLOCK FALLS (SLATE RIVER) 160
SLATE FLUME FALLS (SLATE RIVER) 161
BLACK CASCADES (SLATE RIVER) 162
THE GRADE FALLS HIKE 163
THE GRADE FALLS (UNNAMED TRIBUTARY) 163
THE GRADE CASCADES (UNNAMED TRIBUTARY) 164
VICTORY FALLS HIKE 165
VICTORY FALLS (SLATE RIVER) 165

TIBBETS FALLS AREA 166
TIBBETS FALLS HIKE 166
TIBBETS FALLS (STURGEON RIVER) 167

TIOGA FALLS AREA 168
TIOGA FALLS HIKE 168
TIOGA FALLS (TIOGA RIVER) 168
TIOGA FALLS - UPPER (TIOGA RIVER) 169
TIOGA PARK FALLS HIKE 170
TIOGA PARK FALLS (TIOGA RIVER) 170
TIOGA PARK RAPIDS (TIOGA RIVER) 171

MAPS........
HIKES........
WAVERFALLS........

TABLE OF CONTENT KEY

The Bishop Baraga Shrine overlooks the southern end of Keweenaw Bay between L'Anse and Baraga.

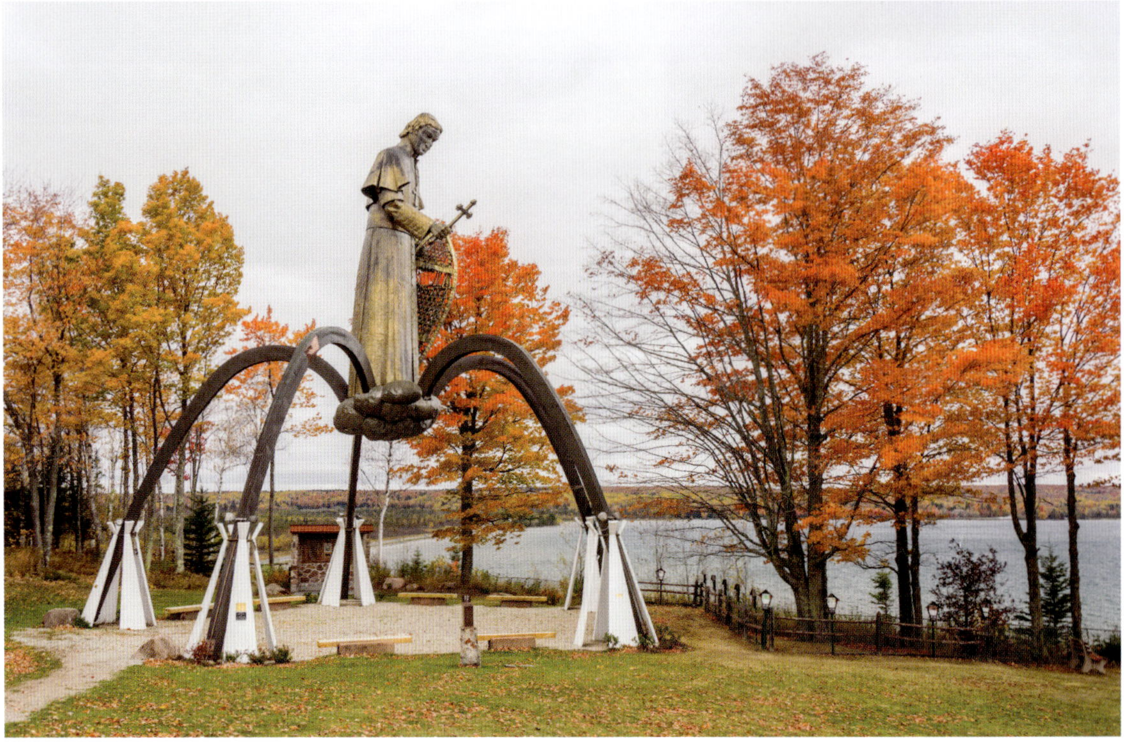

The Arvon Slate Quarry - nature is slowly reclaiming the piles of poor rock that surround this old pit.

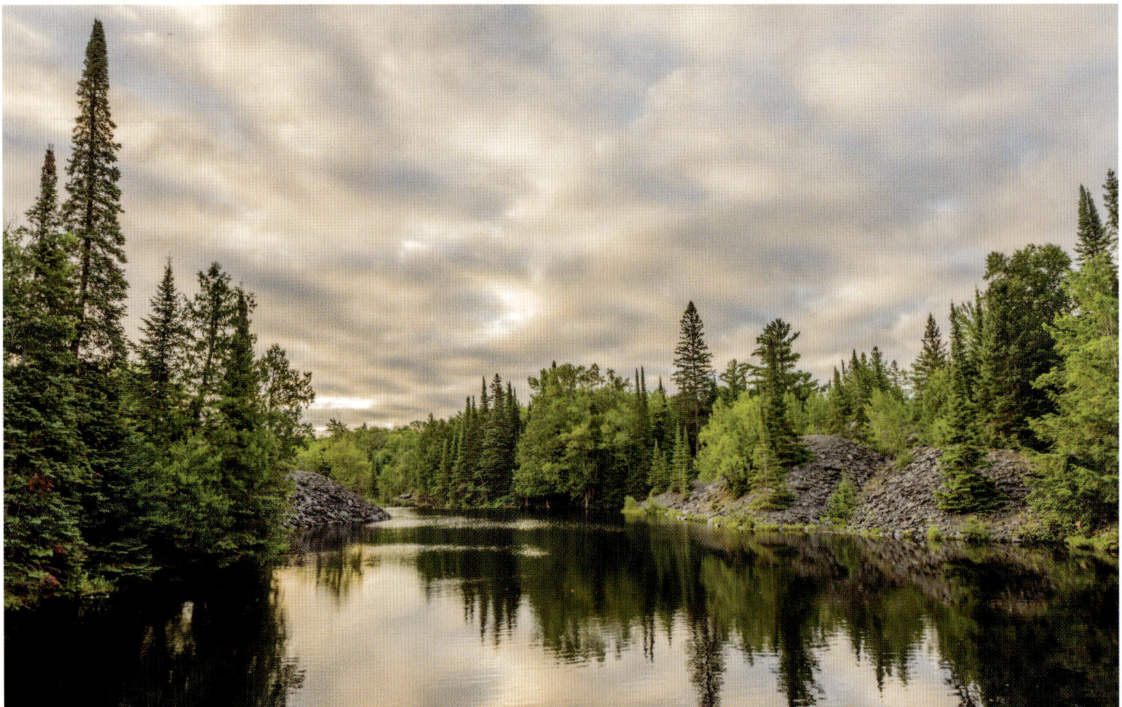

BARAGA COUNTY FACTS

Founded:	1875
Size:	904 square miles
Population (2010):	8,860
County Seat:	L'Anse

Baraga County received its name from Father Frederic Baraga, who started a Catholic mission at Assinins in 1843.

Fur traders and missionaries were the first white people to make their way through Baraga County in the seventeenth century. Later, the lure of lumber, fishing and mining brought entrepreneurs to this rugged portion of Michigan. By the late nineteenth century, lumber had taken over as the dominant natural resource used in the development of the county. As lumbering operations in the area grew and thrived, they caught the attention of Henry Ford. The Ford Motor Company bought the entire holdings of Charles Hebard and Sons in 1923. This included a sawmill and even the town of Pequaming, a community built on a narrow strip of land running parallel to the shoreline on the Abbaye Peninsula. During its peak production, this sawmill cut over 30 million board feet per year. The great depression saw demand for lumber shrink dramatically, and after the United States entered World War II, operations were halted in 1942, and the town of Pequaming was eventually abandoned. Remnants of the Ford Motor Company's historic past can still be seen in Pequaming, as well as further south along US-41 in Alberta.

The lumbering industry still provides many jobs in the county today, but now tourism, casino gambling, and manufacturing brings more economic diversity to the region.

Natural beauty is on display throughout the county. Most of the county lies in a pristine state, with ninety-three percent of the land forested. There are 65 miles of Lake Superior shoreline, 1,080 lakes, 636 miles of rivers and streams and some of the nicest waterfalls in Michigan!

Mount Arvon is the highest point in Michigan at 1,979 feet above sea level (1,380 feet above Lake Superior). For more information on Mt. Arvon check out *http://www.baragacounty.org/wp-content/uploads/2013/02/Mt_Arvon.pdf* on the internet.

Craig Lake State Park is the most remote state park in Michigan. It is a true wilderness area with over 6,900 acres of lakes, rivers and woodlands. Roads and trails in this area are very primitive, and may be impassible. *http://www.stateparks.com/craig_lake.html*

Take time to stop at the information center near the entrance of L'Anse. You will always receive valuable information delivered in a friendly manner. There are also free brochures and tourist guides available.

Baraga County Map

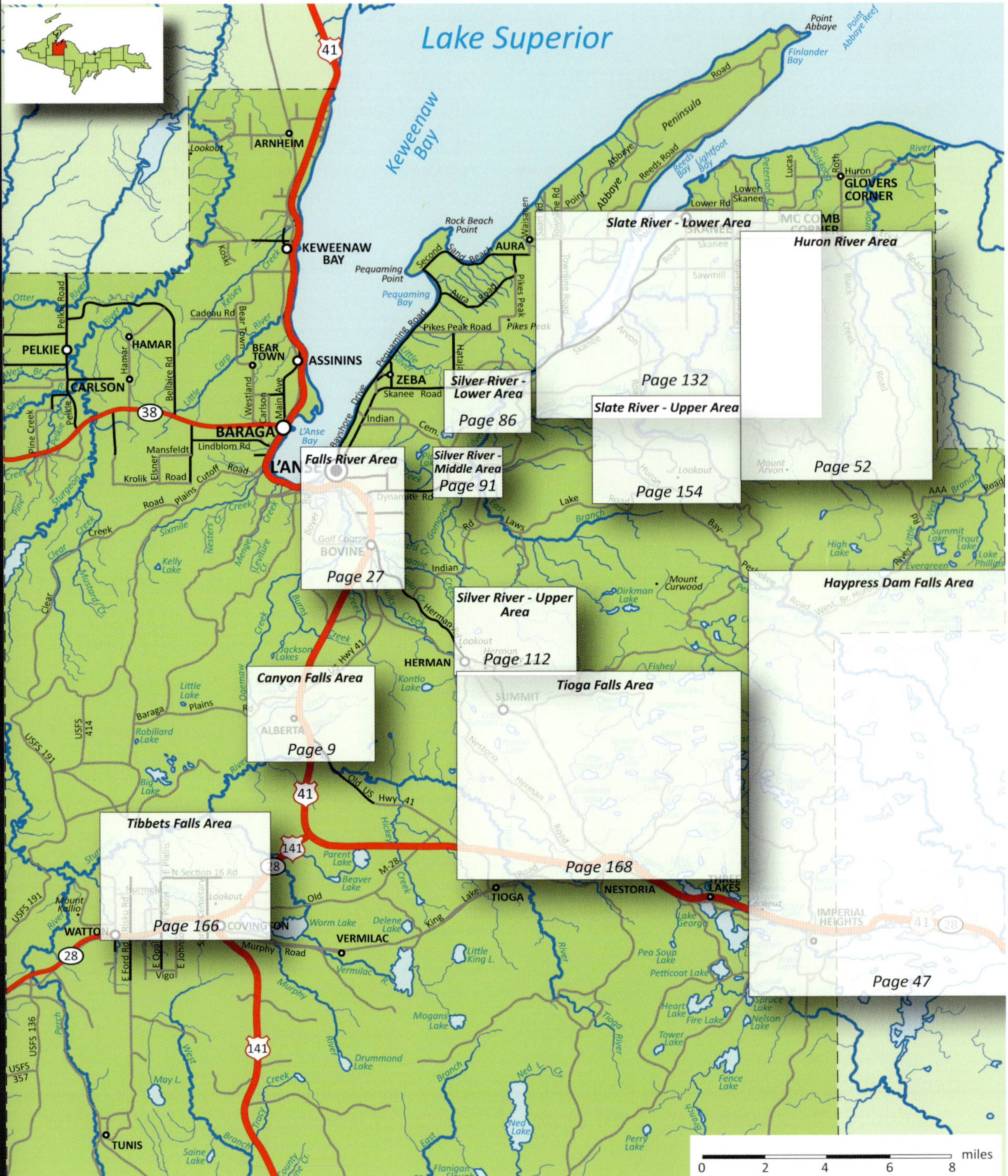

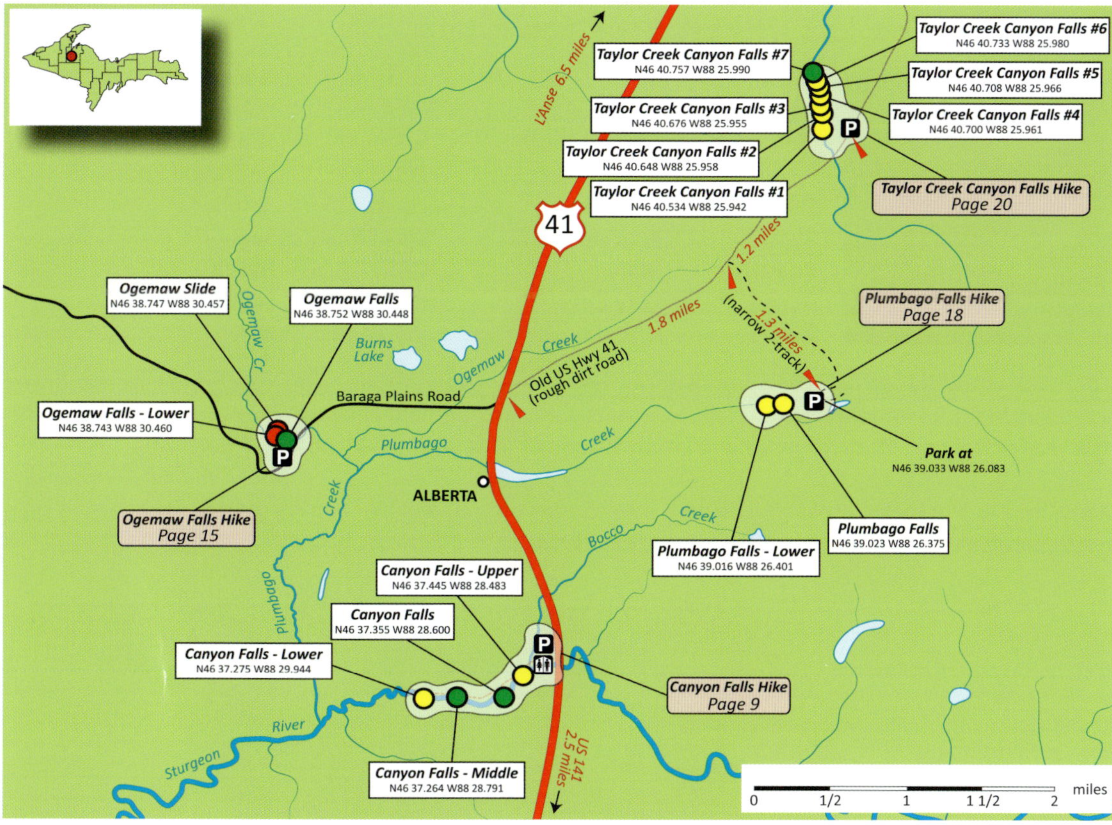

Canyon Falls Hike

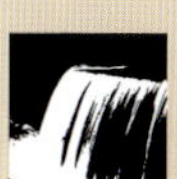

Canyon Falls Roadside Park at the trail head to the falls features drinking water, toilets, picnic tables and charcoal grills. This wonderful facility sets the tone for a hike to Canyon Falls on a semi-improved footpath.

Directions: US-41 crosses the Sturgeon River 2.9 miles north of the intersection of M-28 and 1.4 miles south of Alberta. Just north of the bridge is a very nice roadside park on the west side of the road. The trailhead to the falls is toward the southern end of the parking lot. The trail is fairly flat, although there are a couple low areas that must be crossed. These are covered with planks that are very slippery when wet. About halfway to Canyon Falls the upper falls will be plainly visible from the trail. It is a small cascade that children (and some adults) enjoy playing around. At Canyon Falls there is a nice railed area for viewing the falls. From here, the trail to the lower falls is not kept up, so use extreme caution when hiking the rest of the way. There are no guard rails and the trail runs next to the edge of the canyon. You need to keep a close eye on young children, or safer yet, don't bring them on this portion of the hike.

Clarification: USGS maps call falls downstream of Canyon Falls, "Upper Canyon Falls" even though they are downstream. I haven't been able to find a satisfactory answer as to the reason for this, so I have labeled the cascades below Canyon Falls as the "Lower" falls, and the small cascade above Canyon Falls as the "Upper" falls.

CANYON FALLS - UPPER (STURGEON RIVER)

Private

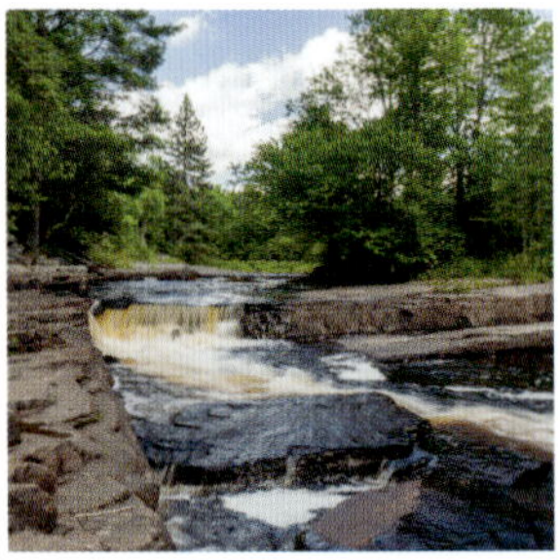

Must See: 4
Height: 2 feet
Time: 15-30 minutes

Driving Information
Signs: Roadside Park
Road: Main
Access: Very Easy
4WD: N/A

GPS: N46 37.445 W88 28.483

Hiking Information
Path: Improved Footpath
Length: .2 miles
Elev. Change: Slight
GPS: Helpful
Danger: Slight
WP Boots: N/A

Stop here at the upper falls for a break about halfway to Canyon Falls. This cute little cascade draws passersby in for an intimate look at a little waterfall. Young and old alike can play around the falls with little fear of danger. This is a very kid-friendly location! This is a nice location for portraits.

Take a look at the rock plates. This is the same formation that will be seen further down river but on a much grander scale as the river enters the short canyon.

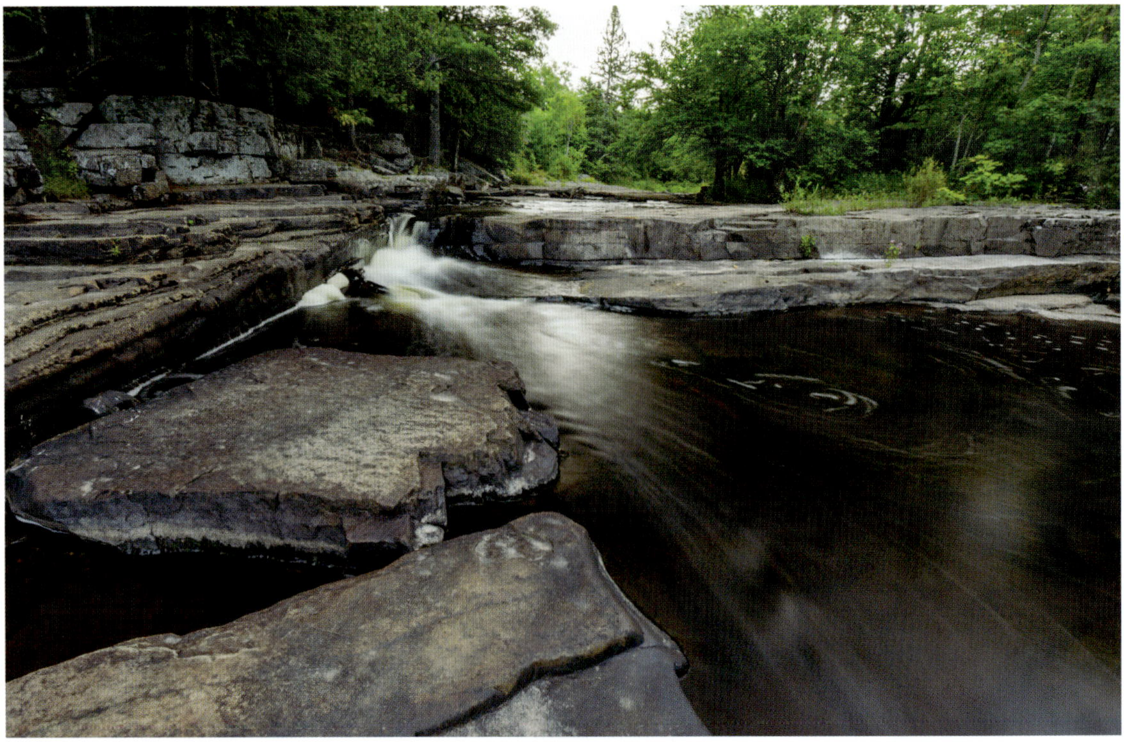

CANYON FALLS (STURGEON RIVER)

Private

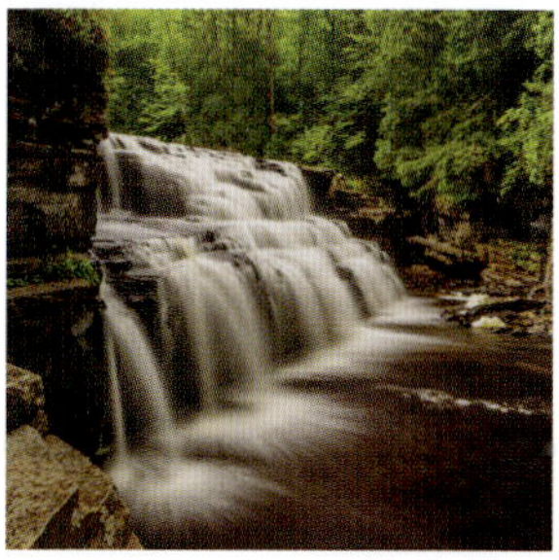

Must See:	8	GPS:	N46 37.355 W88 28.600
Height:	15 feet		
Time:	30-45 minutes	**Hiking Information**	
		Path:	Improved Footpath
Driving Information		Length:	.4 miles
Signs:	Roadside Park	Elev. Change:	Slight
Road:	Main	GPS:	N/A
Access:	Very Easy	Danger:	Slight
4WD:	N/A	WP Boots:	N/A

Canyon Falls has been referred to as "The Grand Canyon of Michigan". Although this comparison is a bit of a stretch, the box canyon that starts at the waterfall is a beautiful natural feature that everyone should make an effort to visit. The incredible rock formations are as intriguing as the falls themselves and are well worth the time it takes to explore them.

Wooden rails line the edge of the main viewing area to provide safety from the raw power of the waterfall and sheer canyon walls. Keep small children close.

The trail to Canyon Falls winds through a beautiful forest. An elevated boardwalk is provided for the portion of the hike that runs through a wet area. Although it keeps your feet dry, be careful as the wood tends to become slippery when wet.

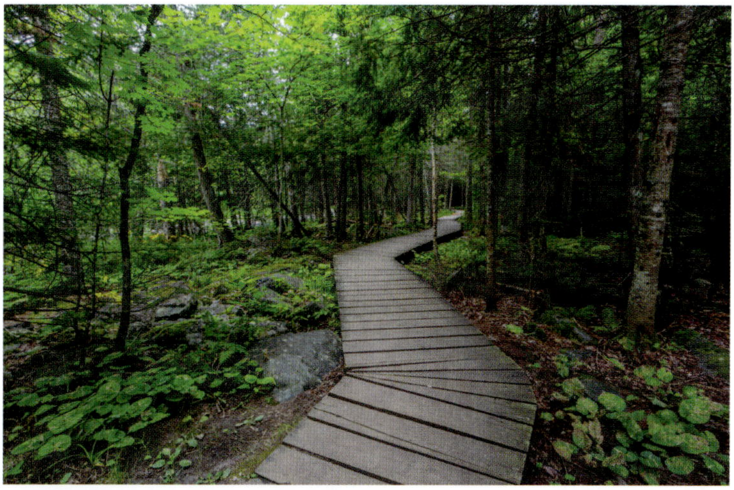

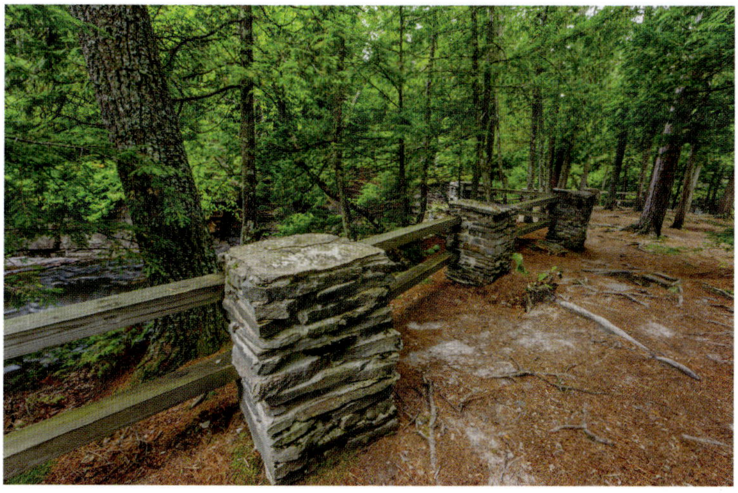

After hiking .4 miles, the trail widens out to a flat, undergrowth free viewing area. On the left side, wooden rails with large, square stone posts stand as sentinels along the canyon edge. At the far end of the clearing the terrain quickly changes. A cut in the bedrock leads down to the river's edge. Also nearby, a set of stone steps leads up, marking the beginning of the unimproved hike along the rest of the canyon and a continuation of the NCT.

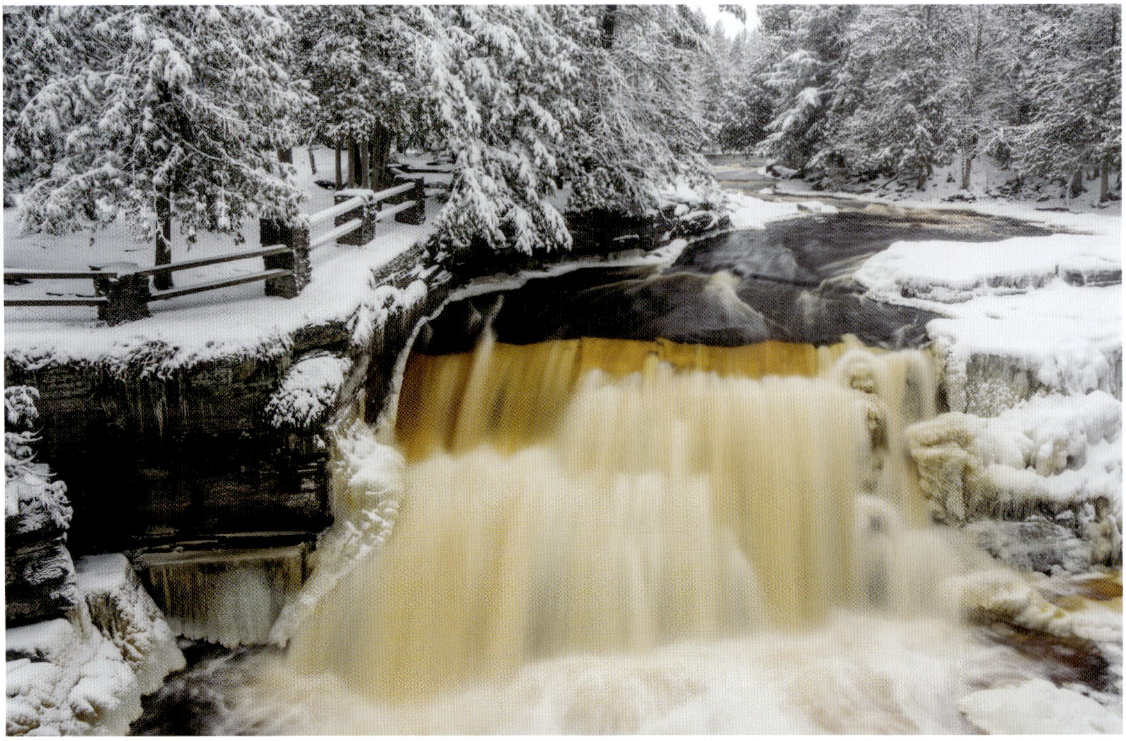

Canyon Falls as seen from the far side of the river during winter. The stonework built by the public works program years ago can be seen along the canyon's edge.

Looking back at Canyon Falls from further along the North Country Trail

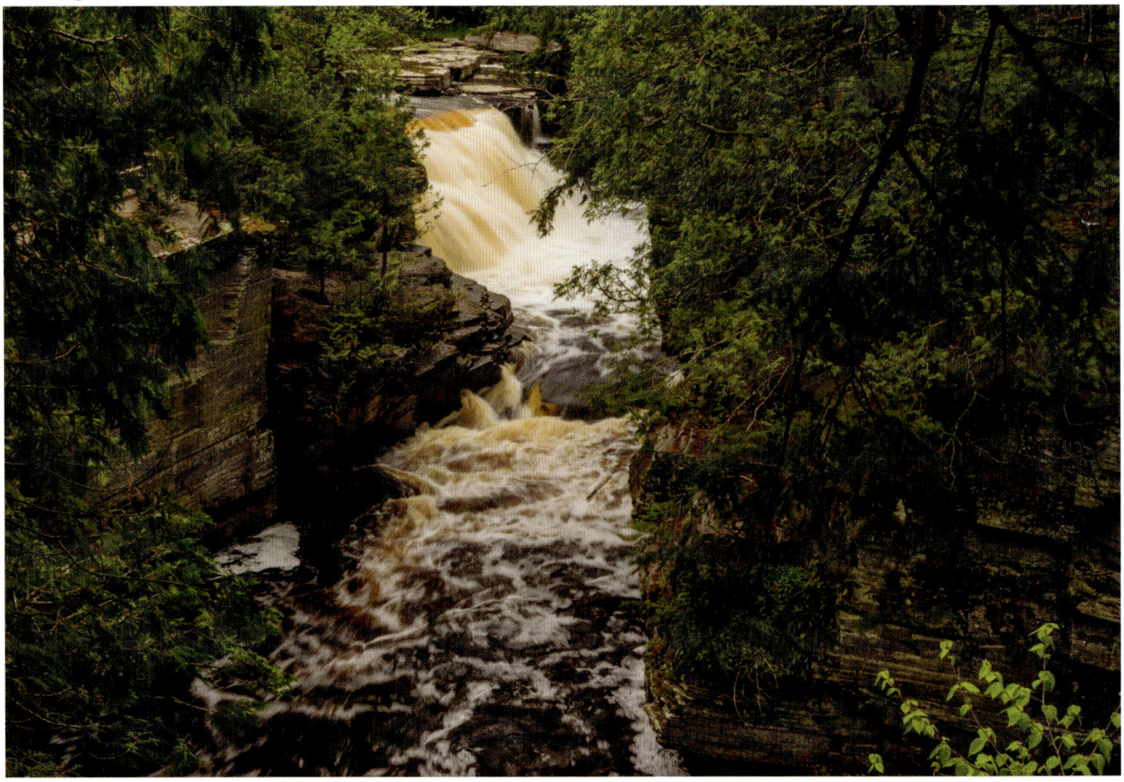

CANYON FALLS - MIDDLE (STURGEON RIVER)

Private

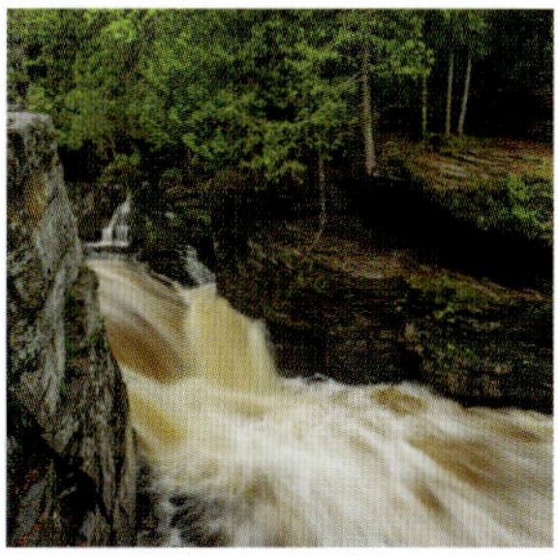

Must See:	7	GPS:	N46 37.264 W88 28.791
Height:	8 feet		
Time:	45-60 minutes		

Driving Information		Hiking Information	
		Path:	Semi-Improved Footpath
		Length:	.8 miles
Signs:	Roadside Park	Elev. Change:	Slight
Road:	Main	GPS:	Helpful
Access:	Very Easy	Danger:	Moderate
4WD:	N/A	WP Boots:	N/A

The canyon narrows to about 15 feet at this point and sports a nice cascading drop in the river. There is not a great way to view this waterfall. Getting close to the canyon edge is the only way to see it properly. Be careful! There are no guardrails in this area and rocks can be unstable.

Looking down on the falls near the brink

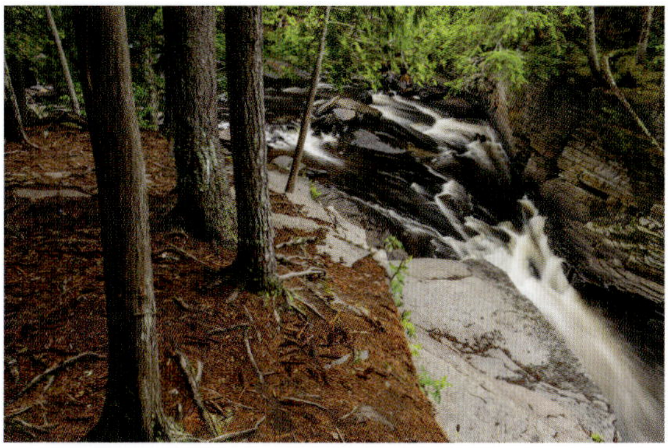

The North County Trail that runs along the canyon

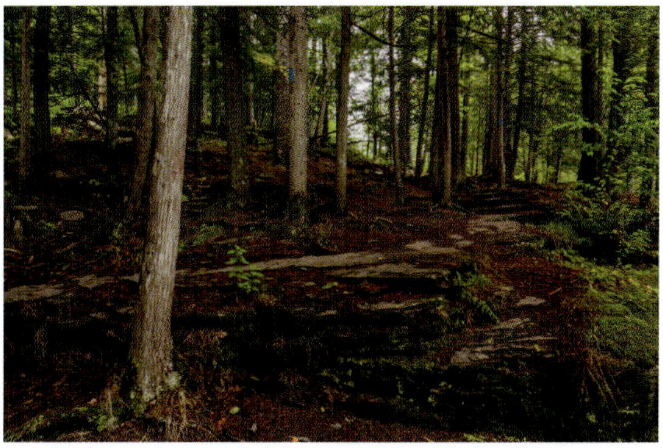

Local youth love to jump into the river at the base of the falls from the far side of the river

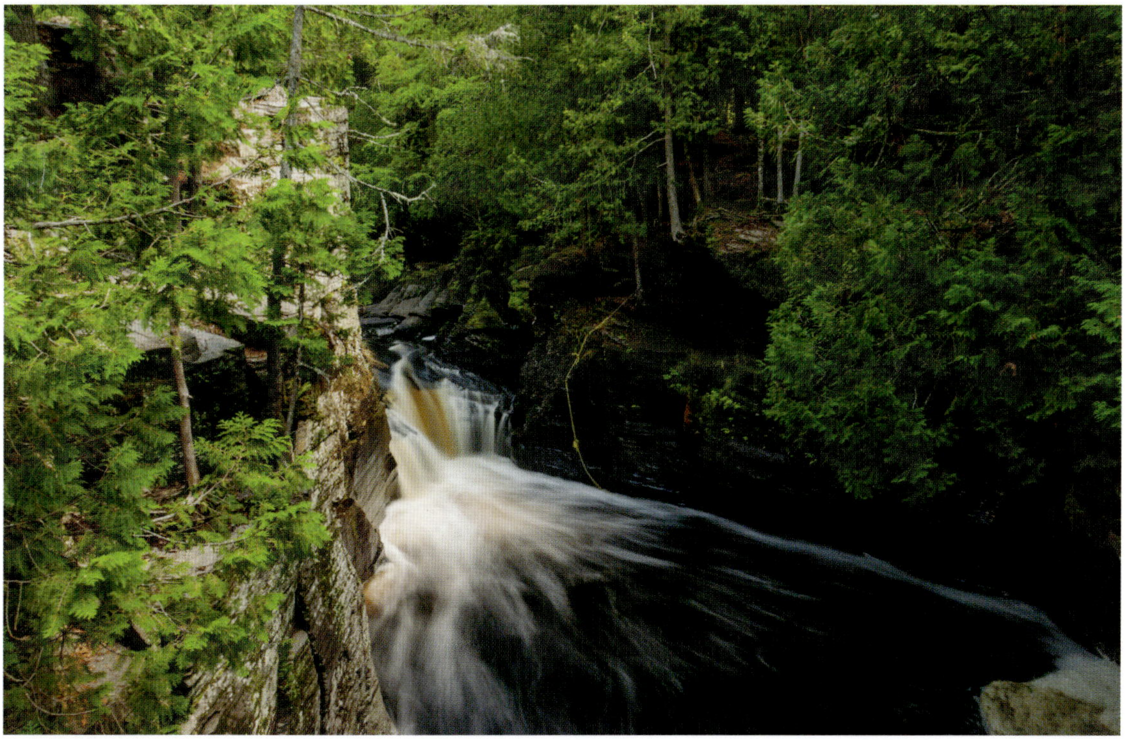

CANYON FALLS - LOWER (STURGEON RIVER)

Private

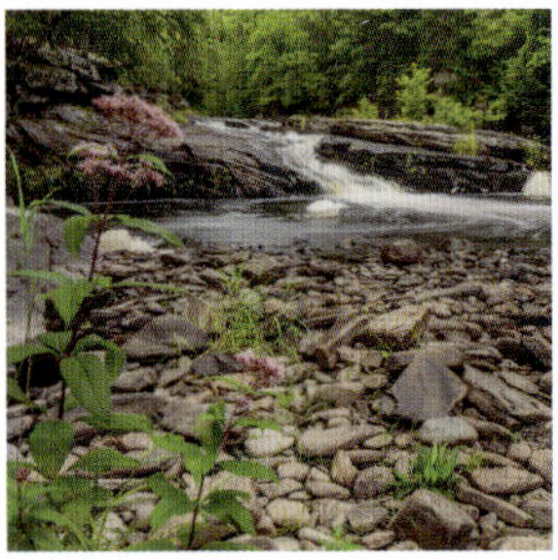

Must See:	6
Height:	15 feet
Time:	45-60 minutes

Driving Information

Signs:	Roadside Park
Road:	Main
Access:	Very Easy
4WD:	N/A

GPS:	N46 37.275 W88 29.944

Hiking Information

Path:	Footpath
Length:	.8 miles
Elev. Change:	Slight
GPS:	Helpful
Danger:	Moderate
WP Boots:	Recommended

The canyon ends here with the second of the lower falls. The river slides over the last portion of the canyon bedrock. It can be nicely viewed from small rocks scattered below the falls. I have been to this waterfall several times. Even though the parking lot was full on more than one of those occasions, I have rarely encountered anyone this far downstream.

A portion of the unimproved trail from Canyon Falls to the lower falls

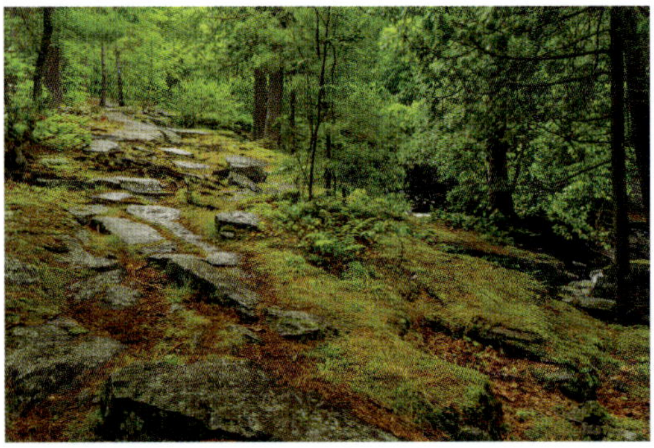

Blue blazed trees mark the trail that basically follows the canyon edge.

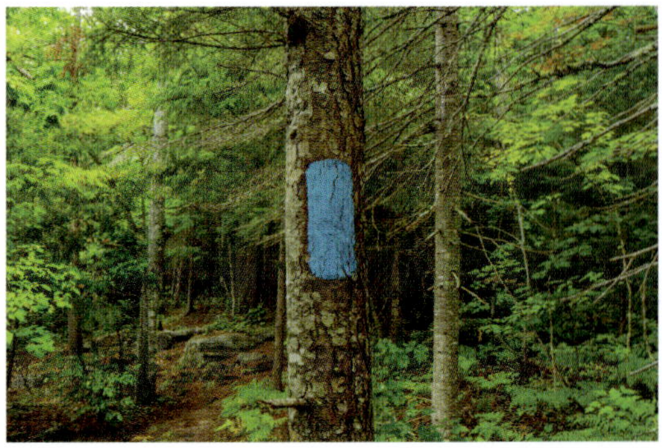

As the river rises, it surrounds the mass in the center of the riverbed, dividing the river in two.

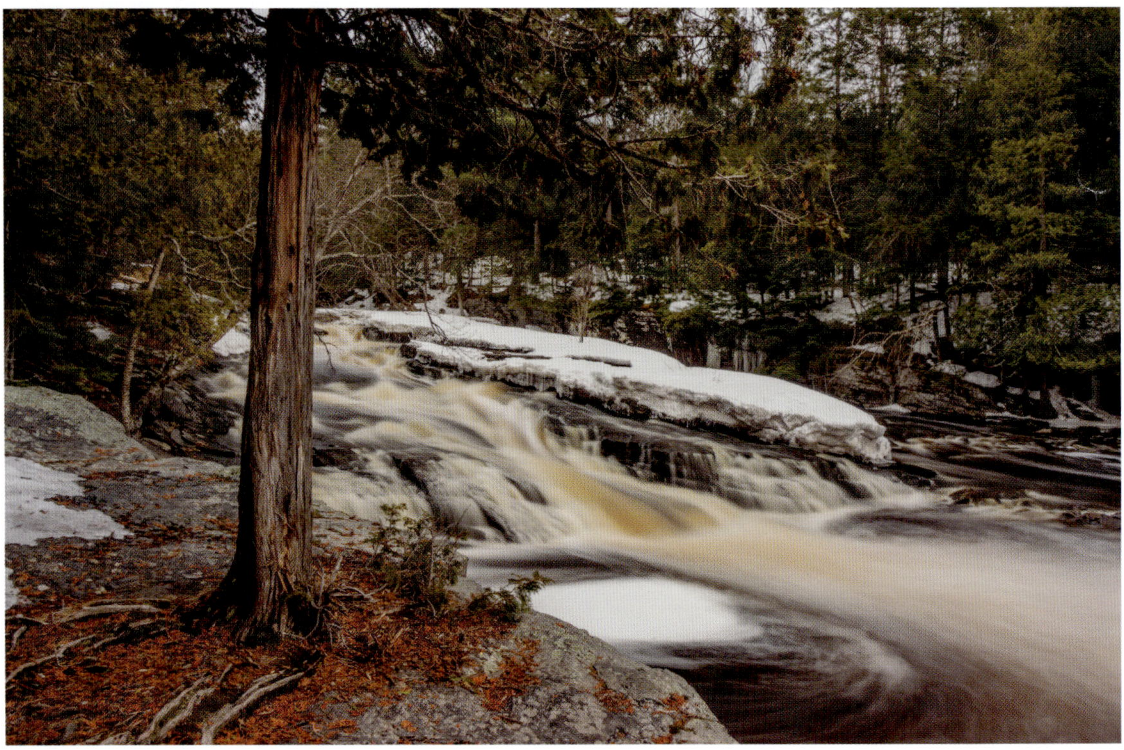

Ogemaw Falls Hike

A short walk followed by a relatively easy climb down a fairly steep embankment ends at this beautiful little waterfall. The main cascade pours into a spill pool with a second, smaller drop emptying out of a narrow, shallow spot between two rocky segments of the pool rim. The creek then turns hard to the right, flowing along an interestingly smooth and rounded hump of bedrock. This creates the Ogemaw Slide. When the creek is running high, overflowing water runs through a fault in the rounded bedrock. This branch of the then divided creek drops over a precipice into a tangle of undergrowth at Ogemaw Falls - Lower.

Directions: From US-41, turn west onto Baraga Plains Road (.5 miles north of Alberta). In 1.5 miles, the road crosses Ogemaw Creek. Just before the bridge, the shoulder of the road widens out. Park by the wooden sign for the waterfall. A faint footpath runs through the woods. The creek is at the base of a short, but somewhat steep, forested hillside. Ogemaw Slide is around the corner and just downstream from Ogemaw Falls. The lower falls (if they are running) are just downstream from Ogemaw Falls and on the other side of the creek.

OGEMAW FALLS (OGEMAW CREEK)

Private

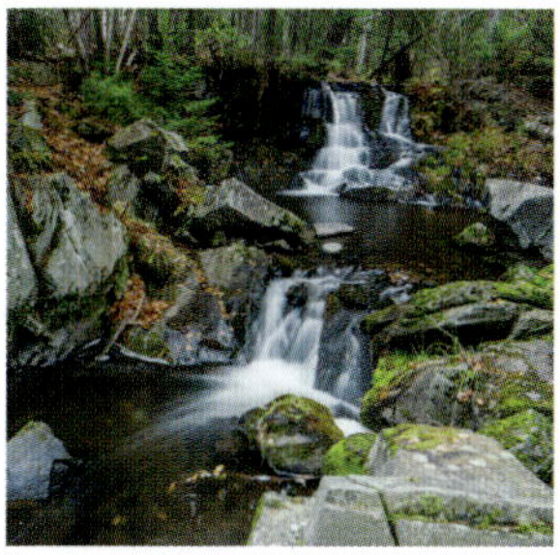

Must See:	7	GPS:	N46 38.752 W88 30.448
Height:	10 feet		
Time:	15-30 minutes	Hiking Information	
		Path:	Unimproved Footpath
Driving Information		Length:	100 yards
Signs:	None	Elev. Change:	Moderate
Road:	Secondary	GPS:	N/A
Access:	Somewhat Easy	Danger:	Moderate
4WD:	N/A	WP Boots:	Recommended

Signs have been placed at various waterfalls around the county by the Baraga County Visitor's Bureau. One of them is here. The trail down to the waterfall has several places that can be slippery and there is a short but steep climb down at the waterfall itself, so do be careful on this short hike. Wade across the shallow creek to view both of the drops from the best vantage point.

Ogemaw Creek widens out into a good sized pond before narrowing down again and flowing through a culvert below Baraga Plains Road on its way to the waterfall. The pond can be easily seen on the left and serves as a good landmark for the waterfall.

The sign for Ogemaw Falls is on the right. Park off the side of the road here.

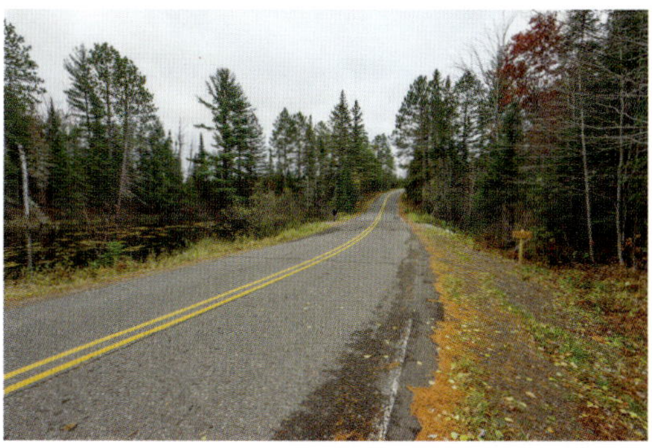

A wintry view of this lovely waterfall

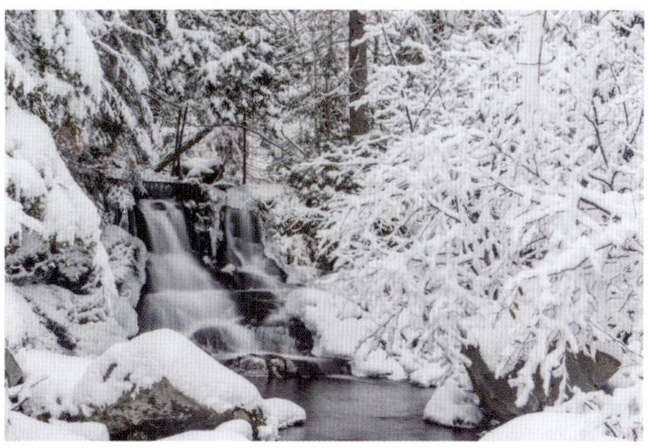

OGEMAW SLIDE (OGEMAW CREEK)

Private

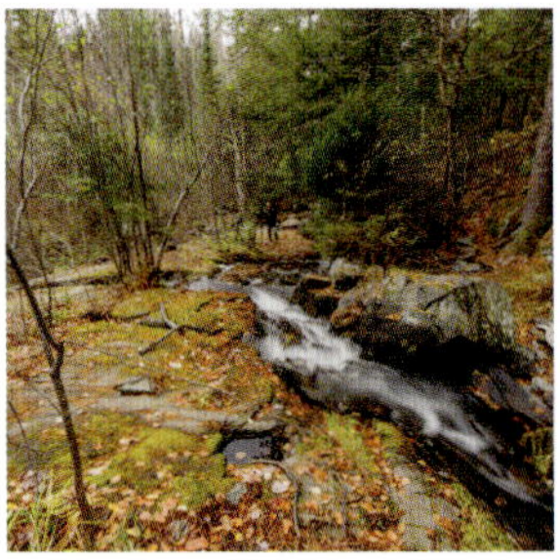

Must See:	3
Height:	8 feet
Time:	20-35 minutes

Driving Information

Signs:	None
Road:	Secondary
Access:	Somewhat Easy
4WD:	N/A

GPS:	N46 38.747 W88 30.457

Hiking Information

Path:	None
Length:	120 yards
Elev. Change:	Moderate
GPS:	N/A
Danger:	Moderate
WP Boots:	Recommended

After the creek leaves the lower drop at Ogemaw Falls, it rushes around a corner and then slides down a narrow wedge created by a large cylindrical mass of bedrock that is snuggled up next to the base of the ravine by the creek. This cylindrical piece is tilted, smooth, and often slippery.

The smooth bedrock mass can be VERY slippery, especially when covered with moss. Take care.

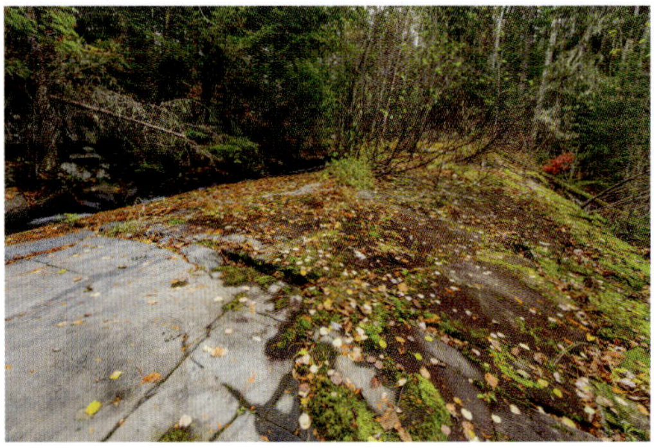

As the creek level rises it spreads out and covers more of the rocky mass.

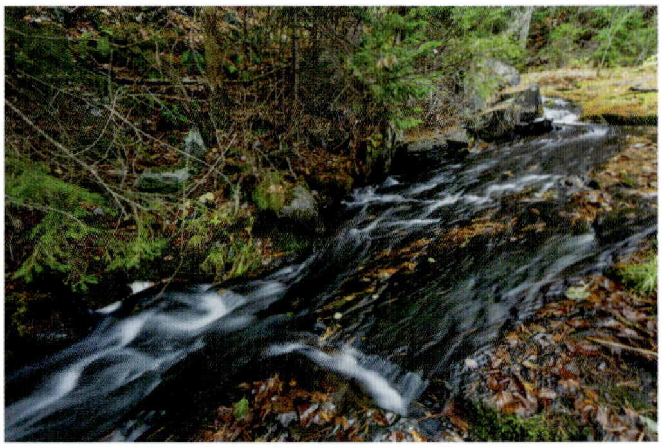

Looking up the long slide - Ogemaw Falls is just around the corner above the top of the slide.

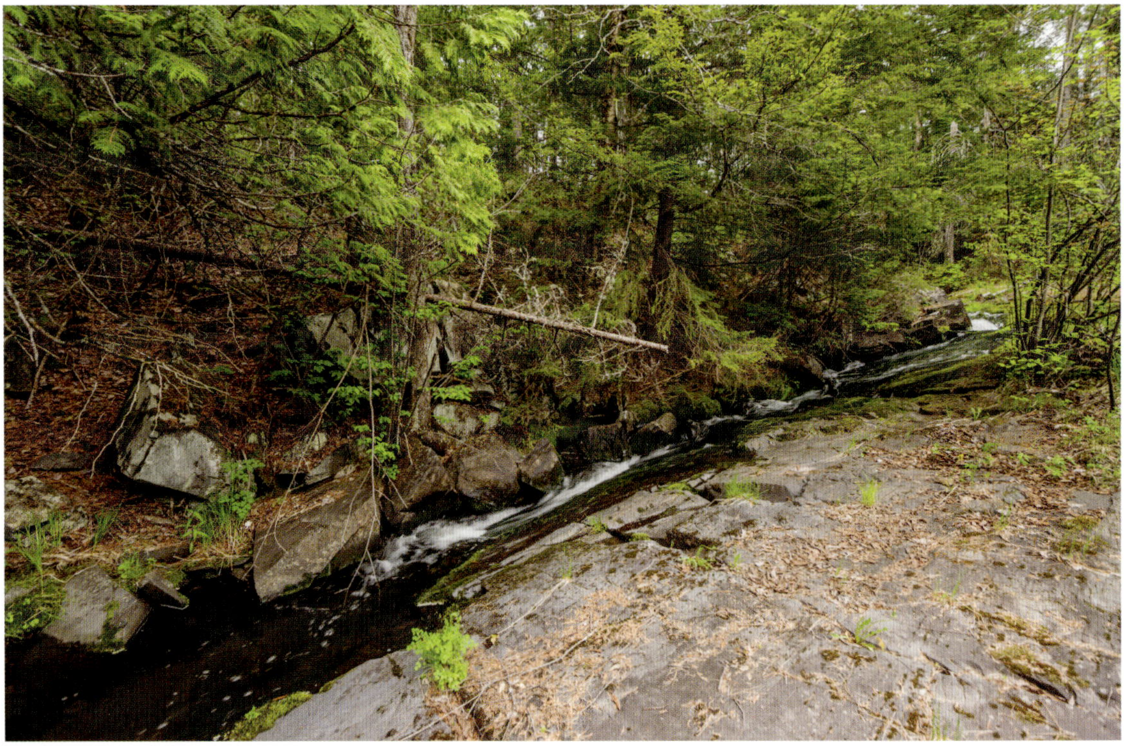

OGEMAW FALLS - LOWER (OGEMAW CREEK)

Private

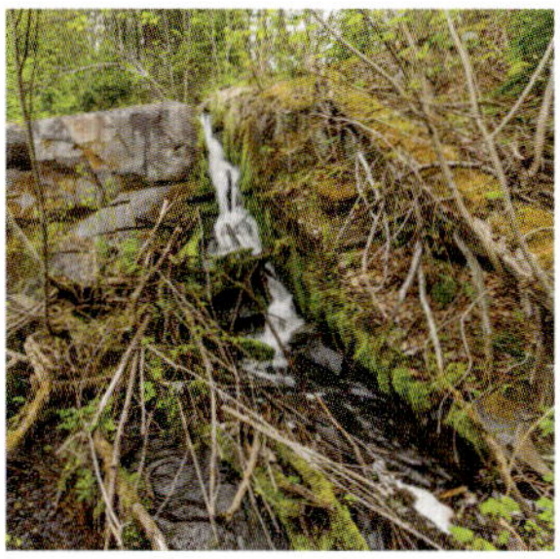

Must See:	3	GPS:	N46 38.743 W88 30.460
Height:	12 feet		
Time:	20-35 minutes	Hiking Information	
		Path:	None
Driving Information		Length:	130 yards
Signs:	None	Elev. Change:	Moderate
Road:	Secondary	GPS:	N/A
Access:	Somewhat Easy	Danger:	Moderate
4WD:	N/A	WP Boots:	Recommended

This waterfall is a "high water" fall. These shots were taken when water levels were above normal. This may dry up during the summer. As seen in the picture, there were downed trees and brush obscuring the waterfall at the time. The creek runs alongside a rounded hump of rock below Ogemaw Falls in the Ogemaw Slide. A portion of the creek splits off when the levels are high enough and runs over the lower falls.

This is the rounded hump of rock. A portion of the creek runs through the crack by the tree.

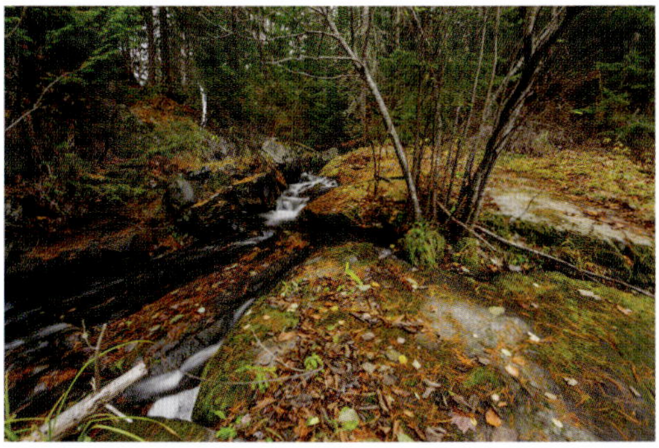

Looking down from the top of the lower falls into the lowlands.

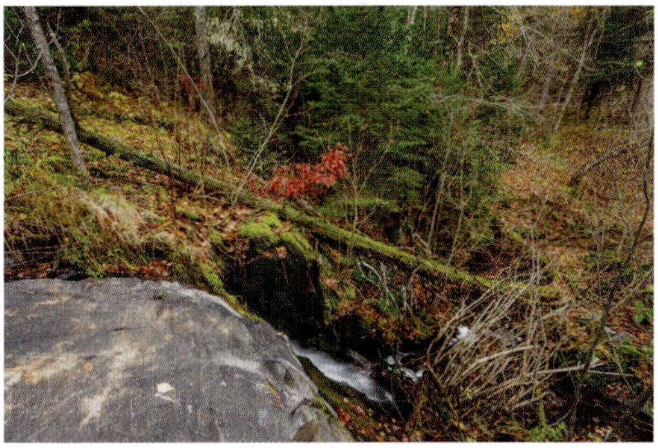

It is thick with undergrowth down here at the base of the falls. Probably prime tick area...

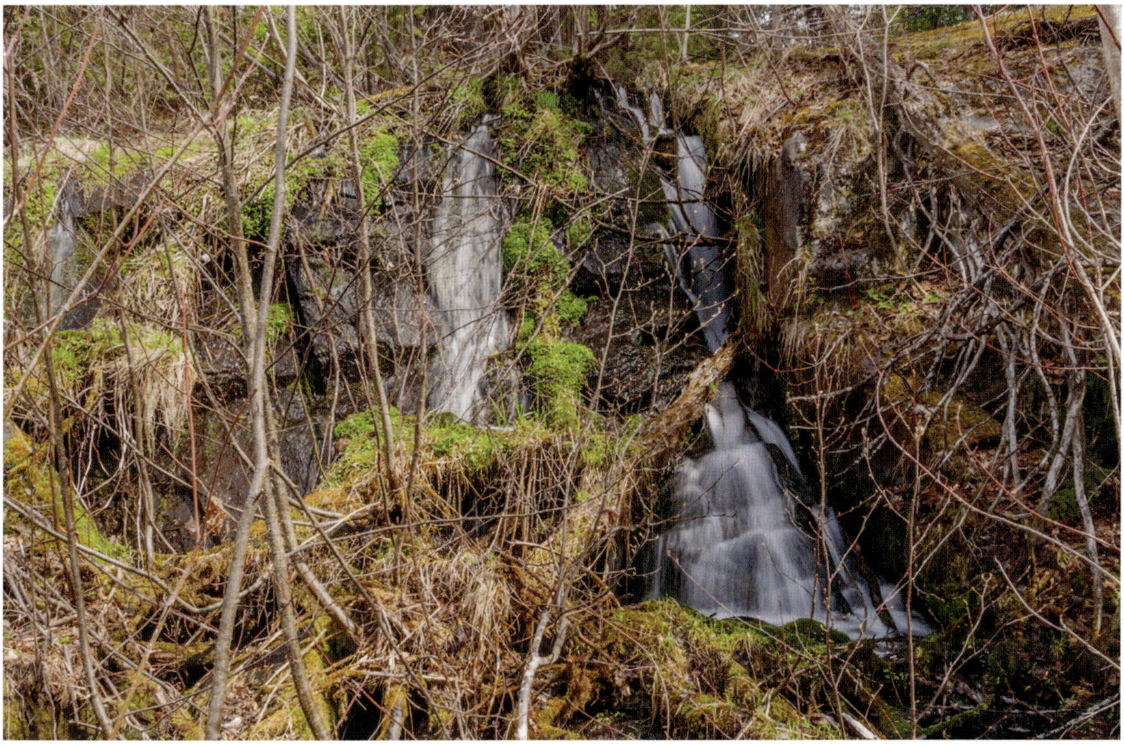

Plumbago Falls Hike

The hike to and from Plumbago Falls ranks as one of the most difficult hikes I have made in Michigan. It is only about 1/3 mile hike, but Plumbago Creek is situated at the base of a very steep and deep ravine. Scrambling down to the bottom then climbing back out is very physically demanding. I don't recommend it unless you are in excellent physical shape and are agile on steep hillsides.

Directions: From US-41, turn northeast onto "Old US HWY 41" - it is a rough dirt road that starts across from Baraga Plains Road, about 6.5 miles south of L'Anse. Follow the dirt road for 1.8 miles. A narrow 2-track turns to the right (south/southeast). A 4WD vehicle with good clearance on this trail is highly recommended. (Recent logging in the area has improved the 2-track.) Follow the 2-track for about 1.3 miles to N46 39.033 W88 26.083. Park here. Hike toward the falls. The gorge that the creek runs through will come into view. Find a "safe" place to climb down to the base of the gorge. Follow the creek to the falls.

PLUMBAGO FALLS (PLUMBAGO CREEK)

Private

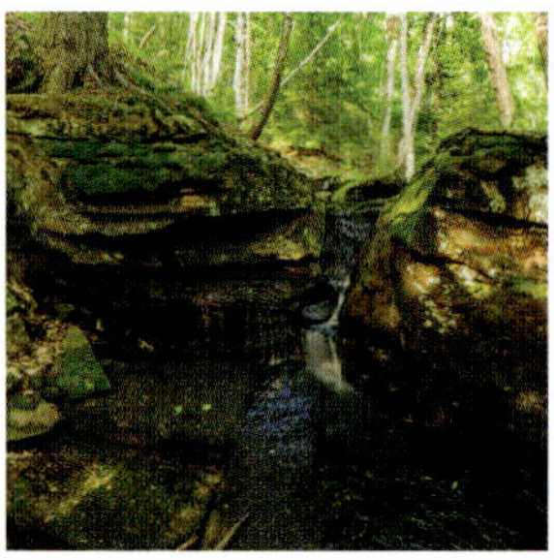

Must See: 5
Height: 6 feet
Time: 1.5-2 hours

Driving Information
Signs: None
Road: 2-track
Access: Difficult
4WD: Required

GPS: N46 39.023 W88 26.375

Hiking Information
Path: None
Length: .3 miles
Elev. Change: Major
GPS: Required
Danger: Elevated
WP Boots: Helpful

Plumbago Creek is nestled in the bottom of the deep gorge surrounding it. The river is channeled down to 1 foot in width at the waterfall. The falls drop between upward thrust rocks that are covered with thick, fuzzy, green moss. Car sized chunks of rocks are scattered around the bottom of this rugged gorge. The creek can drop to a trickle during drier times.

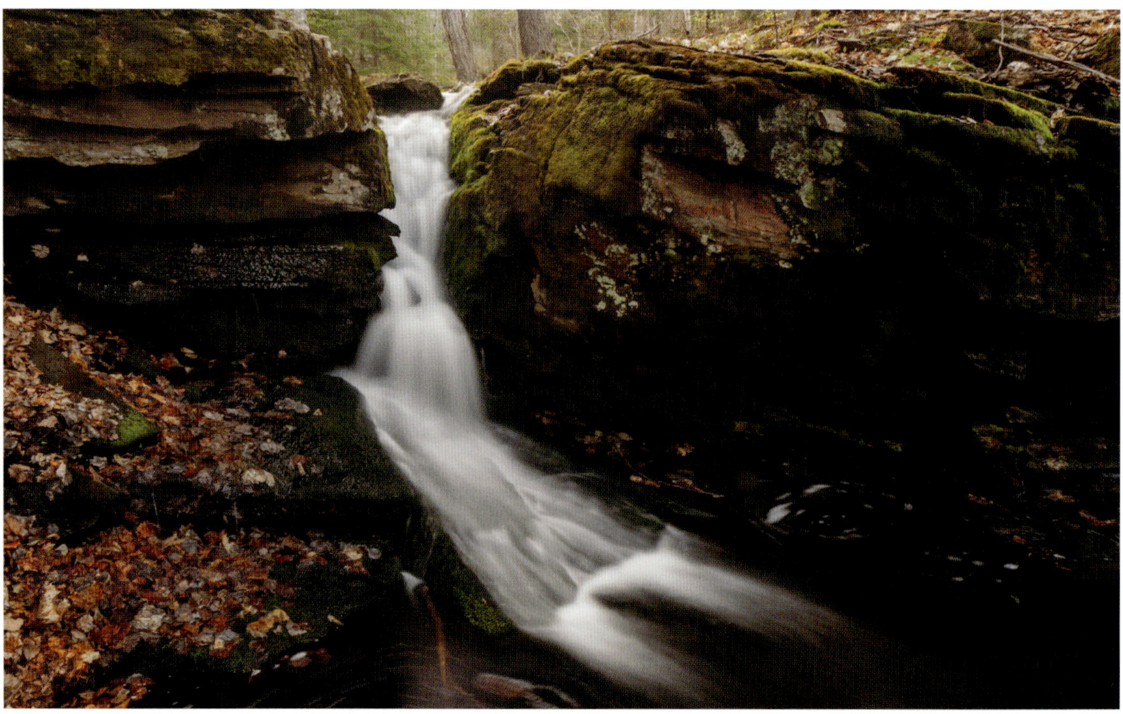

PLUMBAGO FALLS - LOWER (PLUMBAGO CREEK)

Private

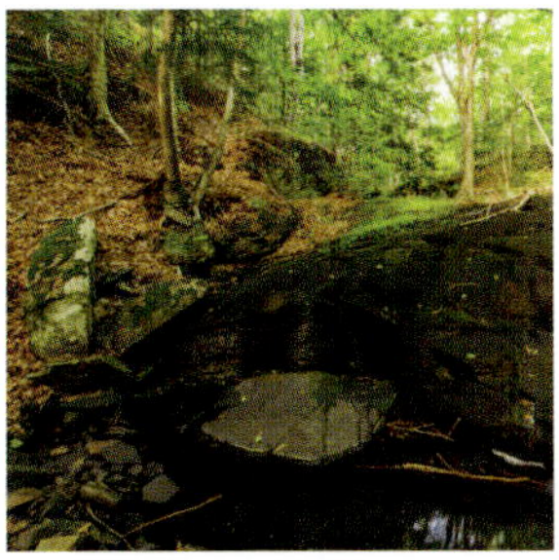

Must See:	4	GPS:	N46 39.016 W88 26.401
Height:	8 feet		
Time:	1.5-2 hours	Hiking Information	
		Path:	None
Driving Information		Length:	.3 miles
Signs:	None	Elev. Change:	Major
Road:	2-track	GPS:	Required
Access:	Very Difficult	Danger:	Elevated
4WD:	Required	WP Boots:	Helpful

Hike 40 yards further down the ever widening gorge from Plumbago Falls to the lower falls. The creek slides down mossy rocks for an 8 foot total drop at the lower falls. Once again, water volume makes all the difference! I have yet to get to this spot during a good water flow. But even these two low water shots vary greatly.

Hiking back out of the ravine requires navigating the rock-strewn hillside of the gorge. Be prepared to rest several times during the climb.

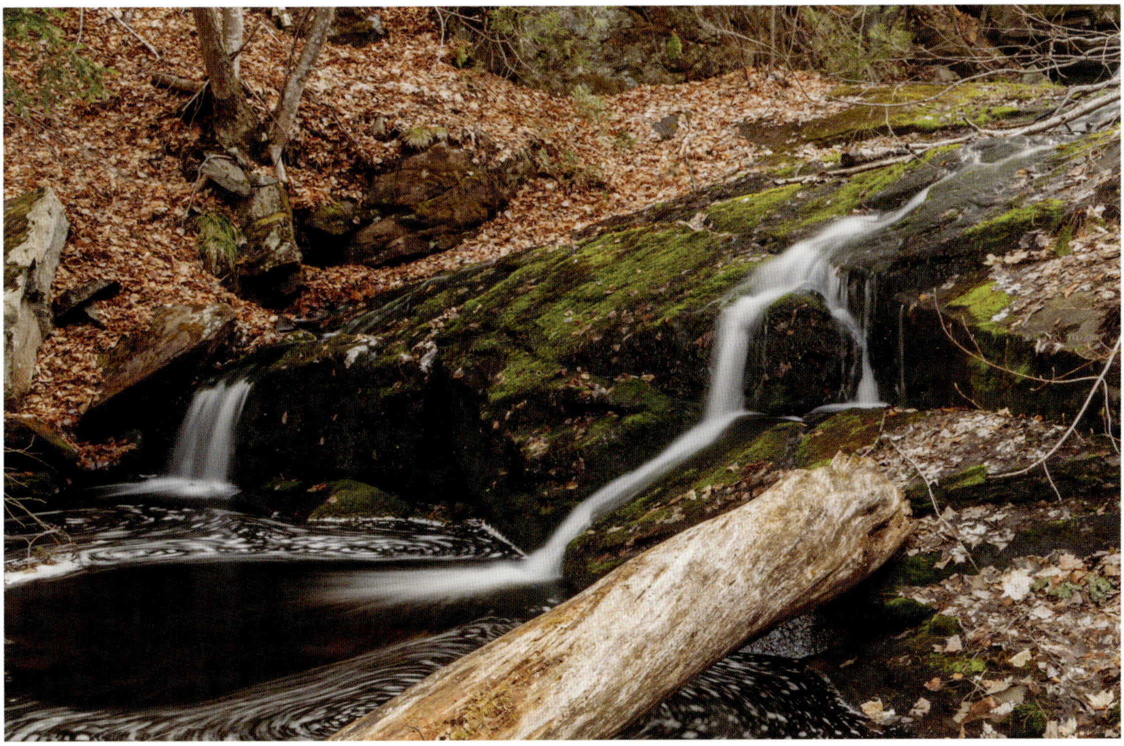

Taylor Creek Canyon Falls Hike

The waterfalls along Taylor Creek occur throughout a canyon that seemingly appears out of nowhere. The terrain is mostly flat with some rolling hills sporting hardwoods and evergreens. Suddenly, increasingly steep rocky banks give way to nearly vertical cliff walls over 20 feet tall with the creek running through the resulting canyon. The floor of the canyon drops several times, a waterfall being created at each elevation change.

Directions: From US-41, turn northeast onto "Old US HWY 41" - it is a rough dirt road that starts across from Baraga Plains Road, about 6.5 miles south of L'Anse. Drive 3.0 miles. Park at N46 40.592 W88 25.777. Hike 200 yards cross country to #1. Follow the creek downstream for another 250 yards. The canyon starts just downstream from here. Follow the near bank. Climb down the steep hillside when possible to enter each section of the canyon to view each of the waterfalls.

TAYLOR CREEK CANYON FALLS #1 (TAYLOR CREEK)

Private

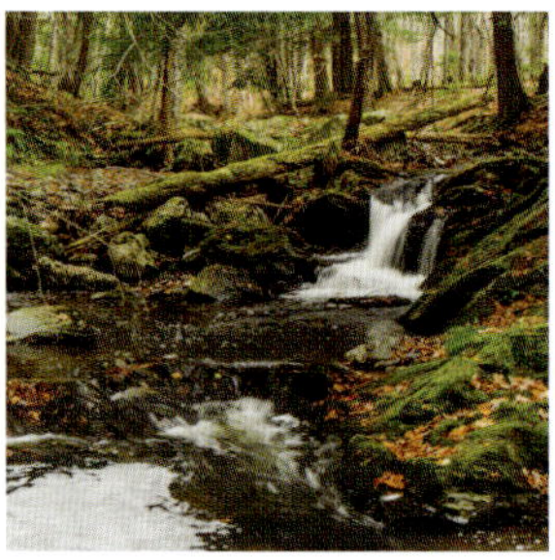

Must See:	4	GPS:	N46 40.534 W88 25.942
Height:	4 feet		
Time:	15-30 minutes	**Hiking Information**	
		Path:	None
Driving Information		Length:	200 yards
Signs:	None	Elev. Change:	Slight
Road:	Gravel	GPS:	Required
Access:	Somewhat Difficult	Danger:	Moderate
4WD:	Helpful	WP Boots:	Helpful

Layered bedrock thrust up at a 45 degree angle dams the creek until a weak point lets the overflowing water pour down onto a flat stone to the creek bed 4 feet below. Large boulders up to 10 feet in length lie in the waterway above the falls.

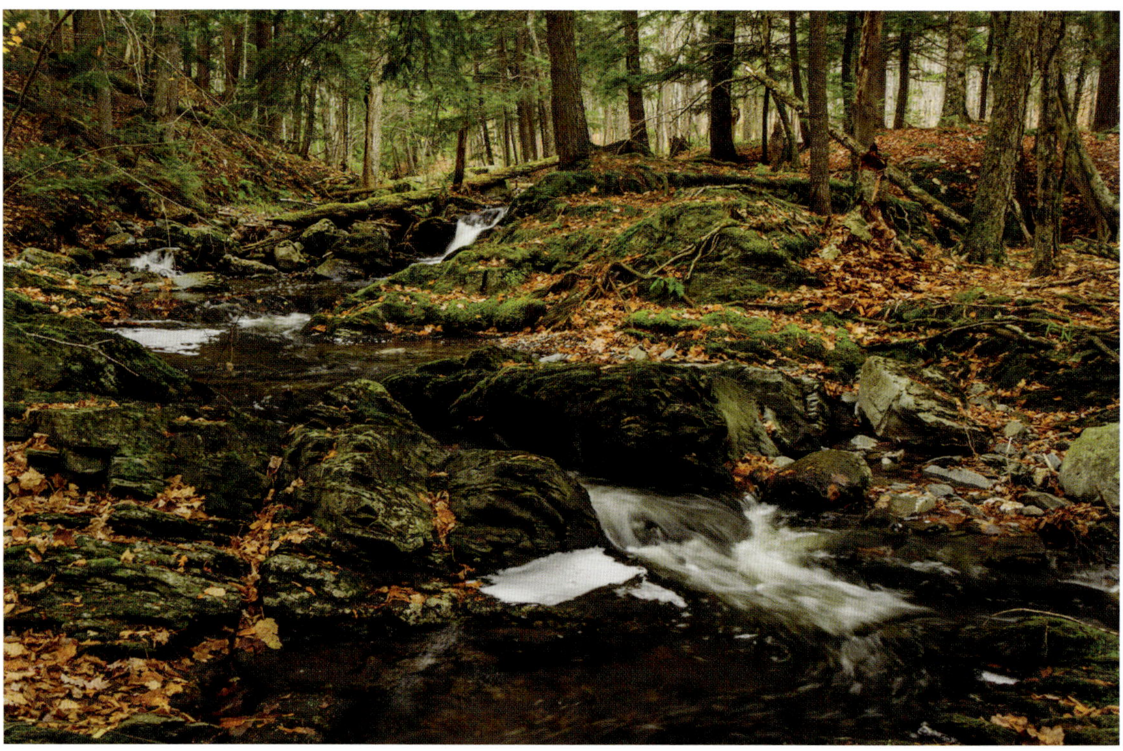

TAYLOR CREEK CANYON FALLS #2 (TAYLOR CREEK)

Private

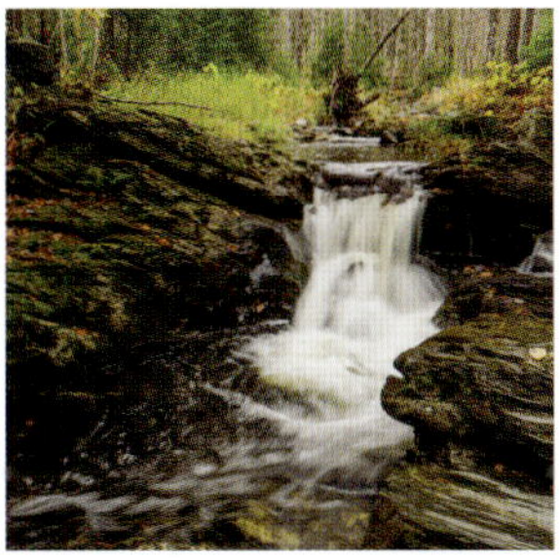

Must See:	4	GPS:	N46 40.648 W88 25.958
Height:	5 feet		
Time:	30-45 minutes	**Hiking Information**	
		Path:	None
Driving Information		Length:	.22 miles
Signs:	None	Elev. Change:	Moderate
Road:	Gravel	GPS:	Required
Access:	Somewhat Difficult	Danger:	Moderate
4WD:	Helpful	WP Boots:	Helpful

There's a big gap between #1 and #2. Hike about 230 yards downstream. Taylor Creek starts its descent into Taylor Creek Canyon with this 5 foot drop over slanted bedrock. This marks the beginning of the creek's tumultuous journey downward. Note the grassy flat area above the waterfall. How quickly the terrain can change in Michigan's rugged Upper Peninsula!

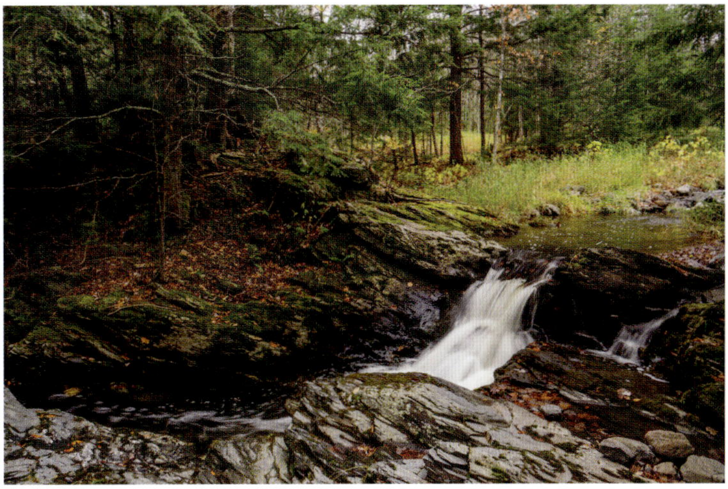

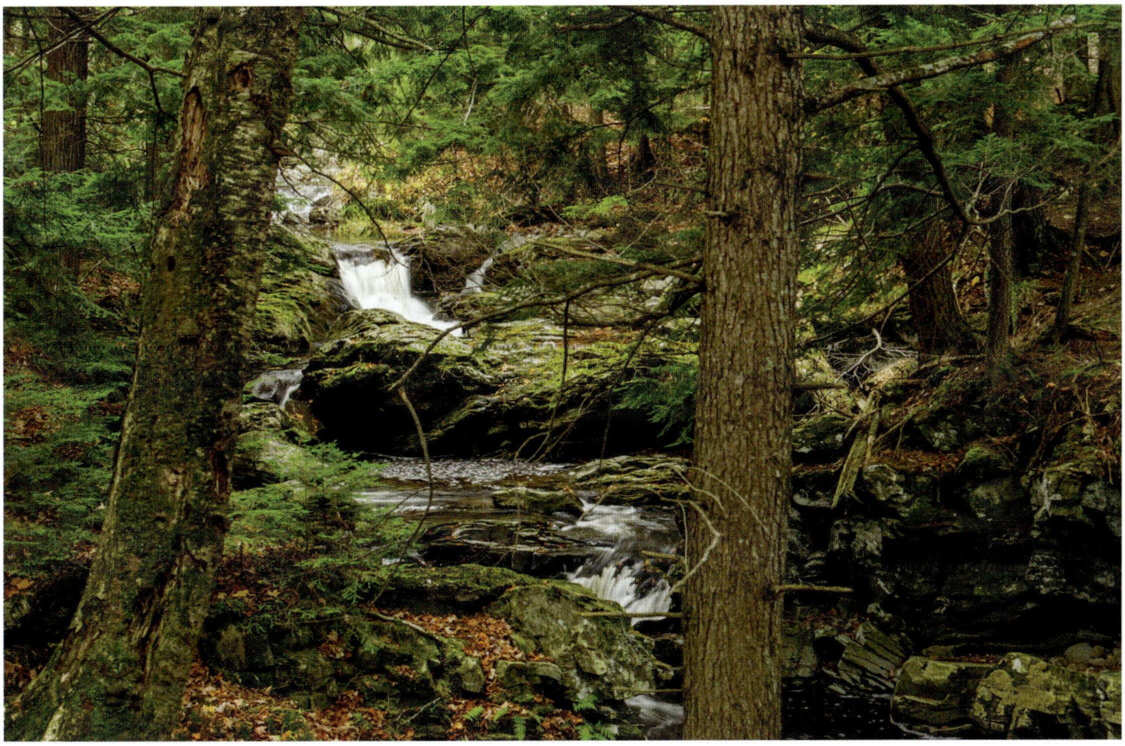

TAYLOR CREEK CANYON FALLS #3 (TAYLOR CREEK)

Private

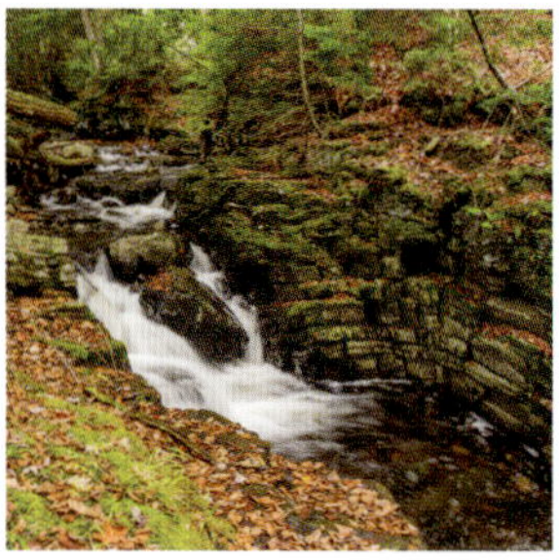

Must See:	4	GPS:	N46 40.676 W88 25.955
Height:	5 feet		
Time:	40-60 minutes	Hiking Information	
		Path:	None
Driving Information		Length:	.26 miles
Signs:	None	Elev. Change:	Moderate
Road:	Gravel	GPS:	Required
Access:	Somewhat Difficult	Danger:	Moderate
4WD:	Helpful	WP Boots:	Helpful

Follow the creek 170 feet downstream from #2 as Taylor Creek Canyon gets more serious with this 5 foot waterfall. The spill pool runs through the 8' wide beginning of the canyon. The creek upstream is filled with rocks and boulders.

There is no "official" trail to the creek, but there is a faint path that may be seen from time to time running along the top of the canyon and back to the parking area.

Kevin, my oldest son, was with me on this trip. He thought he was hiding behind a tree as I took this shot. He needs to find larger trees!

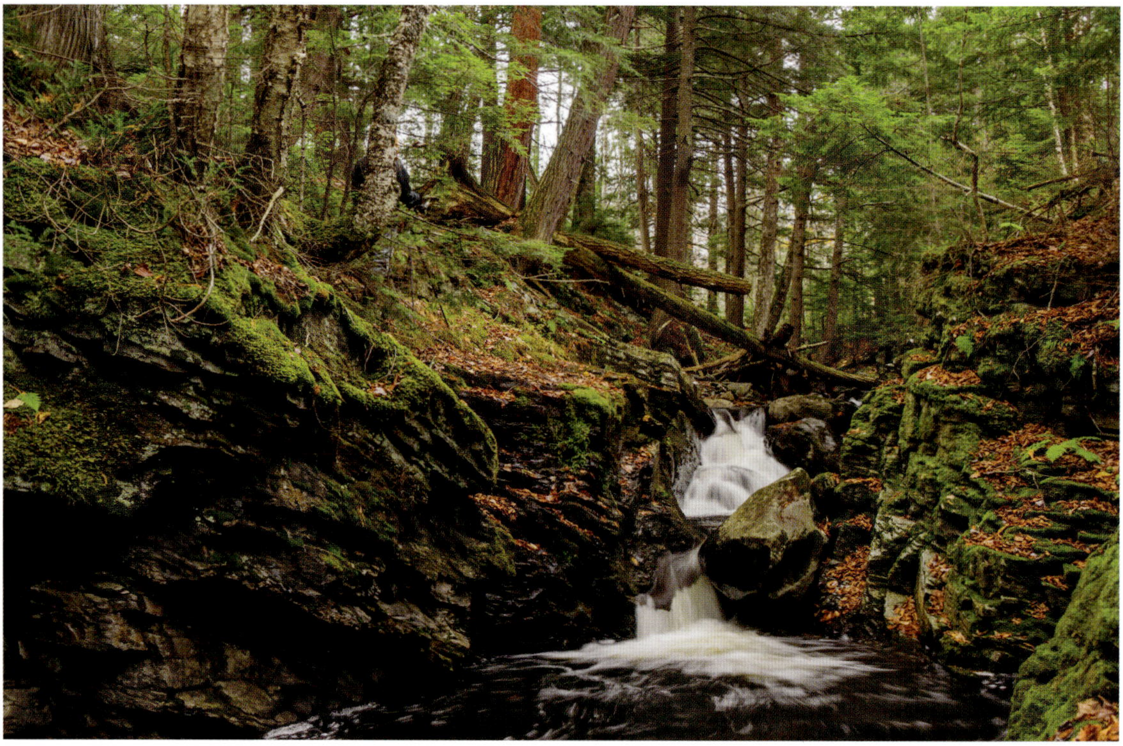

TAYLOR CREEK CANYON FALLS #4 (TAYLOR CREEK)

Private

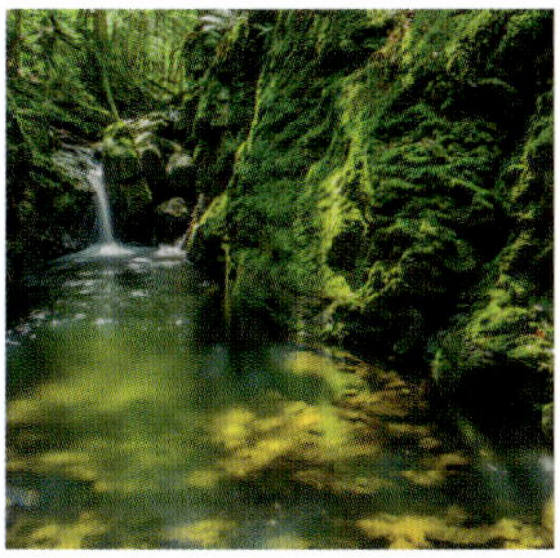

Must See:	4	GPS:	N46 40.700 W88 25.961
Height:	3 feet		
Time:	50-75 minutes	Hiking Information	
		Path:	None
Driving Information		Length:	.31 miles
Signs:	None	Elev. Change:	Moderate
Road:	Gravel	GPS:	Required
Access:	Somewhat Difficult	Danger:	Moderate
4WD:	Helpful	WP Boots:	Required

The canyon gets much taller after this waterfall. The walls are vertical and rise to nearly 20 feet. This section of the canyon is about 80' long and 20' wide. The canyon gets deeper and wider with each successive waterfall.

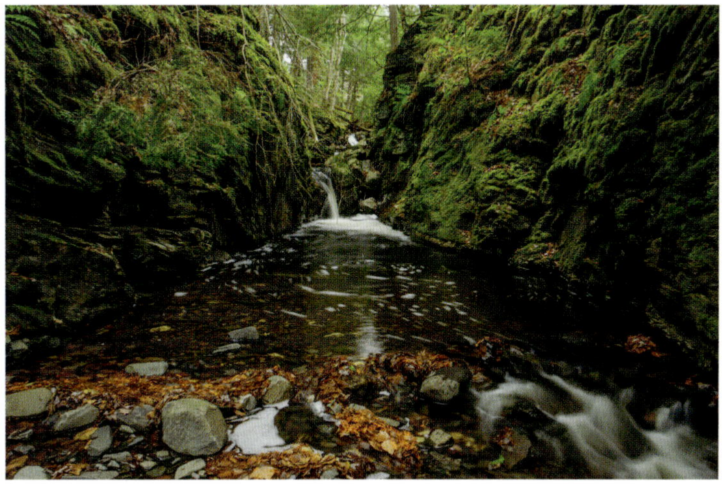

What a beautiful private viewing area for this waterfall! The peaceful creek rushes by, just feet from the cobble stones.

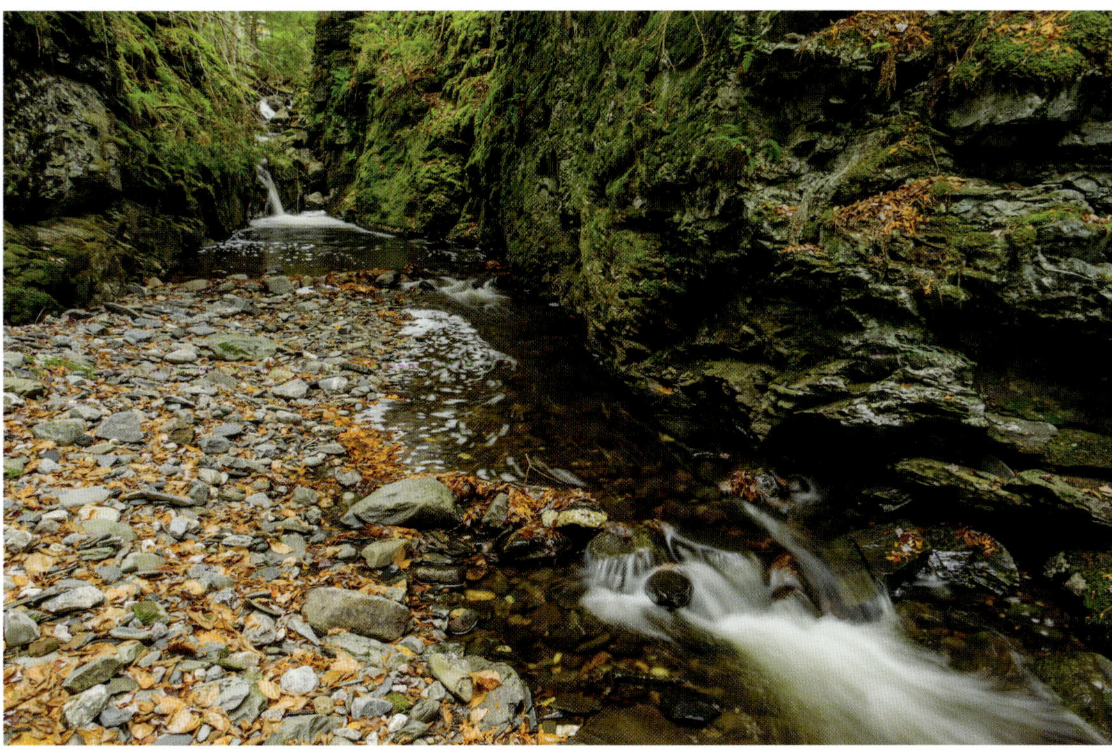

TAYLOR CREEK CANYON FALLS #5 (TAYLOR CREEK)

Private

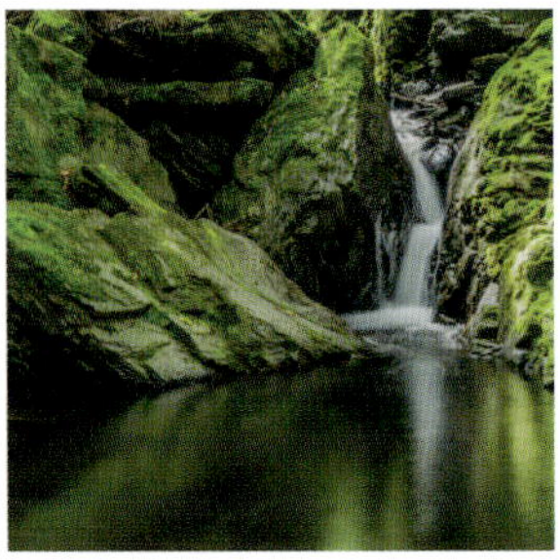

Must See:	5	GPS:	N46 40.708 W88 25.966
Height:	4 feet		
Time:	60-90 minutes	Hiking Information	
		Path:	None
Driving Information		Length:	.33 miles
Signs:	None	Elev. Change:	Moderate
Road:	Gravel	GPS:	Required
Access:	Somewhat Difficult	Danger:	Moderate
4WD:	Helpful	WP Boots:	Required

Slabs of rock fallen from the canyon walls partially block the creek. Narrowed to less than 1' wide, the creek drops along the flat edge of a moss covered boulder. Two more drops can be seen downstream from here! The #7 falls is similar in look, but larger.

Note the rugged, nearly vertical walls that keep access to the creek bed to a minimum.

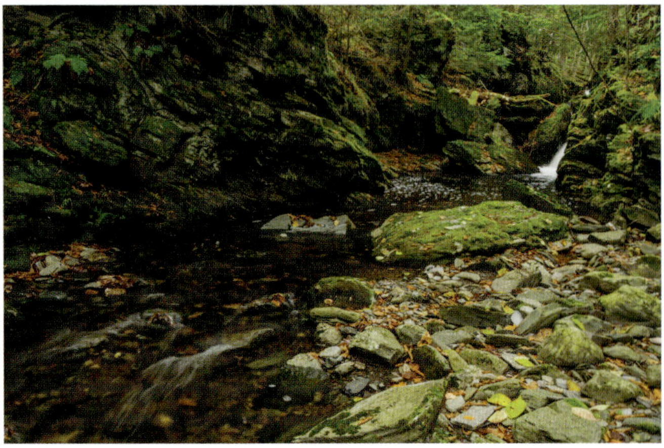

The steep walls and narrow width gives a sense of privacy and intimacy in this canyon.

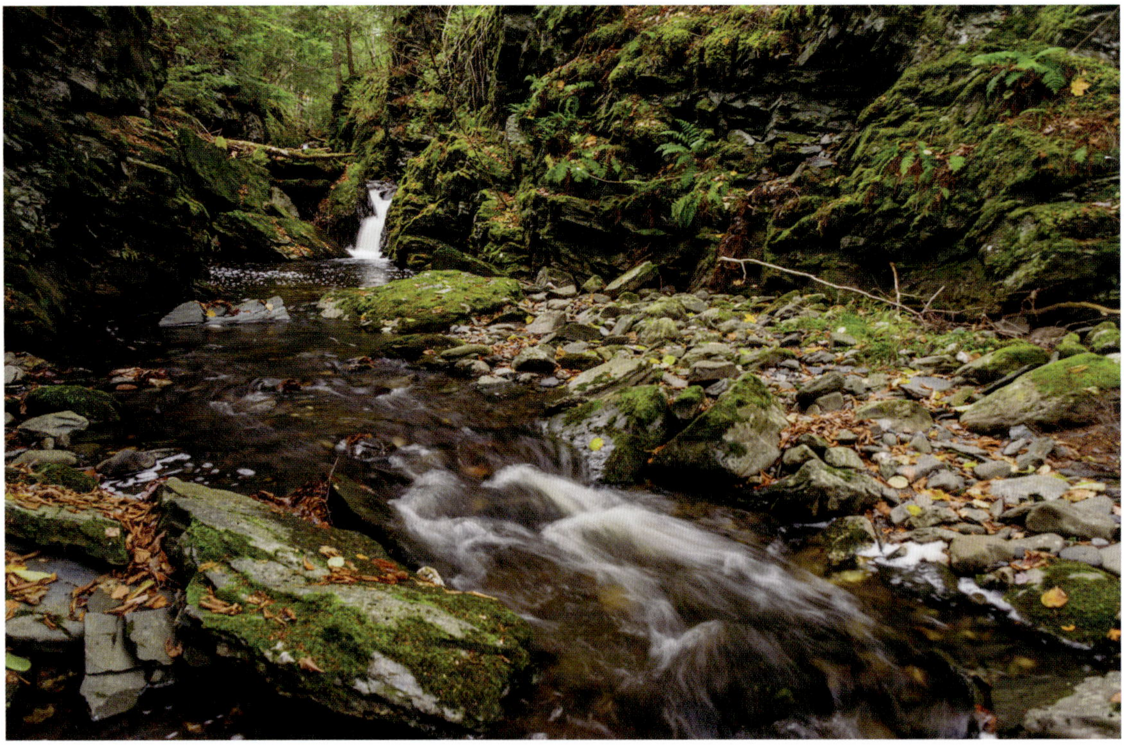

TAYLOR CREEK CANYON FALLS #6 (TAYLOR CREEK)

Private

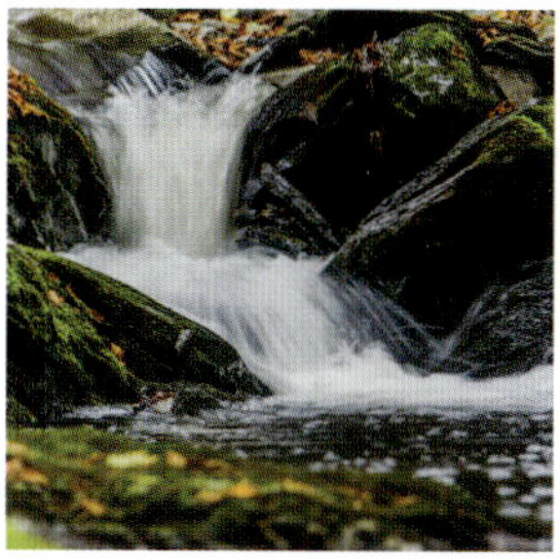

Must See:	4	GPS:	N46 40.733 W88 25.980
Height:	5 feet		
Time:	70-100 minutes	Hiking Information	
		Path:	None
Driving Information		Length:	.35 miles
Signs:	None	Elev. Change:	Moderate
Road:	Gravel	GPS:	Required
Access:	Somewhat Difficult	Danger:	Moderate
4WD:	Helpful	WP Boots:	Required

These are two small drops between the "main" canyon drops, #5 and #7. The first 3 foot drop cascades over several angled mossy boulders. The second, a 2 foot drop, pours over a flattened slab overhanging softer underlying rock. The water rushes in several angles down to the frothing narrow channel below.

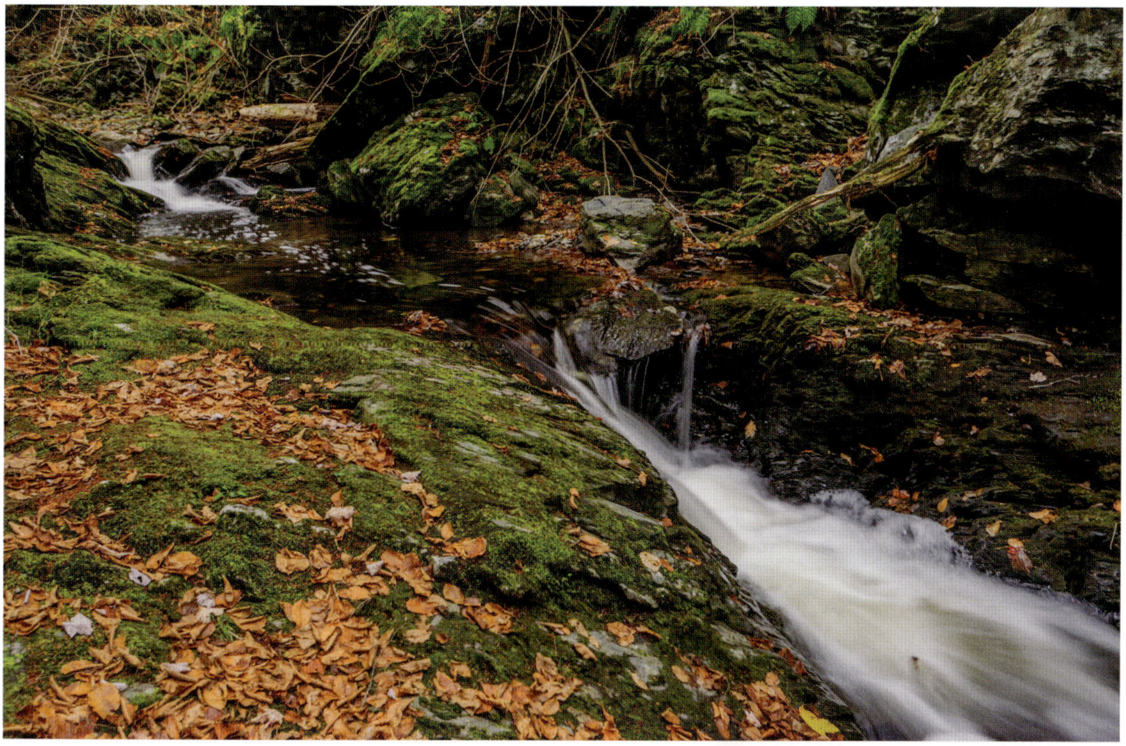

TAYLOR CREEK CANYON FALLS #7 (TAYLOR CREEK)

Private

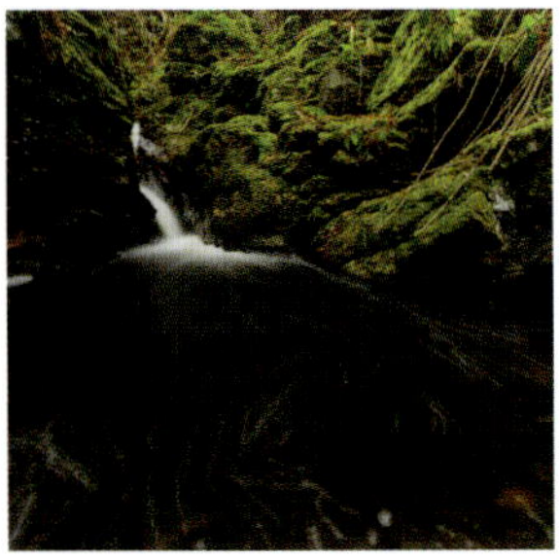

Must See:	7	GPS:	N46 40.757 W88 25.990
Height:	9 feet		
Time:	80-110 minutes	Hiking Information	
		Path:	None
Driving Information		Length:	.39 miles
Signs:	None	Elev. Change:	Moderate
Road:	Gravel	GPS:	Required
Access:	Somewhat Difficult	Danger:	Moderate
4WD:	Helpful	WP Boots:	Required

As the canyon narrows, so does the riverbed until it becomes a 1' wide cleft between the rocky walls. The creek then churns down to a quiet pool below the falls. Ferns and moss cling to 25' tall canyon walls overlooking the rock strewn creek.

To access the base of the falls, follow the top of the cliff until it descends to the creek's edge. Walk back up the creek, stepping from rock to rock into the canyon.

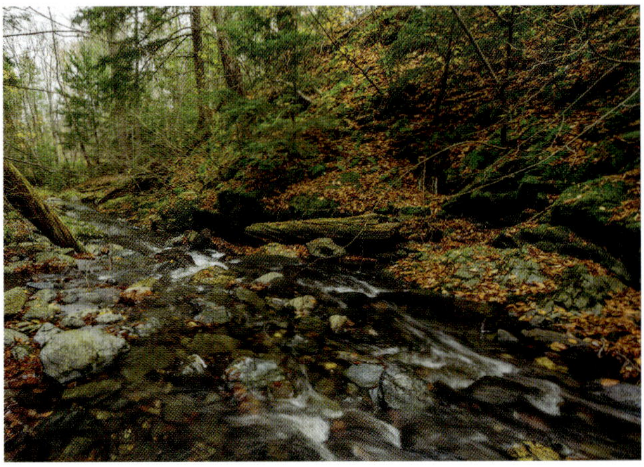

Look how quickly the canyon walls drop away below this, the last of the Taylor Creek Canyon Falls.

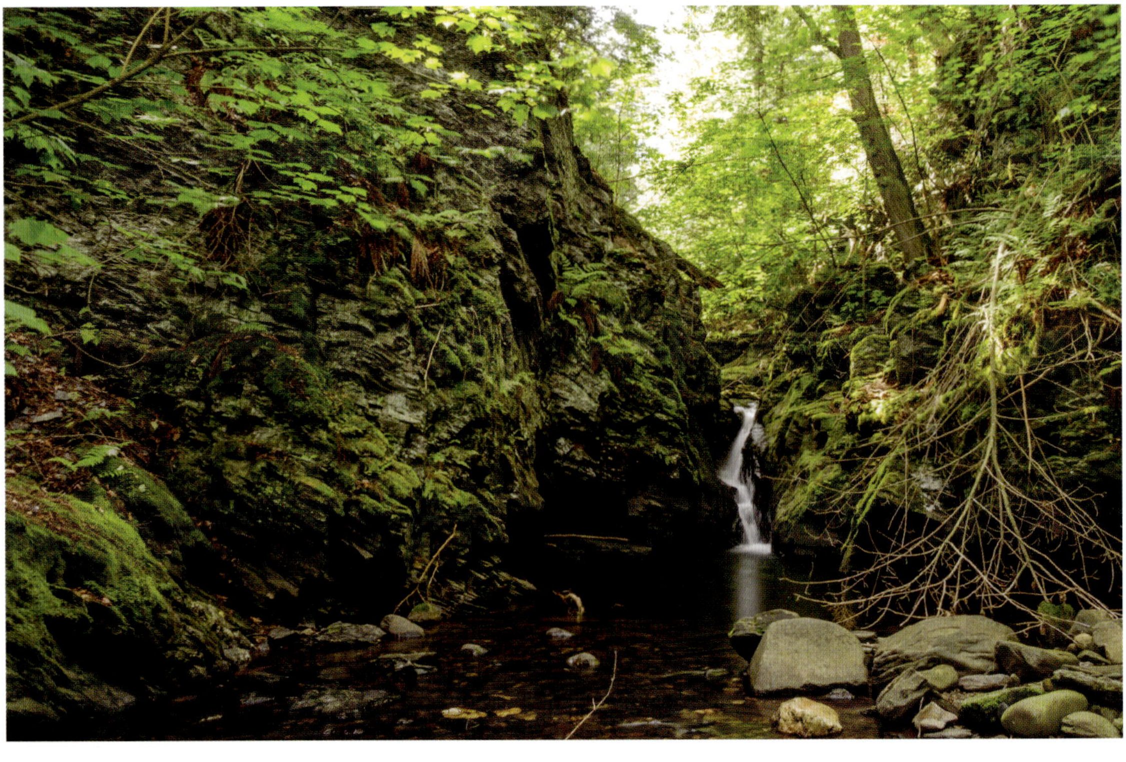

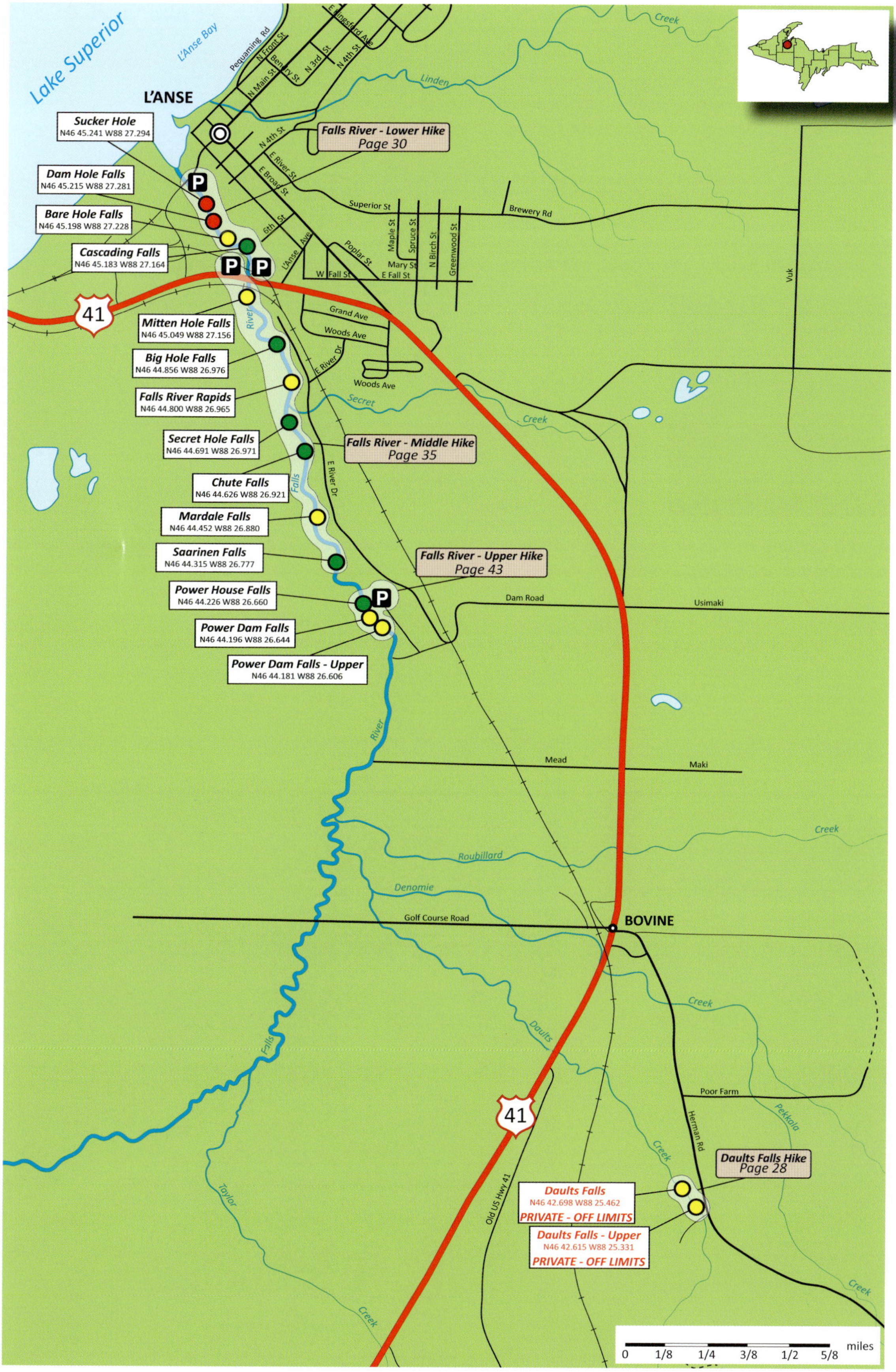
Lake Superior
L'Anse Bay
L'ANSE
Sucker Hole
N46 45.241 W88 27.294
Dam Hole Falls
N46 45.215 W88 27.281
Bare Hole Falls
N46 45.198 W88 27.228
Cascading Falls
N46 45.183 W88 27.164
Mitten Hole Falls
N46 45.049 W88 27.156
Big Hole Falls
N46 44.856 W88 26.976
Falls River Rapids
N46 44.800 W88 26.965
Secret Hole Falls
N46 44.691 W88 26.971
Chute Falls
N46 44.626 W88 26.921
Mardale Falls
N46 44.452 W88 26.880
Saarinen Falls
N46 44.315 W88 26.777
Power House Falls
N46 44.226 W88 26.660
Power Dam Falls
N46 44.196 W88 26.644
Power Dam Falls - Upper
N46 44.181 W88 26.606
Falls River - Lower Hike
Page 30
Falls River - Middle Hike
Page 35
Falls River - Upper Hike
Page 43
Daults Falls Hike
Page 28
Daults Falls
N46 42.698 W88 25.462
PRIVATE - OFF LIMITS
Daults Falls - Upper
N46 42.615 W88 25.331
PRIVATE - OFF LIMITS
41
Superior St
Brewery Rd
Dam Road
Usimaki
Mead
Maki
Golf Course Road
BOVINE
Poor Farm
Herman Rd
Old US Hwy 41
Vuk
Grand Ave
Woods Ave
E River Dr
Linden
Secret
Roubillard
Denomie
Daults
Pekkala
Taylor
Creek
Falls
River
0 1/8 1/4 3/8 1/2 5/8 miles

Daults Falls Hike

Daults Falls: The owner has made this waterfall off limits to the public. Permission must first be obtained. Be respectful of private property. The waterfall is close to the road, but there is no trail. Trees overhang the creek, creating a sense of mystery and discovery upon seeing the tumbling water for the first time.

Directions: Since Daults Falls is not accessible, no directions are given.

DAULTS FALLS (DAULTS CREEK)

Private

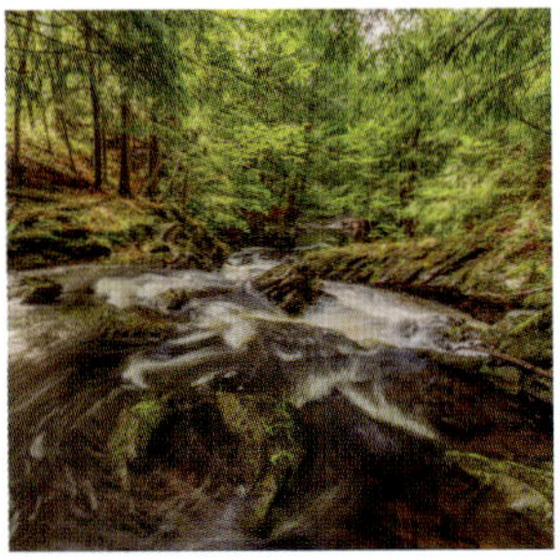

Must See:	6	GPS:	N46 42.698 W88 25.462
Height:	9 feet		
Time:	10-20 minutes	**Hiking Information**	
		Path:	None
Driving Information		Length:	200 yards
Signs:	None	Elev. Change:	Slight
Road:	Secondary Road	GPS:	Required
Access:	Somewhat Easy	Danger:	Slight
4WD:	N/A	WP Boots:	Helpful

A split cascade rushes down 6 feet, narrows as it runs around a mass of rock that protrudes into the river, then drops a final 3 feet.

Daults Falls is on private property. The owner has had trouble with people leaving trash around the waterfall in the past, so it is now off limits to the public. Do not go here without permission.

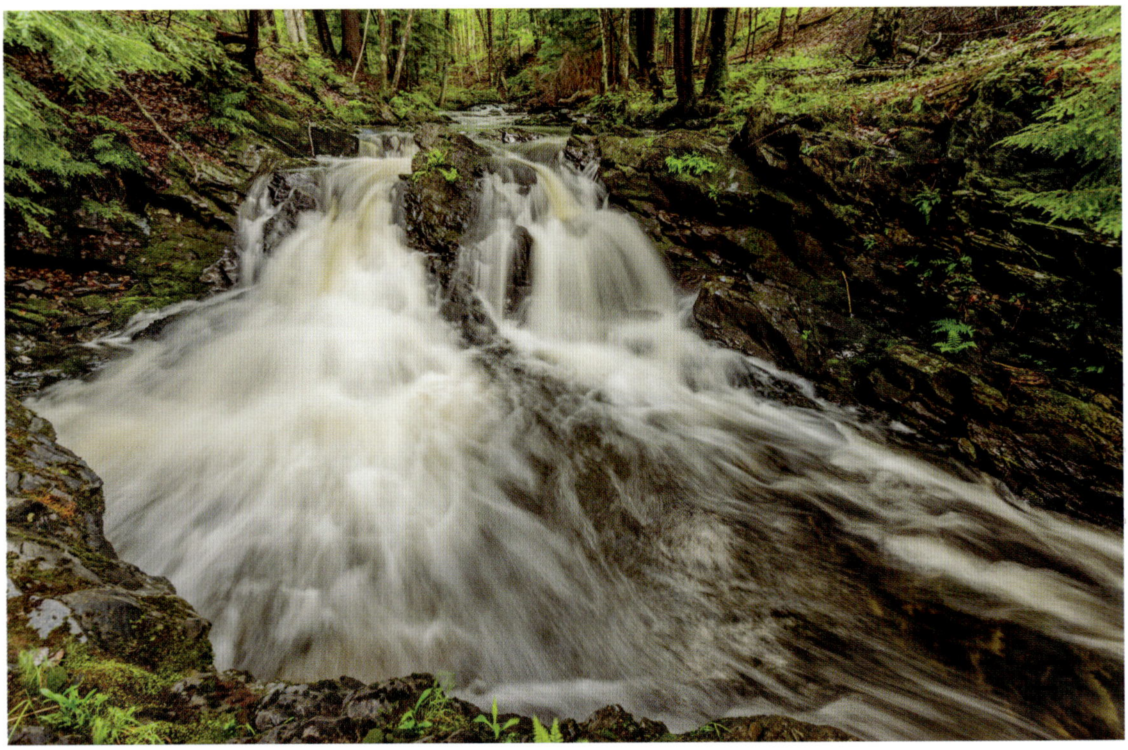

DAULTS FALLS - UPPER (DAULTS CREEK)

Private

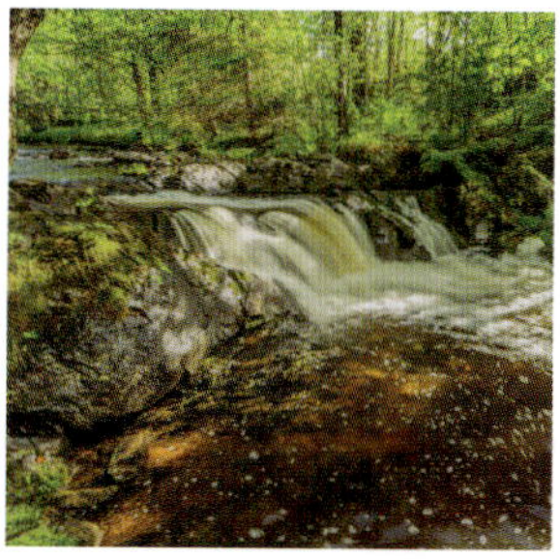

Must See:	5	GPS:	N46 42.615 W88 25.331
Height:	4 feet		
Time:	10-20 minutes		

Driving Information		Hiking Information	
		Path:	None
Signs:	None	Length:	50 yards
Road:	Secondary Road	Elev. Change:	Slight
Access:	Somewhat Easy	GPS:	Required
4WD:	N/A	Danger:	Slight
		WP Boots:	Helpful

Silver River and Daults Creek drain the western slope of Mount Curwood. Silver River heads more northerly, while Daults Creek cuts to the west before emptying into the Falls River.

The Upper waterfall is about .15 miles upstream from Daults Falls. The 3 foot angled drop pours into a spill pool. Below the pool, the creek widens out, splits, and drops another foot.

Daults Falls - Upper is on private property. The owner has had trouble with people leaving trash around the waterfall in the past, so it is now off limits to the public. Do not go here without permission.

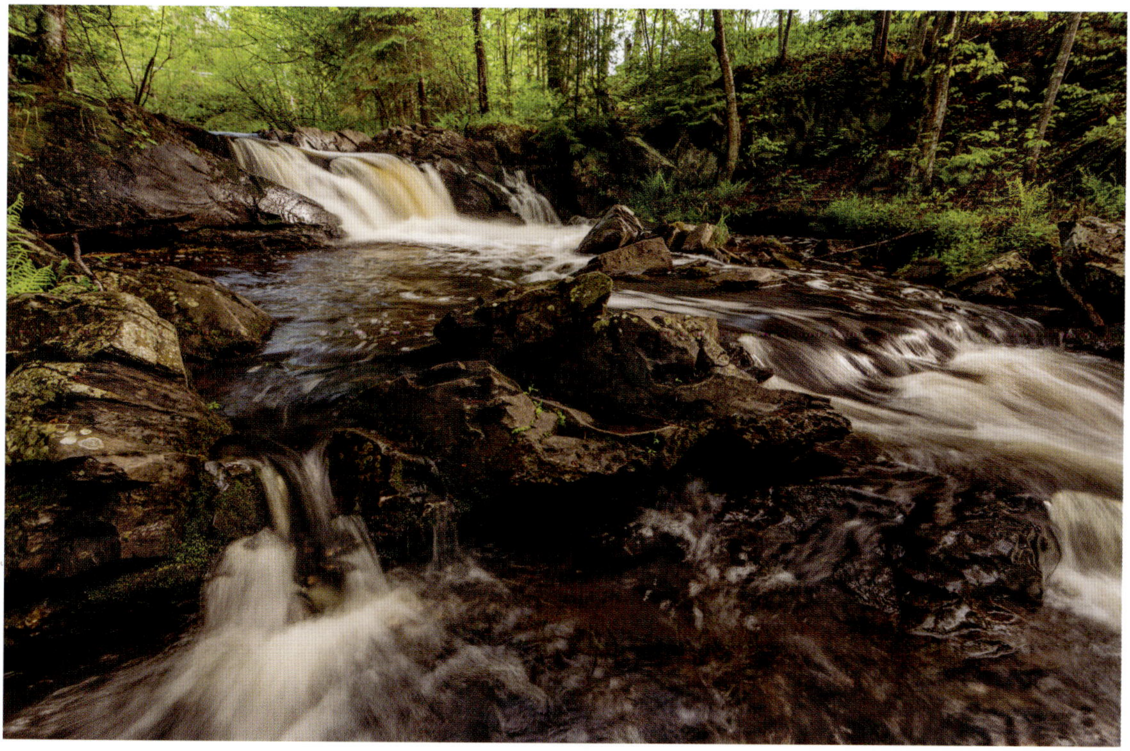

Falls River - Lower Hike

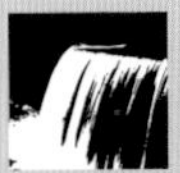

The lower falls on the Falls River are the batch of falls north of US-41. These are the easiest to access on the Falls River, and Bare Hole Falls as well as Cascading Falls are very nice to view! The waterfalls on the Falls River are a local attraction for the youth of the area since they are so close to the village. It is also not uncommon to see fishermen along the banks of the river.

Cascading Falls: A stretch of cascades begins just down river from the train trestle. I prefer to view this waterfall from higher up the hillside, rather than from the river's edge as usual.

Bare Hole Falls: Bare Hole Falls is a complicated "slide waterfall" with cascades falling off of either side of the slide. It lies at the bottom of a steep ravine.

Dam Hole Falls: A small waterfall tumbles from the ruins of an old dam that stretched across the river in years gone by. The river flows through flat terrain down to Lake Superior after it leaves the ravine where Cascading Falls and Bare Hole Falls are located.

Sucker Hole Falls: I have been told that Suckers are stopped at this first tiny waterfall as they attempt to travel upstream from Lake Superior.

Directions: This stretch of river can be reached by several different routes.
1) US-41 crosses the Falls River just west of the Burger King. Park on the east side of the bridge. There is ample room to pull off of the busy highway. Walk north along the river (downstream) following the blue blazed footpath. (This is my favorite parking spot and hiking information is based on this option.)
2) Drive to the center of the L'Anse by taking E. Broad Street from US-41 (you will drive under the "Welcome" sign. Turn left at the light (N. Main Street). Just before crossing the Falls River, the road deteriorates into what seems more like a glorified parking lot. A factory is on the left. Drive over that direction. There will be places to park along the river. Walk south (upstream) along the river to view the waterfalls. This route will take you along the east side of the river. The falls are best viewed from this side.
3) There is a snowmobile trail that winds along the eastern top of the ravine overlooking the Falls River. On the side of this trail there is an iron bench set in the ideal place for viewing Cascading Falls. This is a very scenic location for those not able to traverse hillsides. (This is the route required to allow for wheelchair access.)

Note: Restrooms are available at nearby establishments.

CASCADING FALLS (FALLS RIVER)

Private

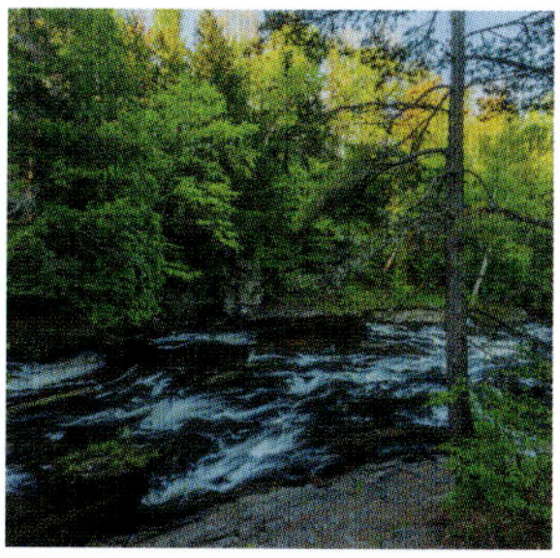

Must See:	7
Height:	20 feet
Time:	10-20 minutes

Driving Information

Signs:	Sign on US-41
Road:	Highway
Access:	Very Easy
4WD:	N/A

GPS: N46 45.183 W88 27.164

Hiking Information

Path:	Footpath
Length:	.13 miles
Elev. Change:	Moderate
GPS:	N/A
Danger:	Moderate
WP Boots:	N/A

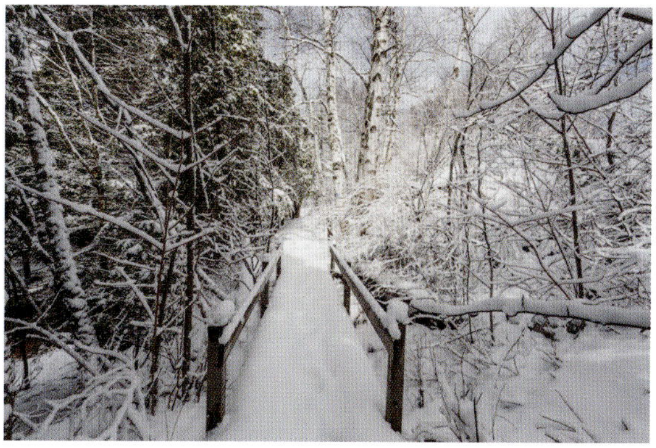

AKA "Lower Falls", Cascading Falls is best viewed from the east side of the river. The western side is more rugged, less accessible, and since the river turns sharply to the west at the base of the waterfall, it is difficult to view the waterfall from that side.

The river widens out after it passes beneath the train trestle and begins its descent down the many cascades that stretch out over nearly 100 yards. The rocky island in the middle of the river is topped when the river is running strong.

From the rough dirt road that runs nearby it is possible to maneuver a wheelchair to the overlook.

** Hiking information is based on parking along US-41*

This is the view from the bench that sits atop the high bank on the eastern side of the river.

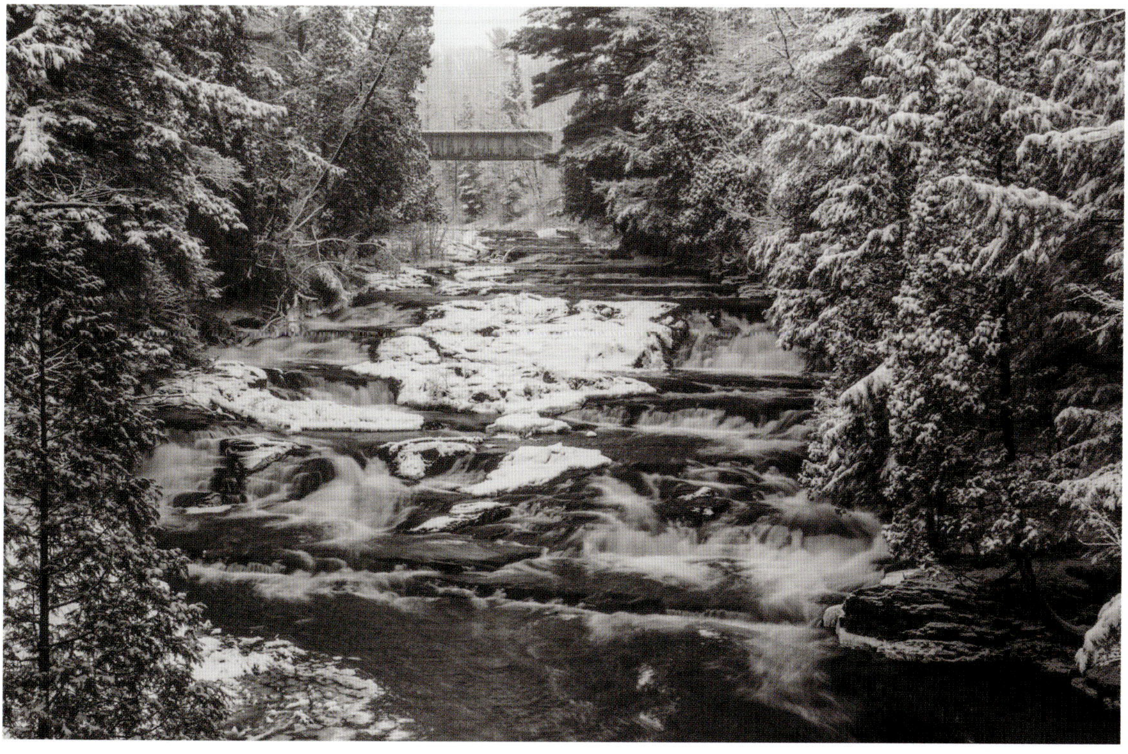

BARE HOLE FALLS (FALLS RIVER)

Private

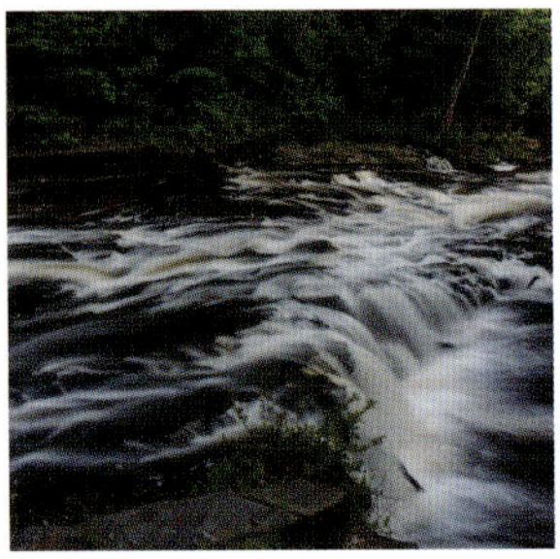

Must See:	6
Height:	15 feet
Time:	20-40 minutes

Driving Information

Signs:	Sign on US-41
Road:	Highway
Access:	Very Easy
4WD:	N/A

GPS:	N46 45.198 W88 27.228

Hiking Information

Path:	Unimproved Footpath
Length:	250 yards
Elev. Change:	Moderate
GPS:	N/A
Danger:	Moderate
WP Boots:	N/A

The river narrows and turns hard to the west below Cascading Falls. It then widens out again while rushing over Bare Hole Falls. This waterfall is a multi-faceted drop, with a plunge on the northern side and a slower, cascading side to the south.

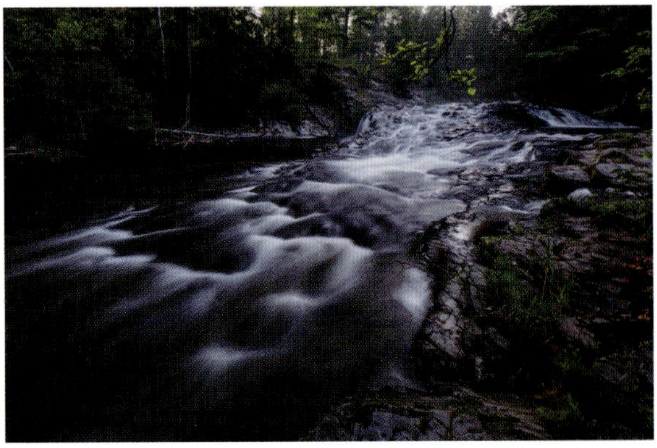

I was informed that young people in the '40s and '50s would skinny dip here, hence the name!

** Hiking information is based on parking along US-41*

The plunge on the northern side of the waterfall can be seen peeking through this gap in the trees .

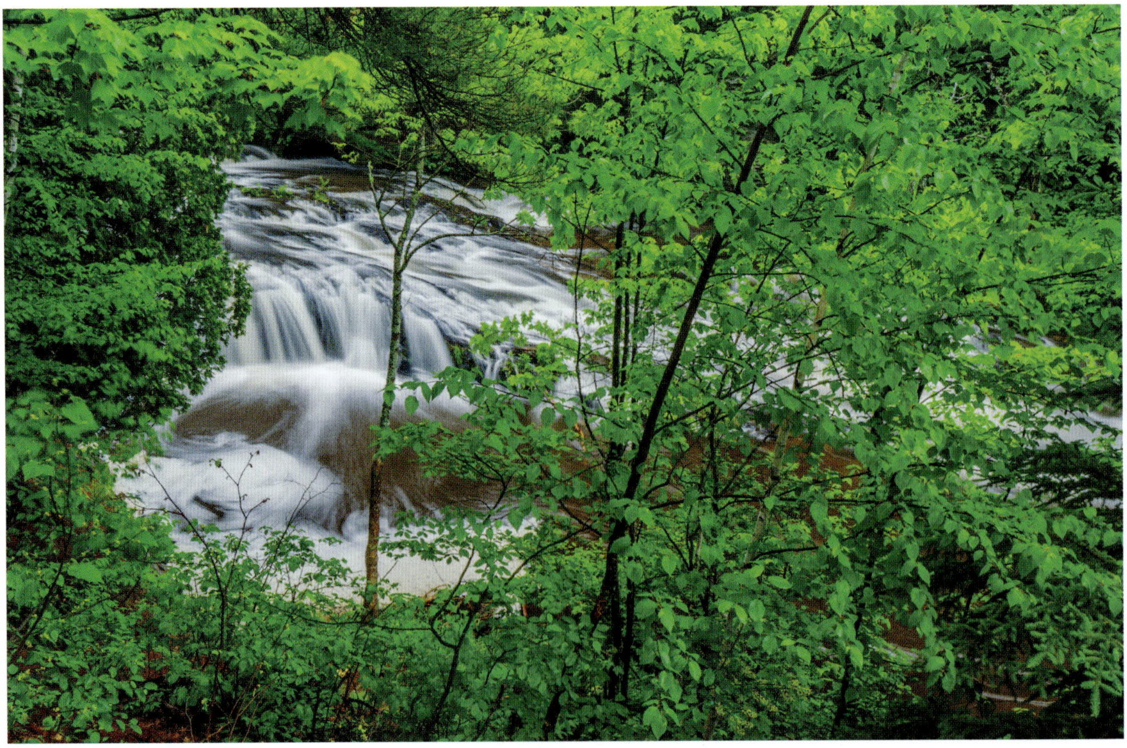

DAM HOLE FALLS (FALLS RIVER)

Private

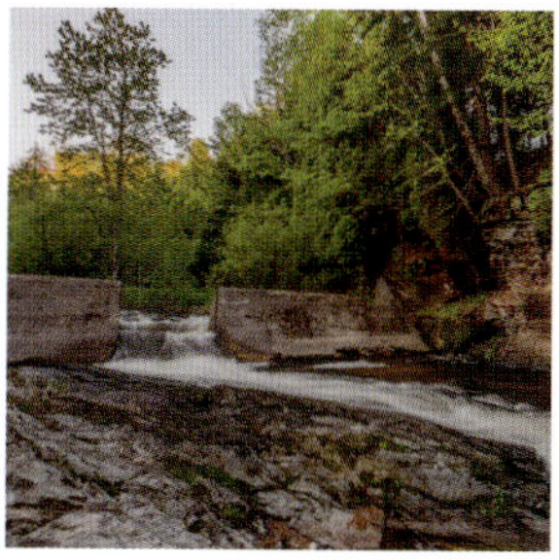

Must See:	2
Height:	2 feet
Time:	30-45 minutes

Driving Information

Signs:	Sign on US-41
Road:	Highway
Access:	Very Easy
4WD:	N/A

GPS:	N46 45.215 W88 27.281

Hiking Information

Path:	Unimproved Footpath
Length:	.23 miles
Elev. Change:	Moderate
GPS:	N/A
Danger:	Moderate
WP Boots:	N/A

Dam Hole Falls is only about 50 yards further upstream from Sucker Hole. This waterfall is just a little drop in the river at the point where a dam once was. Concrete remnants are still on either side of the river as a reminder of days gone by when waterways played a more critical role in the harnessing of energy.

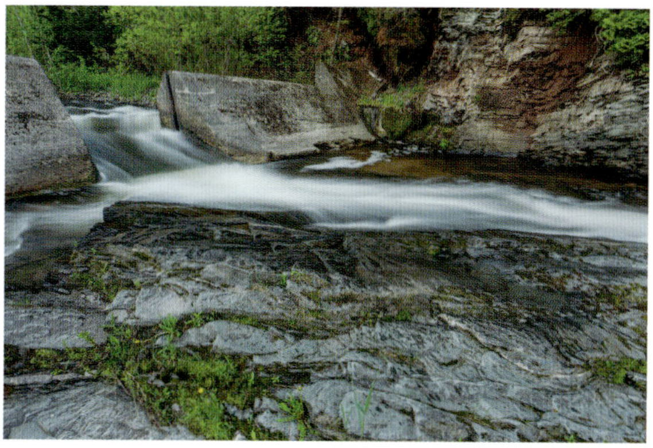

** To keep things simple, I have included Dam Hole Falls and Sucker Hole in the "Lower Hike". If you just want to see these drops, you may want to follow the driving directions #2 from several pages back.*

** Hiking information is based on parking along US-41.*

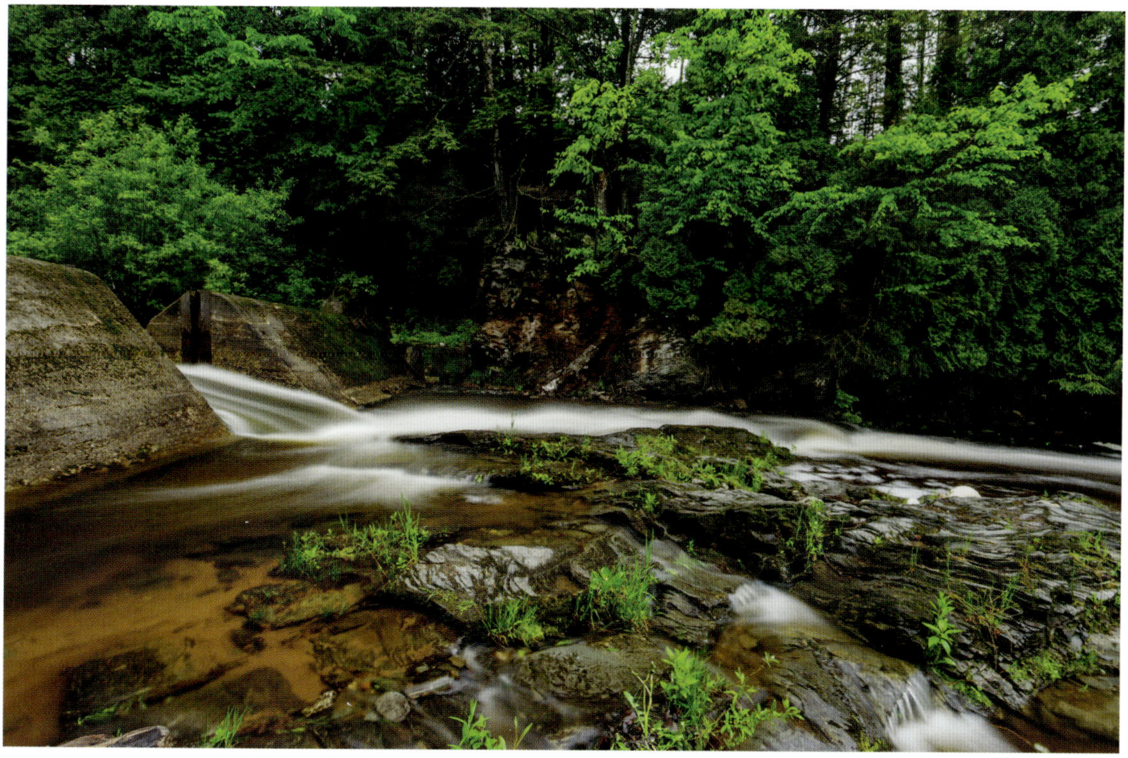

SUCKER HOLE (FALLS RIVER)

Private

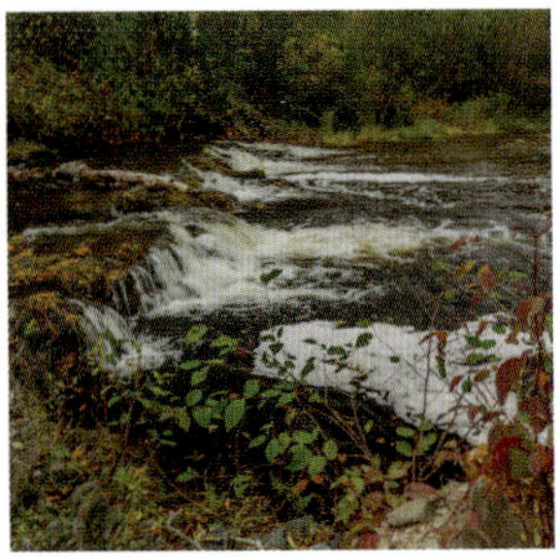

Must See:	3
Height:	2 feet
Time:	40-60 minutes

Driving Information

Signs:	Sign on US-41
Road:	Highway
Access:	Very Easy
4WD:	N/A

GPS:	N46 45.241 W88 27.294

Hiking Information

Path:	Unimproved Footpath
Length:	.26 miles
Elev. Change:	Moderate
GPS:	N/A
Danger:	Moderate
WP Boots:	N/A

It's not much of a drop, but it's enough to keep suckers from getting further upstream. They tend to congregate in the waters here in their attempt to head upstream to spawn.

The left side of Sucker Hole ends with a traditional sheer drop of about 2 feet, while the right side of the river tapers down in a tumbling rapids to calm waters.

** To keep things simple, I have included Dam Hole Falls and Sucker Hole in the "Lower Hike". If you just want to see these drops, you may want to follow the driving directions #2 from several pages back.*

** Hiking information is based on parking along US-41*

This is the view from the snowmobile bridge just downstream from the small drop.

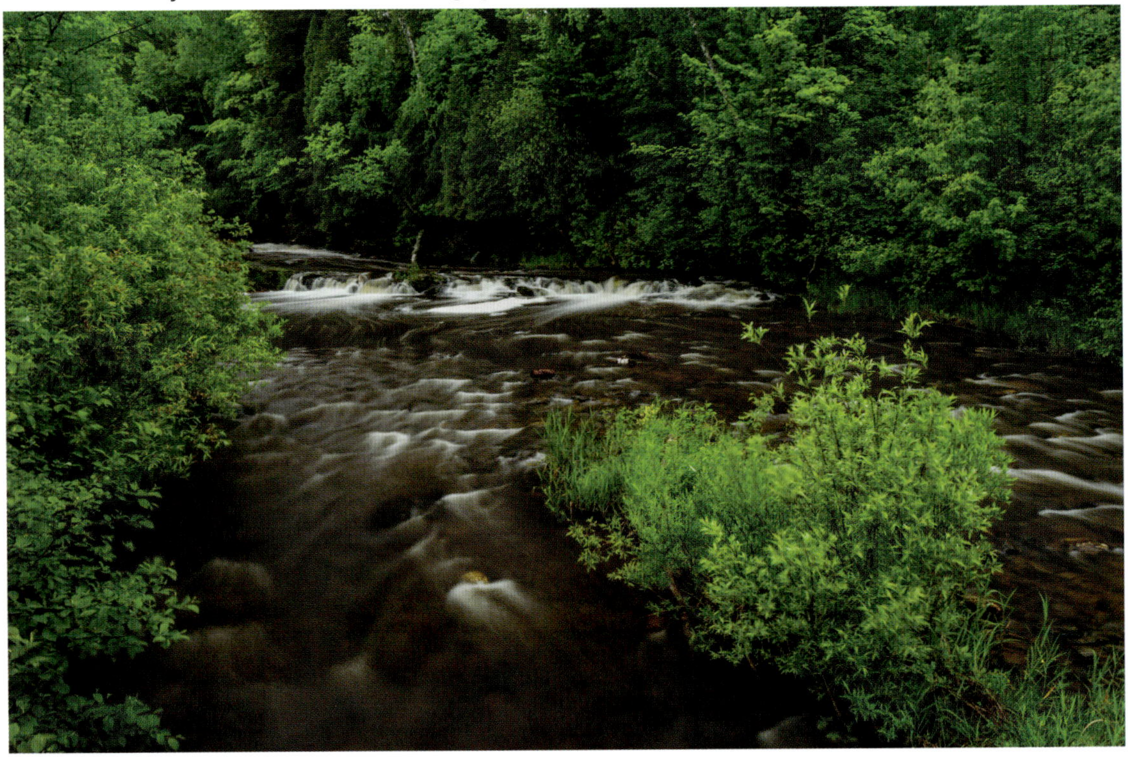

Falls River - Middle Hike

This hike includes the waterfalls south of US-41 and north of Power House Falls. These are all fairly closely spaced together. There are private residences along this stretch of river. Be respectful of the owners. These are beautiful waterfalls to be enjoyed, but please be kind, quiet, and clean. And always obey all "No Trespassing" signs.

Mitten Hole Falls: A glimpse of the waterfall can be had while driving over the Falls River on US-41. After crossing the road and railroad trestle, it is a little climb down to the edge of the river. The falls span the river with a ledge fall of about 4' that is randomly broken up by taller segments of rock.

Big Hole Falls: This large, cascading waterfall is tapered from an 18' drop on the right to about a third of that on the left. A nice fishing hole exists below the falls.

Falls River Rapids: Several exaggerated stretches of rapids make up this drop. There is no one distinguishing drop in this section of rapids.

Secret Hole Falls: Beautiful waterfall! The wonderful cascading drops are perfectly segmented, as though it were engineered by a master waterfall designer!

Chute Falls: Large rock masses on either side of the waterfall constrict the width of the river to about 5' and send the river shooting through the resulting gap.

Mardale Falls: Numerous cascades, more aggressive than the Middle Rapids, are in a beautiful stretch of river.

Saarinen Falls: The river makes a bend and starts cascading down, ending in a final, wide cascade above a small, sandy island.

Directions: Park along the side of US-41 on the western side of the bridge over the Falls River. (This is the same general parking area described in one of the Lower Falls Hikes.) Carefully cross US-41 and the railroad trestle on foot. (The road is normally quite busy.) Walk along the edge of the river. Take care to be considerate as there are houses along the river. Always respect private property. The hike is about 1.1 miles from US-41 to Saarinen Falls.

In the springtime the river flows with so much water that kayakers will put in at Power House Falls and chute the waterfalls all the way to Lake Superior!

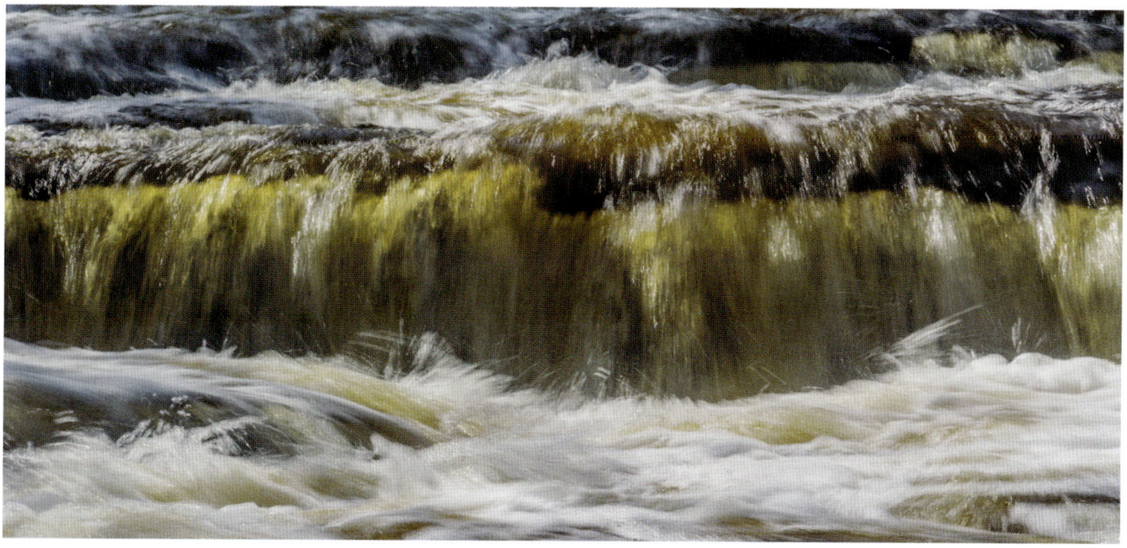

MITTEN HOLE FALLS (FALLS RIVER)

Private

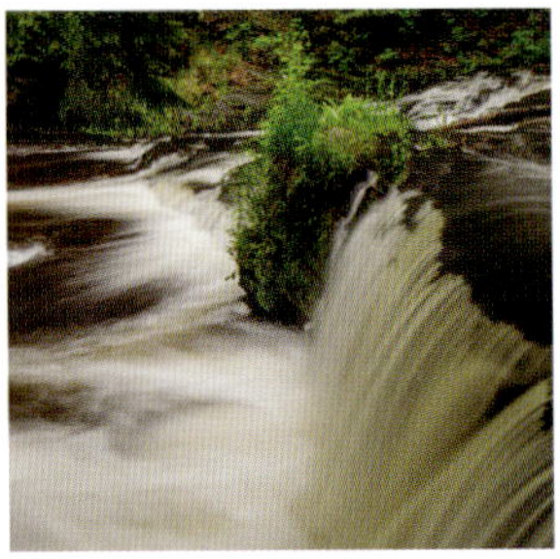

Must See: 6
Height: 6 feet
Time: 10-20 minutes

Driving Information
Signs: None
Road: Main
Access: Very Easy
4WD: N/A

GPS: N46 45.049 W88 27.156

Hiking Information
Path: Unimproved Footpath
Length: 100 yards
Elev. Change: Moderate
GPS: N/A
Danger: Moderate
WP Boots: N/A

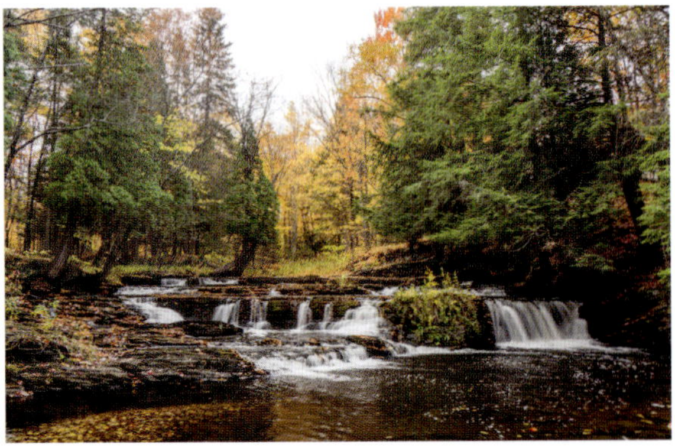

The riverbed is composed of slate, some of which is above water during most of the year. Mitten Hole Falls can be viewed nicely from several of these dry rocks. This is the first of the waterfalls listed in the Middle Falls Hike which starts just 100 yards uphill from here on the other side of US-41.

My youngest son, Luke, was 6 years old when I first took him to this waterfall. He wandered into a nest of yellow jackets while we were there. Neither he, nor I will forget this waterfall which we still refer to as "Yellow Jacket Falls". (I'm thankful to say that I've never encountered any other stinging insects during my hikes in the Upper Peninsula - obviously excluding mosquitoes and ticks which aren't technically stinging insects anyway!)

Note the water level difference between this winter shot and the fall scene above!

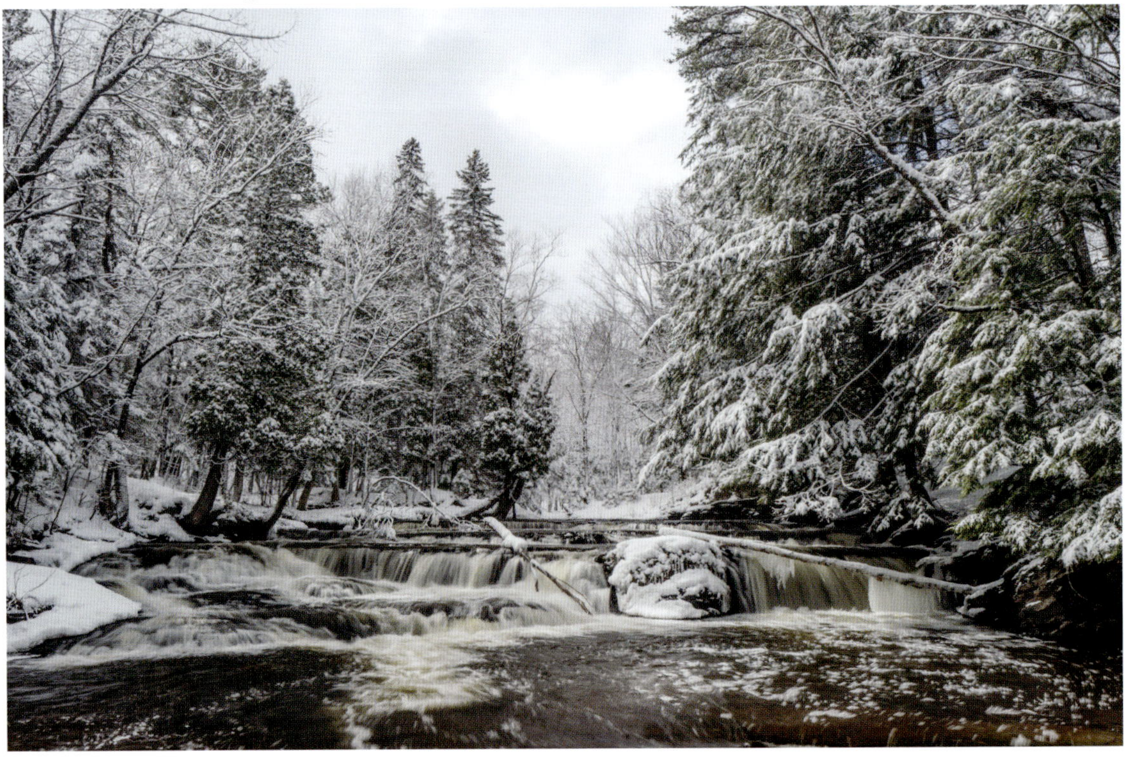

BIG HOLE FALLS (FALLS RIVER)

Private

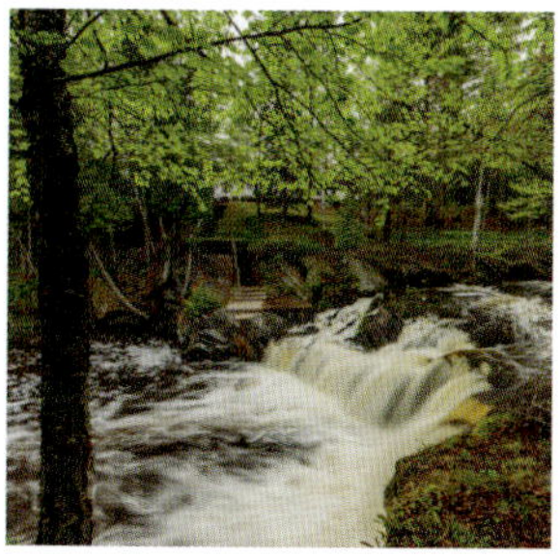

Must See: 7
Height: 18 feet
Time: 30-45 minutes

Driving Information
Signs: None
Road: Main
Access: Very Easy
4WD: N/A

GPS: N46 44.856 W88 26.976

Hiking Information
Path: Unimproved Footpath
Length: .36 miles
Elev. Change: Moderate
GPS: N/A
Danger: Moderate
WP Boots: N/A

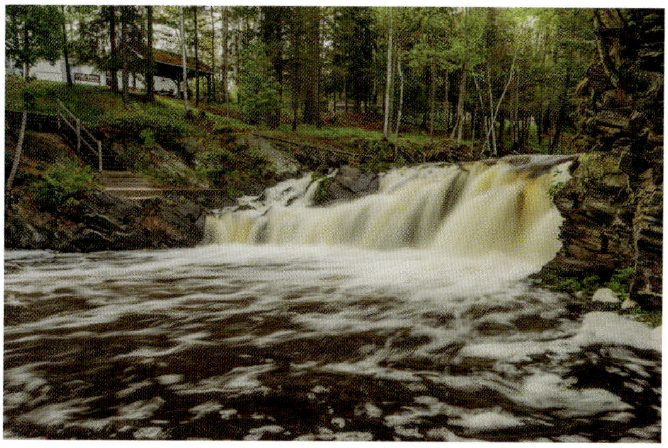

Angled bedrock is suddenly cut away into an increasingly deeper section of the river, fragmented layers of slate glistening black. Along the side of the waterfall the squared off ends are stacked up with tree supporting soil softening the crest of the unrelenting hard slate below.

A promontory stands tall in the center of the waterfall, its glistening black head rising above the white frothy rivulets most of the year. The river cascades down both sides, the left side also tapering away from the center, with that portion of the river running sideways before turning and spilling down the shorter side of the waterfall.

The river runs at one of its lowest levels that I've seen in this November picture.

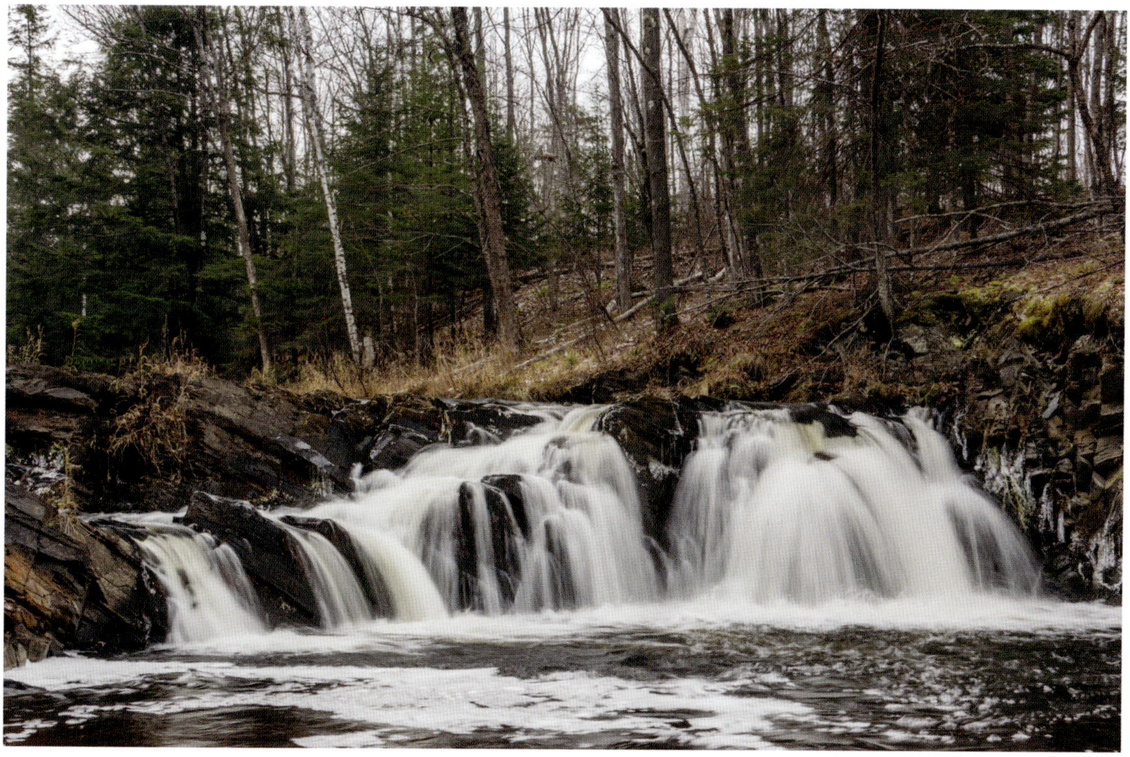

FALLS RIVER RAPIDS (FALLS RIVER)

Private

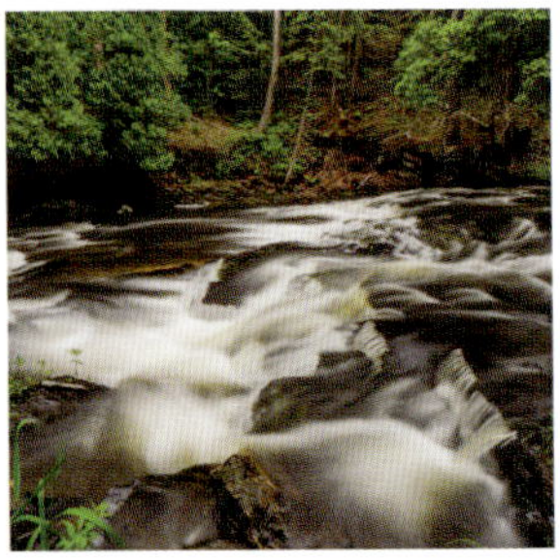

Must See:	5	GPS:	N46 44.800 W88 26.965
Height:	5 feet		
Time:	40-60 minutes		

Driving Information		Hiking Information	
		Path:	Unimproved Footpath
		Length:	.44 miles
Signs:	None	Elev. Change:	Moderate
Road:	Main	GPS:	N/A
Access:	Very Easy	Danger:	Moderate
4WD:	N/A	WP Boots:	N/A

This set of rapids gives you a chance to stop along the hike from Big Hole Falls to Secret Hole Falls and take a break to enjoy the many small cascades that course down the river. It's 125 yards upstream from Big Hole Falls and 230 yards downstream from Secret Hole Falls.

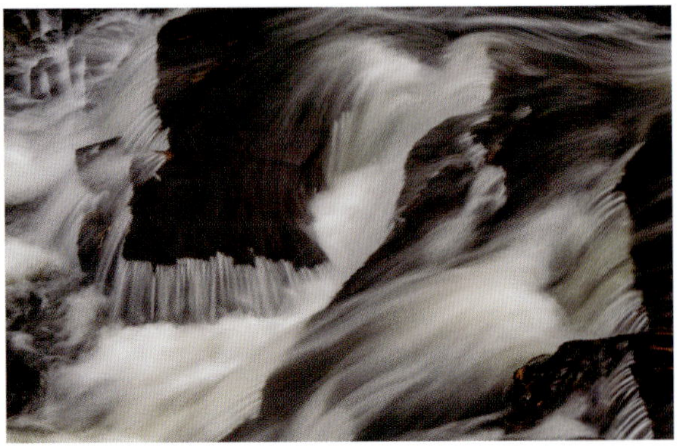

Much of the Falls River (in the waterfall area) runs through a gorge. The rapids here are an exception.

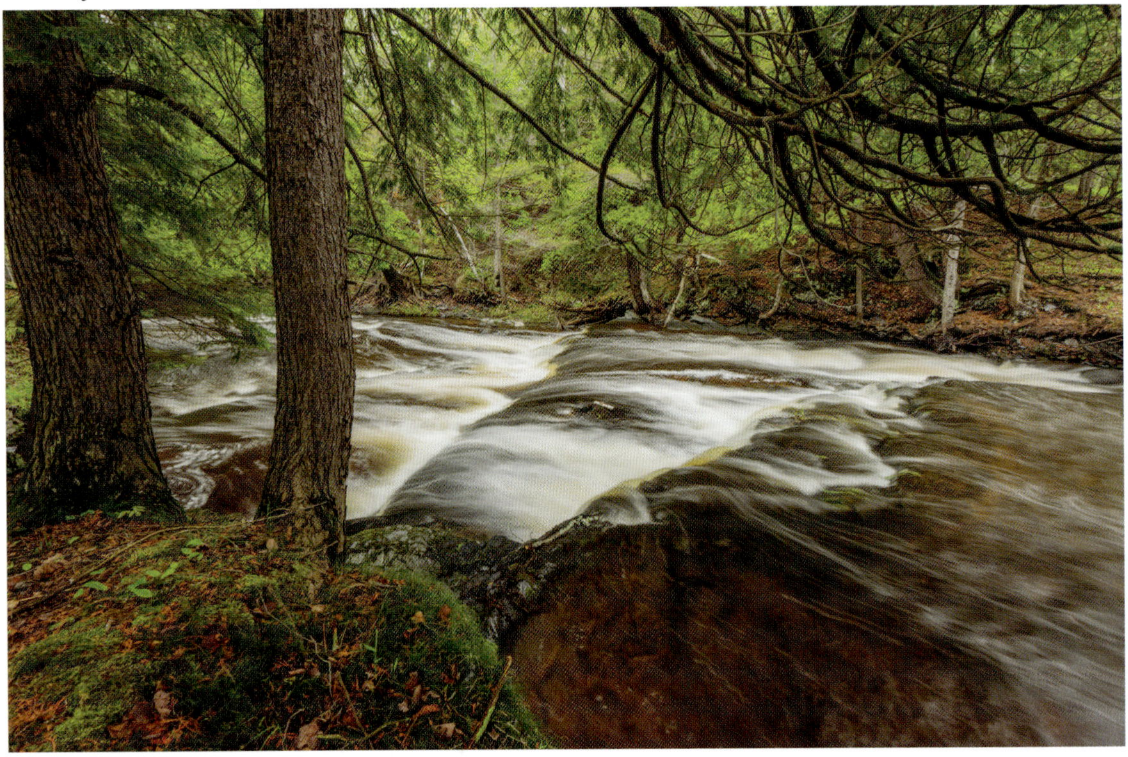

SECRET HOLE FALLS (FALLS RIVER)

Private

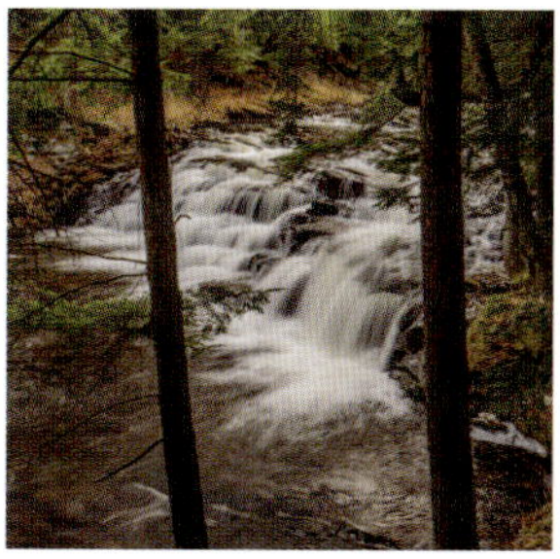

Must See:	8	GPS:	N46 44.691 W88 26.971
Height:	8 feet		
Time:	50-75 minutes	Hiking Information	
		Path:	Unimproved Footpath
Driving Information		Length:	.57 miles
Signs:	None	Elev. Change:	Moderate
Road:	Main	GPS:	N/A
Access:	Very Easy	Danger:	Moderate
4WD:	N/A	WP Boots:	N/A

Hike another .1 miles from the Falls River Rapids to this, my favorite waterfall on the Falls River! The rich, cascading water flows with powerful lines around underlying black bedrock in this slightly rounded waterfall.

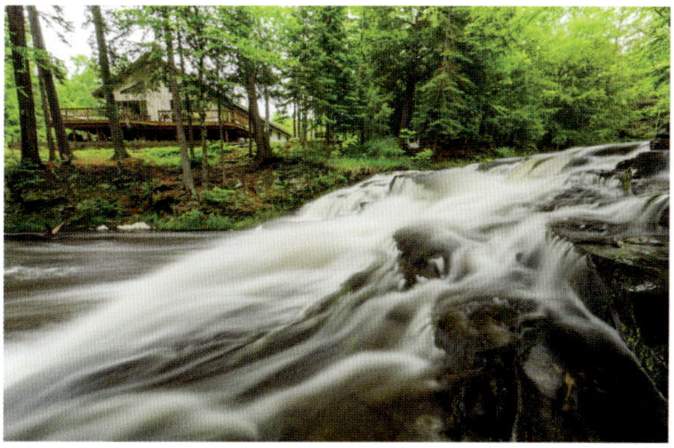

The waterfall gets its name from Secret Creek, which empties into the Falls River nearby. The river starts cascading with small drops, quickly increasing in height and culminating in a nicely defined waterfall situated next to a good sized home on the eastern side on the river.

Early morning light streams through the trees, lighting up the river below the lovely falls.

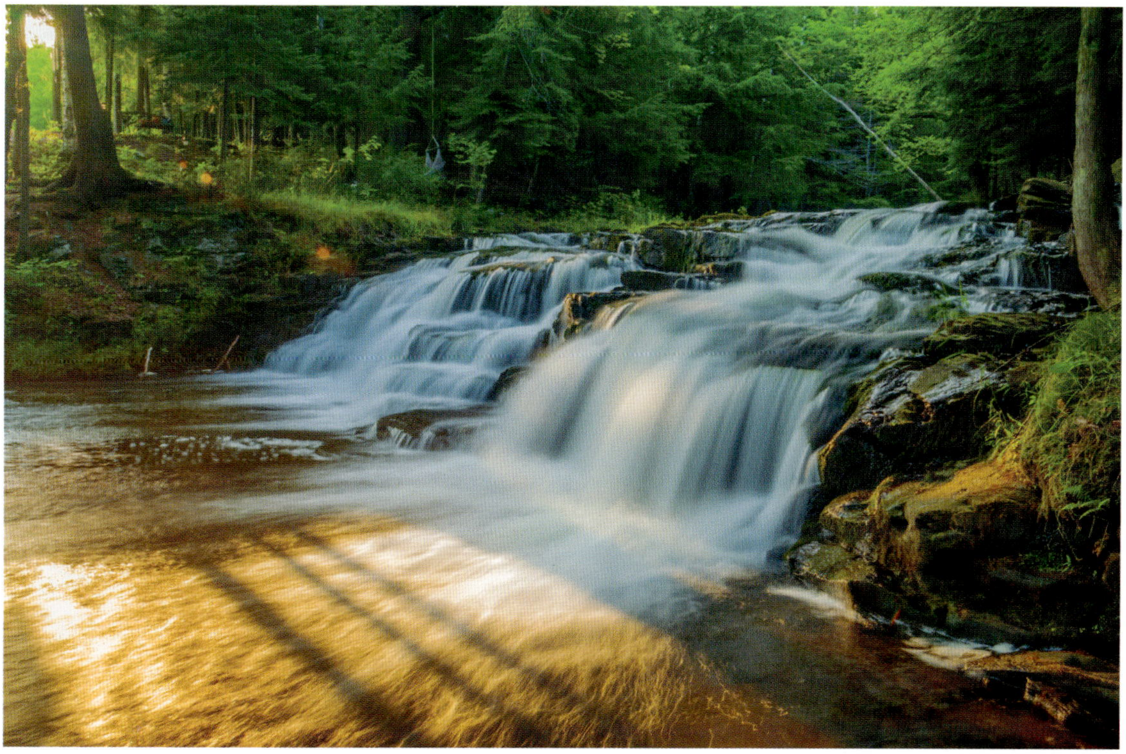

CHUTE FALLS (FALLS RIVER)

Private

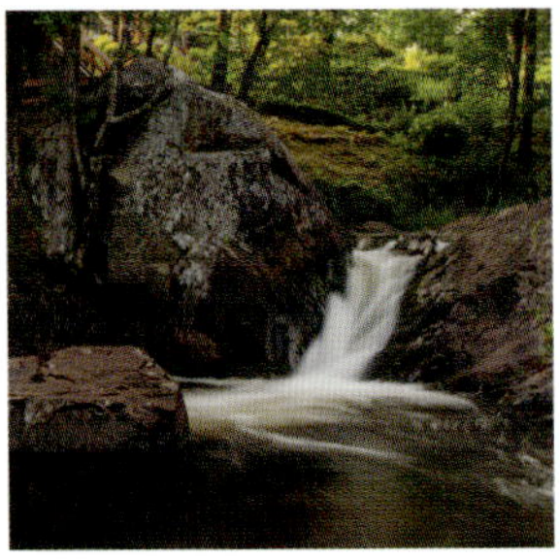

Must See:	7	GPS:	N46 44.626 W88 26.921
Height:	6 feet		
Time:	60-90 minutes	Hiking Information	
		Path:	Unimproved Footpath
Driving Information		Length:	.66 miles
Signs:	None	Elev. Change:	Moderate
Road:	Main	GPS:	N/A
Access:	Very Easy	Danger:	Moderate
4WD:	N/A	WP Boots:	N/A

Hike another .1 miles upstream from Secret Hole Falls to this unique waterfall on the Falls River. The river here is squeezed down to a width of about 5 feet as the water chutes between two large masses of rock. A tangle of rocks below the falls tend to collect tree debris and help to contribute to the always changing look of this waterfall.

A stairway has been built down into the gorge on the eastern side. Several houses can be seen along that side of the river along here.

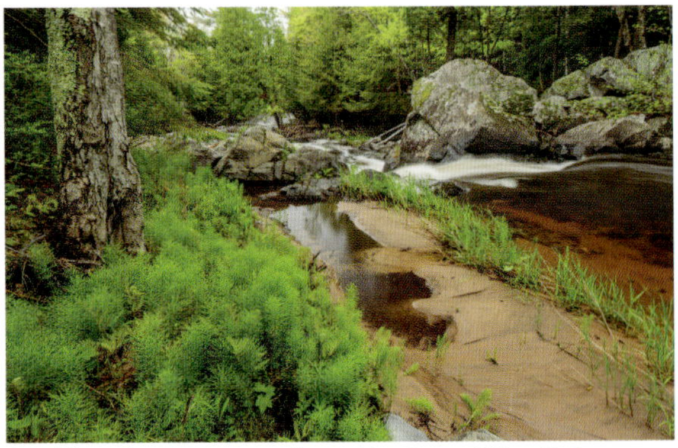

Looking downstream from the top of the falls.

Note: This waterfall has another commonly used name, but isn't appropriate for this family friendly book.

Minor rapids extend downstream from the waterfall.

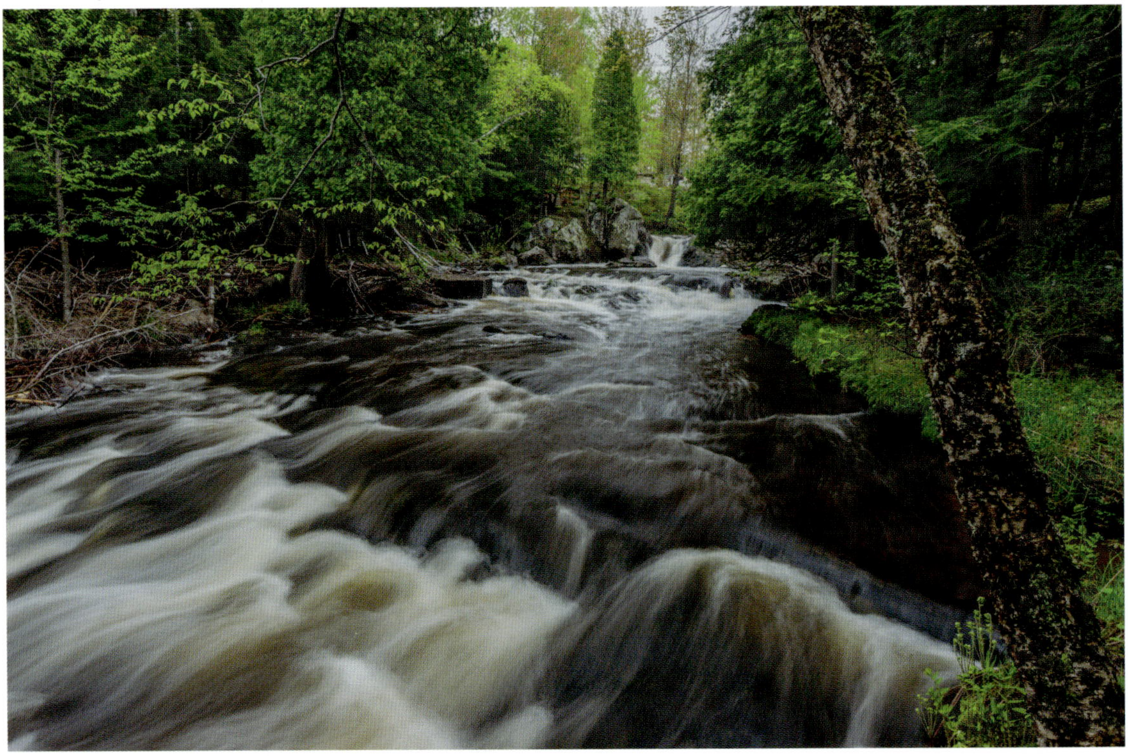

MARDALE FALLS (FALLS RIVER)

Private

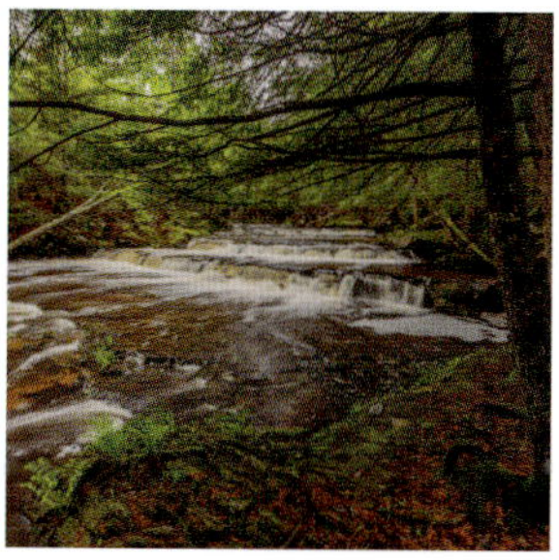

Must See:	6	GPS:	N46 44.452 W88 26.880
Height:	10 feet		
Time:	70-100 minutes		

Driving Information		Hiking Information	
		Path:	Unimproved Footpath
Signs:	None	Length:	300 yards
Road:	Main	Elev. Change:	Moderate
Access:	Very Easy	GPS:	N/A
4WD:	N/A	Danger:	Moderate
		WP Boots:	N/A

About .2 miles further upstream from Chute Falls is the multiple drop waterfall, Mardale Falls. Several cascades scattered over a hundred yards of river culminate in a 3 foot drop. A rugged stone wall 12 feet high rises on the left with a beautiful log house overlooking the falls. The western bank drops down to river level near the base of the falls for a great viewing location.

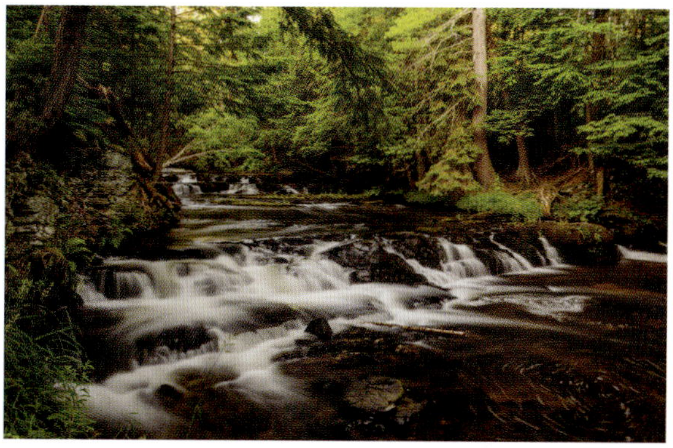

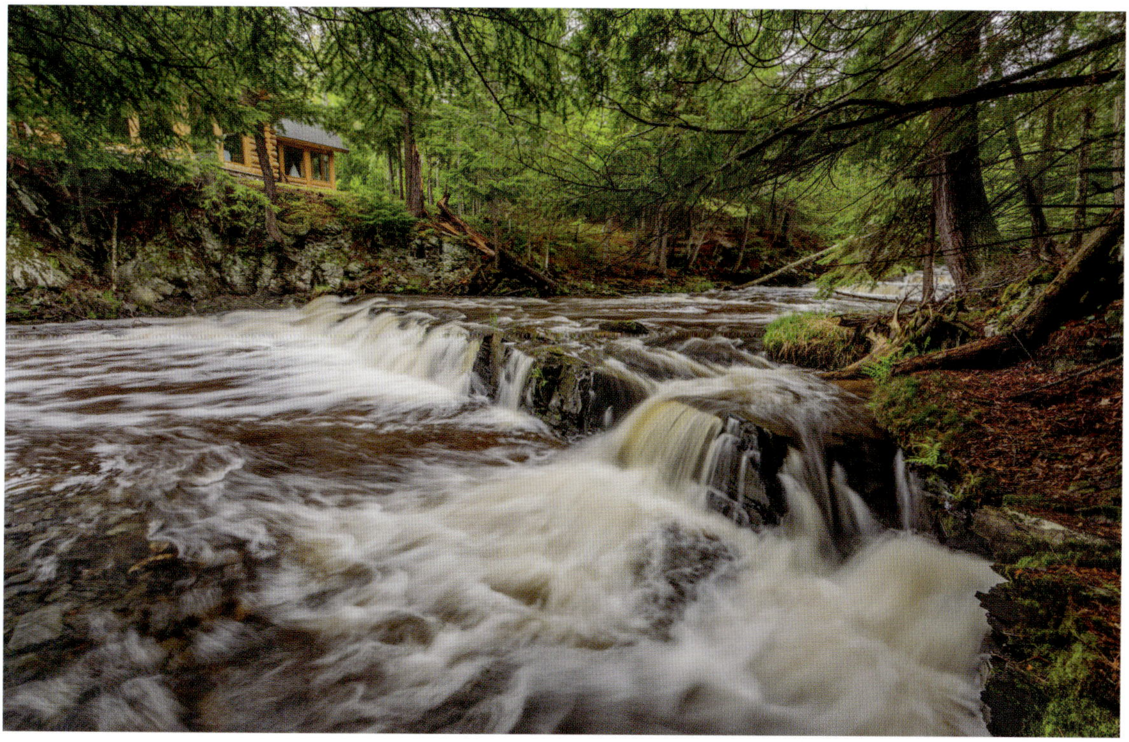

SAARINEN FALLS (FALLS RIVER)

Private

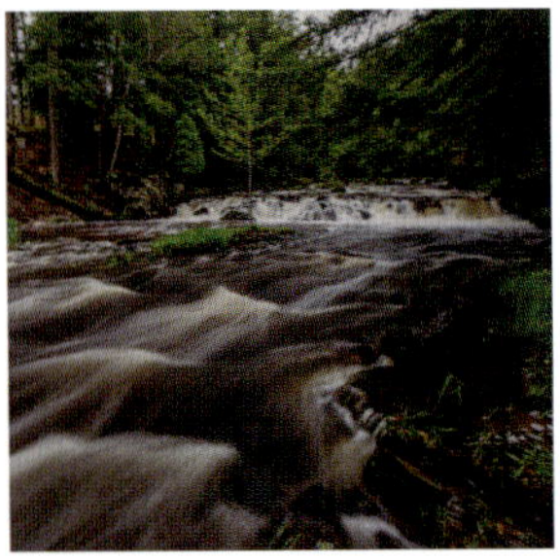

Must See:	7	GPS:	N46 44.315 W88 26.777
Height:	10 feet		
Time:	20-30 minutes	**Hiking Information**	
		Path:	Unimproved Footpath
Driving Information		Length:	250 yards
Signs:	None	Elev. Change:	Moderate
Road:	Main	GPS:	N/A
Access:	Very Easy	Danger:	Moderate
4WD:	N/A	WP Boots:	N/A

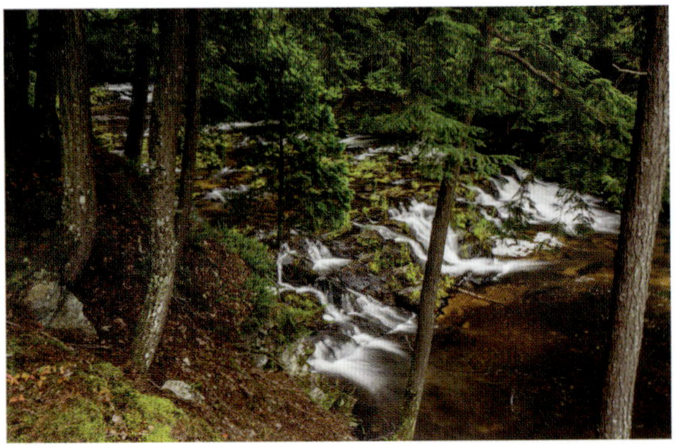

Follow the fishermen's footpath upstream for .21 miles from Mardale Falls. A couple of houses can be seen tucked into the evergreen forest above the falls and the upstream cascades on the eastern side of the river.

Just above Saarinen Falls, the Falls River turns in a sharp hairpin curve before widening out to about 40 feet and then dropping in a multi-tiered variety of water and rock. A final burst sends the river down the last 4 feet in a lovely cascade. Although the bulk of the river flows on the western side of the waterfall, the spill pool is found on the eastern side. Here, the calmer waters swirl before joining up with the stronger current and rushing around a teardrop shaped sandy island centered in the river 30 feet downstream from the base of the waterfall.

There may be more greenery in this waterfall than any other waterfall I have ever seen. Grass and wildflowers cling to rocks that stand above the waterline. These are above the waterfall, below the waterfall, and even down the slant of the cascading face!

The Falls River is cut 15 to 20 feet deep into a gorge at Saarinen Falls.

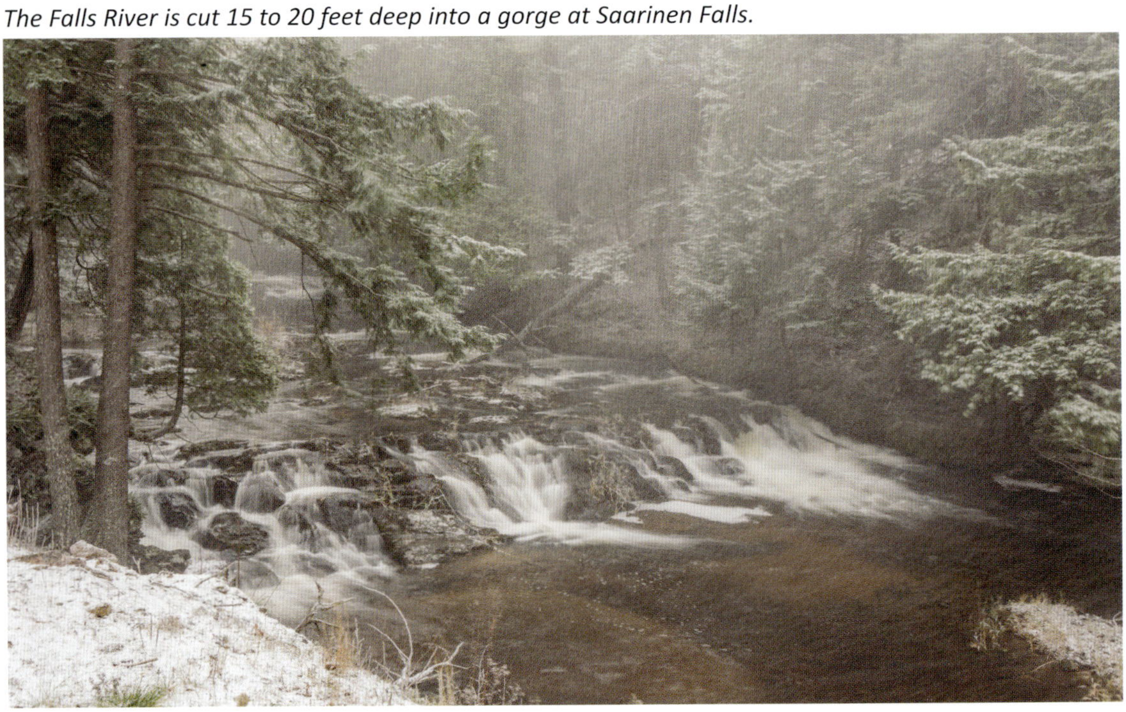

Falls River - Upper Hike

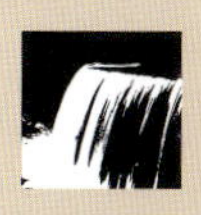

Power House Falls: This is the most easily viewed waterfall in Baraga County. The waterfall is located at the end of the dirt road leading to the abandoned power house. The beautiful, cascading waterfall is adjacent to the power house.

Power Dam Falls: Just 200 feet upstream from Power House Falls are concrete abutments and a short, stone retaining wall. A small cascade is found just upstream from these man-made remnants. Climb the small hill behind the old power house to the river to view this waterfall.

Power Dam Falls - Upper: Continue upstream another 200 feet to view this nice cascading waterfall. Overhanging cedar boughs frame the near side of the river. These little known waterfalls are easily accessed!

Directions: Drive south of L'Anse on US-41 to Power Dam Road. Follow Power Dam Road west. The road will turn hard to the left, then back to the right and cross some railroad tracks. The black top ends with the main road turning to the right, while a dirt road continues on straight. Follow the dirt road. (Sometimes in the spring, the road will be closed by the village when deep ruts develop from spring rains and thawing winter snows.) Another dirt road will intersect from the northwest. Turn right and follow this to its end. The boarded up remains of the electric power house are here, right next to the Power House Falls. Park here. Hike upstream to the Power Dam Falls.

POWER HOUSE FALLS (FALLS RIVER)

Private

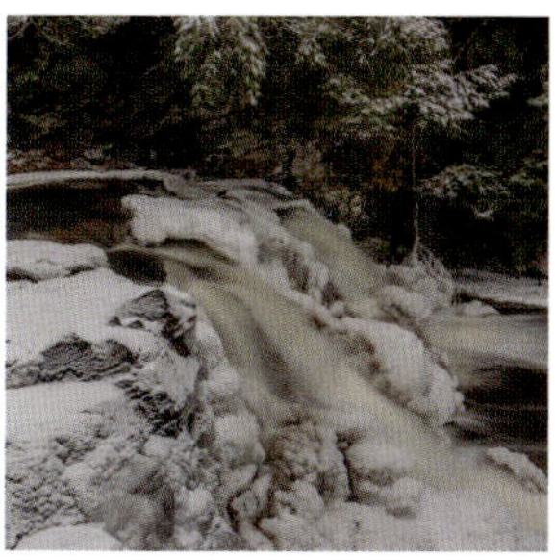

Must See:	8	GPS:	N46 44.226 W88 26.660
Height:	13 feet		
Time:	5-15 minutes	Hiking Information	
		Path:	N/A
Driving Information		Length:	N/A
Signs:	Near Entrance	Elev. Change:	N/A
Road:	Gravel	GPS:	N/A
Access:	Easy	Danger:	N/A
4WD:	N/A	WP Boots:	N/A

The Power House Falls are easily viewed from a vehicle. The old, concrete, boarded up power house doesn't add to the aesthetics of the waterfall, but it does lend a sense of historical significance as many waterfalls have been tapped for their power from years gone by to the present.

Next to the gray building, the Falls River cascades down beautifully in this, the tallest of the waterfalls on the Falls River. The parking lot right next to the river means that it is easily accessible, with no hiking needed to enjoy its beauty.

Note: The dirt road down to the waterfall is not plowed in the winter, so you will need to hike about .3 miles to get to the waterfall then.

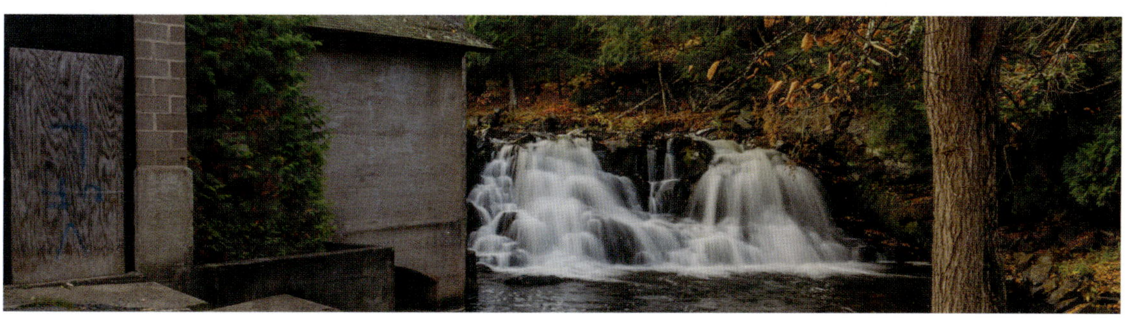

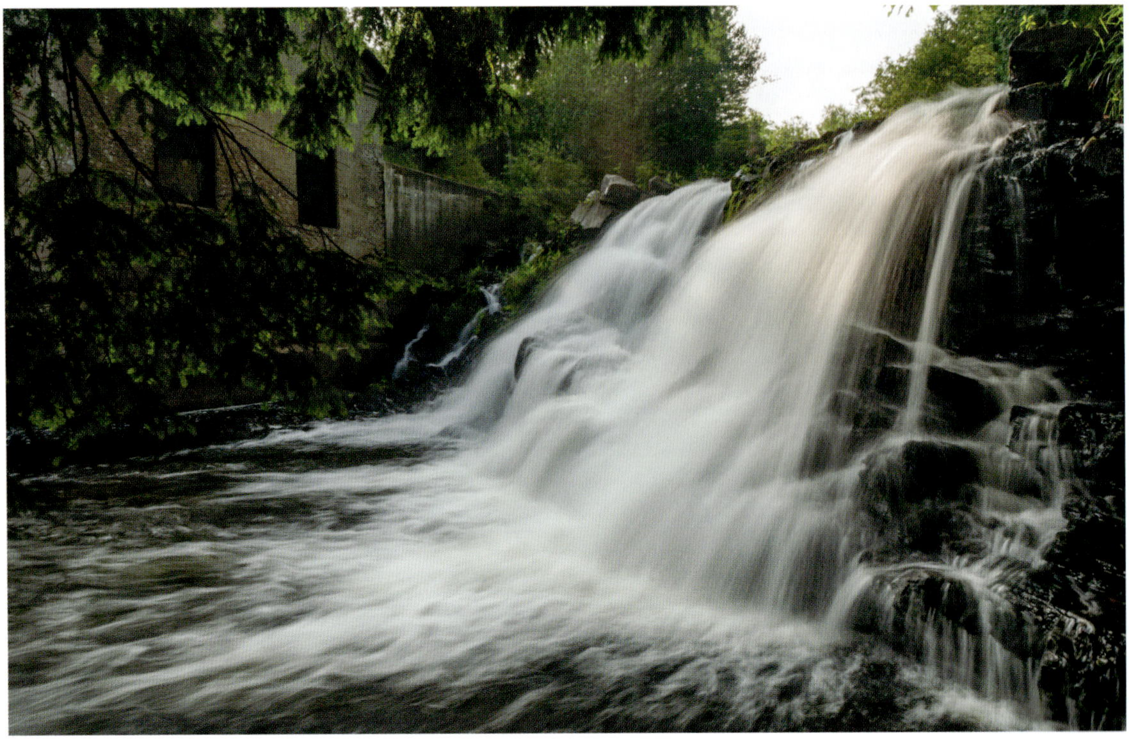

This is the view from the far side of the river. The Power House seems to blend in more naturally when viewed from here.

You can see how close you can park to the waterfall! What a lovely waterfall to be able to view so easily!

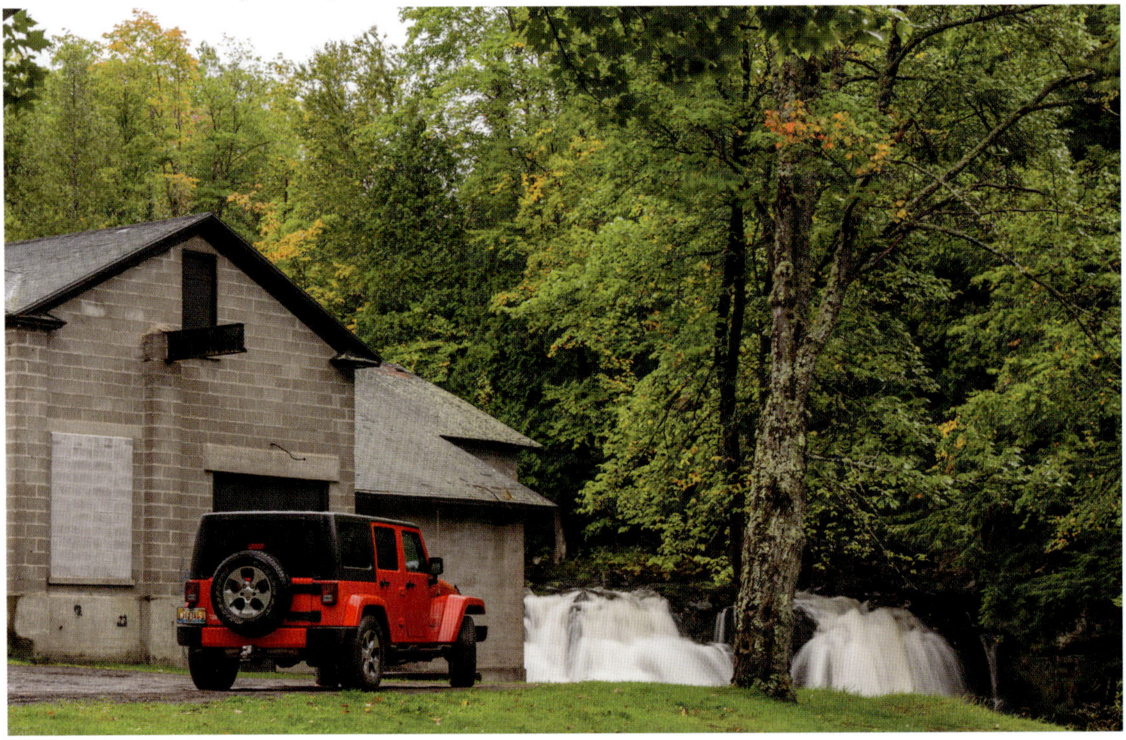

POWER DAM FALLS (FALLS RIVER)

Private

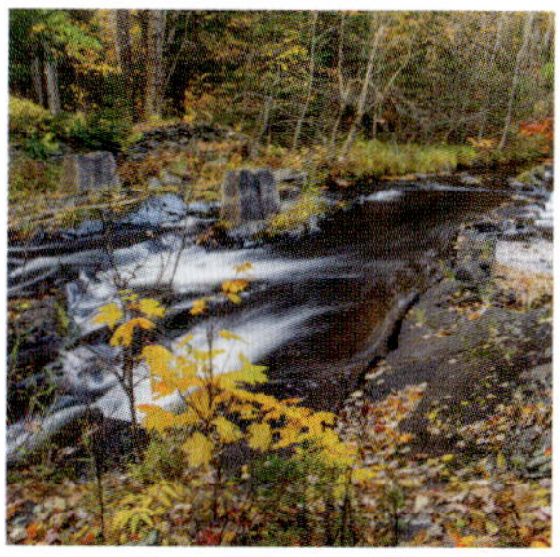

Must See:	4	GPS:	N46 44.196 W88 26.644
Height:	3 feet		
Time:	10-20 minutes		

Driving Information		Hiking Information	
		Path:	None
		Length:	70 yards
Signs:	None	Elev. Change:	Minor
Road:	Dirt	GPS:	N/A
Access:	Somewhat Easy	Danger:	Moderate
4WD:	Helpful	WP Boots:	N/A

Angular bedrock runs across the river, spilling over to make a 3' waterfall. A slate retaining wall lines the far side of the bank below the falls. Concrete remnants are visible just down river from the drop. They are a reminder that the power of this river was once harnessed to produce electricity for the surrounding community.

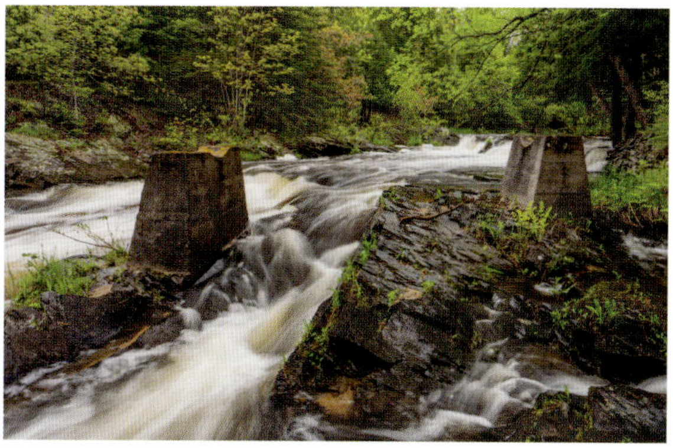

Be careful along the Falls River here. The slanted slate can be very slippery and sits at awkward angles slanting down toward the river.

The river can be beautiful in all seasons!

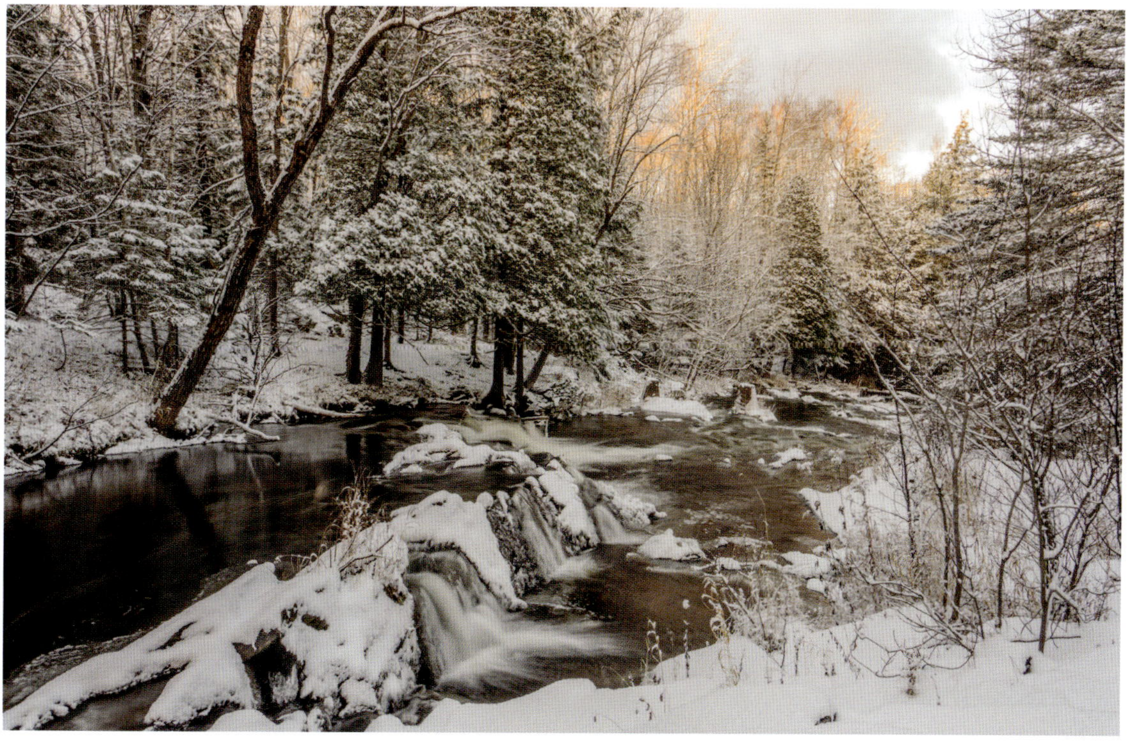

POWER DAM FALLS - UPPER (FALLS RIVER)

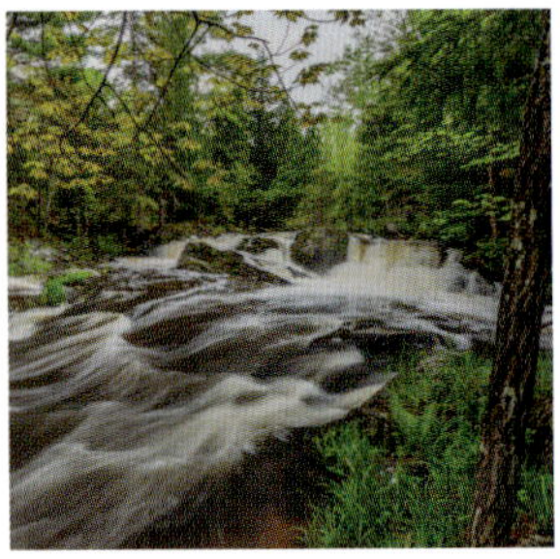

Must See: 4
Height: 4 feet
Time: 10-20 minutes

Driving Information
Signs: None
Road: Dirt
Access: Somewhat Easy
4WD: Helpful

GPS: N46 44.181 W88 26.606
Hiking Information
Path: None
Length: 150 yards
Elev. Change: Minor
GPS: N/A
Danger: Moderate
WP Boots: N/A

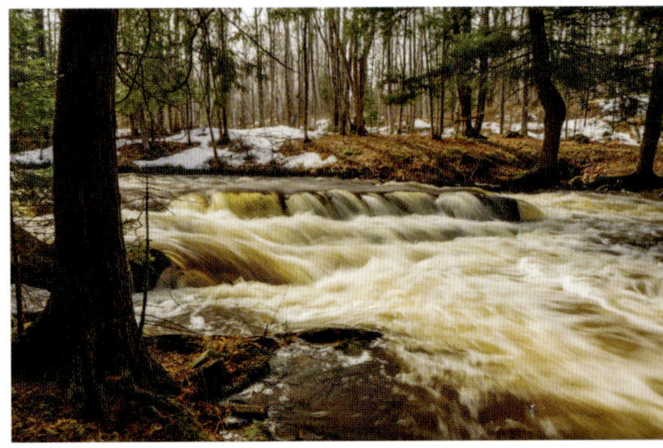

Fifty yards upriver from Power Dam Falls is a nice cascading drop with a plant covered rise splitting the falls toward the western side of the river.

The hike along the river is via a fishermen's trail which can be faint. However, as the undergrowth is not bad, it's not really needed anyway. The more difficult part of hiking between the falls is the slanted bedrock. Here, as at Power Dam Falls, the bedrock is quite tilted and can be very slippery (especially when wet). A crevasse near the upper falls needs to be navigated through. Be careful, as this tends to be one of the most slippery points. A couple of slate quarries can be seen nearby. Holes in the bedrock show where the stone was removed over a century ago. Keep in mind that this is nothing like the massive activity that took place at the Arvon Slate Quarry about 10 miles away.

Note the angled slate bedrock that is so abundant in the area.

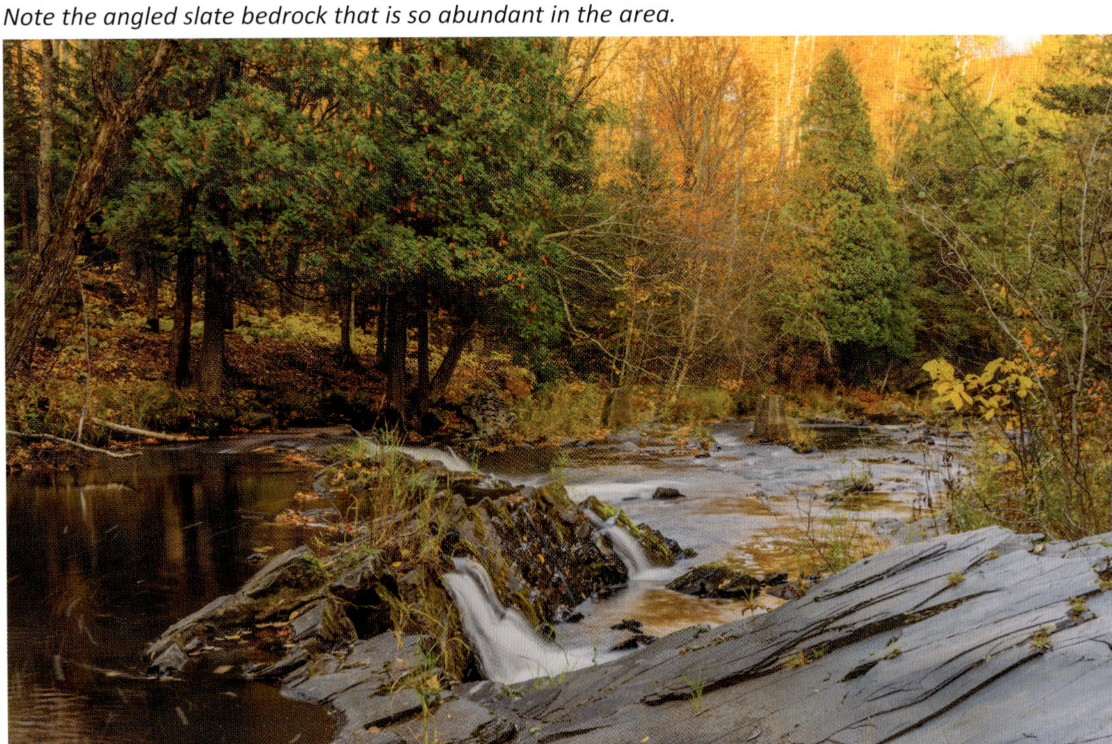

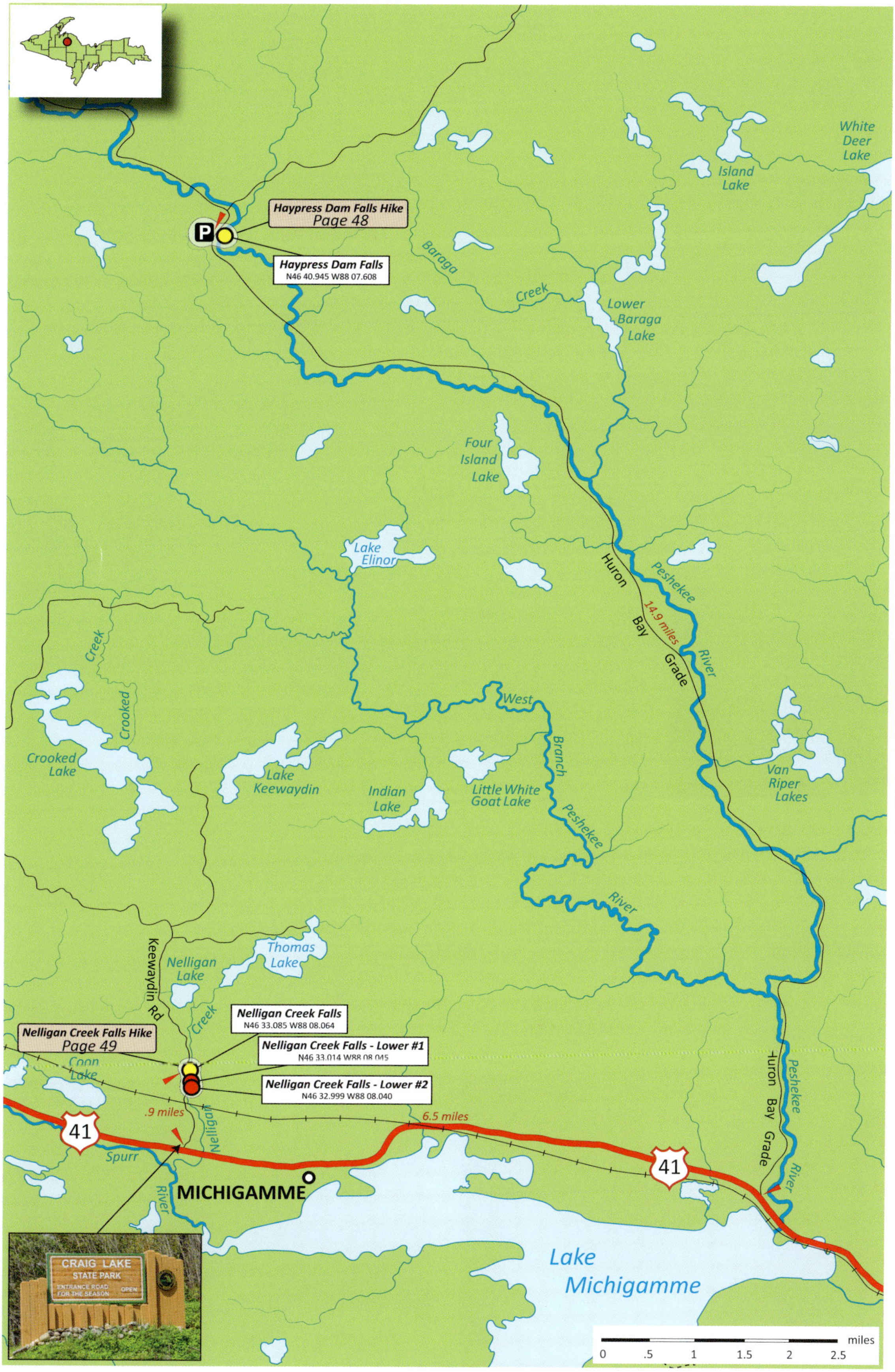
Haypress Dam Falls Hike
Page 48
P
Haypress Dam Falls
N46 40.945 W88 07.608
Baraga Creek
Lower Baraga Lake
Island Lake
White Deer Lake
Four Island Lake
Lake Elinor
Huron Bay Grade
14.9 miles
Peshekee River
West Branch Peshekee River
Crooked Creek
Crooked Lake
Lake Keewaydin
Indian Lake
Little White Goat Lake
Van Riper Lakes
Keewaydin Rd
Nelligan Lake
Thomas Lake
Nelligan Creek
Nelligan Creek Falls
N46 33.085 W88 08.064
Nelligan Creek Falls Hike
Page 49
Nelligan Creek Falls - Lower #1
N46 33.014 W88 08.045
Nelligan Creek Falls - Lower #2
N46 32.999 W88 08.040
Coon Lake
.9 miles
6.5 miles
41
Spurr River
MICHIGAMME
Huron Bay Grade
Peshekee River
Lake Michigamme
CRAIG LAKE
STATE PARK
ENTRANCE ROAD
FOR THE SEASON
OPEN
miles
0 .5 1 1.5 2 2.5

Haypress Dam Falls Hike

The Peshekee River begins as runoff from the eastern slope of Mt. Curwood. This mountain, historically thought to be the highest point in Michigan at 1978 feet above sea level, is actually the second highest. The peak of Mt. Arvon, 5 1/2 miles to the northwest, was recently discovered to be one foot higher, and is now considered Michigan's highest point. The Peshekee River starts at 1883 feet, a high elevation river (in Michigan terms), and flows through a swampy area, dropping only 83 feet in 10 miles before beginning its quicker descent at the waterfall. This makes Haypress Dam Falls the highest elevation waterfall in Michigan at 1,800 feet above sea level.

Directions: Drive north on the Huron Bay Grade (just west of the Peshekee River bridge) from US-41 for 14.9 miles. This is a paved/gravel road that is rough. Plan on 30 to 40 minutes to make this drive. Park along the road at one of the small pull-offs. There is no signage here to indicate that there is a waterfall. A GPS will help you feel confident that you're in the right place. There will be a footpath off to the right of the road (east). It splits into several paths. To the left, the trail ascends to the top of an outcropping overlooking the near side of the waterfall. The trail to the right emerges from the woods at the base of the last slide to the river.

HAYPRESS DAM FALLS (PESHEKEE RIVER)

Private

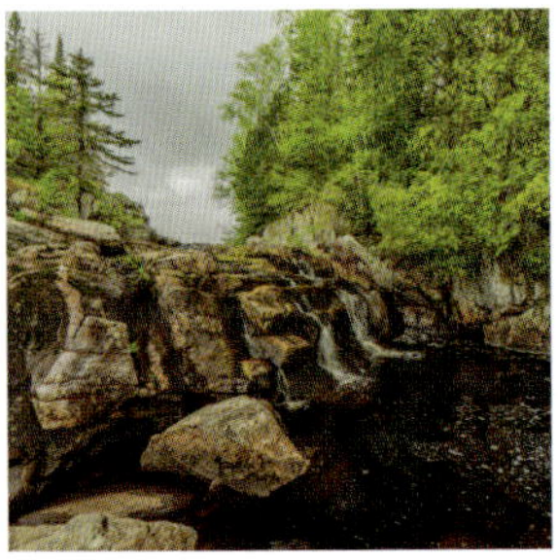

Must See:	6	GPS:	N46 40.945 W88 07.608
Height:	15 feet		
Time:	10-30 minutes	Hiking Information	
		Path:	Narrow Footpath
Driving Information		Length:	50 yards
Signs:	None	Elev. Change:	Minor
Road:	Oversized 2-track	GPS:	Helpful
Access:	Fairly Difficult	Danger:	Moderate
4WD:	N/A	WP Boots:	N/A or Required

After a lengthy journey though the relatively flat highlands, the Peshekee River divides around a tall promontory of rock jutting up 15 feet. The divided river drops several times on both sides of the island. The tall outcropping tapers down on the down river side of the island to a mostly flat picnic area. Lichen and moss in various shades of green cover the island. Wild roses grow in a cluster near the island's far side and stunted pines struggle to find enough soil to support their root system. An overflow stream below the falls runs parallel to the river before joining back in.

Note: Tall waterproof boots are needed to get over to the island/promontory. This is a difficult to view waterfall, but climbing around on the island is the best way to enjoy it.

Looking down from the top of the promontory

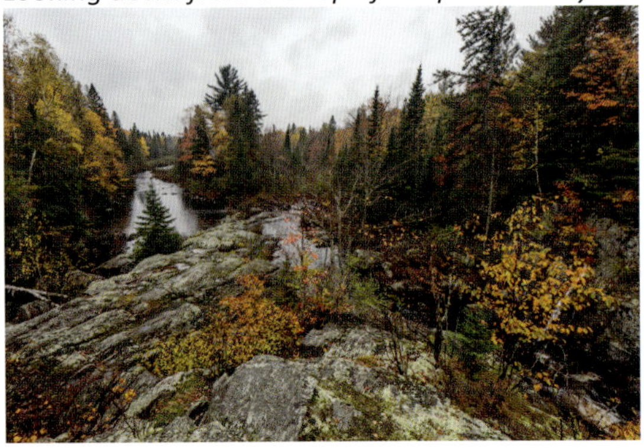

Looking up at the promontory from below

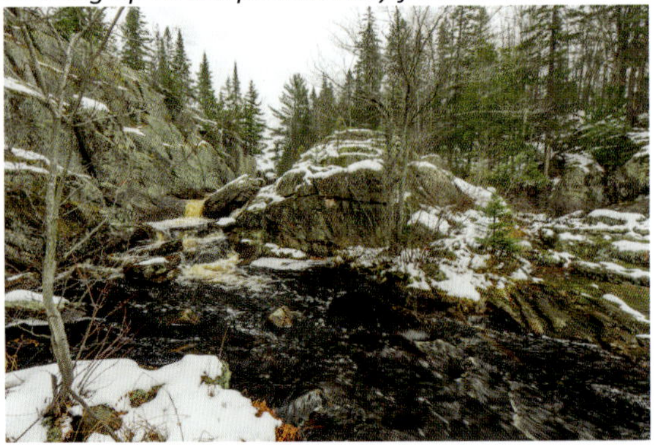

Nelligan Creek Falls Hike

Nelligan Creek is a small waterway that parallels Keewadin Road for over a mile along the entrance road to Craig Lake State Park. About a mile north of US-41 there are 3 small waterfalls that are right by the side of the road.

Directions: Turn north onto Keewadin Road (the gravel entrance road to Craig Lake State Park) off of US-41. This road is just west of Michigamme. Head north for .9 miles. Park on the right (east) side of the road at the small turnoff. Nelligan Creek Falls is just feet to the north of the parking spot. The two lower falls are downstream a short distance. Follow the road back to the south and cut in at the waterfalls, which can be heard and seen from the road. They are not obvious, so be on the lookout.

NELLIGAN CREEK FALLS (NELLIGAN CREEK)

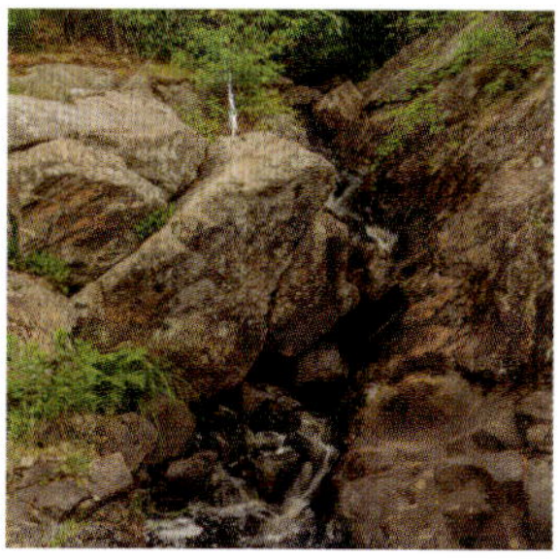

Must See:	4	GPS:	N46 33.085 W88 08.064
Height:	6 feet		
Time:	5-10 minutes	Hiking Information	
		Path:	None Needed
Driving Information		Length:	50 feet
Signs:	None	Elev. Change:	Minor
Road:	Gravel Road	GPS:	Helpful
Access:	Somewhat Easy	Danger:	Minor
4WD:	N/A	WP Boots:	N/A

The small creek tumbles over exposed bedrock. A large rise on the far side of the creek overlooks the babbling stream. Halfway down the cascading waterfall, a lichen covered mass of rock offers a great perch to view the upper portion of the waterfall and small rapids further upstream. The bedrock on the near side of the creek angles in toward the waterway. Sections have loosened over time, having given way to the forces of gravity, time, and water, until they have fallen into the creek bed. Wild raspberries grow at the top of the falls.

Nelligan Creek drains a small section of land. To get good flow, there needs to be spring melt or a very large rain.

Be careful in the winter - the road is NOT plowed

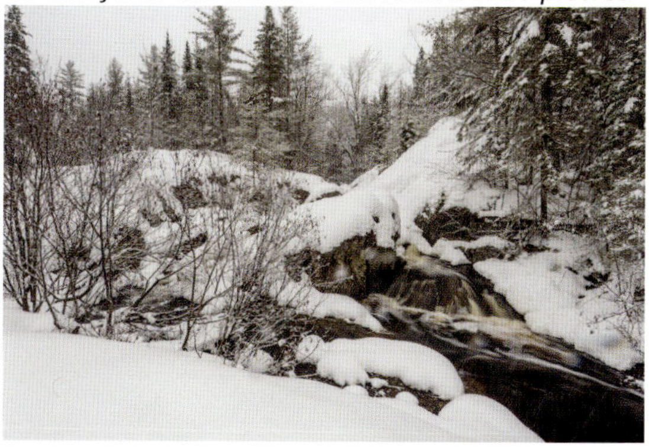

Autumn presents a profusion of color

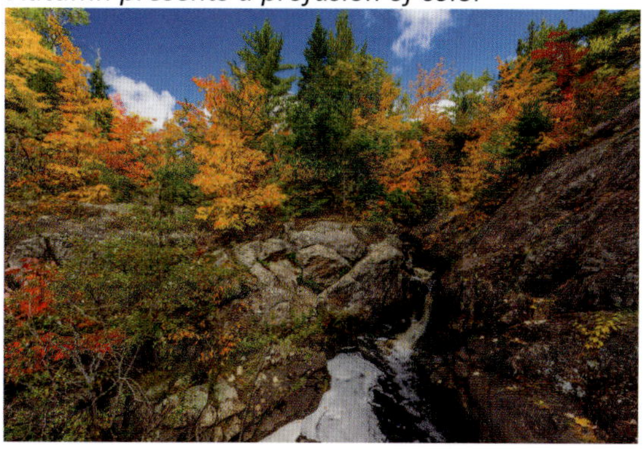

NELLIGAN CREEK FALLS - LOWER #1 (NELLIGAN CREEK) Private

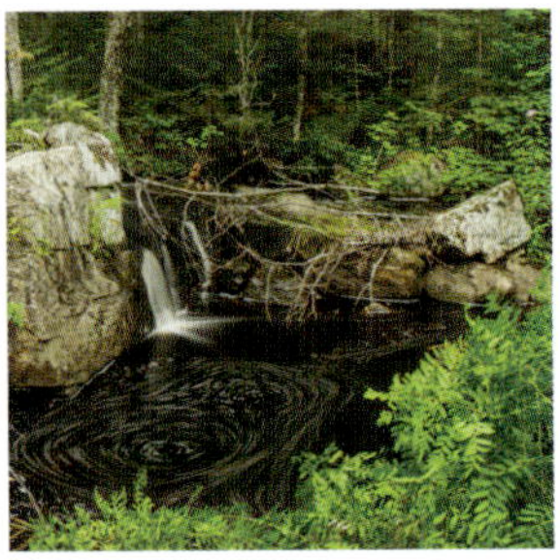

Must See:	3	GPS:	N46 33.014 W88 08.045
Height:	3 feet		
Time:	15-20 minutes	**Hiking Information**	
		Path:	None at waterfall
Driving Information		Length:	175 yards
Signs:	None	Elev. Change:	Minor
Road:	Gravel	GPS:	Helpful
Access:	Somewhat Easy	Danger:	Moderate
4WD:	N/A	WP Boots:	Helpful

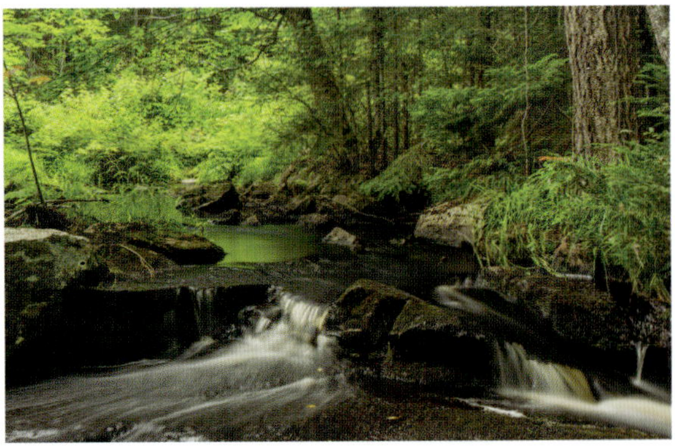

Follow the road back south (downstream) for about 150 yards. The small waterfall is just into the forest and can be seen peeking through the trees from the road.

The creek fans out over the first cascade, a 1 foot drop. It then splits over an angled rock, spreading out further, from 5 feet wide at the top of the waterfall, to 20 feet wide at the base of the top drop. Continuing, the creek flows around a large fractured boulder, falling the final 2 feet on either side. The creek turns back hard on itself below the falls, viewing the small drop as a temporary interruption in the general flow of the stream.

There is a good amount of undergrowth in the forest here. Be careful with your footing.

Notice the long squat ridge that forms the base of the waterfall

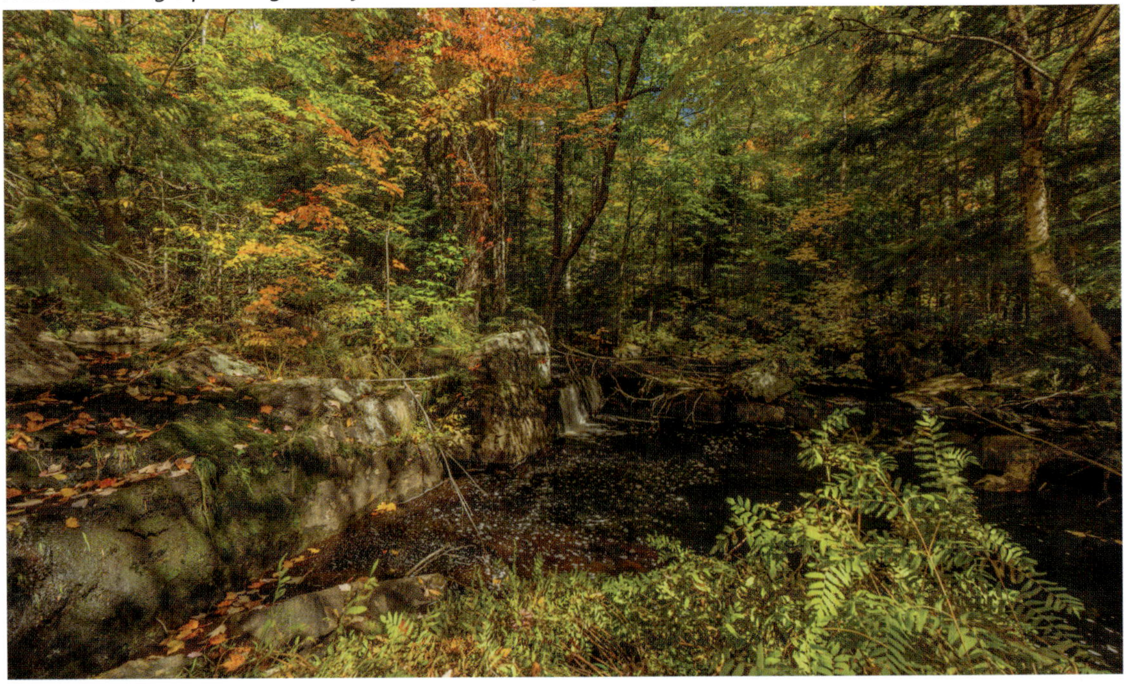

NELLIGAN CREEK FALLS - LOWER #2 (NELLIGAN CREEK) Private

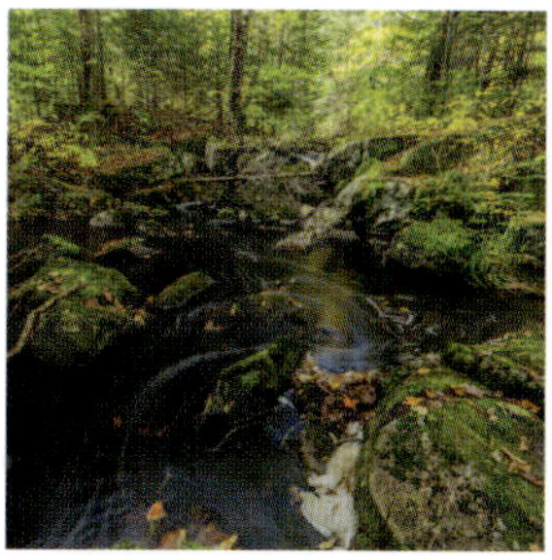

Must See:	2
Height:	3 feet
Time:	20-25 minutes
GPS:	N46 32.999 W88 08.040

Driving Information

Signs:	None
Road:	Gravel
Access:	Somewhat Easy
4WD:	N/A

Hiking Information

Path:	None at waterfall
Length:	200 yards
Elev. Change:	Minor
GPS:	Helpful
Danger:	Moderate
WP Boots:	Helpful

Just 100 feet further downstream from Lower #1 is Lower #2. I'd go back to the road between the waterfalls. The road is much easier to navigate than the undergrowth.

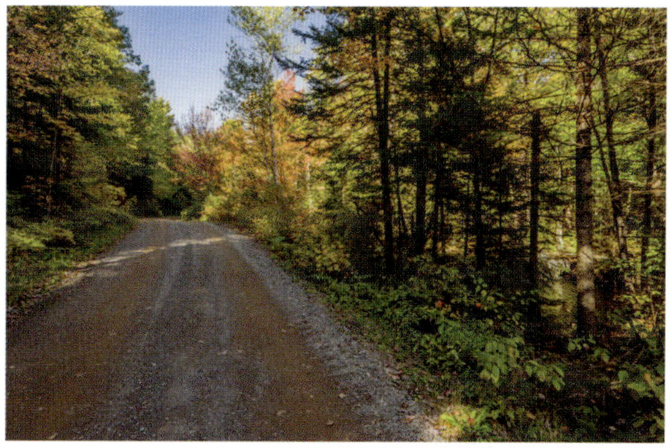

The creek is less than 2 feet wide here. It falls down behind a cluster of large bedrock chunks. In fact, the creek bed below the falls is also full of various sized boulders. The waterfall is difficult to see because of the pile of rocks directly below the waterfall that is choking the channel.

This is the large cluster of bedrock chunks that blocks the view of the waterfall.

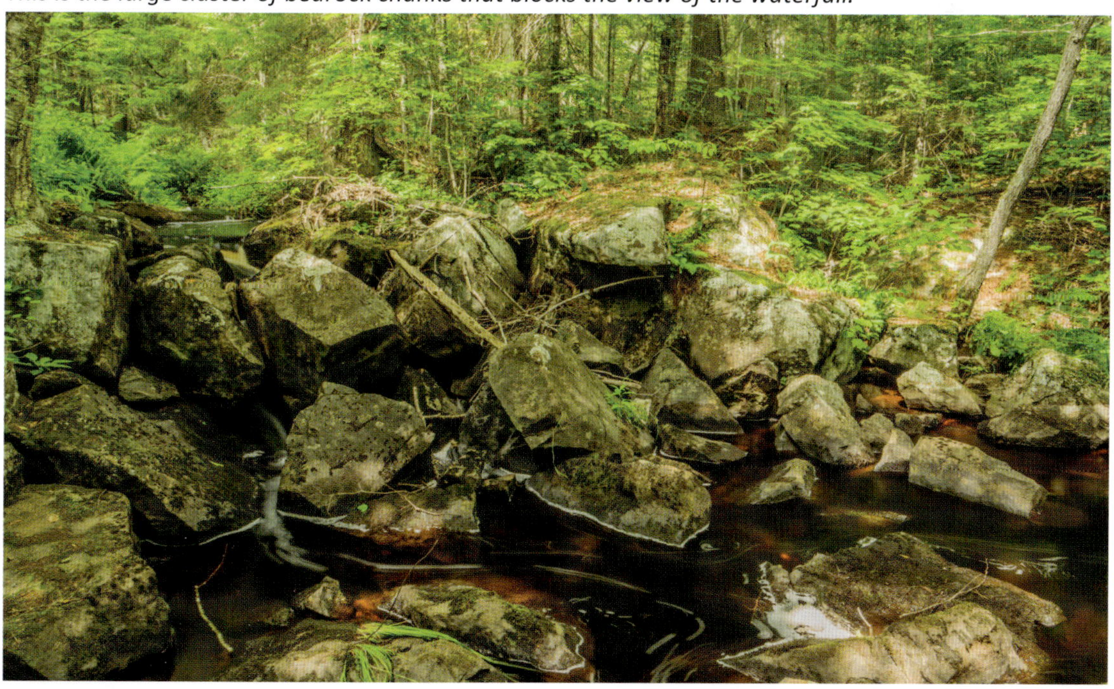

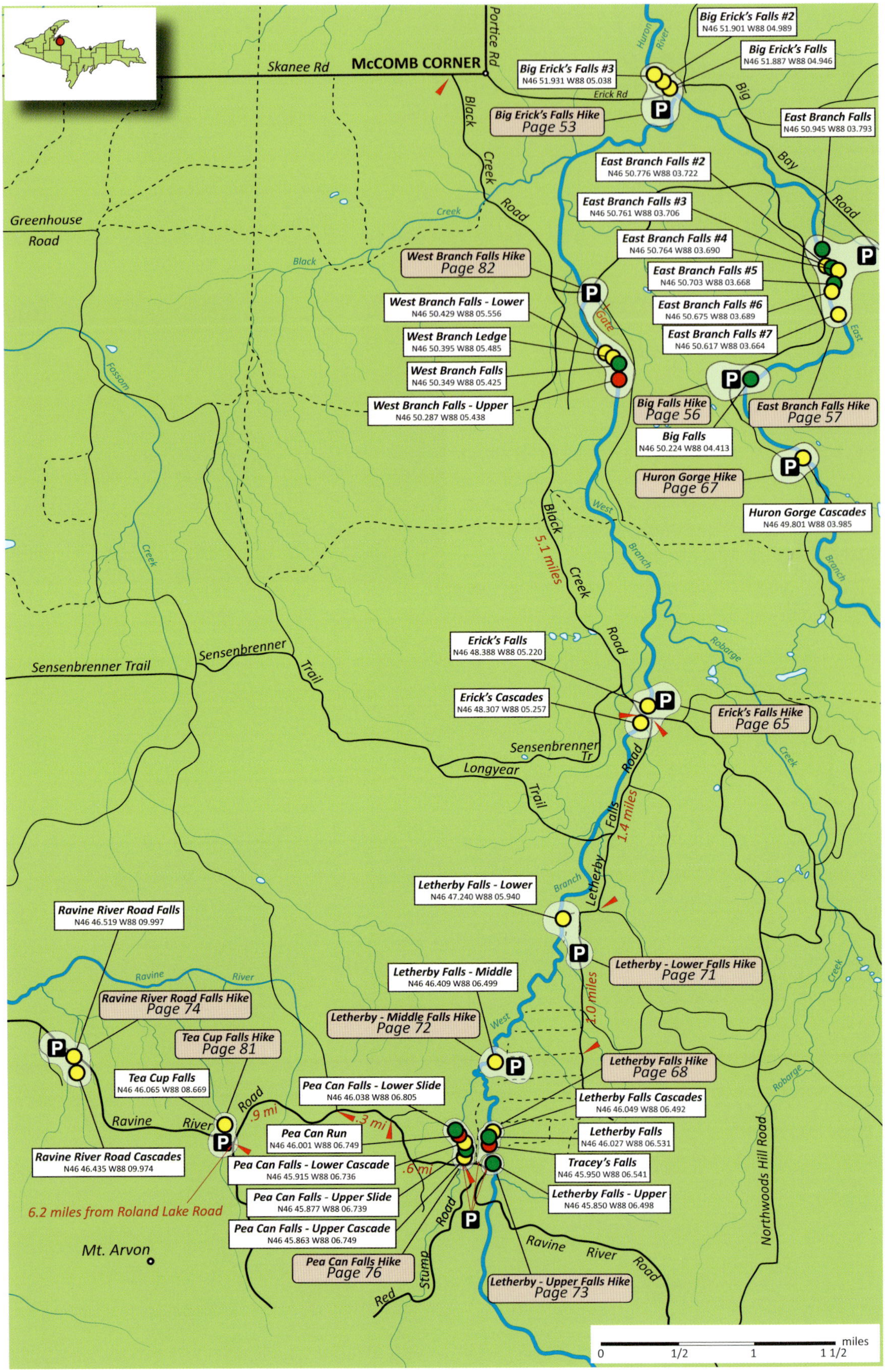
McCOMB CORNER
Skanee Rd
Portice Rd
Erick Rd
Big Bay Road
Black Creek Road
Greenhouse Road
Sensenbrenner Trail
Longyear Trail
Letherby Falls Road
Northwoods Hill Road
Ravine River Road
Red Stump Road
Mt. Arvon
Big Erick's Falls #2
N46 51.901 W88 04.989
Big Erick's Falls
N46 51.887 W88 04.946
Big Erick's Falls #3
N46 51.931 W88 05.038
Big Erick's Falls Hike
Page 53
East Branch Falls
N46 50.945 W88 03.793
East Branch Falls #2
N46 50.776 W88 03.722
East Branch Falls #3
N46 50.761 W88 03.706
East Branch Falls #4
N46 50.764 W88 03.690
East Branch Falls #5
N46 50.703 W88 03.668
East Branch Falls #6
N46 50.675 W88 03.689
East Branch Falls #7
N46 50.617 W88 03.664
West Branch Falls Hike
Page 82
West Branch Falls - Lower
N46 50.429 W88 05.556
West Branch Ledge
N46 50.395 W88 05.485
West Branch Falls
N46 50.349 W88 05.425
West Branch Falls - Upper
N46 50.287 W88 05.438
Big Falls Hike
Page 56
East Branch Falls Hike
Page 57
Big Falls
N46 50.224 W88 04.413
Huron Gorge Hike
Page 67
Huron Gorge Cascades
N46 49.801 W88 03.985
5.1 miles
Erick's Falls
N46 48.388 W88 05.220
Erick's Cascades
N46 48.307 W88 05.257
Erick's Falls Hike
Page 65
1.4 miles
Letherby Falls - Lower
N46 47.240 W88 05.940
Letherby - Lower Falls Hike
Page 71
Ravine River Road Falls
N46 46.519 W88 09.997
Ravine River Road Falls Hike
Page 74
Tea Cup Falls Hike
Page 81
Letherby Falls - Middle
N46 46.409 W88 06.499
Letherby - Middle Falls Hike
Page 72
1.0 miles
Letherby Falls Hike
Page 68
Tea Cup Falls
N46 46.065 W88 08.669
Pea Can Falls - Lower Slide
N46 46.038 W88 06.805
Letherby Falls Cascades
N46 46.049 W88 06.492
.9 mi
.3 mi
.6 mi
Pea Can Run
N46 46.001 W88 06.749
Letherby Falls
N46 46.027 W88 06.531
Ravine River Road Cascades
N46 46.435 W88 09.974
Pea Can Falls - Lower Cascade
N46 45.915 W88 06.736
Tracey's Falls
N46 45.950 W88 06.541
Pea Can Falls - Upper Slide
N46 45.877 W88 06.739
Letherby Falls - Upper
N46 45.850 W88 06.498
6.2 miles from Roland Lake Road
Pea Can Falls - Upper Cascade
N46 45.863 W88 06.749
Pea Can Falls Hike
Page 76
Letherby - Upper Falls Hike
Page 73
Huron River
West Branch
East Branch
Black Creek
Fossom Creek
Robarge Creek
Ravine River
miles
0
1/2
1
1 1/2

Big Erick's Falls Hike

A nice campground, sporting pit toilets and a generous parking lot, is located near the waterfalls. A good section of the grass along the shoreline is mowed, making it relatively easy to walk down the length of the falls.

Big Erick's Falls: The main cascade, located just below the bridge. It is segmented, with regularly spaced sections spilling water over the short ledge.

Big Erick's Falls #2: Just 100 feet further down the river is a second drop of about 3 feet. It is a wide drop, but not spectacular.

Big Erick's Falls #3: As the river continues is course it widens, and flows around an island of sorts. Each branch of the divided river contains a waterfall. On the near side, the west branch, in the shadow of an evergreen, the third drop is similar to the first two; a short, wide, abrupt fall in the river, split into several sections.

Big Erick's Falls #4: On the far side of the island, the east branch drops several feet, bringing a conclusion to the Big Erick's Falls.

Directions: Follow Skanee Road to the east. At the end of the road, Portice Road turns left and Erick Road (gravel) turns to the right. Follow Erick Road east to the bridge that passes over the Huron River. Park next to the bridge in the large parking lot. Walk across the road (north) to the falls. There are several cascades, none of which are spectacular, but since they are easy enough to access, the stop is worth the while.

BIG ERICK'S FALLS (HURON RIVER)

Private

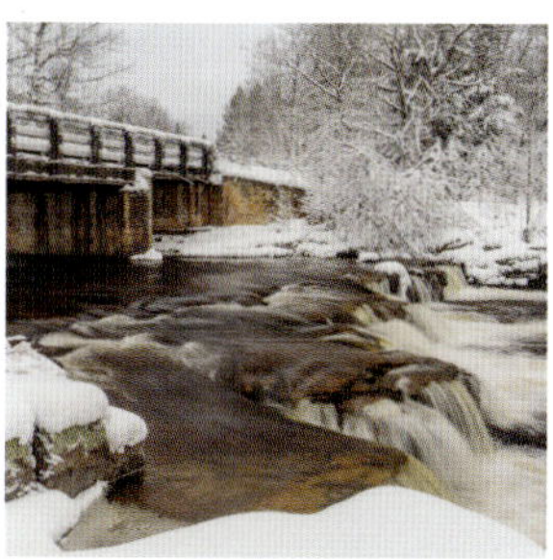

Must See:	6	GPS:	N46 51.887 W88 04.946
Height:	3 feet		
Time:	5-10 minutes	Hiking Information	
		Path:	Unimproved Footpath
Driving Information		Length:	50 yards
Signs:	None	Elev. Change:	Slight
Road:	Gravel	GPS:	N/A
Access:	Easy	Danger:	Slight
4WD:	Helpful	WP Boots:	Recommended

The waterfall is split into 4 separate falls by 3 evenly spaced rock promontories creating nicely proportioned falls. There is a nice gravel parking area adjacent to the bridge. Pit toilets are across the road from the parking lot. Fisherman's trails meander along the river's edge. Follow them down river to the rest of the small drops.

Looking down the river from the bridge

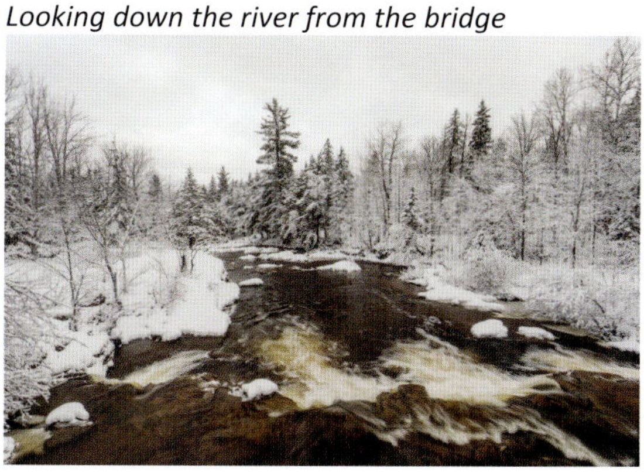

The volume of water can change radically

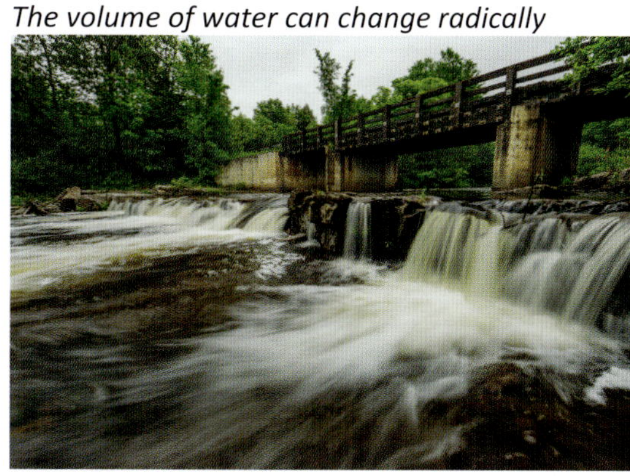

BIG ERICK'S FALLS #2 (HURON RIVER)

Private

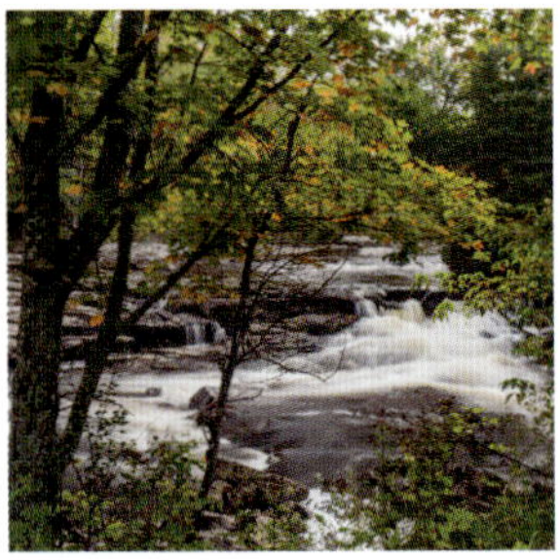

Must See:	4	GPS:	N46 51.901 W88 04.989
Height:	3 feet		
Time:	10-20 minutes	**Hiking Information**	
		Path:	Unimproved Footpath
Driving Information		Length:	125 yards
Signs:	None	Elev. Change:	Moderate
Road:	Gravel	GPS:	Recommended
Access:	Easy	Danger:	Slight
4WD:	Helpful	WP Boots:	Recommended

Follow the footpath that winds along the top of the shallow gorge for about 50 yards downstream from Big Erick's Falls. The river swirls around a narrow point that juts out into the 120 foot wide river. The waterfall is the continuation of that point.

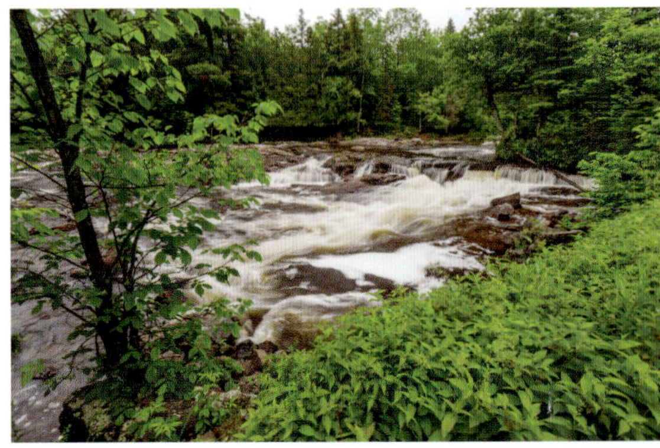

For a better look at the cascade, climb down the steep bank to the river, which is quite shallow.

Fresh snow on a early spring day dresses up the waterfall

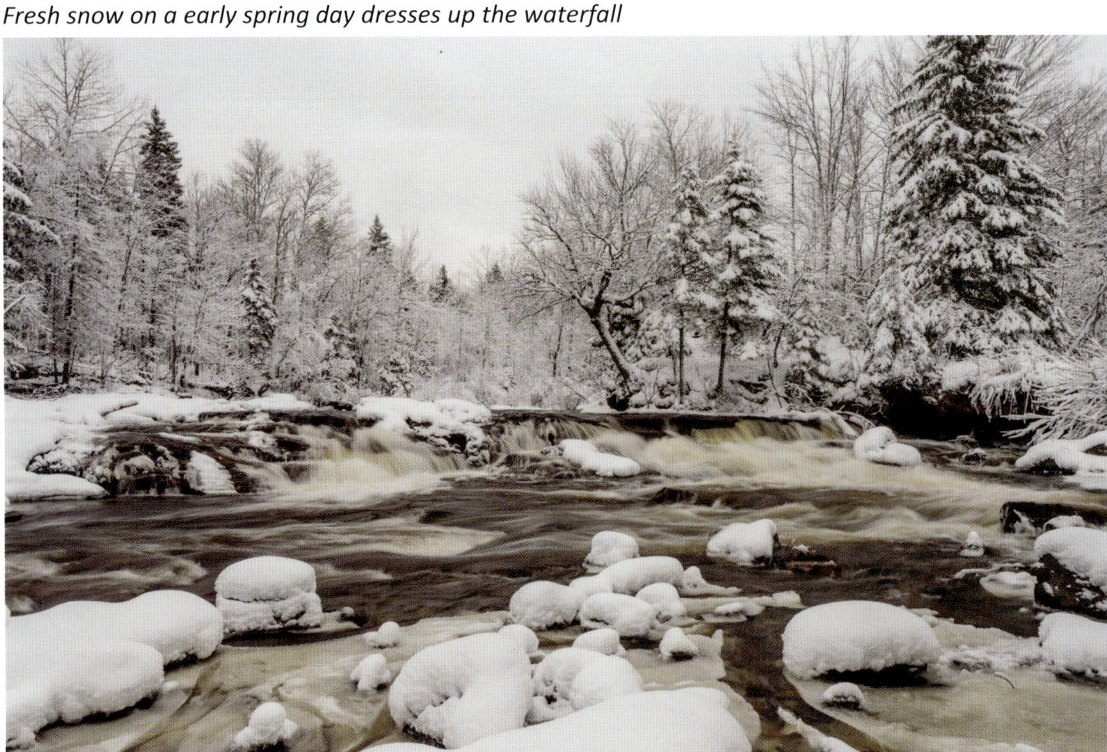

BIG ERICK'S FALLS #3 (HURON RIVER)

Private

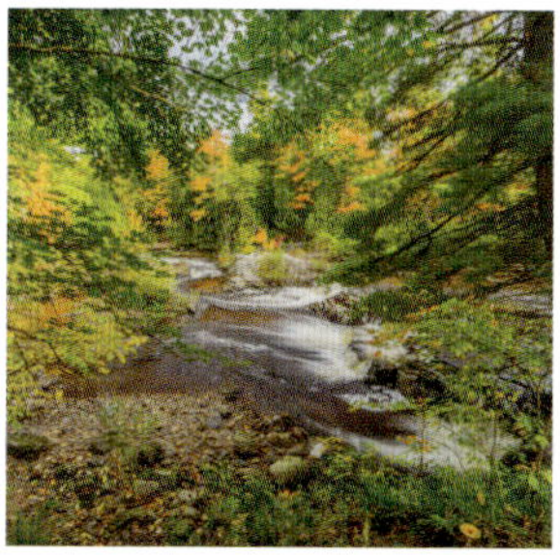

Must See:	5	GPS:	N46 51.931 W88 05.038
Height:	2 feet		
Time:	15-30 minutes	**Hiking Information**	
		Path:	Unimproved Footpath
Driving Information		Length:	200 yards
Signs:	None	Elev. Change:	Moderate
Road:	Gravel	GPS:	Recommended
Access:	Easy	Danger:	Slight
4WD:	Helpful	WP Boots:	Recommended

Another 75 yards downstream you'll find a waterfall that is at the beginning of a large island centered in the Huron River. The two arms of the river that flow around the island are much narrower than the widened river just upstream. The western side is 30 feet wide, while the eastern arm is broader at 50 feet across. Ford the near side of the river to get to the island to see the wider portion of the waterfall.

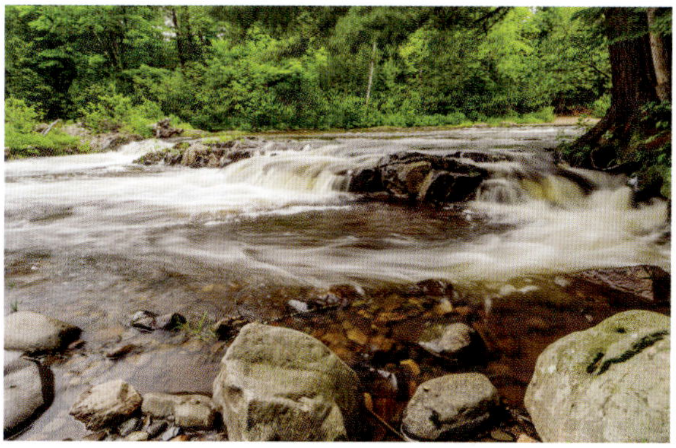

The river is strewn with cobblestones in a wide variety of sizes

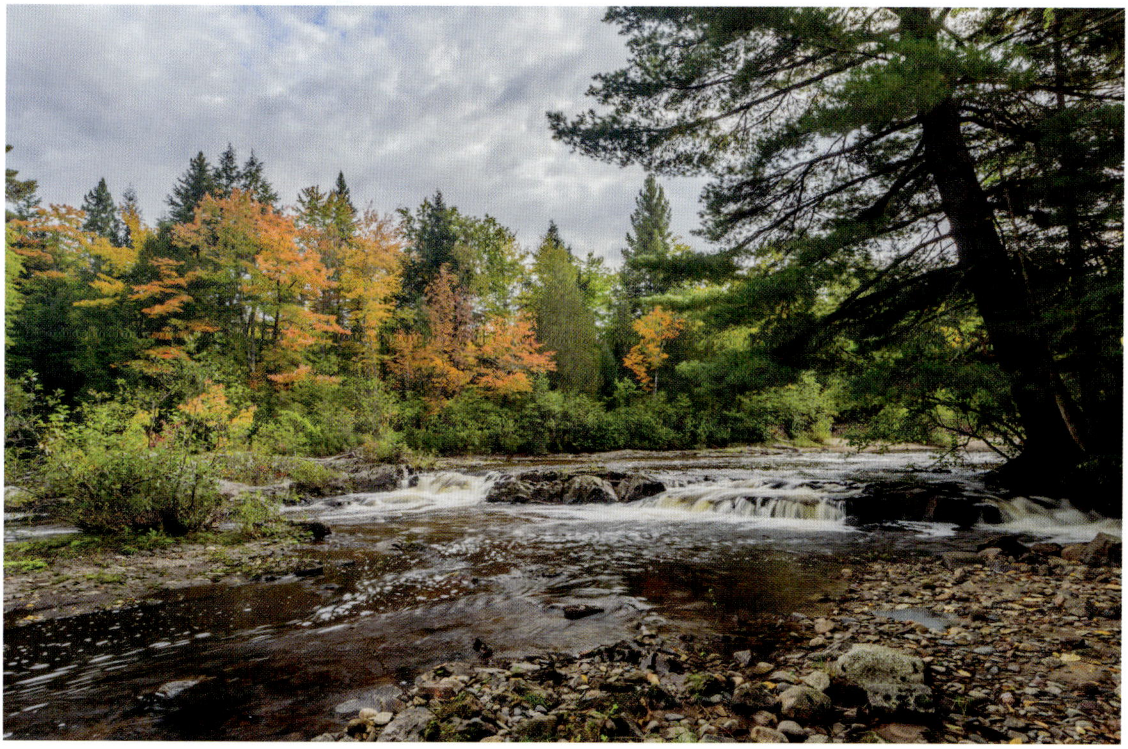

Big Falls Hike

Big Falls: The East Branch of the Huron River widens out and flows around an island situated at the top of the falls. The resultant split waterfall is nicely symmetrical. Remnants of campfires and a flat, pleasing viewing area at the base of the falls show that this is a favorite picnicking area.

Directions: From near the eastern end of Skanee Road turn right (south) onto Black Creek Road. Drive 1.7 miles to N46 50.763 W88 05.956. Turn left (east) onto a good dirt road. Big Falls is 2.1 miles from this intersection. The Western Branch of the Huron River will appear in about .2 miles. Caution! The river must be forded here. If the river is running too high this might not be possible. After crossing the river turn left at the first "Y". Then turn right at the next "Y". Park @ N46 50.241 W88 04.415. There is a small obvious parking spot here. This is just above the waterfall. Climb down the steep 30' tall bank to the base of the falls.

BIG FALLS (HURON RIVER - EAST BRANCH)

Private

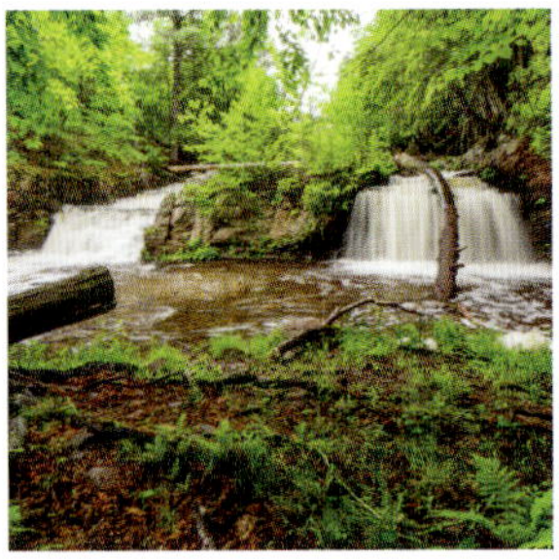

Must See:	9	GPS:	N46 50.224 W88 04.413
Height:	18 feet		
Time:	15-30 minutes	Hiking Information	
		Path:	Unimproved and STEEP
Driving Information		Length:	100 yards
Signs:	None	Elev. Change:	Steep Climb - 30 feet
Road:	Good Dirt	GPS:	Recommended
Access:	Somewhat Difficult	Danger:	Moderate
4WD:	Helpful	WP Boots:	None

A beautiful split cascade surrounds an island in the middle of the 50 foot wide river. There are multi-tiered cascades splashing down either side. A nice spill pool below the waterfall butts up to a flat, pine covered picnic area.

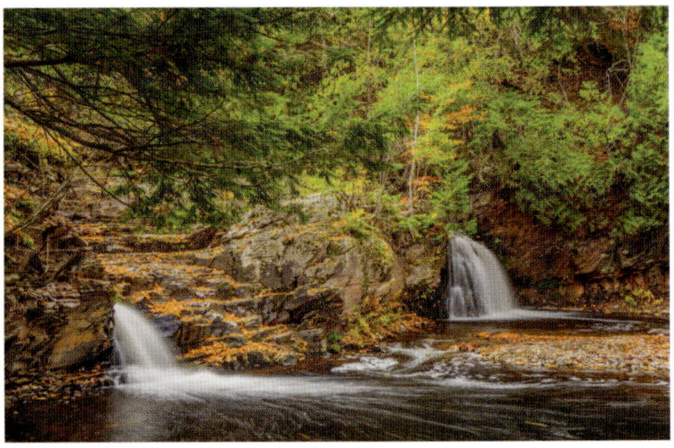

Two channels have been cut through the angular bedrock layers, one on either side of the river. The channels start 40 feet back from the edge of the falls. The eastern side is a series of stair steps, while the western side makes just two small drops before plunging down 10 feet into the spill pool.

More volume pours over the near side of the river

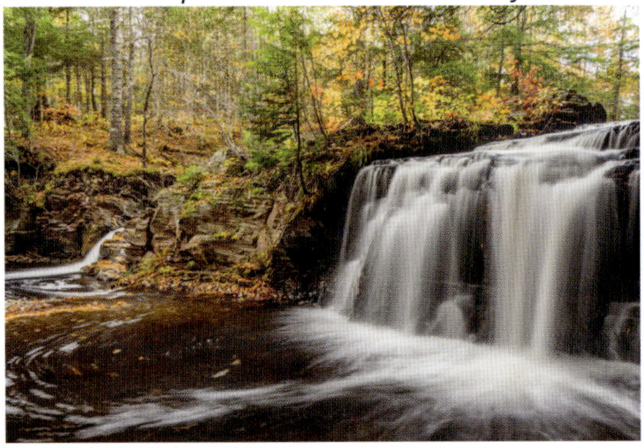

Looking down on the waterfall from the steep hill

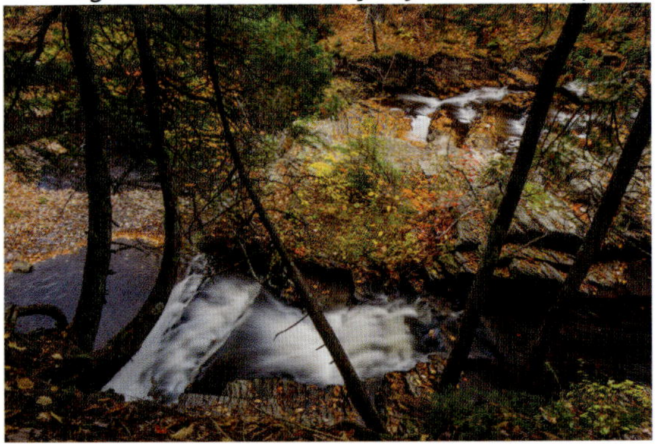

East Branch Falls Hike

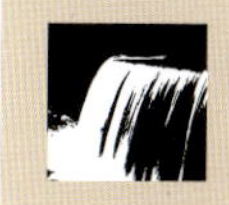

East Branch Falls: The boulder strewn river drops 10 feet in several cascades that ends in the river that is then split in half by a 20 foot wide island. Cedars shroud the rugged rock walls that line the river's sides. The setting, as much as the waterfall, calls for a "Must See" rating of 7.

East Branch Falls - Upper #1: The river seems to appear out of nowhere. A sharp bend in the river turns it almost upon itself. The river is carved through 40 foot high walls of solid rock on either side. The falls consist of 2 cascades. The 1st gently slopes into a pool. The second splits around a high spot in the falls, the main section falling straight down the river, while the smaller cascade runs down the face at a 90 degree angle.

East Branch Falls - Upper #2: Bordered by jagged, thin sheets of bedrock 20 feet high, the falls surge over more layers of the same rock, narrowing to 3 feet at the bottom of the drop, plunging into a small pool. The river turns hard and begins its approach to Upper #1.

East Branch Falls - Upper #3: One hundred feet upstream from #2, several cascades 8-10 inches each fall about 30 feet upstream from the main event, an 18 inch plunge in a roughly circular shaped cavity.

East Branch Falls - Upper #4: Pouring over stone slabs with a frothing rooster tail midway, this hidden waterfall flows into a deep, dark pool. Crumbling rock walls tower overhead.

East Branch Falls - Upper #5: The section of river that can be seen in between bends contains 4 cascades over 400 feet of river length. I have combined them, since they can be viewed all at once, and none of the drops individually are outstanding.

East Branch Falls - Upper #6: A small slide flattens out and cascades down over an arrowhead shaped rocky mass. The ravine is not as steep or quite as close to the river as downstream.

Directions: Follow Erick Road east past the Huron River. Park in a nice sized pullout area by the very nice bridge that crosses an unnamed creek. Cross over the bridge to the turnout large enough for 3 or 4 vehicles and park there. The parking area is at GPS location N46 51.006 W88 03.406. Hike across a berm and small creek. Follow the abandoned roadway. (Old orange/pink ribbons were hanging in strategically placed locations along the way when I was here in 2010.) Use a GPS at the end of the road to navigate through the forest. There is no path here. Scramble down about 20 feet of rock near the falls to the river's edge. Follow the river upstream from East Branch Falls for 1/4 mile. The set of upper falls start here and continue for another 1/4 mile. Caution: There are some steep ravines and sheer drops that must be climbed or avoided. Prepare to cross the river on occasion as the opposite bank will be easier to hike along.

EAST BRANCH FALLS (HURON RIVER - EAST BRANCH)

Private

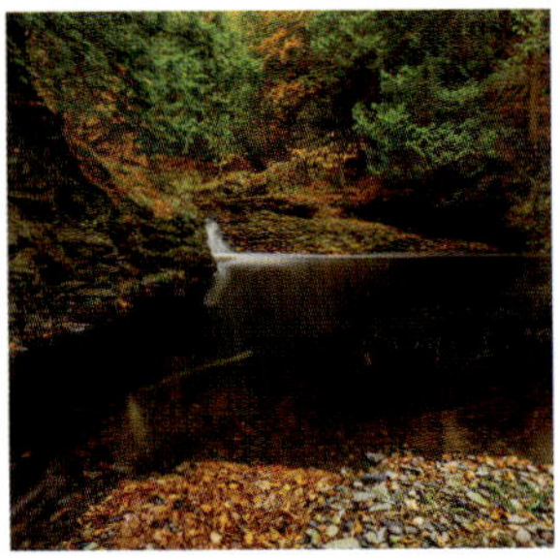

Must See:	7	GPS:	N46 50.945 W88 03.793
Height:	4 feet		
Time:	45-60 minutes	**Hiking Information**	
		Path:	None
Driving Information		Length:	.36 miles
Signs:	None	Elev. Change:	Moderate
Road:	Gravel	GPS:	Required
Access:	Somewhat Difficult	Danger:	Moderate
4WD:	Helpful	WP Boots:	Recommended

Situated with 20 foot tall walls of cracked, layered basalt, the waterfall cascades over a tapered mass of rock, sliding into a pool that splits around an island covered with stones, boulders, and wild flowers. As a backdrop to the waterfall, hardwoods and pines lend their colors.

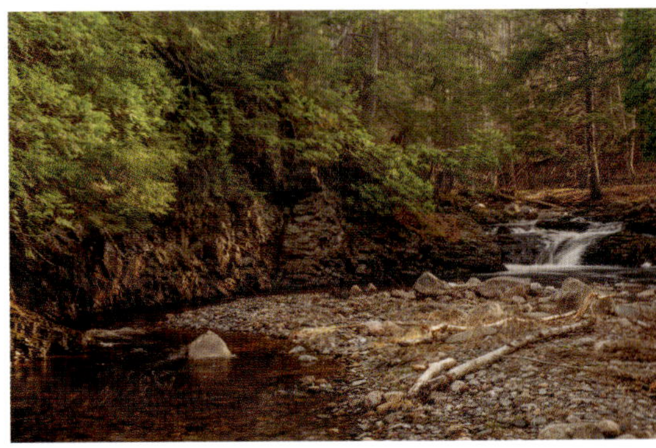

It's a short waterfall, but it presents itself beautifully!

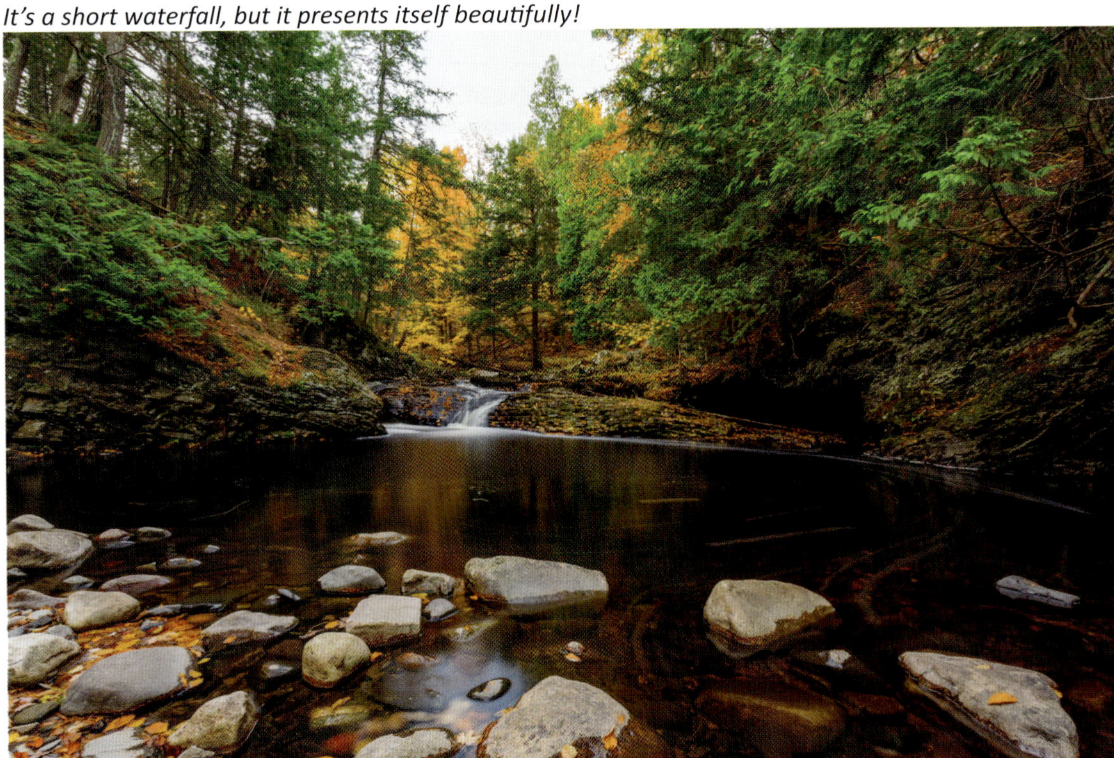

EAST BRANCH FALLS #2 (HURON RIVER - EAST BRANCH)

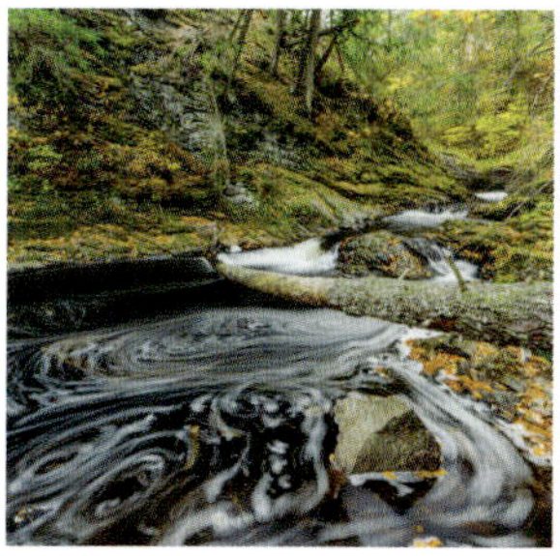

Must See:	6	GPS:	N46 50.776 W88 03.722
Height:	4 feet		
Time:	1-1.5 hours	Hiking Information	
		Path:	None
Driving Information		Length:	.56 miles
Signs:	None	Elev. Change:	Major
Road:	Gravel	GPS:	Required
Access:	Somewhat Difficult	Danger:	Elevated
4WD:	Helpful	WP Boots:	Recommended

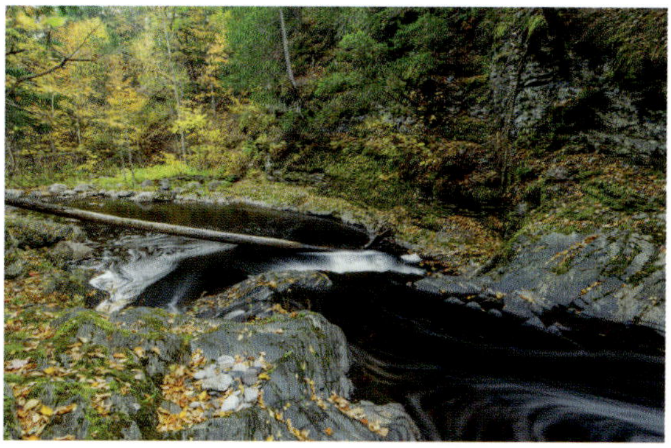

Hike upstream from East Branch Falls for .22 miles through the steep walled ravine following the river, crossing it as needed. A cluster of 3 waterfalls will come on suddenly, all three of them bunched up in 85 yards. They all occur around a large knob of hardened bedrock which forces the river to run around it in a sharp curve. The first waterfall, East Branch Falls #2, is at the end of the curve, #3 is in the center, and #4 is at the beginning.

Hiking up to the first of these waterfalls, the river seems to appear out of nowhere. A sharp bend in the river turns it almost upon itself. The river is carved through 40 foot walls of solid rock on either side. The waterfall contains 2 cascades. The first gently slopes into a pool. The second splits around a high spot in the falls, the main section falling straight down the river, while the smaller cascade runs down the face at a 90 degree angle.

The large rise on the left is the pivot around which the waterfalls occur.

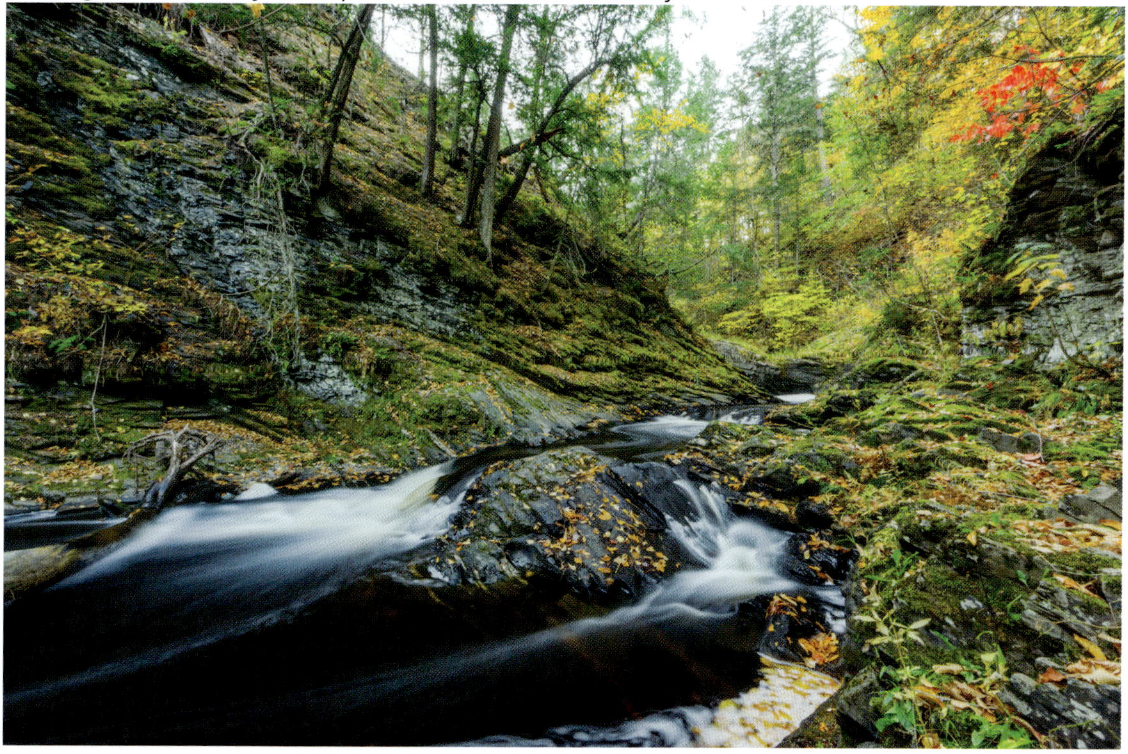

EAST BRANCH FALLS #3 (HURON RIVER - EAST BRANCH)

Private

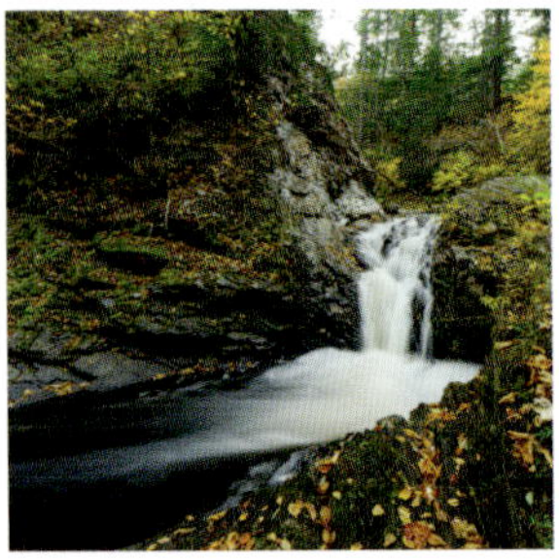

Must See:	8	GPS:	N46 50.761 W88 03.706
Height:	8 feet		
Time:	1-1.5 hours	Hiking Information	
		Path:	None
Driving Information		Length:	.58 miles
Signs:	None	Elev. Change:	Major
Road:	Gravel	GPS:	Required
Access:	Somewhat Difficult	Danger:	Elevated
4WD:	Helpful	WP Boots:	Recommended

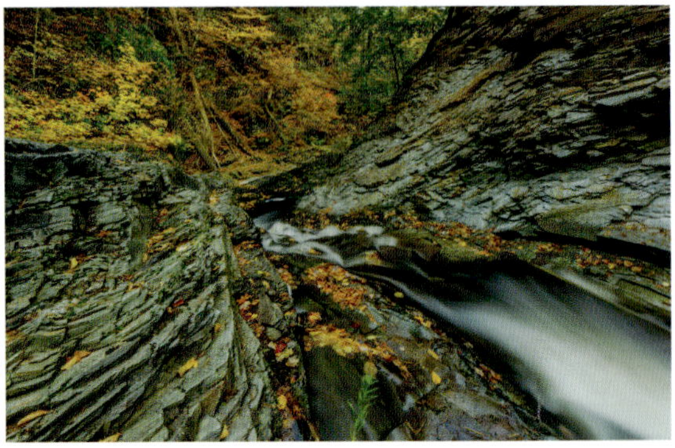

Continue upstream just 50 yards from #2 to see this lovely waterfall that is at the center of the point. Bordered by jagged, thin sheets of bedrock 20 feet high, the falls surge over more layers of the same rock, narrowing to 3 feet wide at the bottom of the drop, plunging into a small pool. The river turns hard and begins its approach to #2.

The picture to the right is looking down the waterfall from the river above. I love this waterfall! The unique geography of the area, coupled with the isolation of the waterfall has this one high on my "got to get back there" list!

The large knob can be easily seen here, the river turning and dropping quickly as it makes the bend.

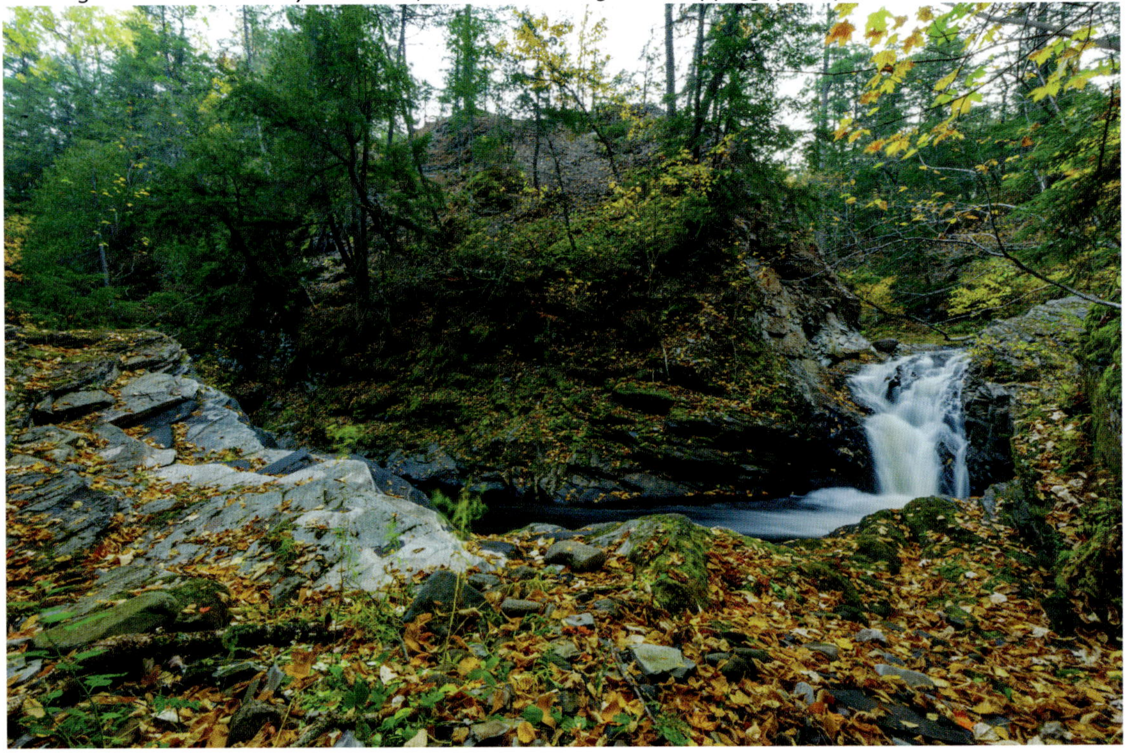

EAST BRANCH FALLS #4 (HURON RIVER - EAST BRANCH) Private

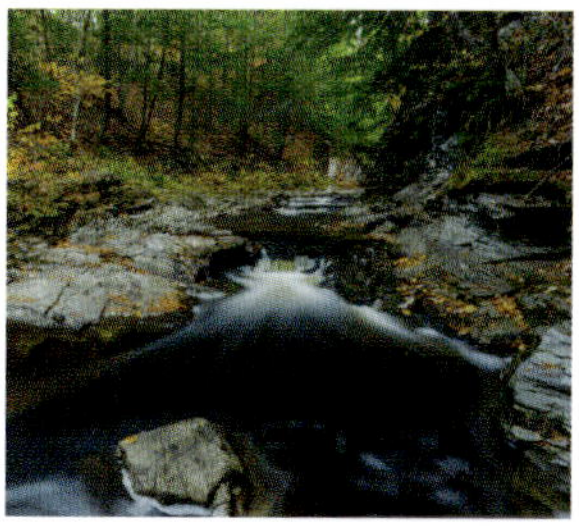

Must See:	4	GPS:	N46 50.764 W88 03.690
Height:	3 feet		
Time:	1.5-2 hours	Hiking Information	
		Path:	None
Driving Information		Length:	.59 miles
Signs:	None	Elev. Change:	Major
Road:	Gravel	GPS:	Required
Access:	Somewhat Difficult	Danger:	Elevated
4WD:	Helpful	WP Boots:	Recommended

Climb on up and around the bend. In about 100 feet you'll find #4. Several cascades 8-10 inches tall fall about 30 feet upstream from the main event, a cute 18 inch plunge into a roughly circular shaped cavity.

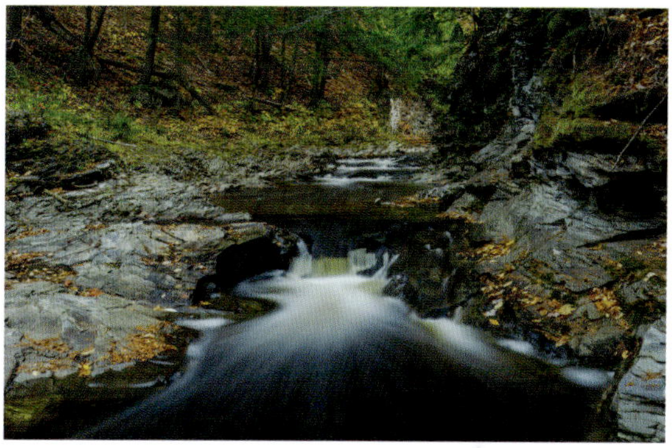

While following the East Branch upstream it is necessary to move from one side of the river to the other. This spot is a case in point. The steep ravine wall on the right side is impassible. At other times the prudent course of action seems to be to leave the riverbed and climb up out of the ravine, navigating along the crest before heading back down to the river again.

Note the gorge wall on the right. Cross to the far side to continue the hike upstream.

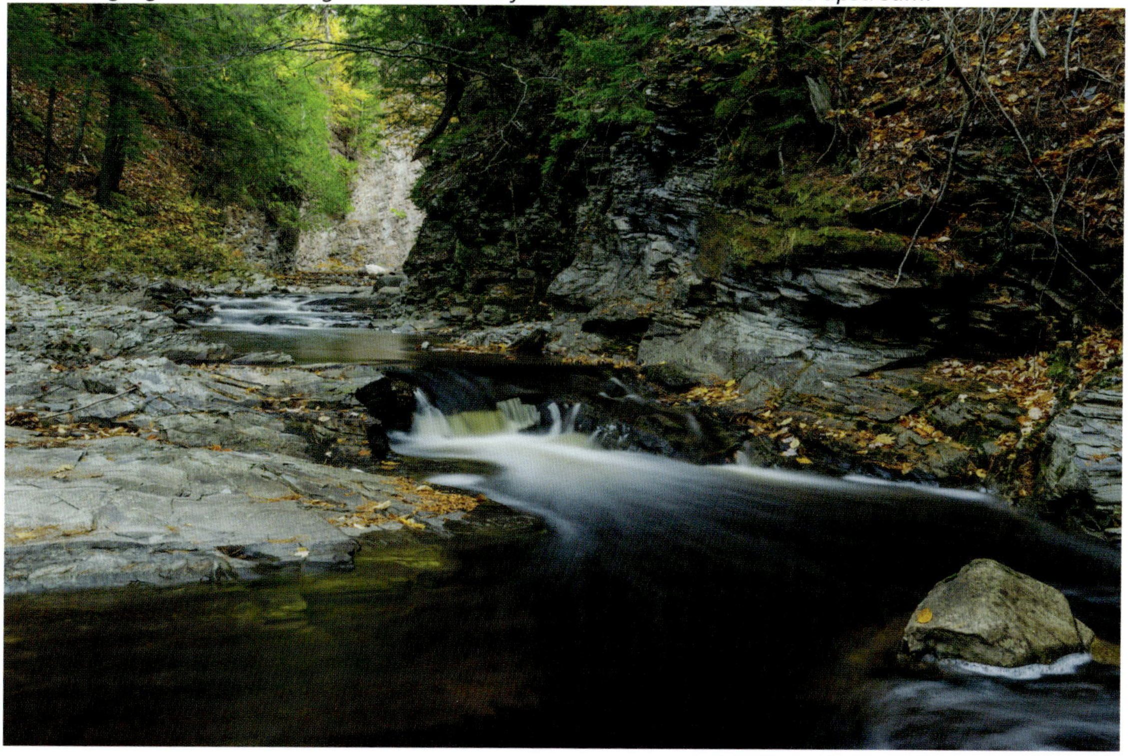

EAST BRANCH FALLS #5 (HURON RIVER - EAST BRANCH) Private

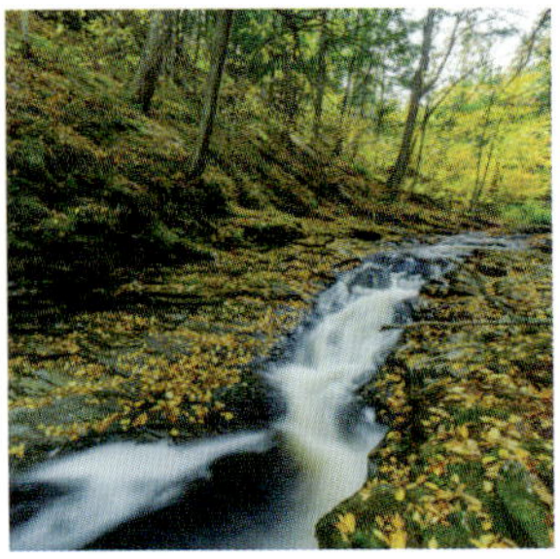

Must See:	7	GPS:	N46 50.703 W88 03.668
Height:	6 feet		
Time:	1.75-2.25 hours	**Hiking Information**	
		Path:	None
Driving Information		Length:	.74 miles
Signs:	None	Elev. Change:	Major
Road:	Gravel	GPS:	Required
Access:	Somewhat Difficult	Danger:	Elevated
4WD:	Helpful	WP Boots:	Recommended

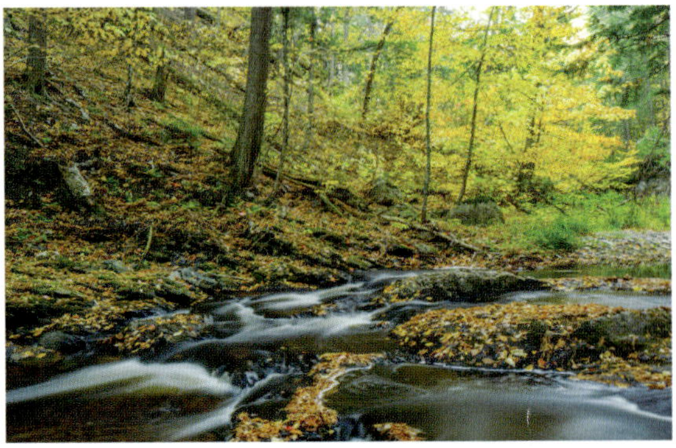

It's .15 miles between #4 and #5 if you follow the river. However, the river makes a large "U" between these waterfalls, so if you climb up out of the gorge after leaving #4 and head directly for the GPS coordinate for #5, the hike is only .10 miles - quite the distance savings!

Pouring over stone slabs with a frothing rooster tail midway, this hidden waterfall flows into a deep, dark pool. Crumbling rock walls tower overhead.

Note how narrow the river is running in the much wider riverbed. I wonder how it looks in the spring?

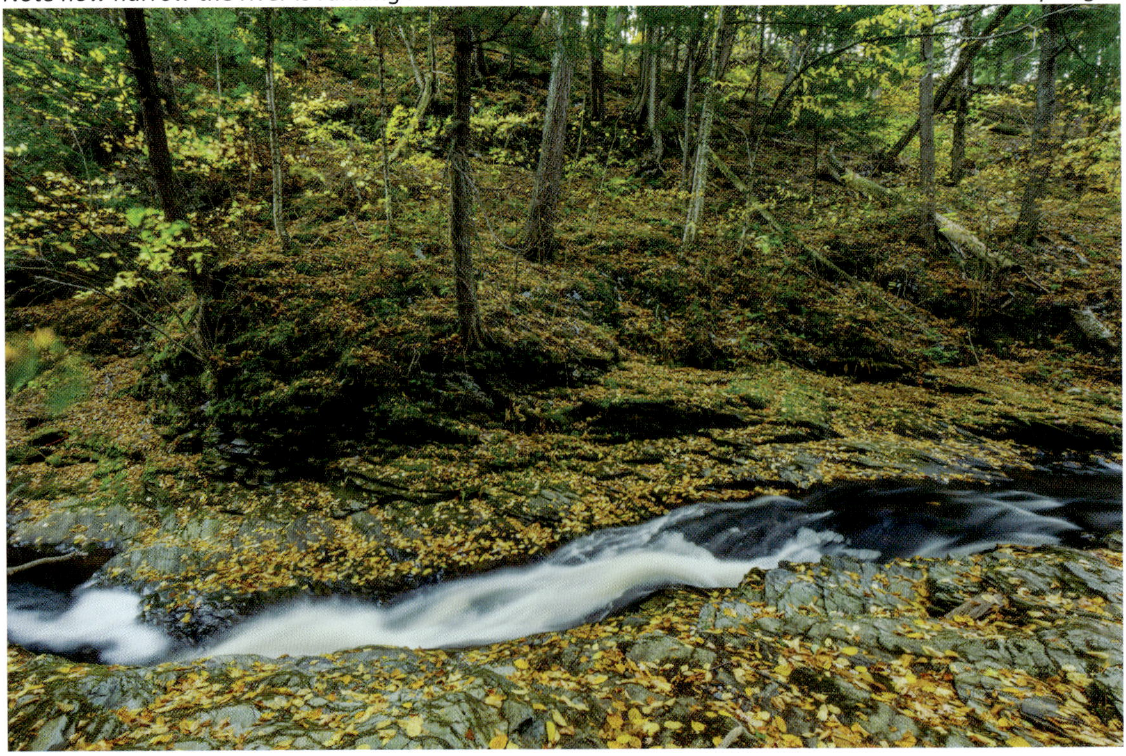

EAST BRANCH FALLS #6 (HURON RIVER - EAST BRANCH) Private

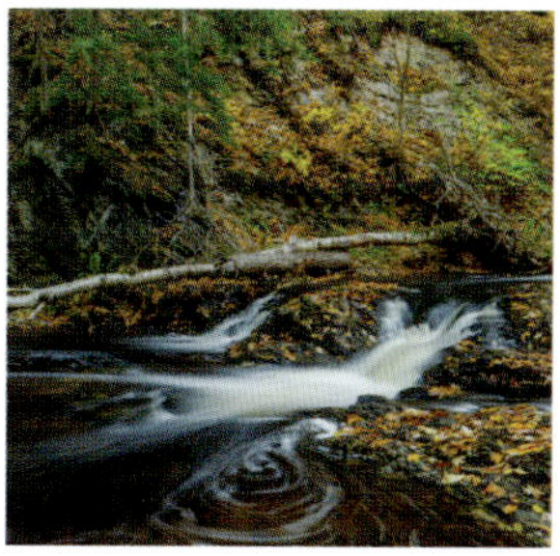

Must See:	5	GPS:	N46 50.675 W88 03.689
Height:	10 feet		
Time:	1.75-2.25 hours	**Hiking Information**	
		Path:	None
Driving Information		Length:	.79 miles
Signs:	None	Elev. Change:	Major
Road:	Gravel	GPS:	Required
Access:	Somewhat Difficult	Danger:	Elevated
4WD:	Helpful	WP Boots:	Recommended

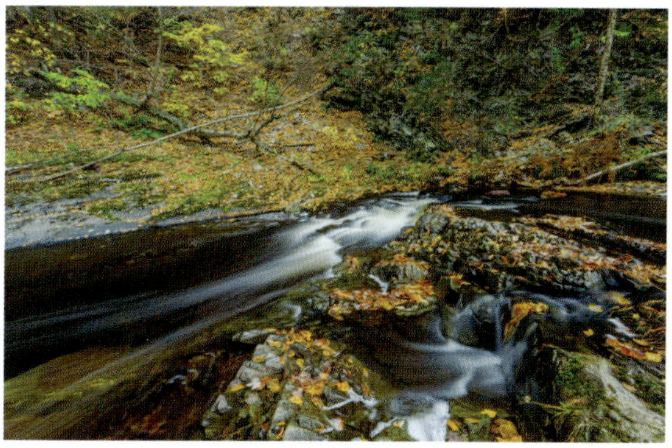

This waterfall is only 65 yards upstream from #5. These last 3 "East Branch Falls" are relatively close, not as close as #2 to #4, but these are all within about 200 yards of each other.

The section of river that can be seen in between bends contains 4 cascades over 150 feet of river length. I have combined them, since they can be viewed all at once, and none of the drops individually are outstanding.

Try to stay down at the river level as much as possible. The ravine walls are about 100 feet high in this area. They rise to this height about 100 yards from either side of the river.

The succeeding cascades can be seen in this wider shot

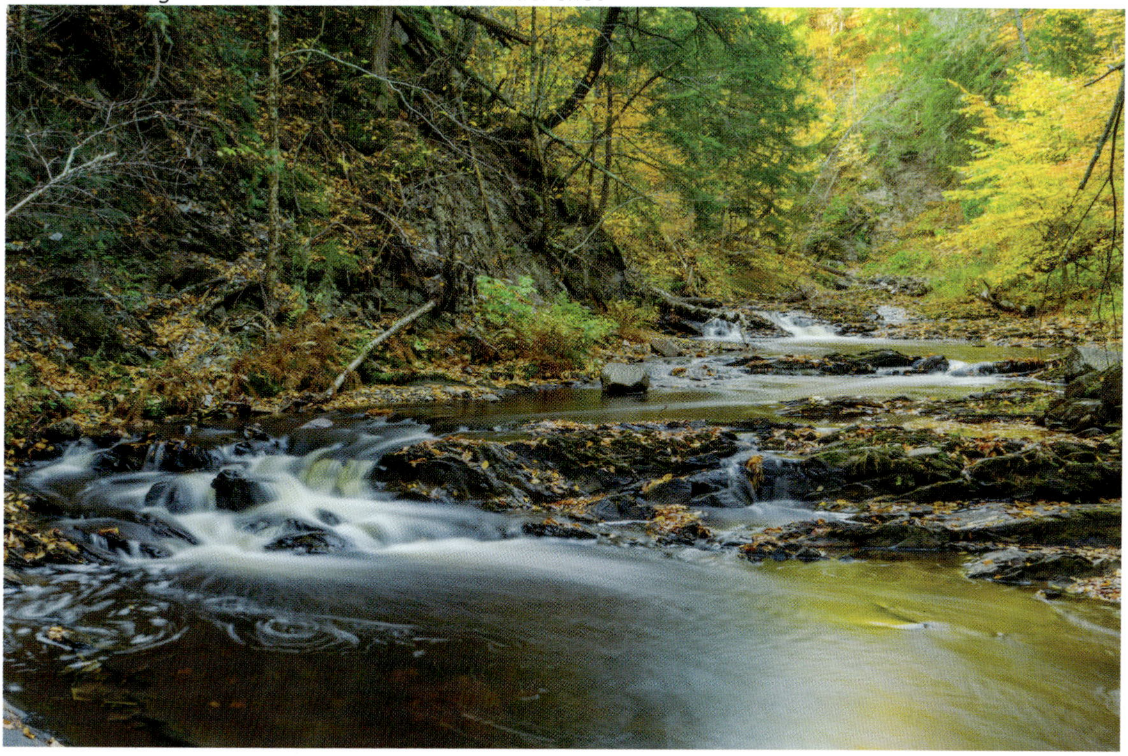

EAST BRANCH FALLS #7 (HURON RIVER - EAST BRANCH) Private

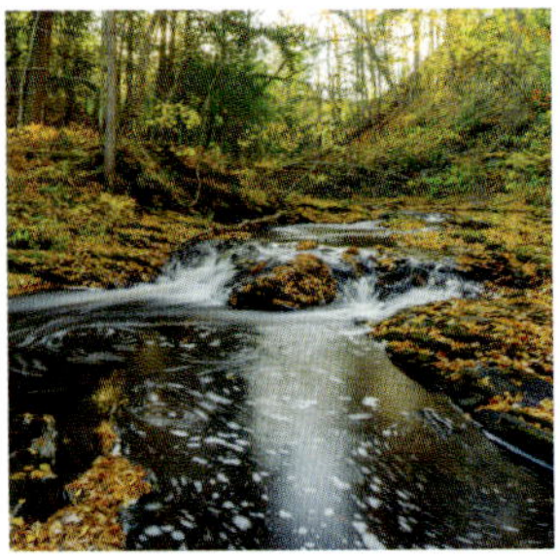

Must See:	5	GPS:	N46 50.617 W88 03.664
Height:	3 feet		
Time:	2-2.5 hours	Hiking Information	
		Path:	None
Driving Information		Length:	.82 miles
Signs:	None	Elev. Change:	Major
Road:	Gravel	GPS:	Required
Access:	Somewhat Difficult	Danger:	Elevated
4WD:	Helpful	WP Boots:	Recommended

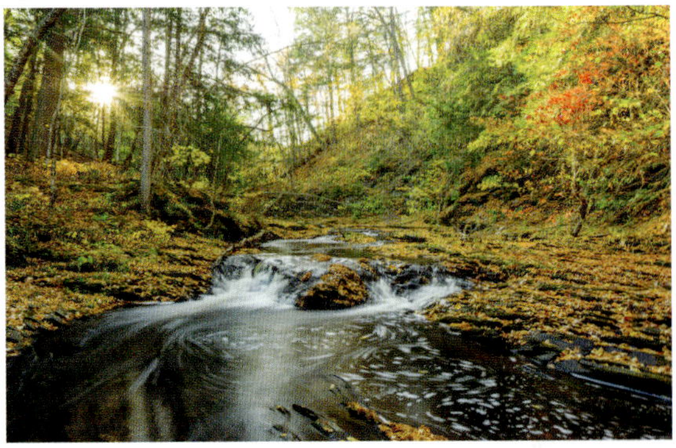

Hike upstream 150 yards from the base of #6 to arrive at the last of this series of small drops. Here, a small slide flattens out and cascades down over an arrowhead shaped rocky mass. The ravine is not as steep or quite as close to the river as downstream.

These woods are full of wildlife. On my hike back to the truck I happened upon several white tail deer. Their ears perked up, heads held aloft, eyes intent. After a few moments they went back to eating, content that I wasn't a threat. You never know what you'll see in the backwoods of Michigan.

There is a shortcut back to the parking spot if you'd like to try it. Cross the river and climb up out of the gorge. Head directly to N46 50.674 W88 03.520. This is about a .14 mile hike with no trail from the waterfall. At that coordinate you will find a 2-track. Follow it to the NE for .36 miles. You will now be back at the road you parked on. Turn left (NW) and hike for .21 miles to the parking spot.

Note how much flatter the bank is on the far side.

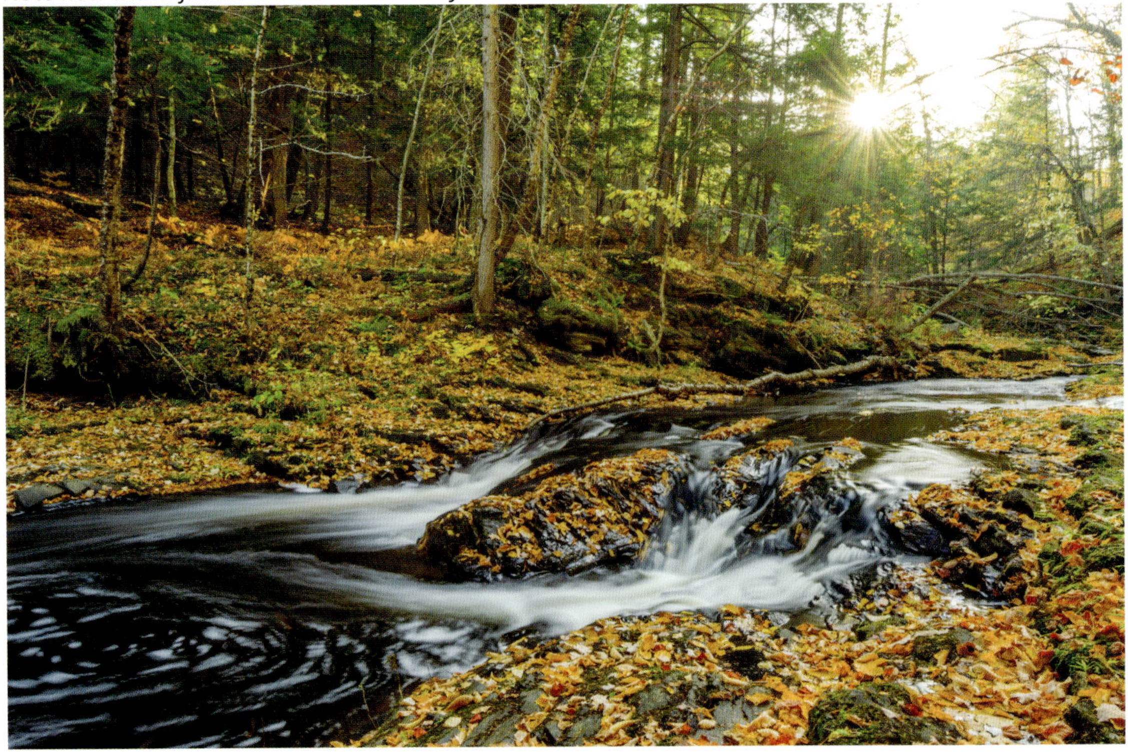

Erick's Falls Hike

Erick's Falls: Black Creek Road is a good gravel road that acts as a main truck route for the logging industry. An unusually nice bridge spans the West Branch of the Huron River just upstream from Erick's Falls. It is sometimes referred to by locals as the "Million Dollar Bridge". The waterfall, cascading over jagged rocks, is close to a gravel parking lot on the east side of the river. This stretch of river is favored by fishermen.

Erick's Cascades: A calm, black pool gives way to a small cascade that spans the river. Although it is a small drop, the setting is idyllic. Pine scented air. Open forest floor. A shallow, babbling river. This is a great family area!

Directions: Turn right on Black Creek Road off of Skanee Road. (This is just west of Erick Road.) Follow the road for 5.1 miles. The road crosses the West Branch of the Huron River on a very nice bridge. Park just east of the bridge. The Erick's Falls are just north of the bridge. The Upper Falls are south of the bridge.

ERICK'S FALLS (HURON RIVER - WEST BRANCH)

Private

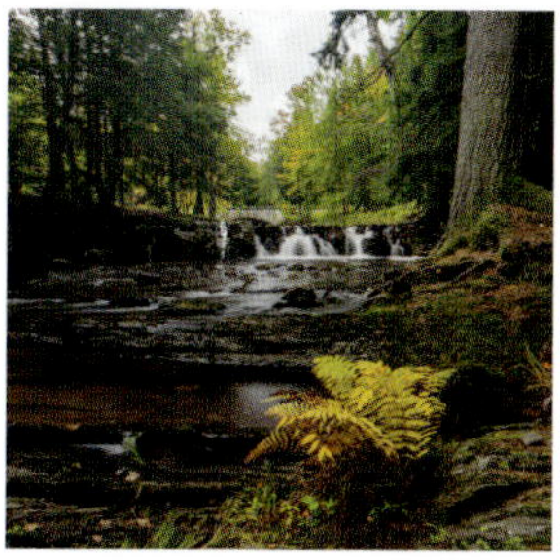

Must See:	6	GPS:	N46 48.388 W88 05.220
Height:	5 feet		
Time:	5-15 minutes	Hiking Information	
		Path:	Unimproved Footpath
Driving Information		Length:	100 feet
Signs:	None	Elev. Change:	Slight
Road:	Gravel	GPS:	N/A
Access:	Somewhat Difficult	Danger:	Slight
4WD:	Helpful	WP Boots:	N/A

Smooth hewn rocks sit quietly by the constantly rushing falls. These falls are just below the bridge.

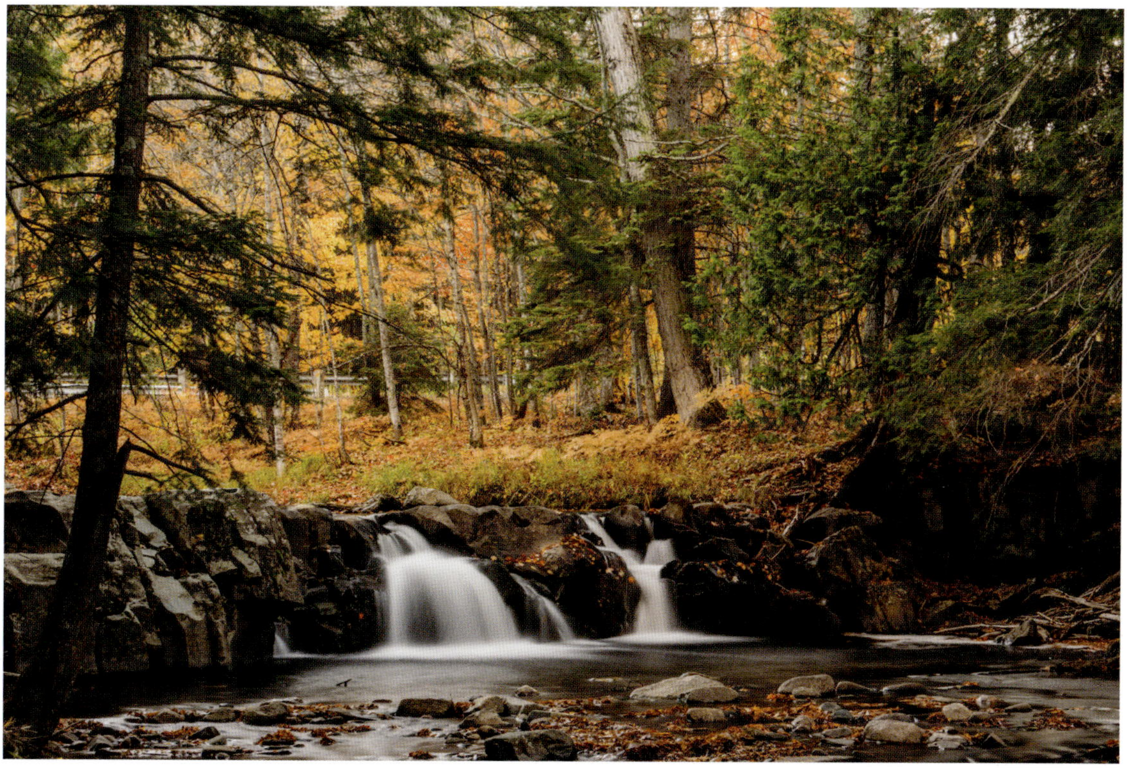

ERICK'S CASCADES (HURON RIVER - WEST BRANCH)

Private

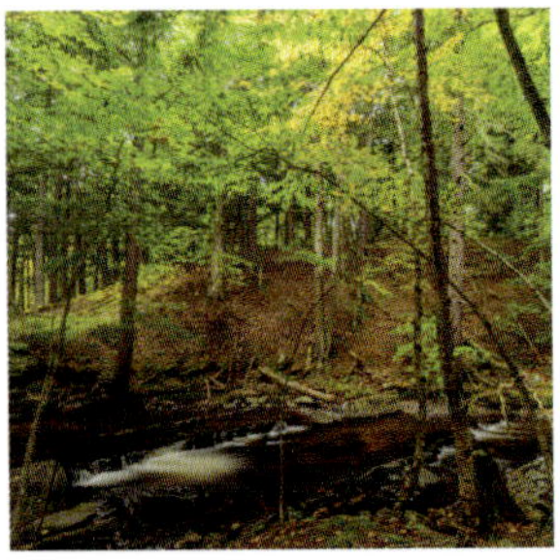

Must See:	4	GPS:	N46 48.307 W88 05.257
Height:	1 feet		
Time:	15-30 minutes	Hiking Information	
		Path:	Unimproved Footpath
Driving Information		Length:	150 yards
Signs:	None	Elev. Change:	Slight
Road:	Gravel	GPS:	N/A
Access:	Somewhat Difficult	Danger:	Slight
4WD:	Required	WP Boots:	Recommended

Two levels of mirrored water are interrupted by a curtain of white with a beautiful rock wall as a backdrop. Hike upstream through a hauntingly silent pine forest to these little falls. Time seems to slow to a crawl in the quiet babble and hushed bowing of the branches above. The thick forest floor cushions the footfall below. Sometimes it's little things that speak more to us in their hushed tones than the cacophony of the majestic ever could.

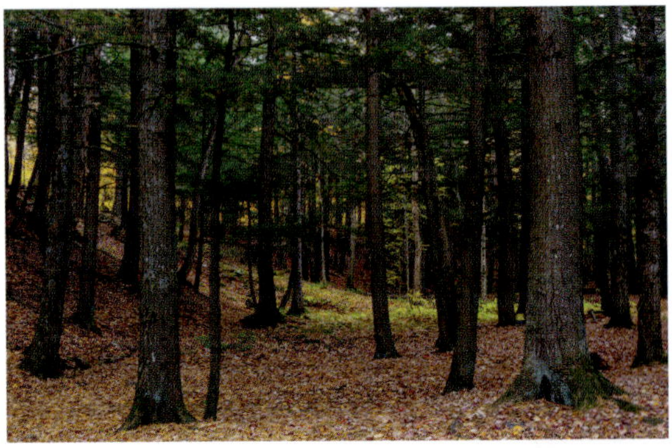

The "main" drop runs in a line across the river - It's a beautiful little cascade.

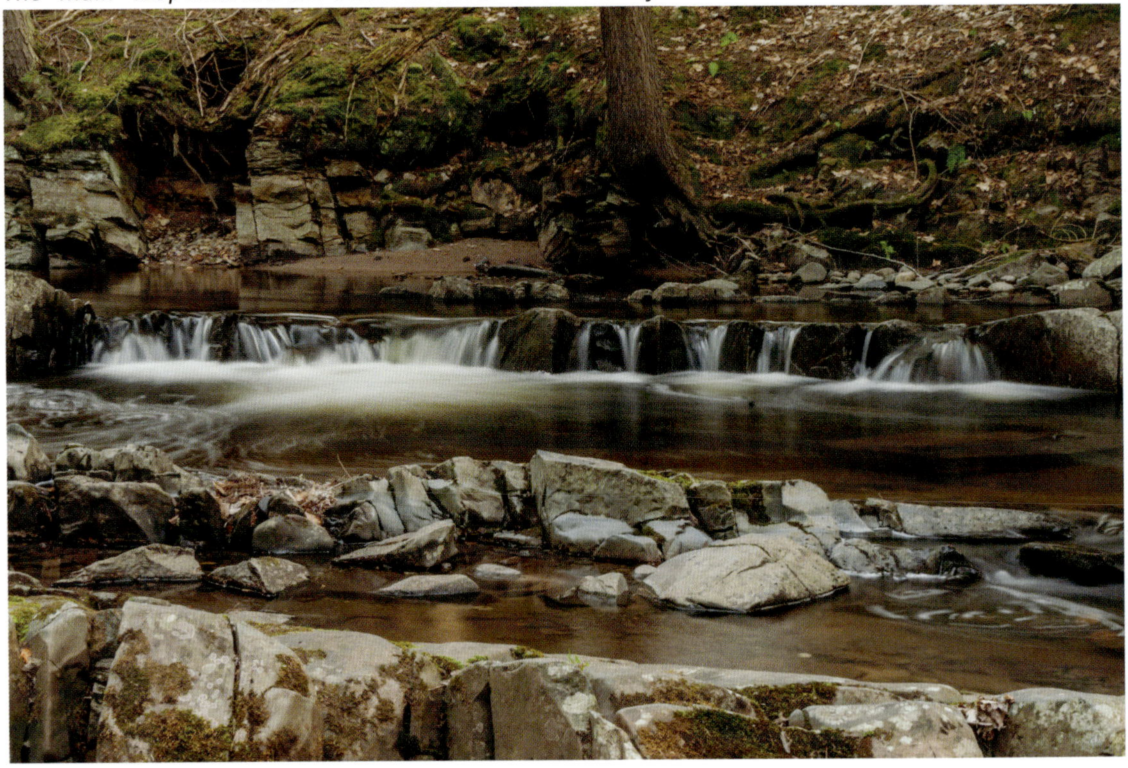

Huron Gorge Hike

Over a mile upstream from Big Falls is the Huron Gorge Cascades. The East Branch of the Huron River here runs through a high walled gorge.

Directions: From near the eastern end of Skanee Road turn right (south) onto Black Creek Road. Drive 1.7 miles to N46 50.763 W88 05.956. Turn left (east) onto a good dirt road. The Western Branch of the Huron River will appear in about .2 miles. Caution! The river must be forded here. If the river is running too high this might not be possible. After crossing the river turn left at the first "Y". Then turn right at the next "Y". After passing Big Falls parking spot, drive 1.25 miles to N46 49.786 W88 04.065. (You will pass by a camp. Be considerate.) Park. Hike to either end of the cascades to climb down into the gorge. There is no way down into the gorge in the middle of the cascades. There is a sheer wall in that area.

HURON GORGE CASCADES (HURON RIVER - EAST BRANCH) Private

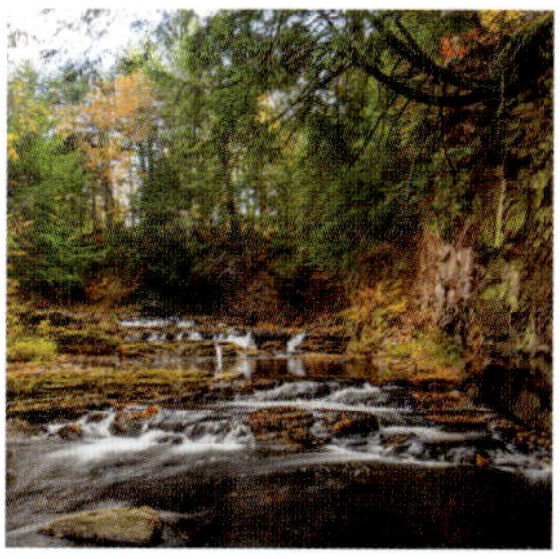

Must See:	4	GPS:	N46 49.801 W88 03.985
Height:	5 feet		
Time:	20-45 minutes	Hiking Information	
		Path:	Old road then none
Driving Information		Length:	.14 miles
Signs:	None	Elev. Change:	Moderate
Road:	Dirt Road	GPS:	Required
Access:	Difficult	Danger:	Moderate
4WD:	Recommended	WP Boots:	Recommended

This is a series of cascades, the highest at 3 feet. They run along the base of a 25 foot sheer walled gorge. Reddish rock, crumbling off of the walls, is piled up here and there at the base of the gorge. Large trees are precariously perched along the edge of the constantly eroding cliff.

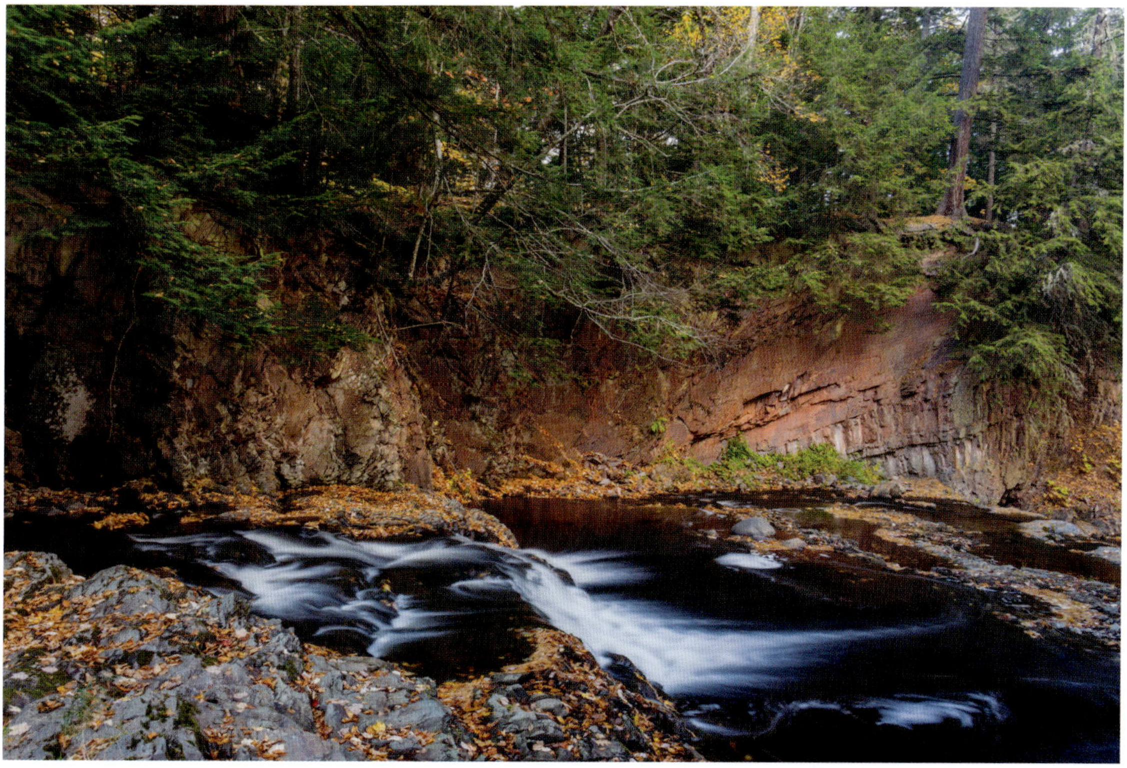

Letherby Falls Hike

Tracey's Falls: Not far down the old, abandoned road that follows the West Branch of the Huron River Tracey's Falls can be found. It is down a bit of a hill and through the forest. A short set of split rocks makes up Tracey's Falls as the river flows through a tame section of woods.

Letherby Falls: You can hear the waterfall before seeing it! Leave the old gravel road at the obvious sound of water falling. Climb down the somewhat steep hill to approach Letherby Falls from the spill pool directly below the falls.

Letherby Falls Cascades: From Letherby Falls, follow the river downstream several hundred feet to see the river tear down a steep section of hillside in a series of cascades.

Directions: Letherby Falls can be accessed from both sides of the river. I prefer the route on the West Side.

Preferred Route (West Side): Turn south off of Skanee Road onto Roland Lake Road (dirt). Follow it to the end (2.9 miles). Turn right (west) onto Ravine River Road for 4.0 miles. Go straight at N46 46.797 W88 10.770 for 2.2 miles. Turn left at N46 45.995 W88 08.627 for .9 miles. Veer right at N46 46.169 W88 07.784 for .3 miles. Veer right at N46 46.120 W88 07.334 for .6 miles. Veer left at N46 45.852 W88 06.741 for .1 miles. Turn onto a connecting "road" @ N46 45.866 W88 06.658 and park. Hike 150 yards (north) to a "T". Hike to the right (east). In 150 feet the road turns to the north. (Tracey's Falls is almost directly ahead, 150 feet through the forest.) Follow the road to the desired waterfalls. The waterfalls are not that far from the road. In fact, Letherby Falls can usually be heard while hiking down the road.

Alternate Route (East Side): Turn south on Black Creek Road off of Skanee Road. Turn right on Letherby Falls Road just past the bridge at Erick's Falls. There is a sign for "Letherby Falls" at this corner. After 2.0 miles the main road turns to the left. Continue on straight for approximately .2 miles. Turn right on the 2nd 2-track on the right. After .4 miles the 2-track comes to a "T". Turn left. The 2-track ends shortly in a clearing. Park. Walk 200 yards down an embankment and across a little creek to the falls. Use a GPS unit as there is no trail.

TRACEY'S FALLS (HURON RIVER - WEST BRANCH)

Private

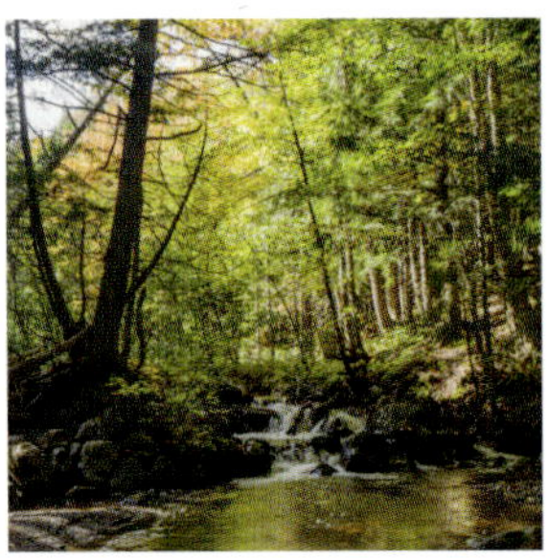

Must See:	4	GPS:	N46 45.950 W88 06.541
Height:	5 feet		
Time:	20-45 minutes	Hiking Information	
		Path:	Old road then none
Driving Information		Length:	.14 miles
Signs:	None	Elev. Change:	Moderate
Road:	Dirt Road	GPS:	Required
Access:	Difficult	Danger:	Moderate
4WD:	Recommended	WP Boots:	Recommended

Tracey's Falls is named after the perennially optimistic and helpful face of the Baraga County Convention and Visitors Bureau. Be sure to stop by the visitor center at 755 E. Broad Street in L'Anse. It's at the corner of US-41 near the large overhead sign welcoming all to L'Anse. If preferred, call (906) 524-7444 for a wealth of information regarding anything in Baraga County.

A jumble of rocks obscures the bulk of the water falling at Tracey's Falls. Maybe check this one out during periods of higher water. Fairly level ground in this vicinity makes for an easier walk.

LETHERBY FALLS (HURON RIVER - WEST BRANCH)

Private

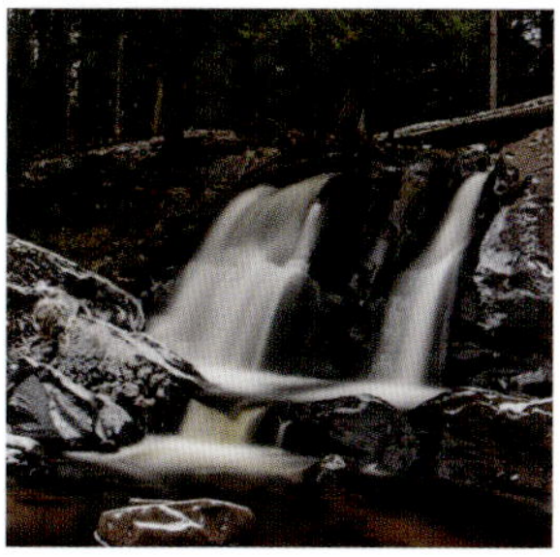

Must See:	8	GPS:	N46 46.027 W88 06.531
Height:	15 feet		
Time:	40-60 minutes	**Hiking Information**	
		Path:	Old road then none
Driving Information		Length:	.22 miles
Signs:	None	Elev. Change:	Moderate
Road:	Gravel Road	GPS:	Required
Access:	Difficult	Danger:	Moderate
4WD:	Helpful	WP Boots:	Recommended

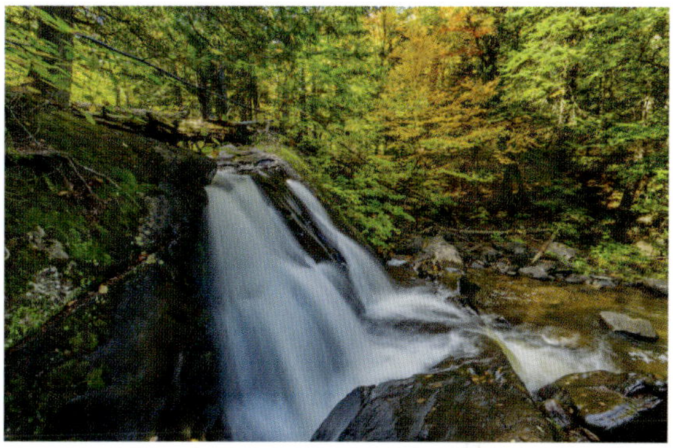

The West Branch of the Huron River flows over a unique igneous mass here at Letherby Falls. Two slits eroded into the basalt disgorge the water in twin tails of frothing white. The rock face has circular and footprint shaped imprints scattered over it. Below the initial spill pool the river drops another 2 feet to finish the waterfall. Continue downstream just another 100 yards to see the Letherby Cascades.

This is a beautiful waterfall, but it is not easily viewed. Uneven rocks and tangled undergrowth run all the way up to the river's edge.

*NOTE: The USGS has "Letherby Falls" located about 1 mile downstream from here. That is NOT ACCURATE! There is no waterfall there. It is one of several such errors found in Michigan USGS maps.

The small drop is the remains of the original waterfall. This layer split away and eroded over time.

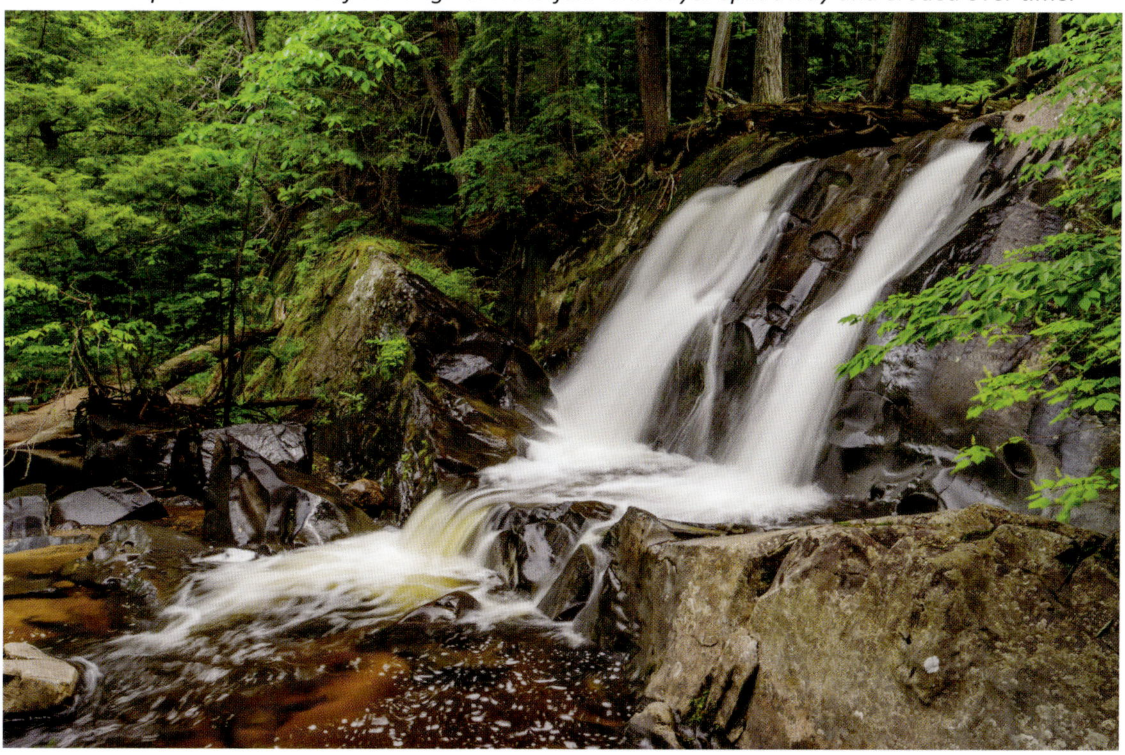

LETHERBY CASCADES (HURON RIVER - WEST BRANCH)

Private

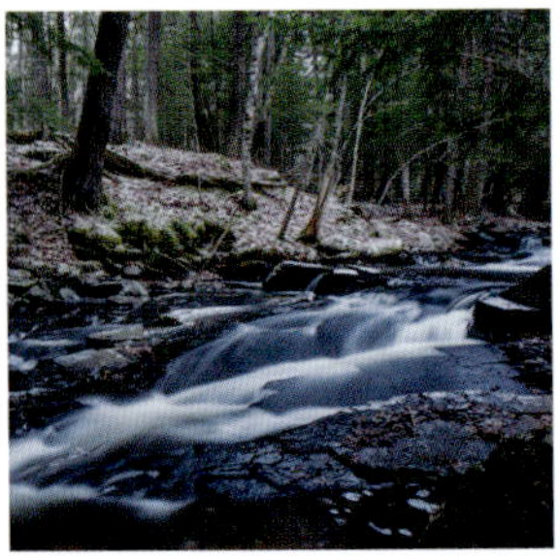

Must See:	6	GPS:	N46 46.049 W88 06.492
Height:	20 feet		
Time:	60-90 minutes	Hiking Information	
		Path:	Old road then none
Driving Information		Length:	.25 miles
Signs:	None	Elev. Change:	Moderate
Road:	Gravel Road	GPS:	Required
Access:	Difficult	Danger:	Moderate
4WD:	Helpful	WP Boots:	Recommended

From the spill pool below Letherby Falls, the river makes a sharp bend. The subsequent quiet portion of river allows for a good area to ford the river if so desired. Letherby Cascades then begins dropping down the hillside in a series of drops and cascades.

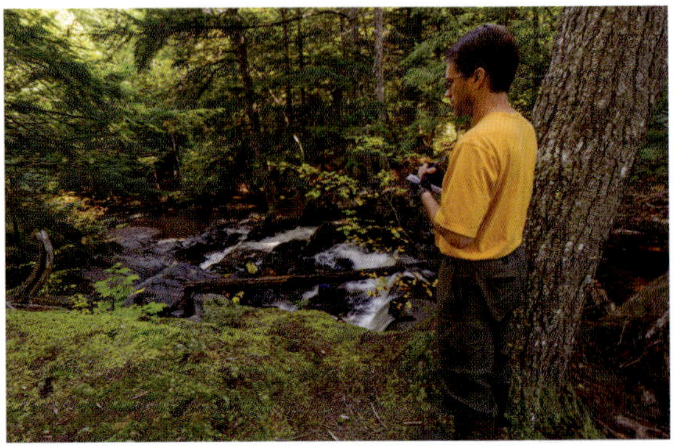

Note the moss covered promontory on the west side of the river up at the top of the cascades. It is a nice place to view both Letherby Cascades and Letherby Falls as it is situated between them. The author used this vantage point to take some field notes.

The cascades have at least 7 drops (depending on how you count them) scattered over 100 feet

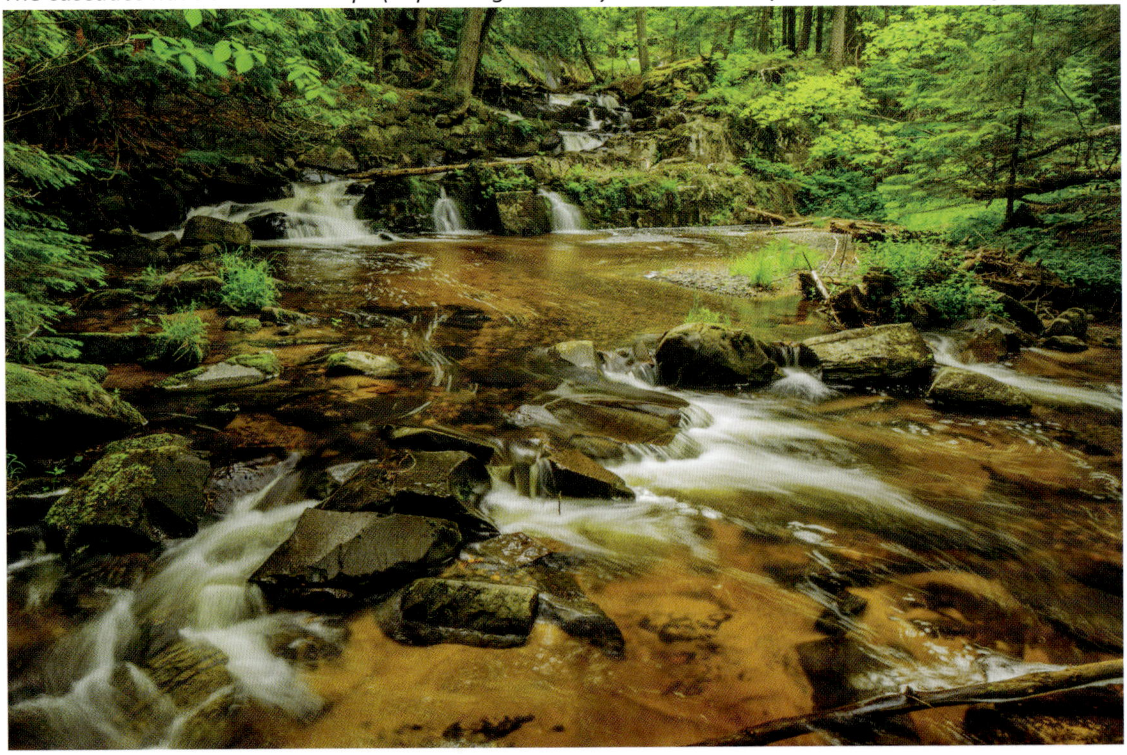

Letherby - Lower Falls Hike

Letherby Falls - Lower: Rounded bedrock drops the river in an angular fashion across the river. A jutting mass of rock in the middle of the falls splits the falls. When the river is running low, all the water flows on the right side of the waterfall.

Directions: Turn south on Black Creek Road off of Skanee Road. Turn right on Letherby Road just past the bridge at Erick's Falls. Drive 1.34 miles. Turn right on an OK dirt road for 150 yards. There is a 2-track here .13 miles long that leads to a hunter's cabin. The falls are about 100 yards down from here. PRIVATE LAND - DO NOT ENTER WITHOUT PERMISSION

LETHERBY FALLS - LOWER (HURON RIVER - WEST BRANCH) Private

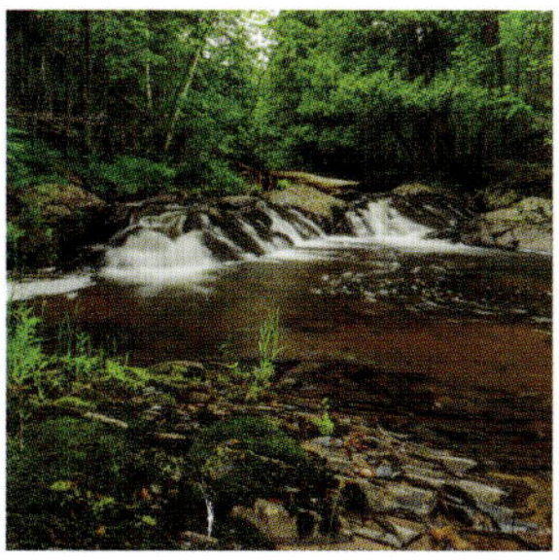

Must See:	4	GPS:	N46 47.240 W88 05.940
Height:	5 feet		
Time:	30-60 minutes	Hiking Information	
		Path:	Unimproved Footpath
Driving Information		Length:	1/2 mile
Signs:	None	Elev. Change:	Moderate
Road:	Gravel	GPS:	Required
Access:	Difficult	Danger:	Moderate
4WD:	Recommended	WP Boots:	Recommended

It was my understanding that this was on publicly accessible land, but after hiking out to the waterfall, I discovered a hunting cabin located at the top of the hill above the waterfall. GET PERMISSION BEFORE ATTEMPTING TO VISIT THIS WATERFALL.

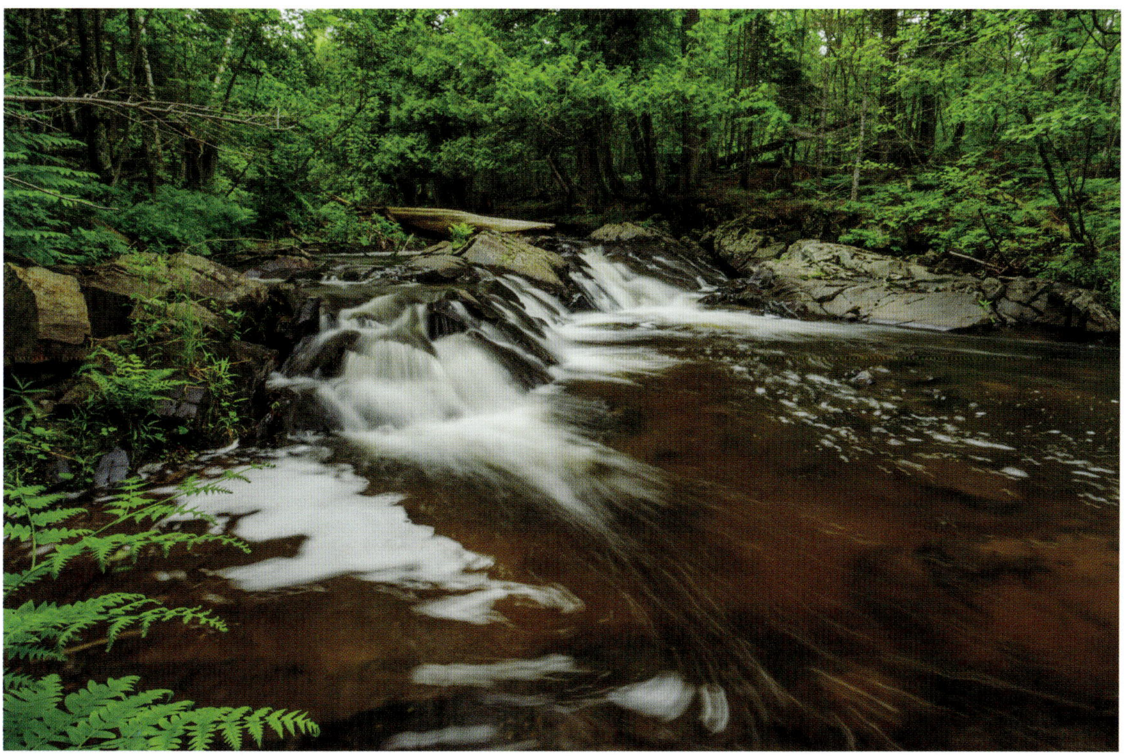

Letherby - Middle Falls Hike

Letherby Falls - Middle: Four main cascades drop over 50 yards of river length. Hike about 150 yards from the parking spot to the waterfall.

Directions: Turn south on Black Creek Road off of Skanee Road. Turn right on Letherby Road just past the bridge at Erick's Falls. Drive 1.34 miles. Turn right (west) onto an OK dirt road (at N46 47.284 W88 05.668) for 1.0 miles. Turn right (west) at (N46 46.479 W88 05.777) for .49 miles to a sharp bend in the trail. Park. Hike through the forest toward the river (which will be audible from the parking area). Shortly, there will be a sharp decline toward the river. Find an "easy" route down (typically off to your left). This portion of the hike lies over soggy ground. Waterproof boots are highly recommended because of this.

LETHERBY FALLS - MIDDLE (HURON RIVER - WEST BRANCH) Private

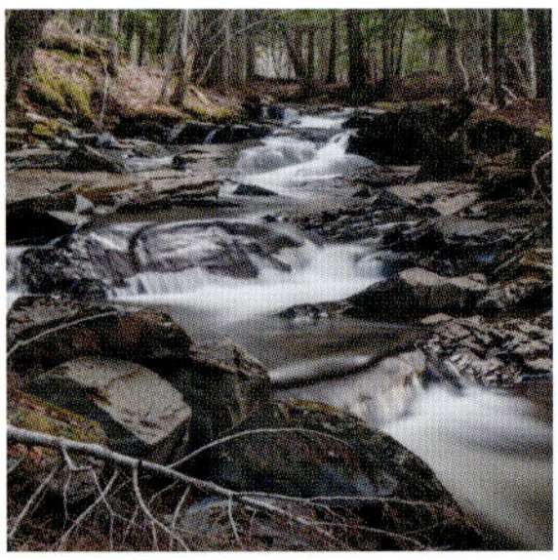

Must See:	5	GPS:	N46 46.409 W88 06.499
Height:	10 feet		
Time:	20-45 minutes	Hiking Information	
		Path:	None
Driving Information		Length:	150 yards
Signs:	None	Elev. Change:	Moderate
Road:	2-track	GPS:	Required
Access:	Difficult	Danger:	Moderate
4WD:	Helpful	WP Boots:	Recommended

You will approach the waterfall from downstream. There will be several small drops before getting to the waterfall proper. The waterfall is made up of four main drops. They are mostly steep slides, anywhere from one to three feet high, and scattered over 100 feet. Birch, hemlock, and cedar trees stretch out feathery arms, sheltering the waterway in an intimate embrace. Large, elongated, grayish boulders lie jumbled along the sides of the waterway, placed there as by a master gardener.

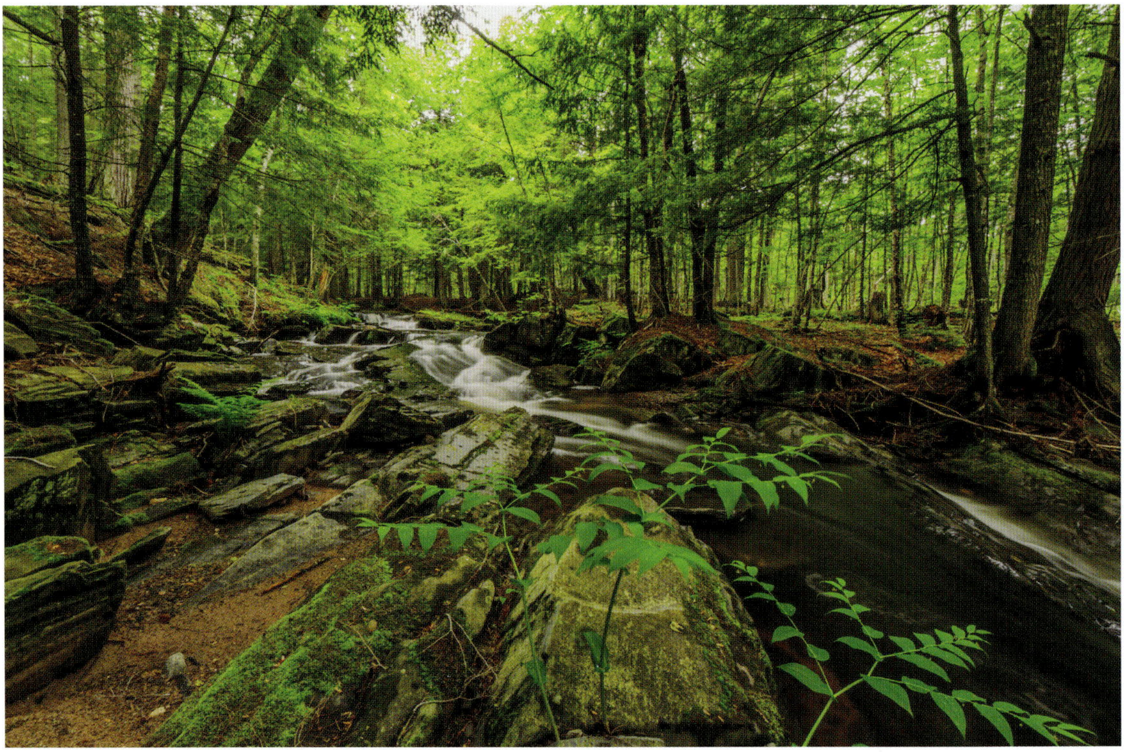

Letherby - Upper Falls Hike

Letherby Falls - Upper: This is the easiest to access out of all the "Letherby" Falls. Park at the entrance to an ATV trail. Hike down the steep trail 100 yards to the base of the waterfall. It is easy to view the waterfall. The terrain is flat and free from undergrowth. This is a locally favorite waterfall.

Directions: Turn south off of Skanee Road onto Roland Lake Road (dirt). Follow it to the end (2.9 miles). Turn right (west) onto Ravine River Road for 4.0 miles. Go straight at N46 46.797 W88 10.770 for 2.2 miles. Turn left at N46 45.995 W88 08.627 for .9 miles. Veer right at N46 46.169 W88 07.784 for .3 miles. Veer right at N46 46.120 W88 07.334 for .6 miles. Veer left at N46 45.852 W88 06.741 for .2 miles. Park at entrance to ATV trail at N46 45.841 W88 06.564. Drive an ATV (or hike) 300 feet down the hill to the base of the falls.

LETHERBY FALLS - UPPER (HURON RIVER - WEST BRANCH) Private

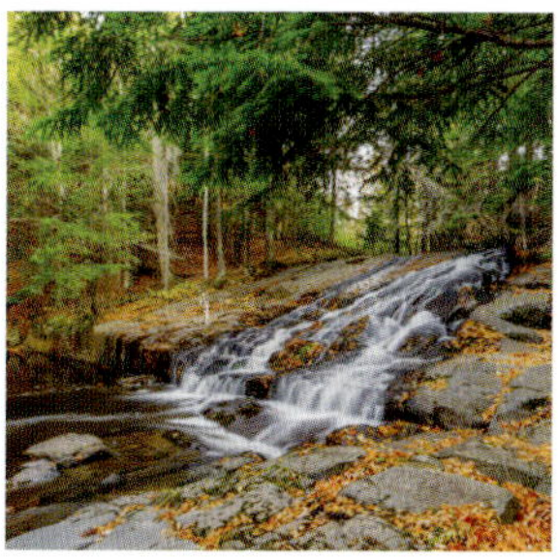

Must See:	8	GPS:	N46 45.850 W88 06.498
Height:	14 feet		
Time:	10-30 minutes	**Hiking Information**	
		Path:	ATV Trail
Driving Information		Length:	100 yards
Signs:	None	Elev. Change:	Moderate
Road:	Gravel	GPS:	Recommended
Access:	Somewhat Difficult	Danger:	Slight
4WD:	Helpful	WP Boots:	Helpful

A long, choppy slide ends with a short 1 foot drop into a 30 foot square spill pool. Cedar trees line the sides of the river.

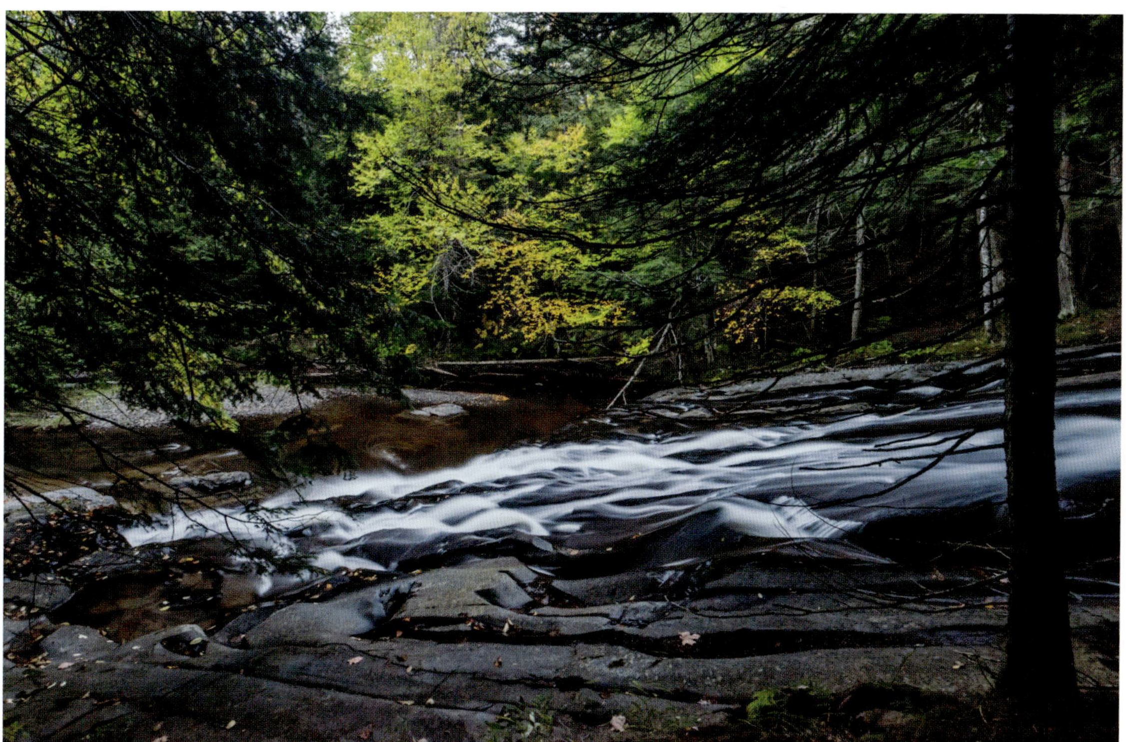

Ravine River Road Falls Hike

Ravine River Road Falls: Watch carefully along the south side of Ravine River Road. The falls can be seen facing the road from about 100 feet upstream.

Ravine River Road Cascades: The small tributary makes a fast descent through a heavily forested hillside 100 yards from Ravine River Road Falls. The fast rapids can be quite pretty, especially when flowers and local greenery are at their best.

Directions: Turn south off of Skanee Road onto Roland Lake Road (dirt). Follow it to the end (2.9 miles). Turn right (west) onto Ravine River Road for 4.0 miles (to N46 46.797 W88 10.770). Go straight for .75 miles. Park alongside Ravine River Road near where a culvert channels the tributary below the road. Ravine River Road Falls are a mere 100 feet upstream. Hike another .1 miles to find the Cascades.

RAVINE RIVER ROAD FALLS (UNNAMED TRIBUTARY)

Private

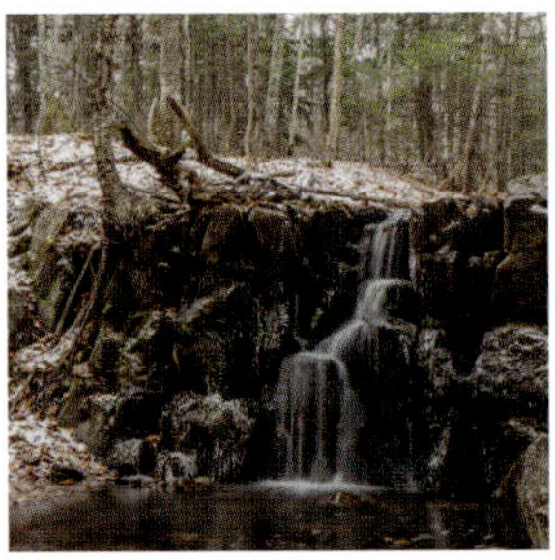

Must See:	6	GPS:	N46 46.519 W88 09.997
Height:	5 feet		
Time:	5-10 minutes	**Hiking Information**	
		Path:	None
Driving Information		Length:	100 feet
Signs:	None	Elev. Change:	Minor
Road:	Gravel	GPS:	Helpful
Access:	Somewhat Difficult	Danger:	Slight
4WD:	Helpful	WP Boots:	N/A

A straight drop into a couple of jutting pieces of bedrock send up rooster tails from this easy to find waterfall. Although it is a bit of a drive to get out to this waterfall, it is one of the closest waterfalls to a road in Baraga County.

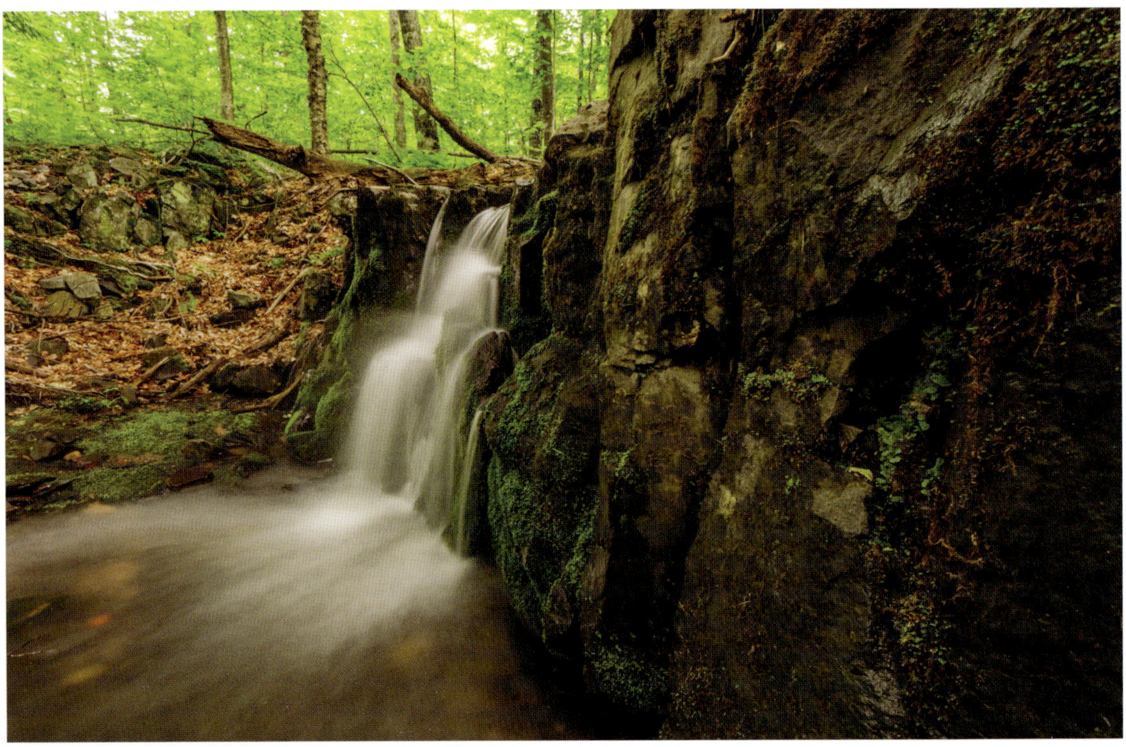

RAVINE RIVER ROAD CASCADES (UNNAMED TRIBUTARY) Private

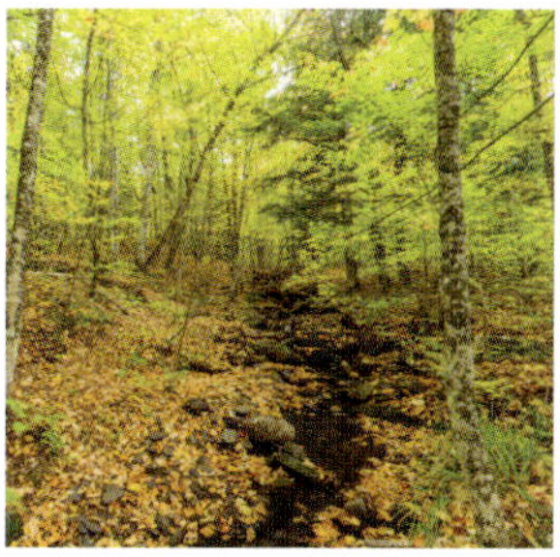

Must See:	4	GPS:	N46 46.435 W88 09.974
Height:	20 feet		
Time:	15-25 minutes	Hiking Information	
		Path:	None
Driving Information		Length:	.1 miles
Signs:	None	Elev. Change:	Minor
Road:	Gravel	GPS:	Helpful
Access:	Somewhat Difficult	Danger:	Slight
4WD:	Helpful	WP Boots:	Helpful

As the small tributary runs down toward the road, it cascades over several small drops. The top one is tallest at 3 feet. It's a pretty setting, especially on a beautiful autumn day with golden leaves all around. The creek is full of nice sized black rocks; pieces of bedrock broken off and now lying exposed in the waterway.

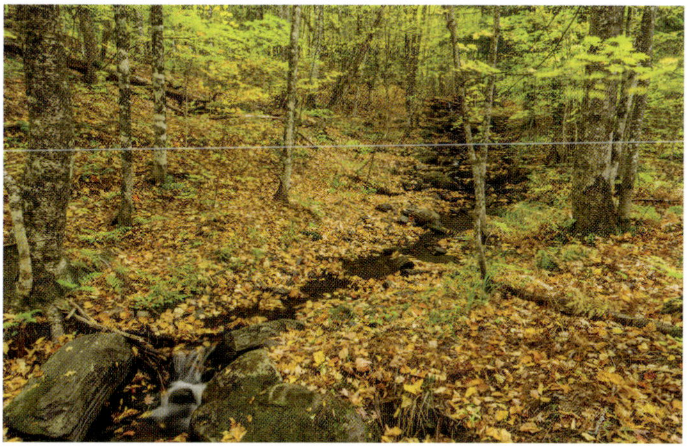

The small tributary runs 1 to 5 feet wide and drops about 20 feet in a 150 foot stretch

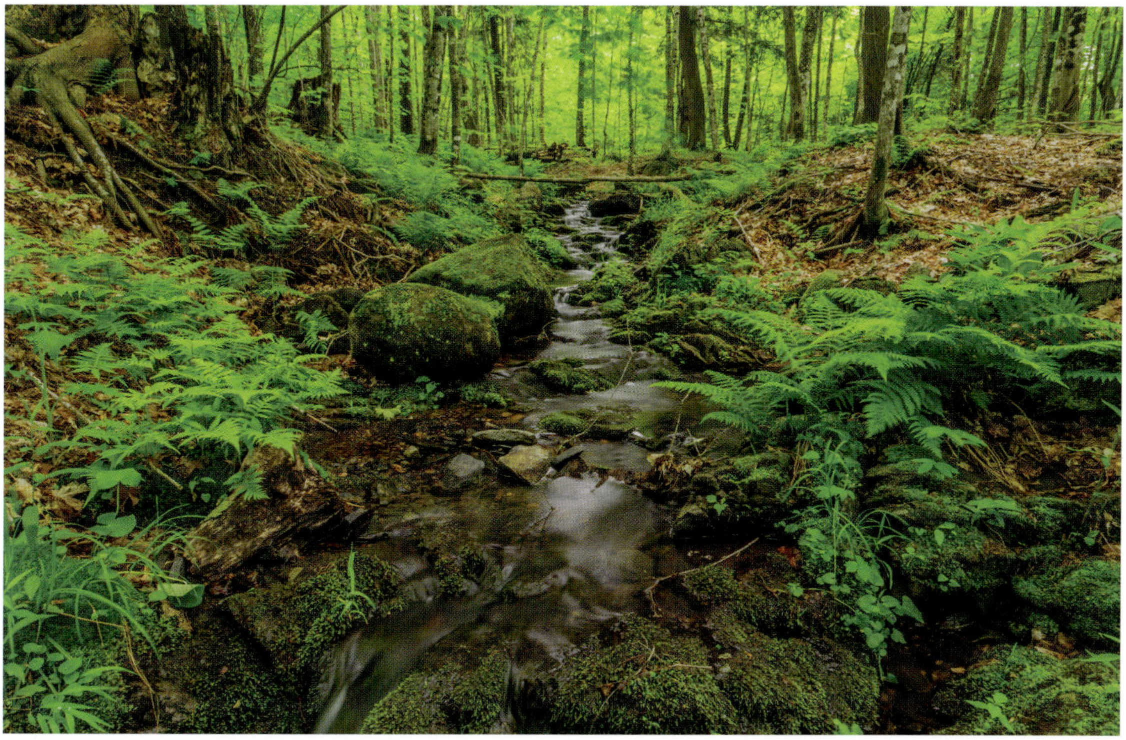

Pea Can Falls Hike

A small tributary to the West Branch of the Huron River has several nice drops just north of Ravine River Road near the intersection of Red Stump Road. The slides are especially noteworthy!

Directions: Turn south off of Skanee Road onto Roland Lake Road (dirt). Follow it to the end (2.9 miles). Turn right (west) onto Ravine River Road for 4.0 miles. Go straight at N46 46.797 W88 10.770 for 2.2 miles. Turn left at N46 45.995 W88 08.627 for .9 miles. Veer right at N46 46.169 W88 07.784 for .3 miles. Veer right at N46 46.120 W88 07.334 for .6 miles. Park off of the side of road near the culvert. Hike downstream about .25 miles to see all the features on this creek.

PEA CAN FALLS - UPPER CASCADE (PEA CAN CREEK) Private

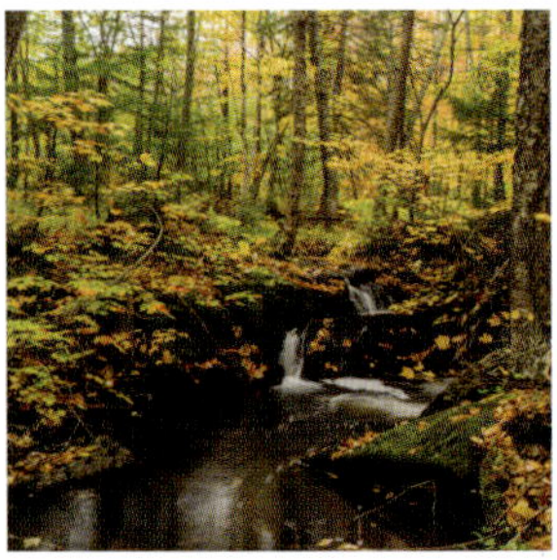

Must See:	4	GPS:	N46 45.863 W88 06.749
Height:	4 feet		
Time:	10-15 minutes	**Hiking Information**	
		Path:	None
Driving Information		Length:	75 feet
Signs:	None	Elev. Change:	Minor
Road:	Gravel	GPS:	Recommended
Access:	Difficult	Danger:	Slight
4WD:	Helpful	WP Boots:	Helpful

The creek divides around a low island, falling as it comes back together through several blackened troughs. Yellow birch surround the falls on this narrow 3-15 foot creek just 75 feet from Ravine River Road near Red Stump Road.

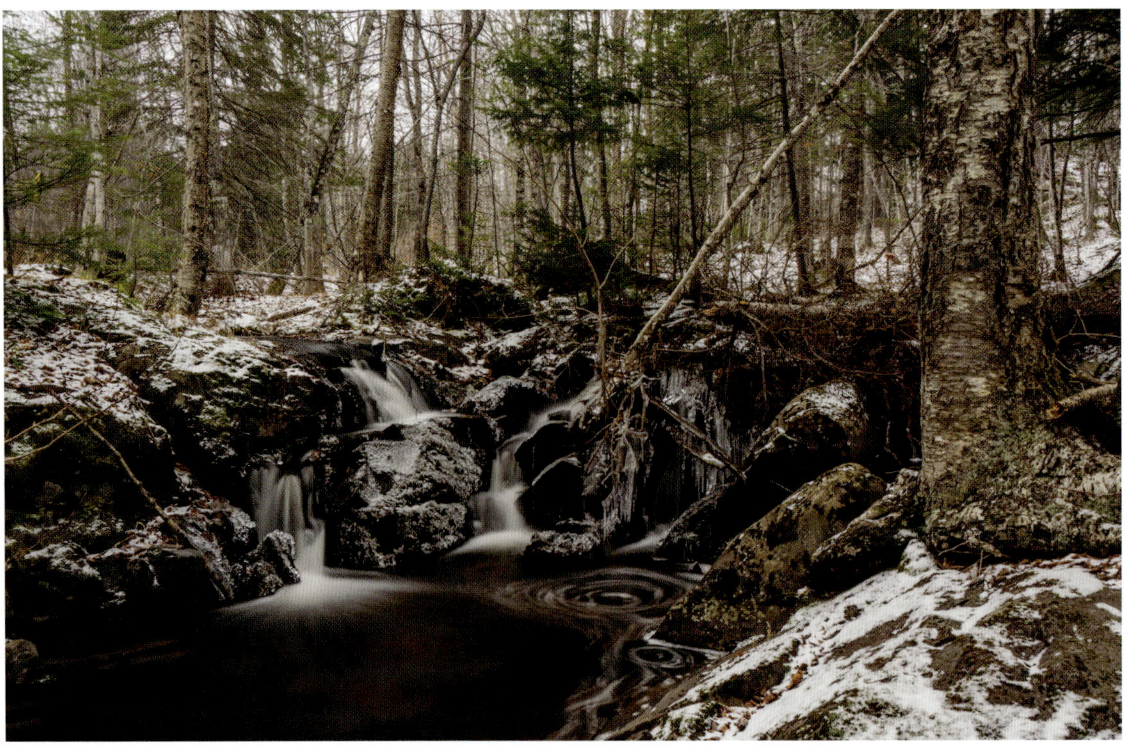

PEA CAN FALLS - UPPER SLIDE (PEA CAN CREEK)

Private

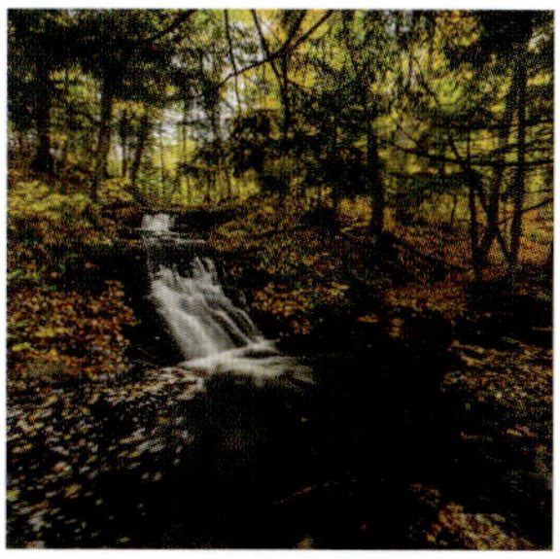

Must See:	7	GPS:	N46 45.877 W88 06.739
Height:	12 feet		
Time:	15-20 minutes		

Driving Information		Hiking Information	
		Path:	None
		Length:	50 yards
Signs:	None	Elev. Change:	Minor
Road:	Gravel	GPS:	Recommended
Access:	Difficult	Danger:	Slight
4WD:	Helpful	WP Boots:	Helpful

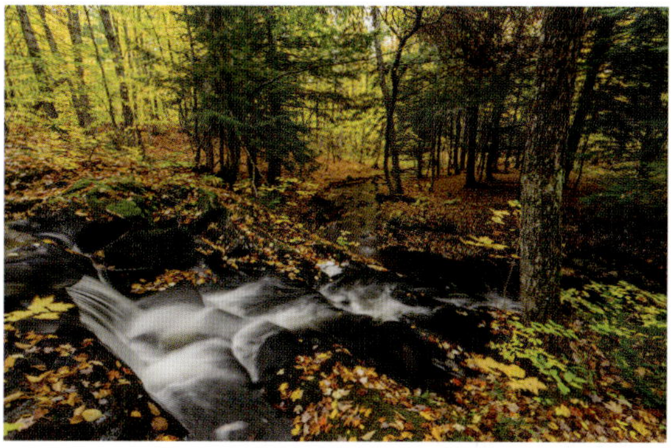

It's a short hike downstream from the Upper Cascade. Follow the creek for just 100 feet to get to this seldom seen beauty!

This is a double drop. There is a 3 foot plunge on top, followed by a 9 foot slide into an elongated spill pool. The slide is mostly smooth, the hard black basalt fractured here and there. The viewing and picnic area below the waterfall is spectacular! An undergrowth free area beneath the overstretched arms of mature trees is quite inviting. And the spill pool looks to be about 2 to 3 feet deep, perfect for wading.

I haven't rated this as "kid friendly", but if they can handle the short hike, this could be a lot of fun!

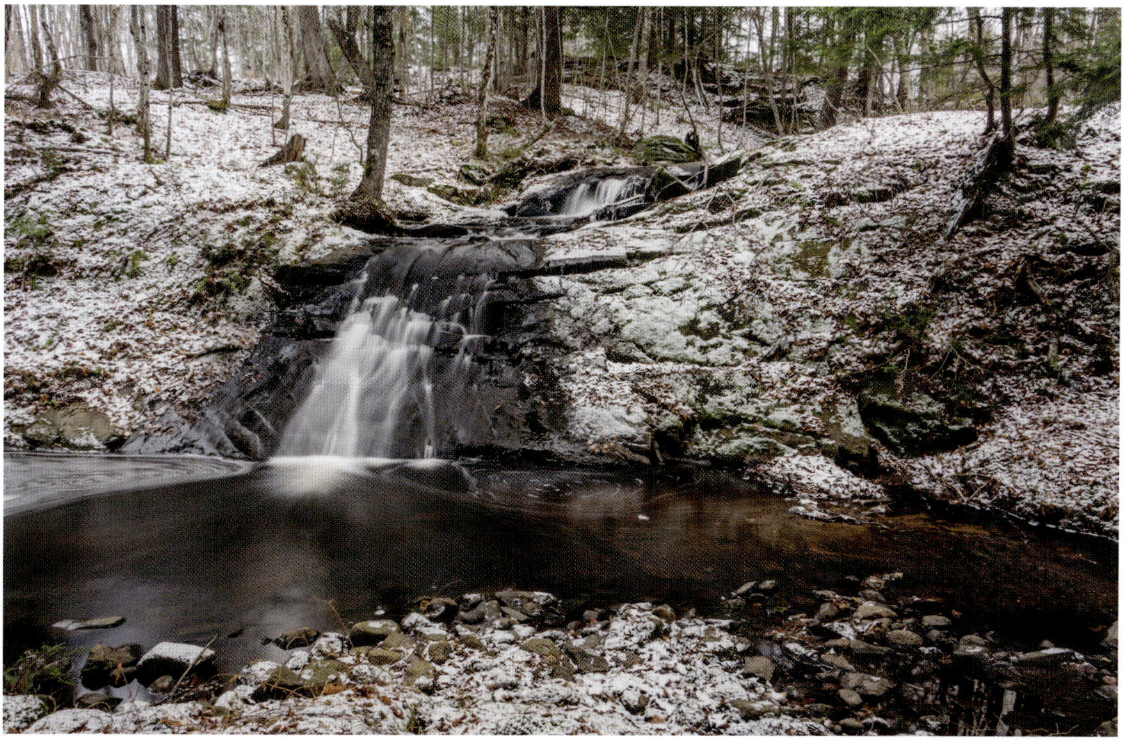

BARAGA COUNTY

PEA CAN FALLS - LOWER CASCADE (PEA CAN CREEK) Private

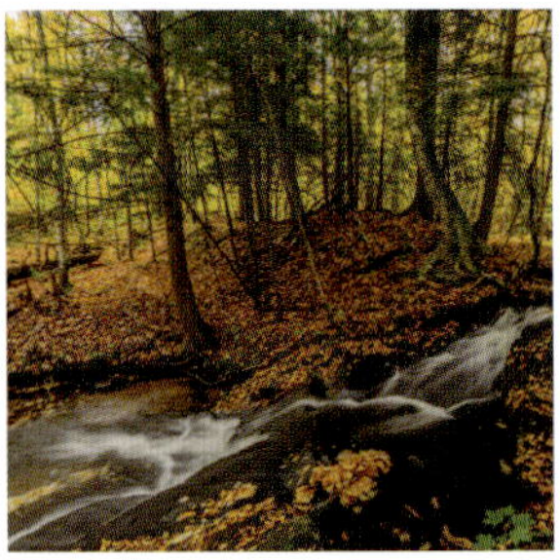

Must See:	5	GPS:	N46 45.915 W88 06.736
Height:	6 feet		
Time:	25-35 minutes	**Hiking Information**	
		Path:	None
Driving Information		Length:	150 yards
Signs:	None	Elev. Change:	Minor
Road:	Gravel	GPS:	Recommended
Access:	Difficult	Danger:	Slight
4WD:	Helpful	WP Boots:	Helpful

There are three segments to this small waterfall. A one foot slide at the top is followed by an angled slide and finishes with yet another slide. For the size of the creek, there is a good sized, 30 foot circular spill pool. Several large trees have fallen across the creek just down stream from the waterfall.

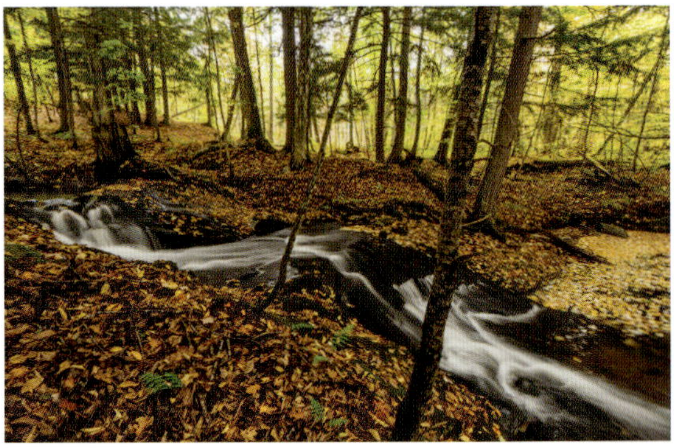

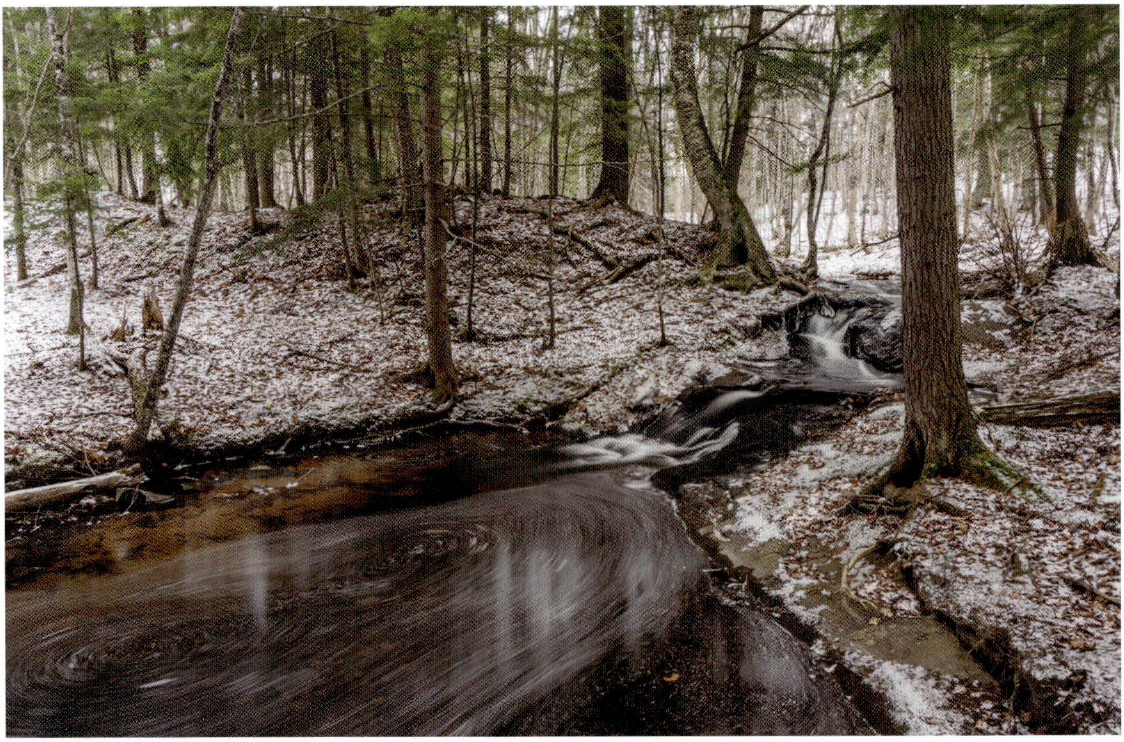

Pea Can - Lower Cascade

PEA CAN RUN (PEA CAN CREEK)

Private

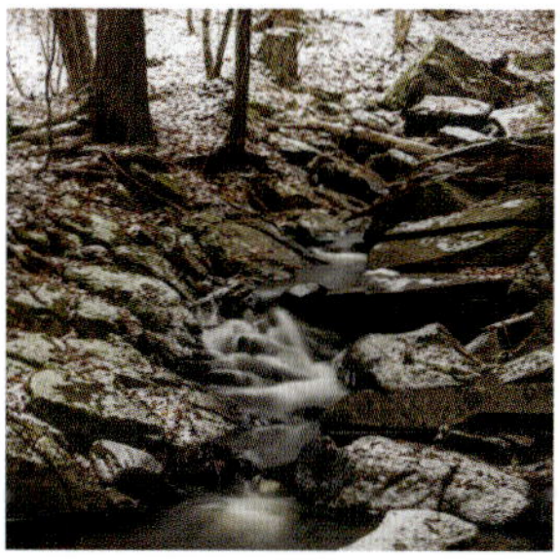

Must See:	3	GPS:	N46 46.001 W88 06.749
Height:	8 feet		
Time:	35-45 minutes	**Hiking Information**	
		Path:	None
Driving Information		Length:	.21 miles
Signs:	None	Elev. Change:	Minor
Road:	Gravel	GPS:	Recommended
Access:	Difficult	Danger:	Slight
4WD:	Helpful	WP Boots:	Helpful

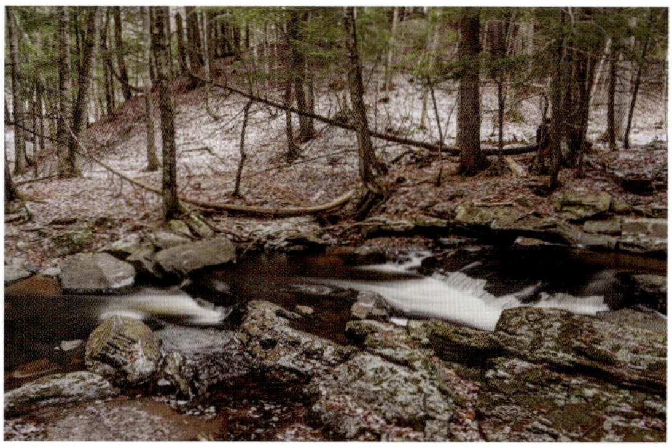

Moss covered bedrock leans in from both sides of the waterway with a large squarish block sitting at a 45 degree angle toward the top of the narrow creek. The creek bounces off of numerous layers of the dark gray stone, running hidden beneath deciduous and evergreen boughs and branches. This small cascade makes for a nice stop between the Lower Cascade and Lower Slide, pausing to listen to the babbling creek's soothing voice. The Run meanders around a couple slight bends in the creek, making it difficult to view all of it from one vantage point.

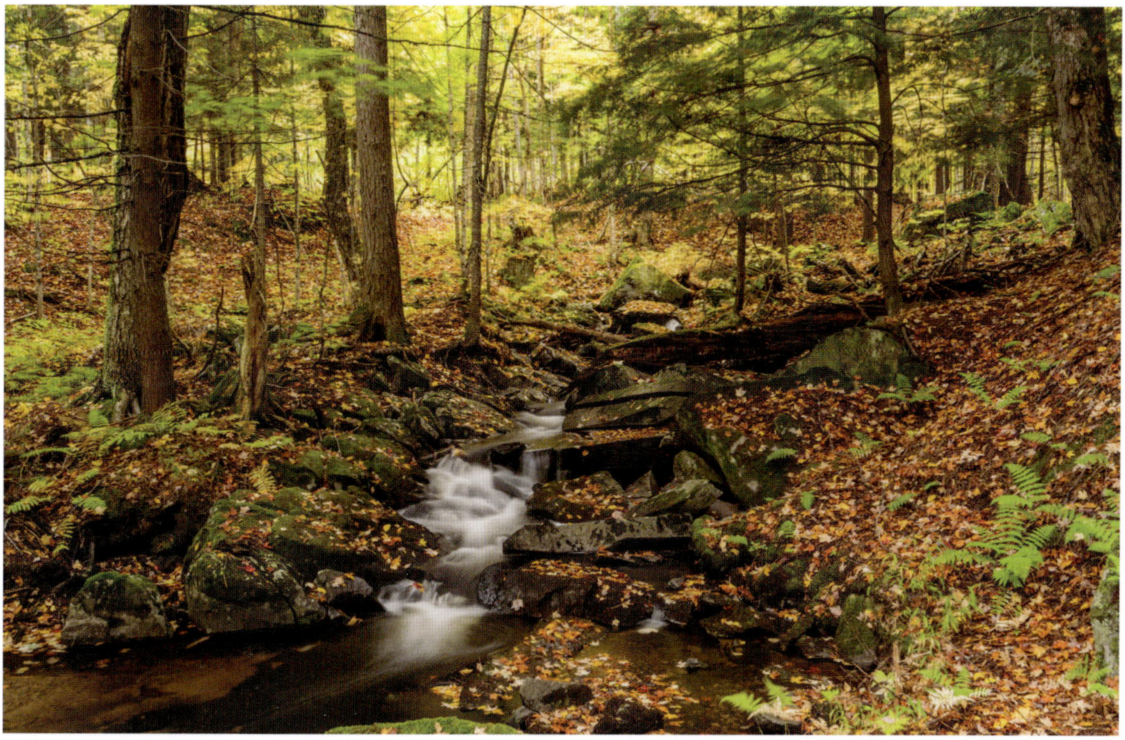

PEA CAN FALLS - LOWER SLIDE (PEA CAN CREEK)

Private

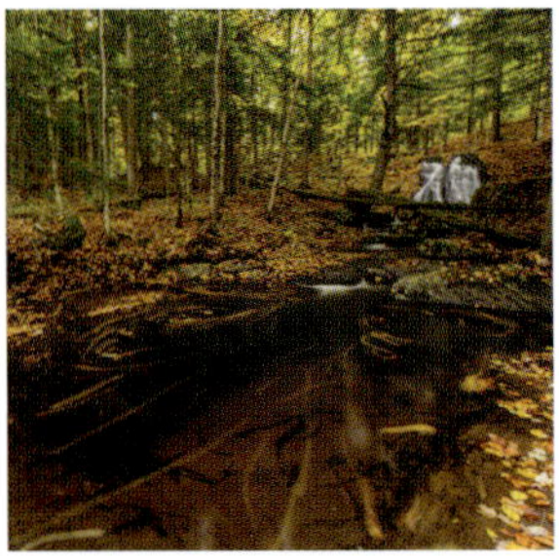

Must See:	7	GPS:	N46 46.038 W88 06.805
Height:	12 feet		
Time:	35-50 minutes	**Hiking Information**	
		Path:	None
Driving Information		Length:	.27 miles
Signs:	None	Elev. Change:	Minor
Road:	Gravel	GPS:	Recommended
Access:	Difficult	Danger:	Slight
4WD:	Helpful	WP Boots:	Helpful

Follow the creek 100 yards downstream from the Run to get to the last of the falls on this creek. This is an amazing slide waterfall! It's about a 45 degree angle slide into a narrow pocket. Small rounded boulders choke the creek just below the falls. Birch and hemlock surround the creek. There is a handful of small cascades just below the falls with boulders scattered throughout.

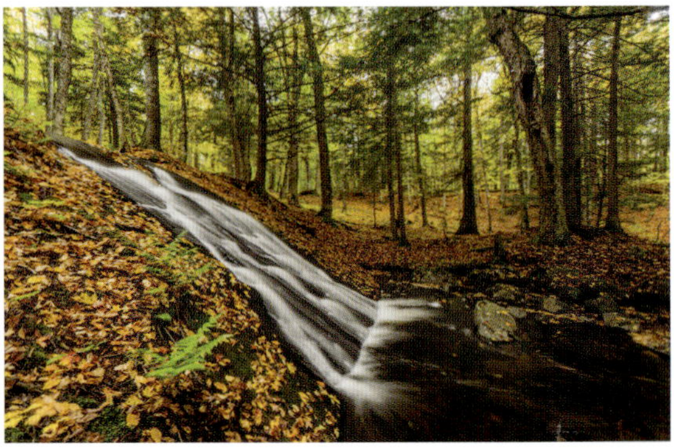

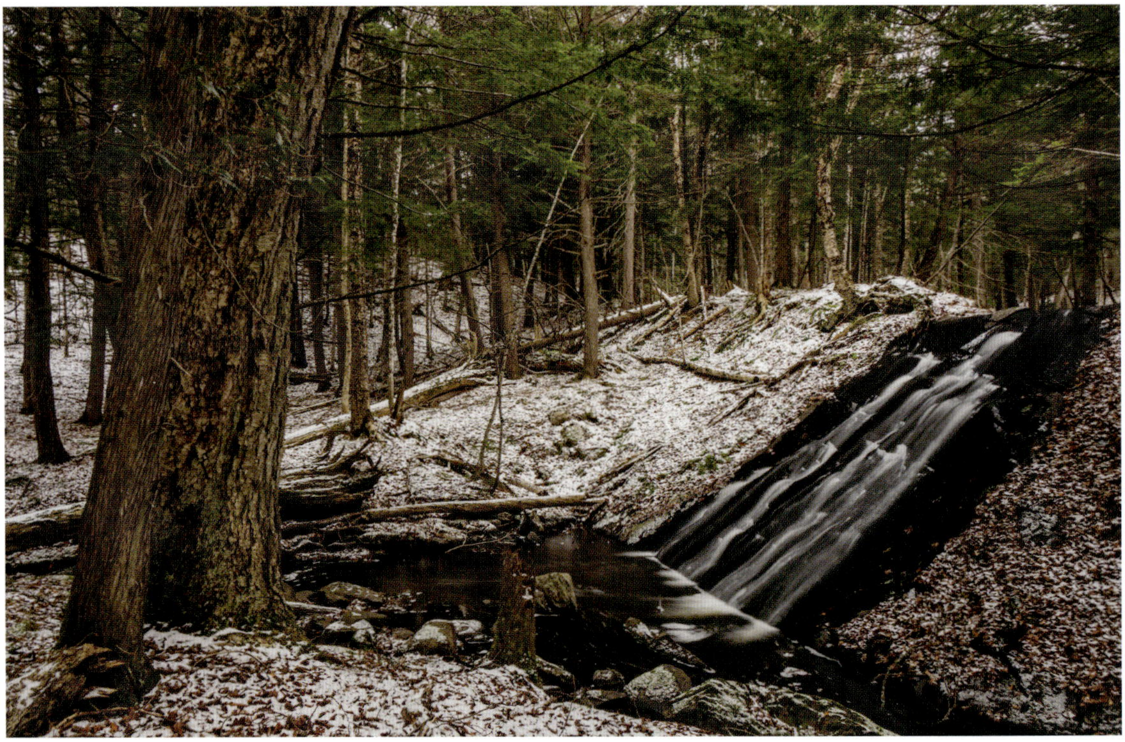

Tea Cup Falls Hike

A small tributary to the West Branch of the Huron River has several nice drops just north of Ravine River Road near the intersection of Red Stump Road. The slides are especially noteworthy!

Directions: Turn south off of Skanee Road onto Roland Lake Road (dirt). Follow it to the end (2.9 miles). Turn right (west) onto Ravine River Road for 4.0 miles. Go straight at N46 46.797 W88 10.770 for 2.1 miles. Park off the side of the road by the culvert. This is about .1 miles west from a "T" in Ravine River Road. Hike along the creek downstream (north) for 160 yards to the waterfall.

TEA CUP FALLS (UNNAMED CREEK)

Private

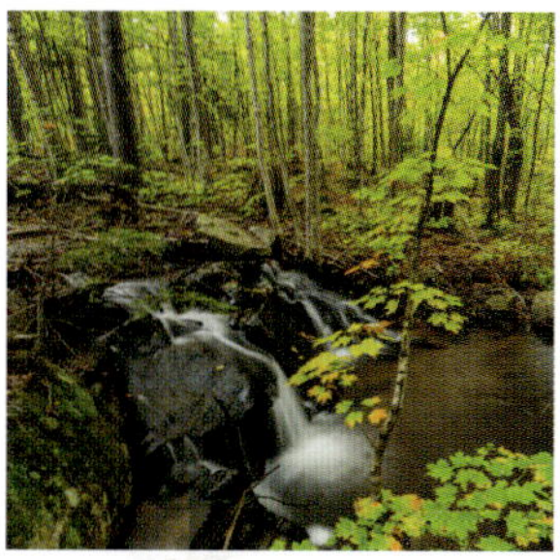

Must See: 4
Height: 5 feet
Time: 15-20 minutes

Driving Information
Signs: None
Road: Gravel
Access: Somewhat Difficult
4WD: Helpful

GPS: N46 46.065 W88 08.669

Hiking Information
Path: None
Length: 160 yards
Elev. Change: Minor
GPS: Recommended
Danger: Slight
WP Boots: N/A

This relatively little known waterfall lies between Ravine River Road Falls and the Letherby series of waterfalls on the West Branch of the Huron River. This easy to access waterfall adds another waterfall stop in the Huron Mountains

Conchoidally fractured black bedrock hosts the 15 foot wide waterfall on the small creek.

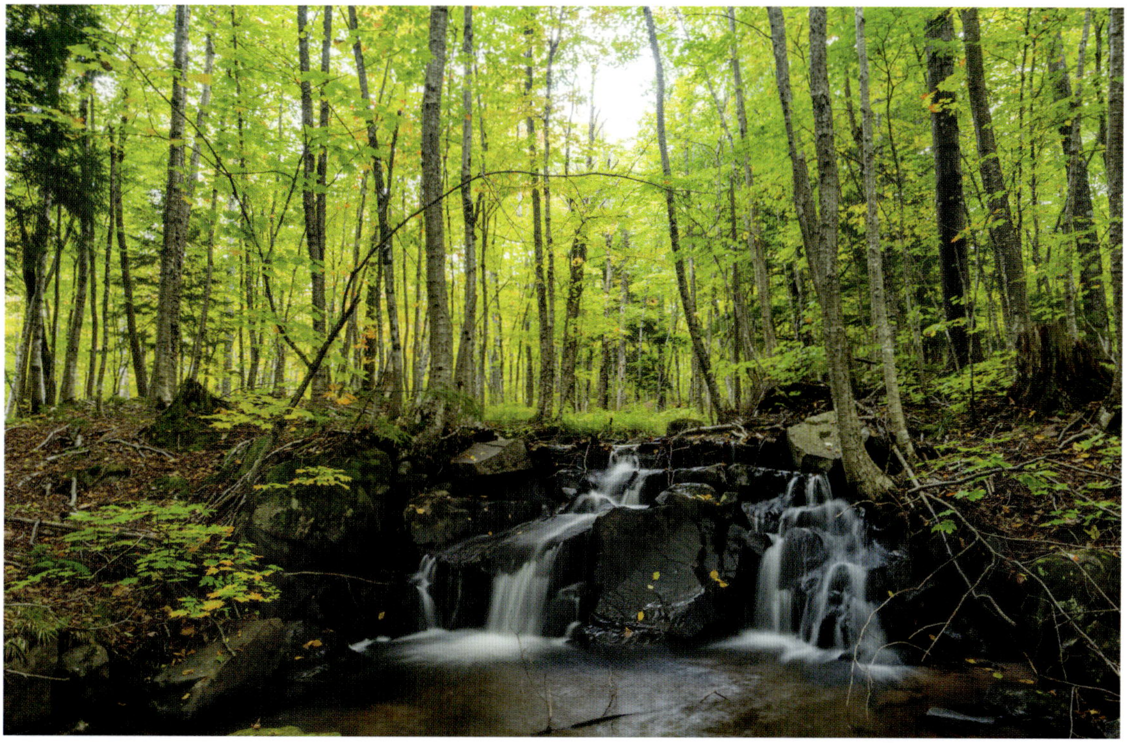

West Branch Falls Hike

West Branch Falls - Lower: Flanked by a rugged 30 foot high wall of rock, the Lower Falls pour down to a widened, quiet spill pool situated at the bottom of a ravine.

West Branch Mini Falls: Between West Branch Falls and the Lower Falls is a small, smooth, angular waterfall; crafted, as it were, as a small dam. The near perfection of the design makes it look almost man-made.

West Branch Falls: Superb! This seldom visited, full bodied, cascading waterfall stretches across a sharp "V" shaped ravine, fully facing the ideal viewing vantage point. A steep footpath leads to the river's edge.

West Branch Falls - Upper: Several cascades upriver from West Branch Falls prime the river for the grand event that will be flowed over shortly. These cascades are most easily viewed from the top of the ravine that the river flows through.

Directions: From near the eastern end of Skanee Road turn right (south) onto Black Creek Road. Drive 1.7 miles to N46 50.763 W88 05.956. Turn left (east) onto a good dirt road. Big Falls is 2.1 miles from this intersection. The Western Branch of the Huron River will appear in about .2 miles. Park. Hike upriver on the west side of the river for a short distance until past the steep hill on the far side of the river. Ford the river and continue upstream on the eastern bank following the fisherman's footpath. Stay near the river as there are several cottages along the way. Be respectful and honor private property.

WEST BRANCH FALLS - LOWER (HURON RIVER - WEST BRANCH) Private

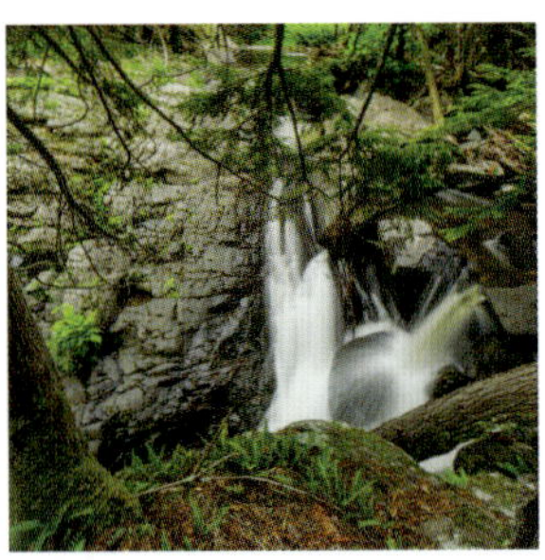

Must See: 5
Height: 8 feet
Time: 1-1.5 hours

Driving Information
Signs: None
Road: Good Dirt
Access: Difficult
4WD: Helpful

GPS: N46 50.429 W88 05.556

Hiking Information
Path: Fisherman's Footpath
Length: .43 miles
Elev. Change: Major
GPS: Recommended
Danger: Elevated
WP Boots: Required

Ford a river, then climb in and out of a ravine to access this waterfall. A rounded mass of rock tries to hide the waterfall on the eastern side while a rugged stone wall lines the western side.

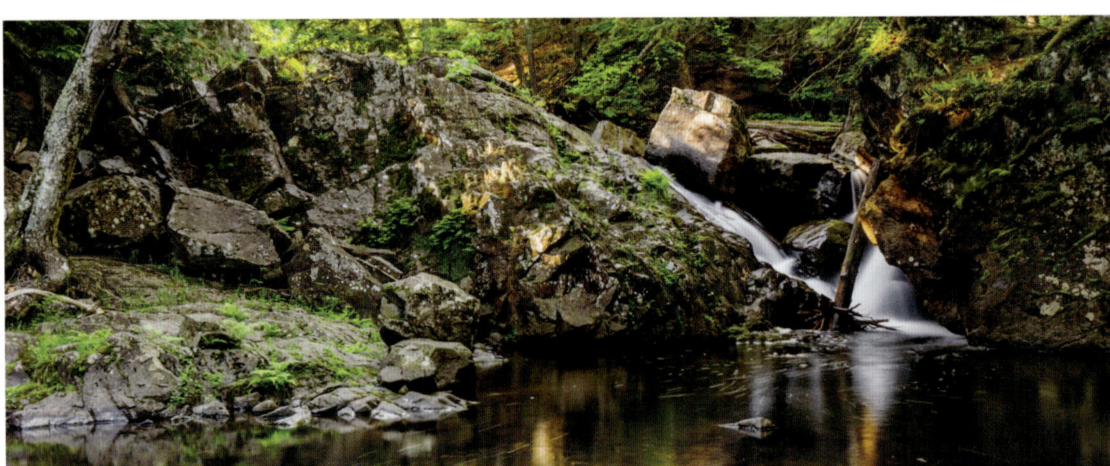

WEST BRANCH LEDGE (HURON RIVER - WEST BRANCH)

Private

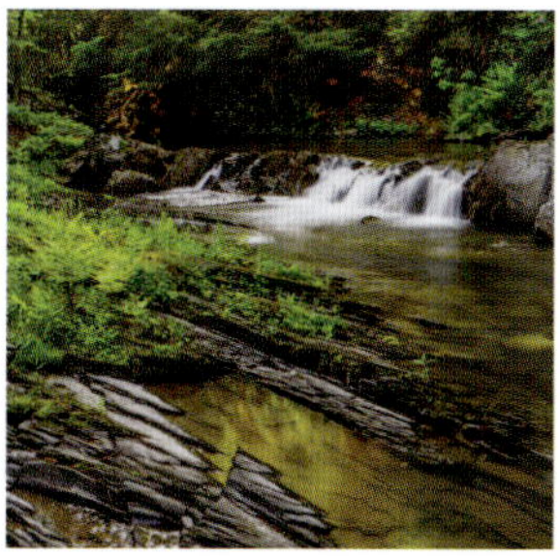

Must See: 5
Height: 2 feet
Time: 1.5-2 hours

Driving Information
Signs: None
Road: Good Dirt
Access: Difficult
4WD: Helpful

GPS: N46 50.395 W88 05.485

Hiking Information
Path: Fisherman's Footpath
Length: .51 miles
Elev. Change: Major
GPS: Recommended
Danger: Elevated
WP Boots: Required

A smooth rock face, nearly vertical, runs diagonally across the river. The center portion has been eroded into a cute cascading waterfall. Some of these unassuming waterfalls hold special interest. This one does for me! You can imagine this wall to be some ancient ruins. It really looks like it could have been hewn by hand, so smooth and symmetrical is the now eroding face.

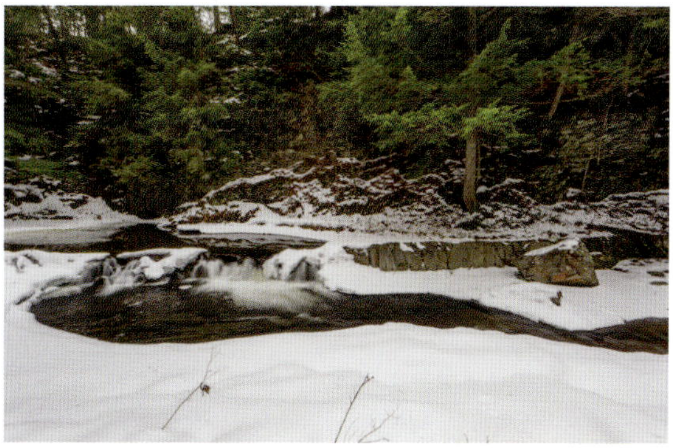

The slanting bedrock layers are covered with delicate wildflowers, thimbleberries, ferns, and moss

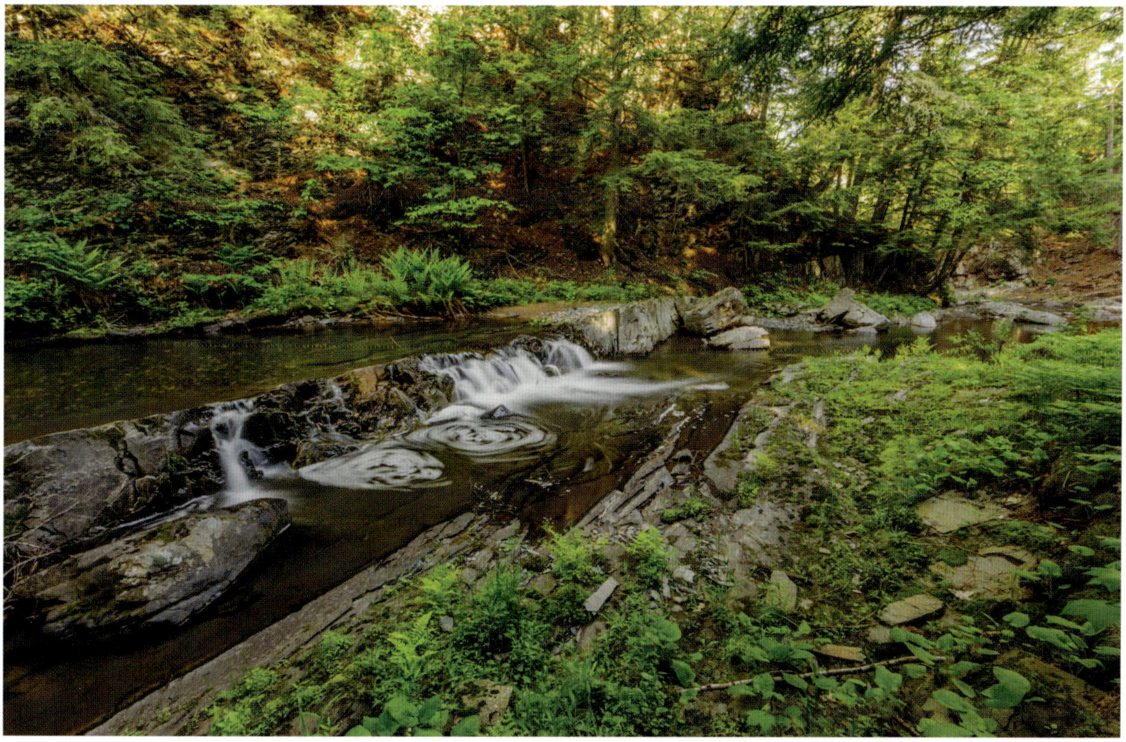

WEST BRANCH FALLS (HURON RIVER - WEST BRANCH)

Private

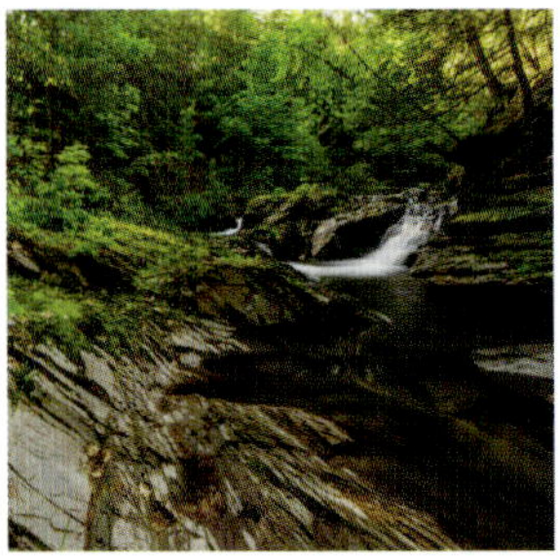

Must See:	8	GPS:	N46 50.349 W88 05.425
Height:	28 feet		
Time:	2-2.5 hours	Hiking Information	
		Path:	Fisherman's Footpath
Driving Information		Length:	.58 miles
Signs:	None	Elev. Change:	Major
Road:	Good Dirt	GPS:	Recommended
Access:	Difficult	Danger:	Elevated
4WD:	Helpful	WP Boots:	Required

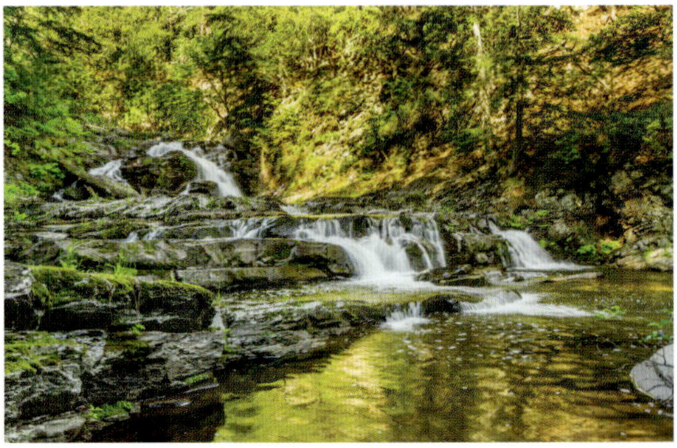

The waterfall is best described in three stages. The river tumbles into a 40 foot gorge over squarish split rock. An outcropping in the middle of the first drop divides the river into two branches in all but the highest of water conditions. Following the initial 13 foot cascade, the river flattens out for 20 yards before tumbling over a 4 foot drop. The river then widens out, passing over smooth, water worn skipping stones for 30 yards. Then the river divides again around a promontory of gray-green bedrock that is covered in wavy hairline grooves etched into the smooth, rounded surfaces. The last drop is 6 feet high. At the base of this drop the river turns 90 degrees immediately, funneled down through a trough of the same gray-green bedrock.

The steep ravine makes it hard to view the waterfall up close. There is a narrow footpath that leads down sharply to the base of the drawn out waterfall. This is the easiest way to view the waterfall. Working your way along the side of the river to the top of the waterfall is more difficult.

Wild roses find a hand hold in the cracks of the red tinged bedrock just downstream from here!

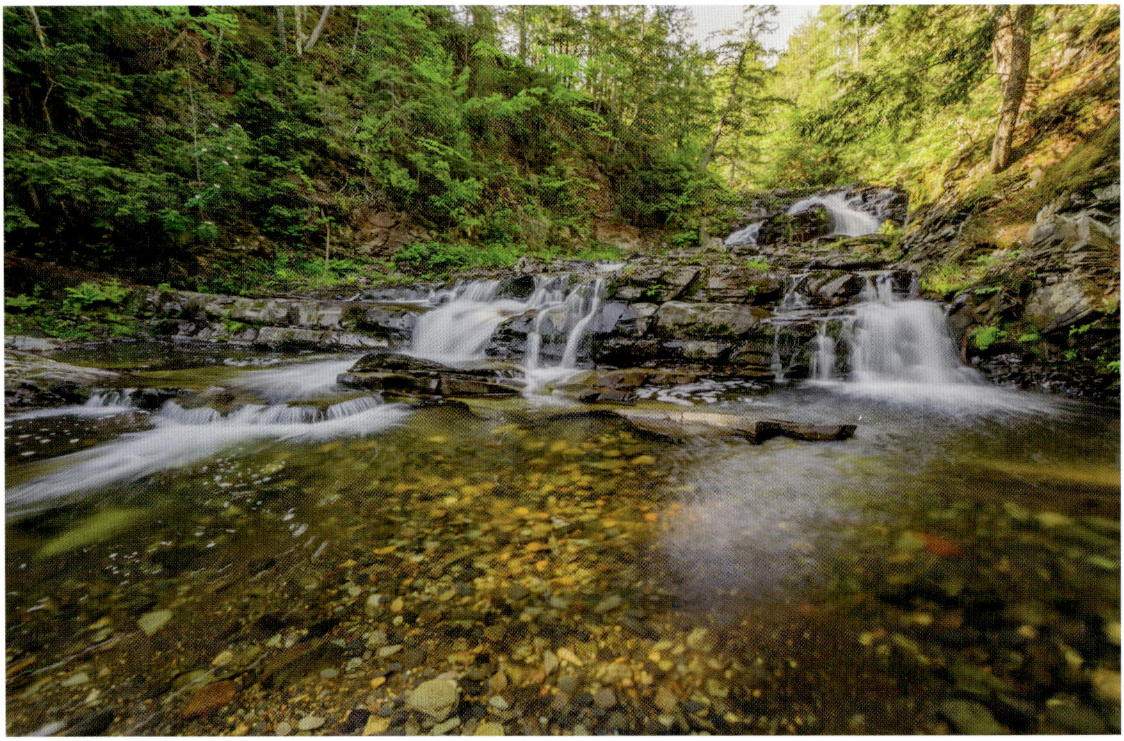

WEST BRANCH FALLS - UPPER (HURON RIVER - WEST BRANCH) Private

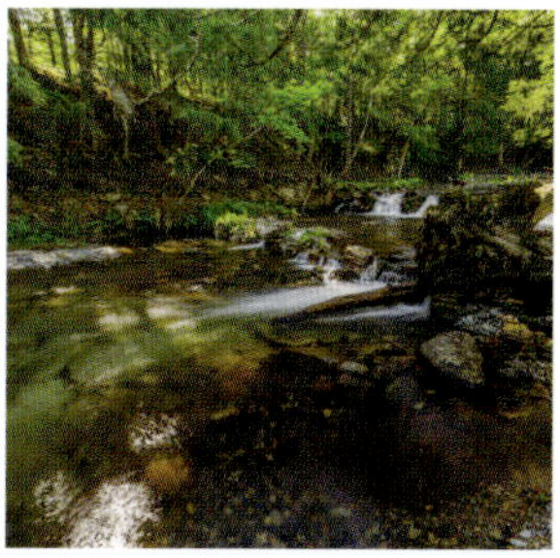

Must See:	5	GPS:	N46 50.287 W88 05.438
Height:	8 feet	Hiking Information	
Time:	2-2.5 hours	Path:	Fisherman's Footpath
		Length:	.67 miles
Driving Information		Elev. Change:	Major
Signs:	None	GPS:	Recommended
Road:	Good Dirt	Danger:	Elevated
Access:	Difficult	WP Boots:	Required
4WD:	Helpful		

There are a series of cascades just upriver from West Branch Falls. They flow between steep 20 foot tall banks. Care must be taken in getting down to the riverbed. The ravine walls tend to drop off quickly near the river.

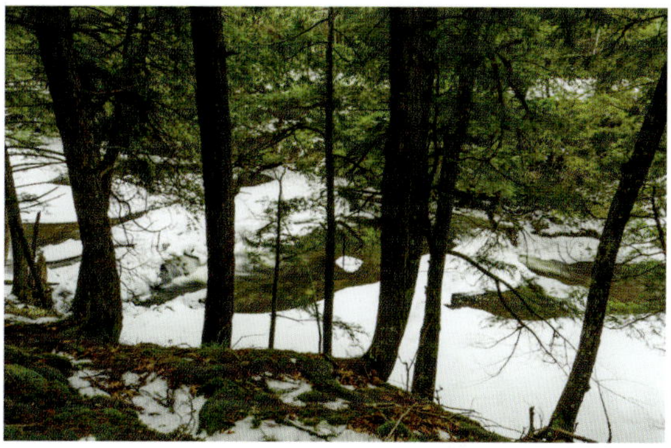

Several small cascades are in a "C" shaped portion of the river. Thin layered sections of bedrock stair step each of the cascades. The river flows through a shallow 20 foot ravine before dropping over West Branch Falls just downstream.

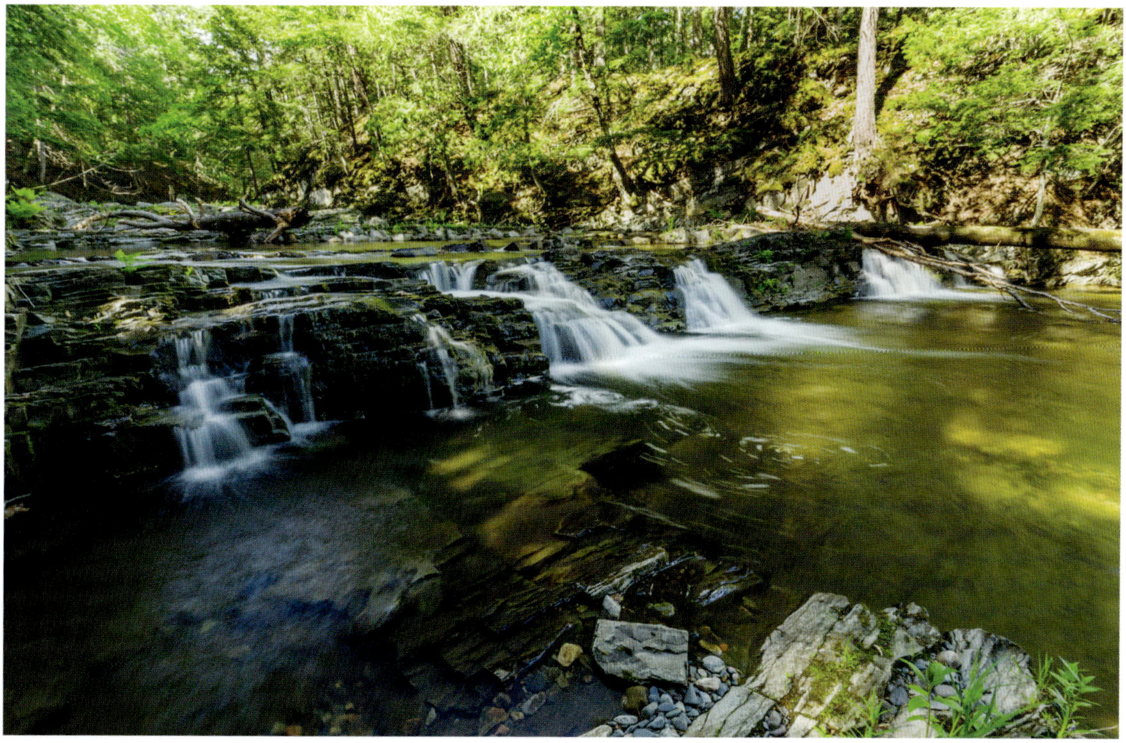

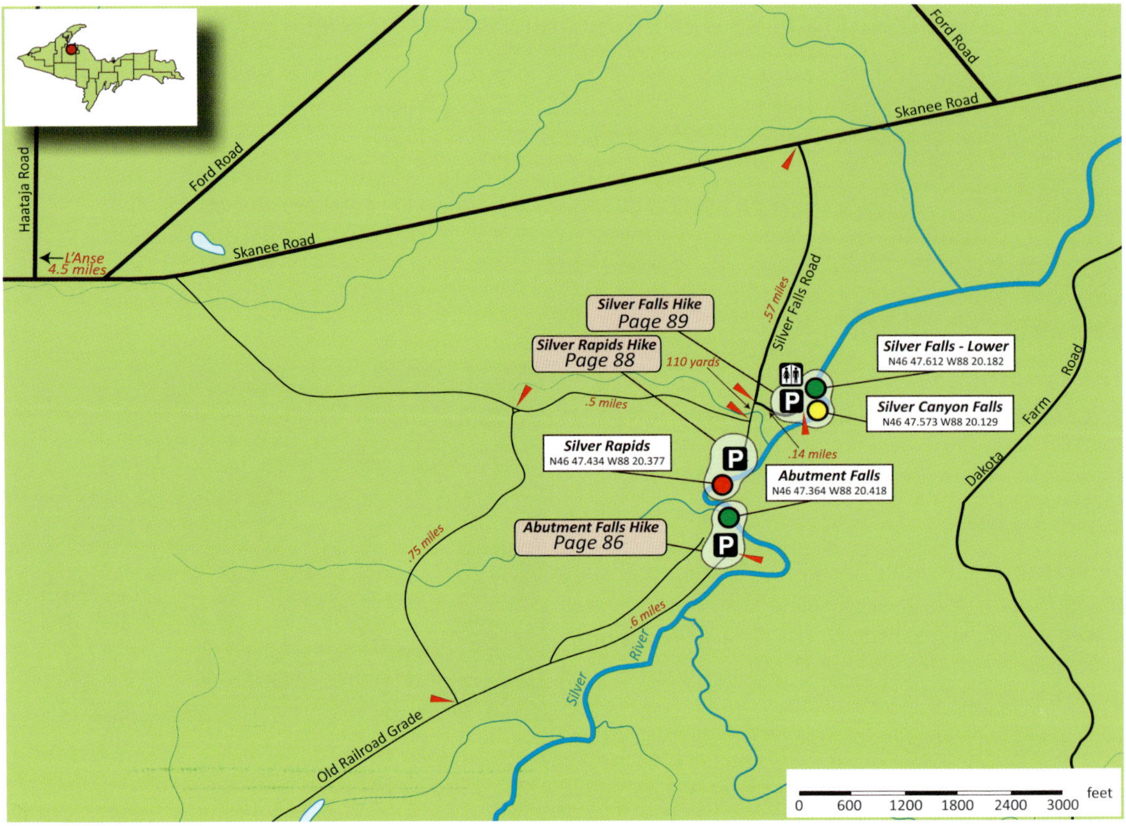

Abutment Falls Hike

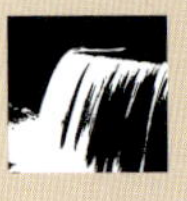

An old railroad grade runs along the Silver River, ending at the waterfall. Old concrete abutments still stand on both sides of the river, helping you to envision where the railroad bridged the waterway.

Directions: From Skanee Road, turn south on Silver Falls Road for .57 miles. Continue on straight for 110 yards. Turn right (west) on a 2-track for .5 miles. Turn left (south) on another 2-track for .75 miles until it reaches a "T". Turn left (east) for .6 miles. Park near the river. (This last .6 miles is along a very narrow 2-track. It's the old railroad grade.) The waterfall is straight ahead and downstream. Hike downstream for some better views. Be careful crossing the exposed bedrock. It can be quite slippery, and it angles down toward the top of the waterfall. A fisherman's trail winds along the shoreline. Follow it a short distance to view the waterfall from the base. The best views of the waterfall are probably from the other side. Either ford the river (I haven't tried yet) or hike in along the far side of the river. I believe it would be quite a long hike with no trail on that side.

ABUTMENT FALLS (SILVER RIVER)

Private

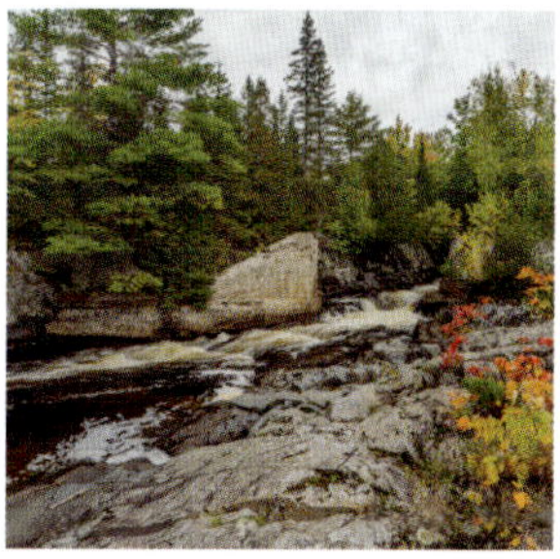

Must See:	8	GPS:	N46 47.364 W88 20.418
Height:	15 feet		
Time:	10-20 minutes	**Hiking Information**	
		Path:	N/A
Driving Information		Length:	50 feet
Signs:	None	Elev. Change:	Minor
Road:	2-track	GPS:	Helpful
Access:	Difficult	Danger:	Moderate
4WD:	Helpful	WP Boots:	N/A

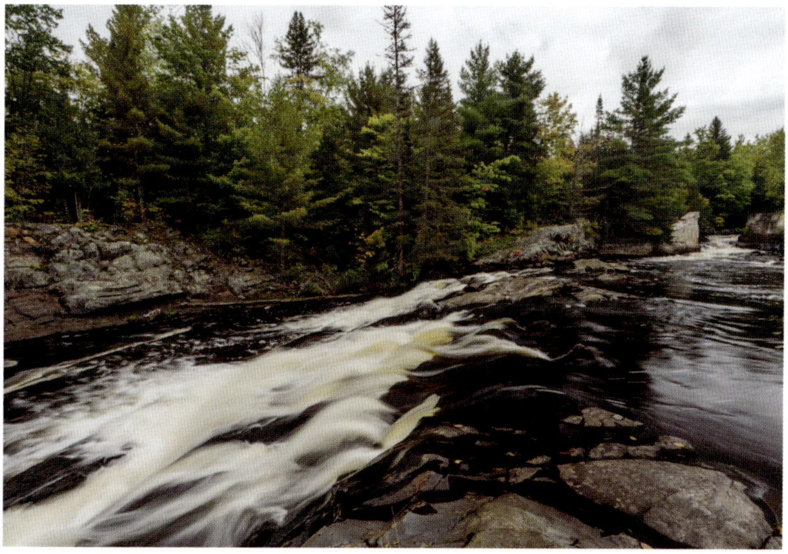

The Silver River rushes through the narrowed river with old concrete abutments squeezing in from either side. It then widens and smooths out, running along the base of slanted, flat, and slippery-when-wet bedrock. The river tilts, sliding down sideways into a gorge in a splashing cascade.

Note the photo below sporting a solitary Spotted Touch-Me-Not, one of my favorite flowers to see at waterfalls. They are so delicate and beautiful! They love water, so they are commonly seen in lowlands. Sometimes they grow in patches, their unique bell-shaped, bright flowers dominating the foreground! There is so much beauty to be enjoyed in this great state of Michigan! If only we look about us...

Slender beauty in a harsh environment

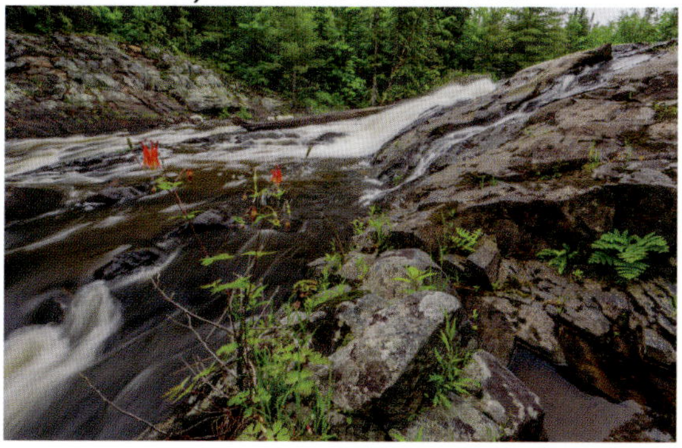

Looking downstream from the abutments

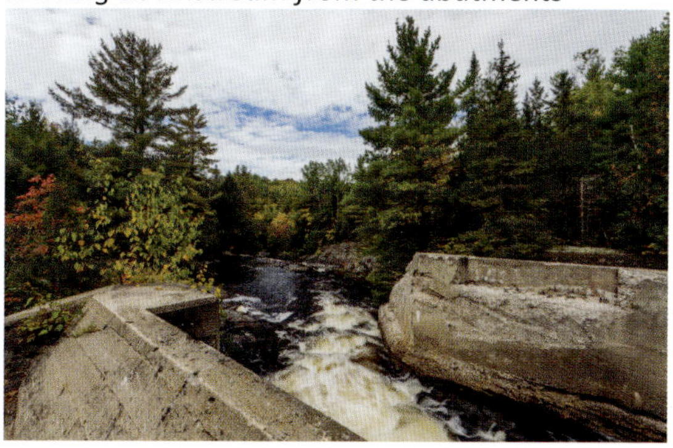

Silver Rapids Hike

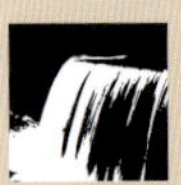

The rapids are not much to look at. Since they are included in other publications, I have added them to my collection.

Directions: From Skanee Road, turn south on Silver Falls Road for .57 miles. Continue on straight for about 200 yards. Park at the top of the hill before the road drops down to the river. Walk down the road to the river. The waterfall, which in reality is a small set of rapids, is just upstream.

SILVER RAPIDS (SILVER RIVER)

Private

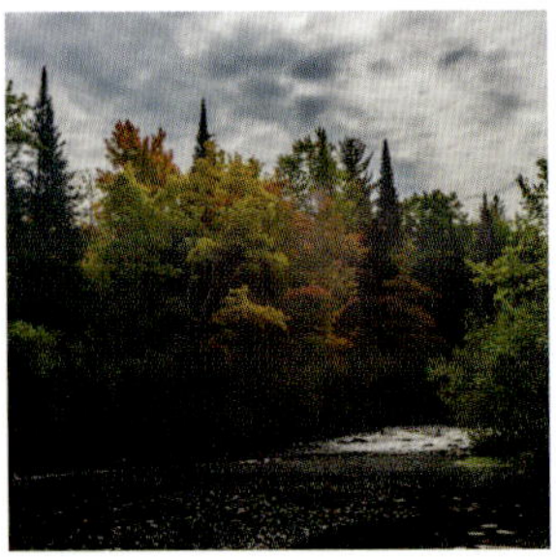

Must See:	2	GPS:	N46 47.434 W88 20.377
Height:	3 feet		
Time:	5-10 minutes	Hiking Information	
		Path:	2-track
Driving Information		Length:	100 feet
Signs:	None	Elev. Change:	Slight
Road:	Dirt	GPS:	Recommended
Access:	Somewhat Easy	Danger:	Slight
4WD:	Helpful	WP Boots:	N/A

After leaving Abutment Falls 1/8 mile upstream from here, the river makes a sharp bend, doubling back on itself. The old railway, crossing Silver River at Abutment Falls, also crossed the river here at the rapids, lining up with the 2-track that you parked on and continuing on northward down Silver Falls Road and beyond.

The 2-track runs right down to the river. Drive as far as you feel comfortable with. Note that it does drop down toward the river into powdery sand and without much room to turn around.

Fishermen enjoy fishing the river below the rapids

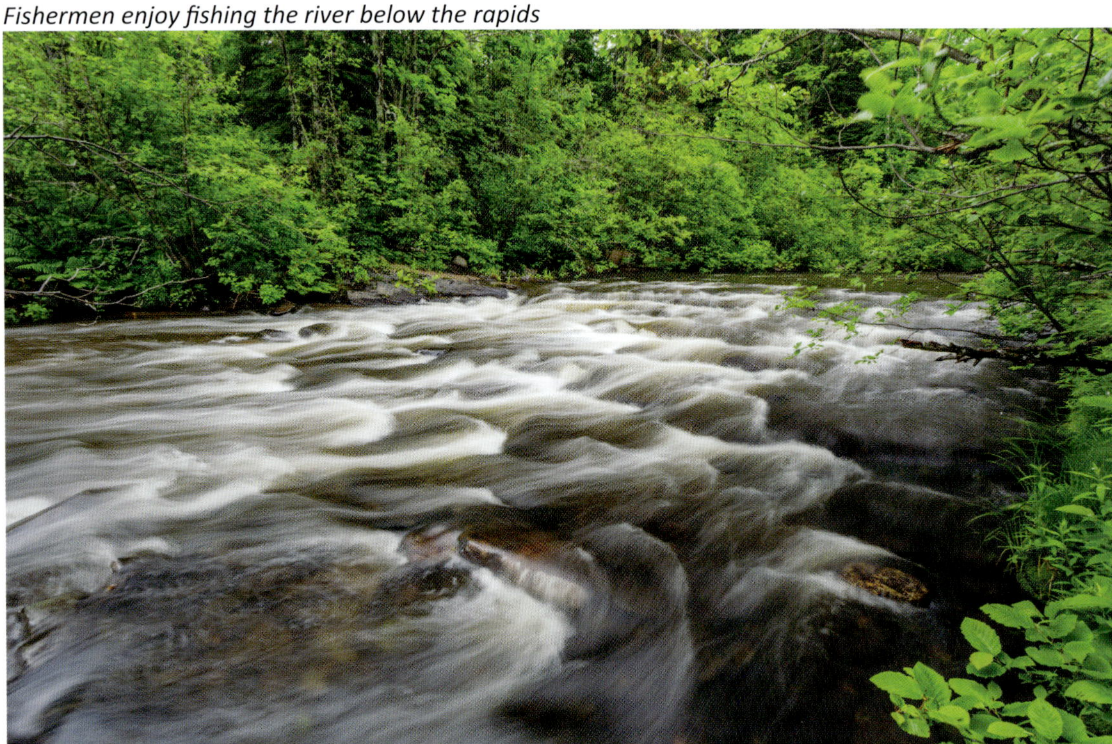

Silver Falls Hike

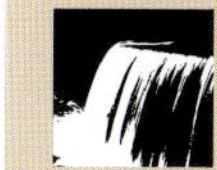

Silver Canyon Falls: From the parking lot a vegetation-less outcropping overlooks Silver Canyon Falls as the river winds through the narrow passage down below.

Silver Falls - Lower: Slippery rocks line the sides of the falls allowing for an intimate view of the falls. Hike down a fairly well used fisherman's trail downstream from the parking lot to the falls.

Directions: From Skanee Road, turn south on Silver Falls Road for .57 miles. The main road turns left, while a lesser travelled road continues straight. Turn left. The road will end in .12 miles at a good sized parking area. There is a vault toilet here. Silver Canyon Falls is on the other side of the rocky outcropping straight ahead of the parking area. Silver Falls - Lower are downstream. Follow the narrow foot trail on the north side of the parking lot to those falls.

SILVER CANYON FALLS (SILVER RIVER)

Private

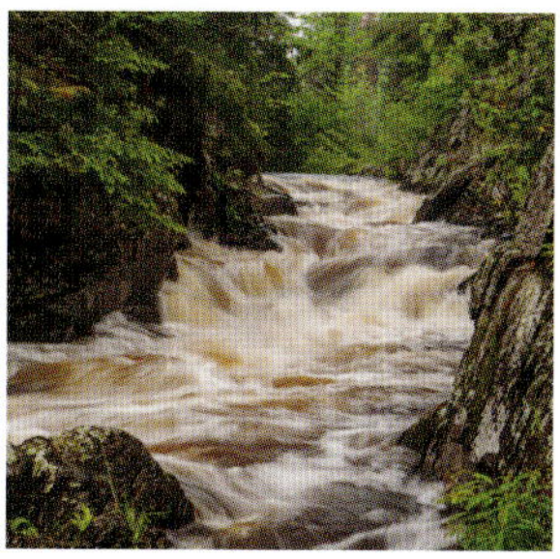

Must See: 6
Height: 8 feet
Time: 10-20 minutes

Driving Information
Signs: None
Road: Dirt
Access: Somewhat Easy
4WD: N/A

GPS: N46 47.573 W88 20.129

Hiking Information
Path: Slight Footpath
Length: 100 yards
Elev. Change: Minor
GPS: N/A
Danger: Minor
WP Boots: N/A

The Silver River cascades through an 8 foot wide canyon with cedar trees growing in 1 to 2 inches of soil on rocky ledges. After passing through the narrow canyon the river divides around sharp pinnacles, thrust up along the steep moss covered wall on the near side. Widening and turning, the river continues on to the top of Silver Falls - Lower, 100 yards downstream.

There used to be a bridge that ran from the top of the bluff across the river. This was an automobile bridge, as opposed to the train trestles that spanned the Silver River just upstream.

Looking down from the top of the shallow canyon

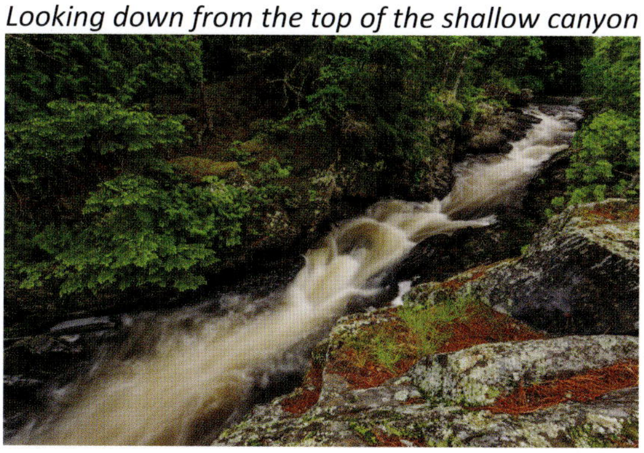

The sharp pinnacles, layered out into the river

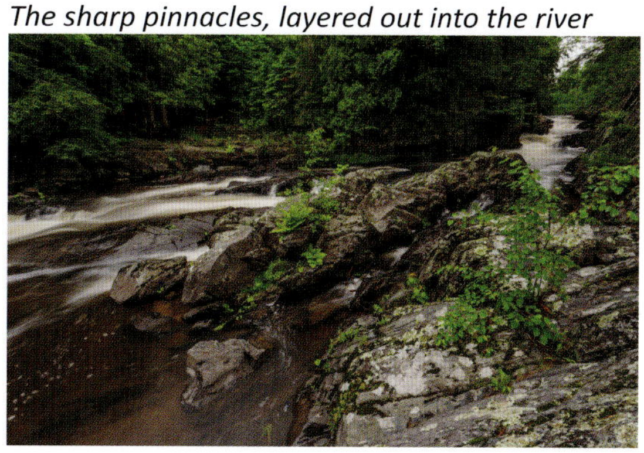

SILVER FALLS - LOWER (SILVER RIVER)

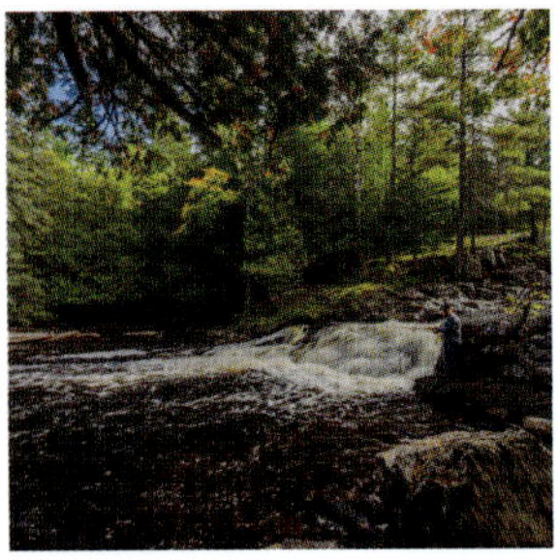

Must See:	7
Height:	20 feet
Time:	20-30 minutes

Driving Information

Signs:	None
Road:	Dirt
Access:	Somewhat Easy
4WD:	N/A

GPS:	N46 47.612 W88 20.182

Hiking Information

Path:	Slight Footpath
Length:	150 yards
Elev. Change:	Minor
GPS:	N/A
Danger:	Slight
WP Boots:	Recommended

The river churns through a narrow channel in a picturesque setting well-loved by local fishermen. A well-worn path leads through a rocky stretch of forest, crossing a wet patch or two on the way to the base of the falls. Both of the waterfalls here are easily accessed from the good sized parking area. A pit toilet built here is testimony to the popularity of this off-the-road "roadside park".

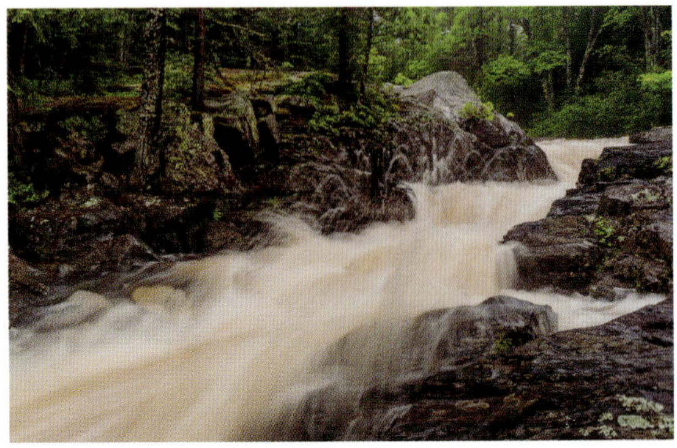

Bare bedrock lies all along the chute, smoothed over time by water and ice

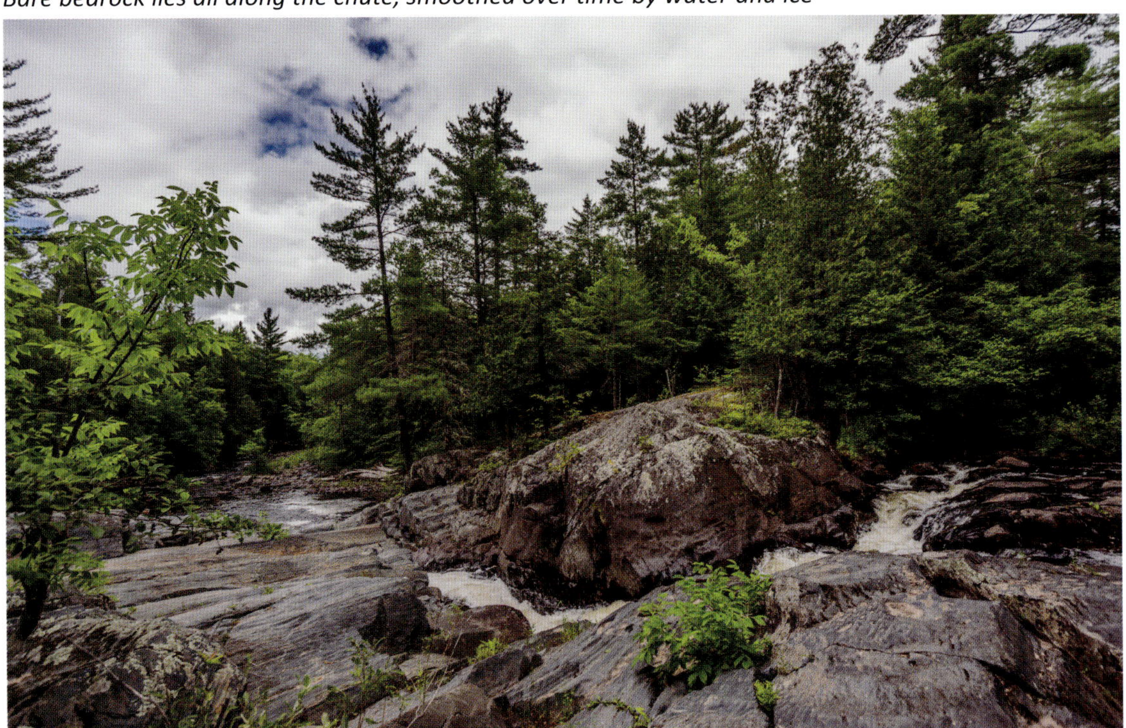

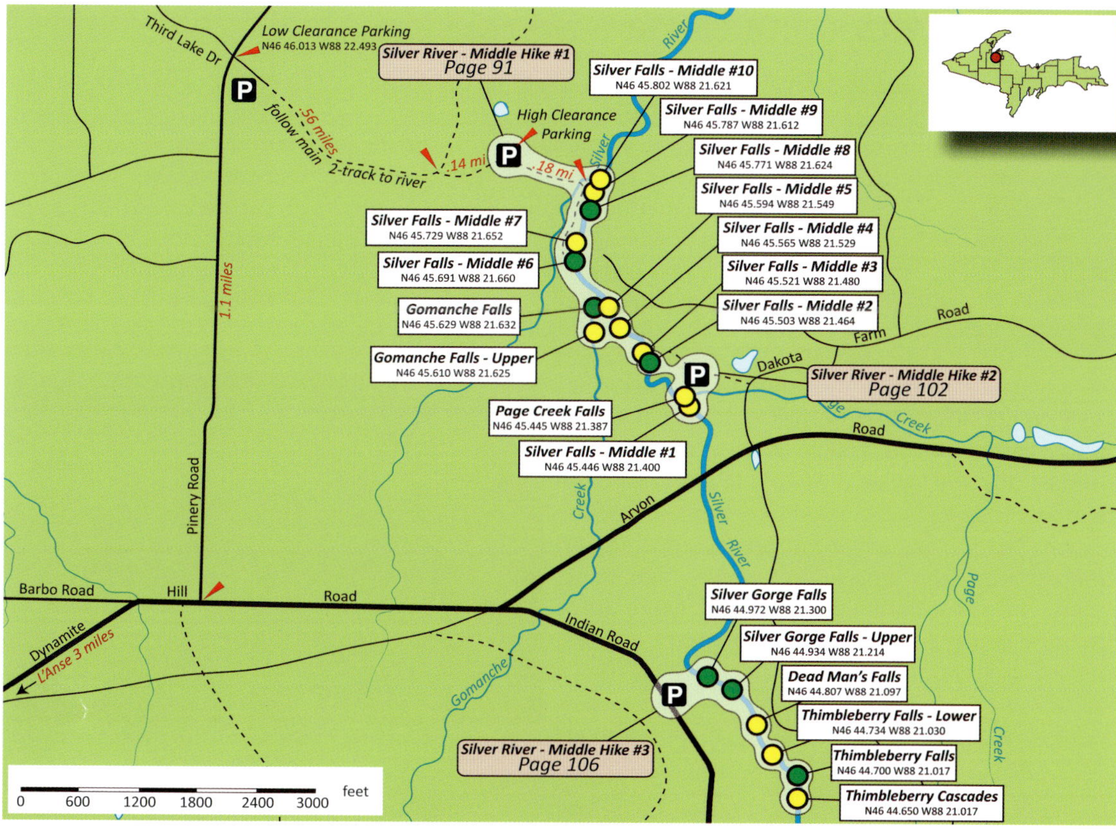

Silver River - Middle Hike #1

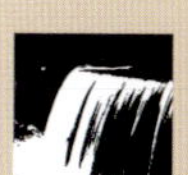

The Silver River runs through a gorge with a steep wall that guards the river from casual observers. Nine waterfalls of varying allure are found along the hike. Fortunately, they can all be seen from the footpath that winds along the top of the gorge wall. At the far end of the hike, Gomanche Creek joins Silver River with a nice set of waterfalls.

Directions: From Dynamite Hill Road turn north onto Pinery Road. Drive 1.1 miles. (The road will jog right and then left again) Third Lake Road is to the left. If you don't have a good clearance vehicle then park on the right (N46 46.013 W88 22.493). High clearance vehicles can drive southeast down the 2-track for .56 miles. The 2-track turns hard to the left. Turn right here onto another 2-track. Follow it for .14 miles. Park on the left of the trail (N46 45.849 W88 21.820). There is room here for 1 vehicle. Hike 1.6 miles down the 2-track past the steep, sandy, rutted area and on to the river. Continue to hike along the river to Gomanche Creek, which empties into Silver River immediately after dropping over Gomanche Falls. Follow Gomanche Creek 100 feet upriver to view the upper Falls. Cross over Gomanche Creek and continue upstream along Silver River to the rest of the waterfalls.

SILVER FALLS - MIDDLE #10 (SILVER RIVER)

Private

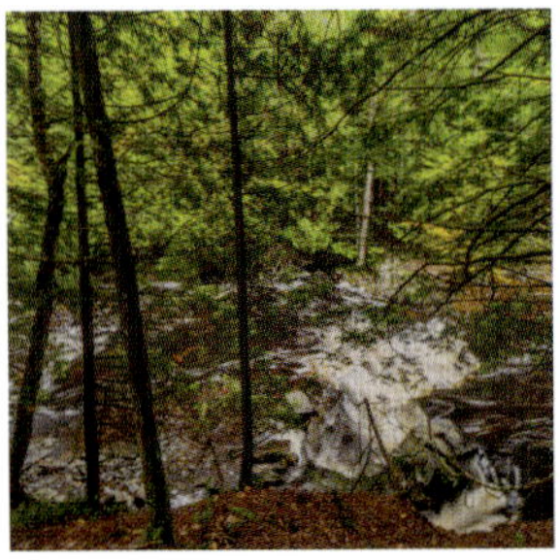

Must See:	4	GPS:	N46 45.802 W88 21.621
Height:	2 feet		
Time:	15-20 minutes	Hiking Information	
		Path:	2-track/ATV trail
Driving Information		Length:	.20 miles
Signs:	None	Elev. Change:	Moderate
Road:	2-track	GPS:	Recommended
Access:	Difficult	Danger:	Moderate
4WD:	Helpful	WP Boots:	N/A

The Silver River rapidly descends over a series of lovely waterfalls. An ATV trail ends toward the bottom of these drops. Follow the river downstream just past this, the lowest drop to find a safe place to get down to the river. Angled bedrock here can be slippery, but the angle helps in getting down the 10 foot rock wall. This drop is just two feet high, but is a sheer drop over hard black split rock. More drops can be seen just a short distance upstream.

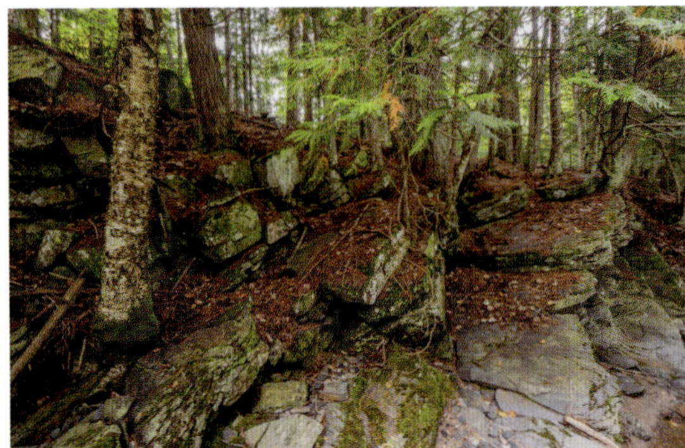

The angled bedrock that slants up from the river

*Note: Hiking Information in the Data Table assumes a high clearance vehicle that parked at the top of the sandy hill along the 2-track. Add .7 miles if parking just off of Pinery Road.

The next waterfall upstream, #9, can be seen peeking around a slight corner in the river

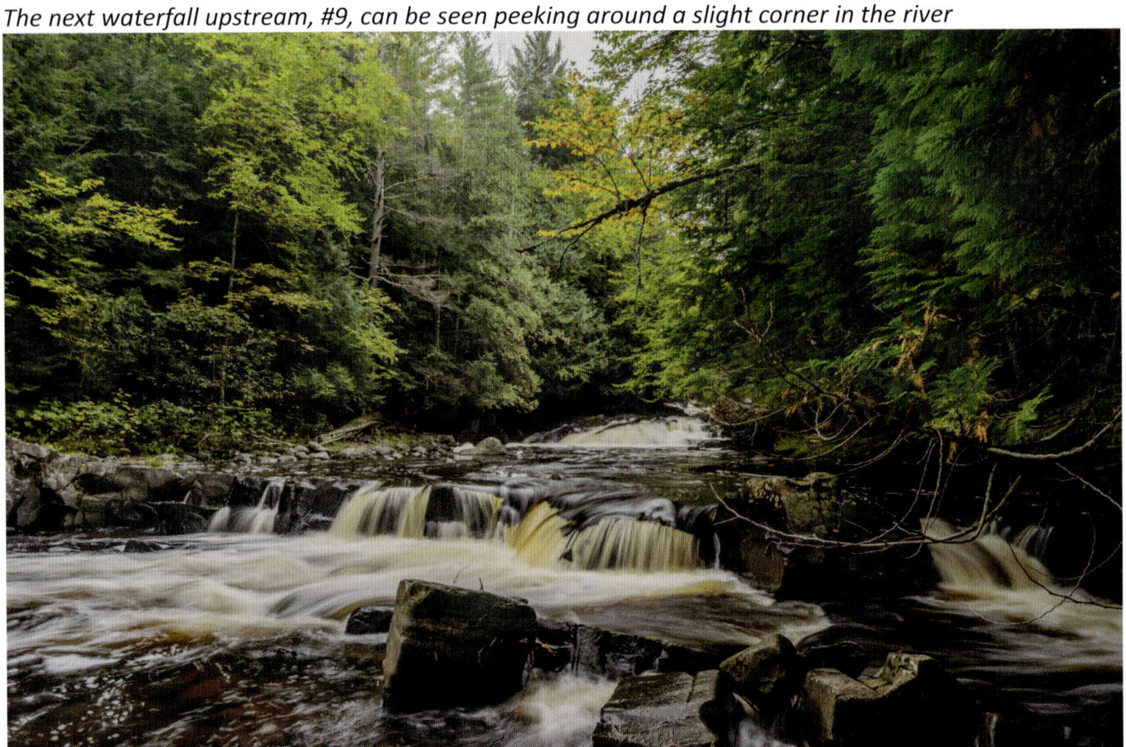

SILVER FALLS - MIDDLE #9 (SILVER RIVER)

Private

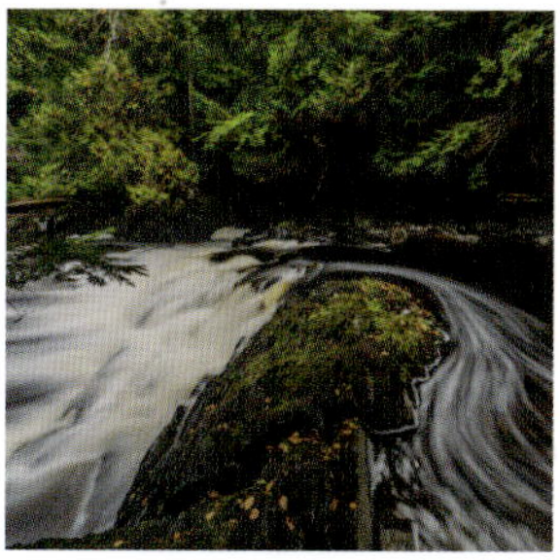

Must See:	6	GPS:	N46 45.787 W88 21.612
Height:	5 feet		
Time:	20-25 minutes	Hiking Information	
		Path:	2-track/ATV trail
Driving Information		Length:	.19 miles
Signs:	None	Elev. Change:	Moderate
Road:	2-track	GPS:	Recommended
Access:	Difficult	Danger:	Moderate
4WD:	Helpful	WP Boots:	N/A

Just 100 feet upstream from #10, the river rumbles down a short but steep cascade. It angles downstream and also toward the far side of the river. This makes for a visually interesting and unique drop. Once again, a couple more drops can be seen upstream. What a beautiful stretch of river!

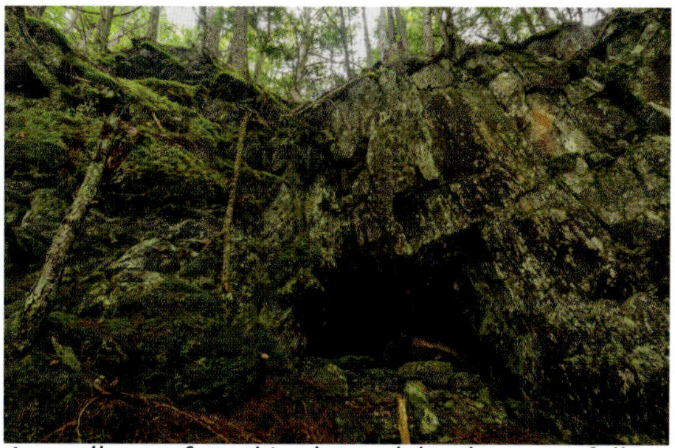

A small cave found in the rock by the waterfall

It is easier to get down to the river at this waterfall. There is a great viewing/picnic spot here. A shallow cave is located in the rock face near the base of the waterfall. Be careful. Large chunks of rock have fallen inside.

*Note: Hiking Information in the Data Table assumes a high clearance vehicle that parked at the top of the sandy hill along the 2-track. Add .7 miles if parking just off of Pinery Road.

This waterfall is down the 15 foot rocky bank from the end of the ATV trail

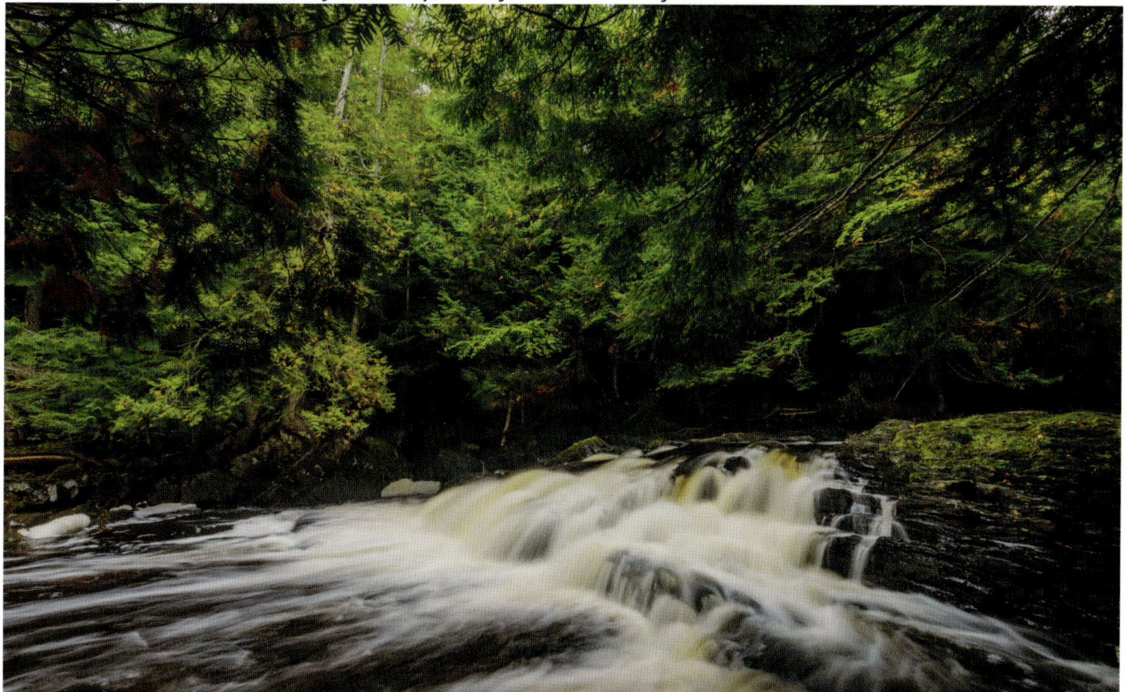

SILVER FALLS - MIDDLE #8 (SILVER RIVER)

Private

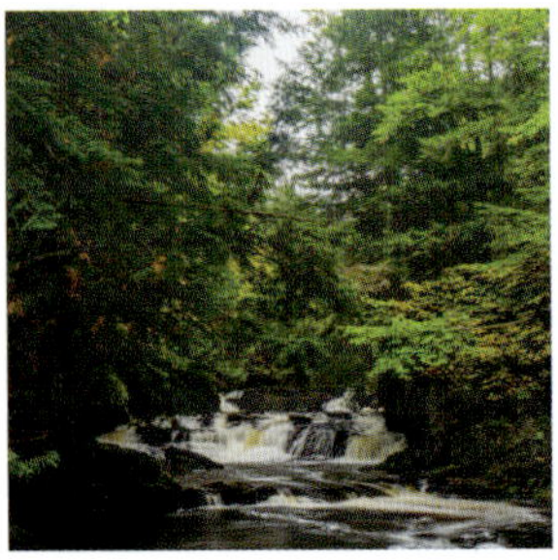

Must See:	7
Height:	15 feet
Time:	25-40 minutes

Driving Information

Signs:	None
Road:	2-track
Access:	Difficult
4WD:	Helpful

GPS:	N46 45.771 W88 21.624

Hiking Information

Path:	ATV trail
Length:	.19 miles
Elev. Change:	Moderate
GPS:	Recommended
Danger:	Moderate
WP Boots:	N/A

About 100 feet upstream from #7 is a lovely 3-drop waterfall. The river starts by dividing and running around a slightly domed mass. It cascades down 8 feet on both sides, pauses for a dozen yards, cascades down a wide and pleasing 6 foot rippled and slightly horseshoe shaped drop and then finishes with a 1 foot drop 25 feet later. A 20 foot bluff is snuggled up next to the center of the waterfall, making it impossible to hike the river's edge up the 3 drops. Climb down the steep bank to the river at the base of the lowest drop.

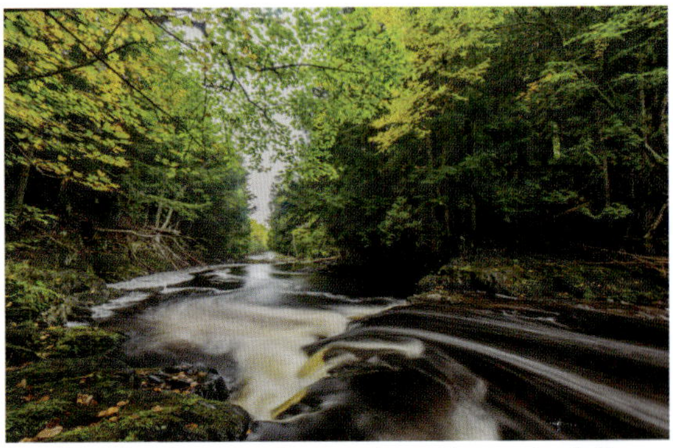

Looking back downstream from the waterfall

*Note: Hiking Information in the Data Table assumes a high clearance vehicle that parked at the top of the sandy hill along the 2-track. Add .7 miles if parking just off of Pinery Road.

Notice the 3 drops, nicely framed in this stretch of river

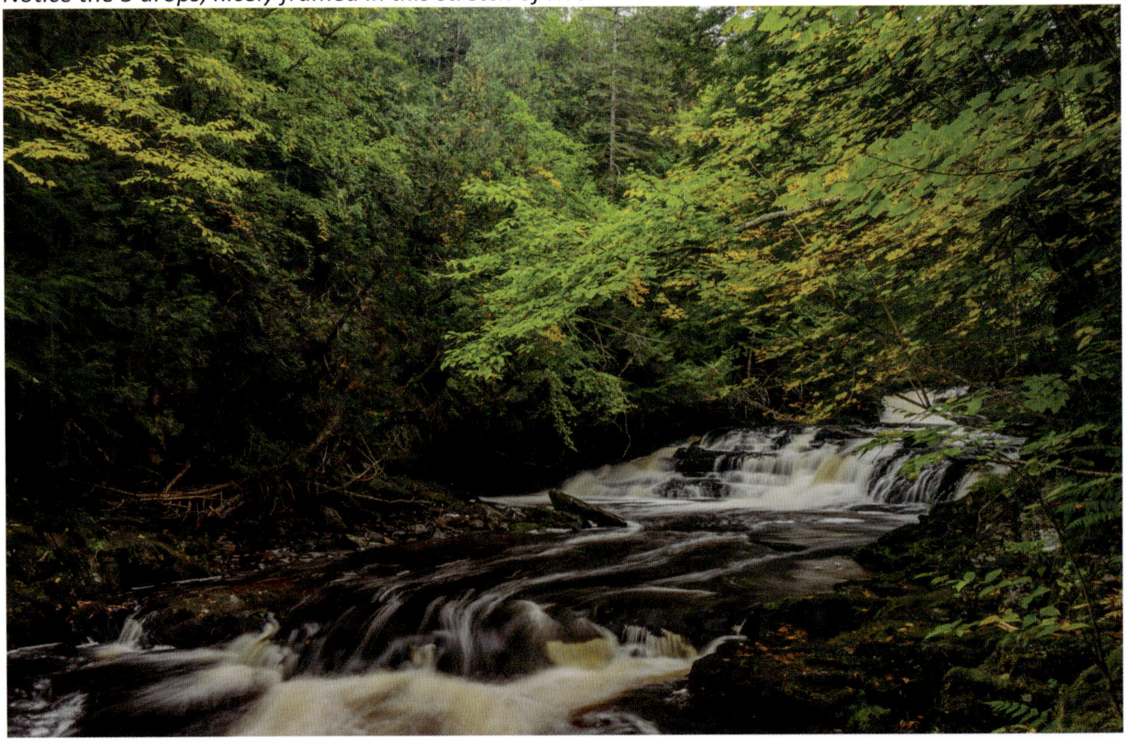

SILVER FALLS - MIDDLE #7 (SILVER RIVER)

Private

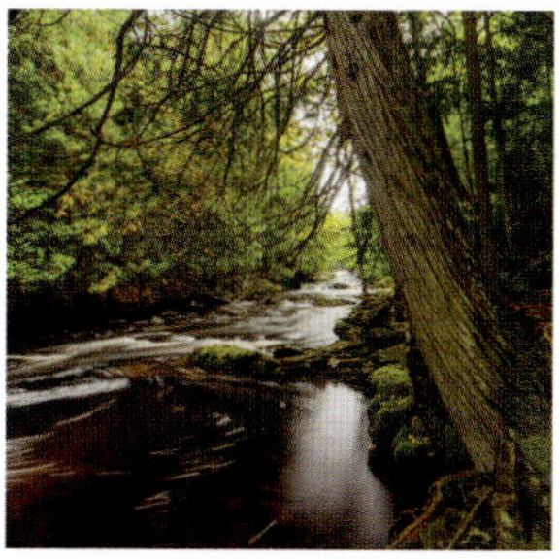

Must See:	4	GPS:	N46 45.729 W88 21.652
Height:	2 feet		
Time:	30-50 minutes	Hiking Information	
		Path:	ATV Trail
Driving Information		Length:	.23 miles
Signs:	None	Elev. Change:	Moderate
Road:	2-track	GPS:	Recommended
Access:	Difficult	Danger:	Moderate
4WD:	Helpful	WP Boots:	N/A

From the top of #8, hike along the top of the gorge to this small drop. Once again, the river is about 20 feet below. Pick your way carefully down the leaf covered steep hillside. The river divides at a waterfall that flows around a small promontory of finely layered black slate. Another smaller drop is 50 feet downstream, not much more than a ripple in the river. This is not a very good viewing area here.

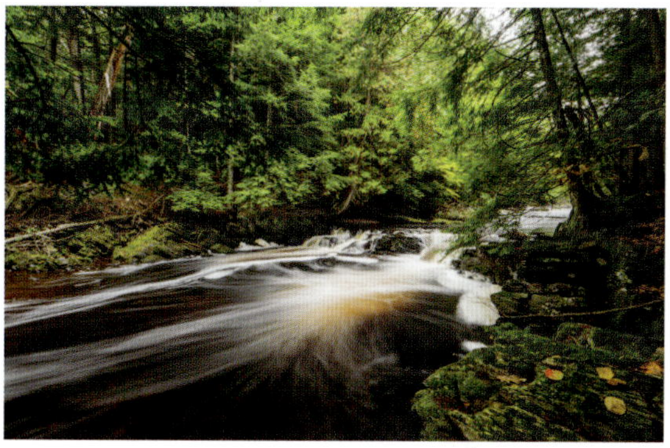

*Note: Hiking Information in the Data Table assumes a high clearance vehicle that parked at the top of the sandy hill along the 2-track. Add .7 miles if parking just off of Pinery Road.

The layered black slate can be easily seen in this shot, looking across the waterfall

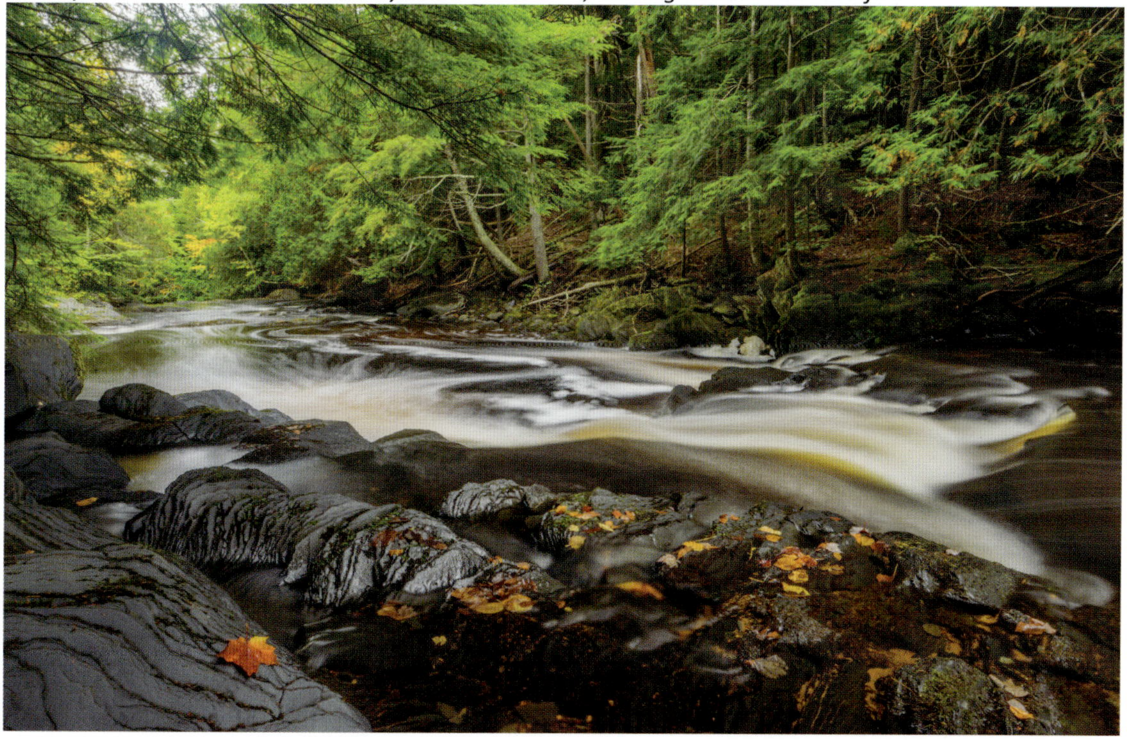

SILVER FALLS - MIDDLE #6 (SILVER RIVER)

Private

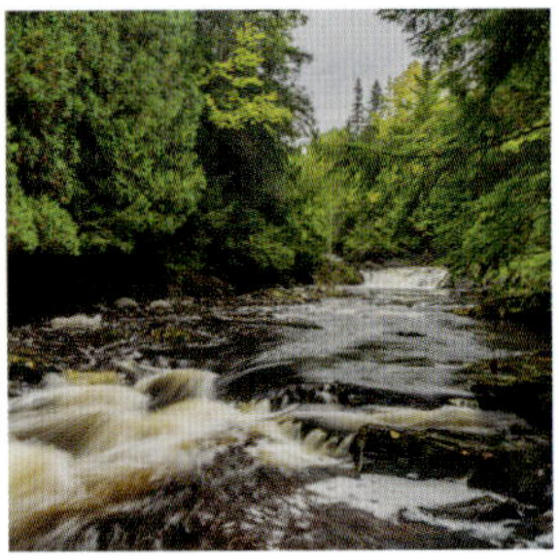

Must See:	8	GPS:	N46 45.691 W88 21.660
Height:	20 feet		
Time:	40-60 minutes	**Hiking Information**	
		Path:	ATV trail
Driving Information		Length:	.28 miles
Signs:	None	Elev. Change:	Moderate
Road:	2-track	GPS:	Recommended
Access:	Difficult	Danger:	Moderate
4WD:	Helpful	WP Boots:	N/A

Multiple cascades run back to back through a picturesque gorge. Sheer rock faces on the near side of the river are reminiscent of Canyon Falls, the flat vertical walls moss covered and standing proudly at the base of the final drop. One hundred yards downstream is #7. Follow the river upstream from #7 along the water's edge. The gorge wall pushes closer and closer to the river until there is no more room to hike along the river. There is a small but lovely place to view the waterfall from about 50 yards downstream.

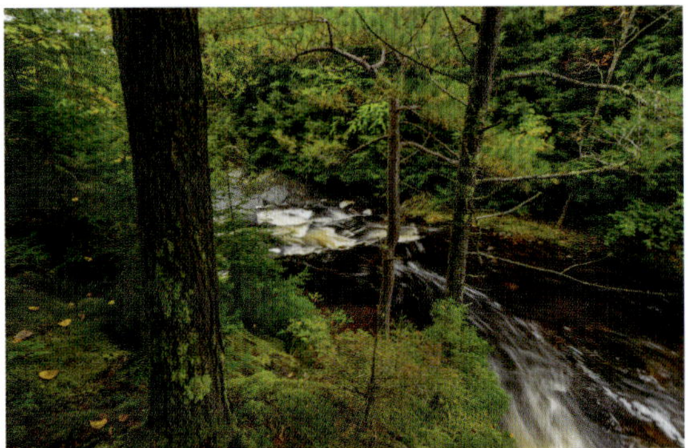

Looking down on #6 from the top of the gorge

*Note: Hiking Information in the Data Table assumes a high clearance vehicle that parked at the top of the sandy hill along the 2-track. Add .7 miles if parking just off of Pinery Road.

The nearly vertical wall stands alongside the Silver River, as though cut by design

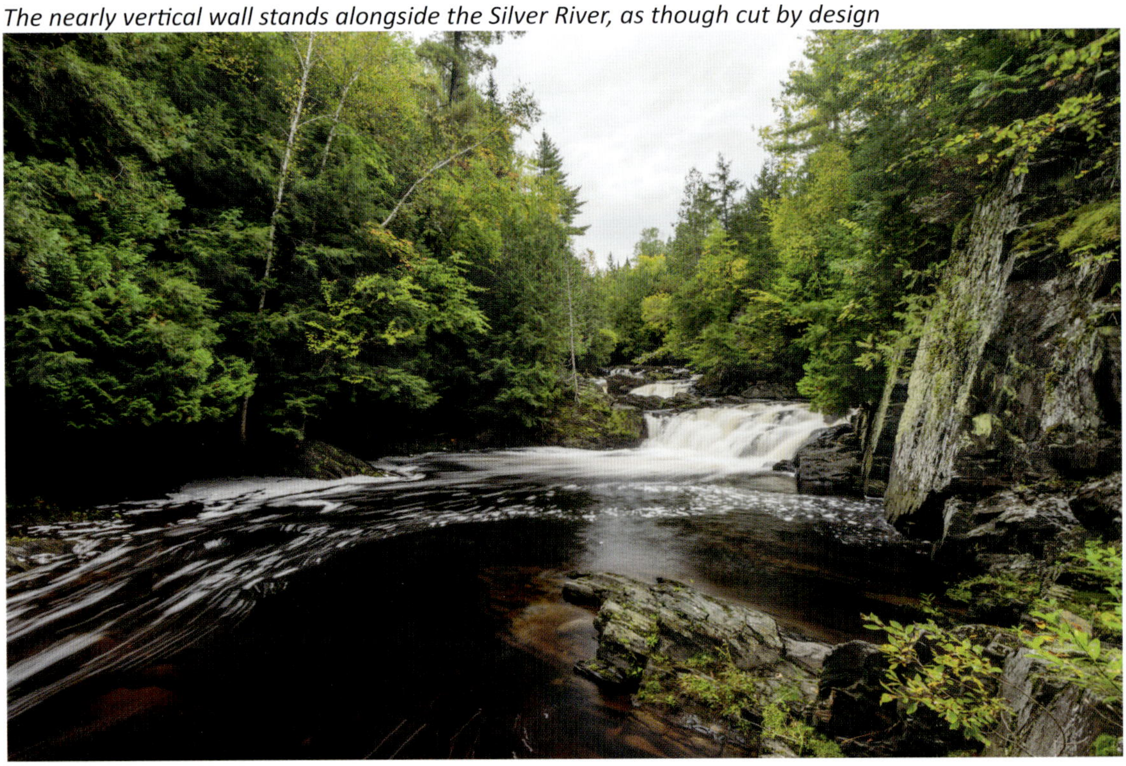

GOMANCHE FALLS (GOMANCHE CREEK)

Private

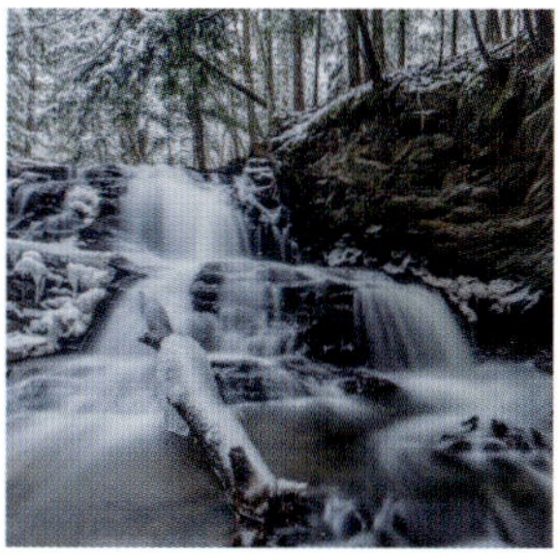

Must See:	7	GPS:	N46 45.629 W88 21.632
Height:	13 feet		
Time:	45-65 minutes	**Hiking Information**	
		Path:	None
Driving Information		Length:	.37 mile
Signs:	None	Elev. Change:	Moderate
Road:	2-track	GPS:	Recommended
Access:	Difficult	Danger:	Moderate
4WD:	Helpful	WP Boots:	Recommended

Gomanche Creek makes a double drop into a narrow gorge just before it falls several more feet as it empties into Silver River. There is a very nice viewing area that would be a perfect spot for a picnic. The entire area is composed of crumbling slate.

The best viewing of Gomanche Falls is from the south side of the creek. This requires wading across from the north. Therefore waterproof boots are recommended if wanting to get over to the far side.

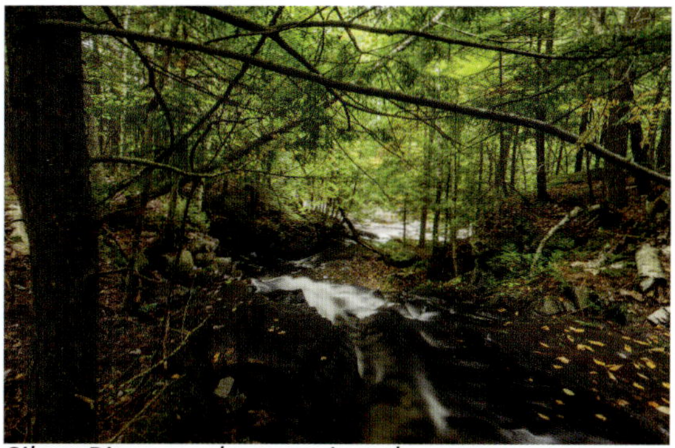

Silver River can be seen just downstream

*Note: Hiking Information in the Data Table assumes a high clearance vehicle that parked at the top of the sandy hill along the 2-track. Add .7 miles if parking just off of Pinery Road.

Amazing fragmented layers of slate splay out on the northern side of the waterfall

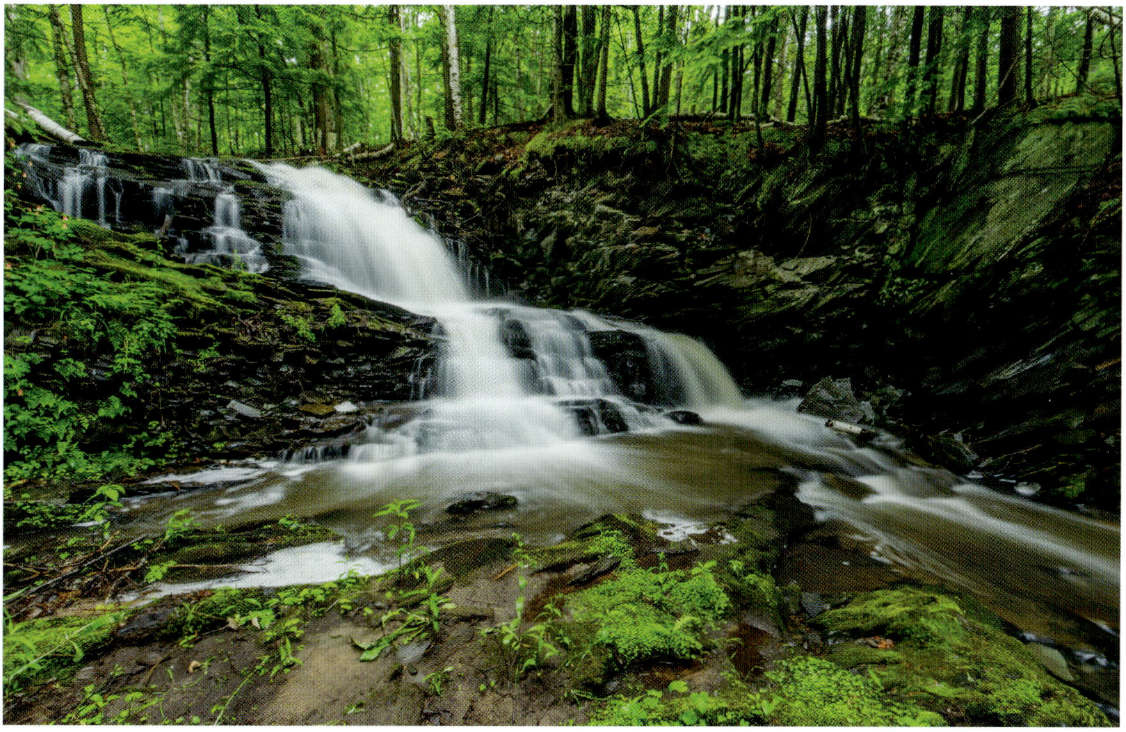

GOMANCHE FALLS - UPPER (GOMANCHE CREEK)

Private

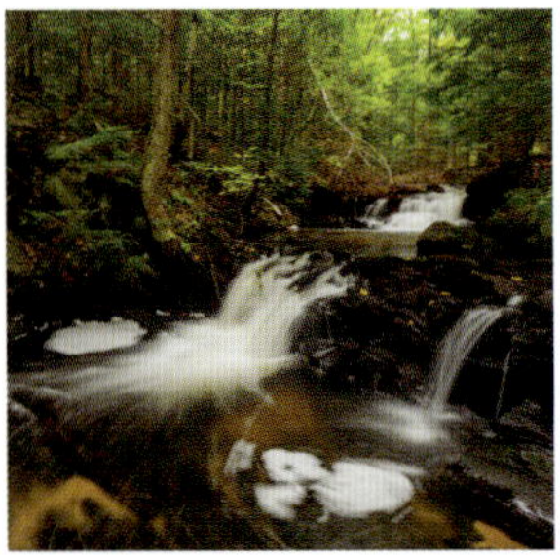

Must See:	6	GPS:	N46 45.610 W88 21.625
Height:	9 feet		
Time:	50-70 minutes	Hiking Information	
		Path:	None
Driving Information		Length:	.39 miles
Signs:	None	Elev. Change:	Moderate
Road:	2-track	GPS:	Recommended
Access:	Difficult	Danger:	Moderate
4WD:	Helpful	WP Boots:	N/A

Hike upstream 100 feet from Gomanche Falls. The 10 feet wide creek makes three successive drops, overshadowed by hardwoods and pines. In the summer, this waterfall offers a visual feast with black rocks, white water, balanced with green leaves and moss.

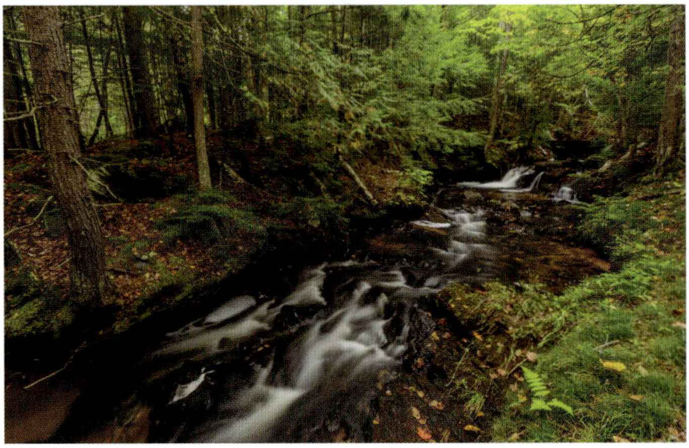

*Note: Hiking Information in the Data Table assumes a high clearance vehicle that parked at the top of the sandy hill along the 2-track. Add .7 miles if parking just off of Pinery Road.

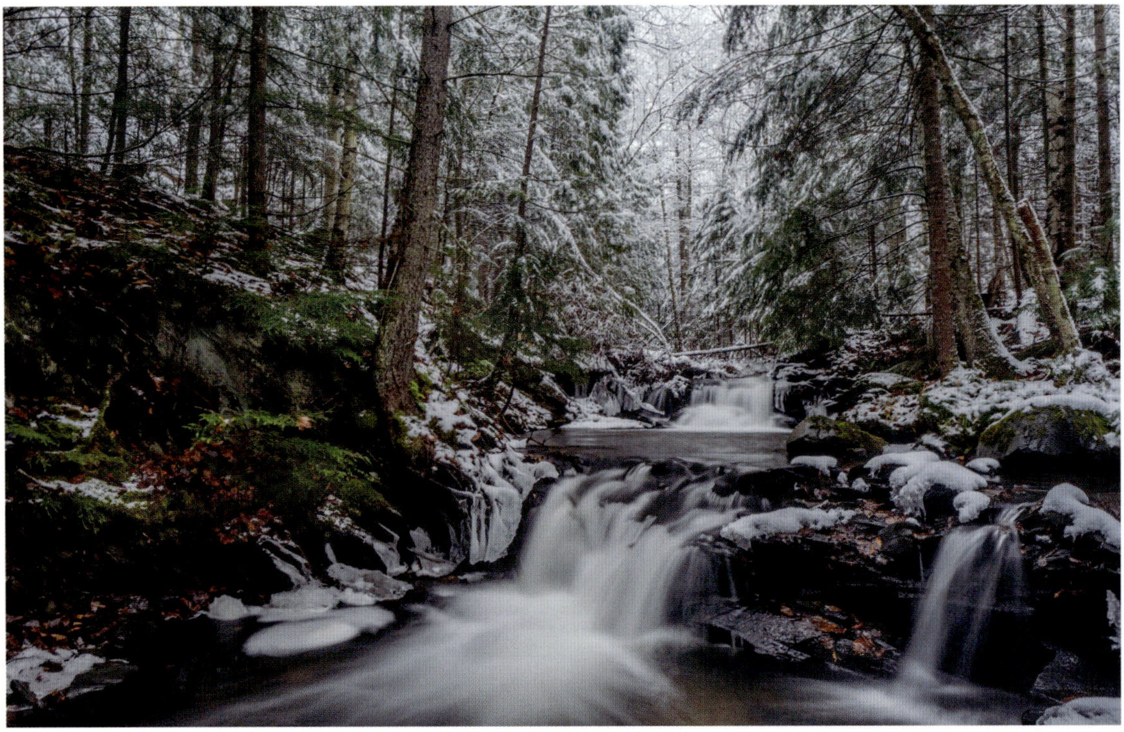

SILVER FALLS - MIDDLE #5 (SILVER RIVER)

Private

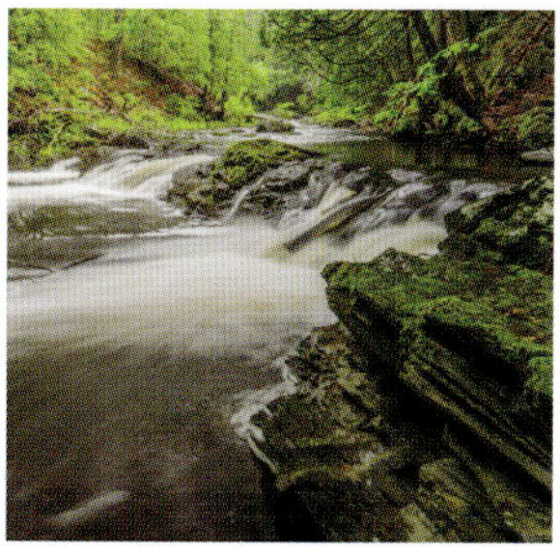

Must See:	5	GPS:	N46 45.594 W88 21.549
Height:	2 feet		
Time:	60-80 minutes		

Driving Information

Signs:	None
Road:	2-track
Access:	Difficult
4WD:	Helpful

Hiking Information

Path:	ATV Trail
Length:	.44 miles
Elev. Change:	Moderate
GPS:	Recommended
Danger:	Moderate
WP Boots:	N/A

Cross over Gomanche Creek. Hike .10 miles up the Silver River and arrive at this short but nicely displayed waterfall. The Silver River widens out to 30 feet. Several upthrust masses of bedrock stick out above the top of the waterfall as it cuts diagonally across the river.

*Note: Hiking Information in the Data Table assumes a high clearance vehicle that parked at the top of the sandy hill along the 2-track. Add .7 miles if parking just off of Pinery Road.

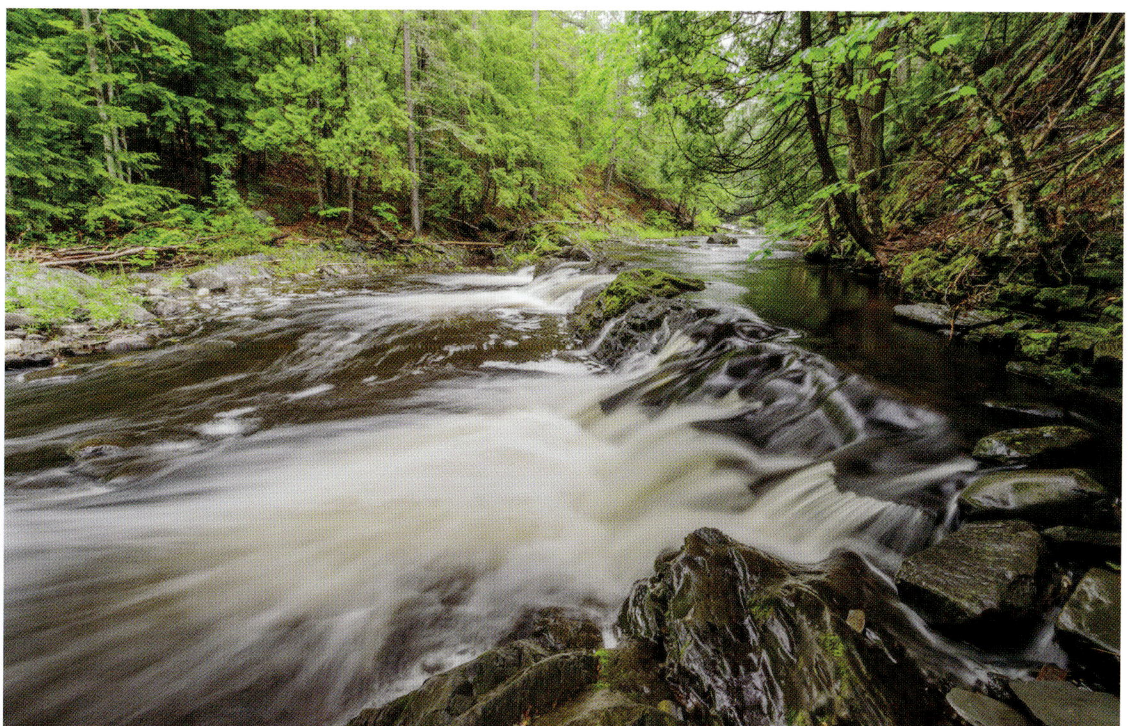

SILVER FALLS - MIDDLE #4 (SILVER RIVER)

Private

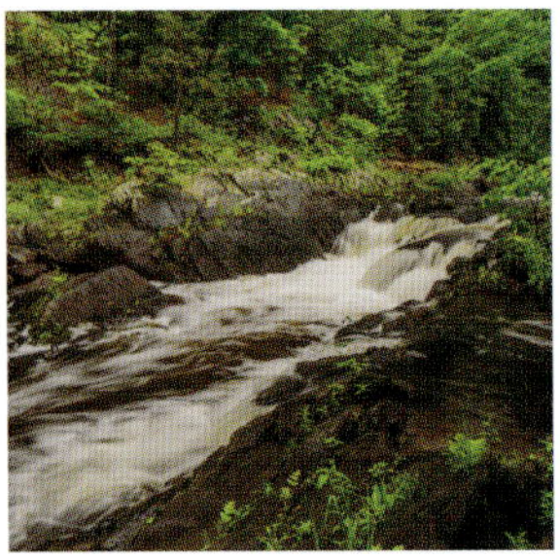

Must See:	5	GPS:	N46 45.565 W88 21.529
Height:	3 feet		
Time:	65-85 minutes	Hiking Information	
		Path:	ATV trail
Driving Information		Length:	.47 miles
Signs:	None	Elev. Change:	Moderate
Road:	2-track	GPS:	Recommended
Access:	Difficult	Danger:	Moderate
4WD:	Helpful	WP Boots:	N/A

Just 200 feet upstream from #5, the river is much narrower. This waterfall lies at the base of the now familiar gorge wall on the near side, while severely angled bedrock on the far side rises menacingly as high as 50 feet above the river, a thin layer of soil giving rise to the ground cover and trees, their intertwined roots holding together in a mesh of sorts, collectively defying gravity on the steep hillside.

The waterfall is separated by a small "island", a mass clustered in the center of the river, twin horse tail shaped arcs of water splaying over churning white water alongside. Along both sides of the river, cleaned by the river after heavy rains, smooth formed rocks line the waterway.

*Note: Hiking Information in the Data Table assumes a high clearance vehicle that parked at the top of the sandy hill along the 2-track. Add .7 miles if parking just off of Pinery Road.

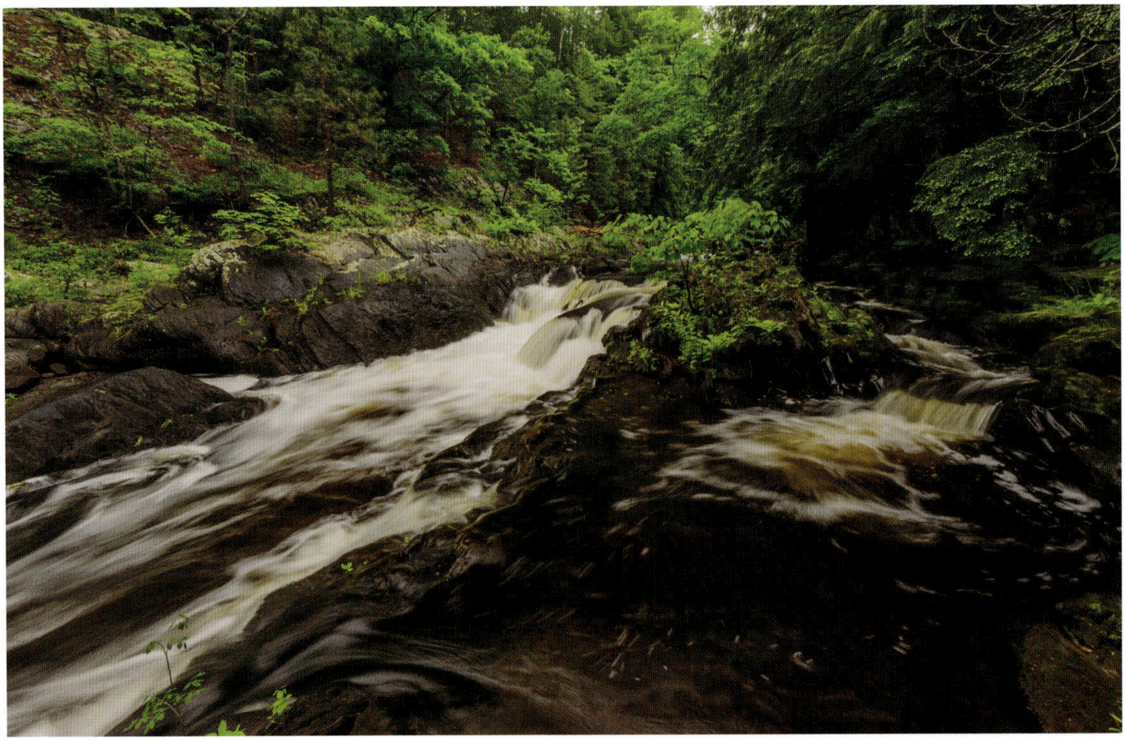

SILVER FALLS - MIDDLE #3 (SILVER RIVER)

Private

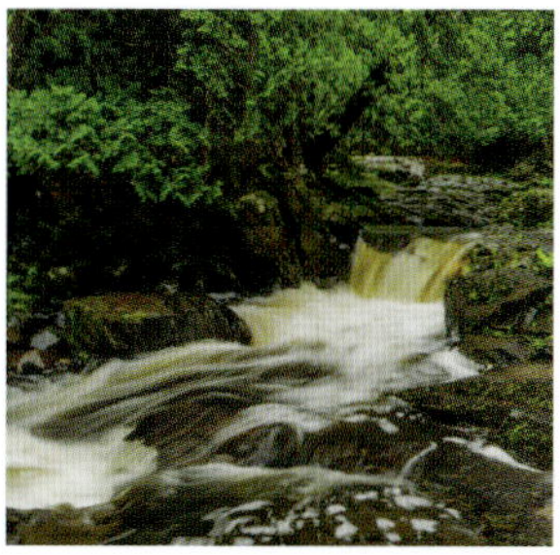

Must See:	5	GPS:	N46 45.521 W88 21.480
Height:	4 feet		
Time:	70-90 minutes	**Hiking Information**	
		Path:	ATV Trail
Driving Information		Length:	.54 miles
Signs:	None	Elev. Change:	Moderate
Road:	2-track	GPS:	Recommended
Access:	Difficult	Danger:	Moderate
4WD:	Helpful	WP Boots:	N/A

It's 125 yards from #4 to #3. The much wider river upstream narrows dramatically down to just 5 feet. It then plunges down 3 feet between moss covered rocks. The frothing spill pool then drops down another foot. A rocky mass and a stone strewn bank make for a good viewing area along the near side.

This waterfall can only be viewed from the west side of the river. Although is only about 100 feet downstream from #2 (which is best viewed from the eastern side), a rapid and high rise on the eastern side blocks the viewing ability from over there.

*Note: Hiking Information in the Data Table assumes a high clearance vehicle that parked at the top of the sandy hill along the 2-track. Add .7 miles if parking just off of Pinery Road.

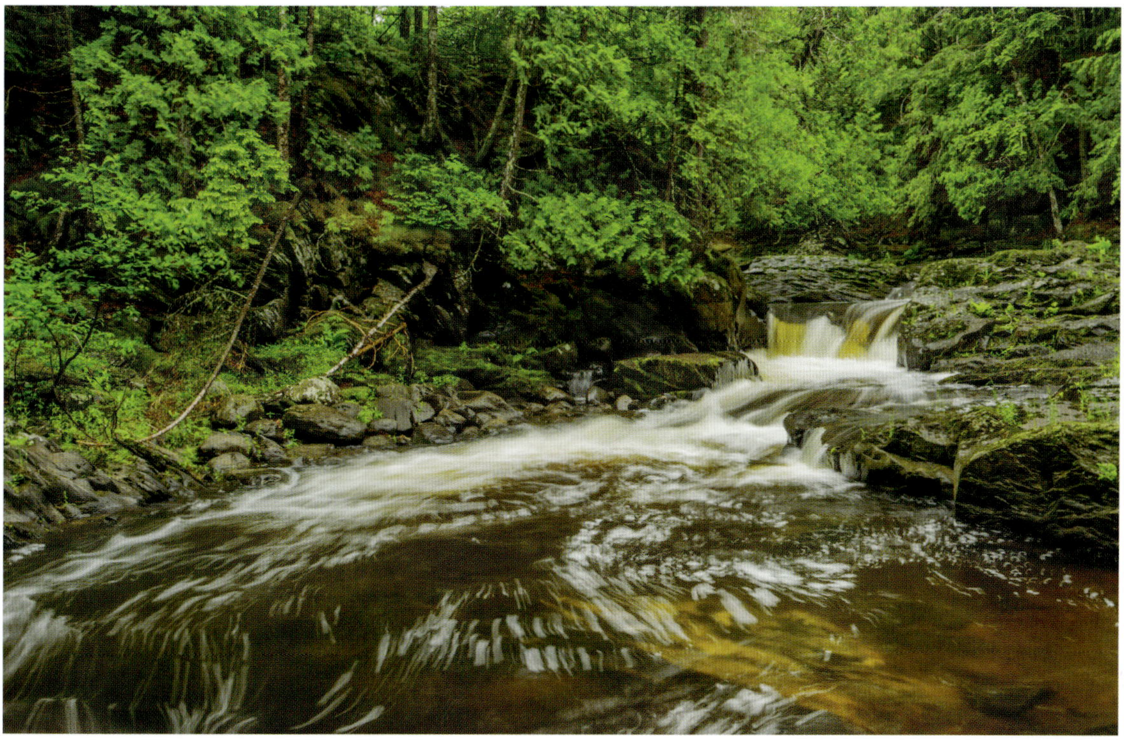

Silver River - Middle Hike #2

The waterfalls between Arvon Road and Gomanche Creek are best seen from the eastern side of the river. Fortunately, there is access to this side of the river through a gravel pit area.

Directions: From US-41, turn left (east) onto Dynamite Hill Road just .3 miles from the big corner in L'Anse. Follow Dynamite Hill Road for 3.8 miles. Turn left onto Arvon Road. Follow it for .5 miles to the bridge over Silver River. Continue on .1 miles. Turn left at the first gravel road (Dakota Farm Road). In .16 miles, upon entering the gravel pit, stay left, heading west. In .15 miles, park up close to the tree line. Hike .1 miles through the forest to the GPS coordinates for Page Creek Falls. This will be at the meeting of Page Creek and Silver River. After viewing these 2 waterfalls, follow the Silver River downstream. The hike will rise up high above the river. There is a fisherman's trail that follows the top of the ridge, offering nice views of the river far below. Upon approaching Silver Falls - Middle #2, the ridge starts descending. Work your way down to the river's edge to view the waterfall.

SILVER FALLS - MIDDLE #1 (SILVER RIVER)

Private

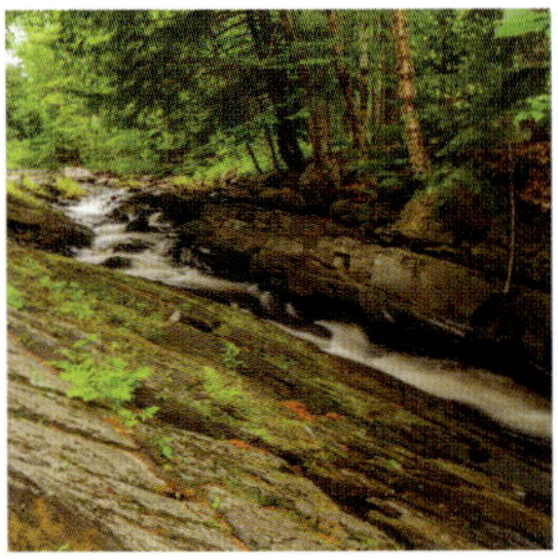

Must See:	4	GPS:	N46 45.446 W88 21.400
Height:	10 feet		
Time:	15-25 minutes	Hiking Information	
		Path:	None
Driving Information		Length:	.1 miles
Signs:	None	Elev. Change:	Minor
Road:	Gravel Road	GPS:	Required
Access:	Somewhat Easy	Danger:	Moderate
4WD:	N/A	WP Boots:	Recommended

The Silver River, filled with good sized boulders above the fast run, narrows dramatically, at one point down to just a couple of feet as it enters a shallow gorge. Slippery angular bedrock slopes down to the river on the near side, with a layered sheer wall on the other side. A nice log home peeks through the trees on the far side. The first 4 foot drop is at the entrance to the gorge. The second drop is one foot high in the center of the run. And the final drop tumbles two feet just upstream from where Page Creek joins the river.

Looking up the run from near Page Creek

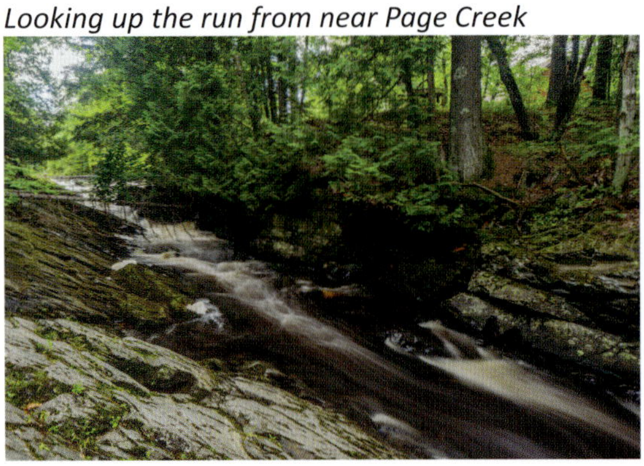

The top of the run as the river narrows

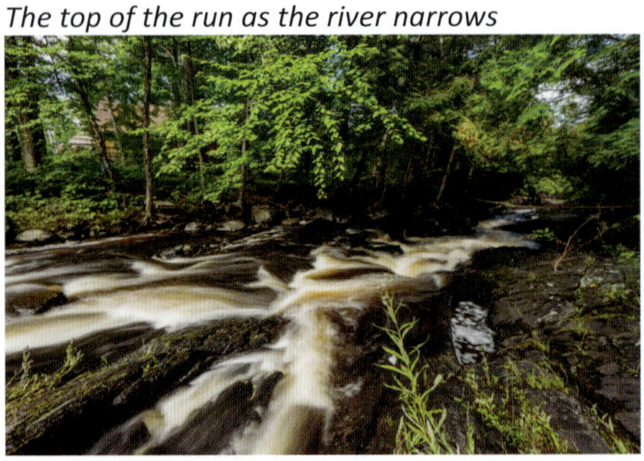

PAGE CREEK FALLS (PAGE CREEK)

Private

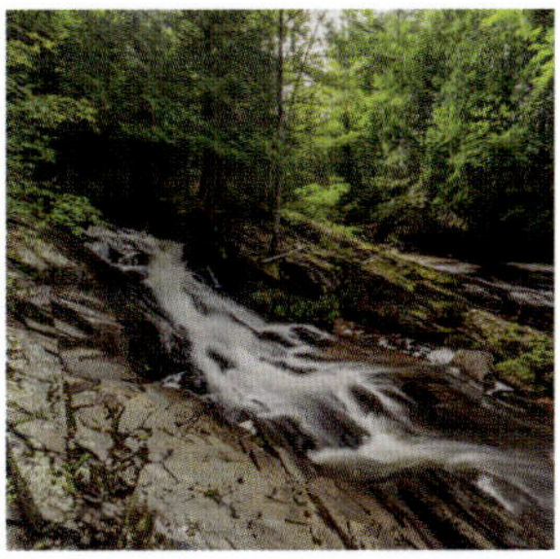

Must See:	6	GPS:	N46 45.445 W88 21.387
Height:	8 feet		
Time:	20-30 minutes	Hiking Information	
		Path:	None
Driving Information		Length:	.1 miles
Signs:	None	Elev. Change:	Minor
Road:	Gravel Road	GPS:	Required
Access:	Somewhat Easy	Danger:	Moderate
4WD:	N/A	WP Boots:	Recommended

Page Creek wanders in from the east, dropping at the end into the river just 100 feet downstream from the first of the middle set of waterfalls on the Silver River. The picture below shows the relationship between the two waterfalls. It's unusual to have the opportunity to see waterfalls from two different waterways from the same location. Enjoy this!

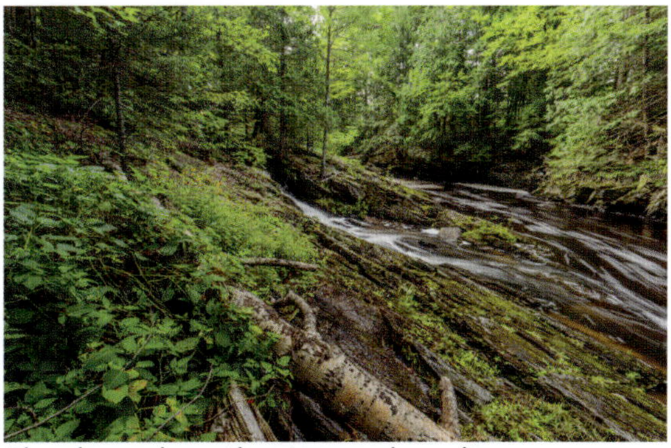

The slope along the river and creek

The four foot wide creek is slightly settled into the blackened bedrock. It joins the much larger Silver River in a rushing cascade, spread out over 30 feet. A small patch of spotted touch-me-nots sits near the base of the waterfall.

Check out Page Creek Falls on the following page during an August dry spell.

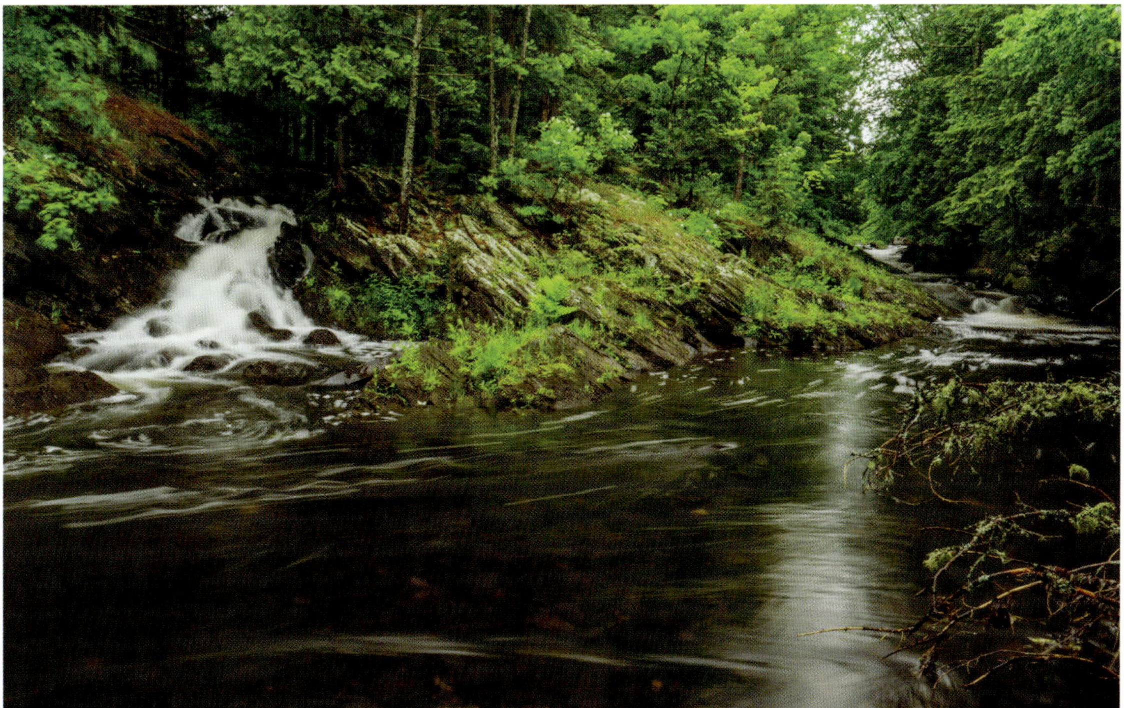

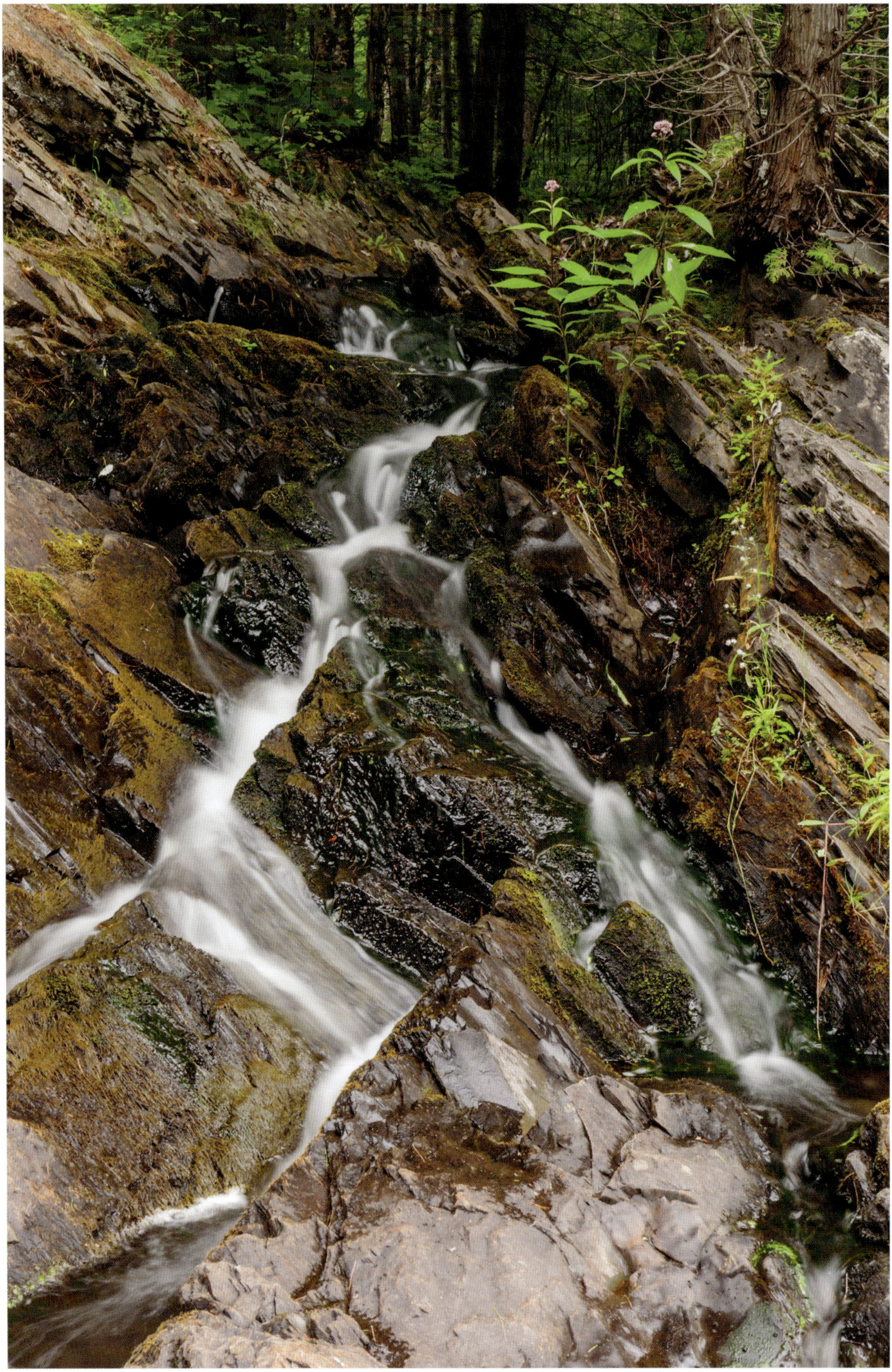

SILVER FALLS - MIDDLE #2 (SILVER RIVER)

Private

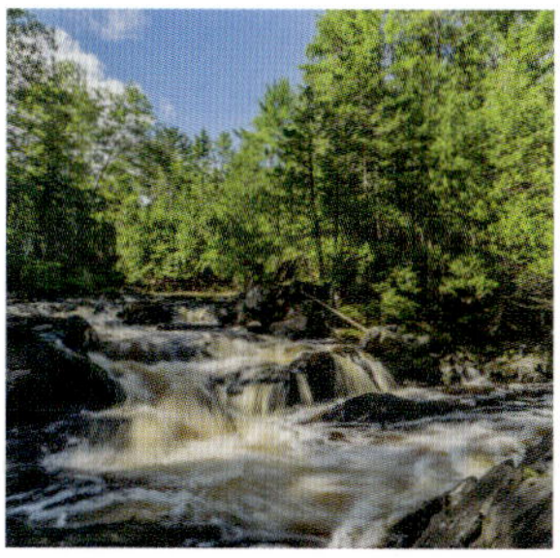

Must See:	7	GPS:	N46 45.503 W88 21.464
Height:	7 feet		
Time:	40-60 minutes	**Hiking Information**	
		Path:	None - then footpath
Driving Information		Length:	.21 miles
Signs:	None	Elev. Change:	Elevated
Road:	Gravel Road	GPS:	Required
Access:	Somewhat Easy	Danger:	Moderate
4WD:	N/A	WP Boots:	Helpful

Between Page Creek and here, the trail rises as it follows the river. There are wonderful views of the river far below. The trail diminishes as you near the waterfall, but the undergrowth is sparse and the grade drops down gently toward the river.

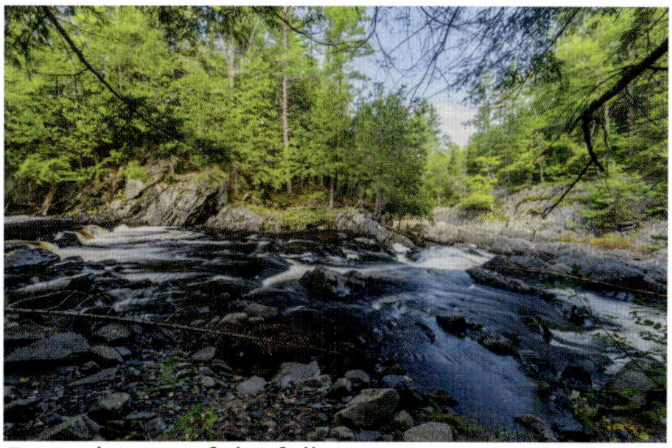

From the top of the falls

Wonderful chimney-like stacks of bedrock rise as nature's theater seating, waiting for an audience to come and view the waterfall, laid out mere feet away. The stair-stepped falls cascade down in the wide (at this point) river. The nicest of the drops is also the last, so the great viewing/picnicking area has a literal front row seat to the best performance!

The "theater seating" can be seen along the left side of the shot

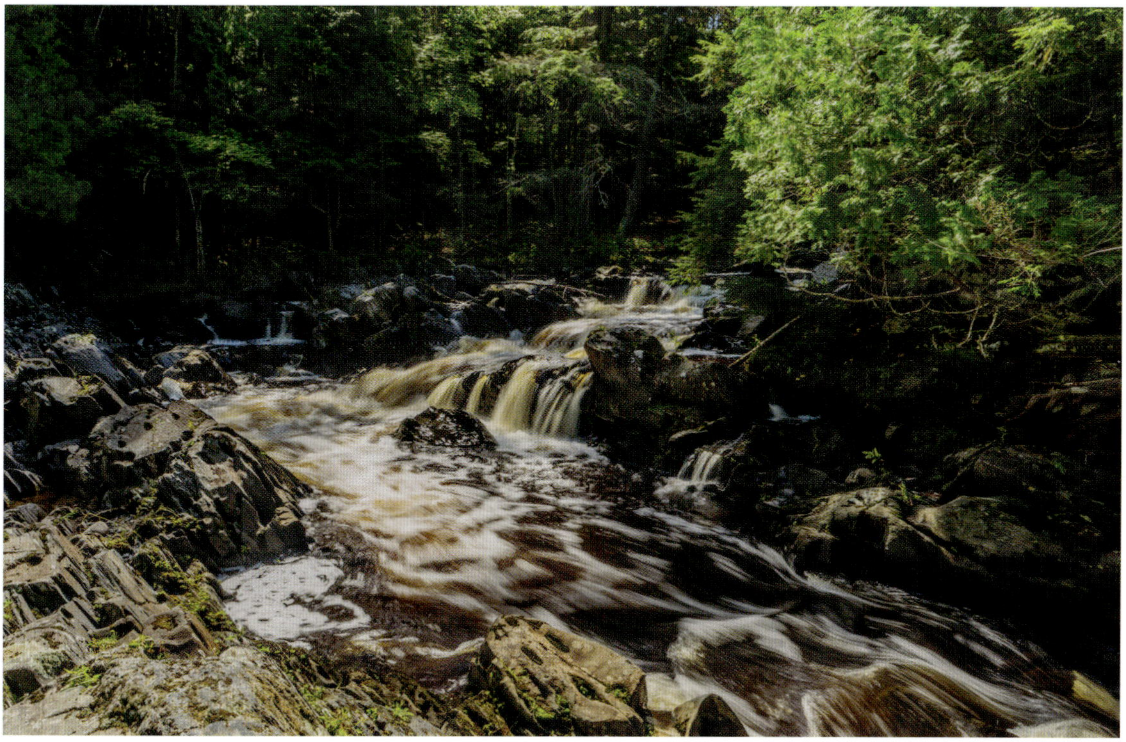

Silver River - Middle Hike #3

The area south of Arvon Road has a number of houses and camps along the Silver River. Always be respectful of private property and obey all "No Trespassing" signs.

Directions: From US-41, turn left (east) onto Dynamite Hill Road just .3 miles from the big corner in L'Anse. Follow Dynamite Hill Road for 3.8 miles. Stay right onto Indian Road (gravel). In .42 miles, park off the side of the road. (There is no obvious parking spot and no signage.) Hike 150 yards northeast through the woods to Silver Gorge Falls (use a GPS - there is no trail). Follow the river upstream for the next .47 miles to see the rest of the waterfalls in this stretch of the Silver River.

SILVER GORGE FALLS (SILVER RIVER)

Private

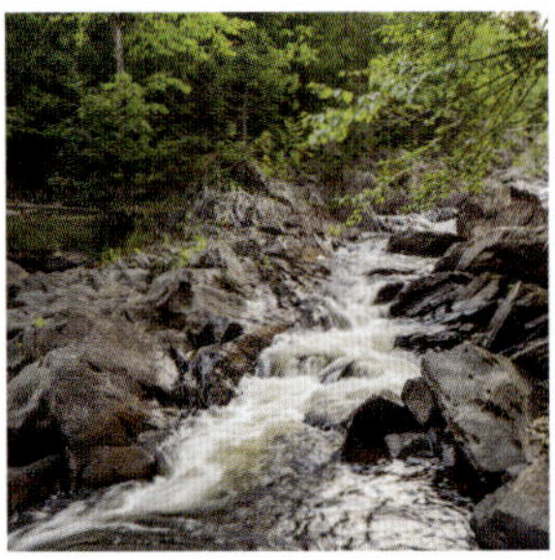

Must See:	7	GPS:	N46 44.972 W88 21.300
Height:	20 feet		
Time:	15-25 minutes	Hiking Information	
		Path:	None
Driving Information		Length:	150 yards
Signs:	None	Elev. Change:	Minor
Road:	Gravel Road	GPS:	Required
Access:	Somewhat Difficult	Danger:	Moderate
4WD:	N/A	WP Boots:	Helpful

Hike 150 yards through the mature forest to the waterfall. There is no trail, so make sure you have a good hand-held GPS and know how to use it.

The gorgeous cascade over fractured gray-brown bedrock gets quickly funneled to the west into a narrow gorge then continues to burst over small cascades for the next 100 yards or so. A bridge has been constructed over the river, but has a "NO TRESPASSING" sign on it. Obey all such signs. Do not go onto the bridge. More cascades upstream from the bridge mark the beginning of the waterfall.

From the base of the cascades, looking upstream

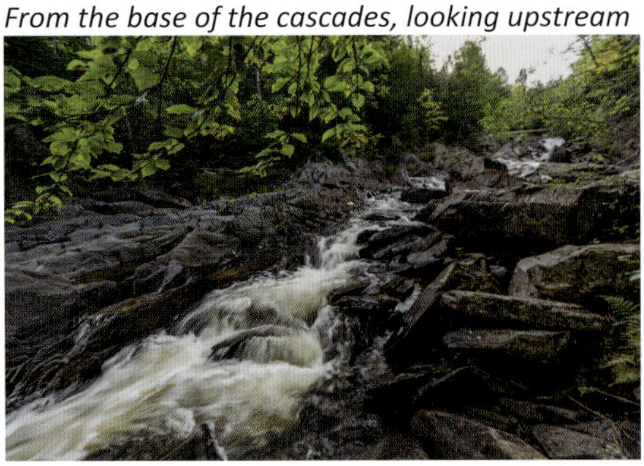

The view from the top of the waterfall

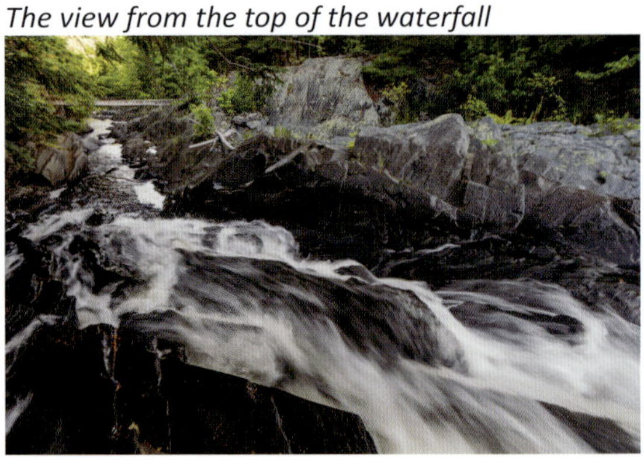

SILVER GORGE FALLS - UPPER (SILVER RIVER)

Private

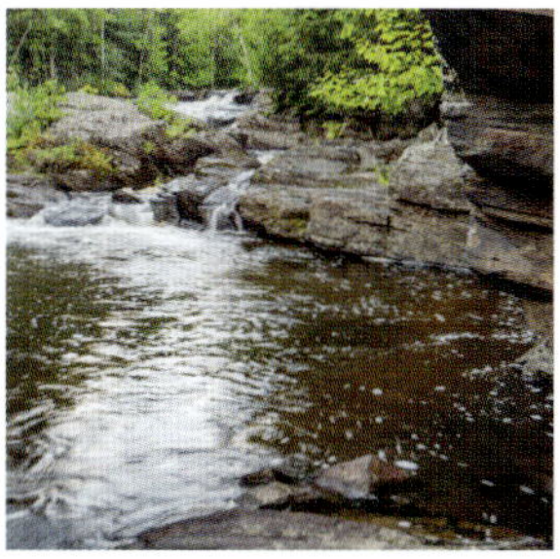

Must See:	7	GPS:	N46 44.934 W88 21.214
Height:	12 feet		
Time:	25-35 minutes	Hiking Information	
		Path:	None
Driving Information		Length:	.17 miles
Signs:	None	Elev. Change:	Minor
Road:	Gravel Road	GPS:	Required
Access:	Somewhat Difficult	Danger:	Moderate
4WD:	N/A	WP Boots:	Helpful

Follow Silver River upstream 150 yards from the base of Silver Gorge Falls to the Upper falls.

The Silver River falls off a short ridge to a wide cascade that deposits the river into a shallow gorge where the waterfall continues its descent in a tight "S" curve, narrowing the river to four feet just before it enters a large, shallow pool. At the far end of the pool, the river starts dropping over the upper portion of Silver Gorge Falls. A cabin sits on the east side of the river at the top of the waterfall. What a beautiful view!

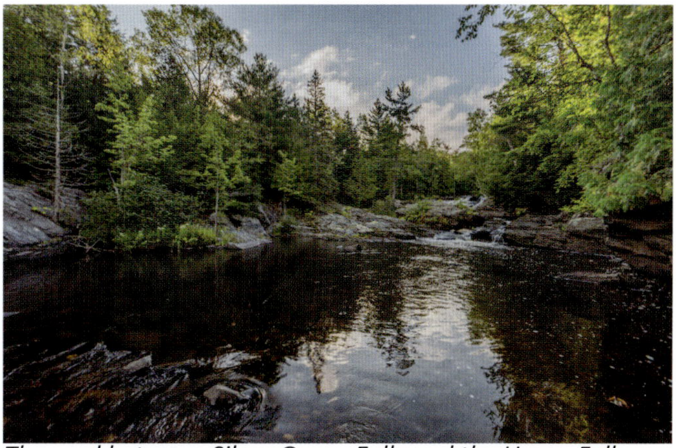

The pool between Silver Gorge Falls and the Upper Falls

Up at the top of the waterfall, the cabin can be seen on the far side

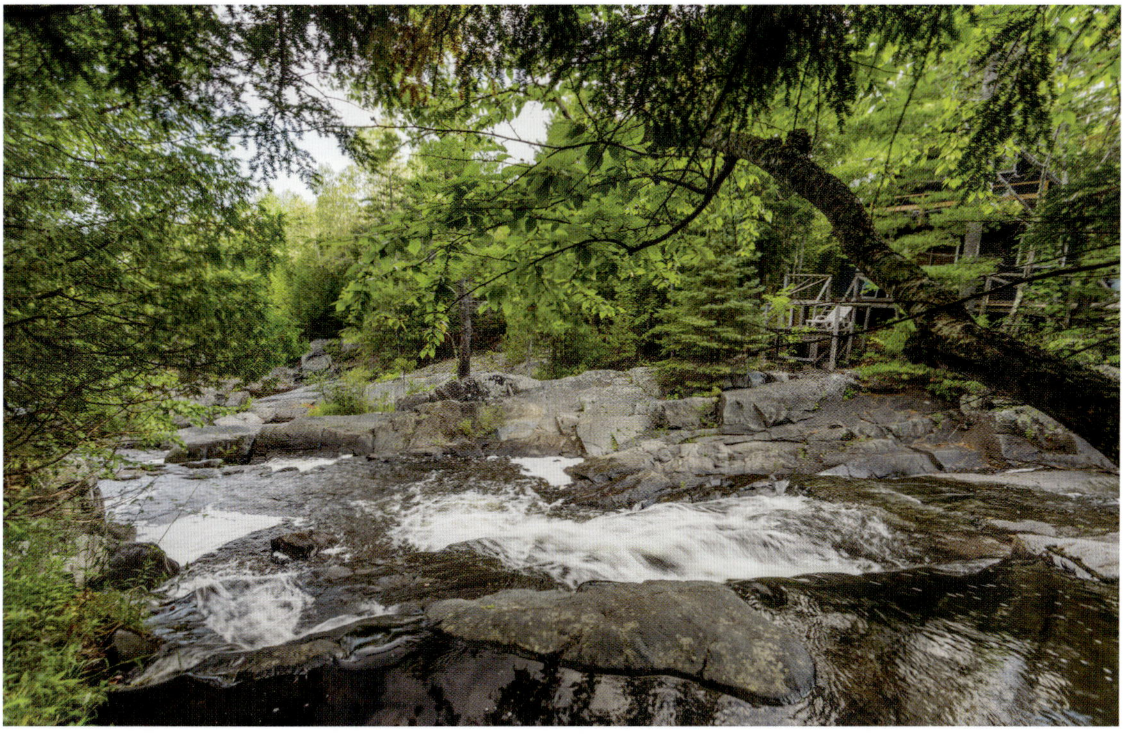

DEAD MAN'S FALLS (SILVER RIVER)

Private

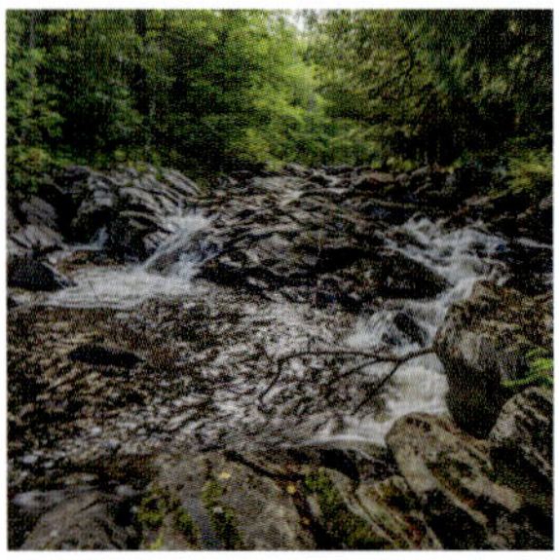

Must See:	4	GPS:	N46 44.807 W88 21.097
Height:	4 feet		
Time:	40-50 minutes	Hiking Information	
		Path:	None
Driving Information		Length:	.34 miles
Signs:	None	Elev. Change:	Minor
Road:	Gravel Road	GPS:	Required
Access:	Somewhat Difficult	Danger:	Moderate
4WD:	N/A	WP Boots:	Helpful

It's a .18 mile hike upstream from Silver Gorge Falls - Upper to Dead Man's Falls. This is this greatest distance between waterfalls on this hike.

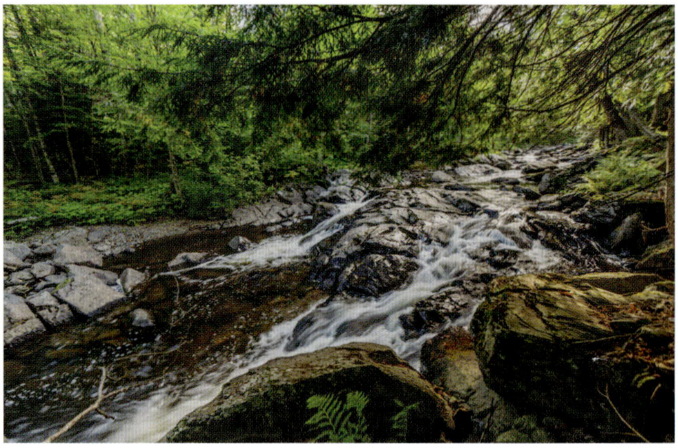

Down the hill from a two story cabin, Dead Man's Falls churns through the boulder choked river, black water-worn bedrock showing itself liberally along the way. Maple, birch, and cedar arch overhead, while squirrels play in the ferns and thimble berries.

The rock strewn river below the waterfall

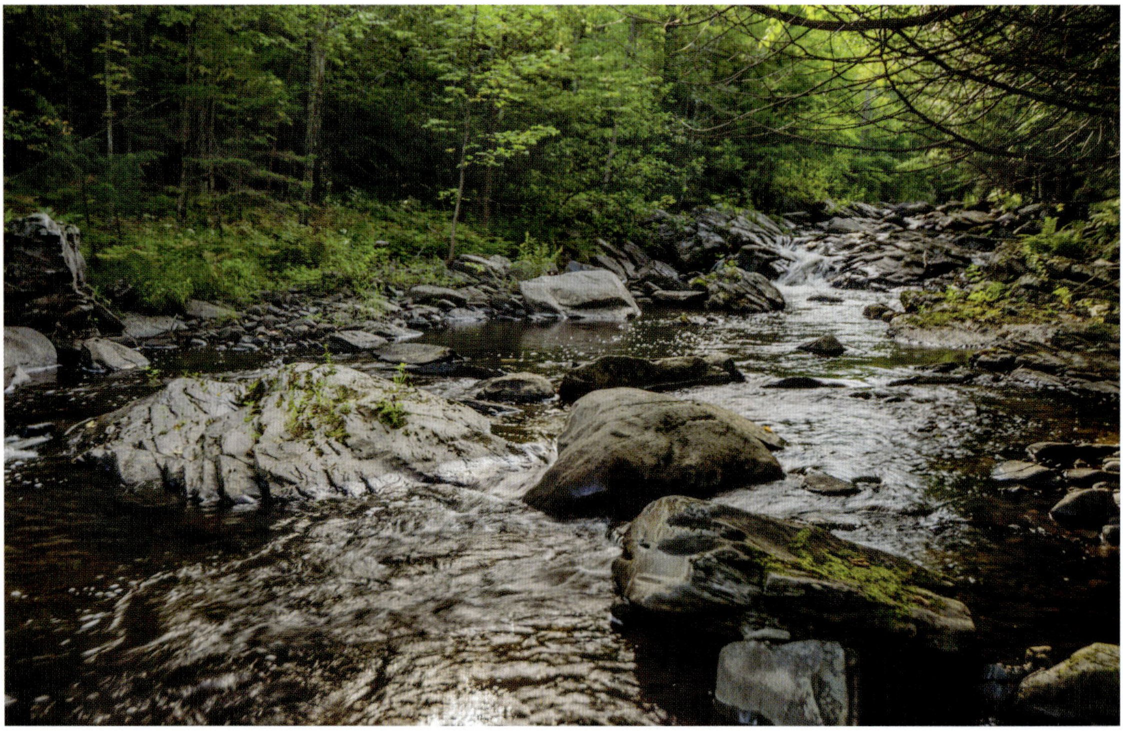

THIMBLEBERRY FALLS - LOWER (SILVER RIVER)

Private

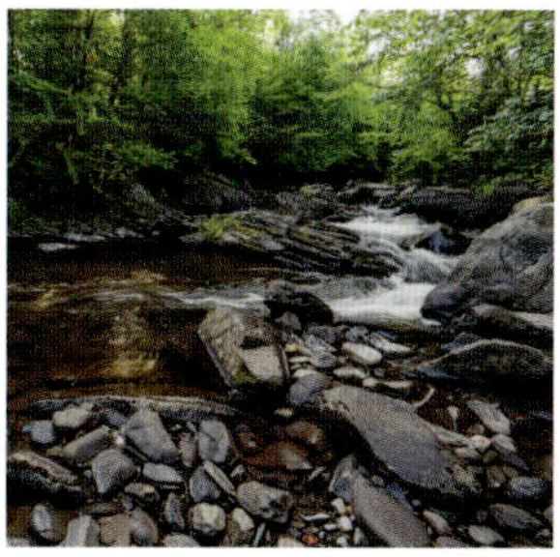

Must See:	4	GPS:	N46 44.734 W88 21.030
Height:	3 feet		
Time:	50-60 minutes	Hiking Information	
		Path:	None
Driving Information		Length:	.46 miles
Signs:	None	Elev. Change:	Minor
Road:	Gravel Road	GPS:	Required
Access:	Somewhat Difficult	Danger:	Moderate
4WD:	N/A	WP Boots:	Helpful

Continue hiking up Silver River .13 miles to Lower Thimbleberry Falls.

Here, the river runs narrow between black boulders and tilted, ribbed bedrock. Sparse wildflowers grow among the moss on the larger rocky masses in the river. The waterway pushes hard to the west, shoving up against a four foot boulder before turning back to the west. As the river rises, it overflows around upthrust, short promontories.

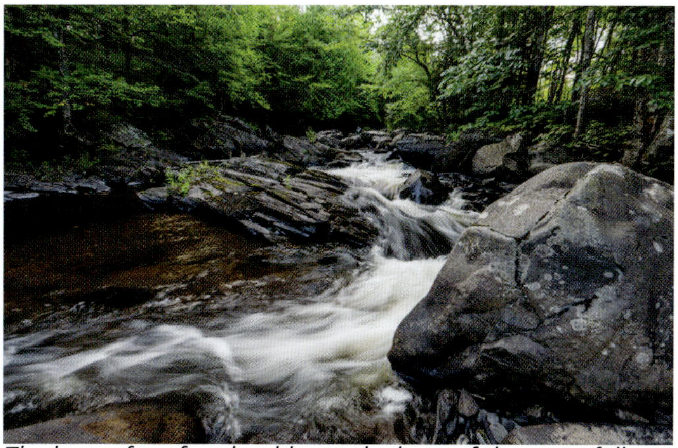

The large, four foot boulder at the base of the waterfall

The playful river runs through the narrowed waterway

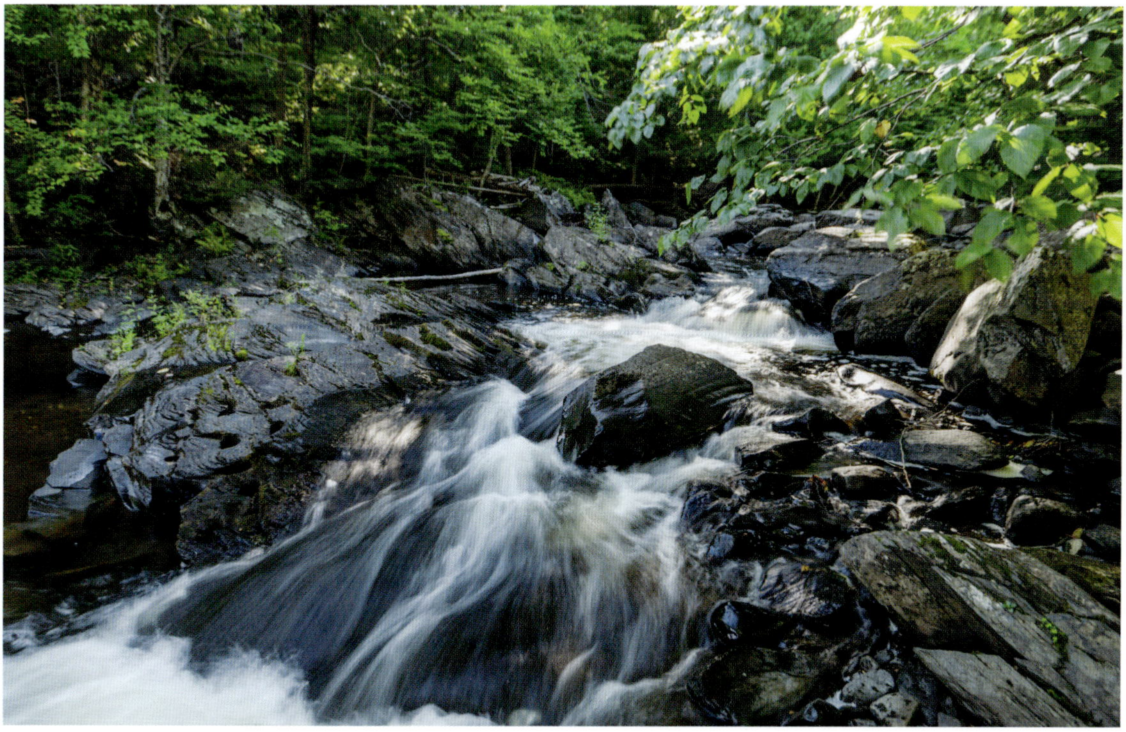

THIMBLEBERRY FALLS (SILVER RIVER)

Private

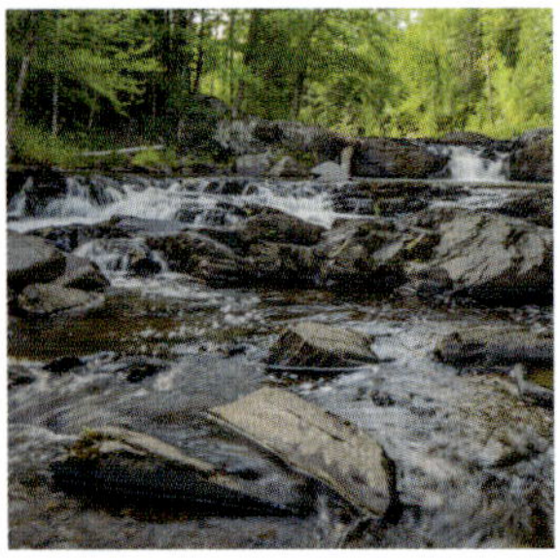

Must See:	7	GPS:	N46 44.700 W88 21.017
Height:	10 feet		
Time:	40-50 minutes	Hiking Information	
		Path:	None
Driving Information		Length:	.49 miles
Signs:	None	Elev. Change:	Minor
Road:	Gravel Road	GPS:	Required
Access:	Somewhat Difficult	Danger:	Moderate
4WD:	N/A	WP Boots:	Helpful

Sixty-five yards upstream from the Lower Falls you'll come upon a very nice waterfall.

This double cascade has a widened spill pool separating the drops. The upper drop has eroded away a section of the 6 foot bluff over the years, turning a sheer drop into a frothing cascade. The lower drop careens over finely layered bedrock to the boulder strewn waterway downstream.

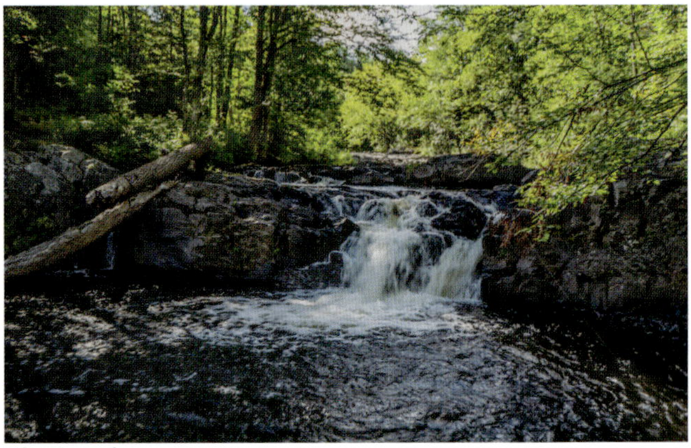

The top drop

The rock strewn river below the waterfall

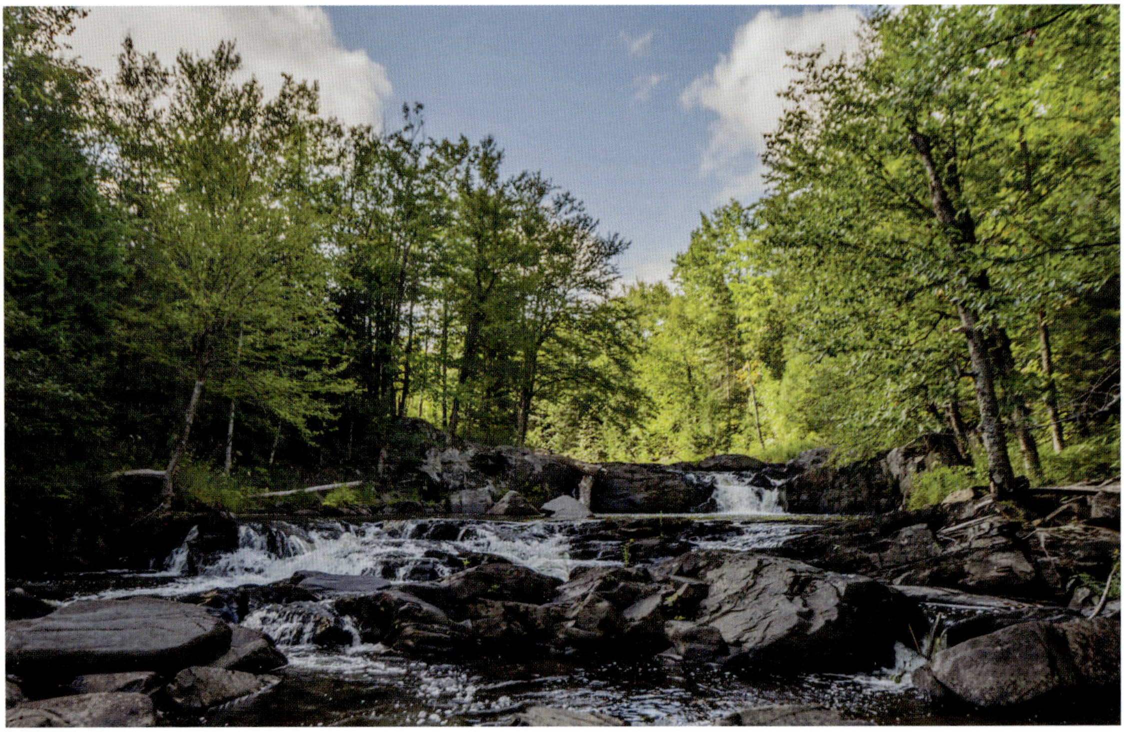

THIMBLEBERRY CASCADES (SILVER RIVER)

Private

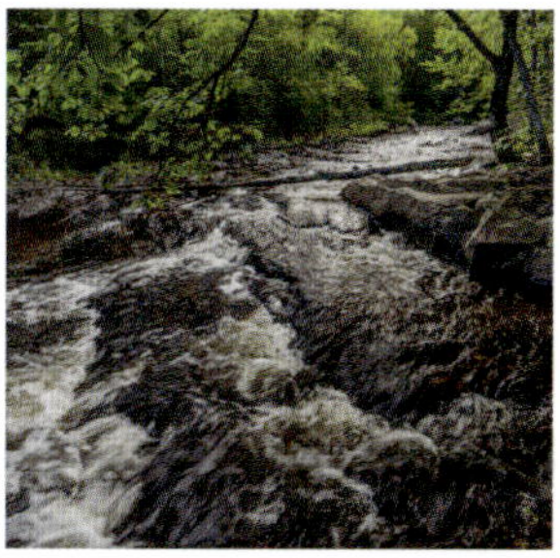

Must See:	3	GPS:	N46 44.650 W88 21.017
Height:	4 feet		
Time:	50-60 minutes	Hiking Information	
		Path:	None
Driving Information		Length:	.55 miles
Signs:	None	Elev. Change:	Minor
Road:	Gravel Road	GPS:	Required
Access:	Somewhat Difficult	Danger:	Moderate
4WD:	N/A	WP Boots:	Helpful

Climb up above Thimbleberry Falls 60 yards to Thimbleberry Cascades, the last of this hike's water features on the Silver River.

The river flows rapidly over rough bedrock. The bluff downstream dams up the river, creating a deeper than normal spill pool at the end of these cascades.

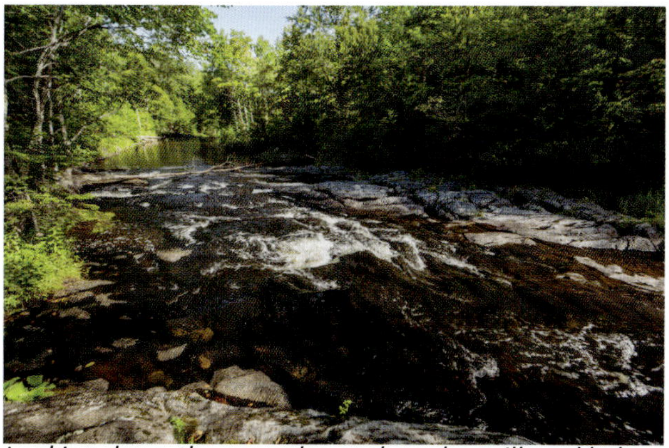

Looking down the cascades at the calm spill pool below

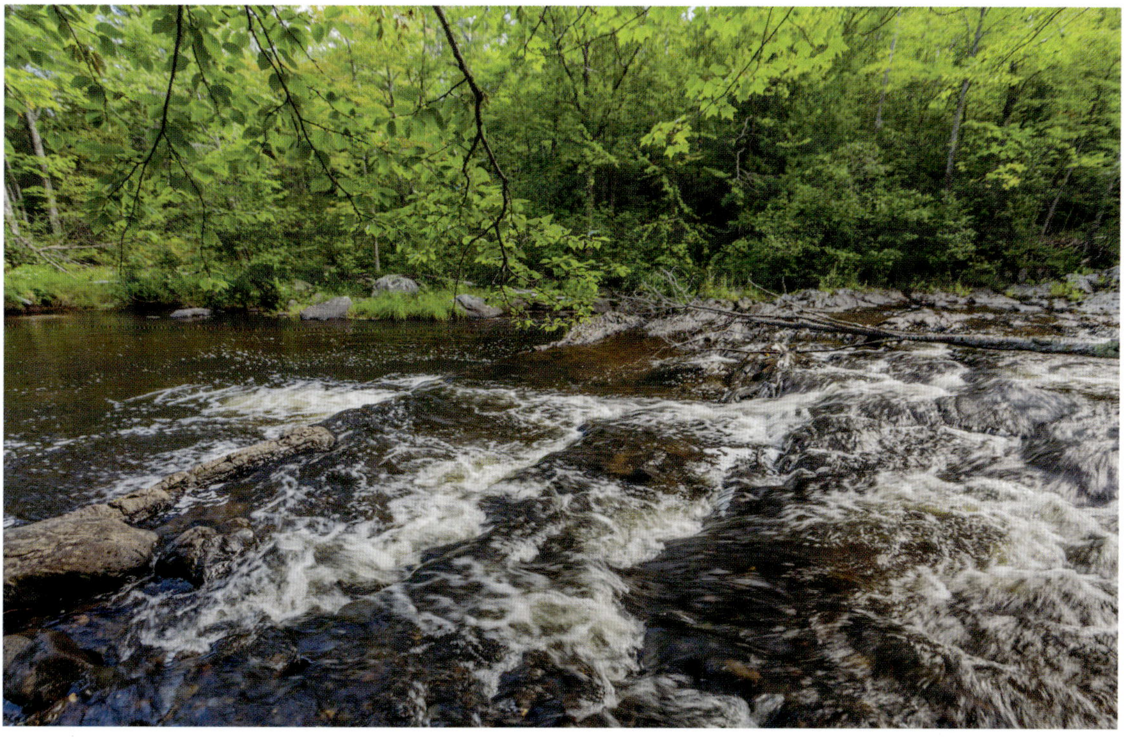

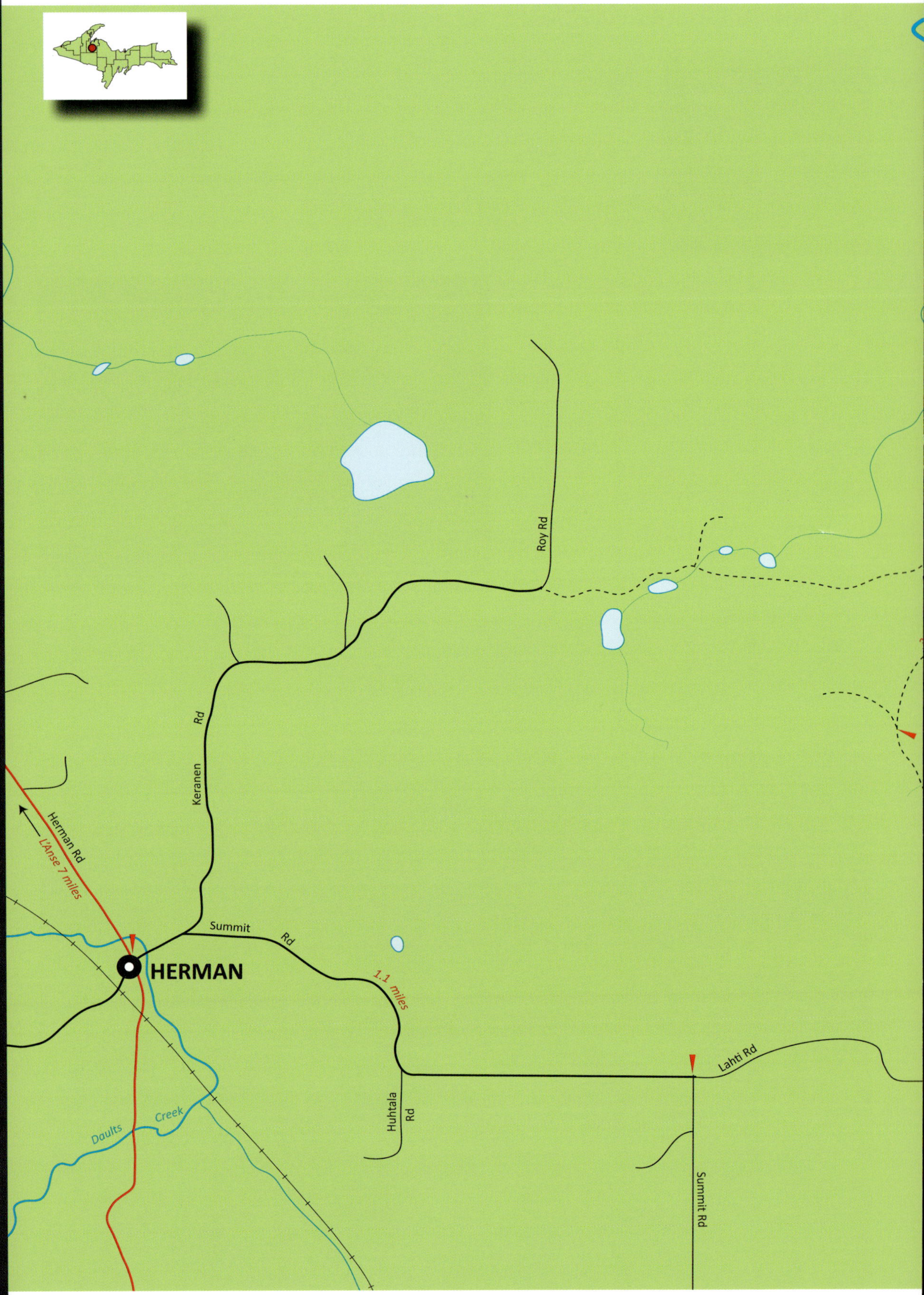
Roy Rd
Keranen Rd
Herman Rd
L'Anse 7 miles
Summit Rd
HERMAN
1.1 miles
Lahti Rd
Huhtala Rd
Daults Creek
Summit Rd

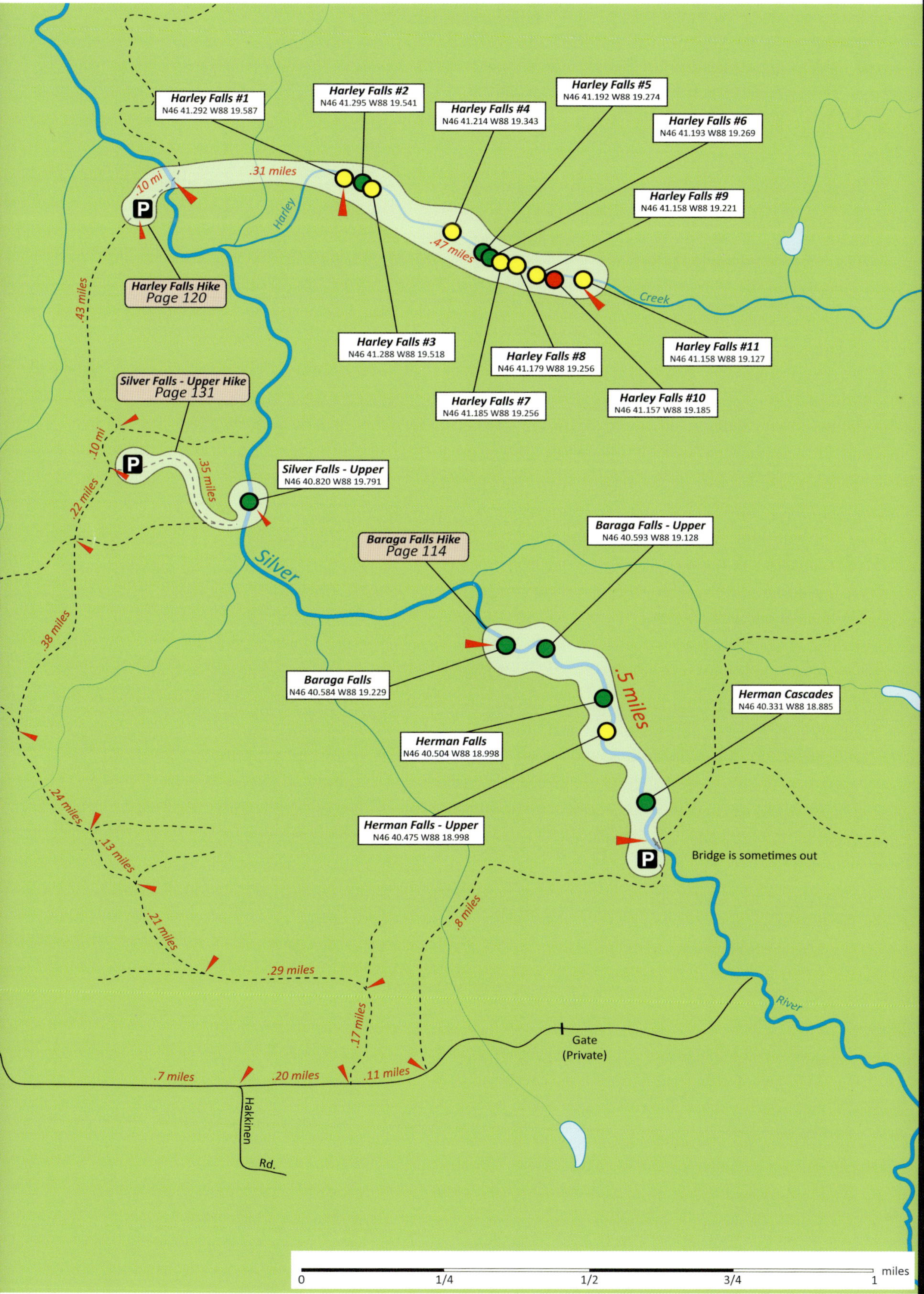

Harley Falls #1
N46 41.292 W88 19.587
Harley Falls #2
N46 41.295 W88 19.541
Harley Falls #3
N46 41.288 W88 19.518
Harley Falls #4
N46 41.214 W88 19.343
Harley Falls #5
N46 41.192 W88 19.274
Harley Falls #6
N46 41.193 W88 19.269
Harley Falls #7
N46 41.185 W88 19.256
Harley Falls #8
N46 41.179 W88 19.256
Harley Falls #9
N46 41.158 W88 19.221
Harley Falls #10
N46 41.157 W88 19.185
Harley Falls #11
N46 41.158 W88 19.127
Harley Falls Hike
Page 120
Silver Falls - Upper Hike
Page 131
Silver Falls - Upper
N46 40.820 W88 19.791
Baraga Falls Hike
Page 114
Baraga Falls - Upper
N46 40.593 W88 19.128
Baraga Falls
N46 40.584 W88 19.229
Herman Falls
N46 40.504 W88 18.998
Herman Falls - Upper
N46 40.475 W88 18.998
Herman Cascades
N46 40.331 W88 18.885
Bridge is sometimes out
Harley
Creek
Silver
River
Gate
(Private)
Hakkinen
Rd.
.10 mi
.31 miles
.47 miles
.43 miles
.10 mi
.35 miles
.22 miles
.38 miles
.5 miles
.24 miles
.13 miles
.21 miles
.29 miles
.8 miles
.17 miles
.7 miles
.20 miles
.11 miles
0
1/4
1/2
3/4
1
miles

Baraga Falls Hike

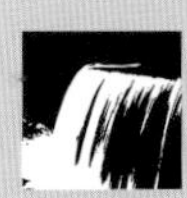

The hike to the five waterfalls downstream from the parking area is one of my favorite secluded waterfall hikes. Even though there is no trail, the hike is not oppressive. This area contains a mature hardwood forest. This means that the undergrowth is kept at bay, and walking is mostly unobstructed. There are, however, rolling hills to be navigated, and very large boulders strewn about at random to be walked around.

Herman Cascades: A short 150 yards down the river from the bridge, Baraga Falls #5 shows off its multiple cascades with random scattered moss covered rocks accenting the presentation.

Herman Falls - Upper: Falling around a large rock situated on top of the waterfall in the center of the river, Baraga Falls #4 pours predominantly over the southern side of the falls.

Herman Falls: The river falls over an amazingly sheer slab of stone. This is not a common sight and begs to be viewed!

Baraga Falls - Upper: Mossy rocks line the river's edge. Solid rock washed clean by the rushing river slides severely halfway down to the foot of the falls before the gushing water abruptly encounters a large slab of stone that creates a large rooster tailed stream of flying water. Continue down the river for a look at one of Michigan's spectacular waterfalls.

Baraga Falls: "Take your breath away!" What a way to end an incredible hike! A gorgeous cascade tumbles down the perfectly proportioned waterfall. Rocks are strewn through the riverbed below the falls with a large, 6 foot boulder situated ideally in the middle of the river as an ideal specimen for a photographic accent. This waterfall should be on the very short list for any serious waterfall enthusiast.

Directions: From Herman, which is 7 miles southeast of L'Anse, drive northeast on Keranen Road and then turn right (east) almost immediately onto Summit Road. When Summit turns to the right (about 1 mile) keep going straight (east) on Lahti Road (dirt) for 1 mile. Turn left. A high clearance vehicle may be required for this stretch of road. Follow the road to the river. A wooden bridge over the river is normally closed. Park here. Follow the river downstream to the waterfalls. I have hiked down both sides of the river. I prefer the eastern side. I think it is any easier hike, although I like to photograph the falls from both sides. During most of the year it is possible to find places to carefully cross the river on exposed rocks.

HERMAN CASCADES (SILVER RIVER)

Private

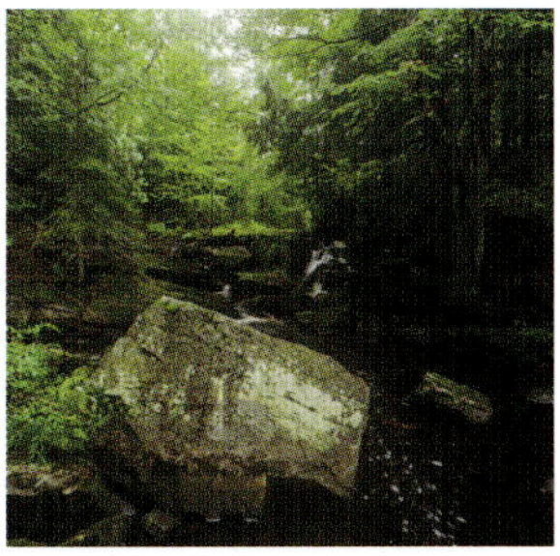

Must See:	7	GPS:	N46 40.331 W88 18.885
Height:	14 feet		
Time:	20-30 minutes		

Driving Information

Signs:	None
Road:	2-track
Access:	Difficult
4WD:	Helpful

Hiking Information

Path:	None
Length:	125 yards
Elev. Change:	Moderate
GPS:	Recommended
Danger:	Minor
WP Boots:	Recommended

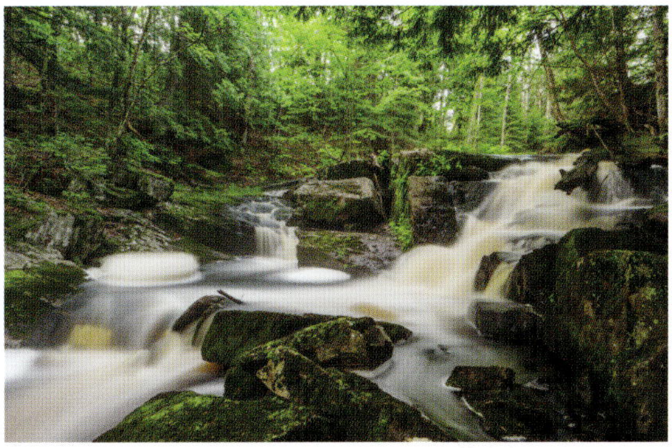

The split waterfall tumbles around the sides of a high mass of rock with a cherry tree growing on top of it. It amazes me how life will flourish in the sparsest of places.

This hike along Silver River is nicely broken up with waterfalls along the way. Pick your way carefully along the banks of the river. It is a remote area, and there are numerous scattered rocks along the way. I grew up downstate where the bedrock isn't exposed like we see in this area. Perhaps that's why I am so enthralled with this rugged terrain! This is one of my favorite hikes. Perhaps it will become yours as well!

The "theater seating" can be seen along the left side of the shot

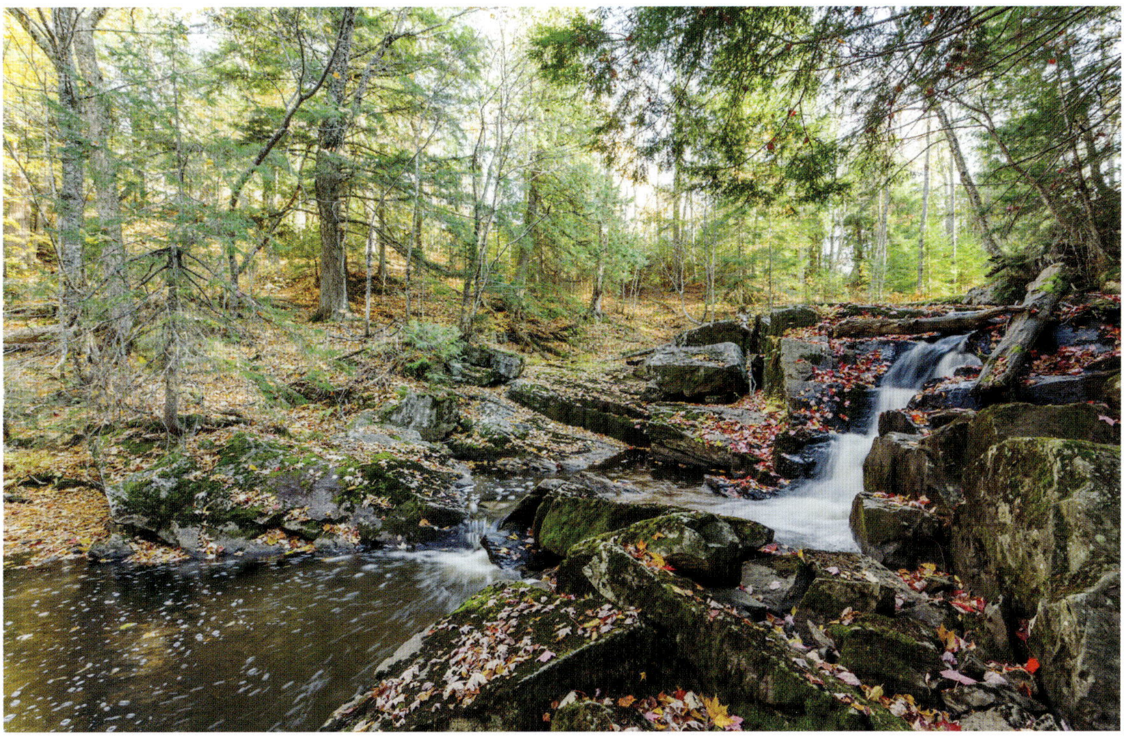

HERMAN FALLS - UPPER (SILVER RIVER)

Private

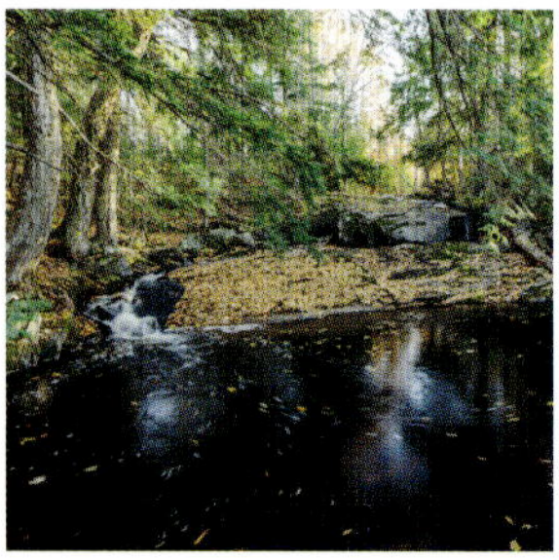

Must See:	6	GPS:	N46 40.475 W88 18.998
Height:	20 feet		
Time:	45-60 minutes	Hiking Information	
		Path:	None
Driving Information		Length:	.29 miles
Signs:	None	Elev. Change:	Moderate
Road:	Dirt	GPS:	Required
Access:	Difficult	Danger:	Minor
4WD:	Helpful	WP Boots:	Recommended

After finding the first waterfall (Herman Cascades) on the hike, continue for another .2 miles to get to this one. Here, the river drops over a top section of bedrock to a flat plate before sliding down a large conical surface to the riverbed below. Changes in water volume dramatically affect the look of this waterfall. As the water level decreases, the flow slides over to the west side of the top rock, moving the fanned out coverage of the bedrock to just a trickle that then runs down to a flat stone plate, crossing the riverbed to the east before it finishes its slide to the spill pool below along the eastern bank.

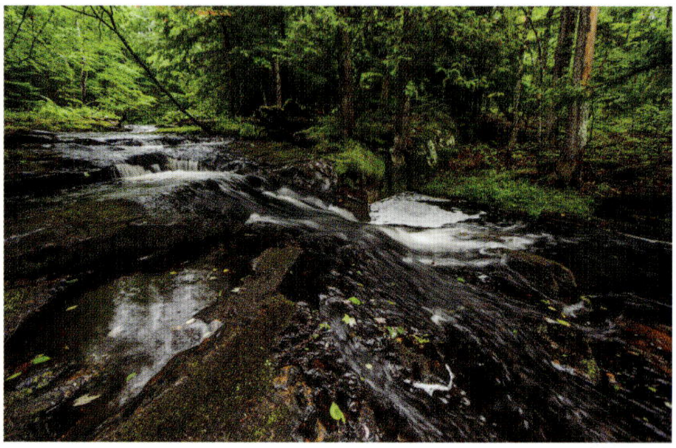

Compare the diminished flow in the autumn scene above with the higher flow in the late June picture below. I think that a greater volume would look even better!

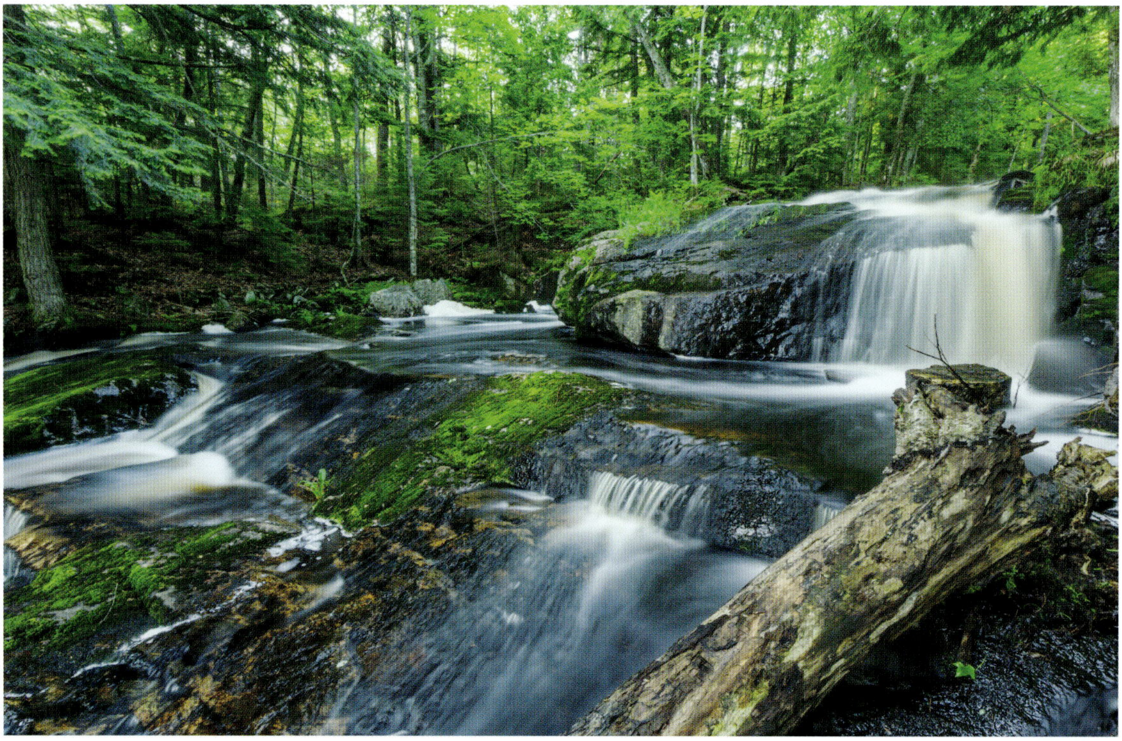

HERMAN FALLS (SILVER RIVER)

Private

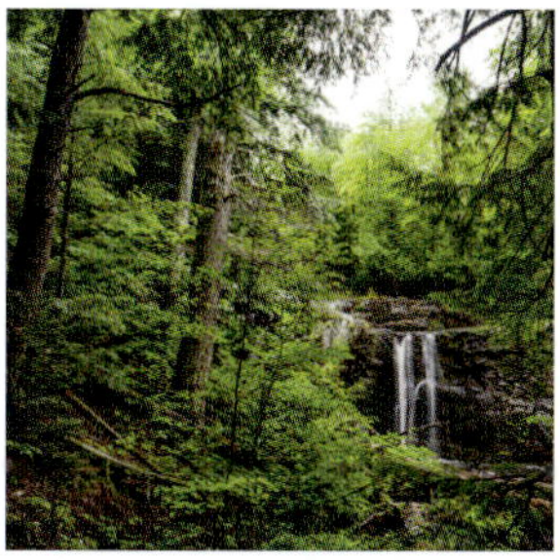

Must See: 8
Height: 18 feet
Time: 1-1 1/2 hours

Driving Information
Signs: None
Road: Dirt
Access: Difficult
4WD: Helpful

GPS: N46 40.504 W88 18.998

Hiking Information
Path: None
Length: .35 miles
Elev. Change: Moderate
GPS: Required
Danger: Minor
WP Boots: Recommended

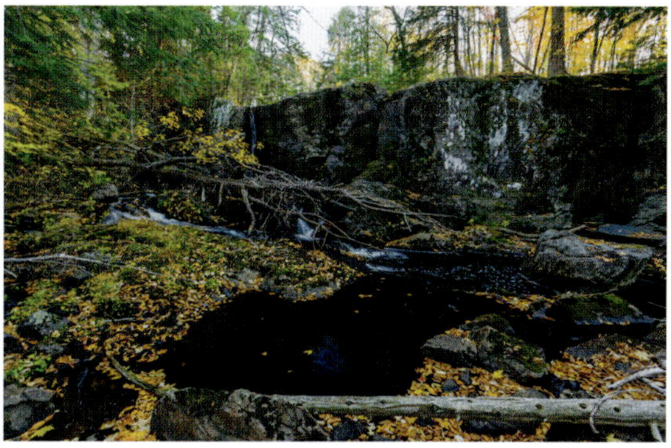

I was shocked the first time I saw this waterfall! I had no idea that there would be a vertical wall waterfall on the Silver River. What a beautiful situation. It reminds me of a miniature Manabezho Falls. Most of the drop is sheer.

Unfortunately, as is often the case, this waterfall acts as a giant garbage collector for tree debris. A large fallen tree lays along the base. It has been diminishing in size over the past several years, and in time, or with some human intervention, it will eventually be gone. This could be a spectacular waterfall to photograph without the distraction.

Just like Herman Falls - Upper, I would love to see this waterfall during spring melt! I suspect that the flow would run wall to wall over this wide face.

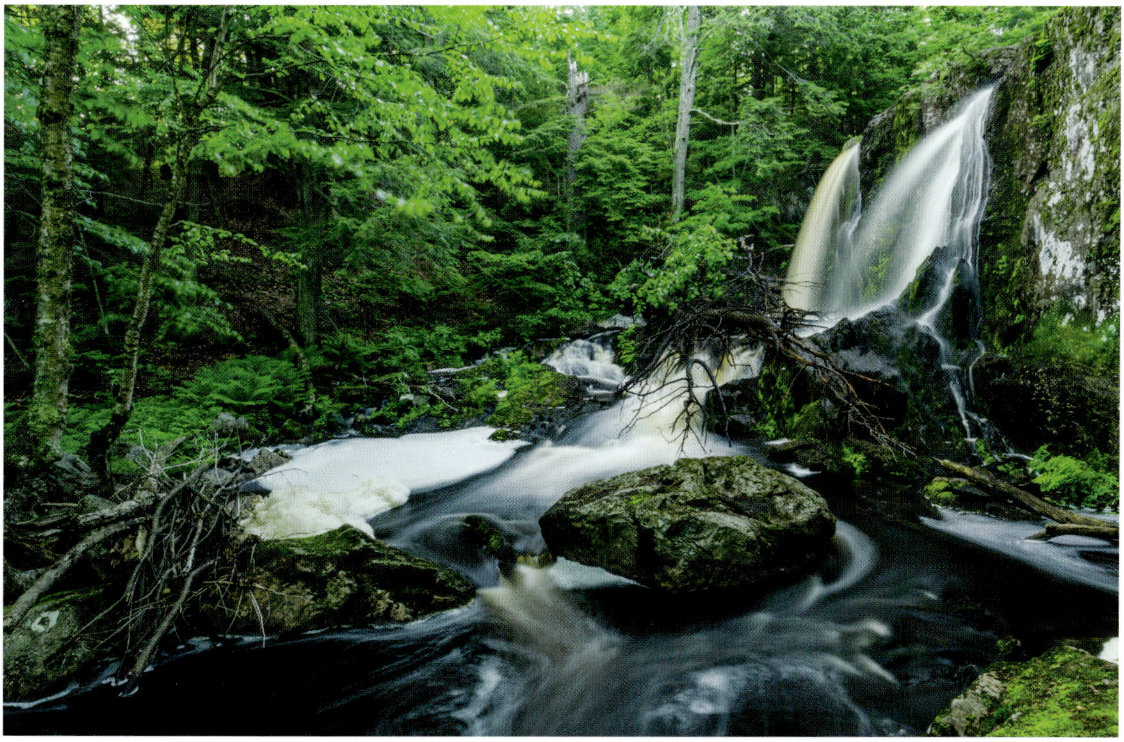

BARAGA FALLS - UPPER (SILVER RIVER)

Private

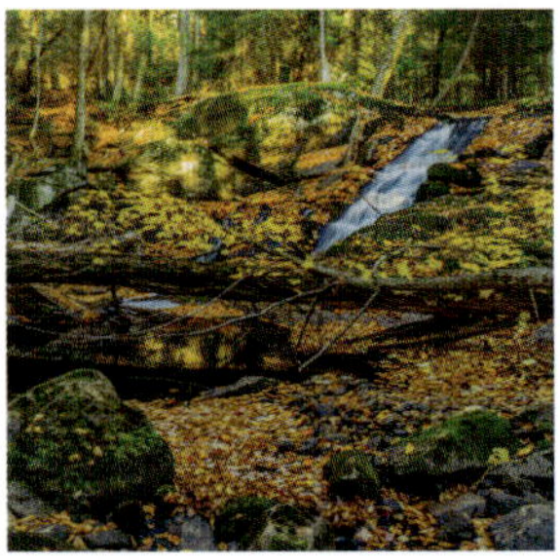

Must See:	7
Height:	10 feet
Time:	1 1/4-1 3/4 hours

Driving Information

Signs:	None
Road:	Dirt
Access:	Difficult
4WD:	Helpful

GPS: N46 40.593 W88 19.128

Hiking Information

Path:	None
Length:	.47 miles
Elev. Change:	Moderate
GPS:	Required
Danger:	Minor
WP Boots:	Recommended

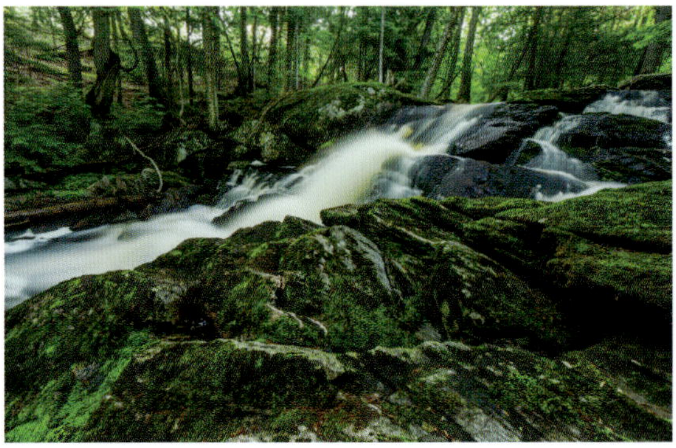

The waterfalls on this hike come in bunches. The first one is just 150 yards from the parking spot. Then, halfway through the hike, the two Herman Falls are within hundreds of feet of each other. Here, at the end of the hike, the last two waterfalls are found 150 yards apart. By now you may be getting tired of picking your way around jumbled rocks and navigating uneven terrain. This waterfall is a great place to rest and enjoy one last waterfall before finishing the outbound portion of the hike.

Most of the river funnels down to 4 feet wide and then dumps into a pocket in the rock sending up a “rooster tail” of water. The river has cut a channel through solid bedrock leaving behind a shallow chasm. The western bank is devoid of soil, the bare rock covered in nothing but thick moss and lichen, perennial favorites at waterfalls in Michigan. They soak up the ever-present moisture, turning dark stone into various shades of green, gray, and red.

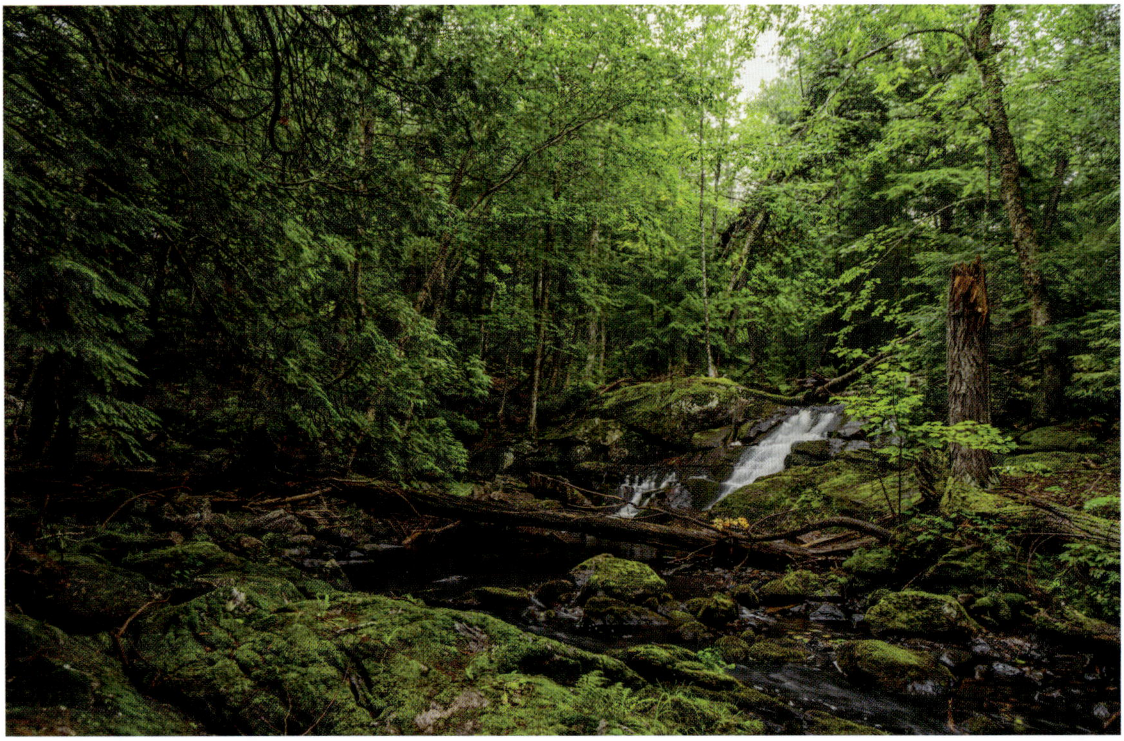

BARAGA FALLS (SILVER RIVER)

Private

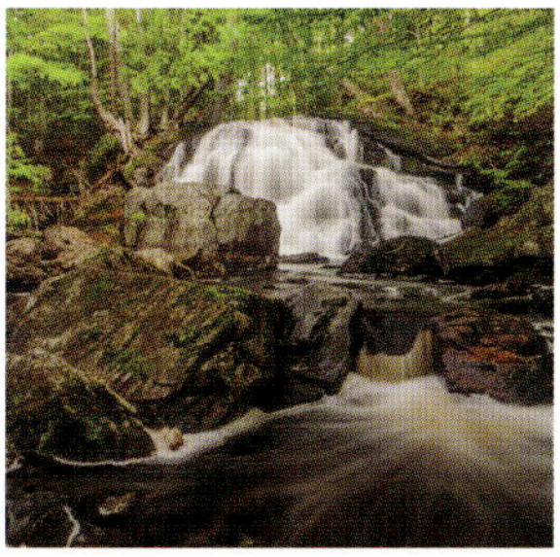

Must See:	9	GPS:	N46 40.584 W88 19.229
Height:	20 feet		
Time:	1 1/2-2 hours	**Hiking Information**	
		Path:	None
Driving Information		Length:	.56 miles
Signs:	None	Elev. Change:	Moderate
Road:	Dirt	GPS:	Required
Access:	Difficult	Danger:	Minor
4WD:	Helpful	WP Boots:	Recommended

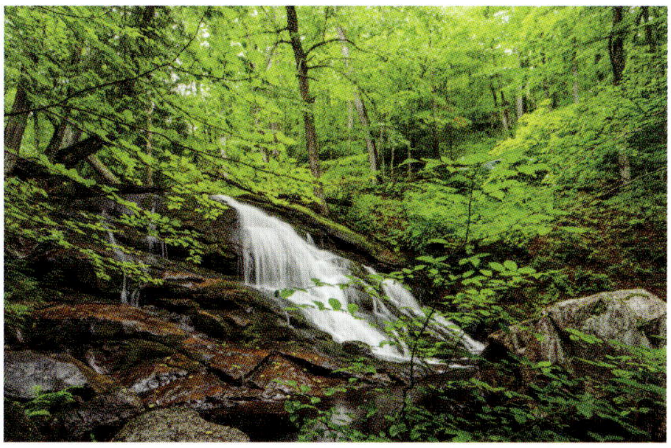

One of my favorite waterfalls in Michigan, Baraga Falls sports a nearly sheer drop, broken up neatly into beautiful cascades. The river winds its way around large boulders strewn throughout the riverbed below the falls. The largest of these is a six foot tall piece of basalt, about the size of a truck, conspicuously placed in the eastern edge of the river just below the waterfall.

The river runs through a steep valley, thick leaves mulching the saplings struggling for light beneath their towering parents. Maple and birch turn the landscape to an earthy gold, nature's Midas returning year after year to touch the land with a crisp display that few can rival! Here and there a cedar tree adds a green accent.

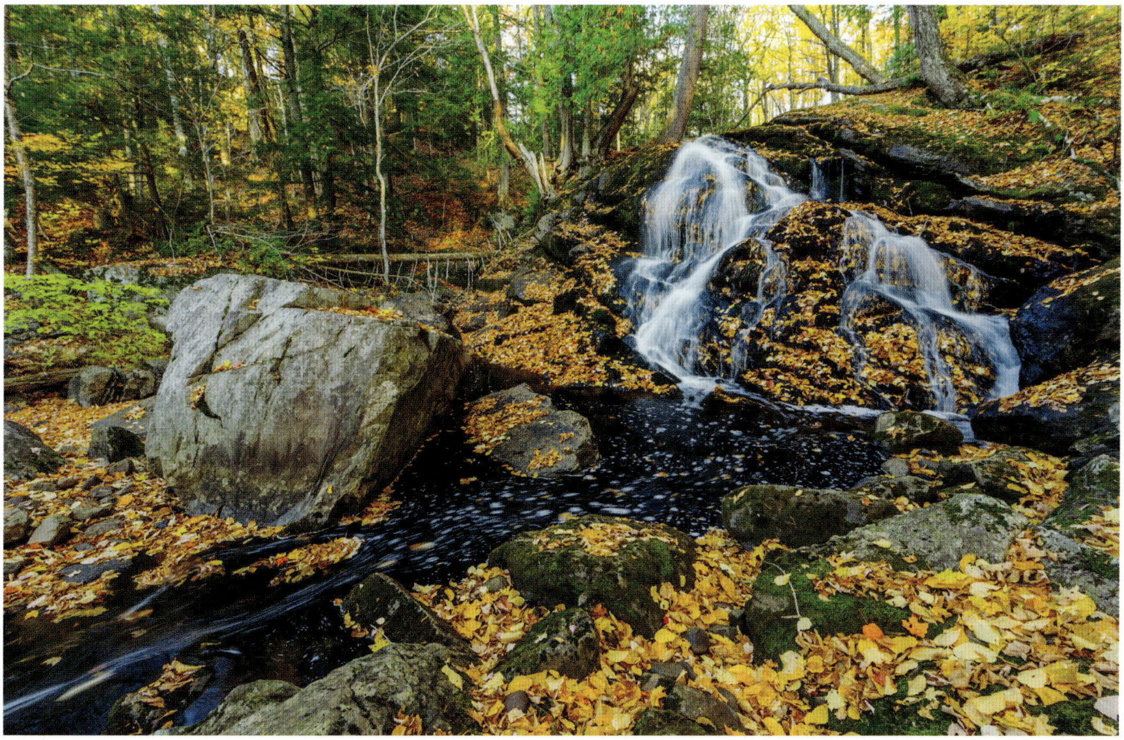

Harley Falls Hike

Harley Creek winds its way through secluded hardwoods and conifers as it drops on its journey to the Silver River. Multiple cascades present themselves in a variety of ways. What an enjoyable way to spend an afternoon!

Directions: After hiking the Harley Creek waterfalls, I found a trail that is to the north of the creek. A lot of logging was recently taking place in the Silver River area, and it looked like the trail found was a drivable logging road. My vehicle was on the other side of the river, so after getting back out of the woods, I tried to find the "easy" trail to Harley Creek - without success. So here is how I get to Harley Creek.

From Herman, drive east/northeast on Summit/Keranen Road. Stay on Summit Road until it turns hard to the right. Continue on straight on Lahti Road for .9 miles. Turn left onto a bumpy road (high clearance recommended). A maze of logging trails heads north from here. Stay on the "main road". Use the area map to help you stay on the correct trail. In 2.1 miles, the trail is blocked by a berm. Park. Hike .10 miles down to the river. Wade across. (Knee high waterproof boots are usually tall enough to keep your feet dry.) Cut cross country .31 miles to Harley Falls #1 using a good handheld GPS. There are a couple seasonal tributaries and their accompanying ravines to cross along the way.

HARLEY FALLS #1 (HARLEY CREEK)

Private

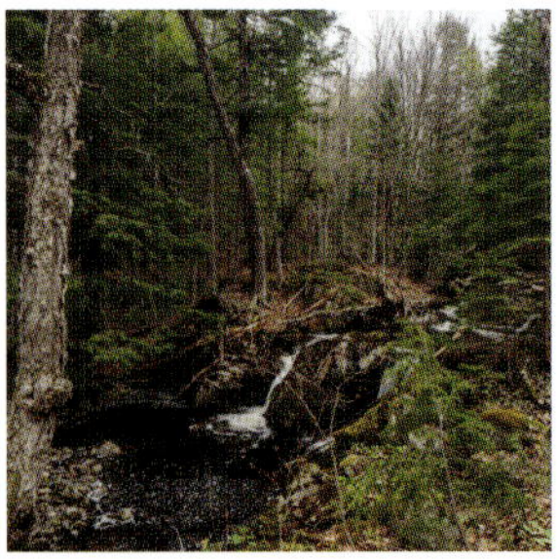

Must See: 6
Height: 15 feet
Time: 45-60 minutes

Driving Information
Signs: None
Road: 2-track
Access: Difficult
4WD: Helpful

GPS: N46 41.292 W88 19.587

Hiking Information
Path: None
Length: .36 miles
Elev. Change: Elevated
GPS: Required
Danger: Moderate
WP Boots: Required

Starting below the slide (Harley Falls #2), the creek cascades down repeatedly, ending with a final, divided 5 foot fall. This main drop is split in half by an 8 foot wide portion of the bedrock rising in the center of the waterway. This natural damming effect is found along the way between #1 and #2. The slide upstream can be seen from the lower cascades, crowning the look from down below.

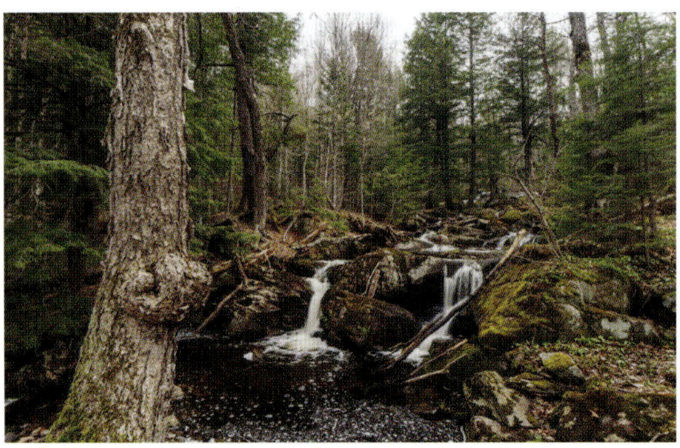

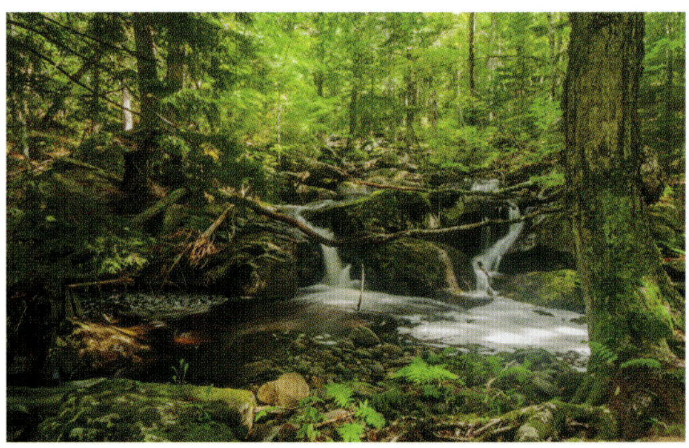

HARLEY FALLS #2 (HARLEY CREEK)

Private

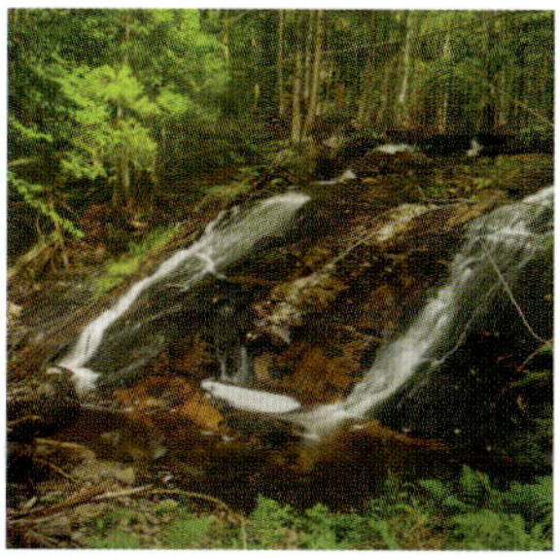

Must See:	7	GPS:	N46 41.295 W88 19.541
Height:	12 feet		
Time:	50-70 minutes	Hiking Information	
		Path:	None
Driving Information		Length:	.39 miles
Signs:	None	Elev. Change:	Elevated
Road:	2-track	GPS:	Required
Access:	Difficult	Danger:	Moderate
4WD:	Helpful	WP Boots:	Required

Follow the creek upstream from #1. Up at the top of the cascades is this wonderful slide! This bare slide sits at about a 45 degree angle, with the creek dividing to flow down both sides. As the water level rises, the waterfall expands to fully cover the 40 foot wide bedrock face.

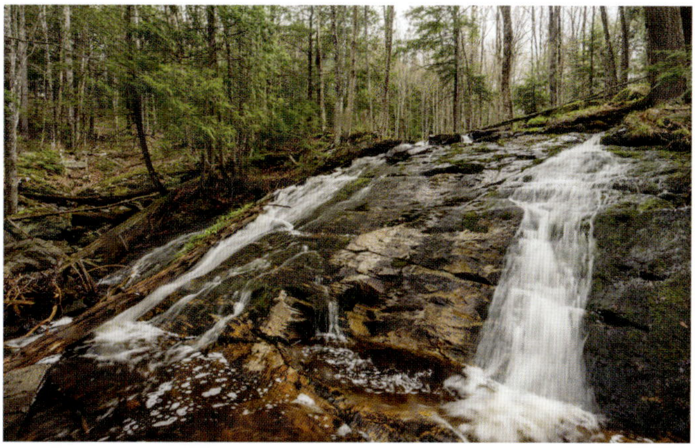

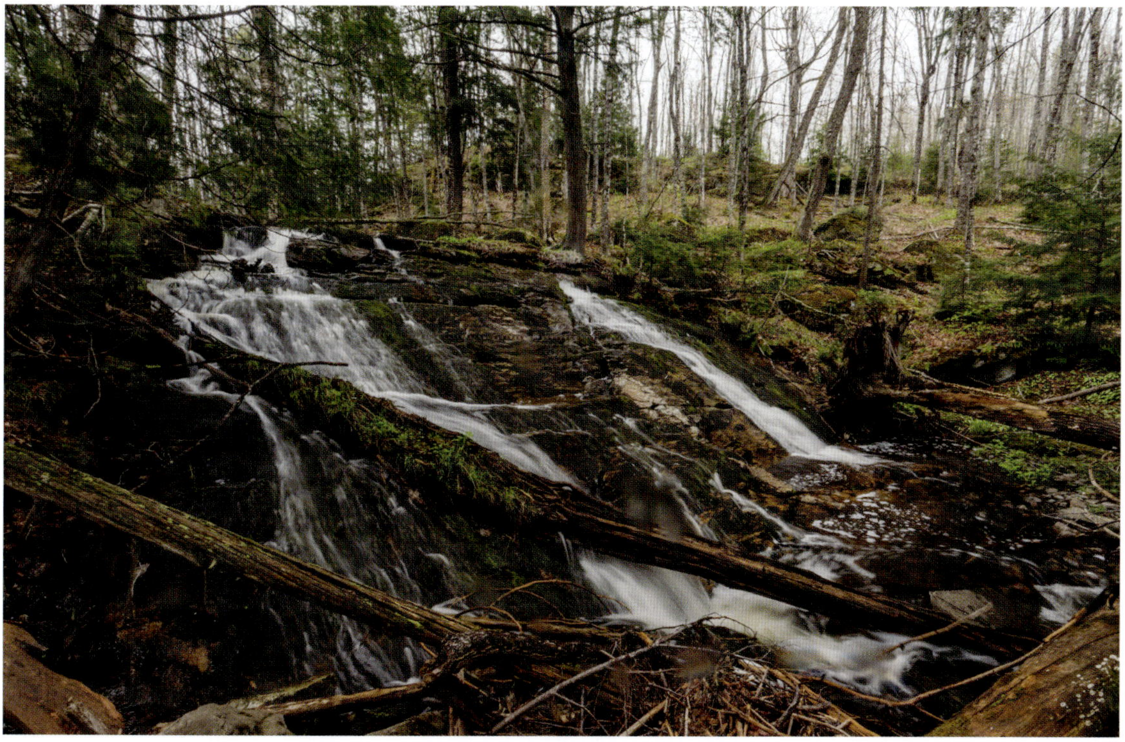

HARLEY FALLS #3 (HARLEY CREEK)

Private

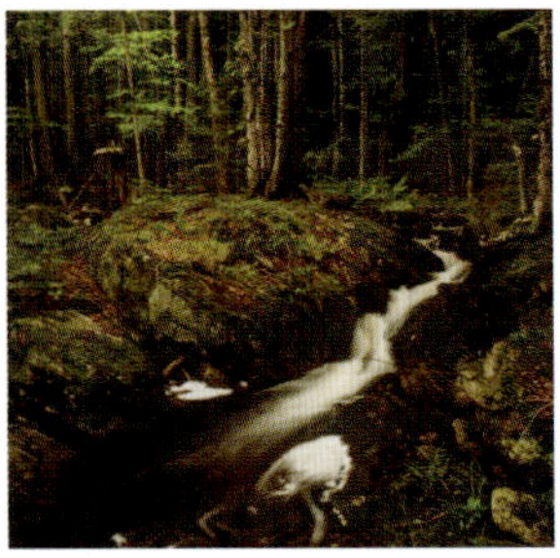

Must See:	6	GPS:	N46 41.288 W88 19.518
Height:	5 feet		
Time:	1-1.5 hours		

Driving Information

Signs:	None
Road:	2-track
Access:	Difficult
4WD:	Helpful

Hiking Information

Path:	None
Length:	.42 miles
Elev. Change:	Elevated
GPS:	Required
Danger:	Moderate
WP Boots:	Required

Hike just 100 feet upstream from #2 to find an amazing difference in the width of these waterfalls! From a 40 foot slide to a 1 foot wide wedge. Here the turbulent creek funnels through a narrow slot of rock, looking like a rocky water slide! The bedrock is tilted. Weaker layers have eroded and the creek runs down 5 feet through the resulting trough.

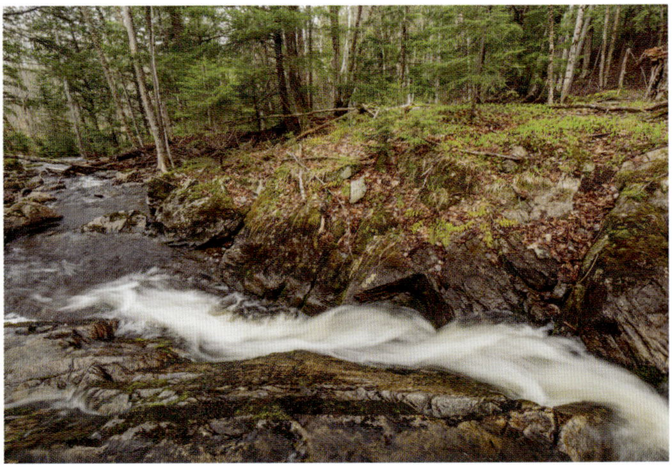

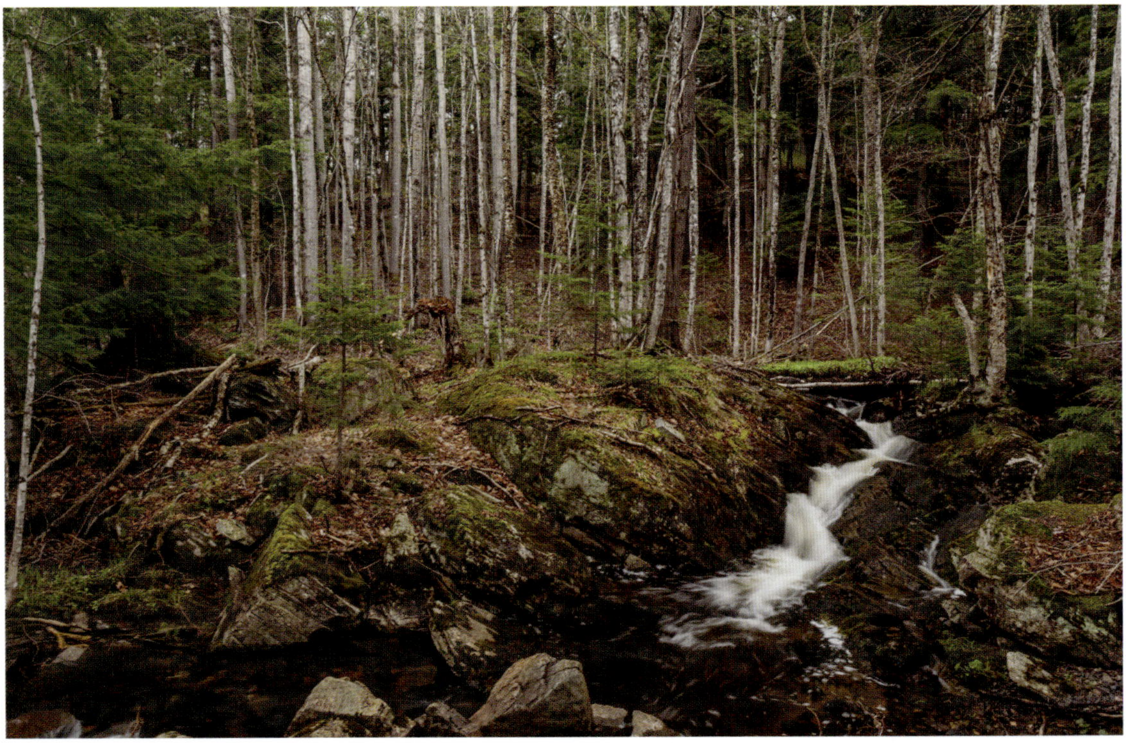

HARLEY FALLS #4 (HARLEY CREEK)

Private

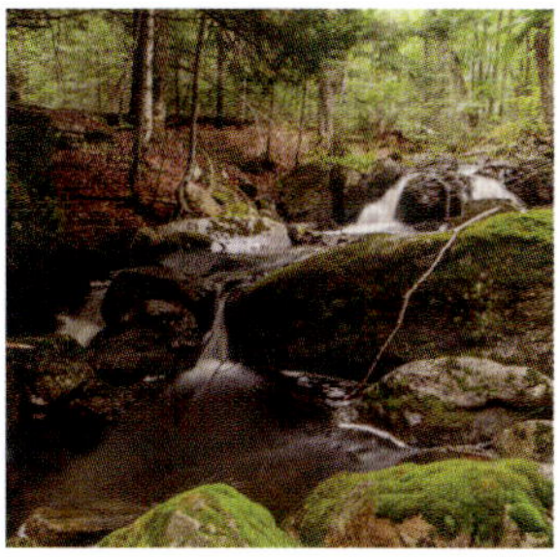

Must See:	6	GPS:	N46 41.214 W88 19.343
Height:	5 feet		
Time:	1.5-2 hours		

Driving Information		Hiking Information	
		Path:	None
		Length:	.61 miles
Signs:	None	Elev. Change:	Elevated
Road:	2-track	GPS:	Required
Access:	Difficult	Danger:	Moderate
4WD:	Helpful	WP Boots:	Required

The first 3 waterfalls on Harley Creek are all clustered closely together. From these, hike a little over 300 yards to find the first of the upper waterfalls on Harley Creek. These upper drops are scattered out over .2 miles.

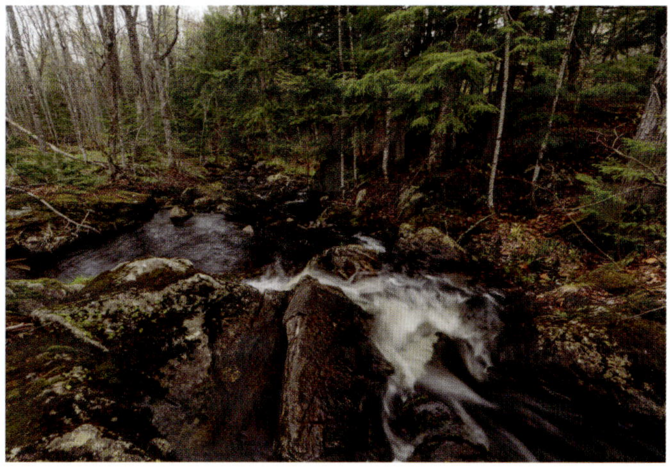

The waterfall splits over a misshapen mass, pushing the 1 foot wide creek up at the top of the waterfall out to 8 feet across at the base. After a rocky spill pool, another divided drop finishes off the waterfall. Tall cedars, birch, and maples overlook the waterfall.

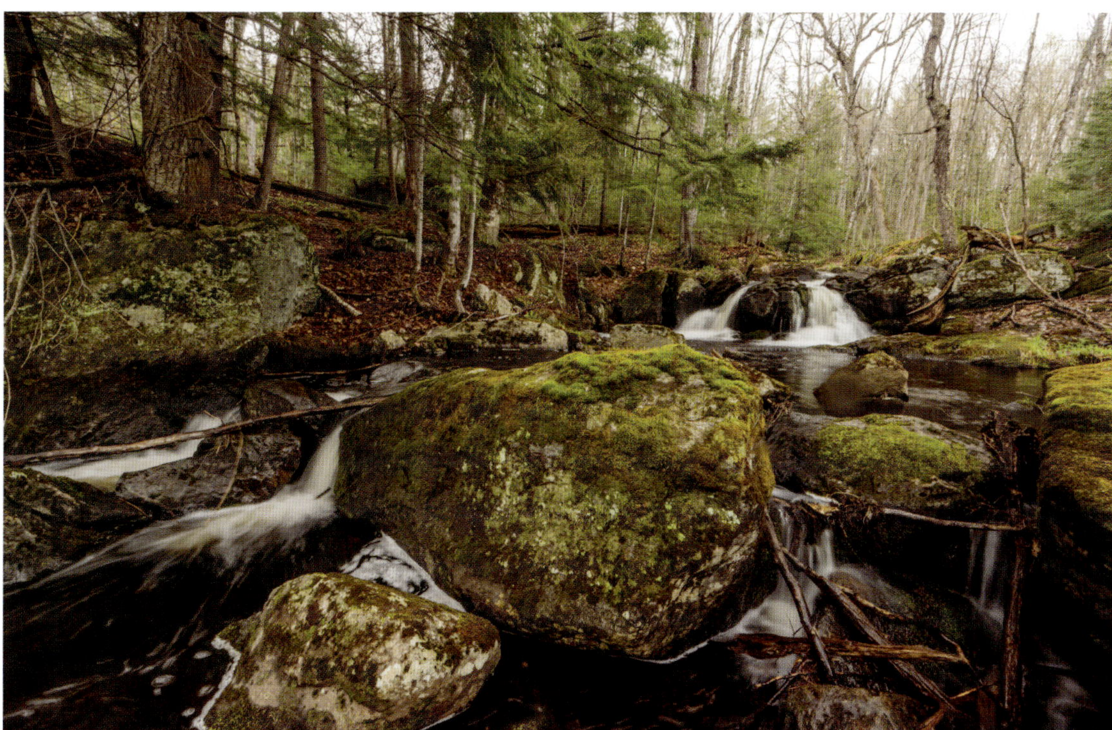

HARLEY FALLS #5 (HARLEY CREEK)

Private

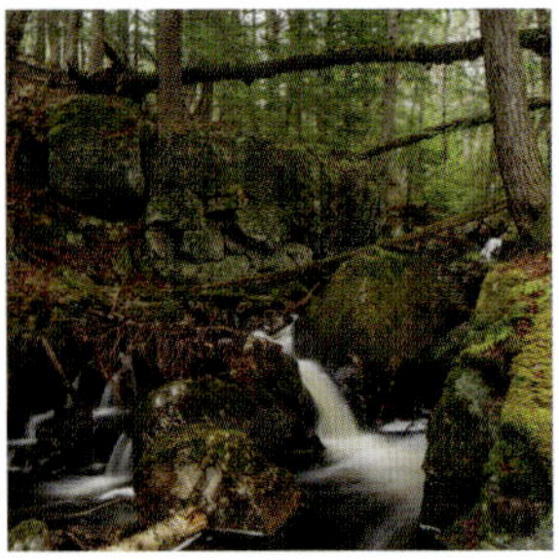

Must See:	7	GPS:	N46 41.192 W88 19.274
Height:	12 feet		
Time:	2-2.5 hours	Hiking Information	
		Path:	None
Driving Information		Length:	.67 miles
Signs:	None	Elev. Change:	Elevated
Road:	2-track	GPS:	Required
Access:	Difficult	Danger:	Moderate
4WD:	Required	WP Boots:	Required

Here is a unique waterfall! The creek flows through a small box canyon with stair stepping bedrock leading the creek down to a semi-calm splash pool. Halfway through the canyon, the walls drop down on both sides - all the way down to the creek on the one side. The waterfall is here also. It is created by the creek flowing around some large boulders that choke the creek bed. It then cascades down while the canyon wall rise back up. Viewed from the bottom end of the canyon, it is a lovely stair-stepped waterfall.

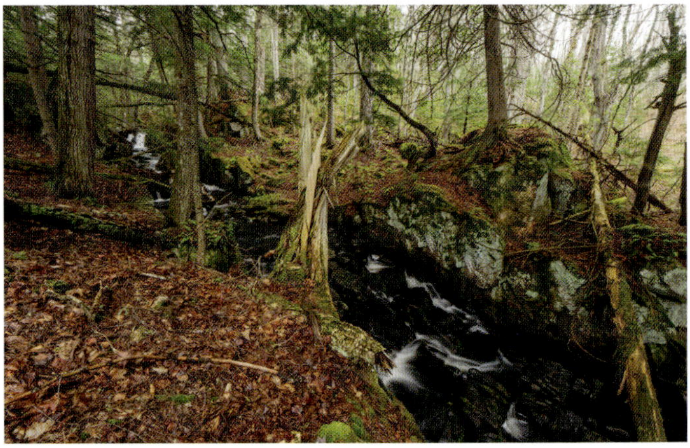

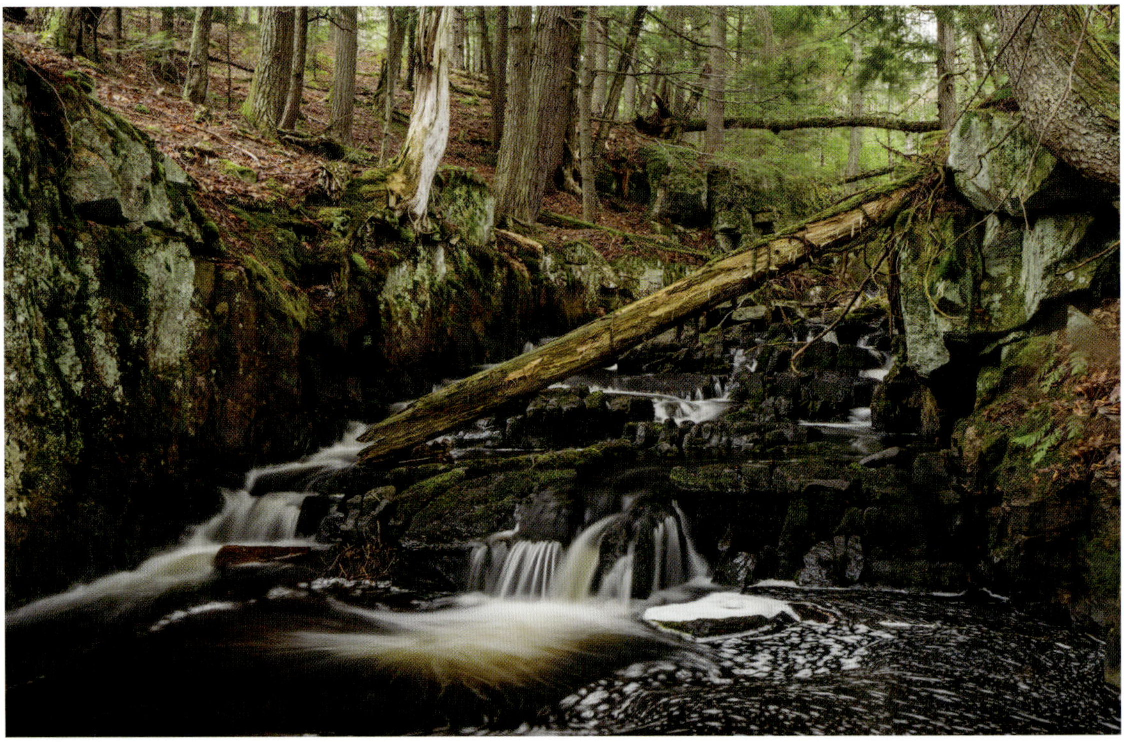

HARLEY FALLS #6 (HARLEY CREEK)

Private

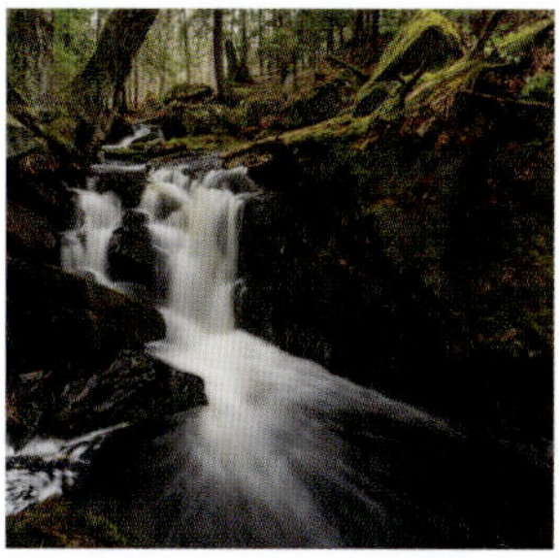

Must See:	7
Height:	4 feet
Time:	2-2.5 hours

Driving Information

Signs:	None
Road:	2-track
Access:	Difficult
4WD:	Required

GPS:	N46 41.193 W88 19.269

Hiking Information

Path:	None
Length:	.68 miles
Elev. Change:	Elevated
GPS:	Required
Danger:	Moderate
WP Boots:	Required

At the head of the canyon, the creek narrows to three feet. It pours over a nearly vertical face, splashing along on blackened rocks. The creek then begins its descent between the steep, 10 foot high canyon walls.

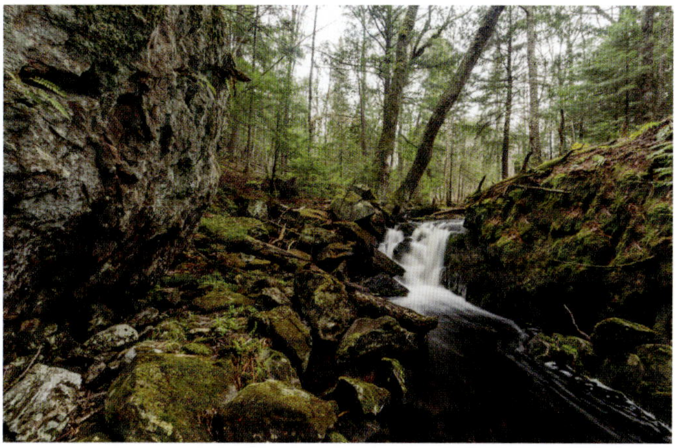

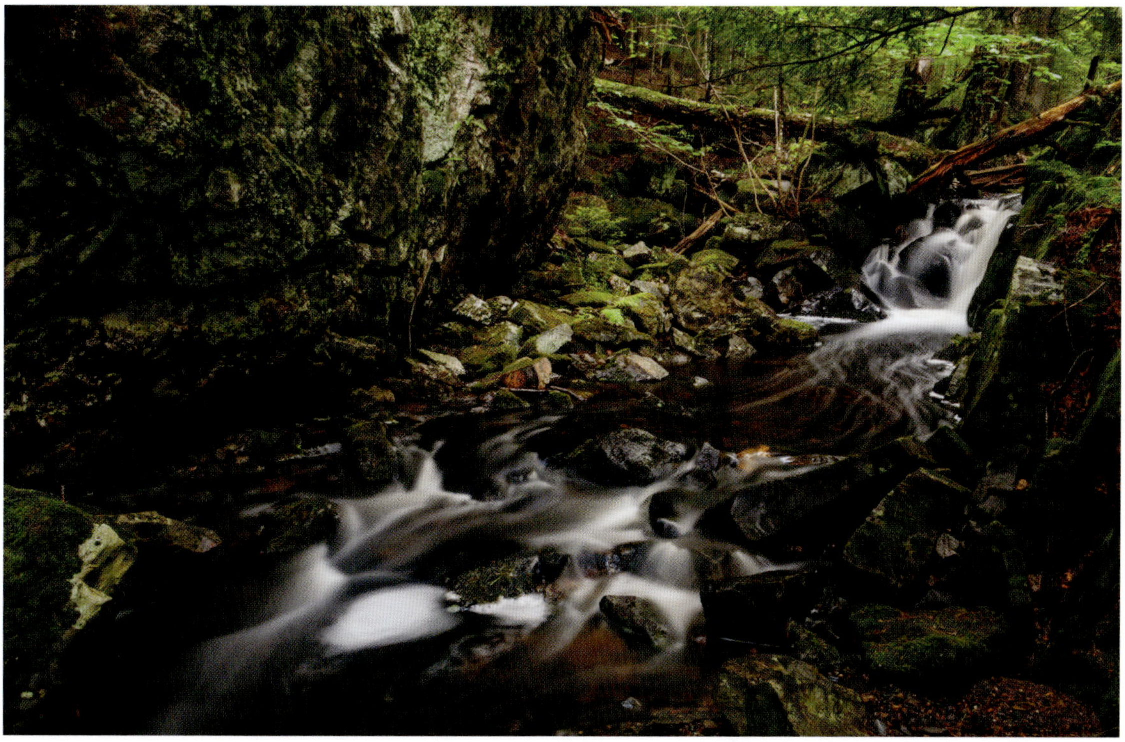

HARLEY FALLS #7 (HARLEY CREEK)

Private

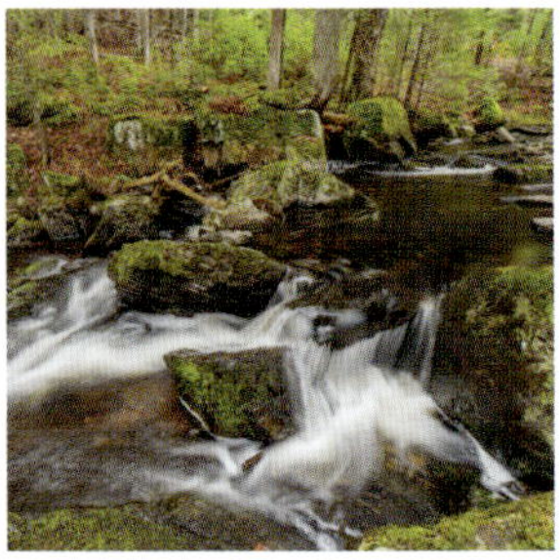

Must See:	4	GPS:	N46 41.185 W88 19.256
Height:	2 feet		
Time:	2-2.5 hours		

Driving Information		Hiking Information	
		Path:	None
		Length:	.69 miles
Signs:	None	Elev. Change:	Elevated
Road:	2-track	GPS:	Required
Access:	Difficult	Danger:	Moderate
4WD:	Helpful	WP Boots:	Required

Seventy-five feet above the canyon, the creek widens out to a dozen feet, a number of large boulders form a crude semi-circle and dam the creek up behind them. The backed up water spills over the low points in a nice, little, 2 foot waterfall.

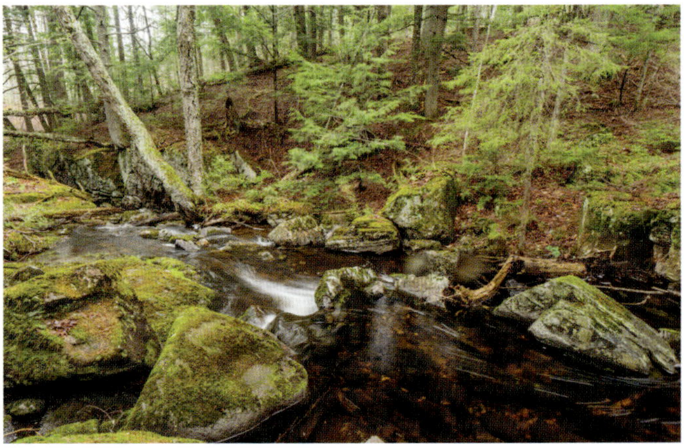

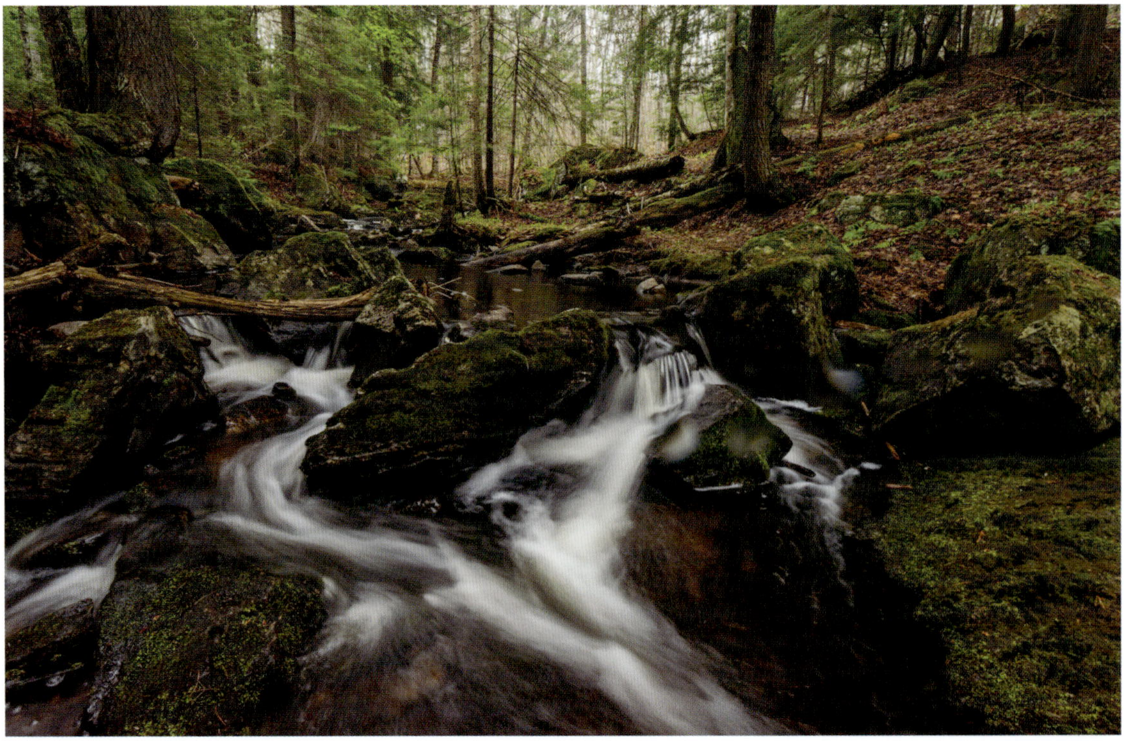

HARLEY FALLS #8 (HARLEY CREEK)

Private

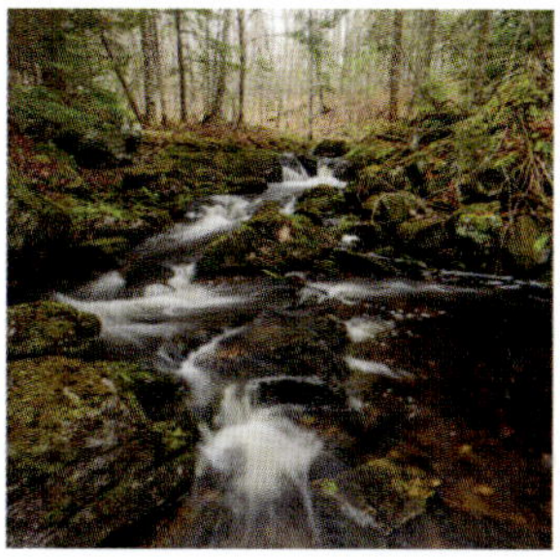

Must See:	6	GPS:	N46 41.179 W88 19.256
Height:	5 feet		
Time:	2-2.5 hours		

Driving Information		Hiking Information	
		Path:	None
		Length:	.69 miles
Signs:	None	Elev. Change:	Elevated
Road:	2-track	GPS:	Required
Access:	Difficult	Danger:	Moderate
4WD:	Helpful	WP Boots:	Required

It's only 35 feet between #7 & #8. These cute little waterfalls are close, yet tucked around a corner in the creek from each other.

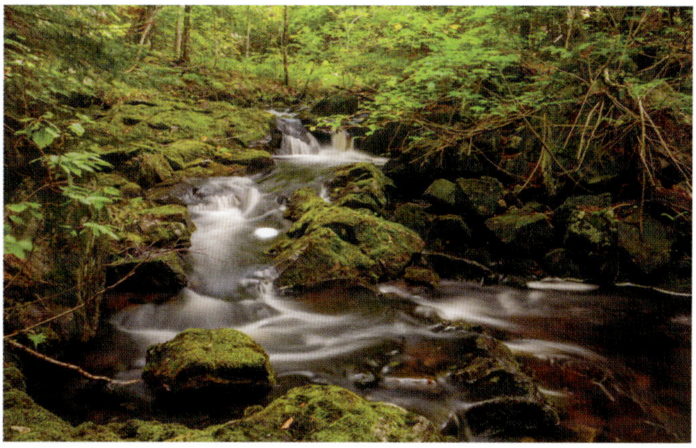

A rocky cascade turns at a mossy shelf and falls over a most picturesque little drop. The 2 foot fall is split around an angled slab of ribbed rock. The creek splashes below, winding and tumbling over more knobby bedrock.

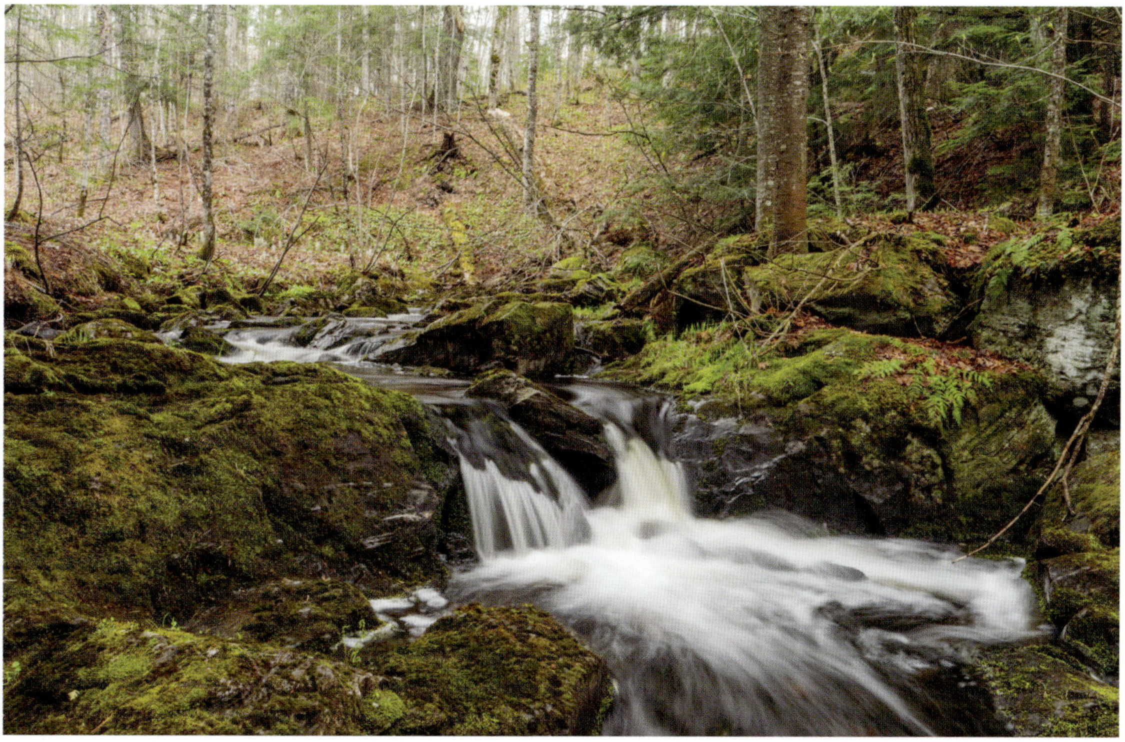

HARLEY FALLS #9 (HARLEY CREEK)

Private

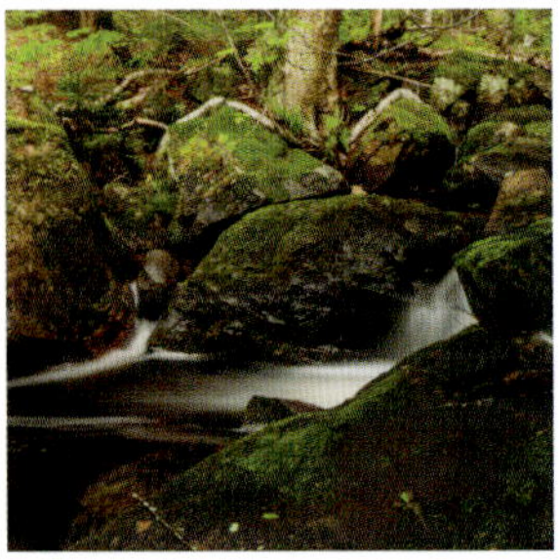

Must See:	5	GPS:	N46 41.158 W88 19.221
Height:	5 feet		
Time:	2.5-3 hours	Hiking Information	
		Path:	None
Driving Information		Length:	.73 mile
Signs:	None	Elev. Change:	Moderate
Road:	2-track	GPS:	Required
Access:	Difficult	Danger:	Moderate
4WD:	Helpful	WP Boots:	Required

Continue hiking upstream 200 feet. Here, the creek bed is overfilled with large mossy boulders. A 20 foot high wall of rock sits off to the side of the waterfall. These boulders split off that wall and tumbled down to the creek over the years. The boulders are actually more impressive than the waterfall!

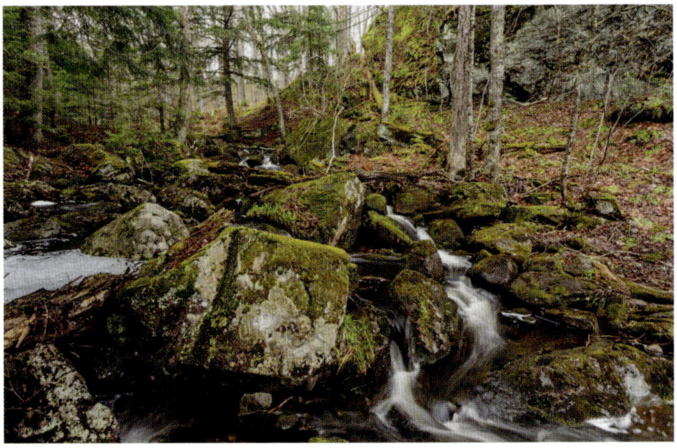

Haphazardly placed green mossy rocks sport frothing white water cascading around them.

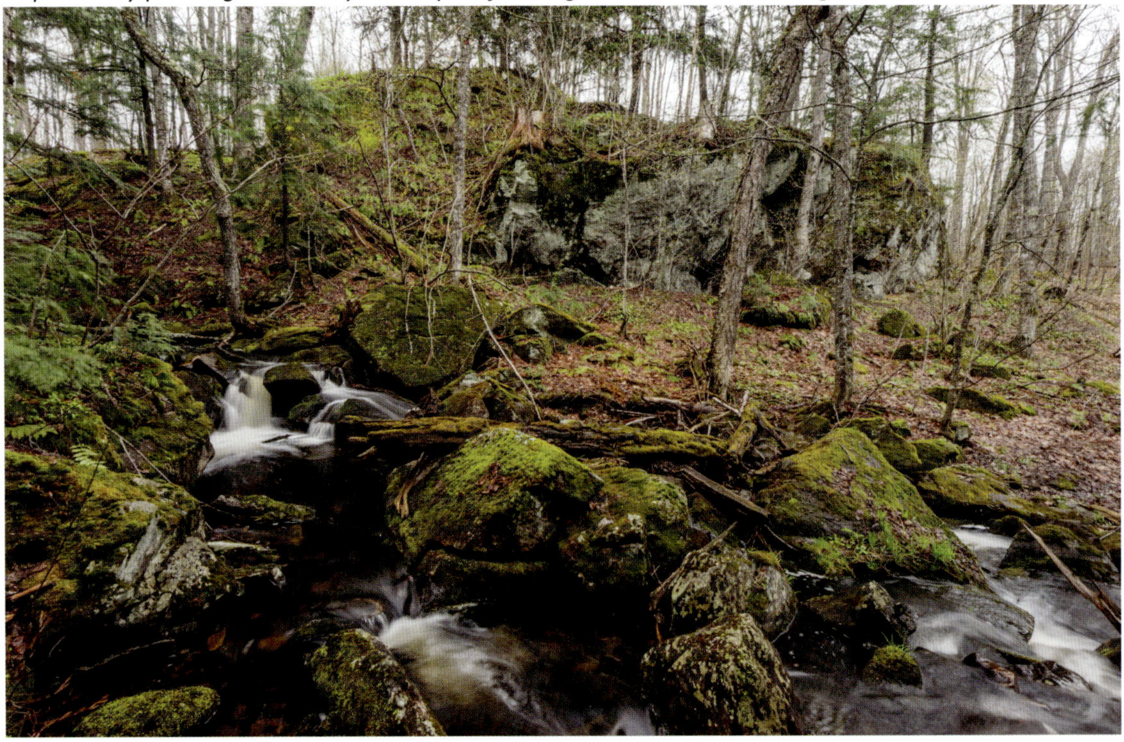

HARLEY FALLS #10 (HARLEY CREEK)

Private

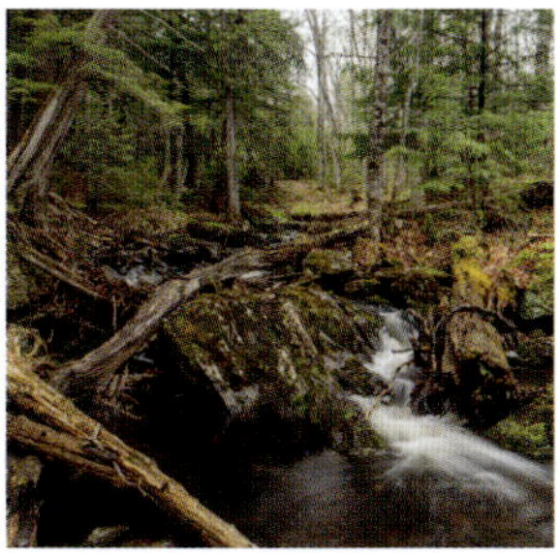

Must See:	3	GPS:	N46 41.157 W88 19.185
Height:	4 feet		
Time:	2.5-3 hours	Hiking Information	
		Path:	None
Driving Information		Length:	.76 mile
Signs:	None	Elev. Change:	Moderate
Road:	2-track	GPS:	Required
Access:	Difficult	Danger:	Moderate
4WD:	Helpful	WP Boots:	Required

About 50 yards upstream from #9, a small batch of cascades will catch your eye. Check out the white rocks along the waterfall. These are similar to the bedrock that will be prevalent upstream at #11. These rocks are much smaller samples, pieces broken off from the bedrock and somehow ending up here. The waterfall cascades down around jagged, large boulders, the most prominent ones standing upright at the base of the waterfall.

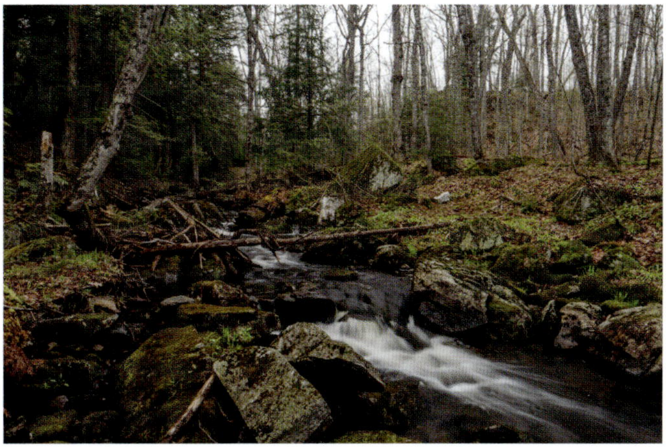

Notice the white boulders on either side of this drop. There will be more upstream.

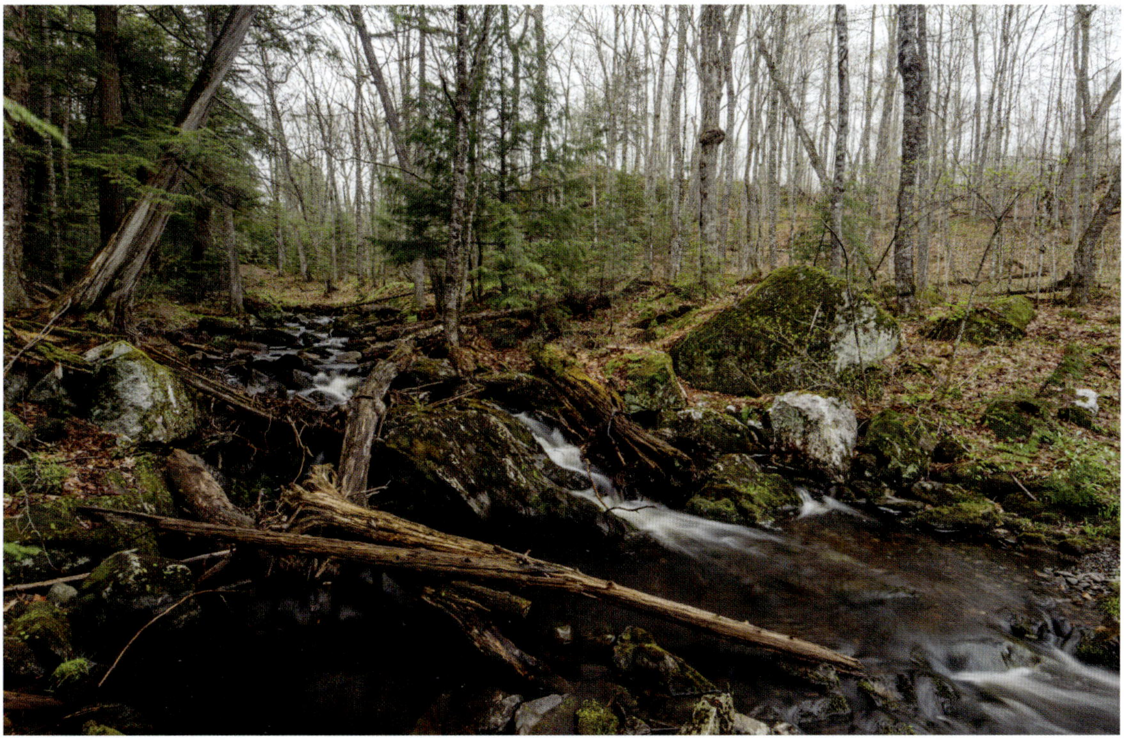

HARLEY FALLS #11 (HARLEY CREEK)

Private

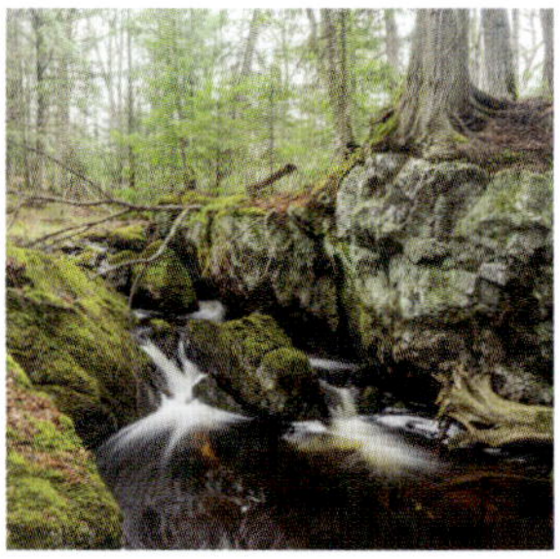

Must See:	5	GPS:	N46 41.158 W88 19.127
Height:	10 feet		
Time:	2.5-3 hours	Hiking Information	
		Path:	None
Driving Information		Length:	.81 mile
Signs:	None	Elev. Change:	Moderate
Road:	2-track	GPS:	Required
Access:	Difficult	Danger:	Moderate
4WD:	Helpful	WP Boots:	Required

About 80 yards above Harley Falls #10 is the upper of the "Harley" drops. The creek runs into a mass of beautiful white bedrock covered in pastel green lichen. The creek has eaten its way into softer rock, with the white mass overhanging the creek. The waterfall splits and tumbles around a number of good sized boulders.

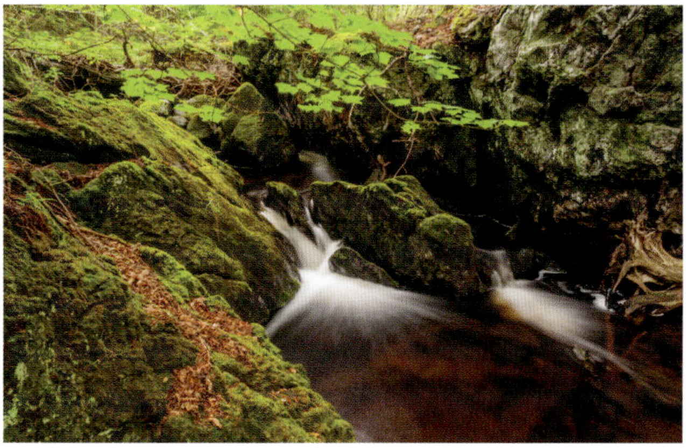

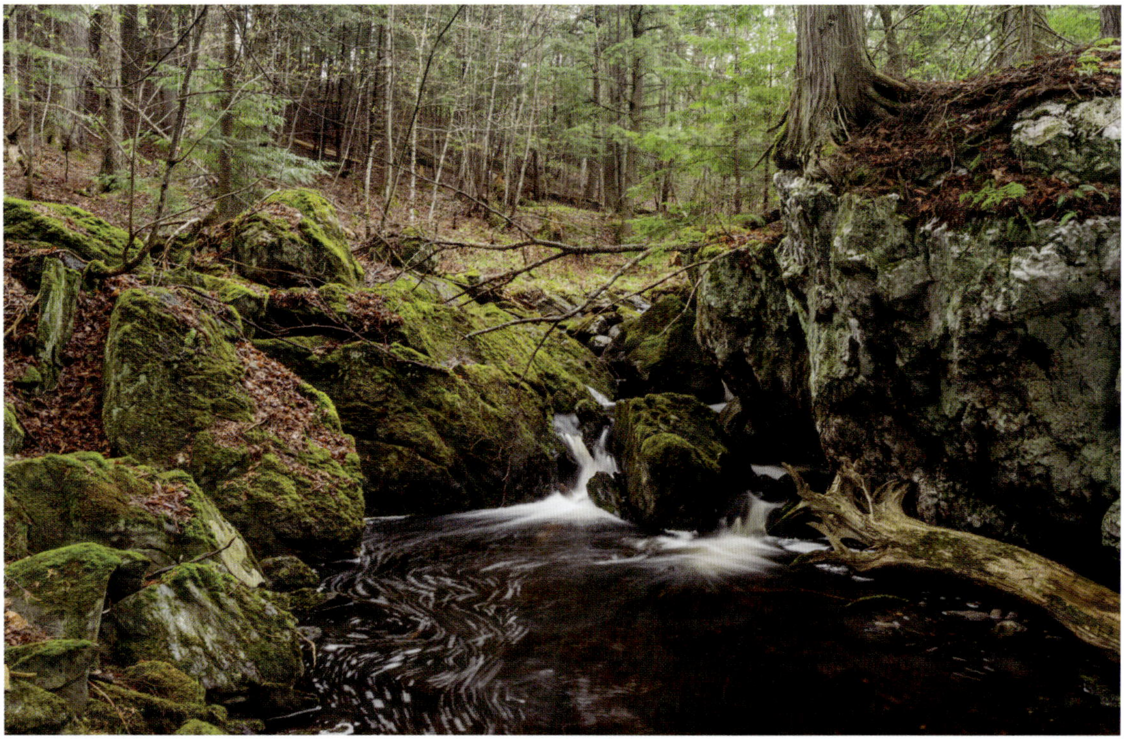

Silver Falls - Upper Hike

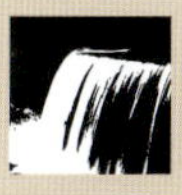

Silver Falls - Upper: The Upper Falls flow over two main cascades. The trail follows the river to the top of the falls, then works its way down to the base. Downed tree debris tends to accumulate among the rocks below the falls.

Directions: From Herman, drive east/northeast on Summit/Keranen Road. Stay on Summit Road until it turns hard to the right. Continue on straight on Lahti Road for .9 miles. Turn left onto a bumpy road (high clearance recommended). A maze of logging trails heads north from here. Stay on the "main road". Use the area map to help you stay on the correct trail. In 1.6 miles, turn right. Park near the berm that shortly blocks the 2-track. Hike down the switchback path for about .35 miles. Fifty yards before the river is a worn down berm. Just before the berm is an old parking spot on the left. Head into that area. A pine tree on the right has red and blue stripes painted on it. That is the trail head. It is a faint path. The path leads to the river and then turns down river to the top of the falls. There is about 100 feet of elevation change on this hike.

SILVER FALLS - UPPER (SILVER RIVER)

Private

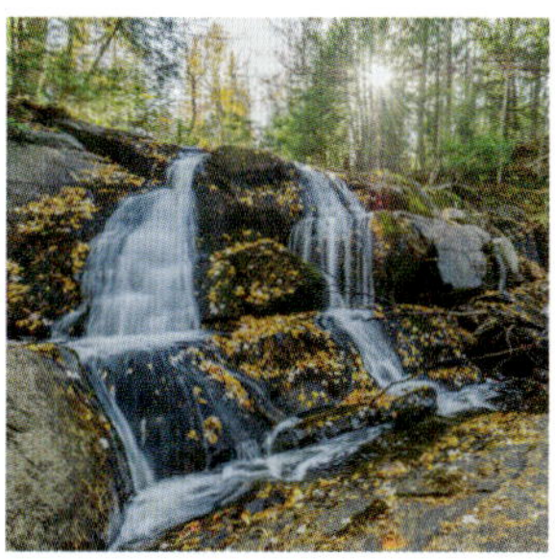

Must See:	8	GPS:	N46 40.820 W88 19.791
Height:	30 feet		
Time:	15-30 minutes	Hiking Information	
		Path:	Unimproved Footpath
Driving Information		Length:	.39 miles
Signs:	None	Elev. Change:	Elevated
Road:	2-track	GPS:	Required
Access:	Difficult	Danger:	Minor
4WD:	Required	WP Boots:	Helpful

Although it is not easy to find, this is a locally popular waterfall destination. Keep in mind that it's about a 100 foot change in elevation from the parking spot. Enjoy the shaded river bank where the footpath winds through mature hardwoods and evergreens.

The 40 foot wide riverbed houses huge rock sections. The river runs through hardwoods, golden yellow in autumn. However, along the side the river, evergreens dominate the foliage. The falls drop 10 feet, splitting around a mounded rock. A pool below the first drop empties on the far side of the river into a narrow crevasse formed between the river bedrock and a large boulder that broke off and is wedged up against the rock face by a number of similarly sized boulders. A narrow pool runs back sideways along the face before the river continues its journey downstream with several small drops added as a parting gift.

Low water level in October

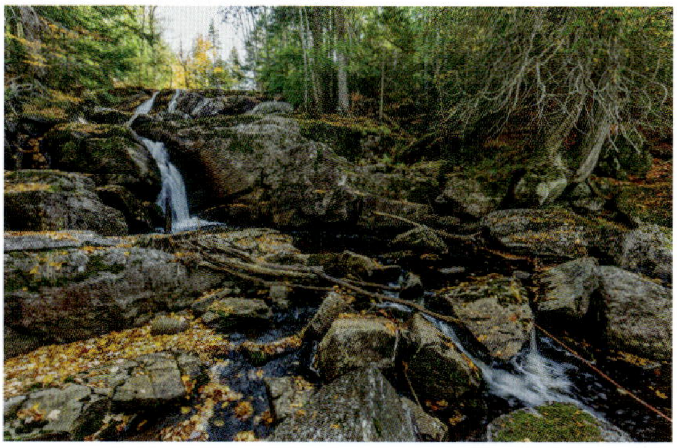

The top cascade can just be seen from down here

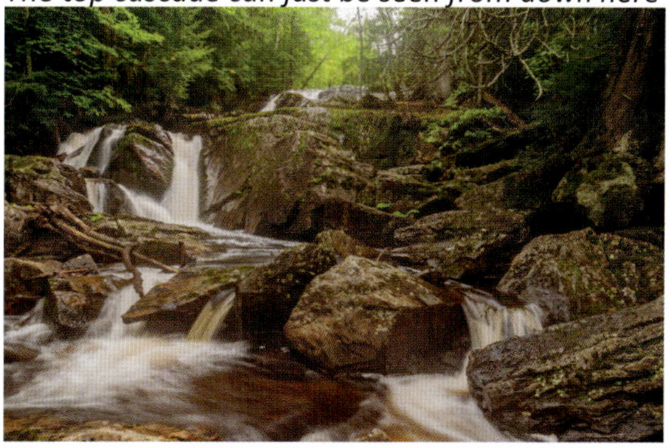

Slate River - Lower Area

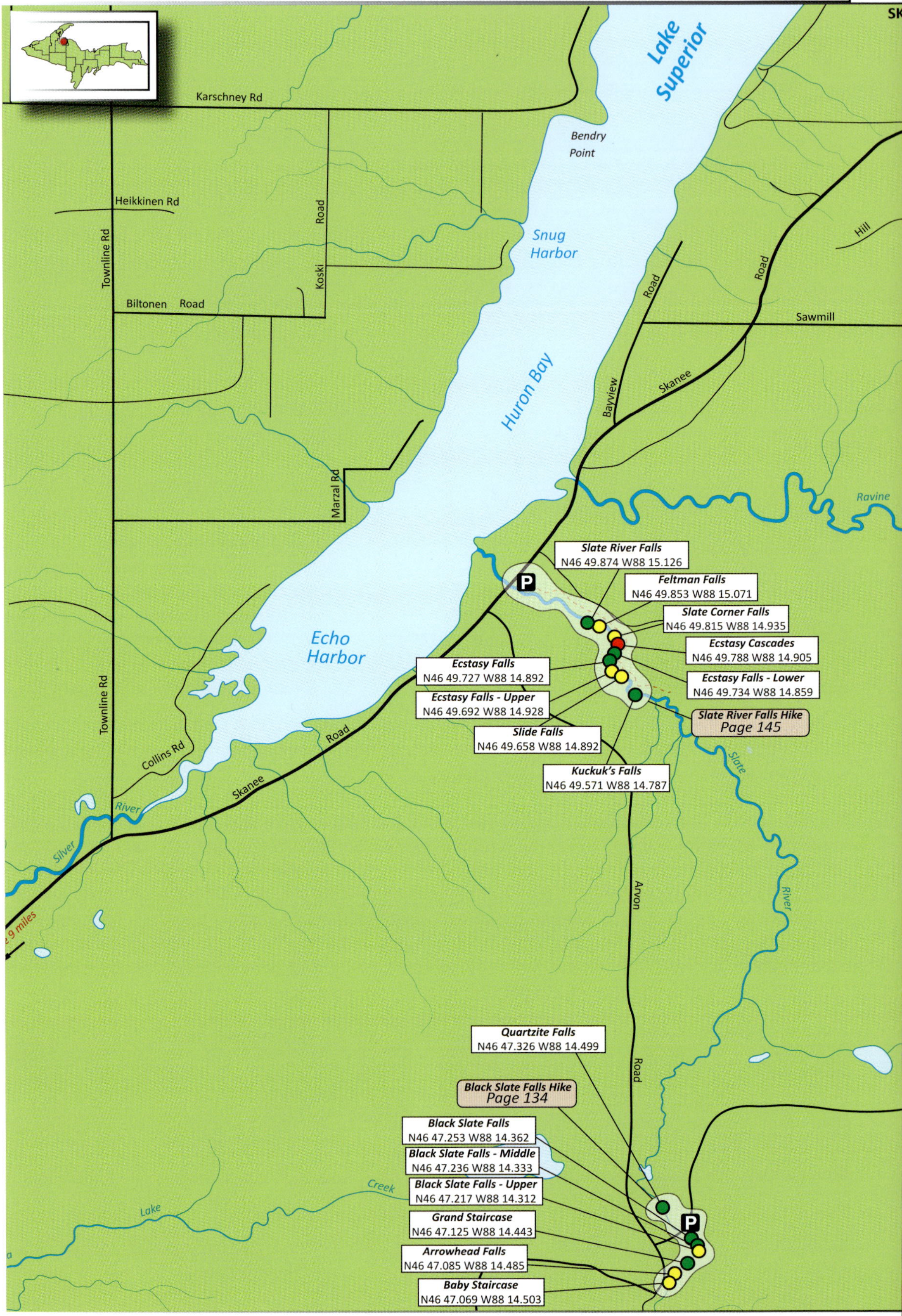

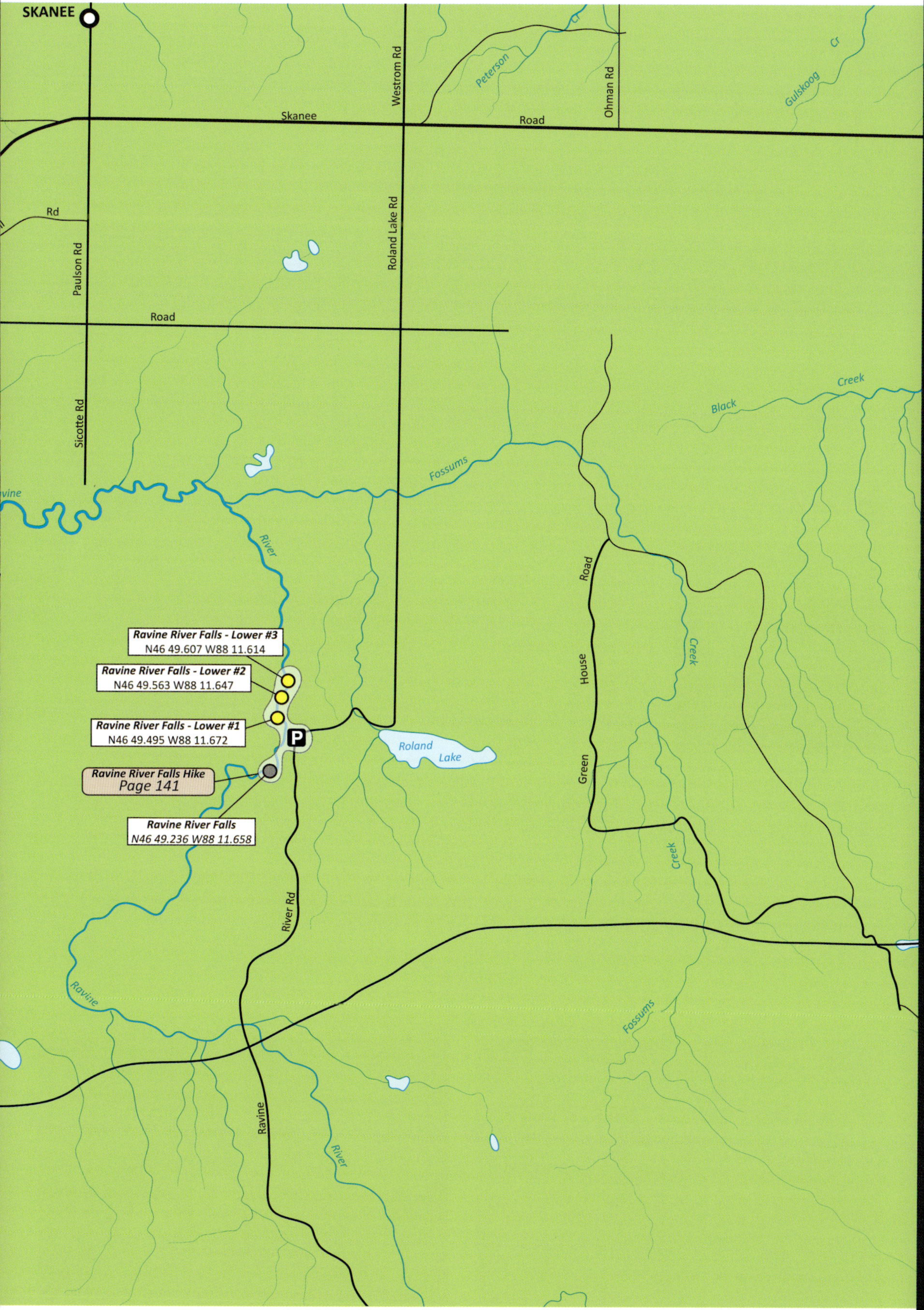
SKANEE
Skanee
Road
Westrom Rd
Ohman Rd
Peterson
Cr
Gulskoog
Cr
Rd
Paulson Rd
Roland Lake Rd
Road
Sicotte Rd
Black
Creek
Fossums
River
Road
House
Green
Creek
Creek
Ravine River Falls - Lower #3
N46 49.607 W88 11.614
Ravine River Falls - Lower #2
N46 49.563 W88 11.647
Ravine River Falls - Lower #1
N46 49.495 W88 11.672
P
Roland
Lake
Ravine River Falls Hike
Page 141
Ravine River Falls
N46 49.236 W88 11.658
River Rd
Ravine
Fossums
Ravine
River

Black Slate Falls Hike

Quartzite Falls and the Black Slate collection of falls are easily accessed and occur in a fairly tame section of the Slate River. An interesting oddity is seen on the short hike to Quartzite Falls. A narrow vein of white rock runs for a ways down the middle of Slate River, looking like a painted center line for dividing water traffic!

Directions: Turn southeast onto Arvon Road off of Skanee Road. (This is the first main dirt road southwest of the Slate River.) Follow Arvon Road in a generally southerly direction for about 3.5 miles. Turn left onto another dirt road. About 200 yards down the road is a bridge that crosses the Slate River. Park on the (far) east side of the bridge. Hike along the ATV trail to the north, following the river downstream to Quartzite Falls. When done, hike back along the trail to the vehicle. Now follow the river (either side) up river from the bridge to Black Slate Falls. I recommend the western side if hiking to all these falls since there is a fairly well travelled footpath on that side.

QUARTZITE FALLS (SLATE RIVER)

Private

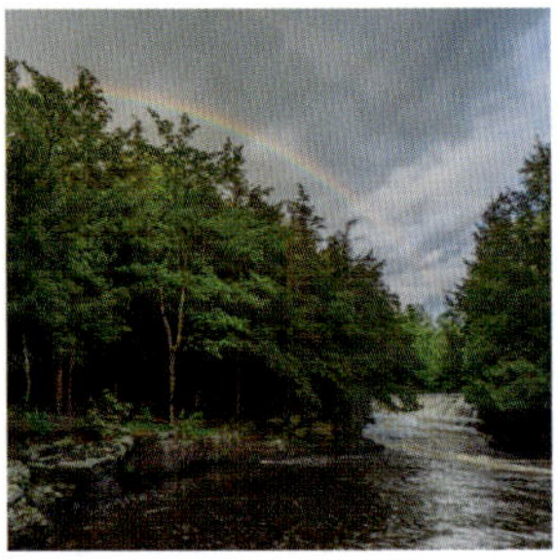

Must See:	7	GPS:	N46 47.326 W88 14.499
Height:	10 feet		
Time:	15-25 minutes	Hiking Information	
		Path:	ATV Trail
Driving Information		Length:	175 yards
Signs:	None	Elev. Change:	Minor
Road:	Gravel	GPS:	N/A
Access:	Somewhat Easy	Danger:	Slight
4WD:	N/A	WP Boots:	N/A

While hiking down the ATV trail to the falls, watch for a unique geological feature. It looks like someone painted a bright, white center line down the river! It's a surprisingly uniform vein of white rock. Of course, it's best to view when the river is low!

The waterfall appears suddenly, as the river cuts deep into the black slate bedrock. A 20 foot wide horseshoe shaped cascade stair-steps the river down into an 8 foot high step-walled gorge. The waterfall continues to slide down flat layers for about 75 feet below the cascade. The river then flushes into a large swimming hole at the base of the slide.

The trail from the bridge to Quartzite Falls

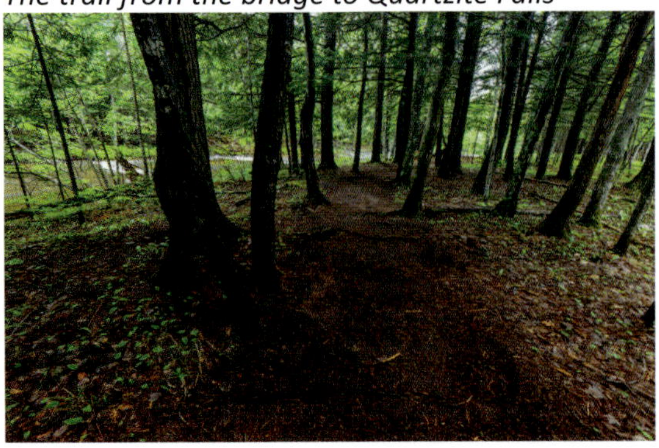

Walking along the side of the waterfall

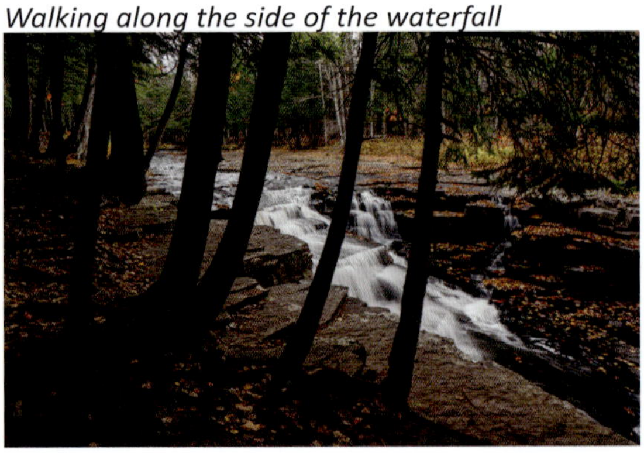

BLACK SLATE FALLS (SLATE RIVER)

Private

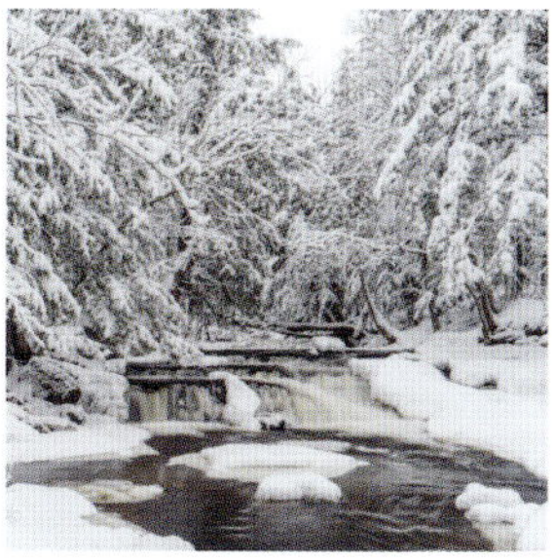

Must See:	7	GPS:	N46 47.253 W88 14.362
Height:	5 feet		
Time:	10-20 minutes	Hiking Information	
		Path:	Slight Footpath
Driving Information		Length:	100 yards
Signs:	East Side of Bridge	Elev. Change:	Minor
Road:	Gravel	GPS:	N/A
Access:	Somewhat Easy	Danger:	Slight
4WD:	N/A	WP Boots:	N/A

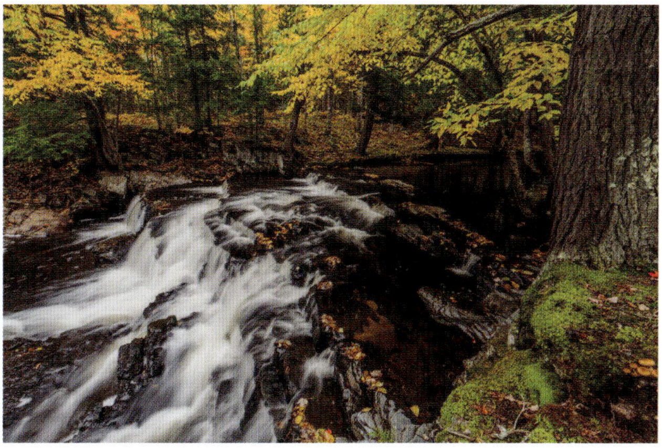

The waterfall can be seen from the bridge, but to view it better, follow the riverbed on either side of the river. The shot to the right was taken from the western bank. It is easier to follow this bank upstream from here. The eastern side gets quite boggy and there are many downed trees as well as thick brush to contend with.

The 30 foot wide river cascades down closely spaced stair steps of slate. Beautiful birch trees on both sides of the river stretch out golden arms each October. Numerous drops occur one after another upstream starting with Black Slate Falls.

A LARGE boulder sits downstream from the waterfall

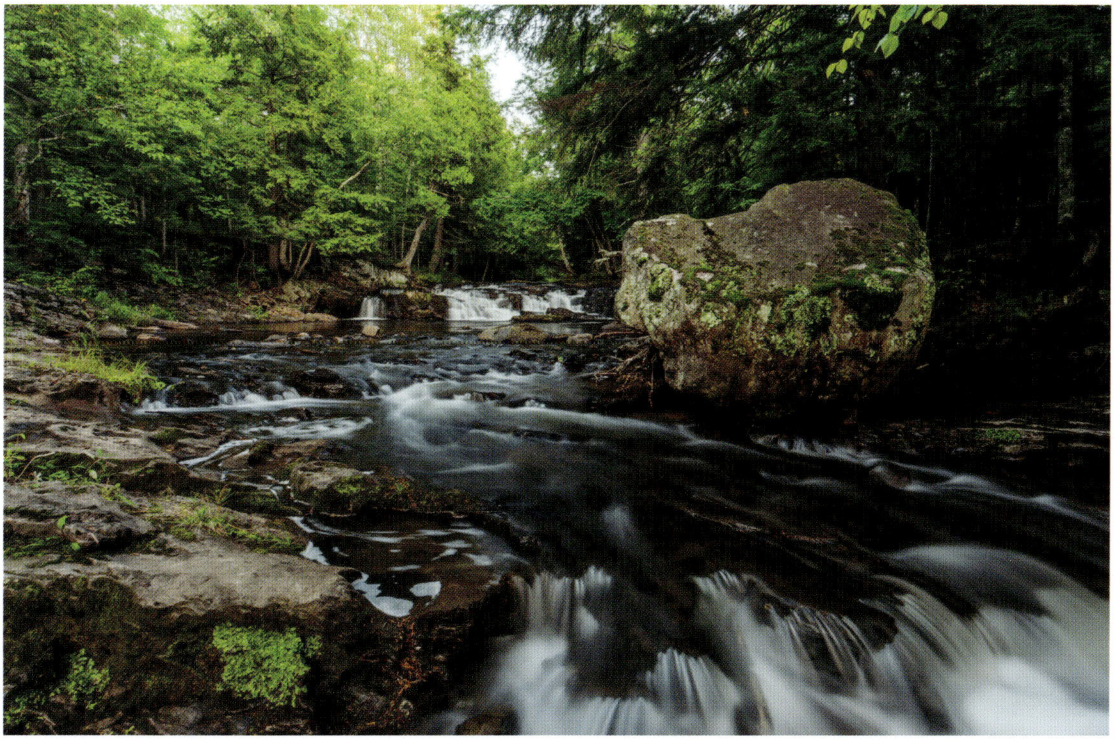

BLACK SLATE FALLS - MIDDLE (SLATE RIVER)

Private

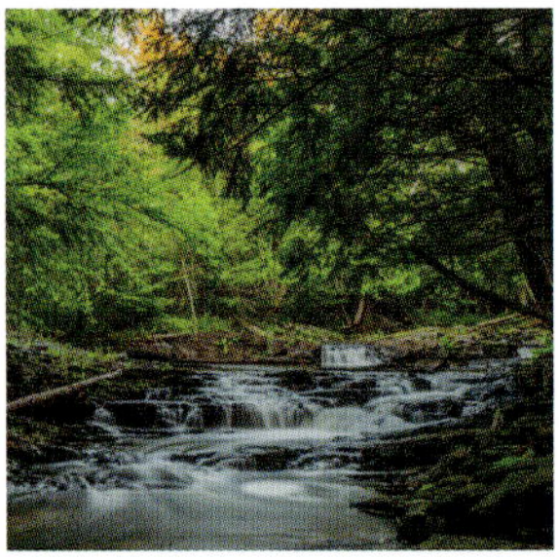

Must See:	7	GPS:	N46 47.236 W88 14.333
Height:	7 feet		
Time:	10-20 minutes	Hiking Information	
		Path:	Slight Footpath
Driving Information		Length:	150 yards
Signs:	None	Elev. Change:	Minor
Road:	Gravel	GPS:	Helpful
Access:	Somewhat Easy	Danger:	Slight
4WD:	N/A	WP Boots:	N/A

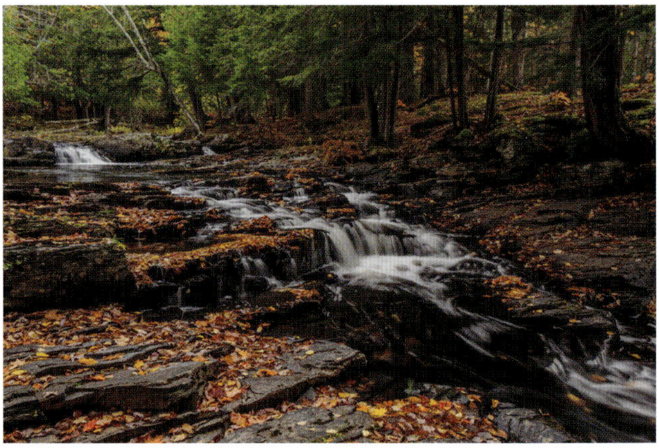

Just 100 feet upstream from Black Slate Falls is another waterfall, just as lovely! It is similar in look and width, but more drawn out, with two more drops above the main one, each about 50 feet apart. There is an interesting baby bluff, 2 feet high, halfway up the waterfall. The river rushes over the middle and around the ends of this short rocky race. The top cascade runs on the western side of the river and drops less than 2 feet.

This waterfall can be viewed nicely from both sides of the river.

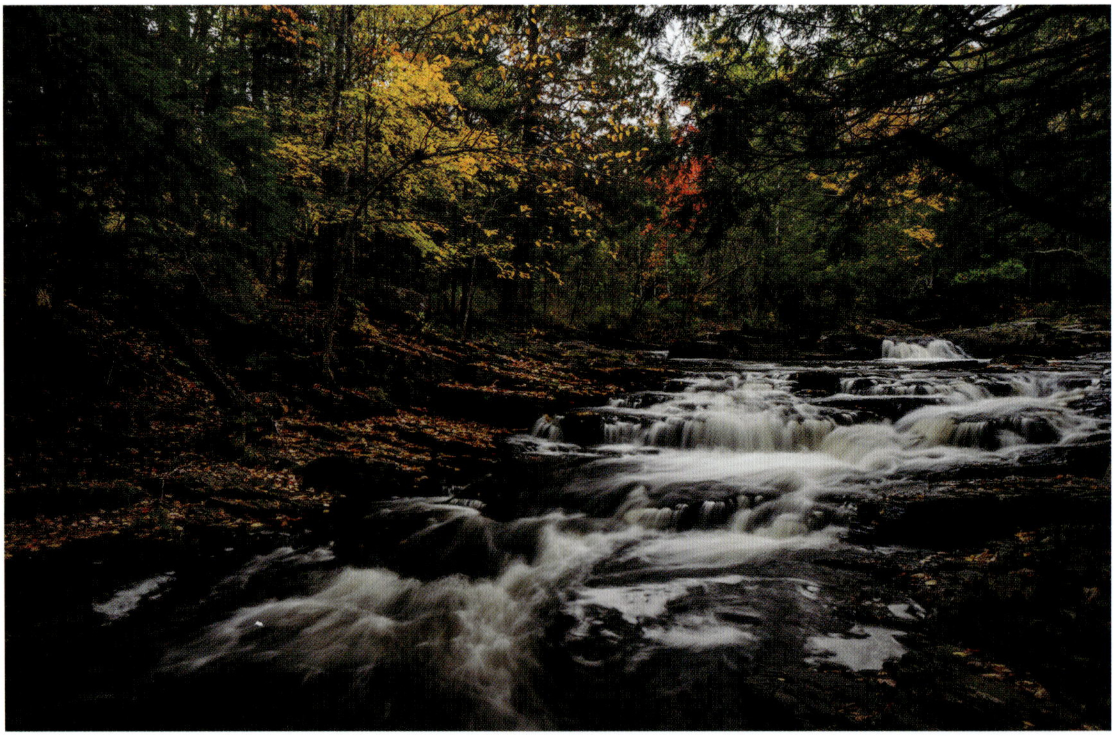

BLACK SLATE FALLS - UPPER (SLATE RIVER)

Private

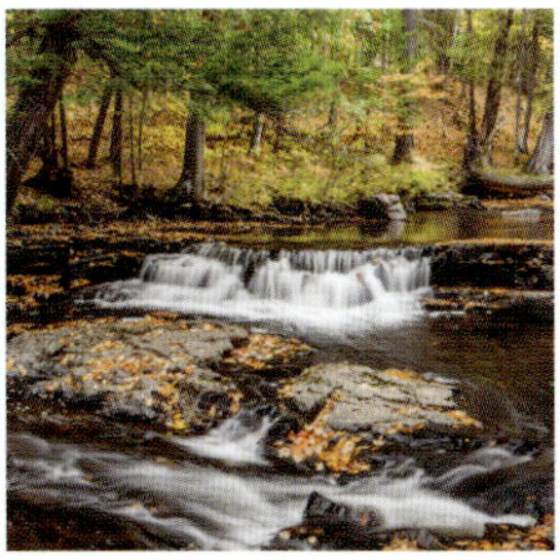

Must See:	6	GPS:	N46 47.217 W88 14.312
Height:	5 feet		
Time:	15-25 minutes	**Hiking Information**	
		Path:	Slight Footpath
Driving Information		Length:	225 yards
Signs:	None	Elev. Change:	Minor
Road:	Gravel	GPS:	Helpful
Access:	Somewhat Easy	Danger:	Slight
4WD:	N/A	WP Boots:	N/A

The next two drops, 150 feet upstream from the Middle Falls, form this waterfall set. A nice, evenly formed 3 foot cascade froths upstream from a 2 foot divided slide. There are predominantly evergreens surrounding these drops, with just several birch and maple mixed in.

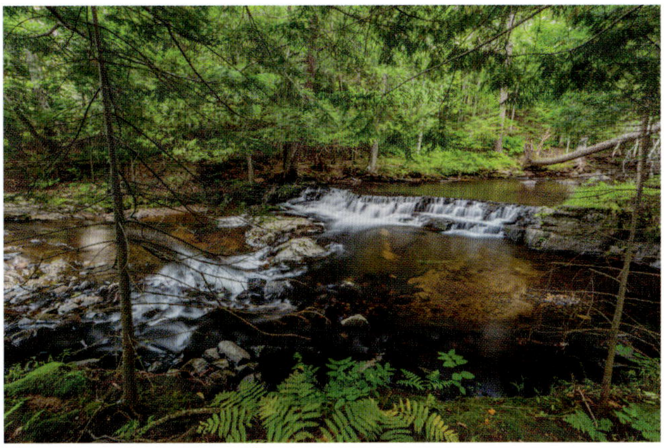

This waterfall also can be viewed nicely from both sides of the river.

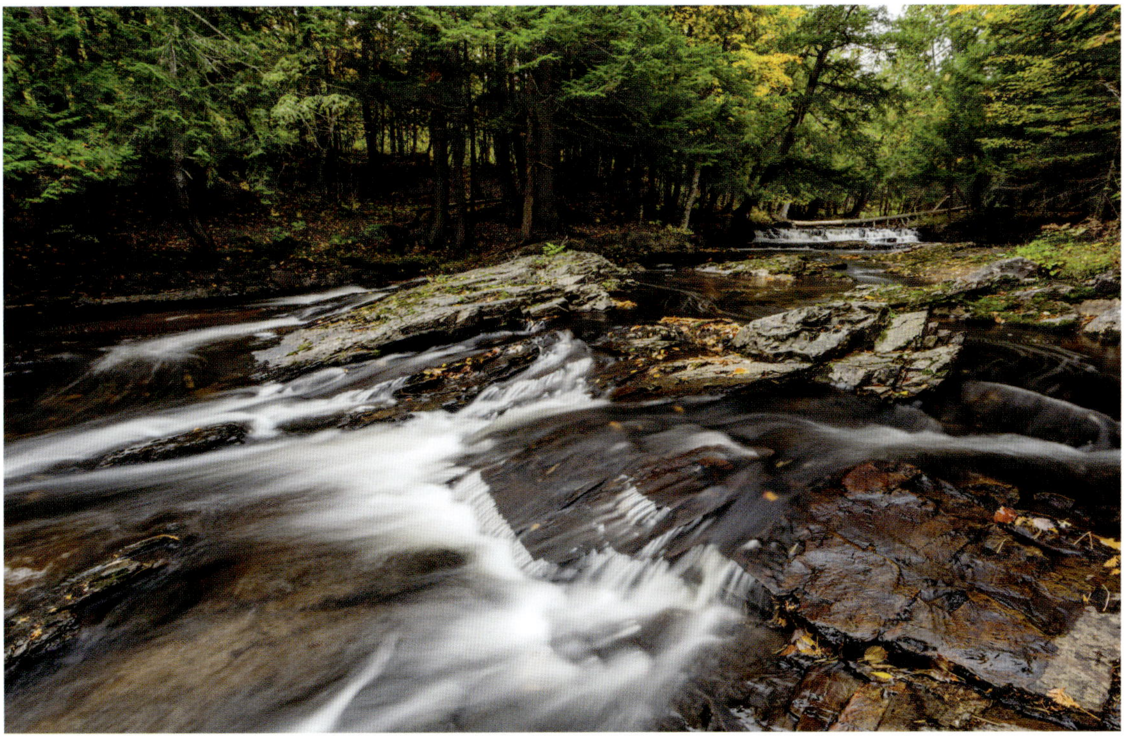

GRAND STAIRCASE (SLATE RIVER)

Private

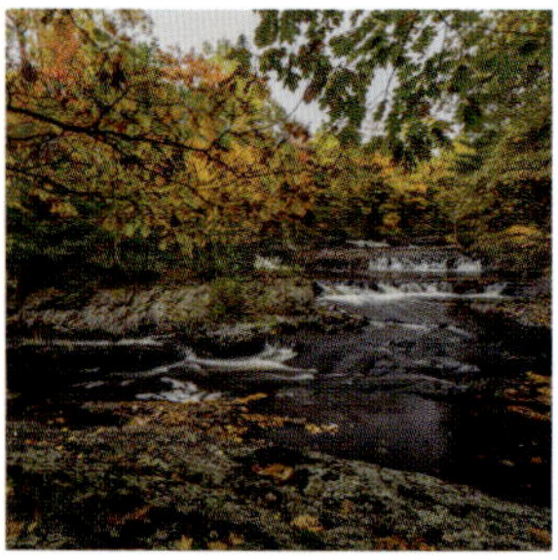

Must See:	7	GPS:	N46 47.125 W88 14.443
Height:	12 feet		
Time:	25-40 minutes	Hiking Information	
		Path:	Slight Footpath
Driving Information		Length:	.28 miles
Signs:	None	Elev. Change:	Minor
Road:	Gravel	GPS:	Helpful
Access:	Somewhat Easy	Danger:	Slight
4WD:	N/A	WP Boots:	N/A

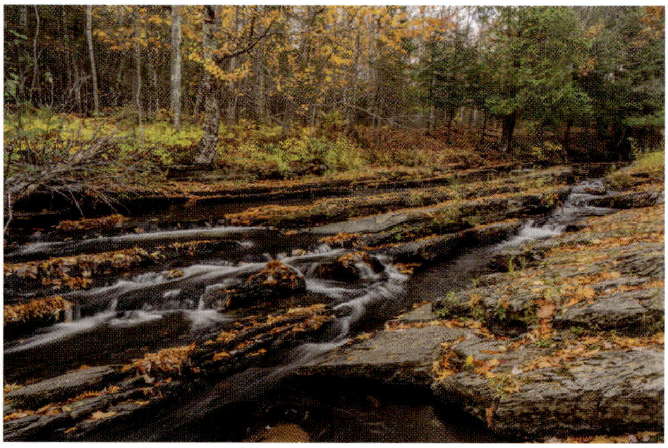

The distance between the Upper Falls and the Grand Staircase is the longest in this hike at .16 miles.

The river widens out to about 50 feet with a number of steps dropping along the way. Thirty feet below the last "step", the river turns 90 degrees and rushes down a narrow, 4 foot wide chute. Up at the top of the waterfall, the river is 20 feet wide, running through several angled layers of slate, channeled beneath a mature birch, getting ready to widen out at the Grand Staircase. When the river's low, the staircase has a lot of its gray bedrock exposed. But during high water times, it runs nearly from side to side, with only the tallest points of the highest layers poking out through the frothing waterfall.

Note the sharp turn in the river at the base of the waterfall - The above shot shows the upper channels

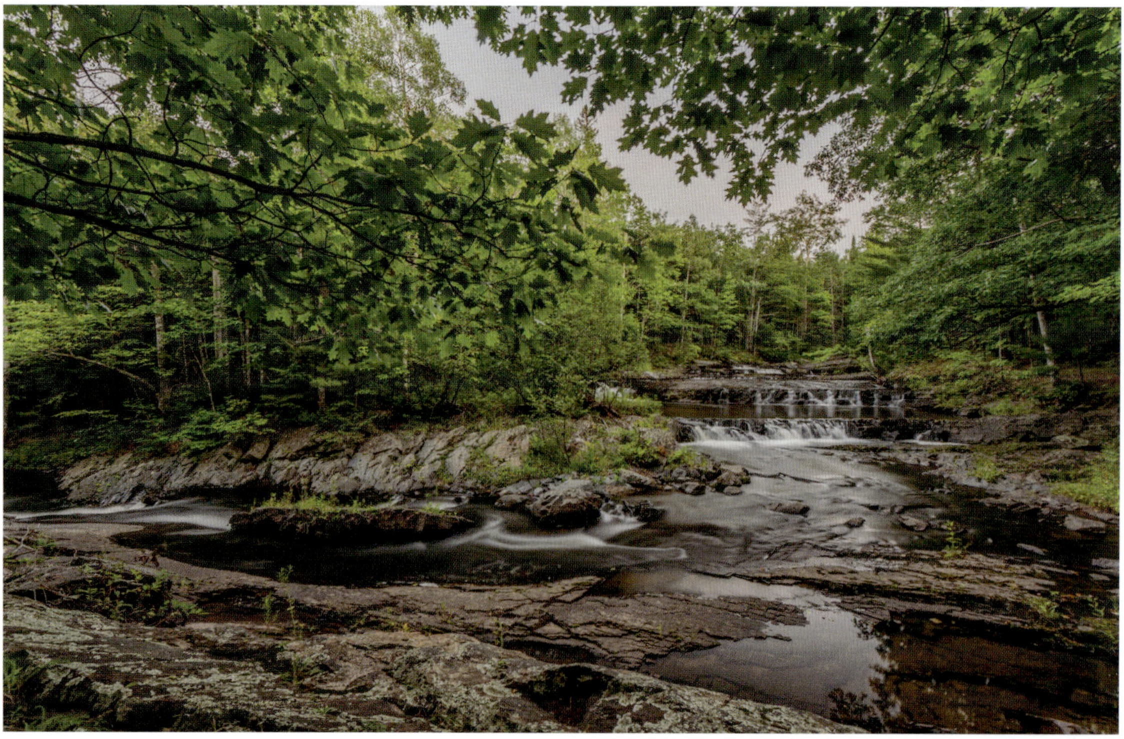

ARROWHEAD FALLS (SLATE RIVER)

Private

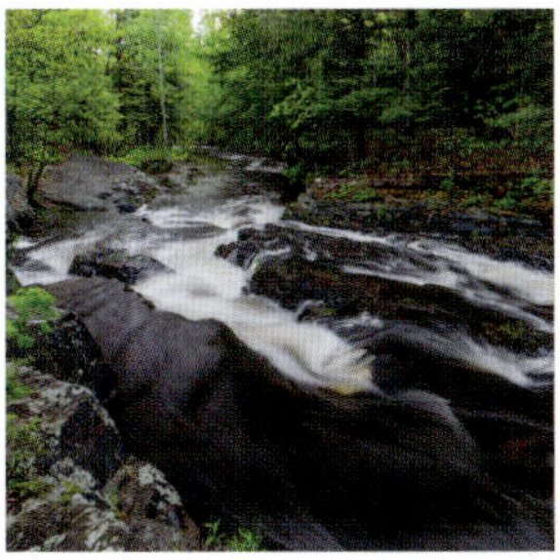

Must See:	4	GPS:	N46 47.085 W88 14.485
Height:	4 feet		
Time:	35-50 minutes		

Driving Information		Hiking Information	
Signs:	None	Path:	Slight Footpath
Road:	Gravel	Length:	.34 miles
Access:	Somewhat Easy	Elev. Change:	Minor
4WD:	N/A	GPS:	Helpful
		Danger:	Slight
		WP Boots:	N/A

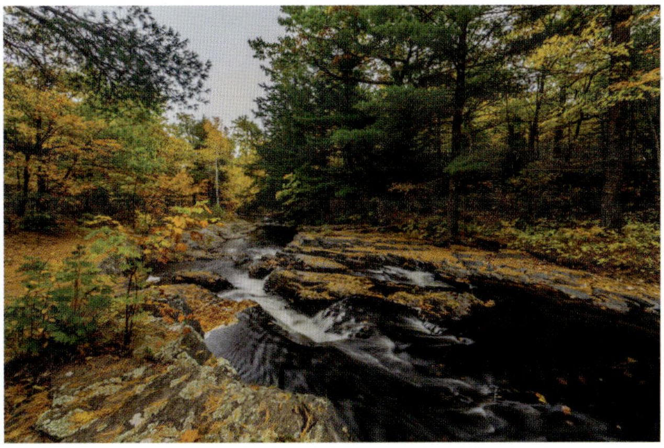

About 150 feet above the top of the Grand Staircase, several interesting channels have been cut through the layers of slate, forming the rough shape of an arrowhead. The multi-layered riverbed can be easily viewed from an outcropping on the west side of the river. The river runs smoothly above the waterfall. Coming into sight around a bend in the river, white air bubbles, hinting at the next waterfall upstream, are the only thing that disturb the black glassy surface. At the base of the waterfall the bedrock squeezes together, narrowing the river to under 4 feet for a moment and then opening back up to a dozen feet or so.

A popular circular pull-off from Arvon Road is just feet away from the waterfall. It's common to see someone camping here.

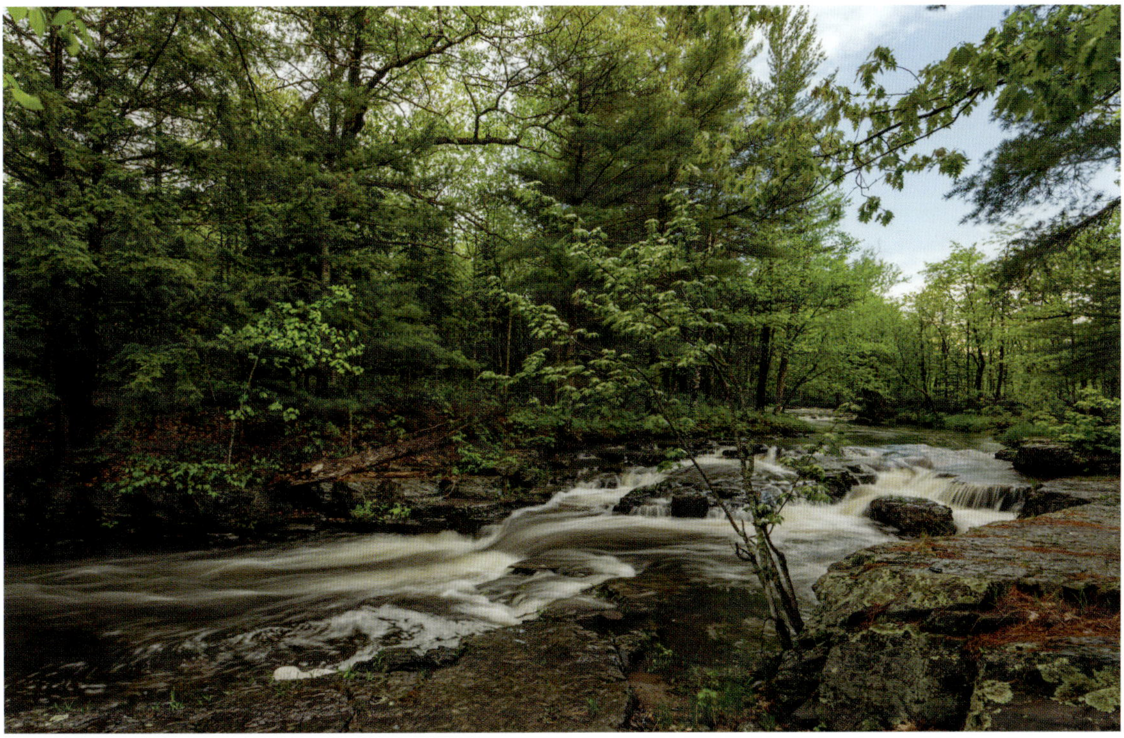

BABY STAIRCASE (SLATE RIVER)

Private

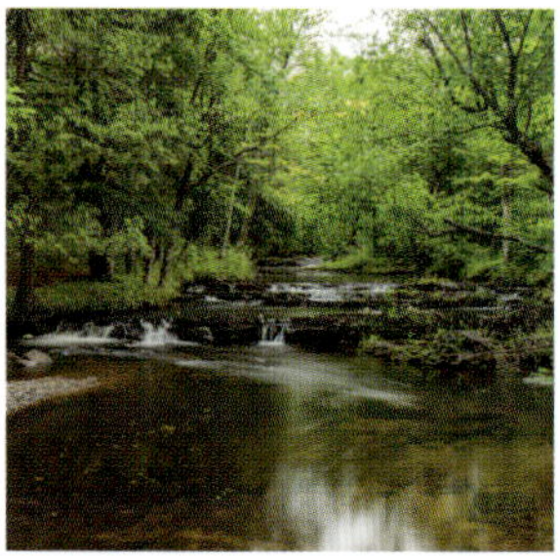

Must See:	5	GPS:	N46 47.069 W88 14.503
Height:	6 feet		
Time:	45-60 minutes	Hiking Information	
		Path:	Slight footpath
Driving Information		Length:	.37 miles
Signs:	None	Elev. Change:	Minor
Road:	Gravel	GPS:	Helpful
Access:	Somewhat Easy	Danger:	Slight
4WD:	N/A	WP Boots:	N/A

A series of cascades, like a miniature Grand Staircase, extends for 200 feet upstream. There are many steps, but none are higher than 1 foot. The base of the cascade is just 75 feet above Arrowhead Falls. There is a gap of about 100 feet in the steps, with about 1/3 of the steps at the top and 2/3 of the steps at the base of the waterfall. Low hanging branches arch gracefully over the white striped waterway. Arvon Road parallels the river, running just 20 yards to the west. A circular pull-off is at the top end of the cascades.

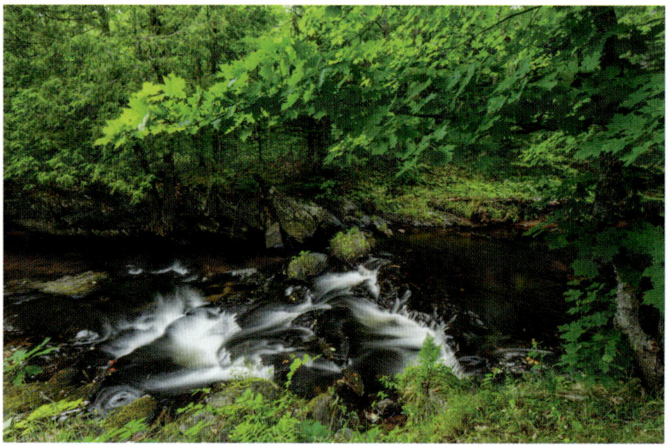

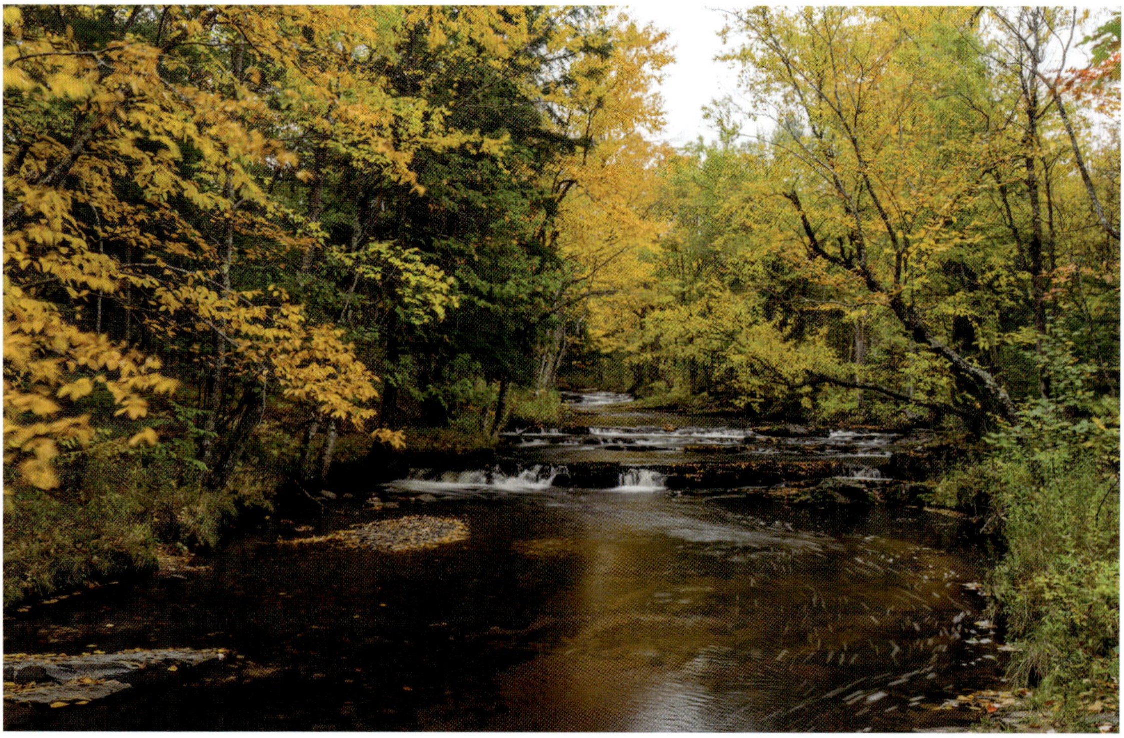

Ravine River Falls Hike

Ravine River Falls is a private waterfall in close proximity to a house with a gated driveway. Respect the "No Trespassing" signs. There are downstream falls that are accessible, however. Enjoy the small cascades and the interesting terrain.

Directions: Turn south off of Skanee Road onto Roland Lake Road (dirt). Follow it to the end (2.9 miles). Turn right onto Ravine River Road for .5 miles (The road turns left (south) at this point). Park on the right by a 2-track (N46 49.370 W88 11.508). Hike the 2-track down close to the river until it turns sharp left and parallels the river. Instead of following the 2-track up-river, hike to the right (down-river) on a faint footpath to the Ravine River Falls. Follow the river downstream to the two lower falls (total hike from the vehicle is .36 miles one way). The river cuts through some higher ground on the way to the lower falls. Hiking along the top of the gorge may be required. It is then a steep climb back down to the river at Lower #3.

RAVINE RIVER FALLS (RAVINE RIVER)

Private

Must See:	?	GPS:	N46 49.236 W88 11.658
Height:	? feet		
Time:	N/A	Hiking Information	
		Path:	Driveway
Driving Information		Length:	250 yards
Signs:	None	Elev. Change:	Minor
Road:	Gravel	GPS:	N/A
Access:	Somewhat Easy	Danger:	Slight
4WD:	N/A	WP Boots:	Helpful

This is a private waterfall. No trespassing.

RAVINE RIVER FALLS - LOWER #1 (RAVINE RIVER)

Private

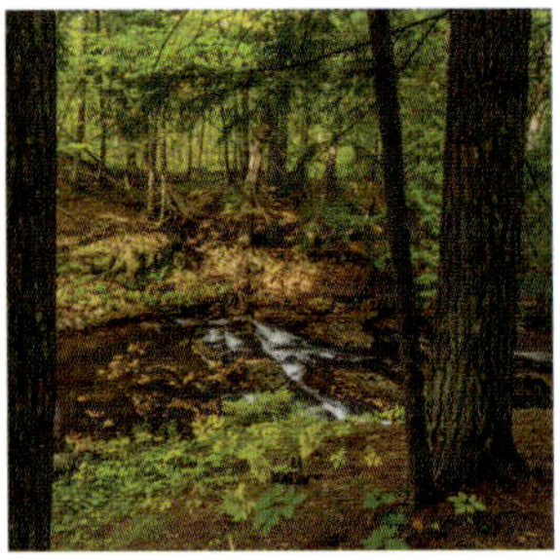

Must See:	5	GPS:	N46 49.495 W88 11.672
Height:	5 feet		
Time:	40-60 minutes	**Hiking Information**	
		Path:	2- track then none
Driving Information		Length:	.22 miles
Signs:	None	Elev. Change:	Moderate
Road:	Gravel	GPS:	Required
Access:	Somewhat Easy	Danger:	Slight
4WD:	N/A	WP Boots:	N/A

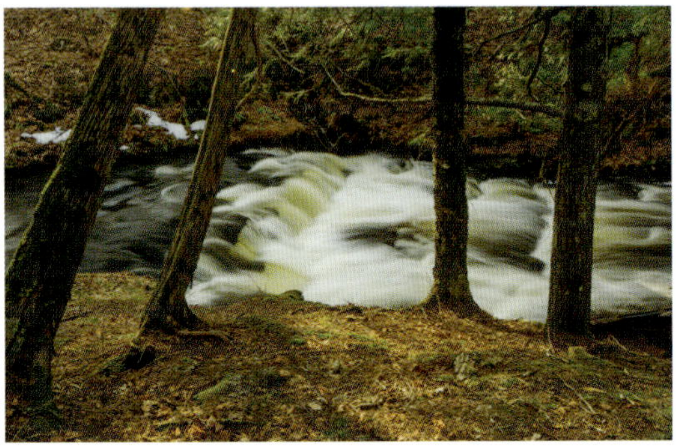

There are several consecutive drops over ledges of basalt. Some of the bedrock is eroded in such a way as to make it look like the bark of petrified trees. The first drop is the largest, at about 2 feet. The last drop, 40 feet down river, is the second largest, at 1 1/2 feet. Above and below the waterfall, the 10 foot wide river flows placidly through a mature forest of maple, beech and cedar trees.

There's not much of a ravine at this point along the Ravine River. Fractured bedrock juts out of the short rock wall on the far side. Gnarled roots are exposed, clinging tenaciously to the steep sides. The river runs through this peaceful setting, cascading down a series of drops.

There's a great viewing spot in the middle of the river, just below the last cascade. It's an elongated stone covered sandbar. In high water it will be covered, however.

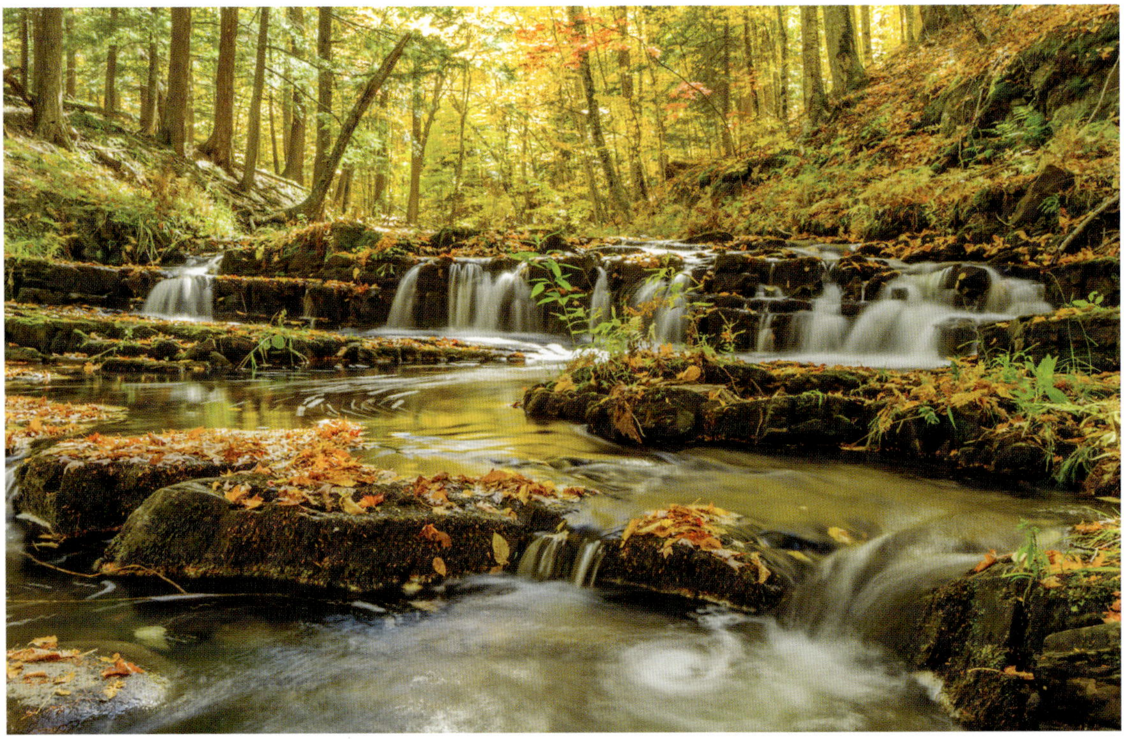

RAVINE RIVER FALLS - LOWER #2 (RAVINE RIVER)

Private

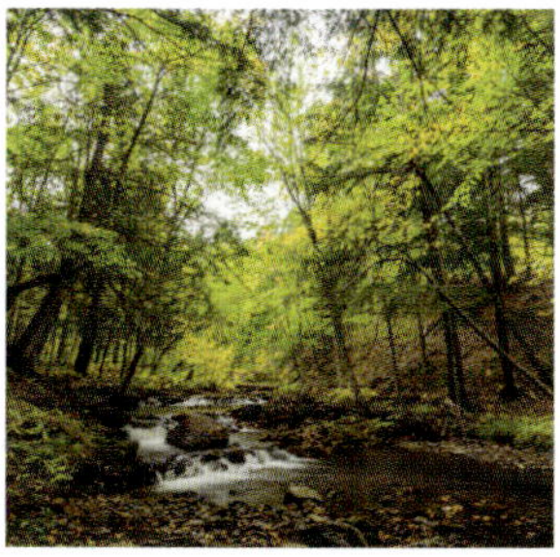

Must See:	4	GPS:	N46 49.563 W88 11.647
Height:	4 feet		
Time:	45-65 minutes	**Hiking Information**	
		Path:	2- track then none
Driving Information		Length:	.30 miles
Signs:	None	Elev. Change:	Moderate
Road:	Gravel	GPS:	Required
Access:	Somewhat Easy	Danger:	Slight
4WD:	N/A	WP Boots:	N/A

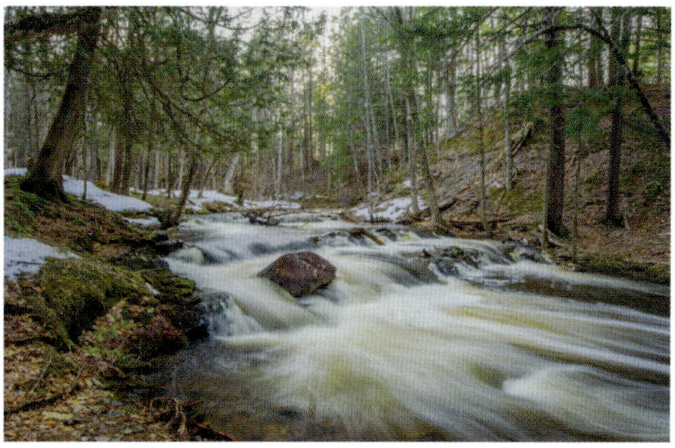

About 170 yards down river from Lower #1, uplifted layers of basalt fight the flow of the water, creating three cascades within 50 feet. A large, faded purple boulder sits in the middle of the last cascade. It feels very much out of place, as though set there by a playful giant. The river narrows a little below these cascades as the far side ravine wall presses in on the river.

Once again, the near side of the river is much easier to hike along than the far side. It's mostly flat and obstruction free from #1, but starts to climb quickly heading downstream.

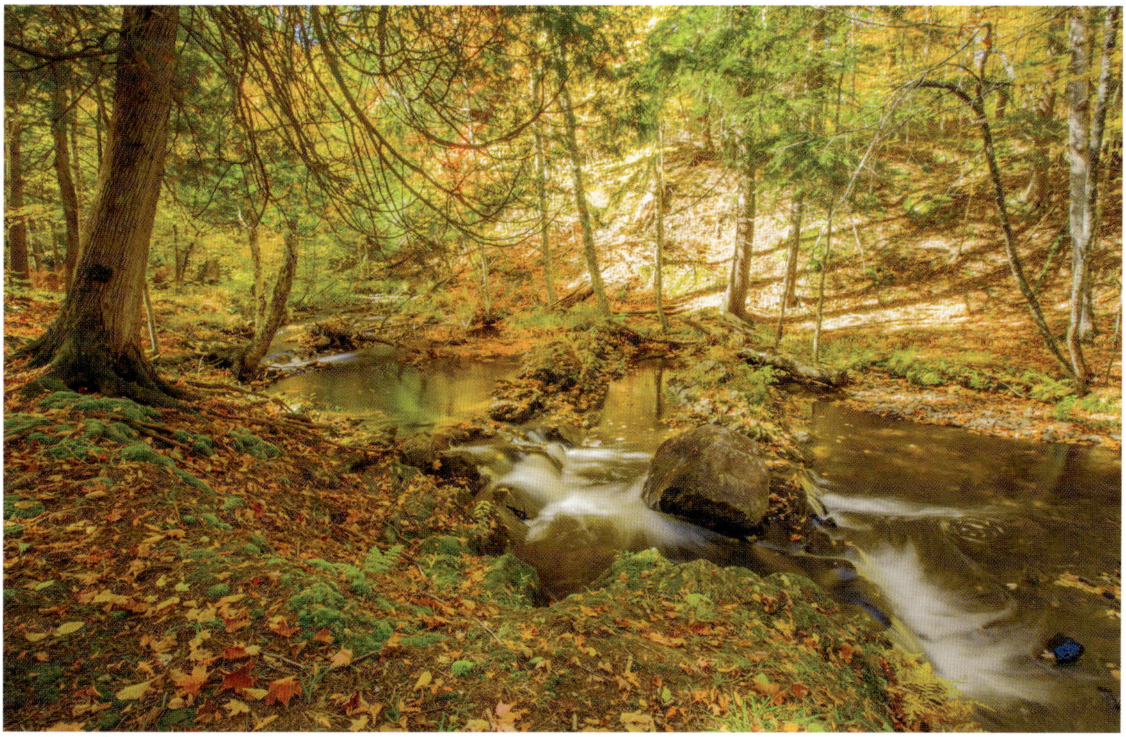

RAVINE RIVER FALLS - LOWER #3 (RAVINE RIVER)

Private

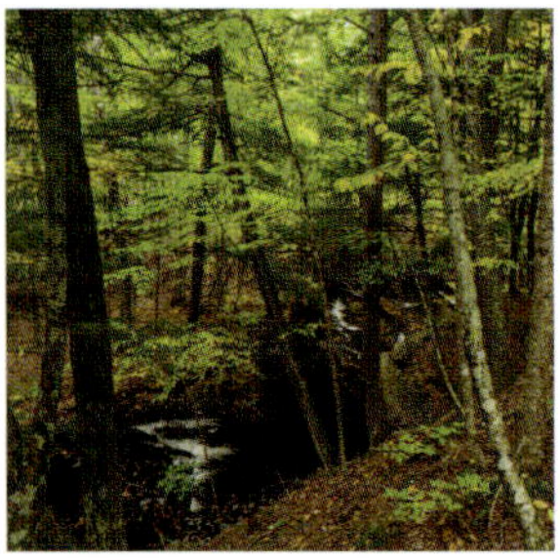

Must See:	4	GPS:	N46 49.607 W88 11.614
Height:	4 feet		
Time:	60-75 minutes	**Hiking Information**	
		Path:	2- track then none
Driving Information		Length:	.37 miles
Signs:	None	Elev. Change:	Moderate
Road:	Gravel	GPS:	Required
Access:	Somewhat Easy	Danger:	Slight
4WD:	N/A	WP Boots:	N/A

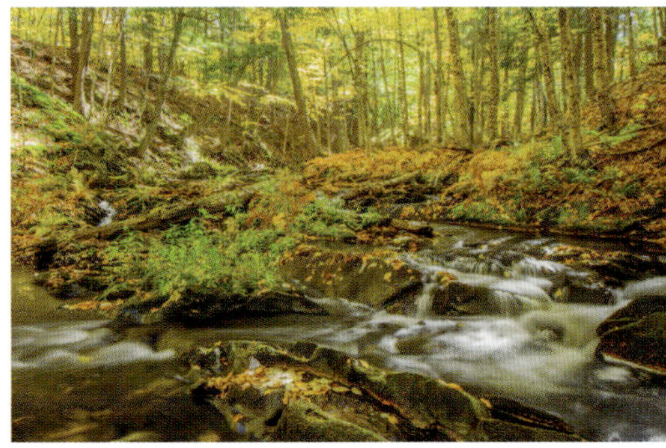

Between #2 and #3, the ravine wall on the near side pushes up against the river, making a walk along the bank impossible. Climb up the 20 foot, relatively steep wall to an old 2-track that runs along the top of the ravine. (Alternately, you can ford the river and walk along the far bank.) It's a short walk along the 2-track before #3 becomes visible down below. The river cascades down segments of the slate bedrock, similar to the waterfalls upstream. This set of drops occurs in a slight "S" curve in the river.

The river makes a slight zig-zag over seven layers of bedrock running back up against the natural flow of the river. This makes for various cascades dropping at various angles. It reminds me of a miniature Bonanza Falls.

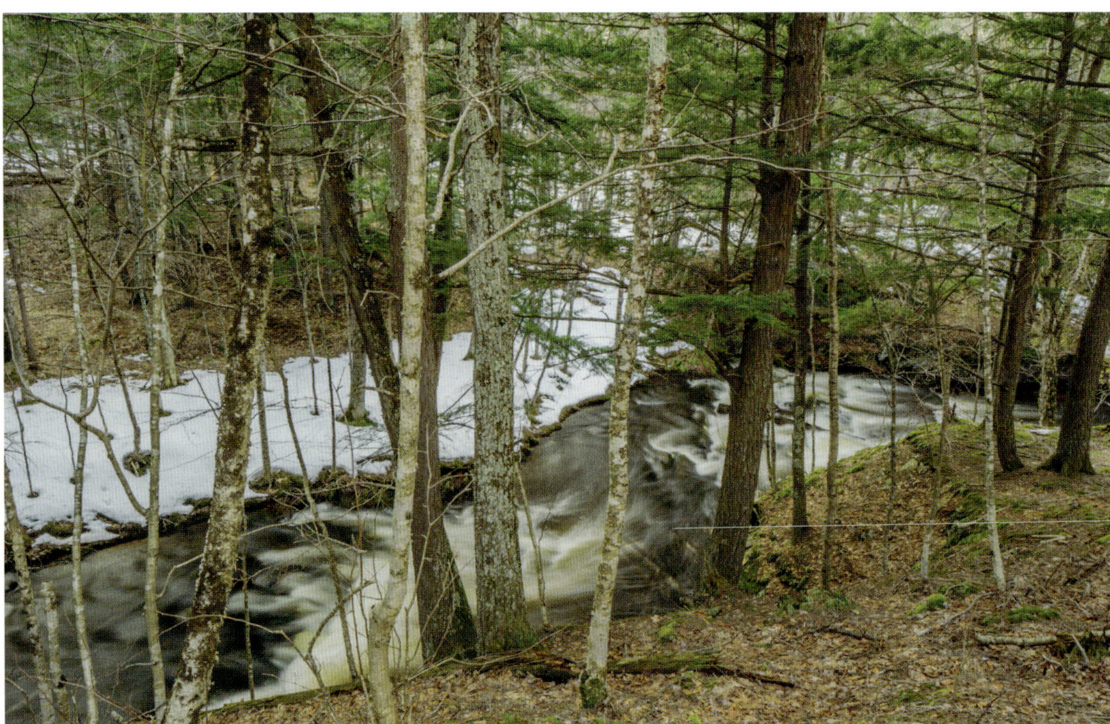

Slate River Falls Hike

Slate River Falls is a wonderful waterfall secreted away at the base of a long, steep, winding ravine. A large sandy area provides for great viewing of the falls and a nice place to take a break after completing this somewhat rigorous hike. Continue upstream when conditions allow to view numerous waterfalls! (The ravine is very steep and runs down to the river in most places, so there is no river's edge to walk along. During high water, the river may be too deep and fast to wade in.)

Directions: Coming from L'Anse on Skanee Road, cross the Slate River bridge (there is a big, wooden sign) and immediately turn right (southeast) on the dirt road. The road doesn't go far, but be looking to your left for a hiking trail that quickly starts climbing the hillside. Park and hike the trail. After 5-10 minutes you will see that you have been paralleling the Slate River, but at a much higher elevation. Nearing the waterfall, the trail dives down into the ravine that it had been running along the top of. This is the most dangerous part of the hike. Be careful on this steep hill, as it seems to be about 100 feet tall and it is easy to start sliding down the hill. With this warning in mind, this is the easiest waterfall to get to on this hike! Climb up above Slate River Falls on the near side of the river and continue upstream, often hiking right up the riverbed to the rest of the falls. After Kuckuk's Falls, I always leave the river, climb up to the top of the ravine (now manageable), and follow the footpath along the top of the ravine back to the vehicle.

SLATE RIVER FALLS (SLATE RIVER)

Private

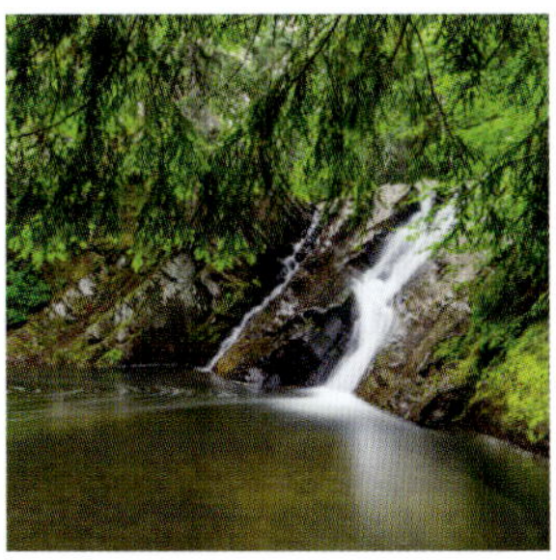

Must See:	8	GPS:	N46 49.874 W88 15.126
Height:	25 feet		
Time:	45-60 minutes	Hiking Information	
Driving Information		Path:	Unimproved Footpath
Signs:	None	Length:	.30 miles
Road:	Dirt	Elev. Change:	Major
Access:	Somewhat Easy	GPS:	Recommended
4WD:	Helpful	Danger:	Moderate
		WP Boots:	Recommended

The walk is fairly strenuous, but the view of the falls is worth it. There is a nice sized landing area to view the falls from. It is a great place for a picnic!

At the end of the trail there is a steep hill (maybe 100 feet high) that needs to be climbed down. There are no steps and only a slight trail. This hike is not for the faint of heart or unsteady of foot.

The viewing area is on the east side of the river

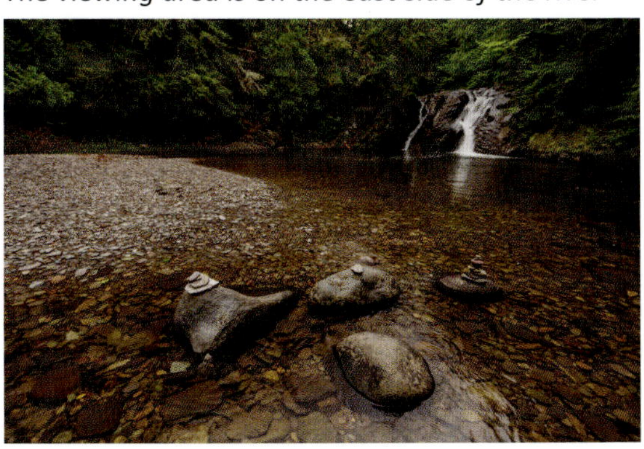

Note the difference in water volume!

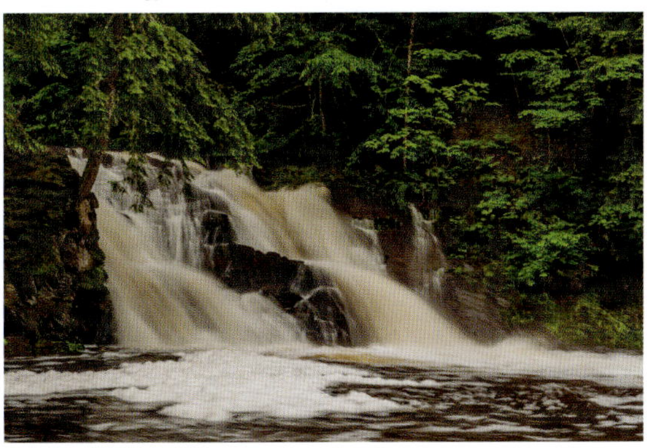

FELTMAN FALLS (SLATE RIVER)

Private

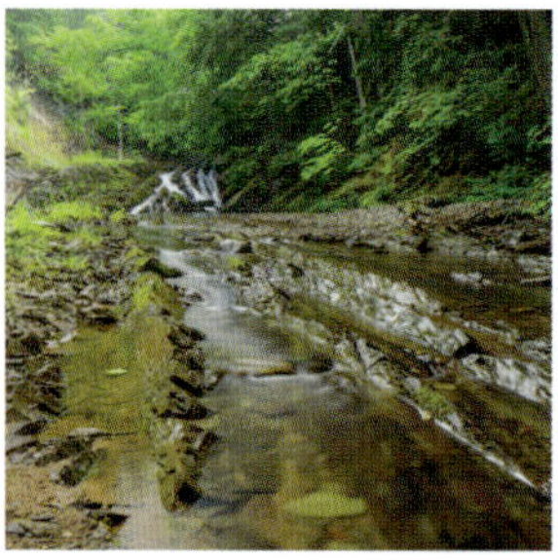

Must See:	6	GPS:	N46 49.853 W88 15.071
Height:	7 feet		
Time:	1-1 1/2 hours	Hiking Information	
		Path:	Footpath then none
Driving Information		Length:	.35 miles
Signs:	None	Elev. Change:	Major
Road:	Dirt	GPS:	Required
Access:	Somewhat Easy	Danger:	Elevated
4WD:	N/A	WP Boots:	Required

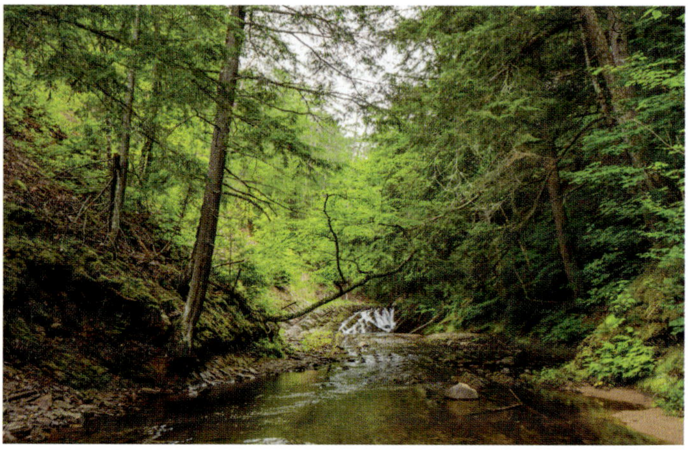

Climb up the left side of Slate River Falls (see the bands of slate on the preceding page just to the left of the waterfall). Layers of slate laid at a 45 degree angle leave exposed ribbons of bedrock running down the riverbed. The river runs through a 70 foot deep ravine with layers of slate exposed nearly to the top. The river was running low when I took these pictures. During high water, this area may too dangerous to hike.

This is named after Douglas Feltman, a fellow waterfall enthusiast, and creator of lovely time-lapse waterfall videos. Check out his Facebook page, "Midwest Waterfalls".

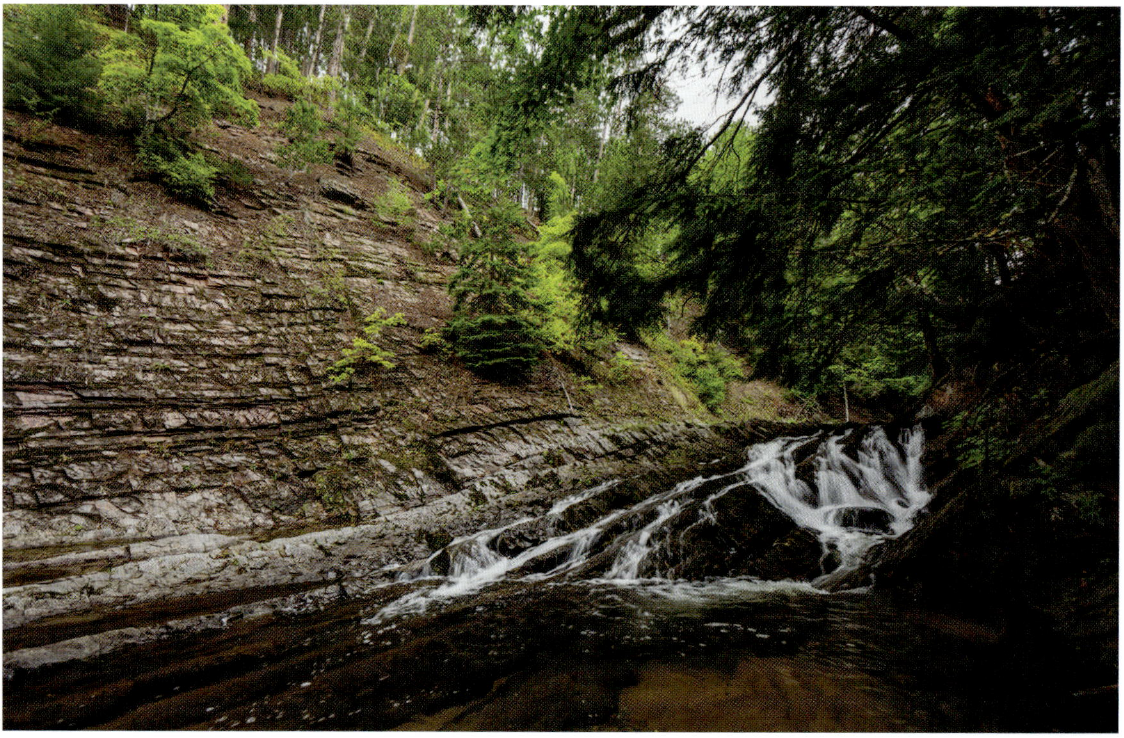

SLATE CORNER FALLS (SLATE RIVER)

Private

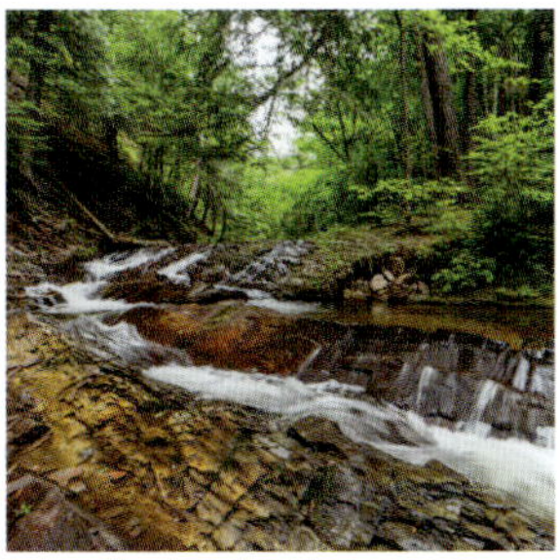

Must See:	5	GPS:	N46 49.815 W88 14.935
Height:	6 feet		
Time:	1 3/4-2 1/4 hours	**Hiking Information**	
		Path:	Footpath then none
Driving Information		Length:	.48 miles
Signs:	None	Elev. Change:	Major
Road:	Dirt	GPS:	Required
Access:	Somewhat Easy	Danger:	Elevated
4WD:	N/A	WP Boots:	Required

Several bends and .13 miles upstream from Feltman Falls, the river slides over slanted bands of slate at about a 45 degree angle. At "normal" river depth, I would guess that two of the bands would be exposed making a double drop. At the base of the falls the river turns hard to the left. There is bedrock to be seen everywhere, and very little vegetation along the waterway - it's rugged terrain.

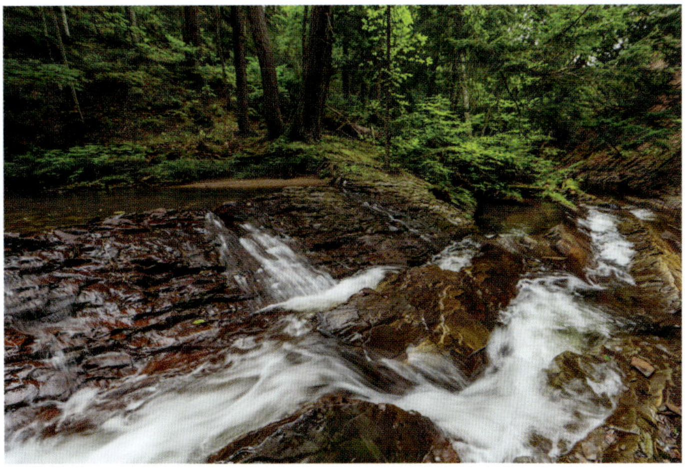

Note the amazing layers - severly angled and twisted around the corner

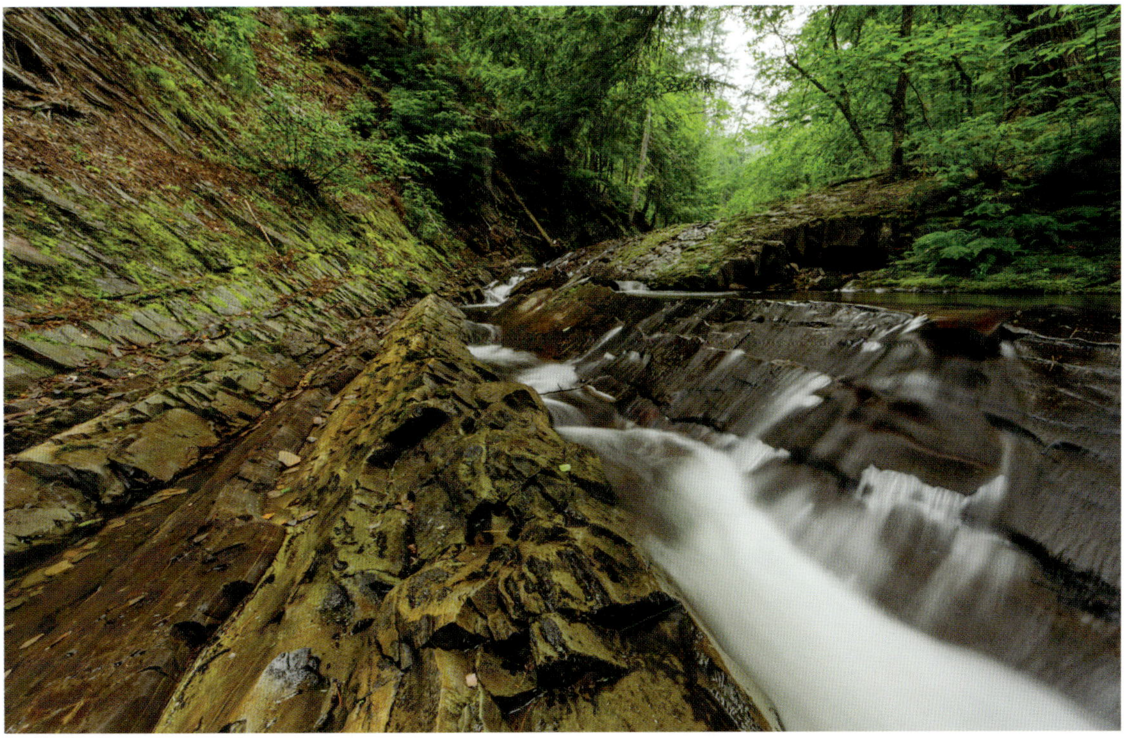

ECSTASY CASCADES (SLATE RIVER)

Private

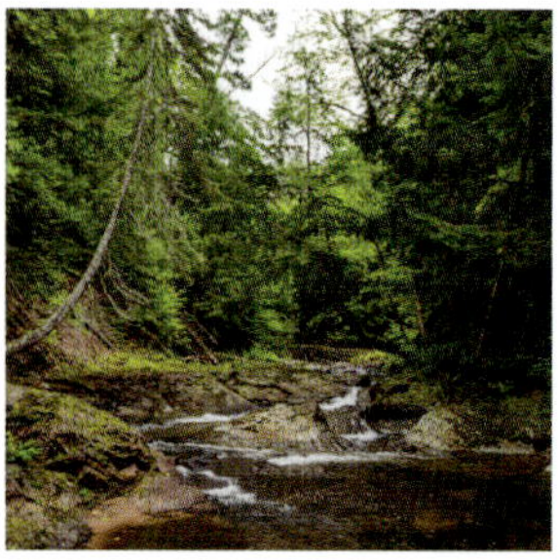

Must See:	3	GPS:	N46 49.788 W88 14.905
Height:	10 feet		
Time:	2-2 1/2 hours	**Hiking Information**	
		Path:	Footpath then none
Driving Information		Length:	.52 miles
Signs:	None	Elev. Change:	Major
Road:	Dirt	GPS:	Required
Access:	Somewhat Easy	Danger:	Elevated
4WD:	N/A	WP Boots:	Required

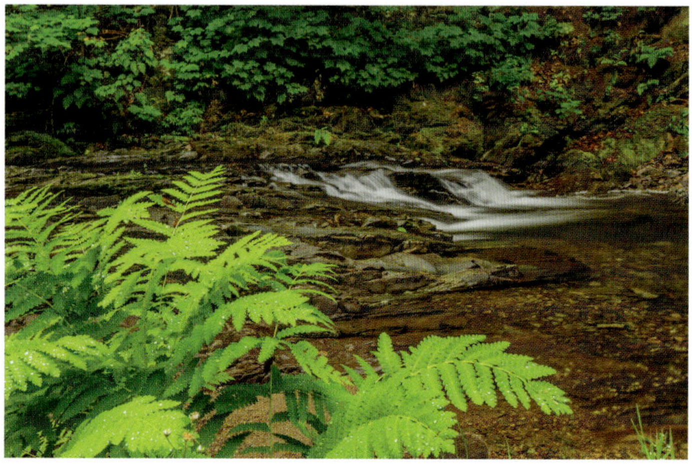

Hike upstream 75 yards from the Slate Corner Falls. It's a straight stretch of river bed and about 1/3 of the way between the Corner Falls and the spectacular Lower Ecstasy Falls.

The cascades start as a series of 6-10 inch high drops with last being a 2 foot drop into a little spill pool. The river then makes an "S" curve with another small drop half way through it. It ends with the main portion of the river channeled through a narrow rock trough. The cascades are situated below a nearly vertical 50 foot tall rock face. A large pine sits precariously at the top, keeping watch over the river far below.

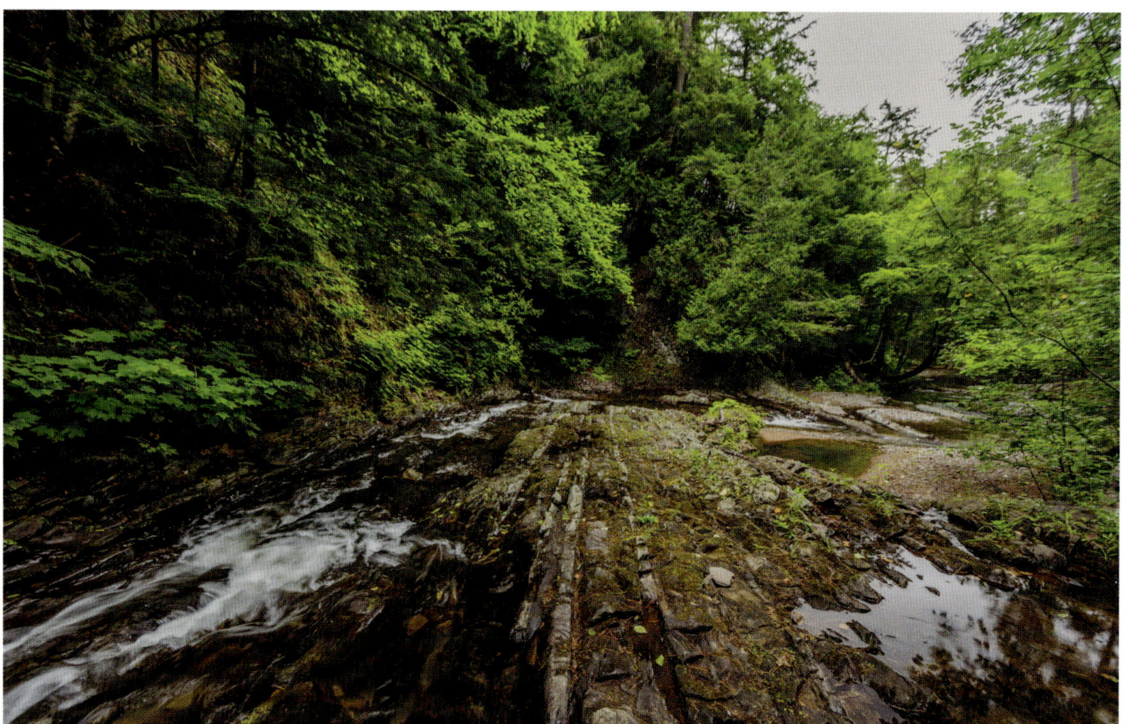

ECSTASY FALLS - LOWER (SLATE RIVER)

Private

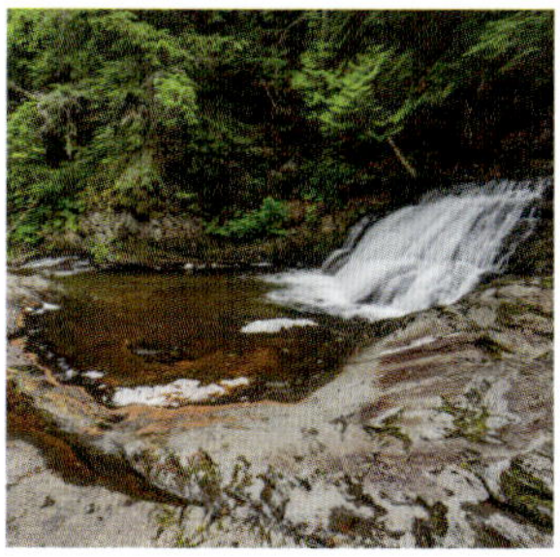

Must See:	8	GPS:	N46 49.734 W88 14.859
Height:	10 feet		
Time:	2 1/4-2 3/4 hours	Hiking Information	
		Path:	Footpath then none
Driving Information		Length:	.61 miles
Signs:	None	Elev. Change:	Major
Road:	Dirt	GPS:	Required
Access:	Somewhat Easy	Danger:	Elevated
4WD:	N/A	WP Boots:	Required

Upstream about 150 yards from the Cascades is the Lower Ecstasy Falls. It is much narrower, and more spectacular during low water periods.

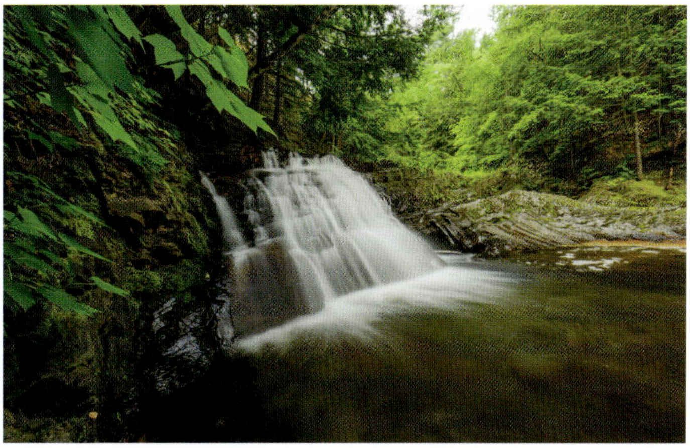

The Lower Ecstasy Falls is a very traditional, 8 foot, slightly rounded cascading waterfall with a small 2 foot drop below the spill pool. There is a convenient stony viewing area along the side and below the main drop. When the river is high it may be under water.

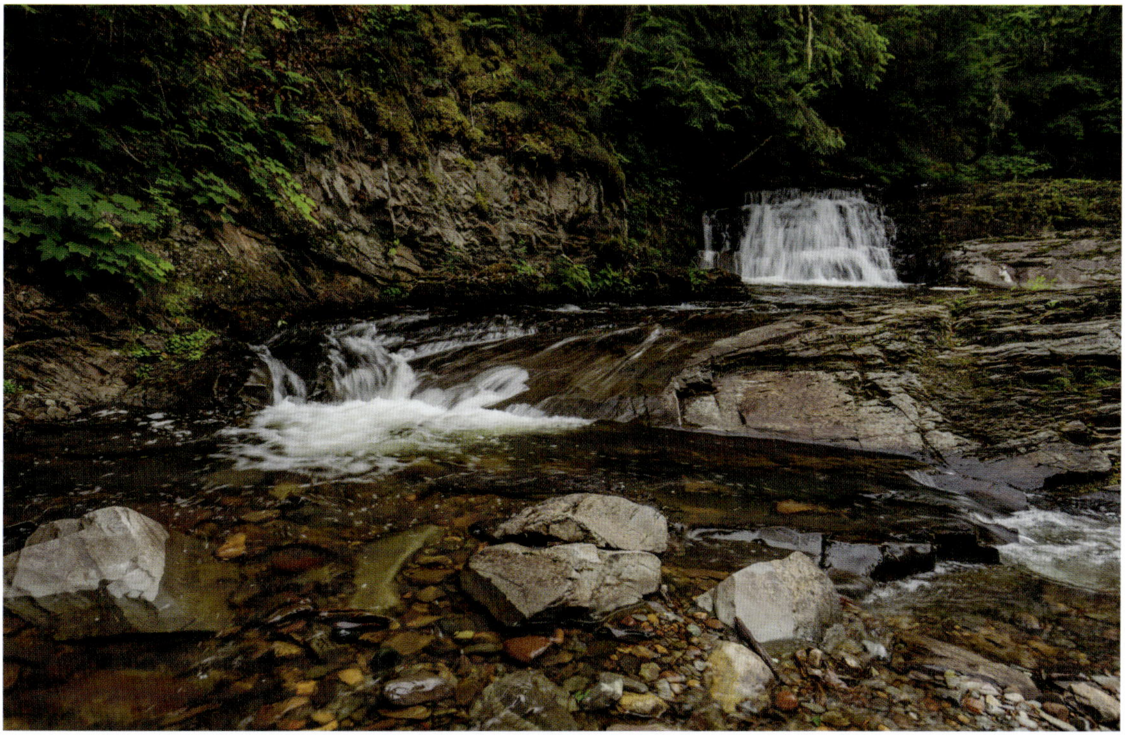

ECSTASY FALLS (SLATE RIVER)

Private

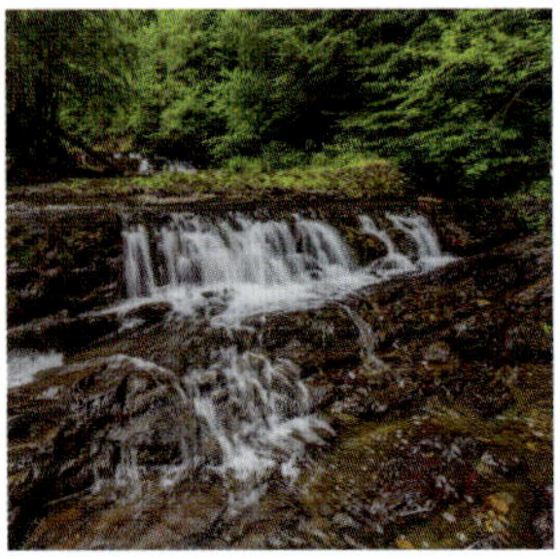

Must See:	7	GPS:	N46 49.727 W88 14.892
Height:	12 feet		
Time:	2 1/2-3 hours	Hiking Information	
		Path:	Footpath then none
Driving Information		Length:	.64 miles
Signs:	None	Elev. Change:	Major
Road:	Dirt	GPS:	Required
Access:	Somewhat Easy	Danger:	Elevated
4WD:	N/A	WP Boots:	Required

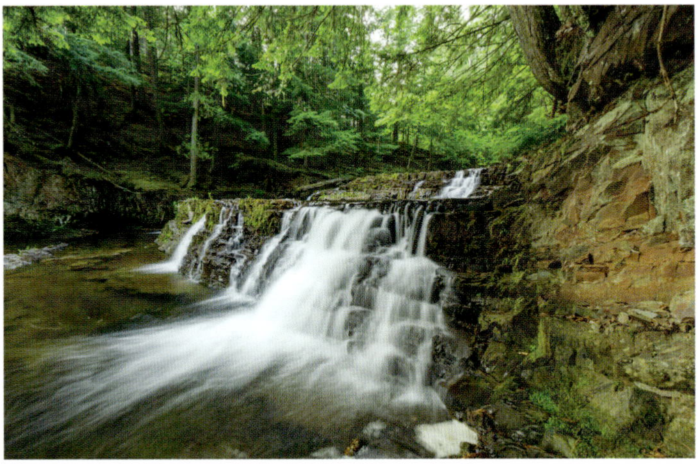

Just 50 yards upstream from Lower Ecstasy Falls, the river runs wall to wall, much wider than at the Lower Falls. It, therefore, takes a lot more water to fill out the wide cascades. I haven't seen it in these conditions yet. A difficulty in viewing this waterfall with high water is getting to it! The river can be dangerous, as much of the hiking needs to take place in the riverbed.

Although there are 4 cascades in this set of falls, the most prominent drops are a parallel batch of cascades that have rounded fronts like dams bulging to the bursting point. Water spills over them at random points when the water level is low, as seen here.

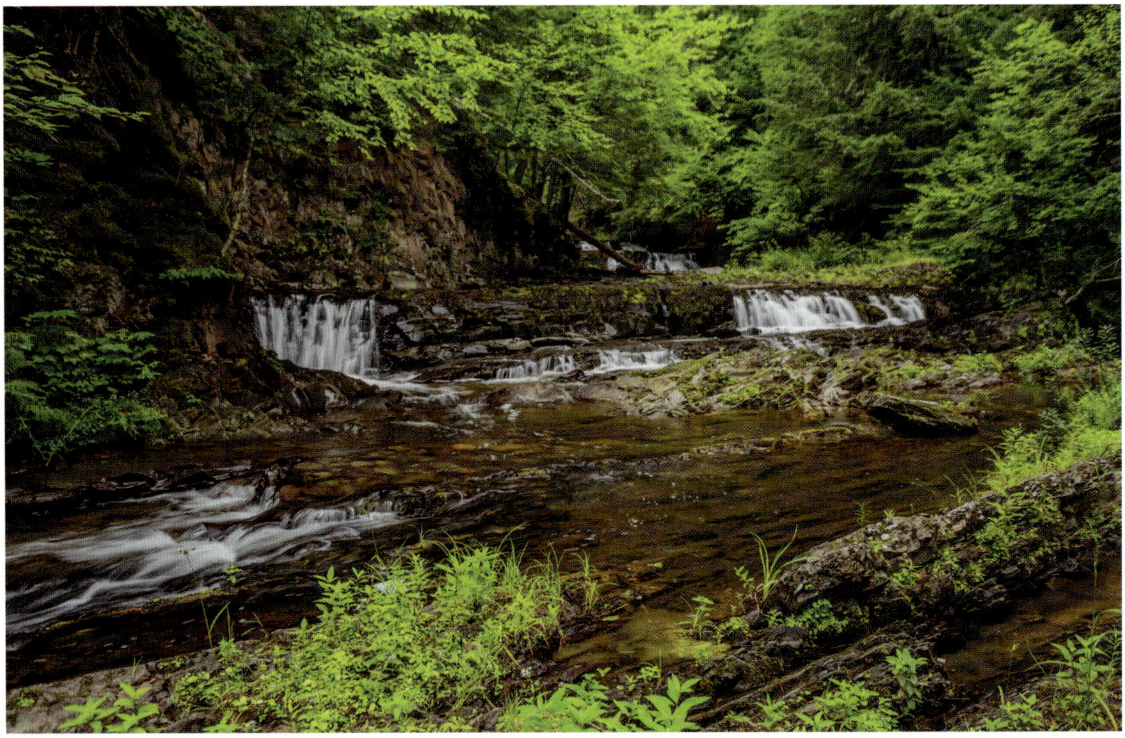

ECSTASY FALLS - UPPER (SLATE RIVER)

Private

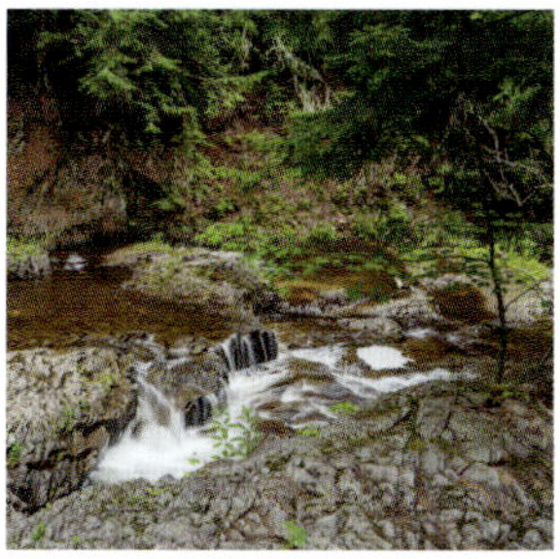

Must See:	4	GPS:	N46 49.692 W88 14.928
Height:	4 feet		
Time:	2 3/4-3 1/4 hours	Hiking Information	
		Path:	Footpath then none
Driving Information		Length:	.69 miles
Signs:	None	Elev. Change:	Major
Road:	Dirt	GPS:	Required
Access:	Somewhat Easy	Danger:	Elevated
4WD:	N/A	WP Boots:	Required

The river runs through a trough below the cliff face. This waterfall is just above Ecstasy Falls. The river hugs the cliff side of the river. Imagine wading up the river in high water conditions. The pocked and layered riverbed would be treacherous to navigate.

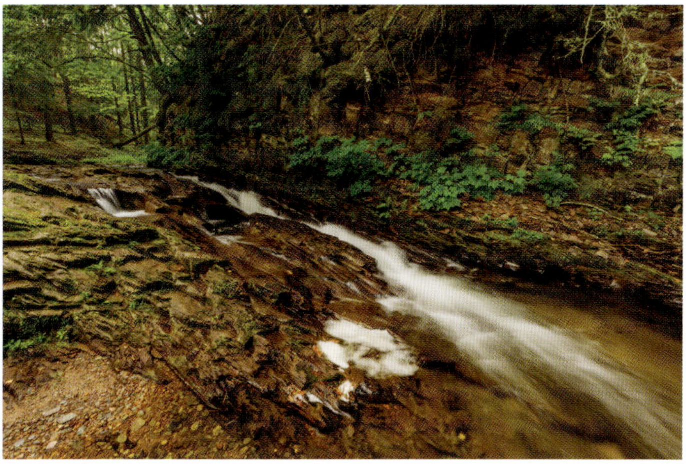

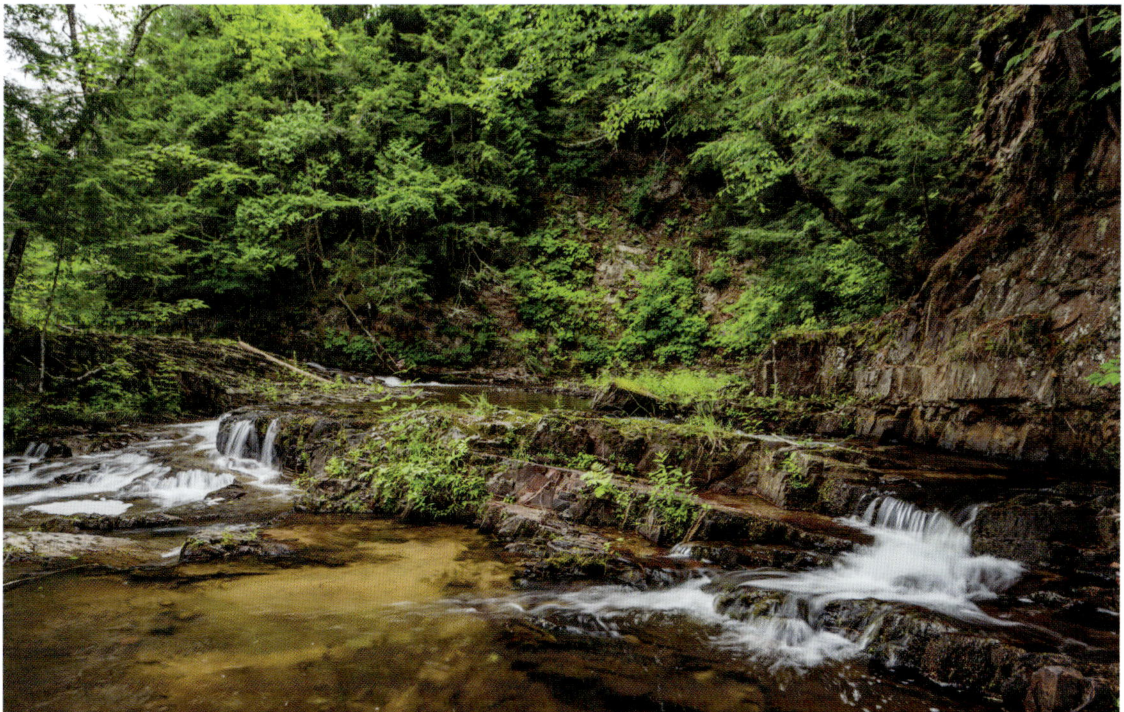

BARAGA COUNTY

SLATE SLIDE (SLATE RIVER)

Private

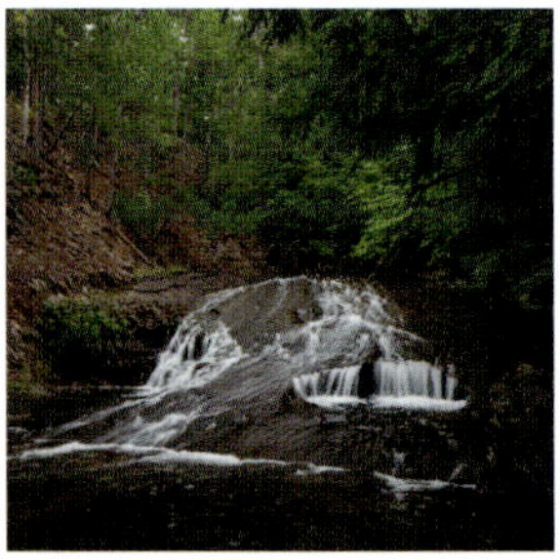

Must See:	6	GPS:	N46 49.658 W88 14.892
Height:	10 feet		
Time:	3 1/2-4 hours	Hiking Information	
		Path:	Footpath then none
Driving Information		Length:	.74 miles
Signs:	None	Elev. Change:	Major
Road:	Dirt	GPS:	Required
Access:	Somewhat Easy	Danger:	Elevated
4WD:	N/A	WP Boots:	Required

Continue .10 miles upstream past a couple of bends for a special treat!

The aptly named waterfall took me by surprise when I first saw it. It is such a smooth, point-to-point face it hardly seemed natural. The edges of the slide have eroded away, leaving drops on either side.

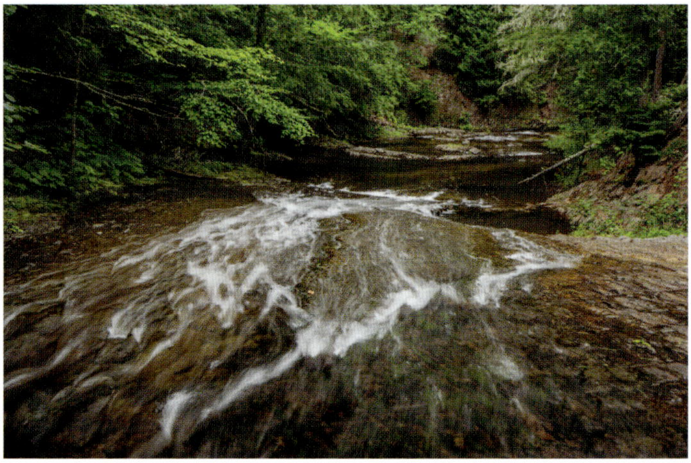

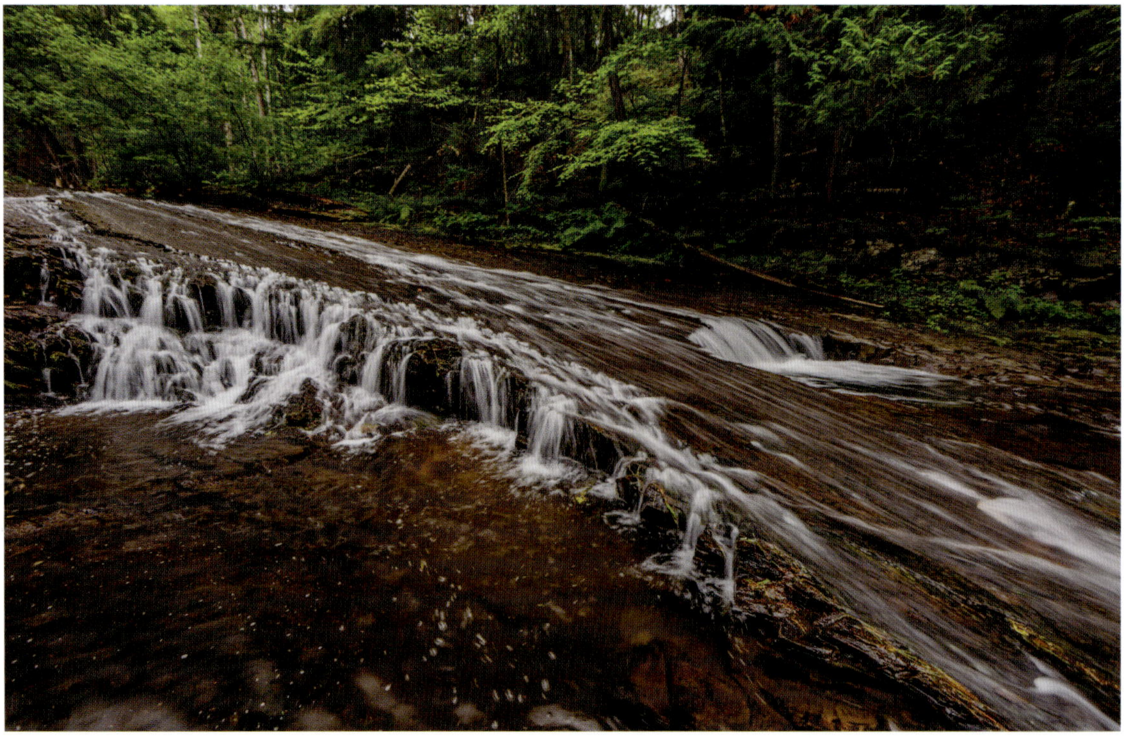

KUCKUK'S FALLS (SLATE RIVER)

Private

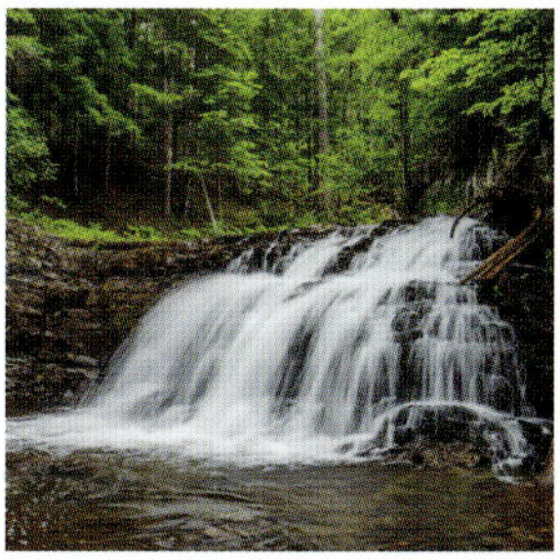

Must See:	8
Height:	14 feet
Time:	4-4 1/2 hours

Driving Information	
Signs:	None
Road:	Dirt
Access:	Somewhat Easy
4WD:	N/A

GPS:	N46 49.571 W88 14.787

Hiking Information	
Path:	Footpath then none
Length:	.92 miles
Elev. Change:	Major
GPS:	Required
Danger:	Elevated
WP Boots:	Required

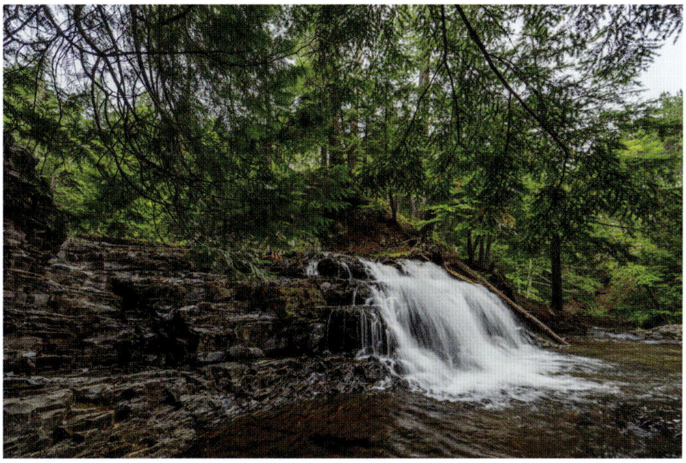

It's quite a stretch between Slate Slide and Kuckuk's Falls. Hike the .18 miles, with just a couple ripples in the river along the way. But the hike ends with this great waterfall!

The river makes a hairpin turn as soon as it falls over the main cascades. It then quickly shoots down another 4 feet of small drops and slides to continue on its way down through a flatter section of riverbed. The steep ravine is much calmer at this point in the river. Climb up the left side of the river to the footpath that follows the top of the ravine. It is a much faster hike back to the vehicle!

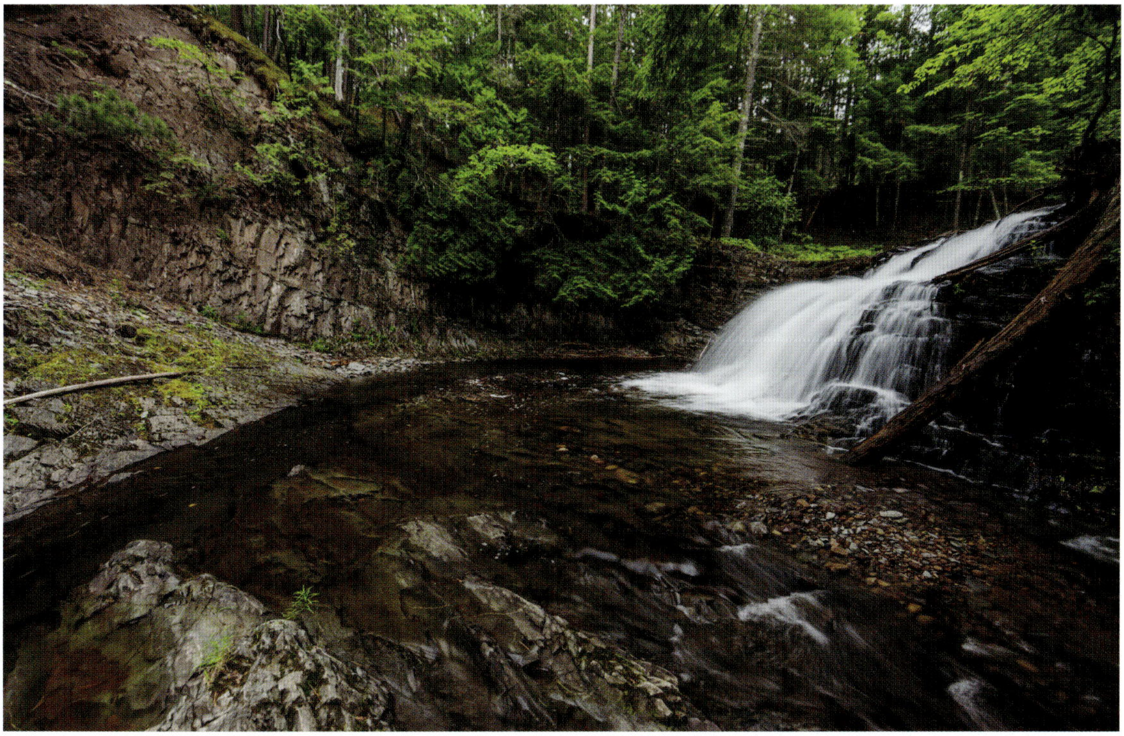

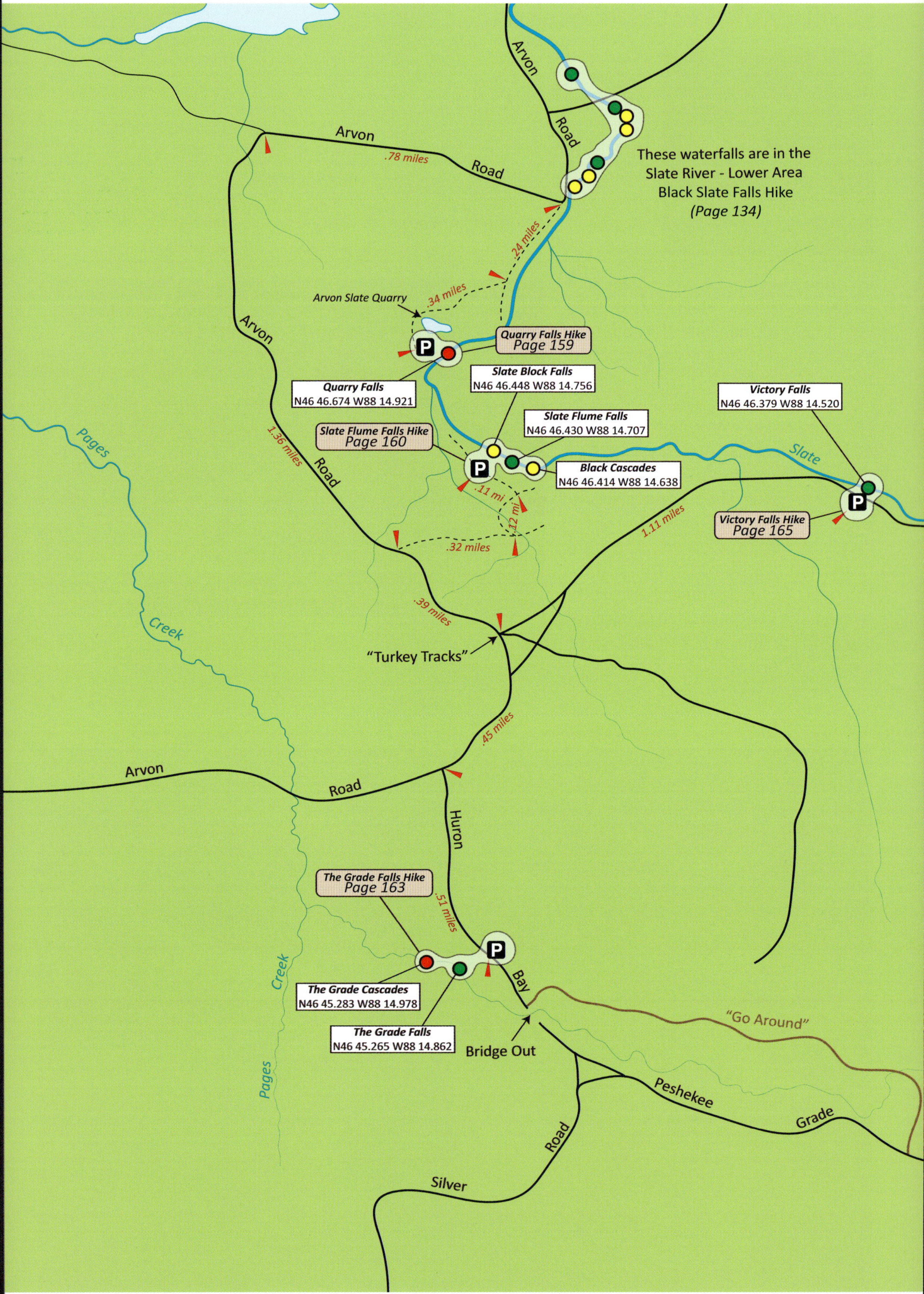
These waterfalls are in the Slate River - Lower Area Black Slate Falls Hike (Page 134)
Arvon Road
.78 miles
.24 miles
.34 miles
Arvon Slate Quarry
Quarry Falls Hike Page 159
Quarry Falls N46 46.674 W88 14.921
Slate Block Falls N46 46.448 W88 14.756
Slate Flume Falls N46 46.430 W88 14.707
Slate Flume Falls Hike Page 160
Black Cascades N46 46.414 W88 14.638
Victory Falls N46 46.379 W88 14.520
Victory Falls Hike Page 165
Slate
1.36 miles
.11 mi
.12 mi
.32 miles
1.11 miles
.39 miles
"Turkey Tracks"
.45 miles
Pages Creek
Huron Bay
.51 miles
The Grade Falls Hike Page 163
The Grade Cascades N46 45.283 W88 14.978
The Grade Falls N46 45.265 W88 14.862
Bridge Out
"Go Around"
Peshekee Grade
Silver Road

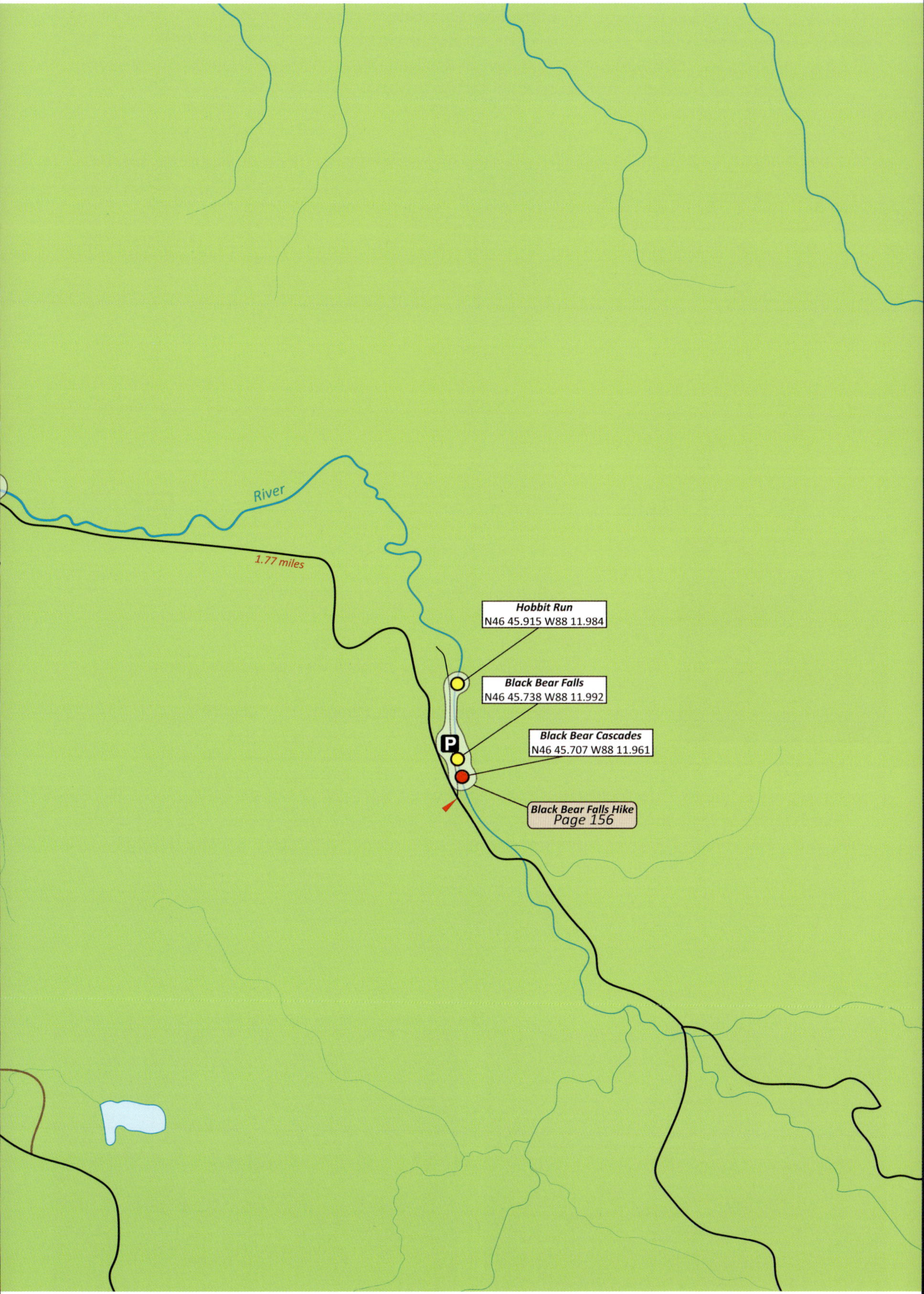
River
1.77 miles
Hobbit Run
N46 45.915 W88 11.984
Black Bear Falls
N46 45.738 W88 11.992
Black Bear Cascades
N46 45.707 W88 11.961
P
Black Bear Falls Hike
Page 156

Black Bear Falls Hike

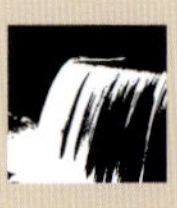

The peak of Mount Arvon, the highest point in Michigan, is just 2 miles to the east. The western side of the mountain drains into the Slate River and its tributaries. In the upper reaches of the river, we have several easy to access waterfalls.

Directions: Turn southeast onto Arvon Road off of Skanee Road. (This is the first main dirt road southwest of the Slate River.) Follow Arvon Road in a generally southerly direction for 3.7 miles. Arvon Road turns to the right (west). Follow it for .78 miles. Arvon turns to the left. Follow it to the "Turkey Tracks" (1.75 miles). Turn left (northeast). Follow the winding road for 2.88 miles. An old 2-track cuts back hard to the left (north). Follow it for .10 miles. Park on the side of the road. Black Bear Falls is easily viewed through the thin tree line. Hike upstream to the cascades or downstream (follow the road) to get to Hobbit Run. (Both are 100 yards from Black Bear Falls.)

BLACK BEAR FALLS (SLATE RIVER)

Private

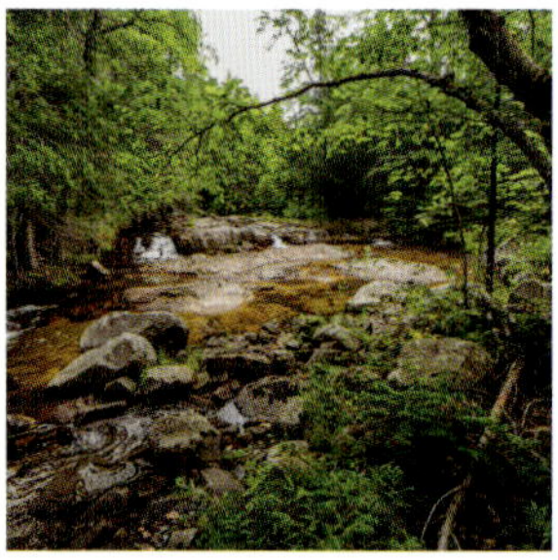

Must See:	6	GPS:	N46 45.738 W88 11.992
Height:	5 feet		
Time:	5-10 minutes	Hiking Information	
		Path:	N/A
Driving Information		Length:	30 feet
Signs:	None	Elev. Change:	Minor
Road:	2-track	GPS:	Helpful
Access:	Somewhat Difficult	Danger:	Slight
4WD:	N/A	WP Boots:	N/A

Dusty brown bedrock is widened out to 100 feet at the waterfall. The uneven mass produces several cascades across its width. After gathering itself together at the base of the 5 foot waterfall, the river turns hard, which gives a great viewing area mere feet from the 2-track amidst scattered boulders, maple, birch, and cedar. The river continues downstream, running through a narrow channel next to the 2-track with Hobbit Run 100 yards downstream.

The view from the road

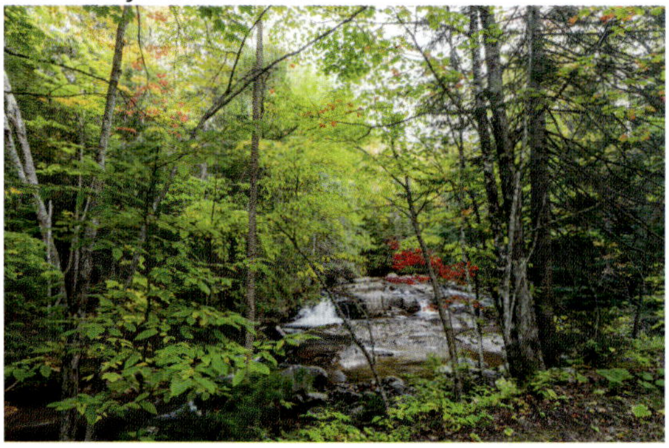

The view from the base of the falls - on dry land

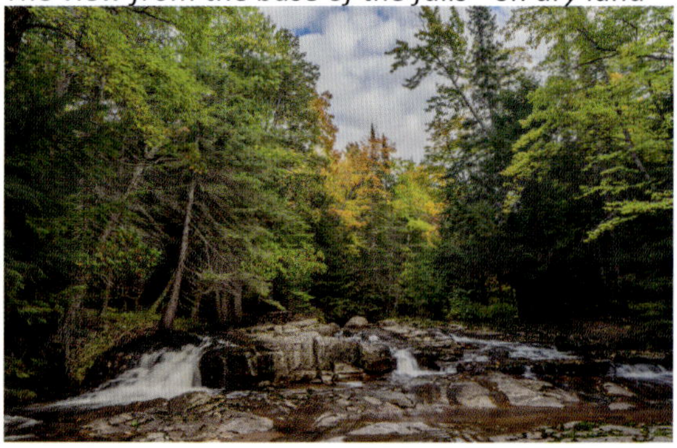

BLACK BEAR CASCADES (SLATE RIVER)

Private

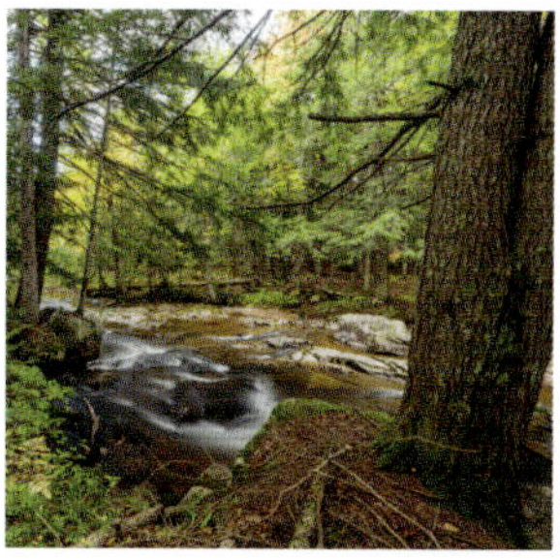

Must See:	2	GPS:	N46 45.707 W88 11.961
Height:	4 feet		
Time:	10-20 minutes	**Hiking Information**	
		Path:	None
Driving Information		Length:	100 yards
Signs:	None	Elev. Change:	Minor
Road:	2-track	GPS:	Helpful
Access:	Somewhat Difficult	Danger:	Slight
4WD:	N/A	WP Boots:	N/A

Hike 100 yards upstream along the side of the river. There is some undergrowth along the way, but its manageable. An alternate route is to hike (or drive) back down the 2-track (south) 75 yards to a small gravel pit. Go to the back of the gravel pit. You'll see the river 50 feet through the trees. That is the bottom end of the cascades.

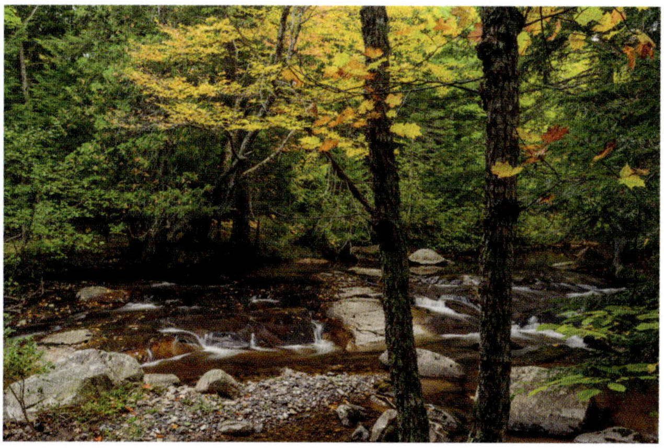

The widened river flows over undulated masses of brown bedrock. Interestingly, this far upstream, the Slate River does NOT flow over slate! Fist sized rocks piled up at the base of the cascades form an island topped with tall wildflowers.

Hike upstream another 125 yards for more small cascades

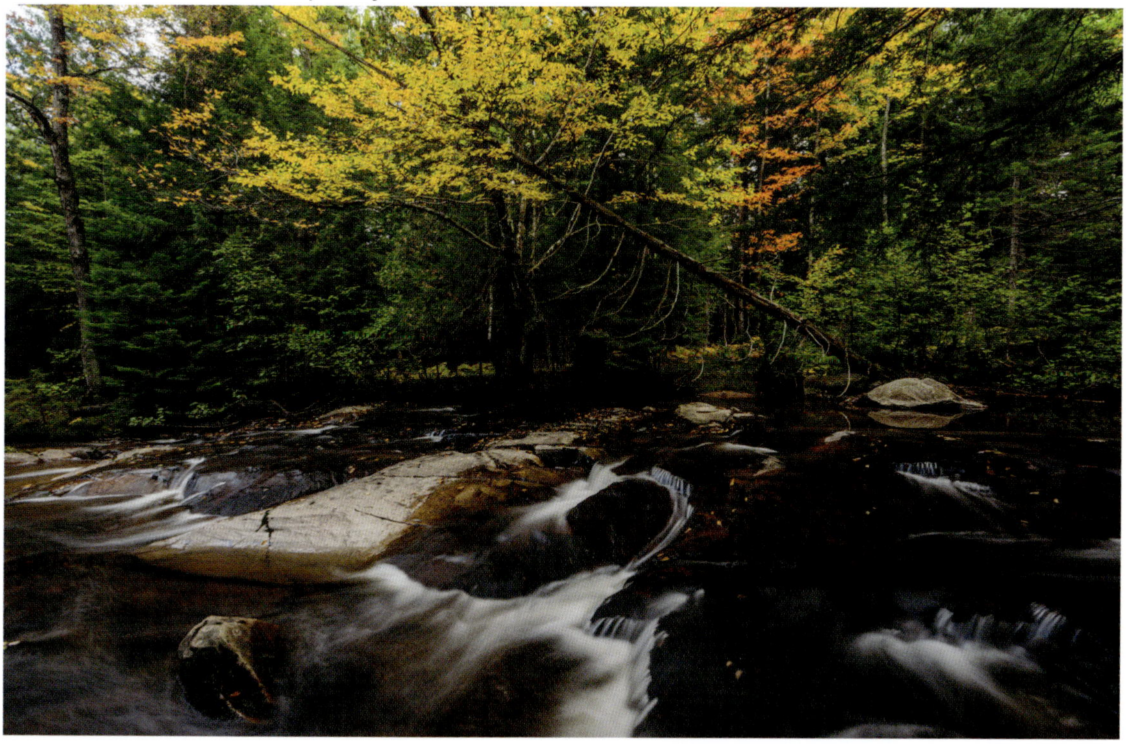

HOBBIT RUN (SLATE RIVER)

Private

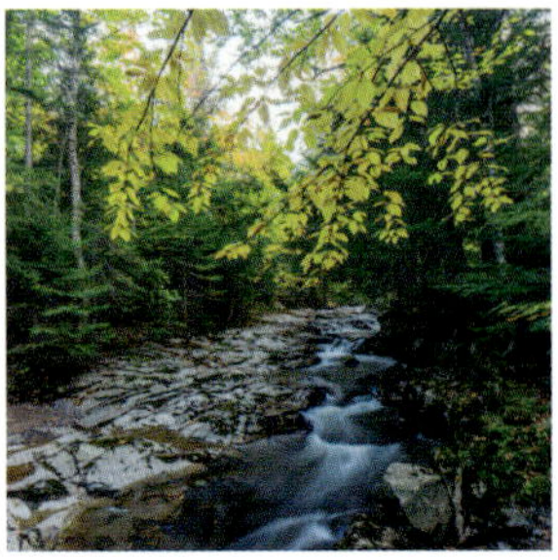

Must See:	5	GPS:	N46 45.915 W88 11.984
Height:	4 feet		
Time:	10-20 minutes	**Hiking Information**	
		Path:	None
Driving Information		Length:	100 yards
Signs:	None	Elev. Change:	Minor
Road:	2-track	GPS:	Helpful
Access:	Somewhat Difficult	Danger:	Slight
4WD:	N/A	WP Boots:	N/A

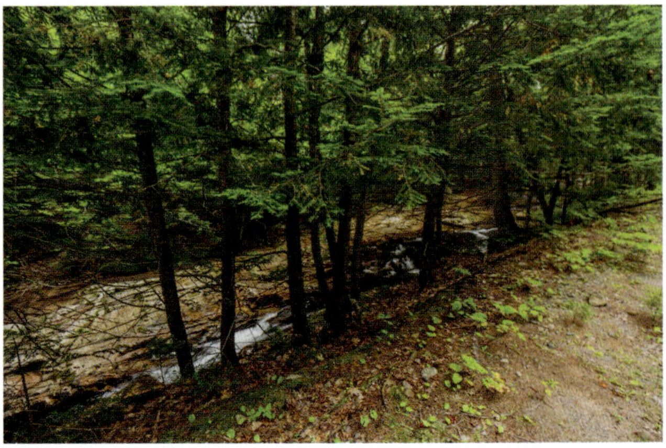

Follow the 2-track downstream (north) 100 yards from Black Bear Falls. The river, once again, is just feet away. There is a short climb down to the river, with a limited viewing area.

Out here in the heart of the Huron Mountains, Hobbit Run (named by my wife for its peaceful, idyllic setting) is shrouded beneath over arching hemlock, cedar and birch trees. The river, only 20 feet wide at this point, is lined with stately gray boulders. The Run is generally divided into two sections. The first tier, on the far side of the river, is the taller of the drops, a squared face running at a sharp angle. A large triangular boulder sits at the far end, as though wedged in place by a youthful giant, seeing if he could dam up the river. The second tier, which is on the near side, is shorter in length. It parallels the first with multiple cascades pouring along its length. The river is calm below the Run, a mossy bank the perfect place for a picnic lunch.

This shot shows the two tiers well. The picture just above was taken from the 2-track.

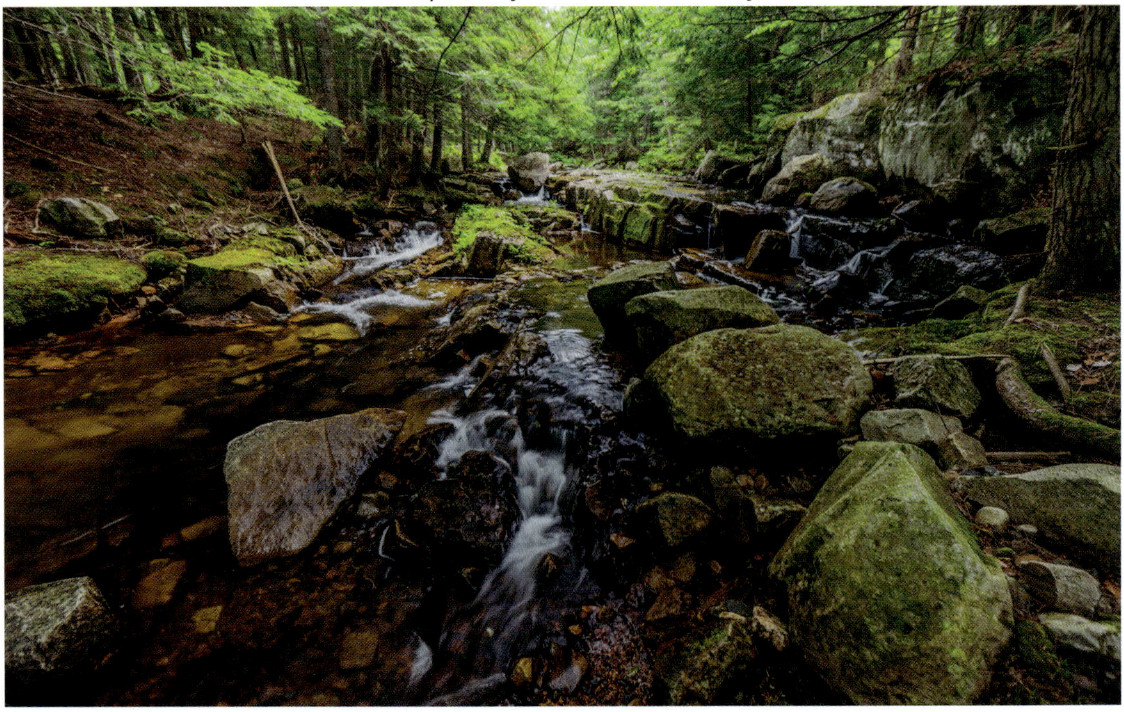

Quarry Falls Hike

The Arvon Slate Quarry, once a bustling site, is now a calm pond surrounded by mountains of waste rock. The houses are gone, but some apple trees remain. Alongside one of the many slate piles the Slate River runs and a small waterfall gurgles.

Directions: Turn southeast onto Arvon Road off of Skanee Road. (This is the first main dirt road southwest of the Slate River.) Follow Arvon Road in a generally southerly direction for 3.7 miles. Arvon Road turns to the right (west), but continue on straight on a 2-track for .24 miles. Turn right (west) onto another 2-track. Follow it for .34 miles. (You will pass the Arvon Quarry Pond). Park by the waste rock. Hike along the side of the slate piles and over to the waterfall. (It's possible to drive right up to the waterfall on the 1st 2-track that follows the river, but this 2-track has some VERY deep holes that may bury your vehicle.)

QUARRY FALLS (SLATE RIVER)

Private

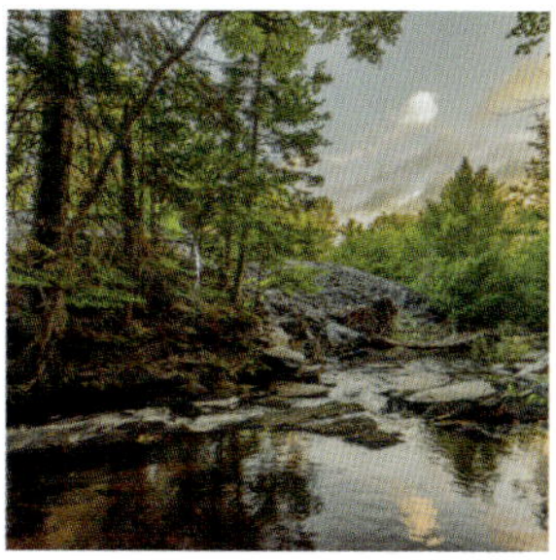

Must See:	3	GPS:	N46 46.674 W88 14.921
Height:	2 feet		
Time:	20-30 minutes	Hiking Information	
		Path:	N/A
Driving Information		Length:	150 yards
Signs:	None	Elev. Change:	Minor
Road:	2-track	GPS:	Recommended
Access:	Somewhat Difficult	Danger:	Slight
4WD:	Recommended	WP Boots:	N/A

A 2 foot drop lies at the base of a broken slate pile, outcasts from the Arvon Quarry that has long since closed. Slate shingles and chalkboards have been replaced with more economical products. The angular waterfall runs through the rock-choked riverbed.

The 2-track along the Slate River

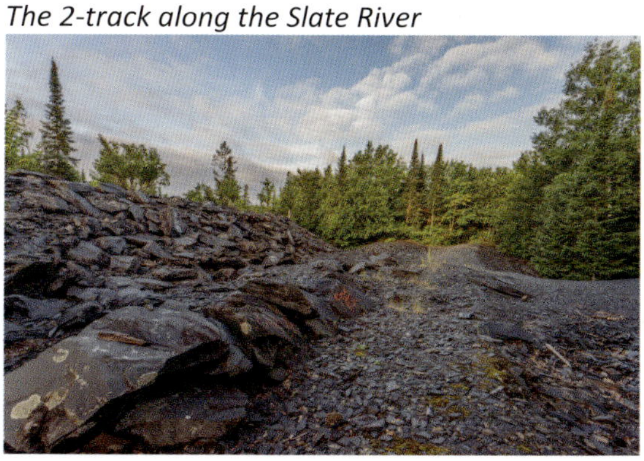

Looking upstream past the small cascade

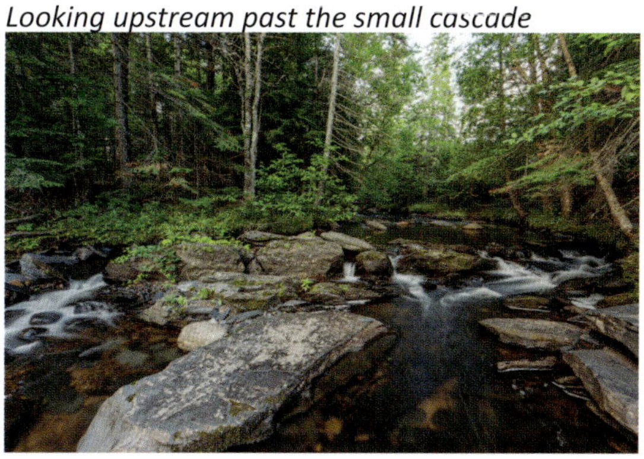

Slate Flume Falls Hike

This hike is unique. It starts by passing by lovely stacked slate from a long ago abandoned quarry. Soon after, the river appears with a trio of interesting waterfalls bunched together and ripe for exploring.

Directions: Turn southeast onto Arvon Road off of Skanee Road. (This is the first main dirt road southwest of the Slate River.) Follow Arvon Road in a generally southerly direction for 3.7 miles. Arvon Road turns to the right (west). Follow it for .78 miles. Arvon turns to the left. Follow it for 1.36 miles to a narrow 2-track on the left. Turn left (east) for .32 miles. Turn left (north) onto another 2-track. Follow it for .12 miles to a 2-track that intersects from the left (northwest). Park, unless you have a high clearance vehicle. Hike or drive down the intersecting 2-track for .11 miles. Pull off of the 2-track and park (no obvious parking spot here). Hike through the woods past meticulously piled slate and over to Slate Block Falls. (Use a GPS) Follow the river upstream to the rest of the falls.

SLATE BLOCK FALLS (SLATE RIVER)

Private

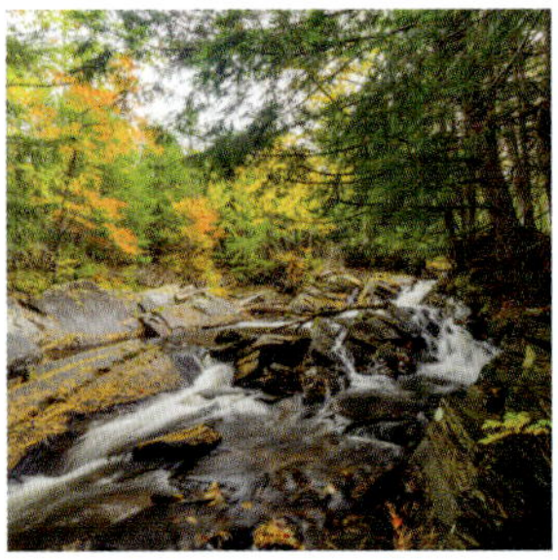

Must See:	5	GPS:	N46 46.448 W88 14.756
Height:	8 feet		
Time:	20-30 minutes	Hiking Information	
		Path:	N/A
Driving Information		Length:	80 yards
Signs:	None	Elev. Change:	Minor
Road:	2-track	GPS:	Required
Access:	Difficult	Danger:	Minor
4WD:	Recommended	WP Boots:	N/A

This rugged section of the Slate River contains a 2-stage waterfall. The top half, a 5 foot cascade, tumbles around squarish black slate blocks. The river settles into a short pool and then cascades down another 3 feet through severely angled slate sheets. The narrow, 20 foot wide riverbed is shrouded by cedar boughs, the trees growing close along the shallow banked river. A smattering of birch, maple, oak, and ironwood complete the thick forest.

Looking down from the top of the waterfall

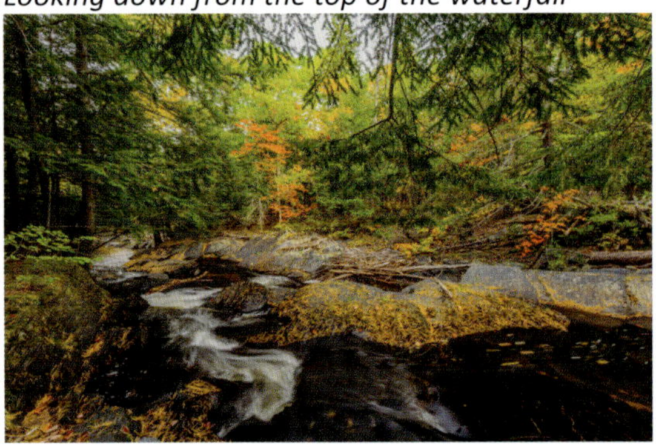

The slate piles from an old quarry

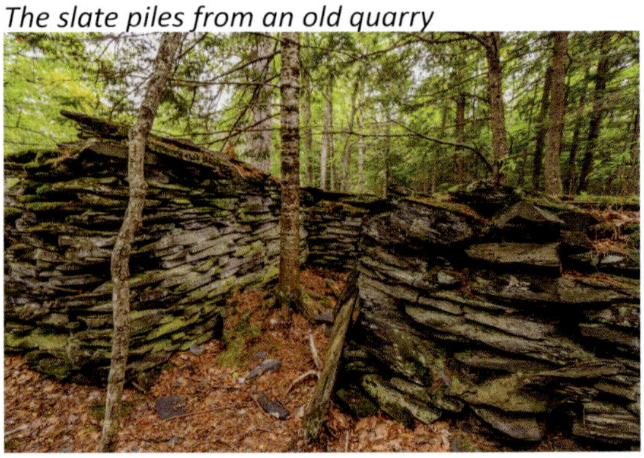

SLATE FLUME FALLS (SLATE RIVER)

Private

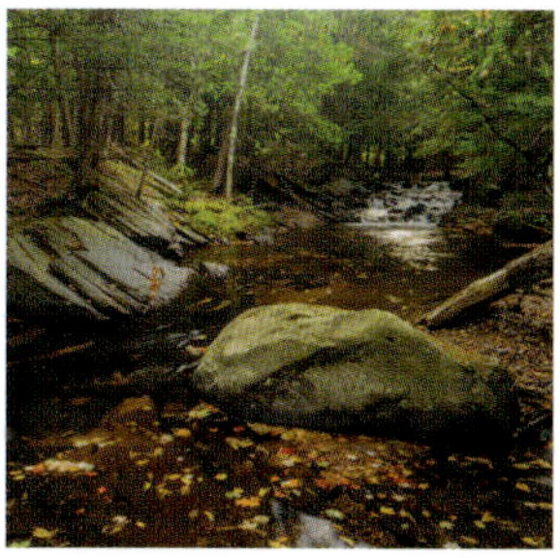

Must See:	7	GPS:	N46 46.430 W88 14.707
Height:	8 feet		
Time:	30-40 minutes	**Hiking Information**	
		Path:	None
Driving Information		Length:	175 yards
Signs:	None	Elev. Change:	Minor
Road:	2-track	GPS:	Required
Access:	Difficult	Danger:	Minor
4WD:	N/A	WP Boots:	N/A

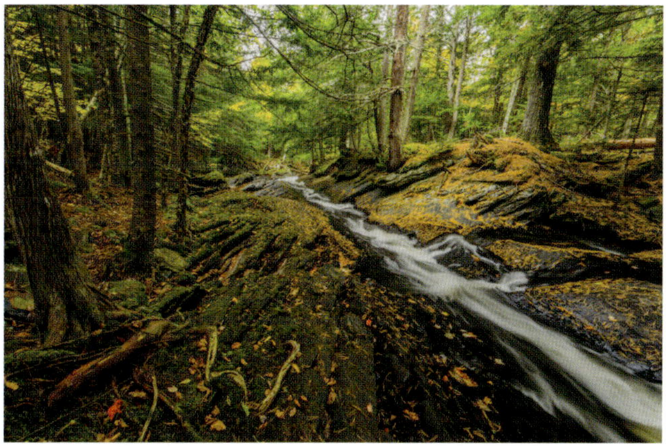

Climb up the 5 foot bank at Slate Block Falls and follow the river upstream for 65 yards. Climb back down the short, steep bank to the rocky riverbed.

A long trough guides the Slate River down a narrow "V", ending in a short plunge. As the river level rises, it overflows the flume, spilling excess water into a surprisingly deep chasm that is well below the level of the riverbed.

Along the side of the rugged Slate River, a host of hemlock and cedar look on. The severely angled bedrock present a striking contrast to the numerous vertical tree trunks set in the mature forest.

The look from the base - the shot above was taken looking down the narrow flume from the top

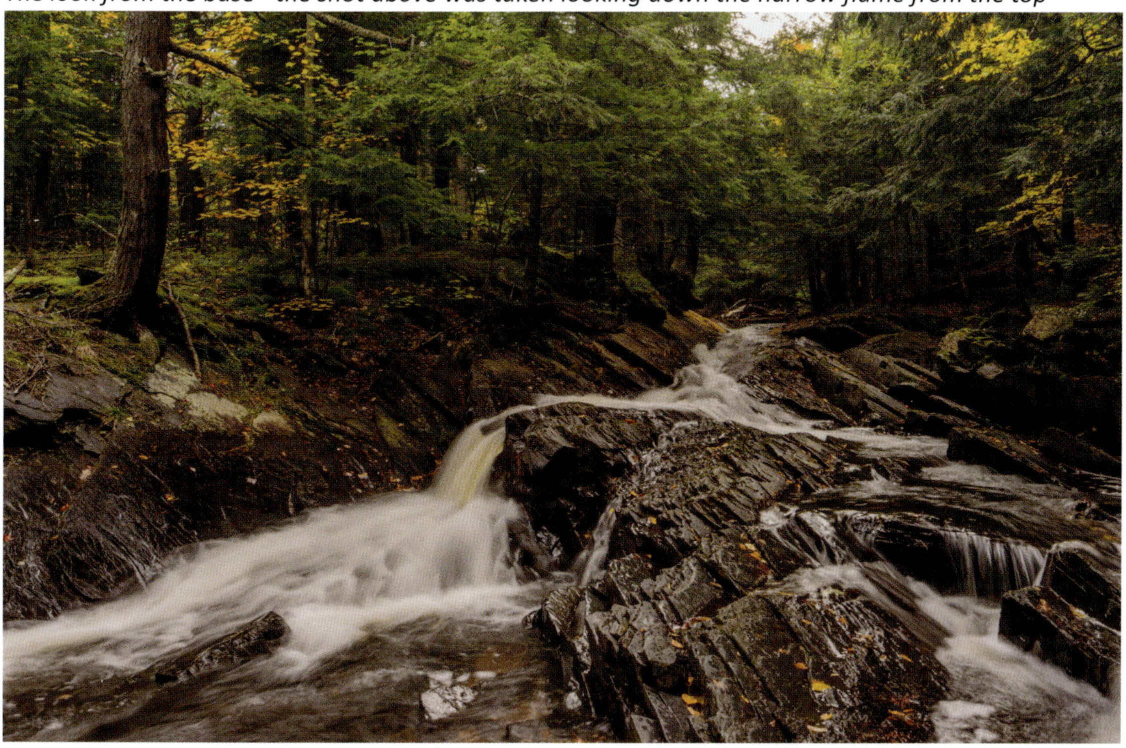

BLACK CASCADES (SLATE RIVER)

Private

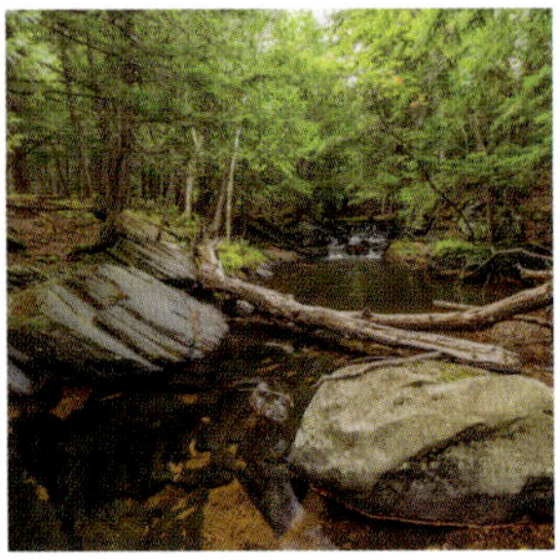

Must See:	5	GPS:	N46 46.414 W88 14.638
Height:	6 feet		
Time:	40-50 minutes	**Hiking Information**	
		Path:	None
Driving Information		Length:	.15 miles
Signs:	None	Elev. Change:	Minor
Road:	2-track	GPS:	Required
Access:	Difficult	Danger:	Minor
4WD:	N/A	WP Boots:	N/A

Continue upstream from Slate Flume Falls for 100 yards. Up ahead you'll see that the Slate River makes a bend. The river starts cascading down toward you from there over rough slate bedrock. Rugged black layers on both sides of the river add to the mystique. The river channel is 10 feet wide and is cut through angled black stone. The river churns through the fractured waterway to a relatively deep spill pool. Colored pebbles form a crescent shaped sandbar for a pleasant viewing experience at the far end of the pool.

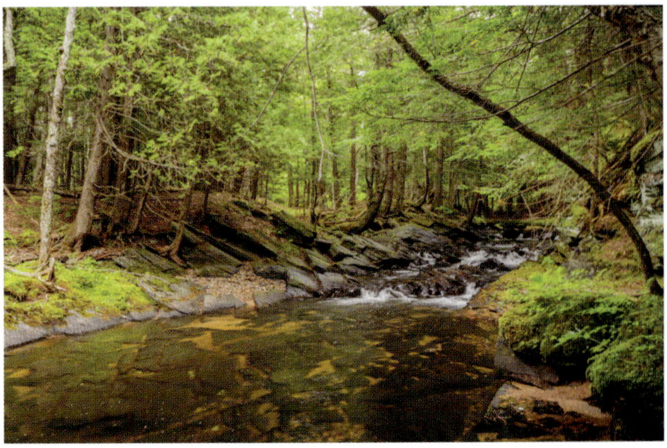

Rugged bedrock is abundant. Fortunately, the river is only cut several feet deep into the forest floor.

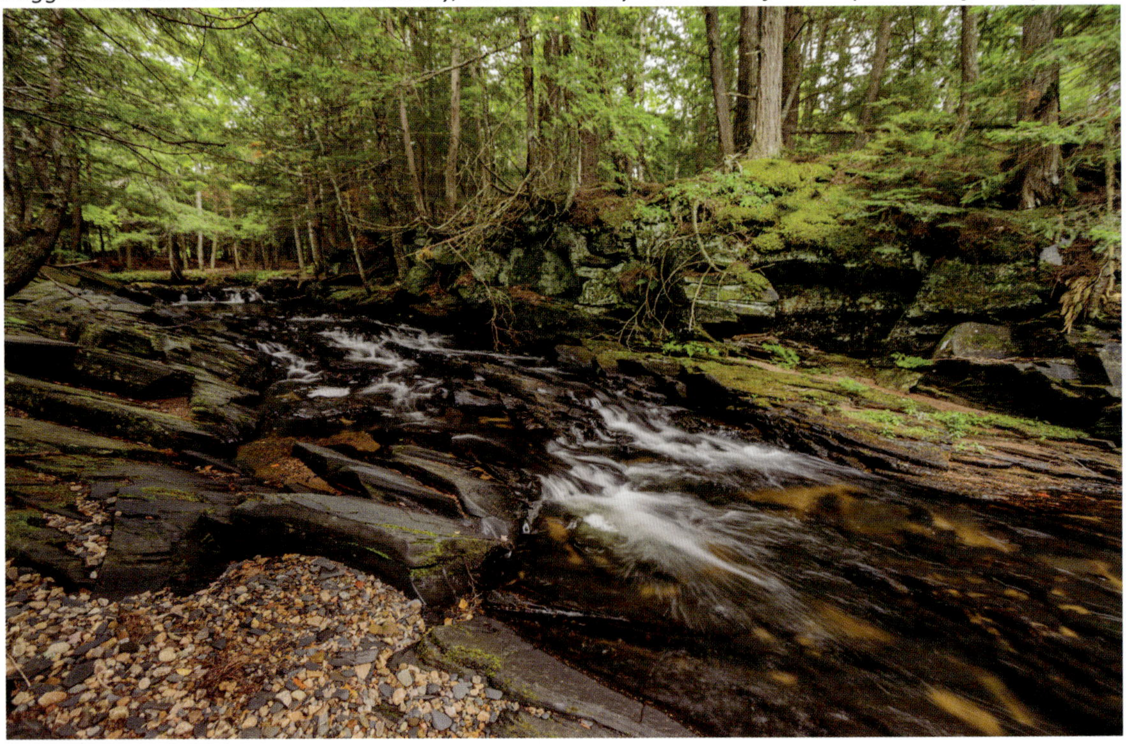

The Grade Falls Hike

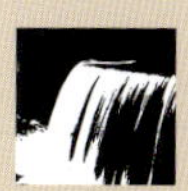

The Huron Bay - Peshekee Grade is an old railroad grade turned into road. This portion of the grade follows the southern side of a mountain that is 3 miles west of Mount Arvon. The runoff from this unnamed mountain is carried into Pages Creek via a small tributary. This is where The Grade Falls and Cascades are found.

Directions: Turn southeast onto Arvon Road off of Skanee Road. (This is the first main dirt road southwest of the Slate River.) Follow Arvon Road in a generally southerly direction for 3.7 miles. Arvon Road turns to the right (west). Follow it for .78 miles. Arvon turns to the left. Follow it for 1.75 miles. Turn right (south) at the Turkey Tracks. In .45 miles turn left onto another gravel road (Huron Bay - Peshekee Grade). In .51 miles park on the left (northeast) side of the road. There is an old 2-track and a bit of a clearing here - probably from logging activity. Hike southwest to the GPS coordinates for The Grade Falls. There are some old overgrown logging trails that may be of help on the short hike downhill toward the waterfall. It's only 130 yards, but there is no trail or signage.

THE GRADE FALLS (UNNAMED TRIBUTARY)

Private

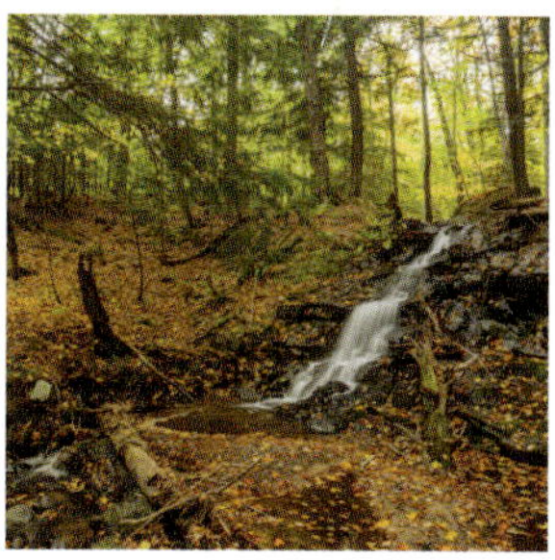

Must See: 7
Height: 12 feet
Time: 20-40 minutes

Driving Information
Signs: None
Road: Gravel
Access: Difficult
4WD: N/A

GPS: N46 45.265 W88 14.862

Hiking Information
Path: None
Length: 130 yards
Elev. Change: Minor
GPS: Required
Danger: Minor
WP Boots: N/A

After parking, cross the road and hike the faint logging trail down toward the waterfall. It's about 350 feet with mostly no trail and a fair amount of undergrowth along the way.

A large boulder sits to the side of the rocky stream just above the waterfall. The tributary then pours over a solid rock ridge and enters a gently sloped ravine. It flows through the stone-filled waterway that meanders in the midst of a peaceful, open forest. It's a great place to enjoy a waterfall!

This tributary can dry up during summer months. Try to go after a good rain.

The waterway up above the waterfall

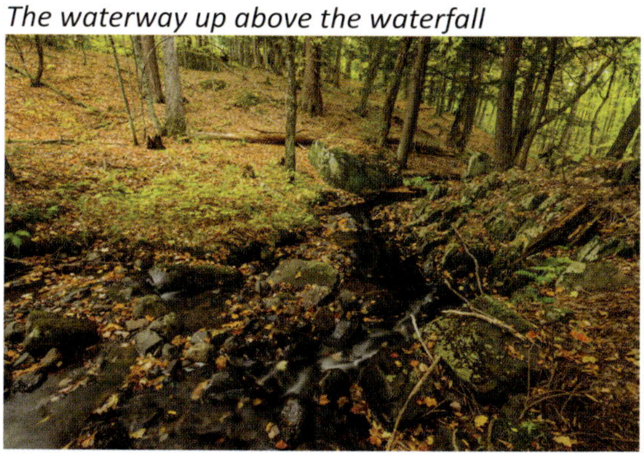

The beautiful, open forest below the waterfall

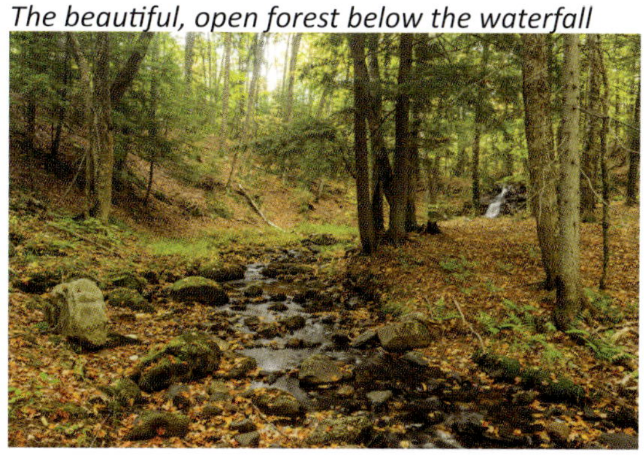

THE GRADE CASCADES (UNNAMED TRIBUTARY)

Private

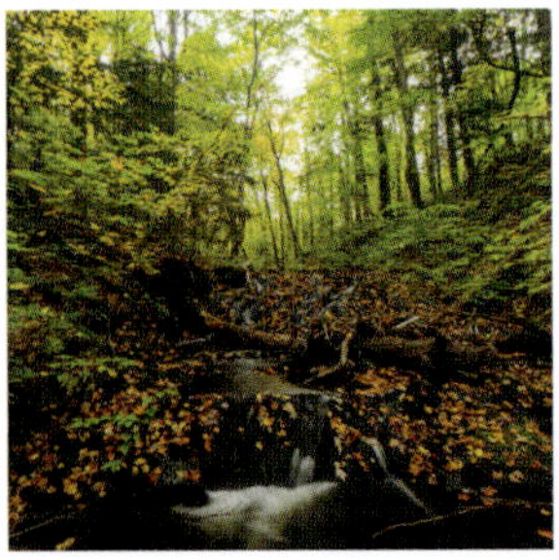

Must See:	2	GPS:	N46 45.283 W88 14.978
Height:	12 feet		
Time:	40-50 minutes	**Hiking Information**	
		Path:	None
Driving Information		Length:	.17 miles
Signs:	None	Elev. Change:	Moderate
Road:	Gravel	GPS:	Required
Access:	Difficult	Danger:	Minor
4WD:	N/A	WP Boots:	N/A

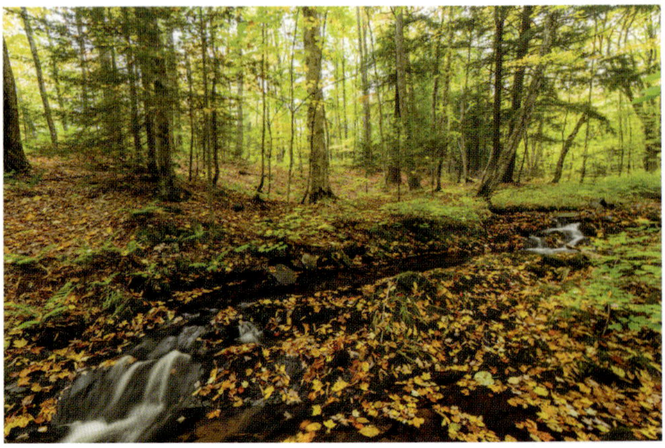

Follow the shallow tributary downstream from The Grade Falls for 175 yards. Toward the cascades, the waterway will enter a ravine, with the far side rising up somewhat aggressively.

The Grade Cascades have several cascades and end with a double segmented slide. Up at the top there is a 2.5 foot drop. The Cascades continue with several smaller drops and then end with a 6 foot double slide. A 4.5 foot slide flattens out and then continues with a second 1.5 foot slide, both angled at about 45 degrees.

It's not much to look at in low water, but can be quite interesting during spring runoff. (Just remember that the road is not plowed during the winter, so it takes a while for it to be passable in the spring.)

The upper end of the Cascades - The thumbnail shot above is the larger, lower end, double slide

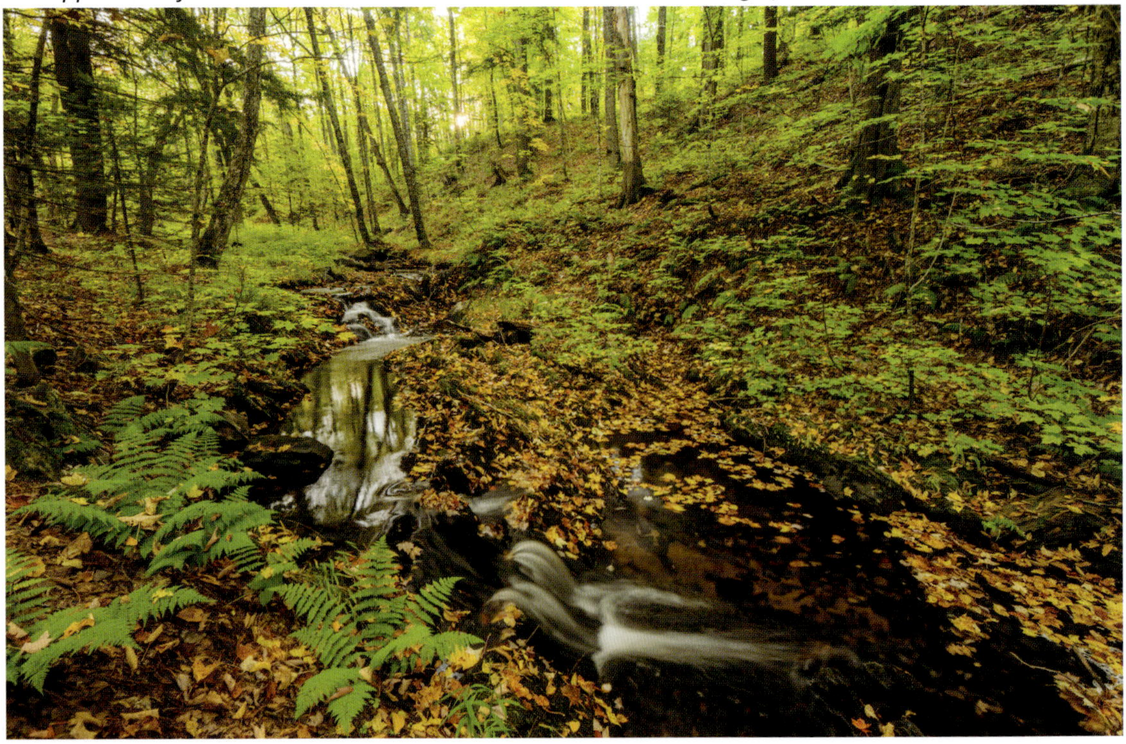

Victory Falls Hike

About halfway between Slate Flume Falls Hike and Black Bear Falls Hike is Victory Falls. It's another waterfall on the Slate River. Fortunately, there is a good gravel road that runs close to the river at this point.

Directions: Turn southeast onto Arvon Road off of Skanee Road. (This is the first main dirt road southwest of the Slate River.) Follow Arvon Road in a generally southerly direction for 3.7 miles. Arvon Road turns to the right (west). Follow it for .78 miles. Arvon turns to the left. Follow it for 1.75 miles. Turn left (northeast) at the Turkey Tracks. In 1.11 miles pull off the side of the road (N46 46.342 W88 13.537). There is no obvious parking spot or trail here. Hike through the woods to the north for 85 yards to N46 46.379 W88 13.520.

VICTORY FALLS (SLATE RIVER)

Private

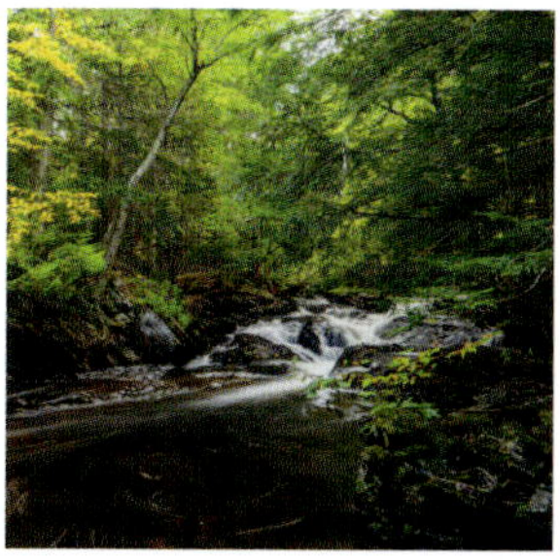

Must See:	6	GPS:	N46 46.379 W88 13.520
Height:	8 feet		
Time:	15-25 minutes	Hiking Information	
		Path:	None
Driving Information		Length:	85 yards
Signs:	None	Elev. Change:	Minor
Road:	Gravel	GPS:	Required
Access:	Difficult	Danger:	Minor
4WD:	N/A	WP Boots:	N/A

There is no trail to the falls, but it is a short 85 yard hike to the river.

Angular sheets of slate lie fractured across the 20 foot wide river. Passages have been cut on either side of the river at the top of the waterfall. They taper in toward each other, meeting near the base of the waterfall where the "V" shaped waterfall plunges a final 2 feet into a shallow channel. Eight feet later, the rocky mass that makes up the 40 foot long cascading waterfall gives way to a pleasant spill pool (possibly nice for swimming), shrouded by birch and cedar.

As the water level rises, the "V" becomes submerged, and the waterfall widens out, filling out more of the rocky riverbed.

The obvious "V" in the river

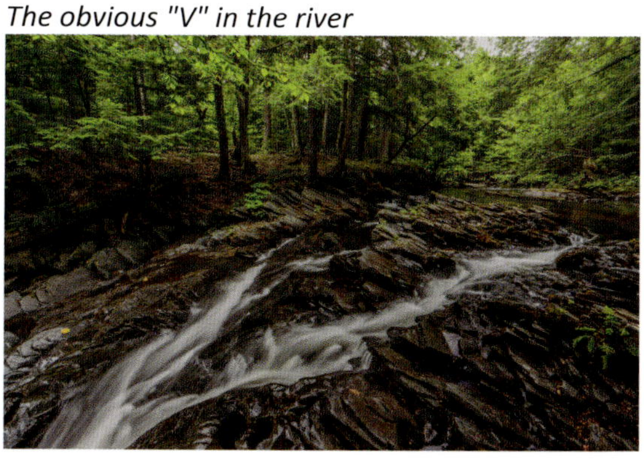

The rugged bedrock creates unique patterns

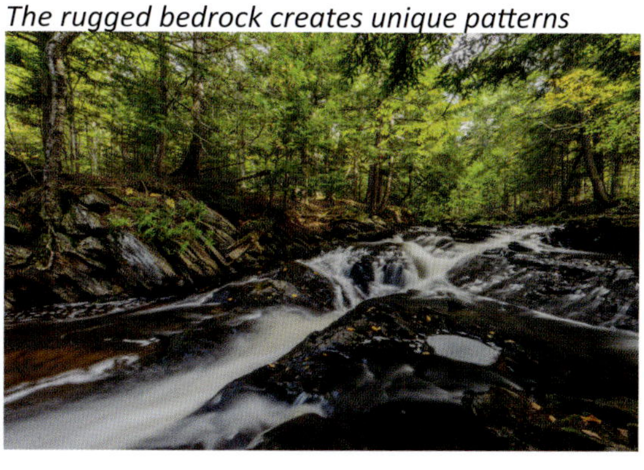

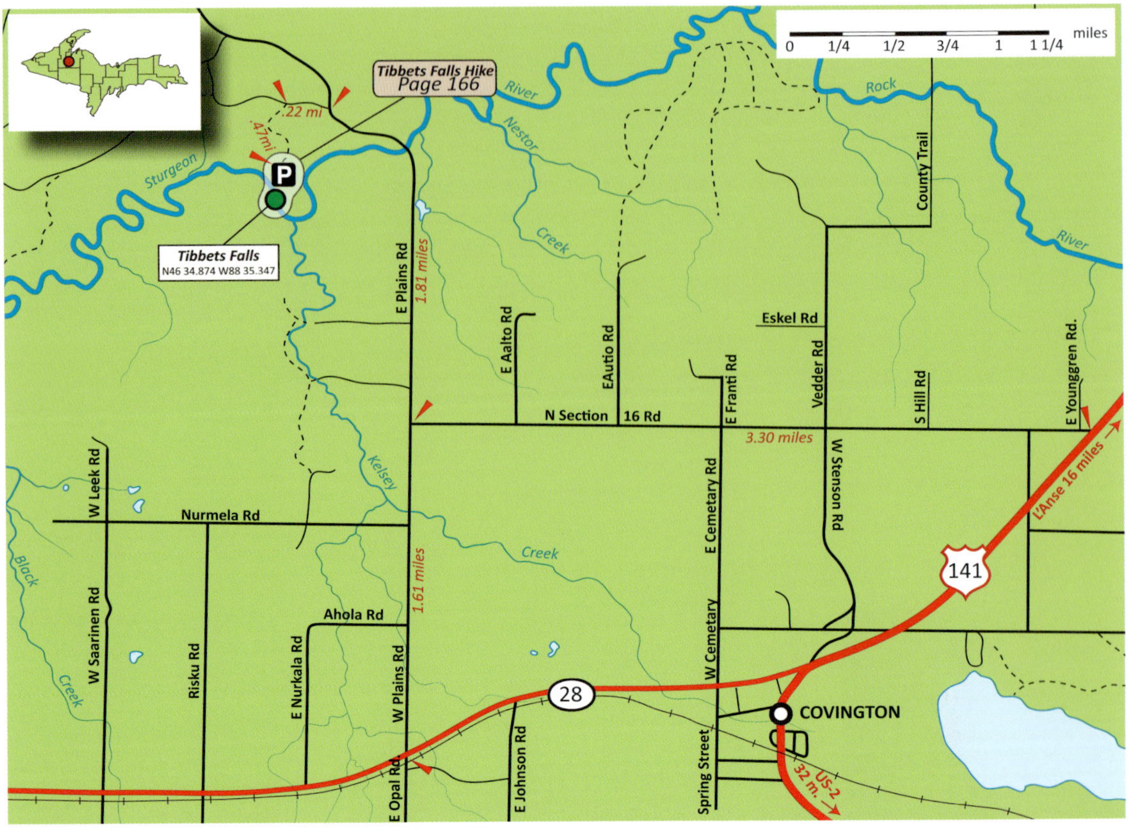

Tibbets Falls Hike

Tibbets Falls: There are no highly-defined drops in this stretch of river. Instead, the bedrock of the river is tilted at an awkward angle, creating interesting lines and patterns. The waterfall begins with a cascading drop and continues in a series of aggressive rapids.

Directions: Drive north on W Plains Road off of M-28 or west on N Section 16 Road from US-141. Drive north from the intersection of E Plains Road and N Section 16 Road 1.81 miles. A white post with "Tibbets Falls" is located by a gravel road on the left (west). Turn left and drive .22 miles. Turn left on a NARROW 2-track. Follow it .47 miles to a parking area at the end of the road. There is a steep downhill trail to the falls. (Be prepared to park short of the end of the road and walk the rest of the way if your vehicle has clearance issues.)

TIBBETS FALLS (STURGEON RIVER)

Private

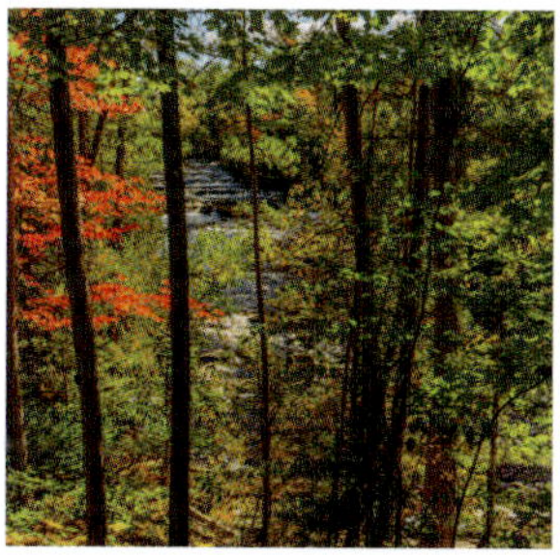

Must See:	6	GPS:	N46 34.874 W88 35.347
Height:	8 feet		
Time:	Series	Hiking Information	
		Path:	Unimproved Footpath
Driving Information		Length:	100 yards
Signs:	Small	Elev. Change:	Moderate
Road:	2-track	GPS:	Helpful
Access:	Difficult	Danger:	Moderate
4WD:	Recommended	WP Boots:	Recommended

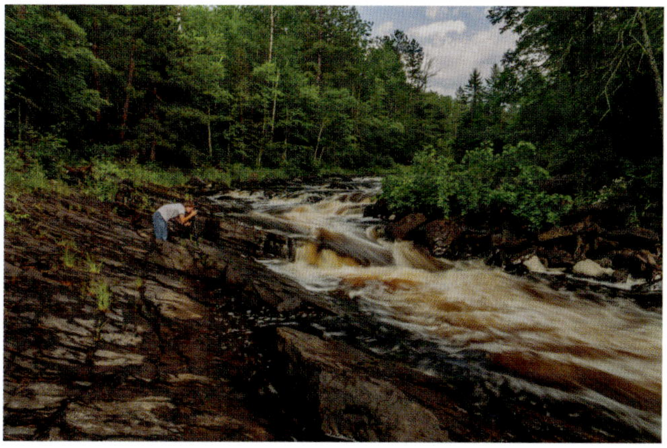

It's a 100 yard hike from the circular parking area to the river. The North Country Trail winds along the top of the gorge up above the Sturgeon River. A spur trail connects the parking lot to the NCT. There are several places along the NCT that you can get down to the river's edge. Most of these are quite steep descents. The easiest way down is to follow the NCT downstream past the main cascades. When the river turns more northerly the trail has dropped down closer to the river. Find a safe way down to the river and follow it back upstream to the falls.

The main falls are upstream. A series of nice cascades continue downstream for several hundred yards. Follow the river downstream for several hundred yards to view them. There is a short, but difficult climb down to the river, and not an easy hike along the river's edge.

The "main" drop - up above the corner cascades

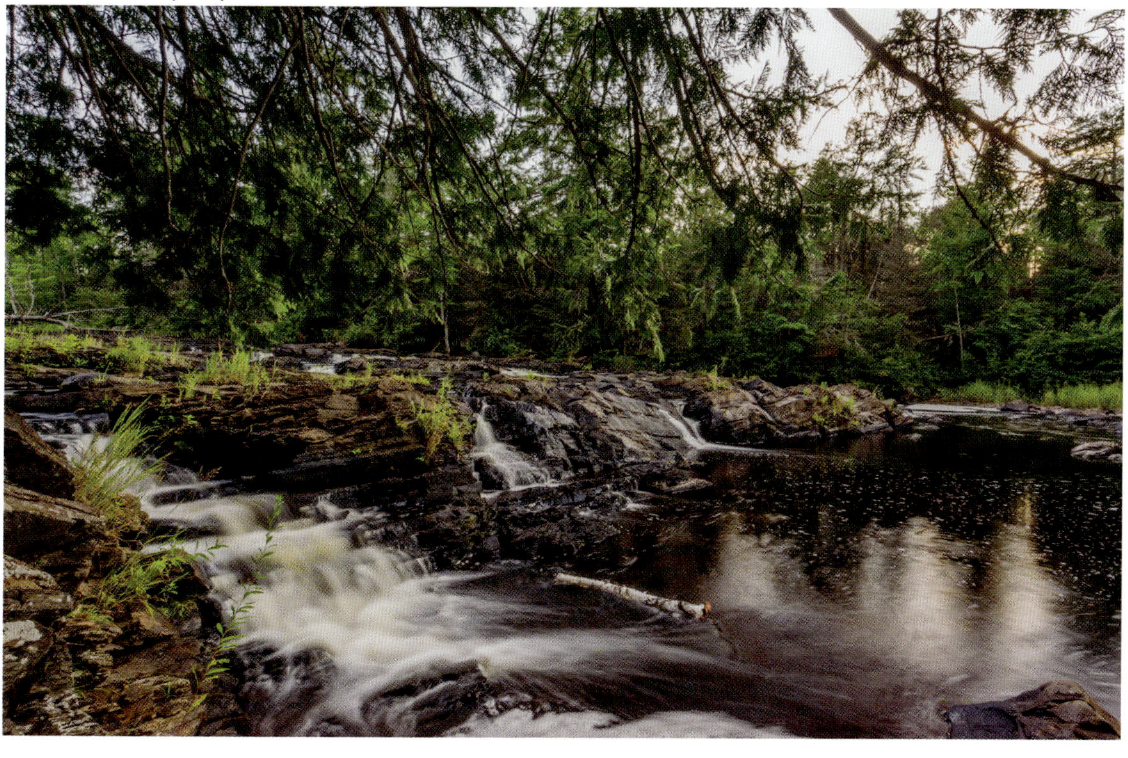

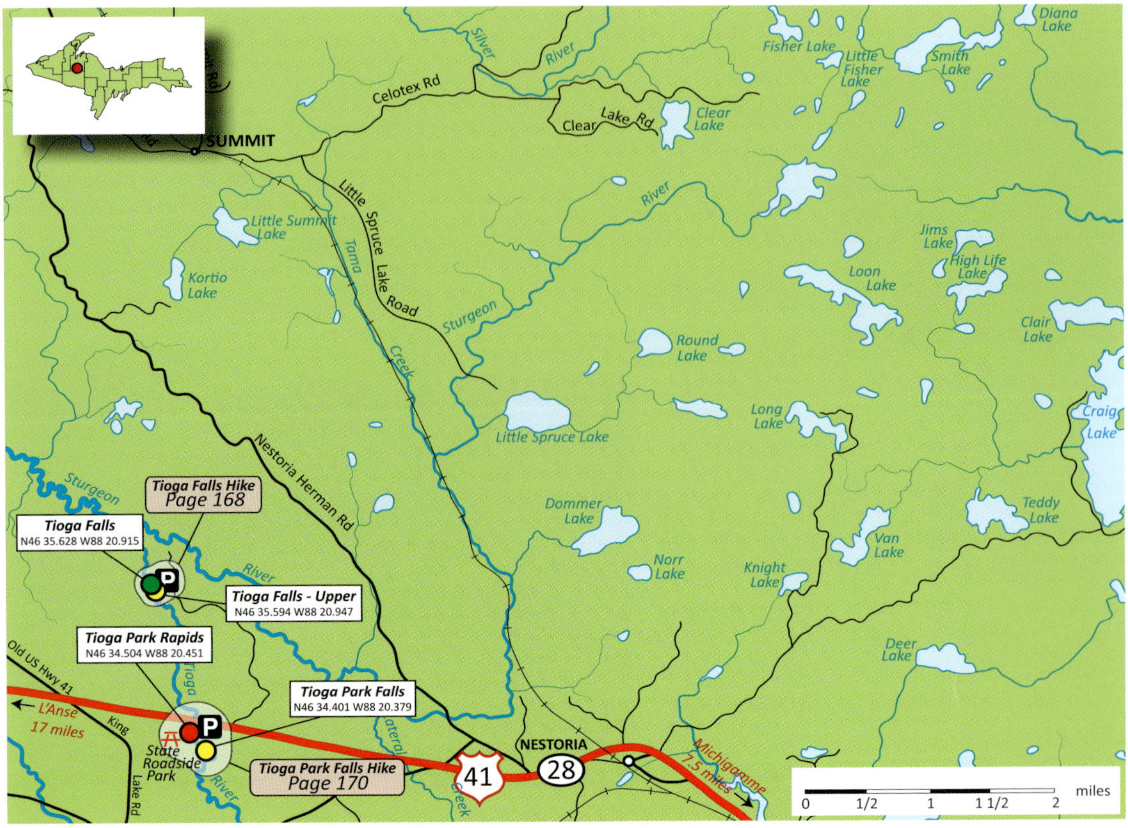

Tioga Falls Hike

*A*t the end of a long, rough 2-track is a house overlooking Tioga Falls. It has recently become available for daily (or longer) rental.

Directions: The Tioga River passes beneath US-41 at the Tioga Roadside Park. Drive east from the park. A 2-track heads north in .3 miles. Follow the rough 2-track for 2.3 miles through the woods, across a rocky stretch and back into close grown evergreens. The road is gated near the cabin. Enter only with permission. The falls are at the base of a 20 foot ravine next to the cabin, with the upper falls about 200 feet upstream.

TIOGA FALLS (TIOGA RIVER)

Private

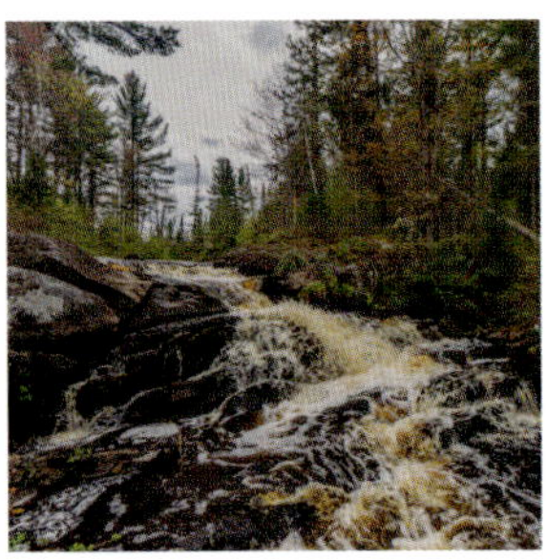

Must See:	7	GPS:	N46 35.628 W88 20.915
Height:	10 feet		
Time:	5-10 minutes	Hiking Information	
		Path:	N/A
Driving Information		Length:	50 yards
Signs:	None	Elev. Change:	Minor
Road:	2-track	GPS:	Recommended
Access:	Difficult	Danger:	Minor
4WD:	Helpful	WP Boots:	Helpful

The river cascades over jagged rocks just below a nice log cabin. No entry without permission.

TIOGA FALLS - UPPER (TIOGA RIVER)

Private

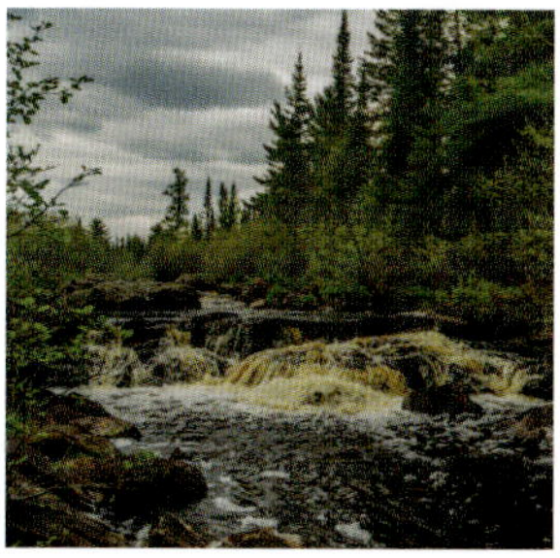

Must See:	6	GPS:	N46 35.594 W88 20.947
Height:	5 feet		
Time:	10-20 minutes	**Hiking Information**	
		Path:	Slight Footpath
Driving Information		Length:	65 yards
Signs:	None	Elev. Change:	Minor
Road:	2-track	GPS:	Recommended
Access:	Difficult	Danger:	Minor
4WD:	Helpful	WP Boots:	N/A

A faint footpath leads along the top of the ravine upstream to the upper falls.

Coming out of a marshy area, the Tioga River narrows and bursts through a section of blackened, mossy rocks. It cascades over a 3 foot ledge where it widens out to about 20 feet. A series of small cascades follow as the river prepares to drop over Tioga Falls.

Once again, this is on private land, and permission must be obtained to view.

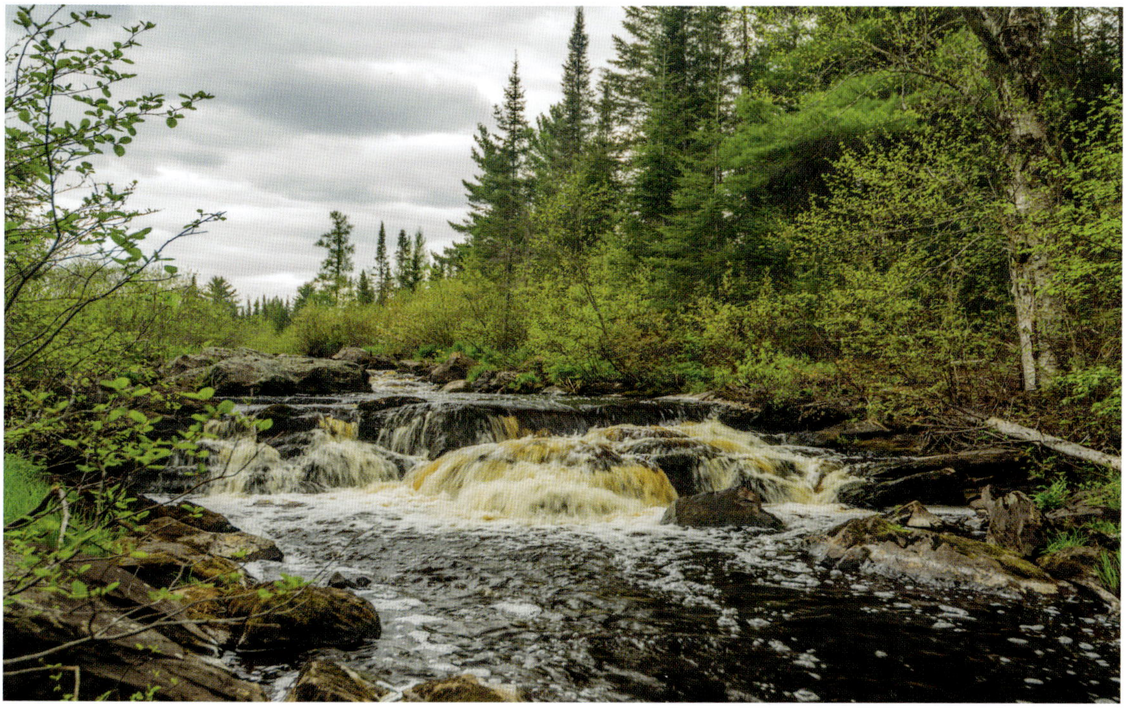

Tioga Park Falls Hike

The roadside park has vault toilets and a water hand pump. There is also a nice sign describing many of the unique features in Baraga County. A unique footbridge spans the Tioga River and offers a nice view of the cascades from there.

Tioga Park Falls: Hike from the parking lot down a somewhat rough footpath. It quickly enters an old forest with little undergrowth. The trail then meets up with the river and follows it upstream. The undergrowth here is thicker. The falls will be around a bend in the river. The lazy river is fairly wide and slow below the falls.

Tioga Park Rapids: Medium sized rocks fill the riverbed throughout this stretch of the river. There are no abrupt drops, merely a fast set of rapids.

Directions: From US-41, turn south into the roadside park next to the bridge over the Tioga River. Park here. The rapids are wheelchair accessible and just 50 yards away. Follow the path to the footbridge that is visible from the parking lot. There are signs from the parking lot giving directions to Tioga Park Falls. Follow the trail at the rear of the park that winds through the woods and then to the left, where the trail then meets the river and follows it upstream to the falls.

TIOGA PARK FALLS (TIOGA RIVER)

Private

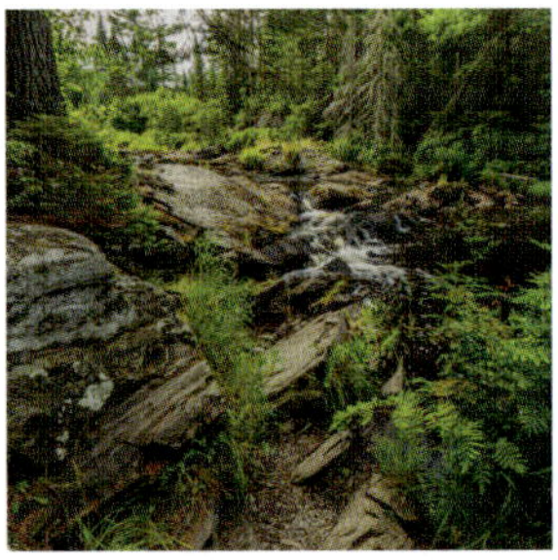

Must See:	4	GPS:	N46 34.401 W88 20.379
Height:	3 feet		
Time:	15-30 minutes	Hiking Information	
		Path:	Unimproved Footpath
Driving Information		Length:	.17 miles
Signs:	Roadside Park	Elev. Change:	Slight
Road:	Main	GPS:	N/A
Access:	Very Easy	Danger:	Slight
4WD:	N/A	WP Boots:	N/A

Hike along the faint trail found at the back of the roadside park along Tioga River upstream and around a corner in the river. An old, gnarly tree sits next to the waterfall. Its roots sprawl along the rocky river bank, looking for soil. Above the falls is an outcropping of rock that can be climbed on for a closer look at the river and waterfall.

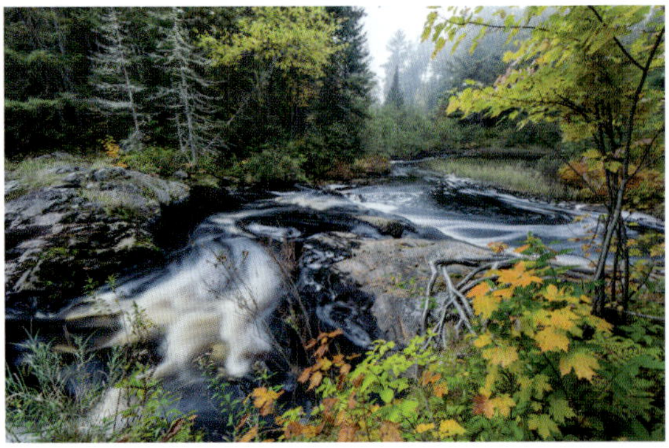

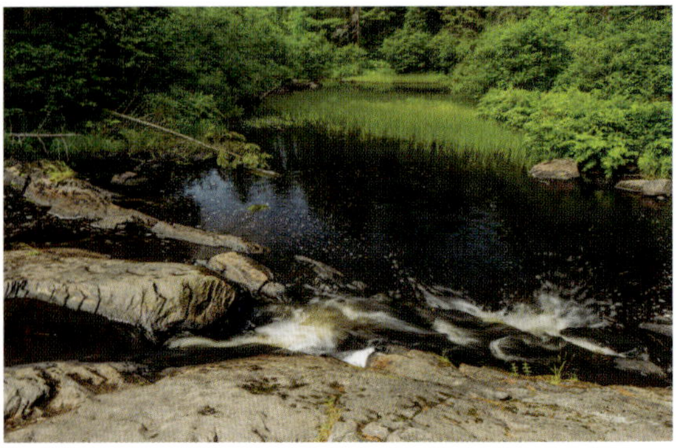

TIOGA PARK RAPIDS (TIOGA RIVER)

Private

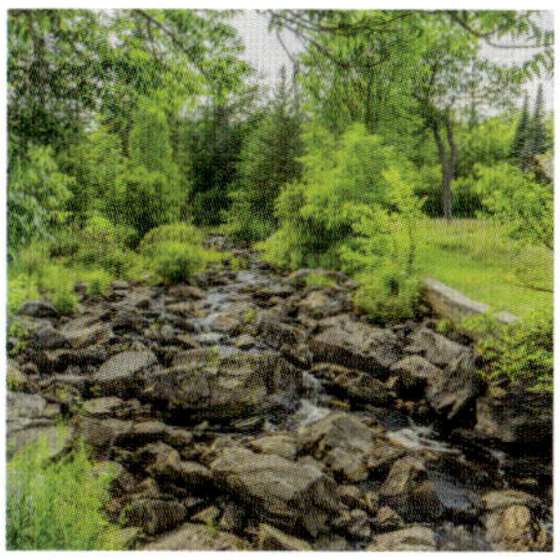

Must See:	3	GPS:	N46 34.504 W88 20.451
Height:	6 feet		
Time:	5-15 minutes	**Hiking Information**	
		Path:	Improved Footpath
Driving Information		Length:	50 yards
Signs:	Roadside Park	Elev. Change:	Slight
Road:	Main	GPS:	N/A
Access:	Very Easy	Danger:	Slight
4WD:	N/A	WP Boots:	N/A

The river can be seen from the parking lot. Look to the west to see the cute footbridge that spans the Tioga River. The lower falls features rapids tumbling around large boulders in a nicely manicured portion of the park. Expanses of green on both sides of the river provide plenty of room for children to run and play. A sidewalk connects the bridge to the parking area, making the bridge wheelchair accessible.

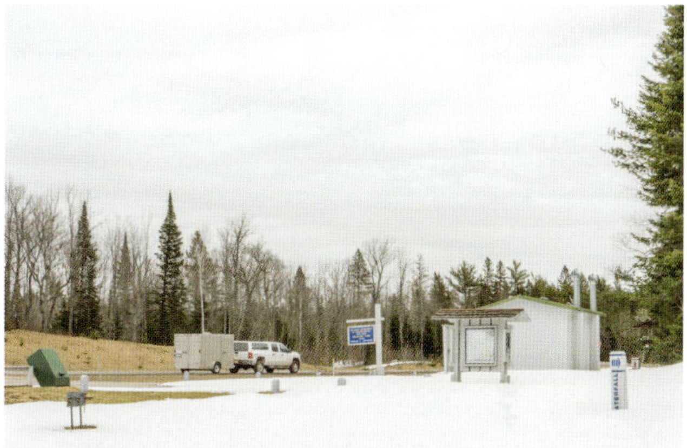

The roadside park alongside US-41

The bridge over the Tioga River at the Rapids

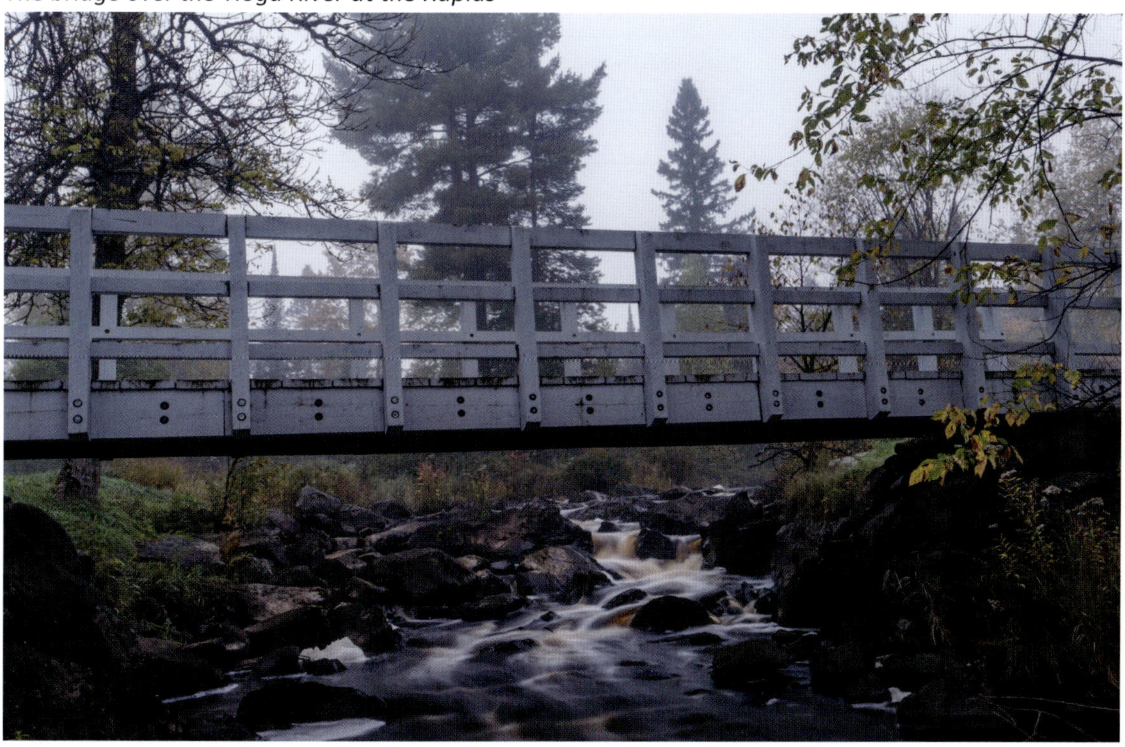

Alberta, an old Ford sawmill town 8 miles south of L'Anse, was donated to Michigan Technological University in 1954. It is now home to the Ford Forestry Center and Research Forest and includes a museum and gift store with gorgeous birdseye maple furniture and related products. For more information go to www.birdseye-connection.com or call (906) 524- 5268.

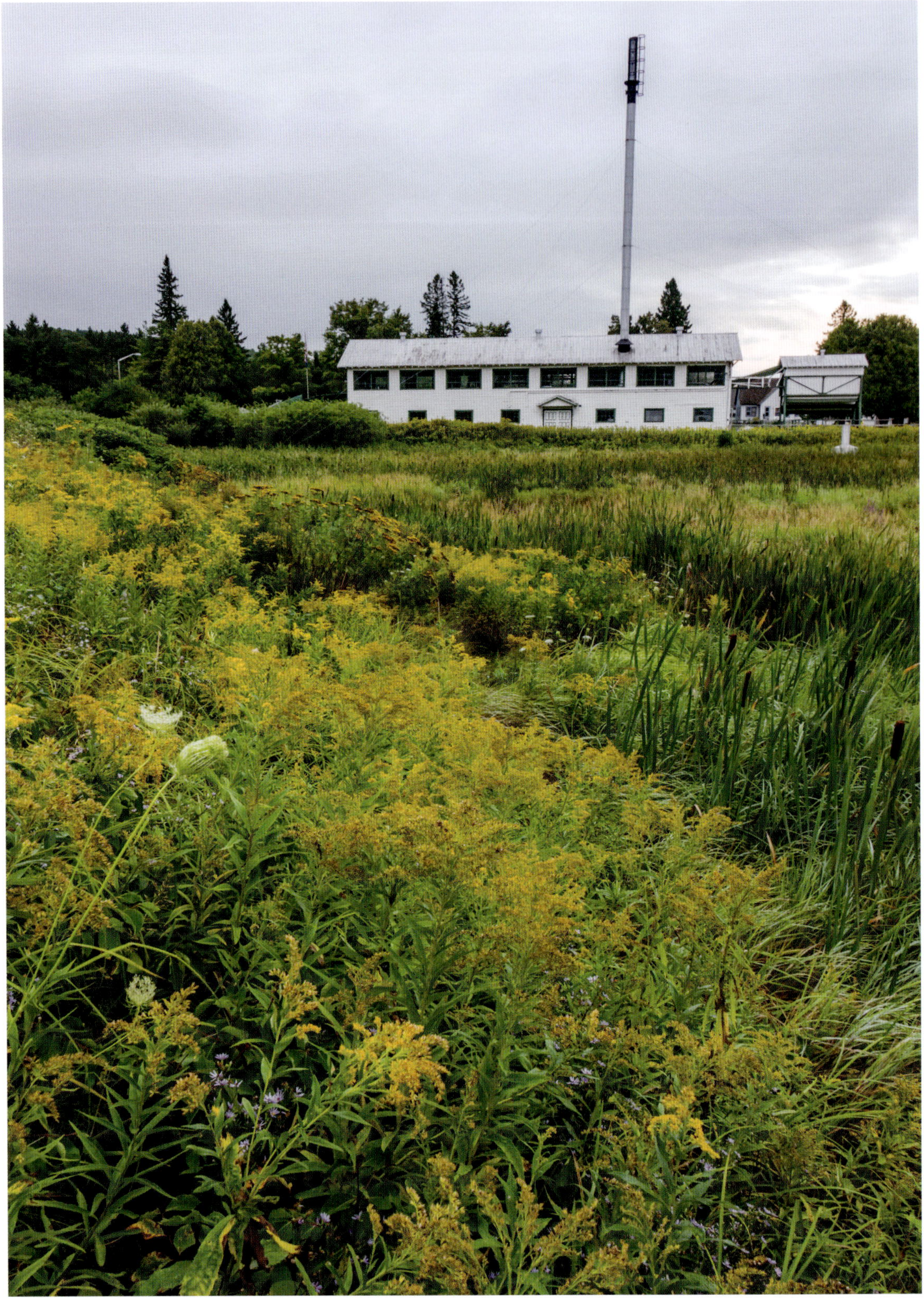

CHAPTER 2
HOUGHTON COUNTY

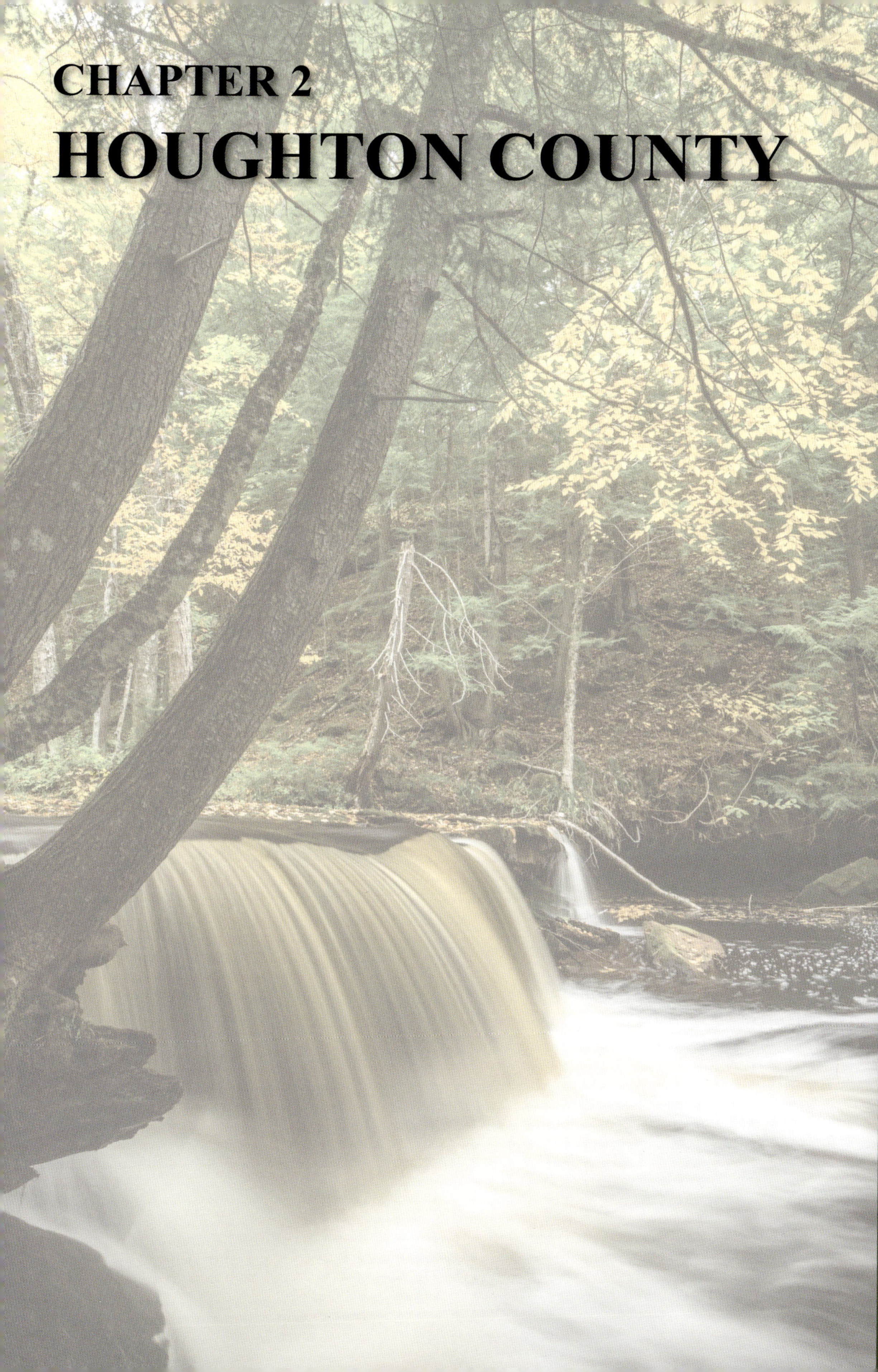

HOUGHTON COUNTY CONTENTS

HOUGHTON COUNTY MAP 178

HOGGER FALLS AREA 179
HOGGER FALLS HIKE ... 180
STURGEON FALLS - WB #1 (WEST BRANCH - STURGEON RIVER) ... 180
STURGEON FALLS - WB #2 (WEST BRANCH - STURGEON RIVER) ... 181
STURGEON FALLS - WB #3 (WEST BRANCH - STURGEON RIVER) ... 182
STURGEON FALLS - WB #4 (WEST BRANCH - STURGEON RIVER) ... 183
STURGEON FALLS - WB #5 (WEST BRANCH - STURGEON RIVER) ... 184
HOGGER FALLS (WEST BRANCH - STURGEON RIVER) ... 185

HUNGARIAN FALLS AREA 186
DOUGLASS HOUGHTON FALLS HIKE ... 187
DOUGLASS HOUGHTON FALLS (HAMMELL CREEK) ... 187
HUNGARIAN FALLS HIKE ... 188
HUNGARIAN GORGE FALLS (UNNAMED CREEK) ... 188
HUNGARIAN LOWER FALLS (DOVER CREEK) ... 189
HUNGARIAN MIDDLE FALLS (DOVER CREEK) ... 190
HUNGARIAN TINY FALLS (DOVER CREEK) ... 191
HUNGARIAN DAM OVERFLOW (DOVER CREEK) ... 192
HUNGARIAN DAM (DOVER CREEK) ... 193
HUNGARIAN UPPER FALLS (DOVER CREEK) ... 194
QUINCY FALLS HIKE ... 195
QUINCY FALLS #4 (QUINCY CREEK) ... 195
QUINCY FALLS #3 (QUINCY CREEK) ... 196
QUINCY FALLS #2 (QUINCY CREEK) ... 197
QUINCY FALLS #1 (QUINCY CREEK) ... 198

JUMBO FALLS AREA 199
JUMBO FALLS HIKE ... 199
JUMBO FALLS (JUMBO RIVER) ... 200

ONION FALLS AREA 201
ONION FALLS HIKE ... 201
ONION FALLS (ONION CREEK) ... 202
ONION FALLS - LOWER (ONION CREEK) ... 203

OTTER FALLS AREA 204
OTTER FALLS HIKE ... 205
OTTER FALLS (OTTER RIVER - WEST BRANCH) ... 205

QUEEN ANNE'S FALLS AREA 206
QUEEN ANNE'S FALLS HIKE ... 206
QUEEN ANNE'S FALLS (SLAUGHTERHOUSE CREEK) ... 207
ST. LOUIS FALLS HIKE ... 208
ST. LOUIS FALLS (UNNAMED CREEK) ... 208
TRAP ROCK RIVER FALLS HIKE ... 209
TRAP ROCK RIVER FALLS (TRAP ROCK RIVER) ... 209

MAPS ...
HIKES ...
WATERFALLS ...

TABLE OF CONTENT KEY

REDRIDGE DAM FALLS AREA **210**
REDRIDGE DAM FALLS HIKE 210
REDRIDGE DAM FALLS (SALMON TROUT RIVER) 210

STURGEON FALLS AREA **211**
STURGEON FALLS HIKE 212
STURGEON FALLS (STURGEON RIVER) 212
STURGEON FALLS - UPPER #1 (STURGEON RIVER) 213
STURGEON FALLS - UPPER #2 (STURGEON RIVER) 214
VISTA FALLS HIKE 215
VISTA FALLS (STURGEON RIVER - WEST BRANCH) 215

WYANDOTTE FALLS AREA **216**
WYANDOTTE FALLS HIKE 216
WYANDOTTE FALLS (MISERY RIVER) 217

MAPS........
HIKES........
WATERFALLS........
TABLE OF CONTENT KEY

The Houghton-Hancock Bridge spans Portage Lake. This is the only bridge that connects the top portion of the Keweenaw Peninsula with the rest of the state.

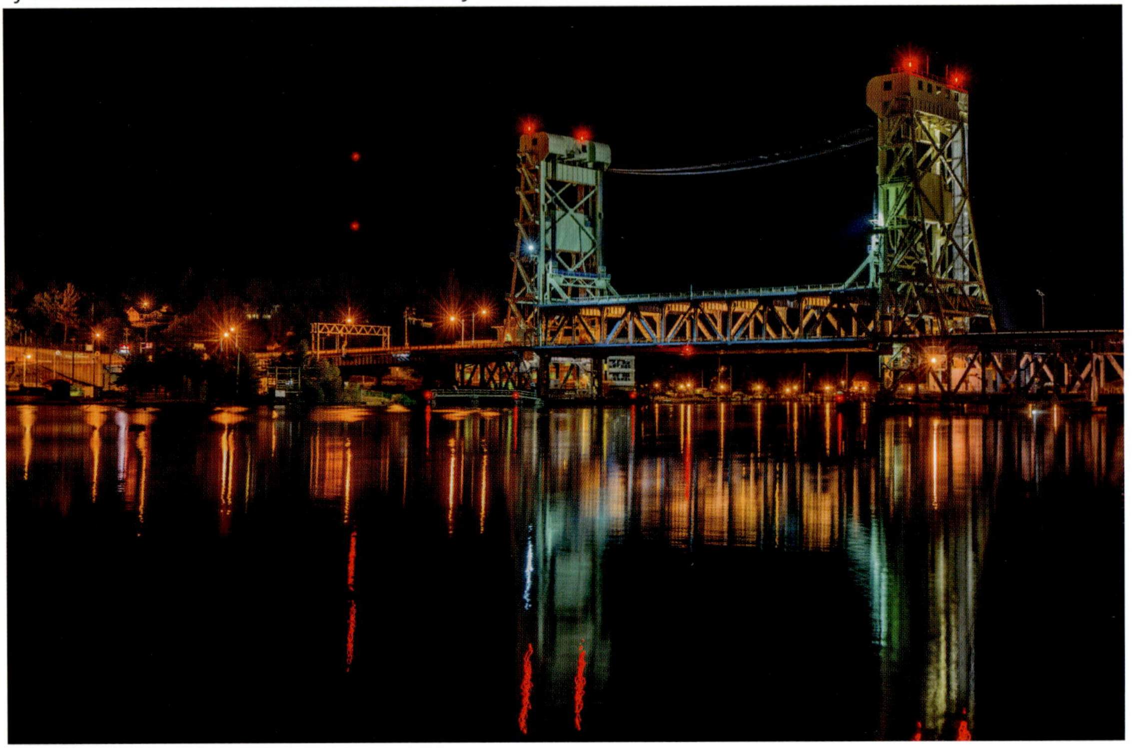

The Quincy Mine (just north of Hancock) offers guided tours and a gift shop. For more information check their website at www.quincymine.com or call (906) 482-3101.

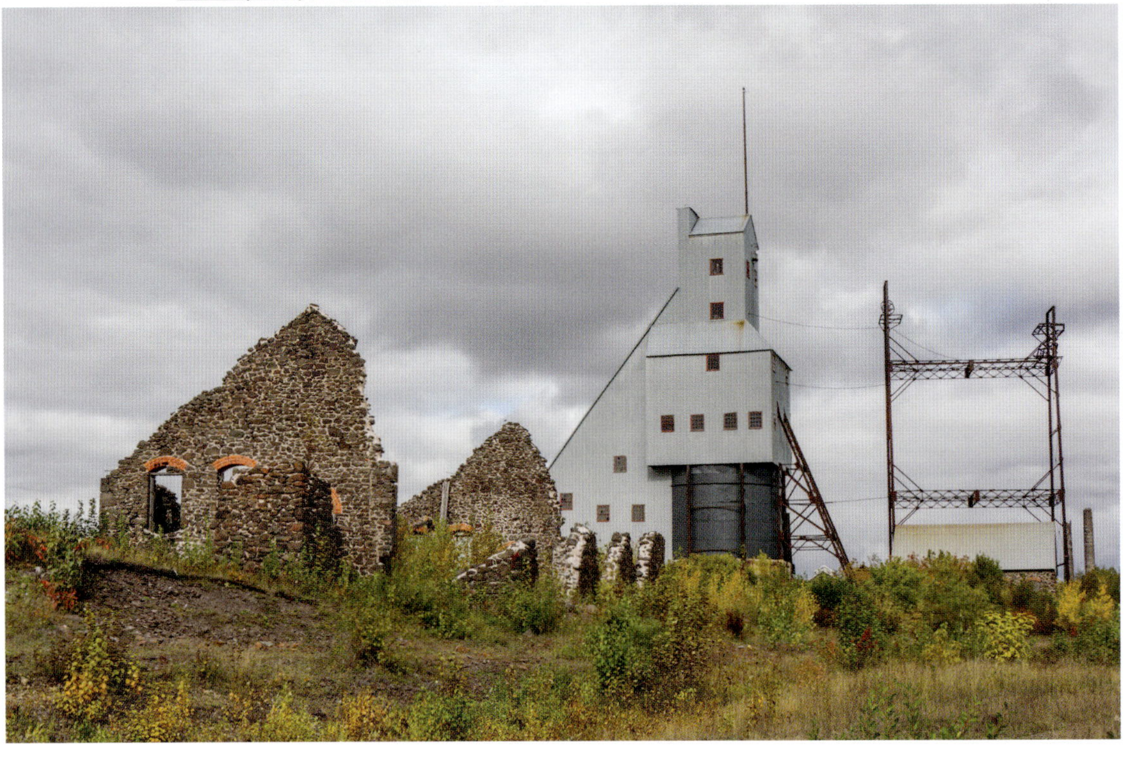

HOUGHTON COUNTY FACTS

Founded:	1845
Size:	1,044 square miles
Population (2010):	36,628
County Seat:	Houghton

While Douglass Houghton was Michigan's State Geologist he surveyed the Keweenaw Peninsula. The ensuing report, delivered in 1841, documented the rich copper deposits. This started a "Copper Rush" and soon Michigan was by far the greatest producer of copper in America, with nearly 80% of Michigan copper pulled up from Houghton County's rocky depths. At that time Houghton County also included Baraga County.

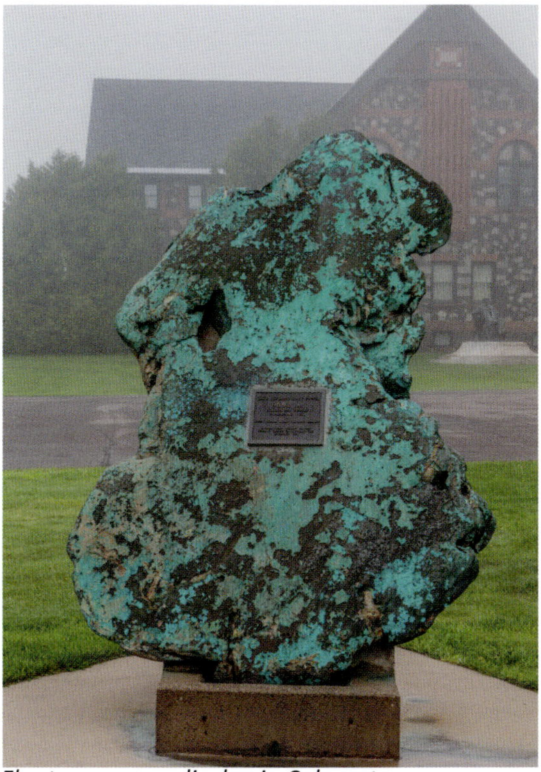

Float copper on display in Calumet

Although the copper mines are now closed, Houghton County still boasts having one of the country's premier engineering universities: Michigan Technological University, located in Houghton, the largest city in the county.

The population in Houghton County was only around 700 in 1850. It rose dramatically with the discovery of copper and by 1910 there were over 88,000 residents. It steadily declined thereafter until the 1950's and has varied little since then.

The Portage Lift Bridge *(opposite page)* is an amazing structure. Built in 1959, it is both the widest and the heaviest double-deck vertical lift bridge in the world.

Snowmobilers flock to the area each winter, eager to have fun on the trails that crisscross the county. Snowfall is typically between 150 and 250 inches each year. The most snow recorded fell during the winter of 1978/1979 when 355.9 inches blanketed the county.

Houghton County Map

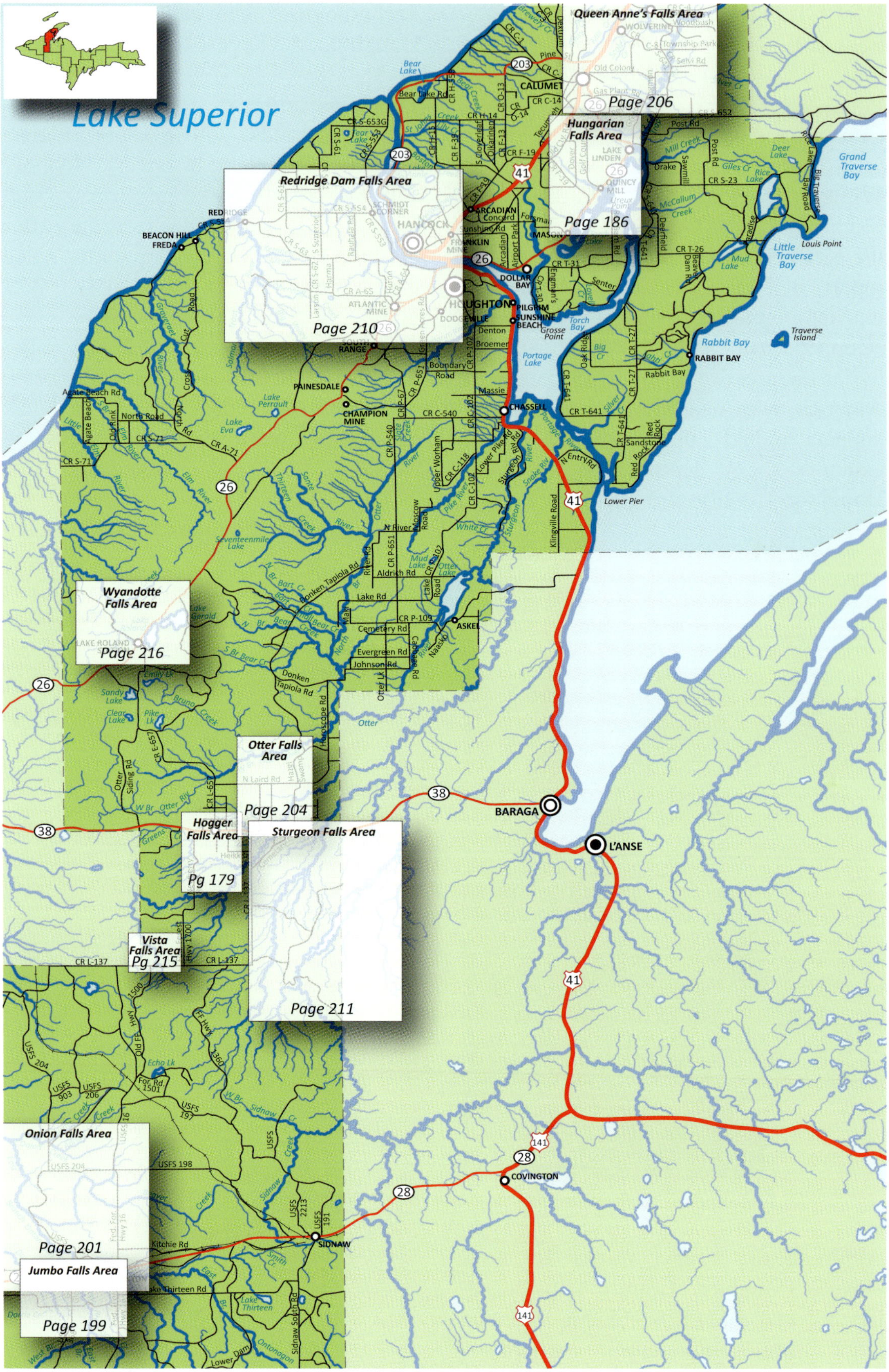

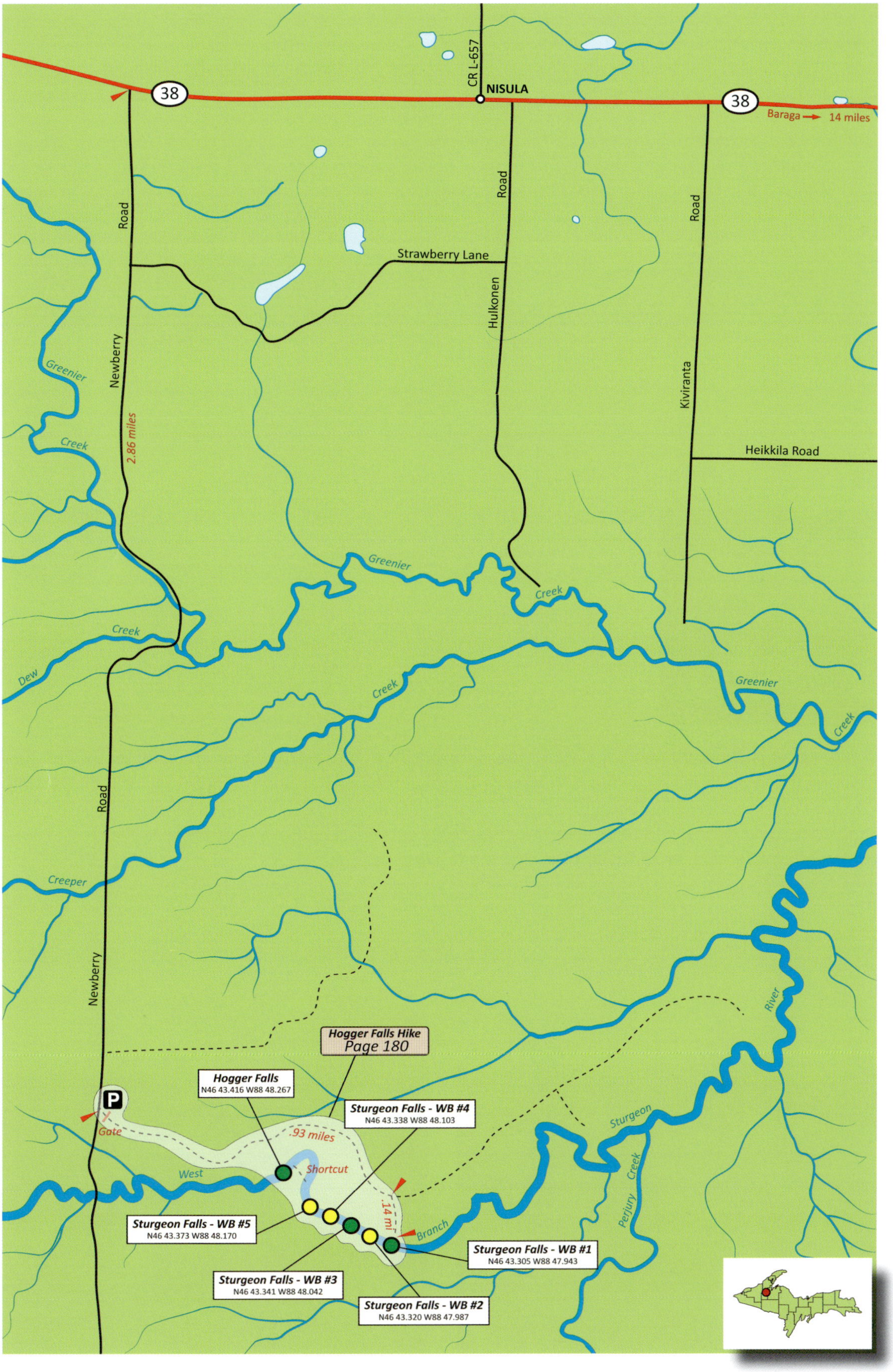
38
CR L-657
NISULA
38
Baraga → 14 miles
Newberry Road
Strawberry Lane
Hulkonen Road
Kiviranta Road
Heikkila Road
2.86 miles
Greenier Creek
Dew Creek
Creeper Creek
Sturgeon River
Perjury Creek
West Branch
Hogger Falls Hike
Page 180
Hogger Falls
N46 43.416 W88 48.267
Sturgeon Falls - WB #4
N46 43.338 W88 48.103
Sturgeon Falls - WB #5
N46 43.373 W88 48.170
Sturgeon Falls - WB #3
N46 43.341 W88 48.042
Sturgeon Falls - WB #2
N46 43.320 W88 47.987
Sturgeon Falls - WB #1
N46 43.305 W88 47.943
.93 miles
Shortcut
.14 mi
Gate
P

Hogger Falls Hike

The West Branch of the Sturgeon River hosts some lovely waterfalls. It takes a little hiking, and they are not the easiest to traverse between, but for those willing and able there are great rewards.

Directions: From Nisula, head west for .9 miles on M-38. Turn left (south) onto Newberry Road. In 2.9 miles turn left into a short 2-track that is now a parking spot. The 2-track has been blocked to keep vehicles from entering the Ottawa National Forest. The parking area is just before a bridge over the West Branch of the Sturgeon River. Hike the 2-track .93 miles to another 2-track to the right (south). Follow it .14 miles to the river and Sturgeon Falls - WB #1. Hike directly up the river as much as possible to keep from having to climb up and down the steep gorge walls between waterfalls. The only exception to this is between #5 and Hogger Falls. Cut cross country for a considerable shortcut. After Hogger Falls, use your GPS and hike back toward the parking spot. There will be no trail through the forest. In about .13 miles you should be back to the 2-track. Follow it about .4 miles to the vehicle.

STURGEON FALLS - WB #1 (WEST BRANCH - STURGEON RIVER) Private

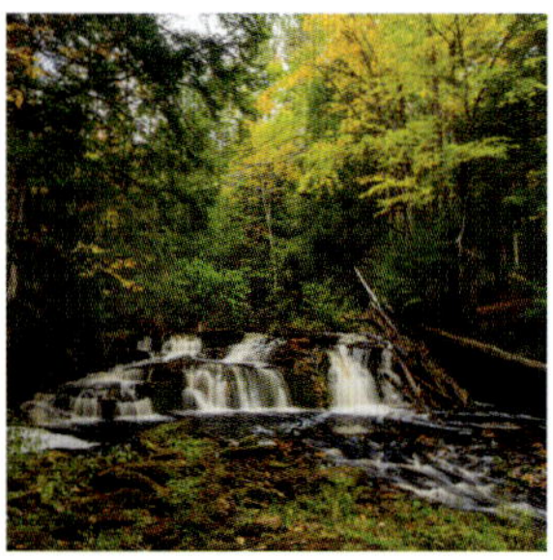

Must See:	7	GPS:	N46 43.305 W88 47.943
Height:	6 feet		
Time:	1-1.5 hours	Hiking Information	
		Path:	2-track
Driving Information		Length:	1.1 miles
Signs:	None	Elev. Change:	Moderate
Road:	Gravel	GPS:	Recommended
Access:	Somewhat Easy	Danger:	Moderate
4WD:	N/A	WP Boots:	Recommended

The river starts about 25 feet wide above the waterfall. It then widens out, particularly on the far side, tapering down on that side, while falling more sharply in the center and the near side of the waterfall. The base of the waterfall is about 40 feet wide, narrowing again quickly between sandbars covered with sandstone, river debris, and thick undergrowth. Large chunks of bedrock have broken off of the 12 foot high gorge wall and fallen in toward the river on the near side.

Beautiful wildflowers grow below the spill pool. The river can often be waded easily, allowing the falls to be explored from both banks.

The 2-track to the falls

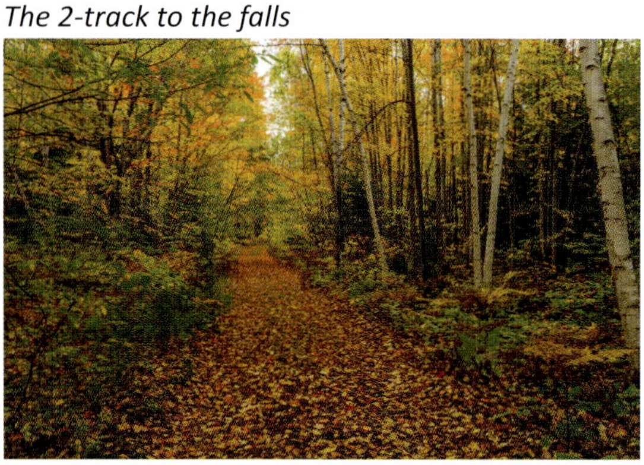

Spotted touch-me-nots cluster below the waterfall

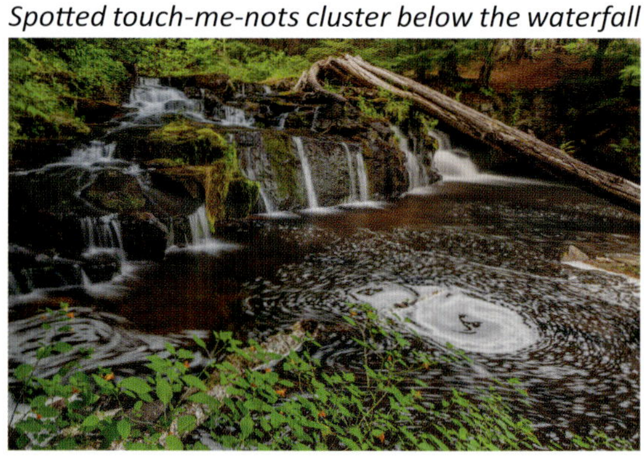

STURGEON FALLS - WB #2 (WEST BRANCH - STURGEON RIVER) Private

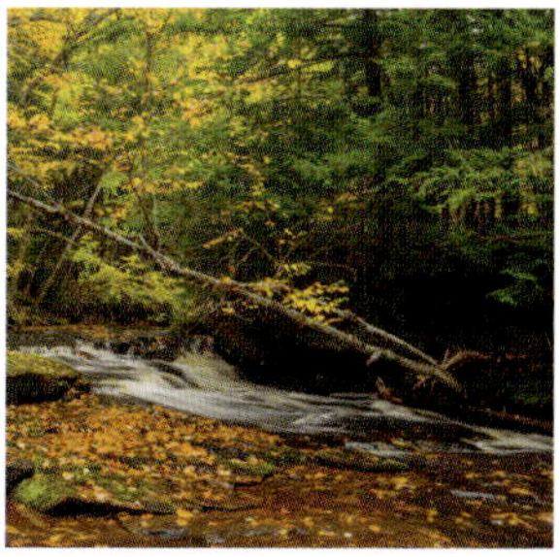

Must See:	5	GPS:	N46 43.328 W88 47.997
Height:	6 feet		
Time:	1-1.5 hours	Hiking Information	
		Path:	2-track
Driving Information		Length:	1.13 miles
Signs:	None	Elev. Change:	Moderate
Road:	Gravel	GPS:	Recommended
Access:	Somewhat Easy	Danger:	Moderate
4WD:	N/A	WP Boots:	Recommended

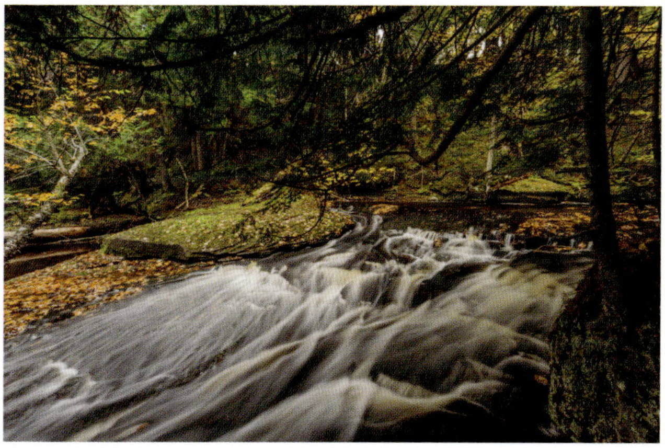

A faint but followable footpath between #1 and #2 follows the top of the gorge wall. It is only about 75 yards between the waterfalls. Feel free to hike up the river if it feels safe.

The river slants back hard to the near bank, rushing down in a slide/cascade. The river compresses from a 50 foot wide river to just 20 feet at the waterfall in normal conditions. It's a little tough to view the waterfall easily, as it snuggles up against the 10 to 20 foot bluff that you are standing on. If you can ford the river, there's a good viewing area on the far side, above and below the waterfall. After the slide, the river slows down and flows calmly around a corner downstream.

Shot of the waterfall - taken from the far side of the river

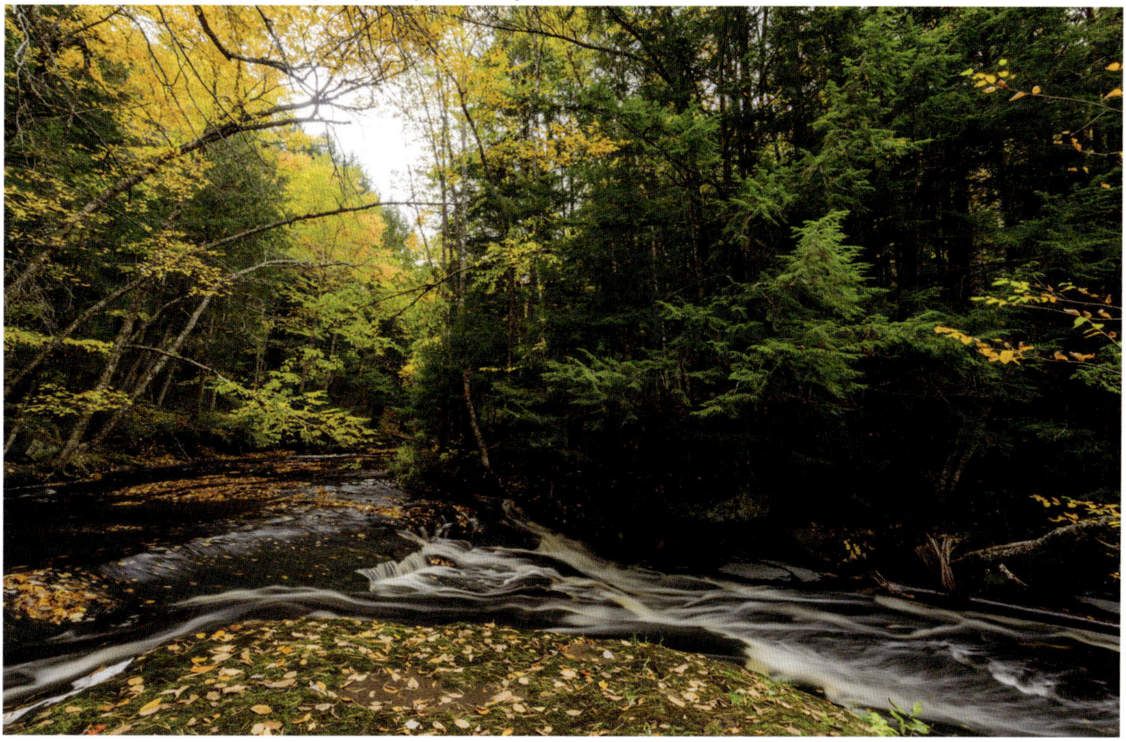

STURGEON FALLS - WB #3 (WEST BRANCH - STURGEON RIVER) Private

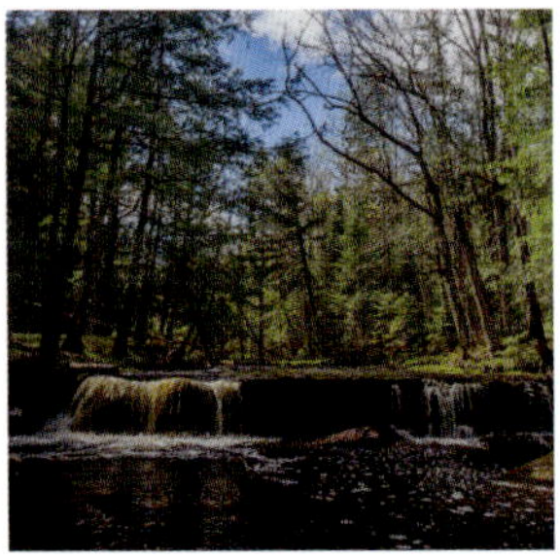

Must See:	7	GPS:	N46 43.341 W88 48.042
Height:	3 feet		
Time:	1.25 to 1.75 hours	**Hiking Information**	
		Path:	2-track
Driving Information		Length:	1.19 miles
Signs:	None	Elev. Change:	Moderate
Road:	Gravel	GPS:	Recommended
Access:	Somewhat Easy	Danger:	Moderate
4WD:	N/A	WP Boots:	Recommended

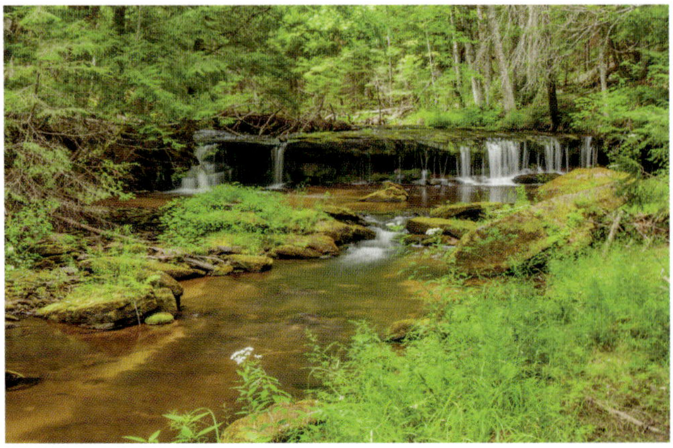

The gorge wall dramatically rises between #2 and #3. It is often easier to walk the 100 yards right up the normally shallow river between these falls.

It's not tall, but this waterfall has a lot of character. The 50 foot wide waterfall is a sandstone ledge that is constantly being undercut. When the ledge becomes too thin, a section breaks off and the undercutting starts over. It somewhat looks like a miniature Tahquamenon Falls. A slow moving spill below the falls narrows and then cascades down another foot or so. Numerous moss covered fragments of broken off sandstone line the sides of the waterway, forcing it ever narrower below the waterfall.

This is from the far side of the river

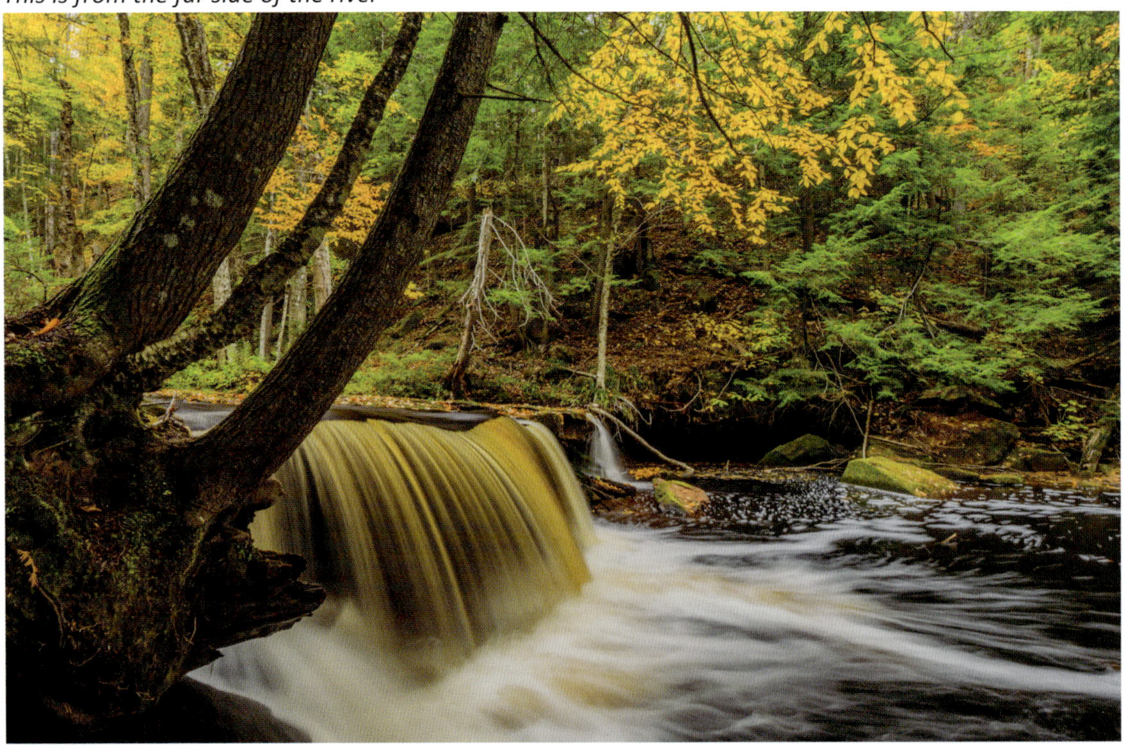

STURGEON FALLS - WB #4 (WEST BRANCH - STURGEON RIVER) Private

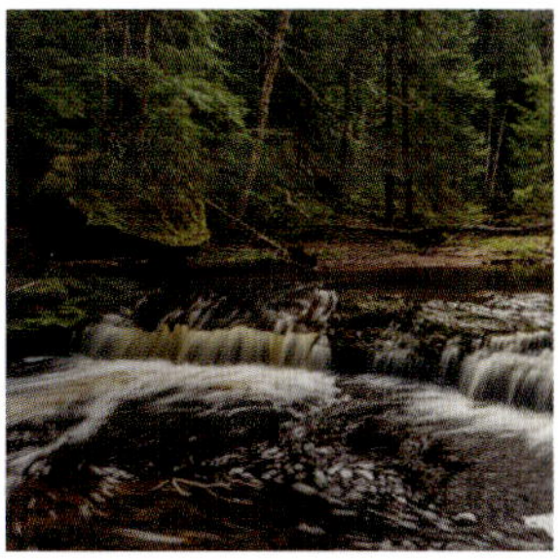

Must See:	5	GPS:	N46 43.338 W88 48.103
Height:	2 feet		
Time:	1.5-2 hours	Hiking Information	
		Path:	2-track then none
Driving Information		Length:	1.23 miles
Signs:	None	Elev. Change:	Aggressive
Road:	Gravel	GPS:	Recommended
Access:	Somewhat Easy	Danger:	Moderate
4WD:	N/A	WP Boots:	Recommended

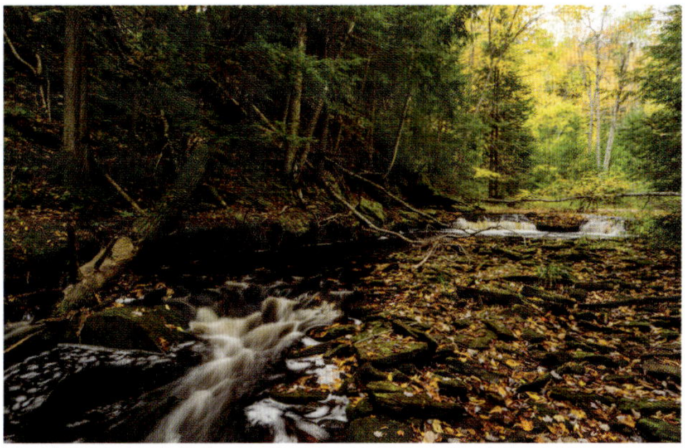

Cross over the river (if possible) to the far side below #3. Climb up above the waterfall. Hike along the flat bank on the far side most of the way to #4. Otherwise you'll need to climb up to the top of the 40 foot gorge wall between the falls. It's 100 yards to #4.

This is another wide, but short waterfall. A high bluff overlooks the far side of the waterfall. Chunks of sandstone, broken off of the bedrock litter the riverbed below the spill pool. A nice viewing/picnic area presents itself above and below the waterfall.

This is quite similar to #3, just shorter and narrower, and with a softer top layer. This waterfall is eroding through the top layers, making a cascade then plunge. It runs mostly over two lower sections of the shelf, filling a wide but short spill pool before narrowing and flowing along the base of the far gorge wall. A large sandstone debris field makes a great viewing area just below the waterfall.

Note the encroaching gorge wall on the far side of the river

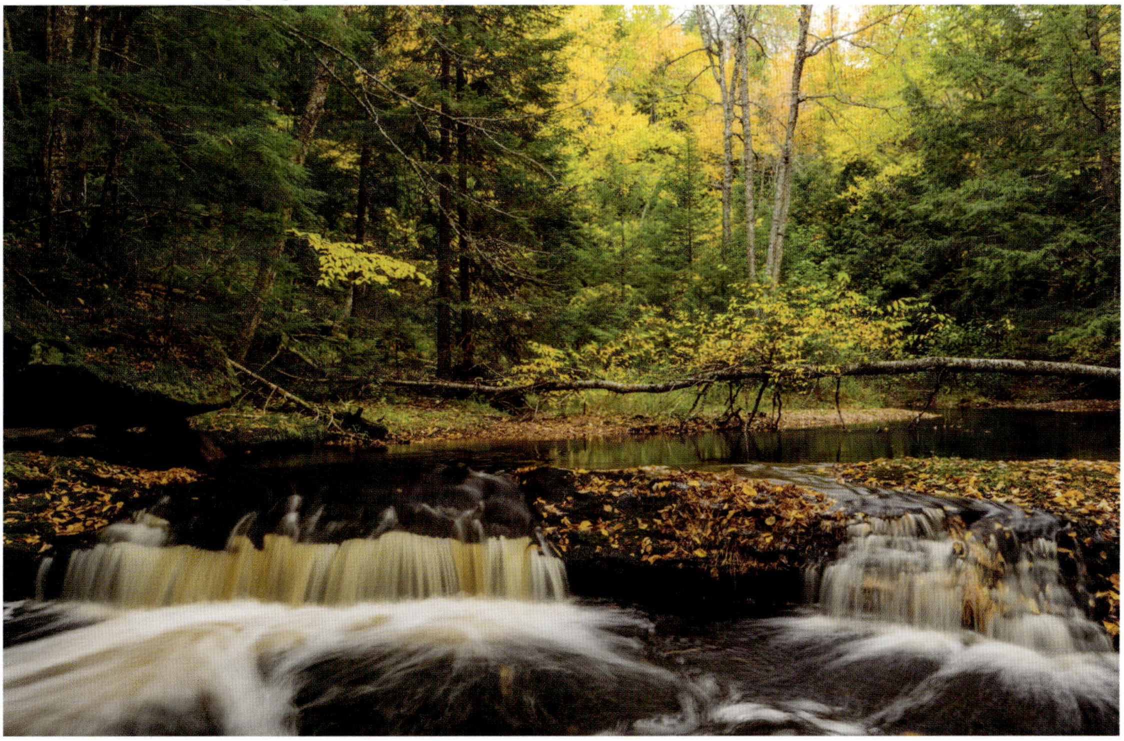

STURGEON FALLS - WB #5 (WEST BRANCH - STURGEON RIVER) Private

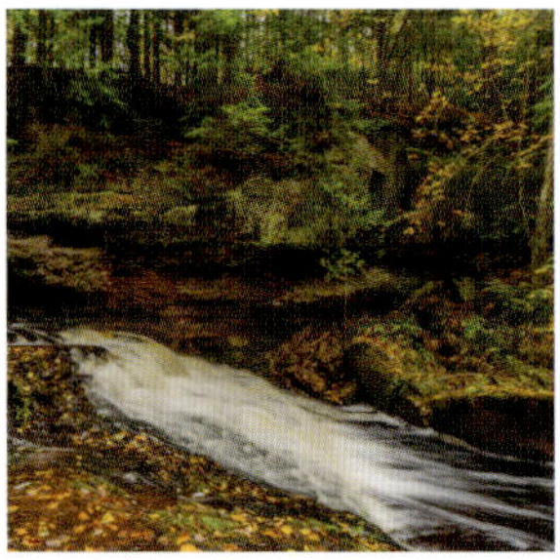

Must See:	7	GPS:	N46 43.373 W88 48.170
Height:	6 feet		
Time:	1.75-2.25 hours	Hiking Information	
		Path:	2-Track Then None
Driving Information		Length:	1.27 miles
Signs:	None	Elev. Change:	Aggressive
Road:	Gravel	GPS:	Recommended
Access:	Somewhat Easy	Danger:	Moderate
4WD:	N/A	WP Boots:	Recommended

Once again, hike along the river's edge at the base of the gorge on the near side upstream to the waterfall. Ford the river over to the "island" below the waterfall and then to the far side and upstream to the base of the waterfall. The near side rises up tall with a 20 foot wall directly above the waterfall.

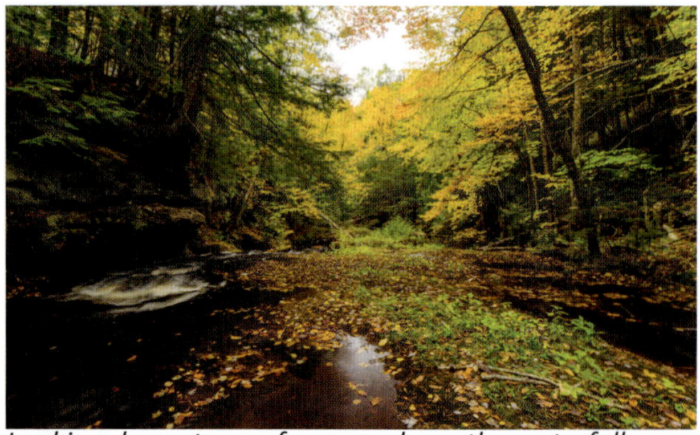

Looking downstream from up above the waterfall

The river has carved out a path through a rocky outcropping, with the remaining rock guarding the left side of the river. The waterfall runs down over a multitude of thin rock layers, each one sticking out slightly further than the one above it, something like a deck of cards fanned out.

The waterfall is a lovely cascade rushing down layers of sandstone. Although the riverbed is 75 feet across, the waterfall snuggles up against the near side, widening out as the river rises.

Eroded sandstone has made a small "island" below the waterfall

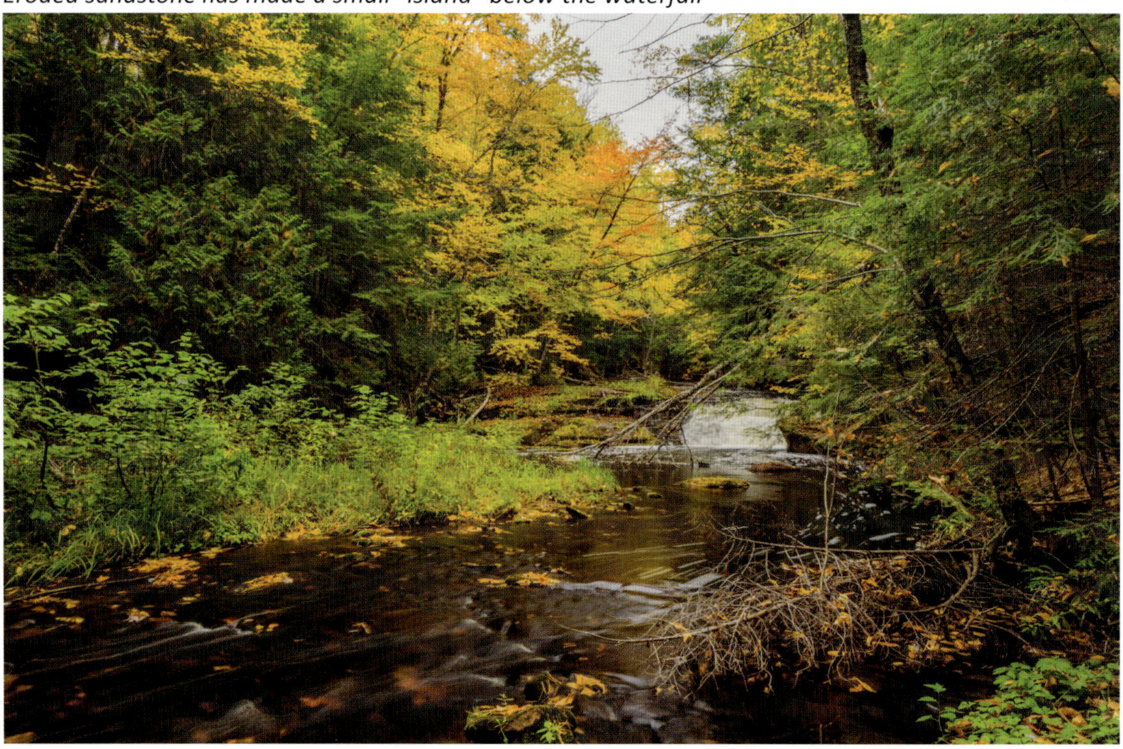

HOGGER FALLS (WEST BRANCH - STURGEON RIVER)

Private

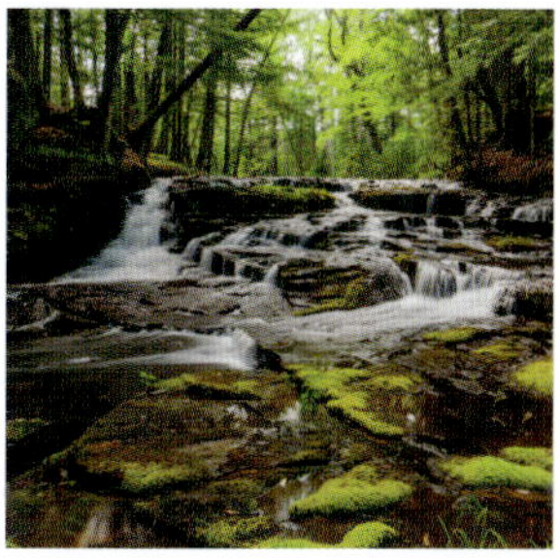

Must See:	8	GPS:	N46 43.416 W88 48.267
Height:	8 feet		
Time:	2-2.5 hours	**Hiking Information**	
		Path:	2-Track Then None
Driving Information		Length:	1.41 miles
Signs:	None	Elev. Change:	Aggressive
Road:	Gravel	GPS:	Recommended
Access:	Somewhat Easy	Danger:	Moderate
4WD:	N/A	WP Boots:	Recommended

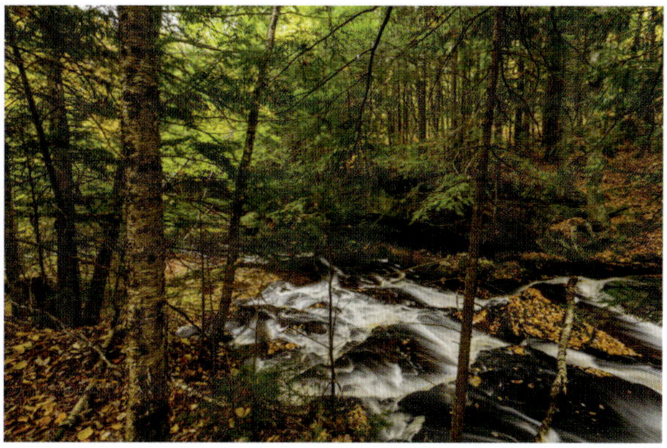

If possible, hike the river upstream from #5 until the bank on the far side looks inviting. Hike along the bank a little ways. The river is going to make a huge "U", doubling back on itself. If you see the tall sand bank across the river, cut straight away from the river and take the shortcut to the other side of the "U". You don't have to climb up the gorge wall as you cut across. If you're tempted to do so, turn a bit to the right and stay on the low ground until you reach the river again. Continue upstream. You should hear the waterfall almost instantly. Cross the river when possible and follow the "near" bank to the waterfall.

The gorgeous waterfall cascades down with the backdrop a 15 foot rock gorge wall on the far side. A sheet of solid sandstone arches over space vacated below the waterfall where softer, fractured stone has now eroded away. Trees grow thick on this precarious formation. It's a beautiful setting for a beautiful waterfall!

The softer layers below the harder rock are eroding away below the waterfall

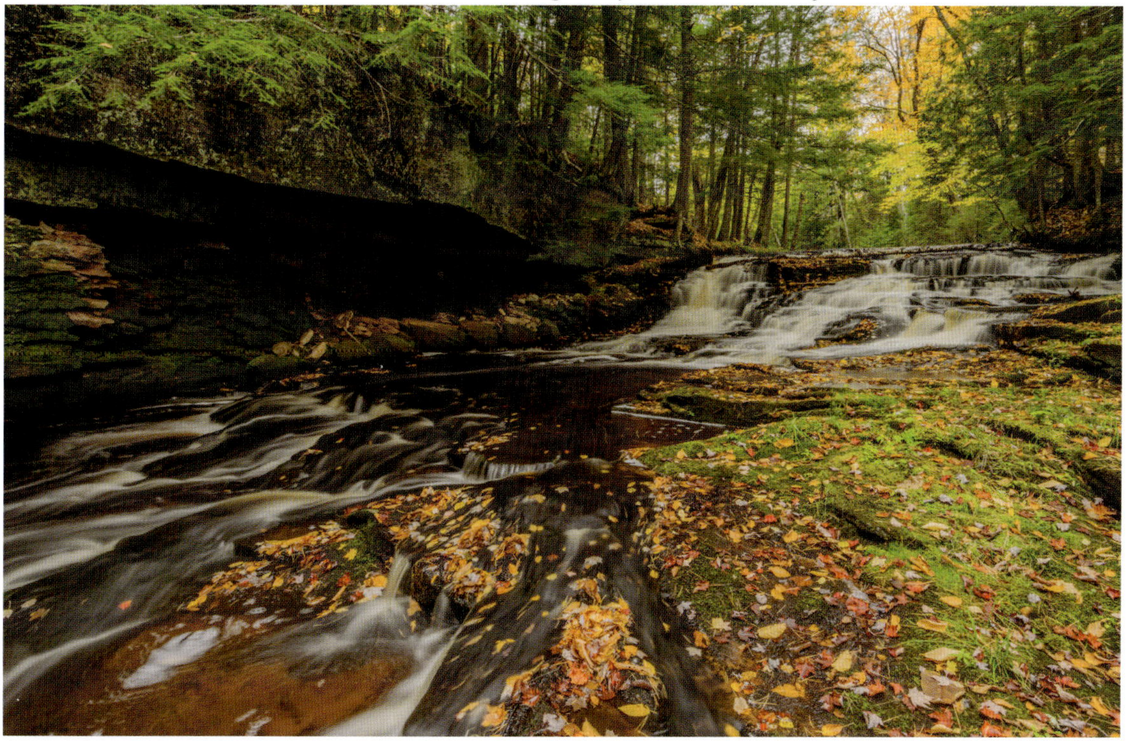

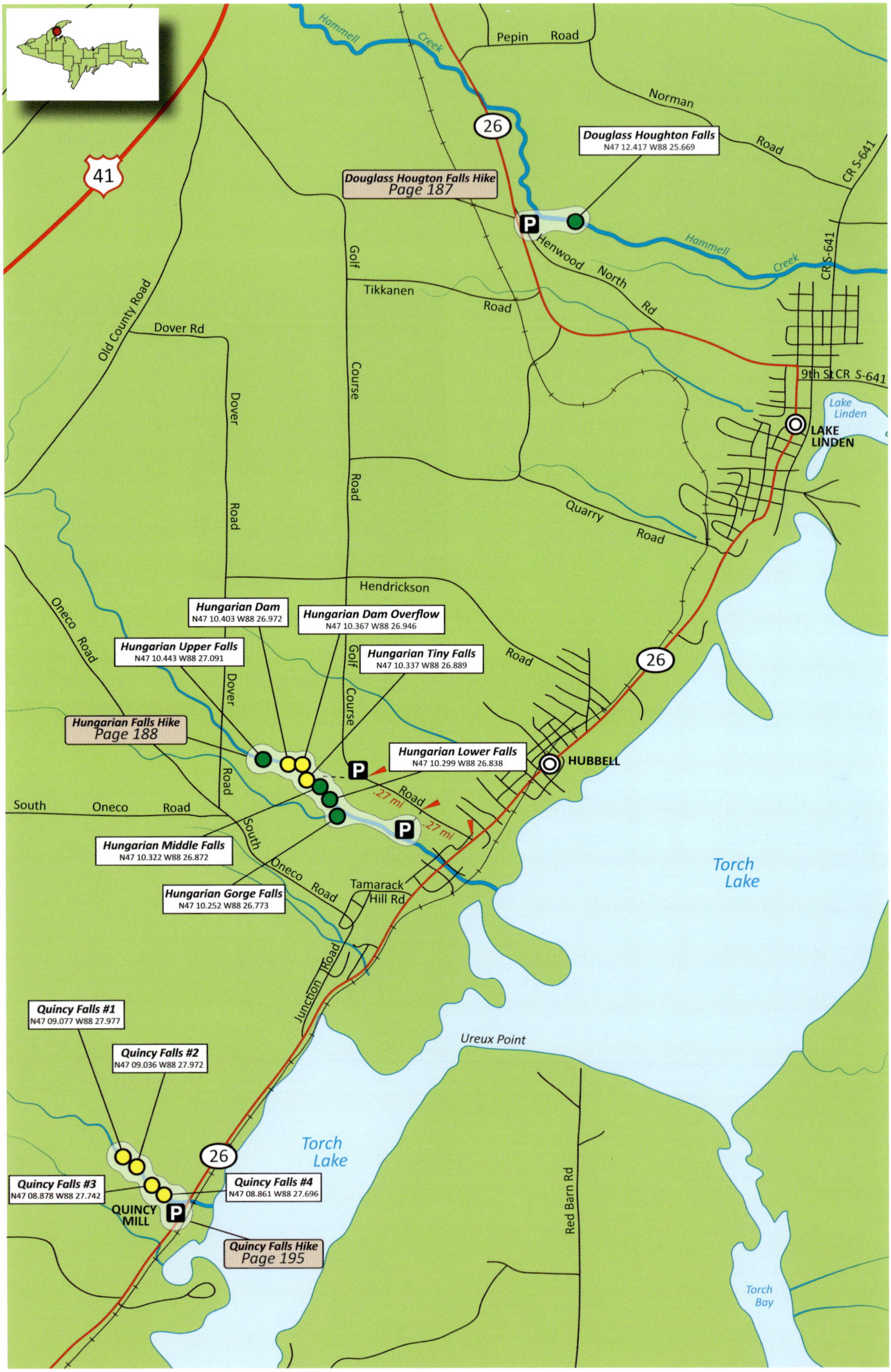
Douglass Houghton Falls
N47 12.417 W88 25.669
Douglass Hougton Falls Hike
Page 187
Hungarian Dam
N47 10.403 W88 26.972
Hungarian Dam Overflow
N47 10.367 W88 26.946
Hungarian Upper Falls
N47 10.443 W88 27.091
Hungarian Tiny Falls
N47 10.337 W88 26.889
Hungarian Falls Hike
Page 188
Hungarian Lower Falls
N47 10.299 W88 26.838
Hungarian Middle Falls
N47 10.322 W88 26.872
Hungarian Gorge Falls
N47 10.252 W88 26.773
Quincy Falls #1
N47 09.077 W88 27.977
Quincy Falls #2
N47 09.036 W88 27.972
Quincy Falls #3
N47 08.878 W88 27.742
Quincy Falls #4
N47 08.861 W88 27.696
Quincy Falls Hike
Page 195
QUINCY MILL
HUBBELL
LAKE LINDEN
Lake Linden
Torch Lake
Torch Bay
Ureux Point
41
26
Hammell Creek
Pepin Road
Norman Road
CR S-641
9th St CR S-641
Henwood North Rd
Golf Course Road
Tikkanen Road
Old County Road
Dover Rd
Dover Road
Quarry Road
Hendrickson Road
Oneco Road
South Oneco Road
Tamarack Hill Rd
Junction Road
Red Barn Rd
.27 mi

Douglass Houghton Falls Hike

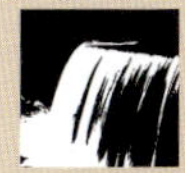

Douglass Houghton Falls: The highest waterfall in Michigan, Douglass Houghton Falls was a favorite haunt of Michigan Tech students for years. I remember my brother taking me to see it back in the 1980's while he was attending college in Houghton. However, since the 1990's it has been closed to the public. Trash was being left behind. Individuals were rappelling down the unstable, crumbling face down into the gorge. Several people had died by falling over the edge to the unforgiving rock floor below. The gorge walls seem to have become steeper and more dangerous over time.

Hammell Creek, the small creek that feeds the falls, runs through a flat field before suddenly plunging over the cliff. Multiple cascades send the creek tumbling over one rock face after another. The creek gathers itself together again at the base of the gorge. It follows the relatively narrow split in the earth, eventually merging with Trap Rock River before dumping into the northern end of Torch Lake.

As of this printing, the State of Michigan has approved funding to purchase the waterfall and surrounding land. It is hoped that the transfer will take place in the spring of 2017. Afterwards, there will need to be construction of appropriate safeguards before public access will be allowed.

Directions: From Lake Linden, head west on M-26 about 1 mile. After the DNR has opened the waterfall to the public, I'm assuming that there will be appropriate signage to the parking area and waterfall.

As of this printing, this waterfall is still on private land, and the landowner has expressly forbidden trespassing. As always, respect landowners' wishes. Do not enter without permission.

DOUGLASS HOUGHTON FALLS (HAMMELL CREEK)

Private

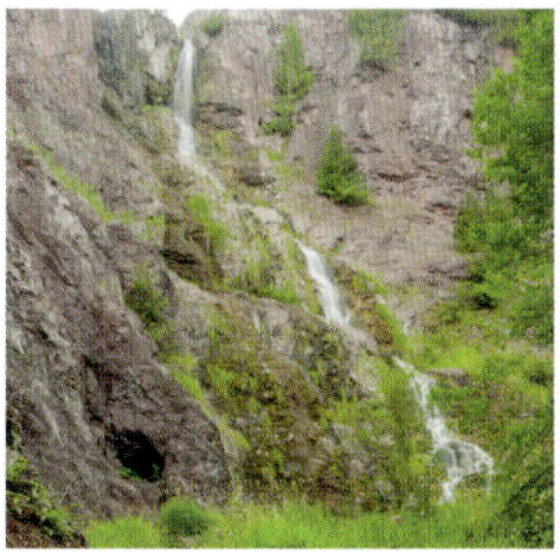

Must See:	8	GPS:	N47 12.428 W88 25.684
Height:	143 feet		
Time:	20-60 minutes	Hiking Information	
		Path:	Overgrown Footpath
Driving Information		Length:	.2 miles from the road
Signs:	None	Elev. Change:	Extremely Steep Gorge
Road:	Secondary	GPS:	N/A
Access:	N/A	Danger:	Extreme
4WD:	N/A	WP Boots:	Recommended

The State of Michigan is in the process of purchasing Douglass Houghton Falls. After it is opened to the public, it stands to be a great tourist draw, with waterfall lovers and geologists alike flocking to enjoy this wonderful Michigan treasure.

Note the black oval shaped hole near the base of the waterfall. This is all that remains of an old mining attempt.

Do not attempt to visit this waterfall until it is owned by the State of Michigan and made available to the public. Until then, it is private, and access is strictly prohibited.

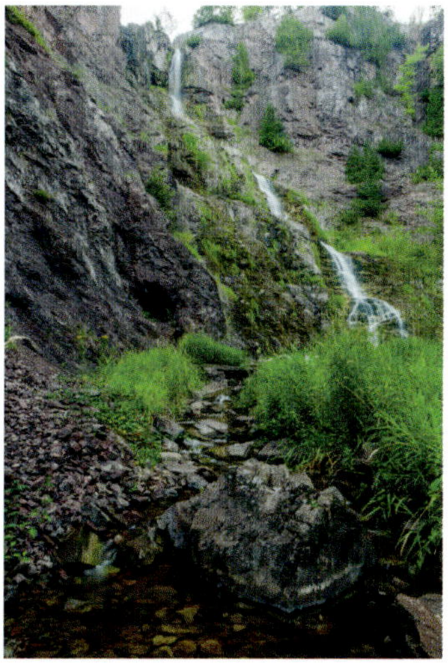

Hungarian Falls Hike

The Hungarian Falls are a very popular set of waterfalls to visit. Many rock climbers enjoy rappelling down the face of the lower falls, they are fairly easy to access, and they are clustered together over only about .3 miles.

Directions: From M-26, near Hubbell, turn northwest onto Golf Course Road (dirt). The road splits almost immediately. Take the left branch. The road rises up quickly into the highlands. About .25 miles up from M-26, turn left (southwest) onto a 2-track. Follow it for about .10 miles. There is a widened out parking area along the 2-track. Park. Follow the 2-track to the edge of the gorge. A footpath follows the gorge. Hike upstream (northwest). Soon, a spur trail "Y"s off down into the gorge. If desiring to get to the base of the gorge to view the Gorge Falls and the Lower Falls from their base, follow this trail. (Note: This is a VERY steep and narrow trail. Beware!) Otherwise, stay on the top path to get to the top of the Lower Falls as well as the rest of the Hungarian waterfalls upstream.

Alternate route: About .5 miles up from M-26 there is a gate on the left. Park off of the side of the road (not blocking the gate). Hike past the gate (southwest) for about .2 miles. There is lacework of dirt roads here. The general idea is to find the creek and follow the road that leads along it. Hiking in should bring you about to the middle of the waterfall area. Hike both directions to see all the waterfalls.

HUNGARIAN GORGE FALLS (UNNAMED CREEK)

Private

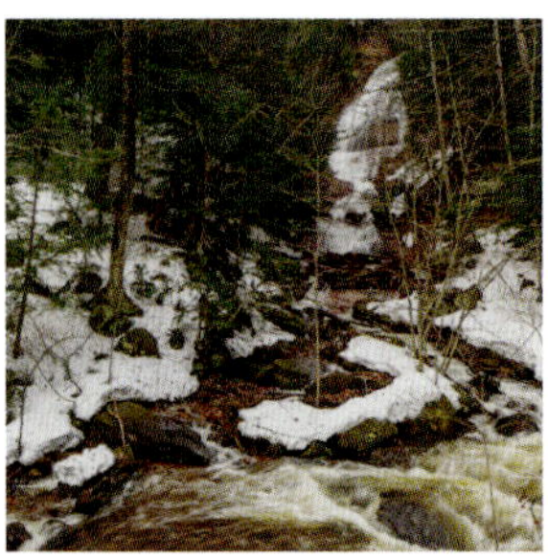

Must See:	8	GPS:	N47 10.252 W88 26.773
Height:	60 feet		
Time:	60-90 minutes	Hiking Information	
		Path:	Steep, Narrow Footpath
Driving Information		Length:	.27 miles
Signs:	None	Elev. Change:	Extremely Steep Gorge
Road:	2-track	GPS:	Helpful
Access:	Somewhat Easy	Danger:	Extreme
4WD:	N/A	WP Boots:	Recommended

An unnamed creek pours down into the gorge in a torrent from the far side during spring melt and after heavy rains. It cascades off of ribbed layers of bedrocks. Small densely packed trees obscure some of the view, adding mystique to the seasonal waterfall.

Note: Hiking Information is based on parking down the 2-track, not by the gate.

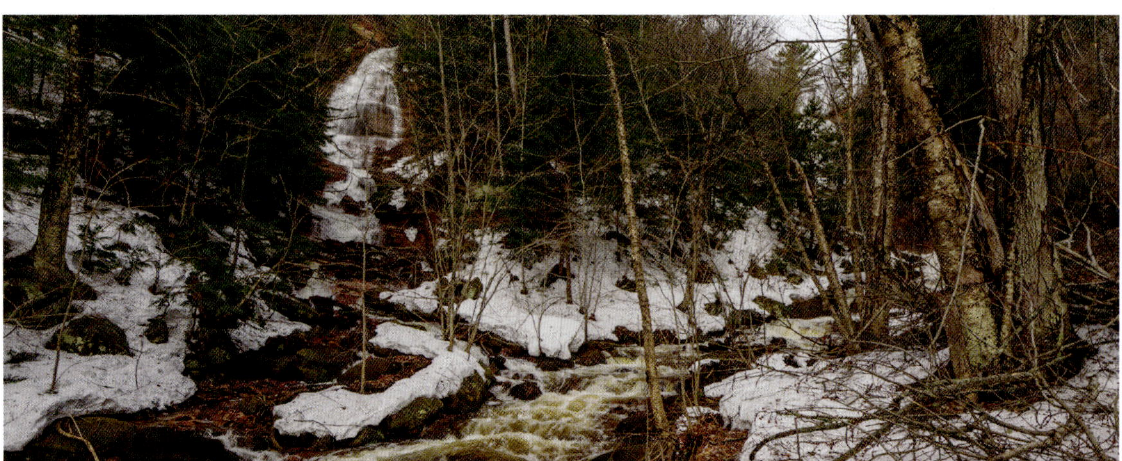

HUNGARIAN LOWER FALLS (DOVER CREEK)

Private

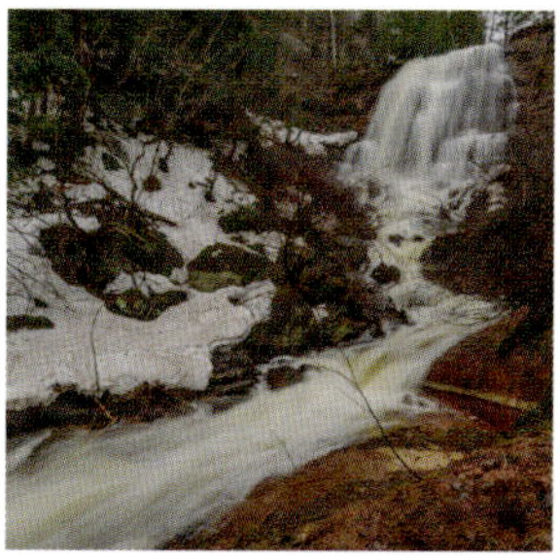

Must See:	9	GPS:	N47 10.299 W88 26.838
Height:	50 feet		
Time:	60-90 minutes	Hiking Information	
		Path:	Steep, Narrow Footpath
Driving Information		Length:	.36 miles
Signs:	None	Elev. Change:	Extremely Steep Gorge
Road:	2-track	GPS:	Helpful
Access:	Somewhat Easy	Danger:	Extreme
4WD:	N/A	WP Boots:	Recommended

The highest waterfall in the Hungarian Falls is also the furthest downstream. It sports a fanned out, bridal veil look over a solid rock face. A jumbled pile of rock slabs and dead tree trunks lie at the foot of the falls. The deep ravine is guarded with steep side walls, making it very difficult to access the base of the falls. Unfortunately, this is the best way to view the waterfall, since there is very little to see from the top. Water seeps down from the surrounding land, saturating the seemingly sheer walls, making for a muddy and slippery climb. It is recommended to take the "mountain goat" footpath from downstream as described in the "Hungarian Falls Hike" on the previous page. Keep in mind that the trail can be washed out by mud slides.

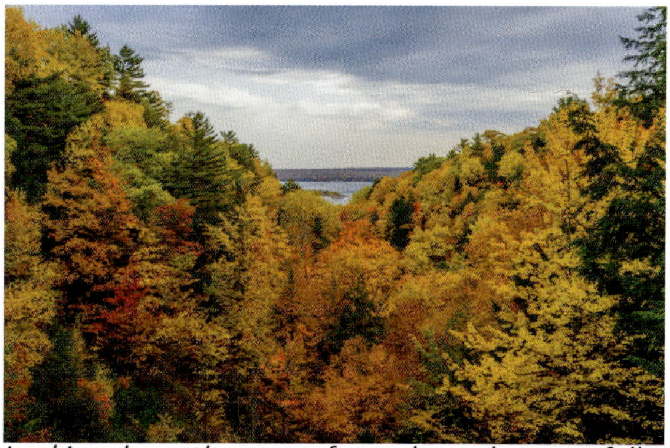

Looking down the gorge from above the waterfall

Note: Hiking Information is based on parking down the 2-track, not by the gate.

The view from the base of the waterfall

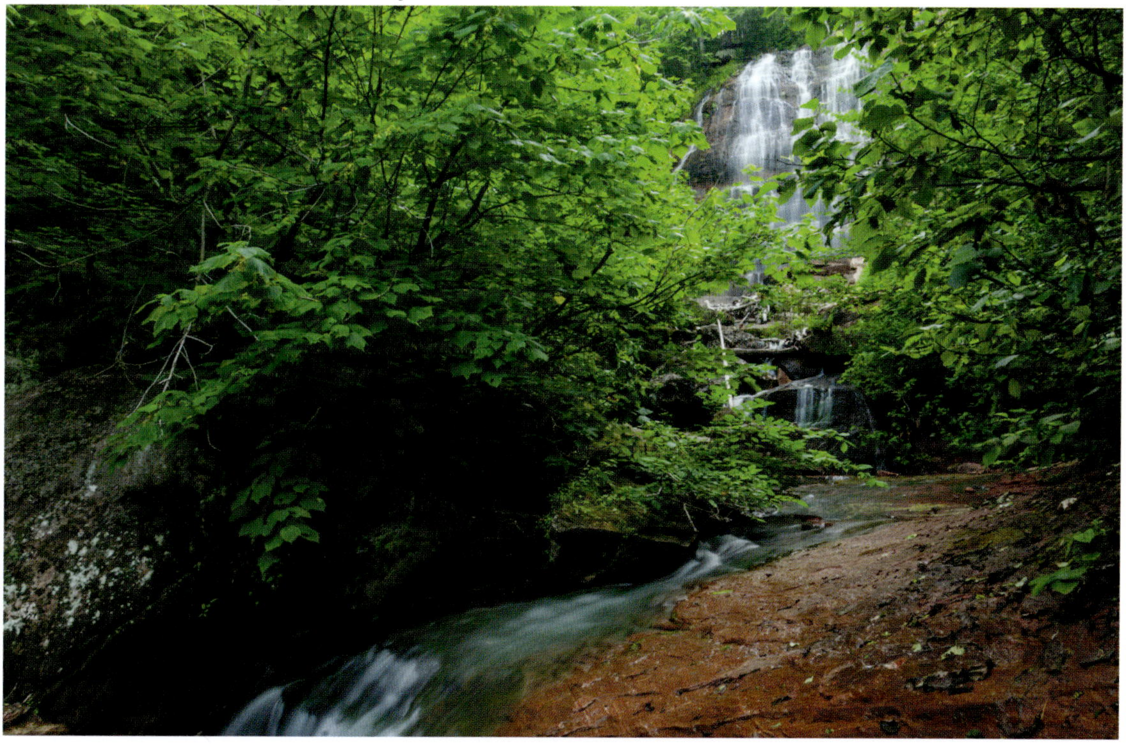

HUNGARIAN MIDDLE FALLS (DOVER CREEK)

Private

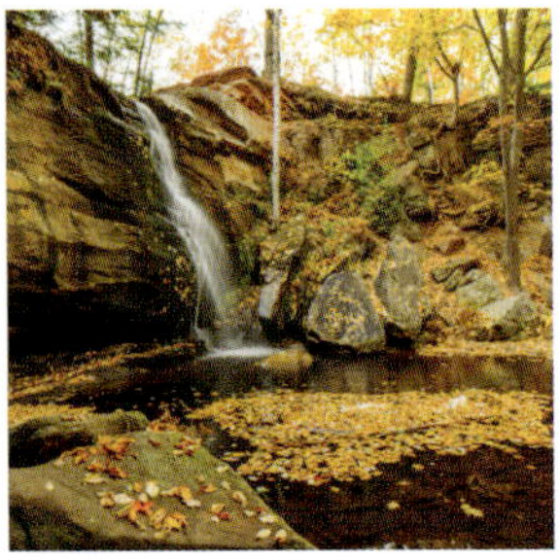

Must See:	9	GPS:	N47 10.322 W88 26.872
Height:	20 feet		
Time:	30-120 minutes	Hiking Information	
		Path:	Narrow Footpath
Driving Information		Length:	.38 miles
Signs:	None	Elev. Change:	Moderate
Road:	2-track	GPS:	Helpful
Access:	Somewhat Easy	Danger:	Moderate
4WD:	N/A	WP Boots:	Recommended

The Middle Falls are only about 200 feet upstream from the Lower Falls. It requires a little bit of climbing (nothing like the Lower Falls, however) to get down to the base of the waterfall, but the view is wonderful, and with the spill pool ringed by rock walls, it feels like the ultimate, intimate, private garden. What a great place for a family picnic! The spill pool is shallow enough for children to splash around in. Just be careful in getting them down the rocky edge to this little piece of paradise.

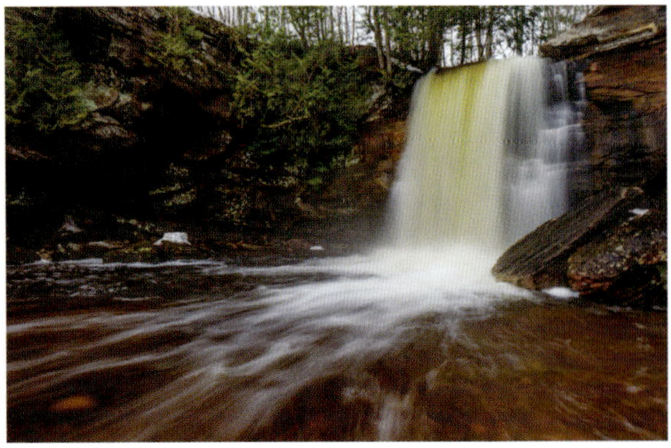

Note: Hiking Information is based on parking down the 2-track, not by the gate.

Note the many looks during the seasons!

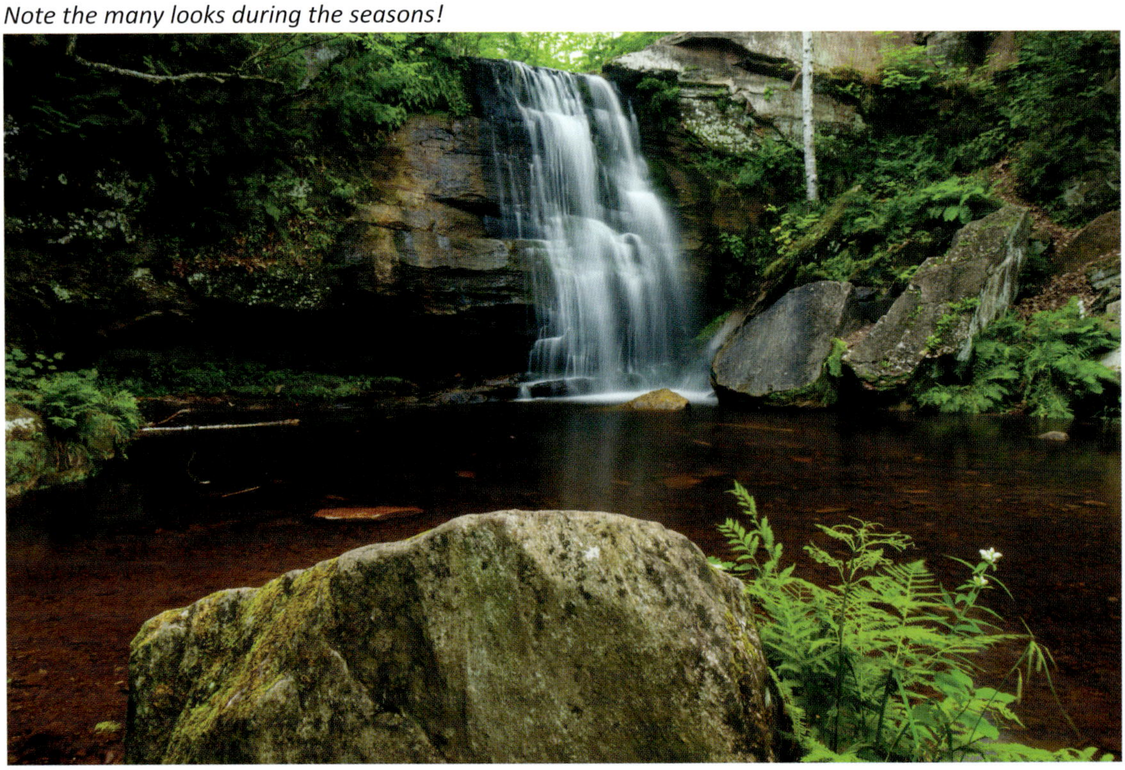

HUNGARIAN TINY FALLS (DOVER CREEK)

Private

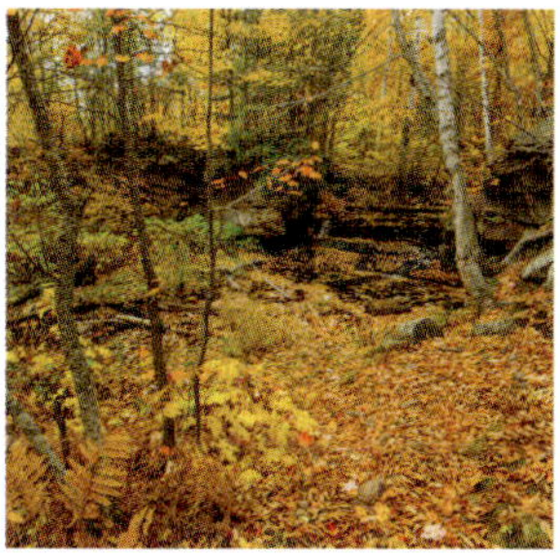

Must See:	6	GPS:	N47 10.337 W88 26.889
Height:	7 feet		
Time:	45-135 minutes	Hiking Information	
		Path:	Narrow Footpath
Driving Information		Length:	.40 miles
Signs:	None	Elev. Change:	Moderate
Road:	2-track	GPS:	Helpful
Access:	Somewhat Easy	Danger:	Moderate
4WD:	N/A	WP Boots:	Recommended

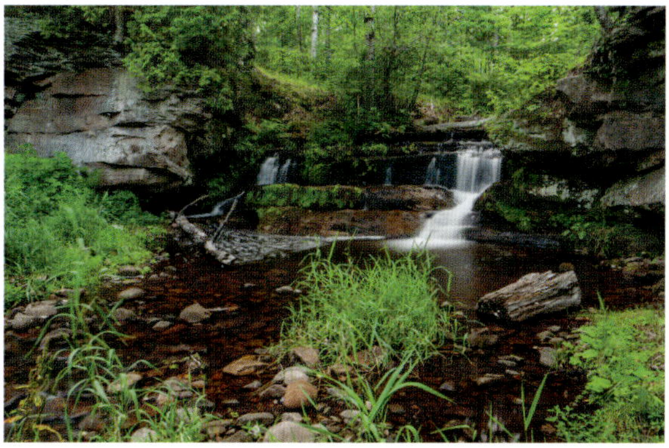

Hike upstream 130 feet from the Middle Falls to get to this very nice, although shorter waterfall. This one is not quite as kid friendly as the Middle Falls, but rock buttresses on either side of the falls frames it very nicely!

The waterfall is situated between two overlooking points of rock, the one on the left looking like the prow of a ship protruding from a rocky mass with several trees growing out of it. With full water flowing, the falls look like a 3-stepped frothing stairway running down to surround an island in the middle of the creek.

Note: Hiking Information is based on parking down the 2-track, not by the gate.

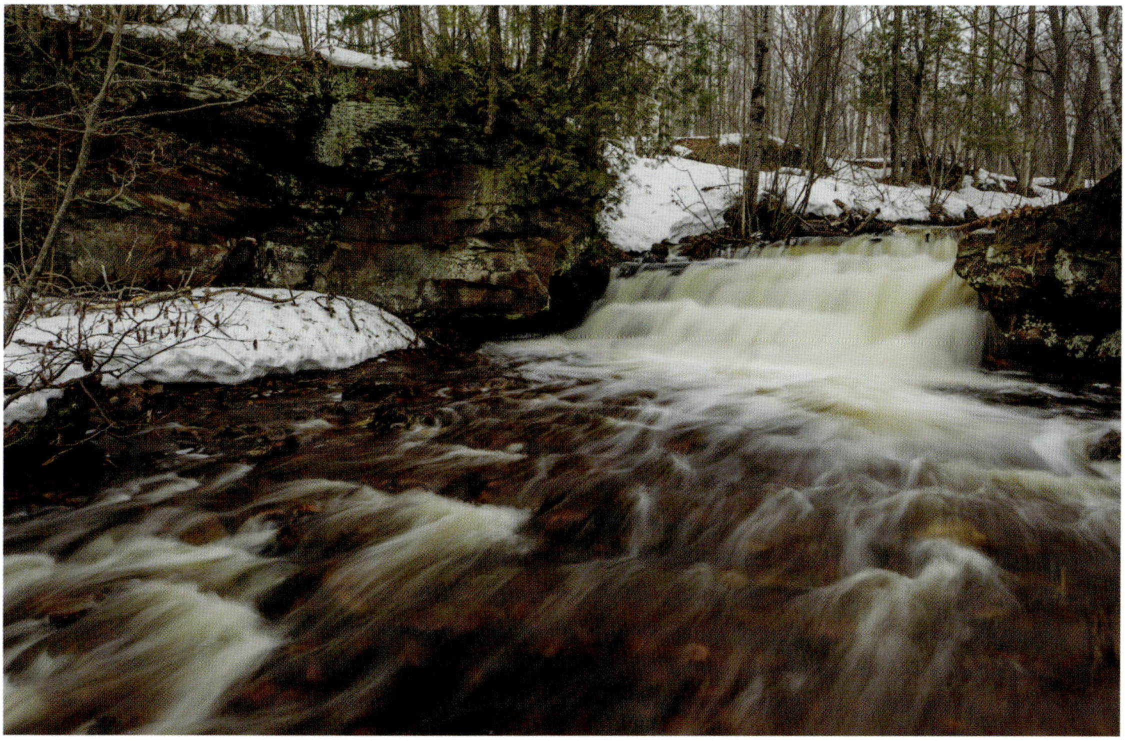

HUNGARIAN DAM OVERFLOW (DOVER CREEK)

Private

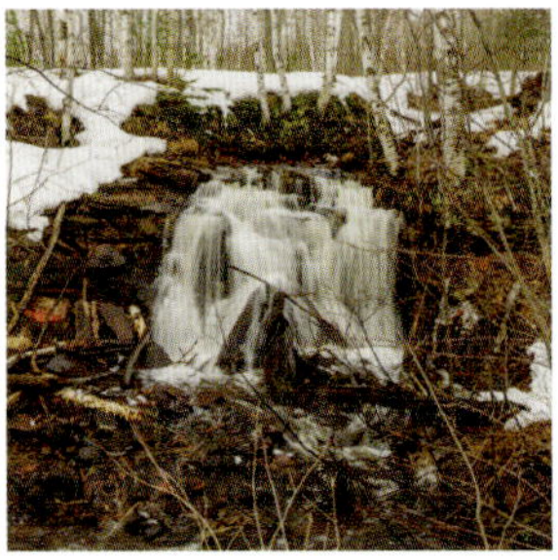

Must See:	5
Height:	10 feet
Time:	60-145 minutes

Driving Information

Signs:	None
Road:	2-track
Access:	Somewhat Easy
4WD:	N/A

GPS:	N47 10.367 W88 26.946

Hiking Information

Path:	2-track
Length:	.47 miles
Elev. Change:	Slight
GPS:	Helpful
Danger:	Slight
WP Boots:	N/A

Continue upstream for about 125 yards from Tiny Falls, around a sharp bend in the creek and just past an old wooden bridge that spans the creek. On the far side of the creek, there is a seasonal waterfall. It flows when the dam is over capacity. The excess water then flows through a concrete channel. The water runs down the channel, drops over a 2 foot ledge, around a slight bend, then cascades down quickly over loose sheets of rock before joining the main water flow.

Note: Hiking Information is based on parking down the 2-track, not by the gate.

The creek is along the right side of the picture - the overflow along the left

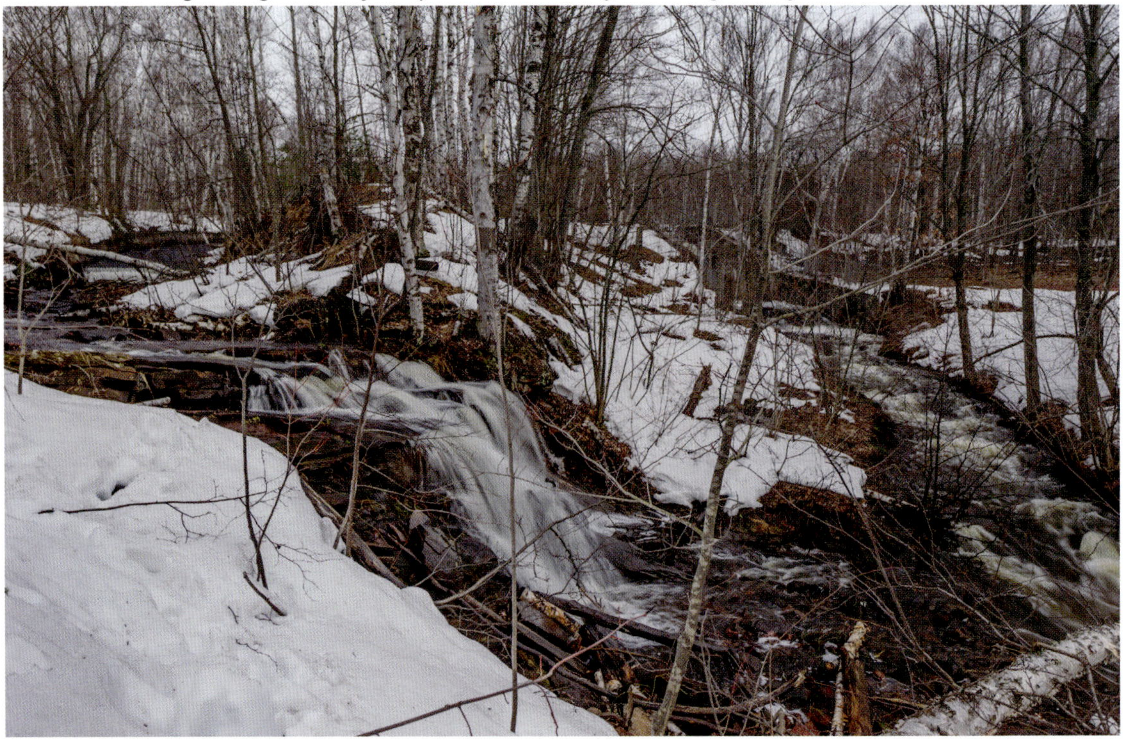

HUNGARIAN DAM (DOVER CREEK)

Private

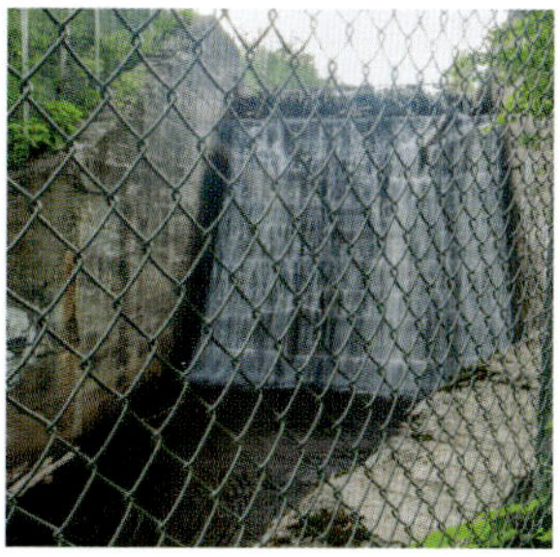

Must See:	4	GPS:	N47 10.403 W88 26.972
Height:	12 feet		
Time:	70-150 minutes	Hiking Information	
		Path:	Dirt Roads
Driving Information		Length:	.51 miles
Signs:	None	Elev. Change:	Slight
Road:	2-track	GPS:	Helpful
Access:	Somewhat Easy	Danger:	Slight
4WD:	N/A	WP Boots:	N/A

The dam is just upstream (250 feet) from the Overflow Falls. The artificial lake drains over the dam spillway about halfway between Tiny Falls and Upper Falls. The concrete walls and steel fence seem somehow out of place amongst all the natural beauty found up and down the creek.

Note: Hiking Information is based on parking down the 2-track, not by the gate.

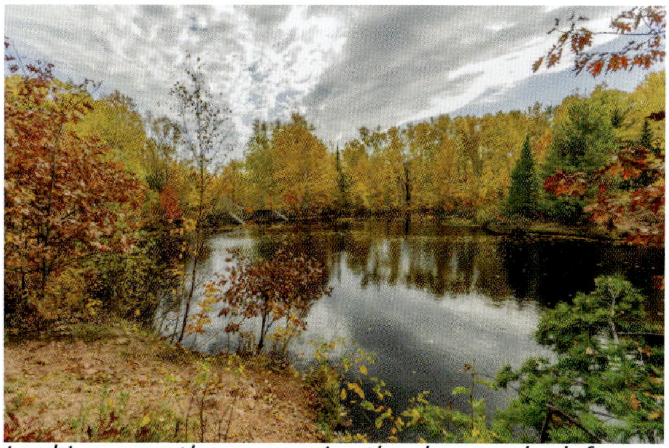

Looking over the reservoir - the dam to the left

The Dam Overflow is to the left of this shot

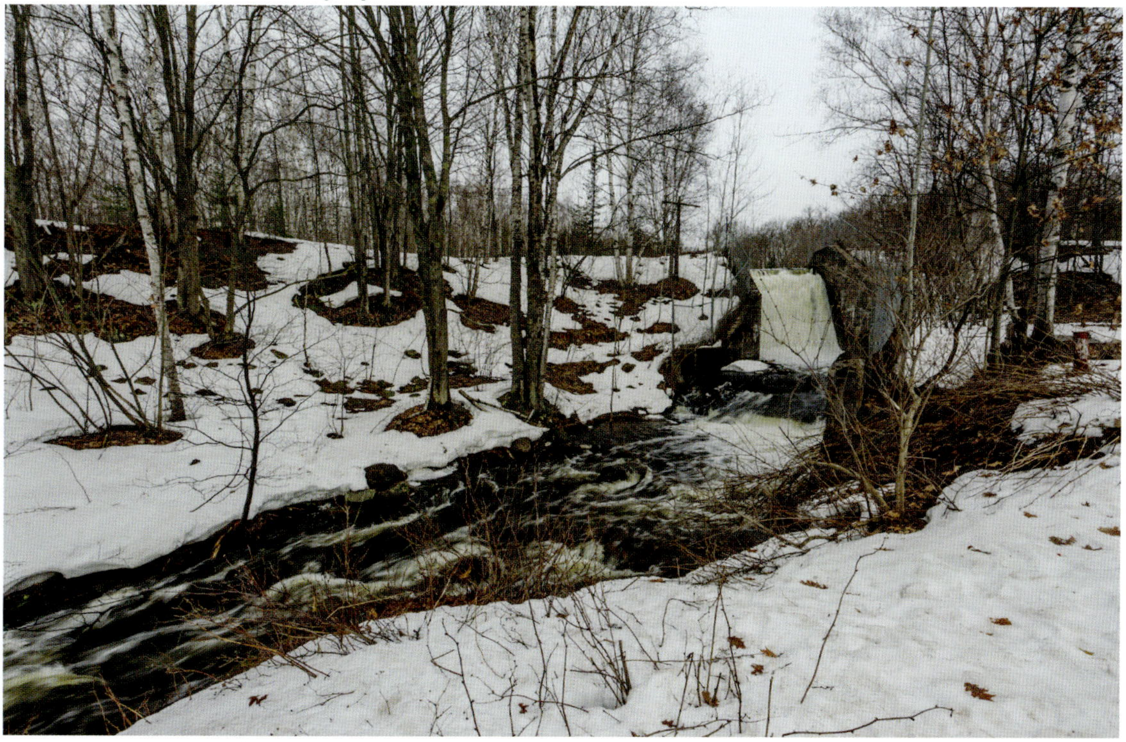

HUNGARIAN UPPER FALLS (DOVER CREEK)

Private

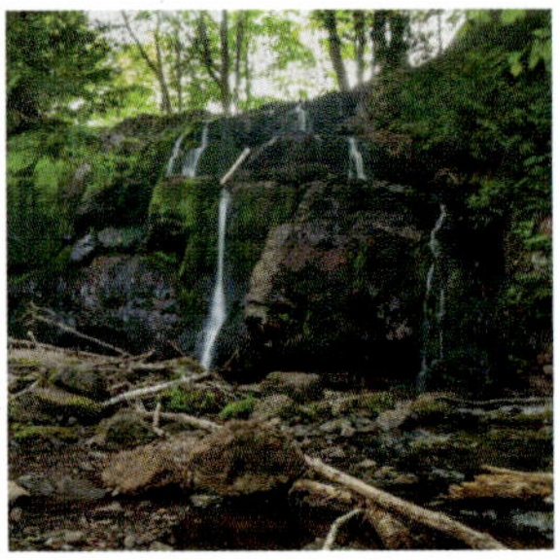

Must See:	7	GPS:	N47 10.443 W88 27.091
Height:	20 feet		
Time:	60-145 minutes	**Hiking Information**	
		Path:	2-track
Driving Information		Length:	.62 miles
Signs:	None	Elev. Change:	Moderate
Road:	2-track	GPS:	Helpful
Access:	Somewhat Easy	Danger:	Moderate
4WD:	N/A	WP Boots:	N/A

From the dam, follow the northern side of the reservoir. About 200 yards upstream from the dam, the Upper Falls cascade down just above the top of the back waters. This is a two-tiered waterfall. The top tier is a 15 foot nearly sheer plunge over a rocky face. The creek flattens out over a debris field for 20 yards, then drops another 5 feet (the second tier) over cascades. It fills the creek bed from side to side during spring melt. The waterfall is much less impressive during dry summer months.

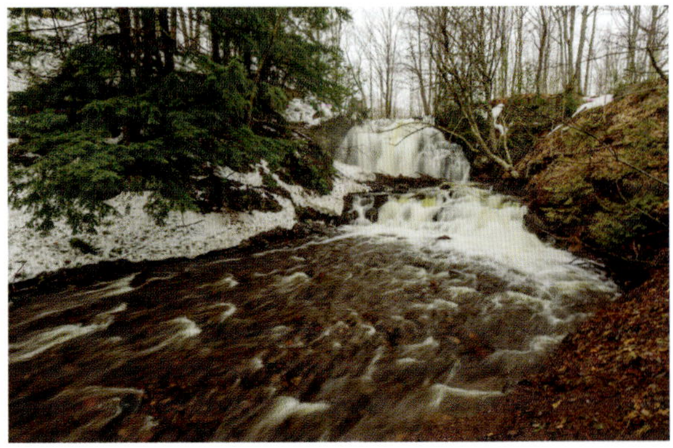

Note: Hiking Information is based on parking down the 2-track, not by the gate.

This waterfall needs a good deal of water to present itself well. Compare these widely different looks!

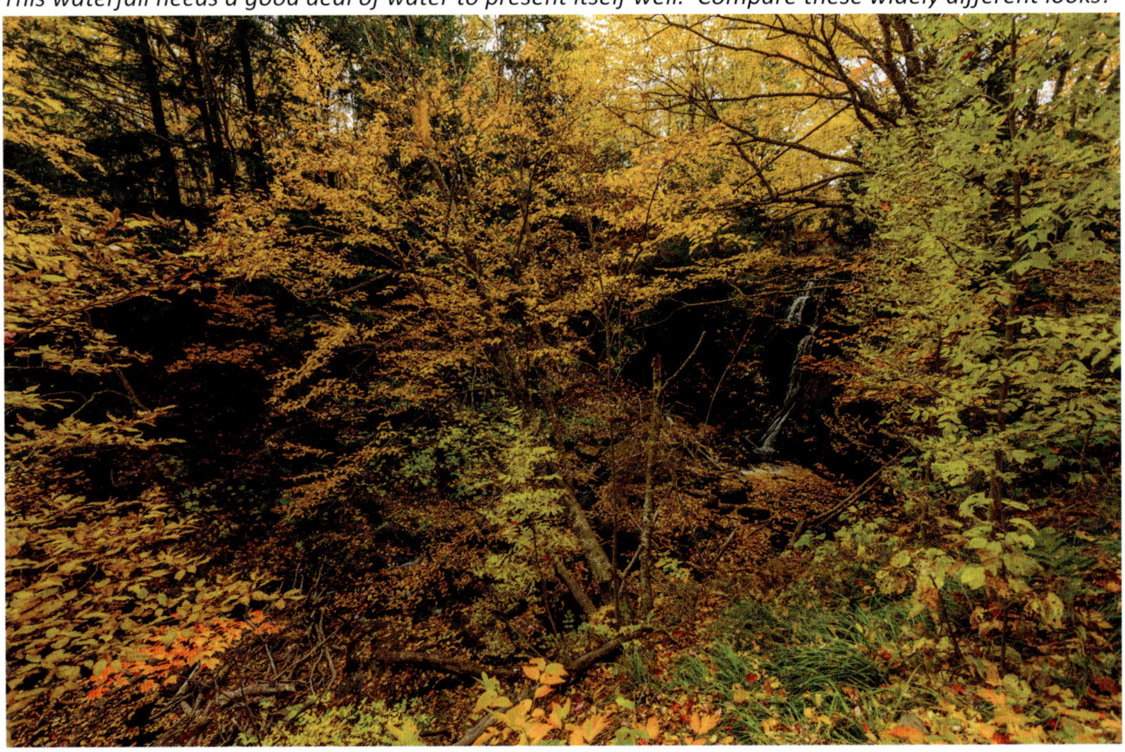

Quincy Falls Hike

Quincy Falls are found along Quincy Creek, which tumbles down through a steep gorge as the creek approaches Torch Lake. The Quincy Stamp Mill ruins can be seen along M-26 near Quincy Creek. The stamp mills crushed copper-bearing rocks taken from deep underground by the Quincy Mine. Large amounts of water were needed to properly operate the stamp mills, so this location on Torch Lake with a creek running through the mill was perfect. (Initially, in 1860, the Quincy Mine had its milling operations on Portage Lake, but over time the massive amount of tailings produced by the mill was restricting navigation and the mine was forced to find a new location.) The mill on Torch Lake operated from the late 1800's until 1931 during the Great Depression and again on a limited basis from 1937 until the close of World War II.

Directions: Cross the drawbridge from Houghton to Hancock, heading north on US-41. (Immediately after crossing the bridge, US-41 turn left to the west. Don't follow this natural inclination.) Turn right (east) instead to head onto M-26. Follow M-26 for 6.2 miles. The old remains of the Quincy Mill are on the left. There is a parking area just before the buildings. Park. Carefully walk west/ northwest back past the building foundations. There is much debris to avoid. Behind the buildings is an access road (dirt 2-track) that runs basically parallel to M-26. Hike to the right (northeast) along the road. It crosses Quincy Creek. Once over the creek look for a faint footpath that follows the creek upstream. The creek is in a steep sided gorge with greenery clinging to the walls where it can. The easiest route to the bottom of the gorge at each waterfall is evidenced by spur trails that leave the "main" trail that follows the top of the gorge from the access road to the end of the gorge (which is at the #1 falls). The #4 falls are just upstream from the access road.

QUINCY FALLS #4 (QUINCY CREEK)

Private

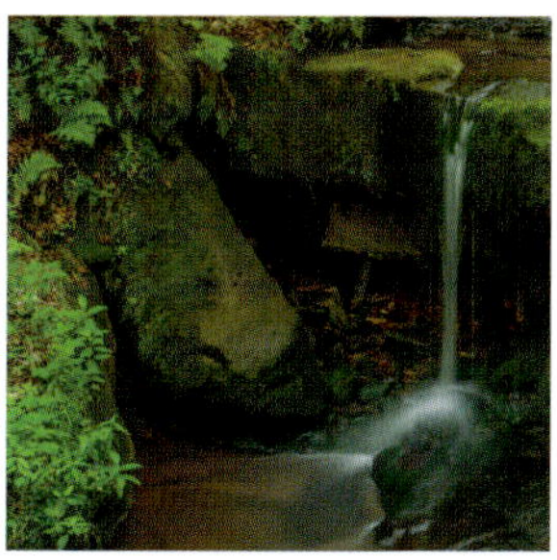

Must See:	6	GPS:	N47 08.861 W88 27.696
Height:	7 feet		
Time:	20-30 minutes	Hiking Information	
		Path:	Unimproved Footpath
Driving Information		Length:	.12 miles
Signs:	None	Elev. Change:	Steep gorge
Road:	Main	GPS:	Recommended
Access:	Somewhat Easy	Danger:	Elevated
4WD:	N/A	WP Boots:	Required

This selection of waterfalls is located in a wild creek. The steep ravine must be repeatedly navigated to access each of the waterfalls. Be prepared for the climbs.

Large moss covered boulders hide the water flowing under them. Remnants of mining equipment are strewn downstream.

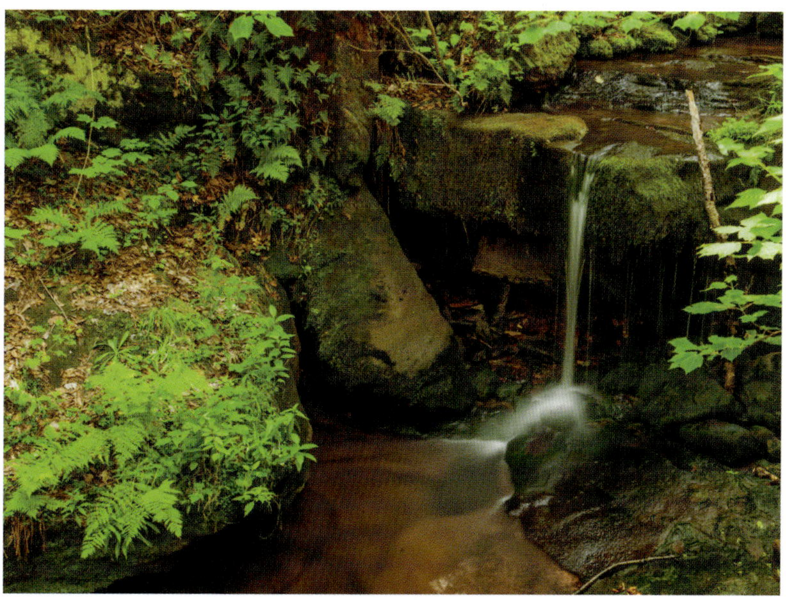

QUINCY FALLS #3 (QUINCY CREEK)

Private

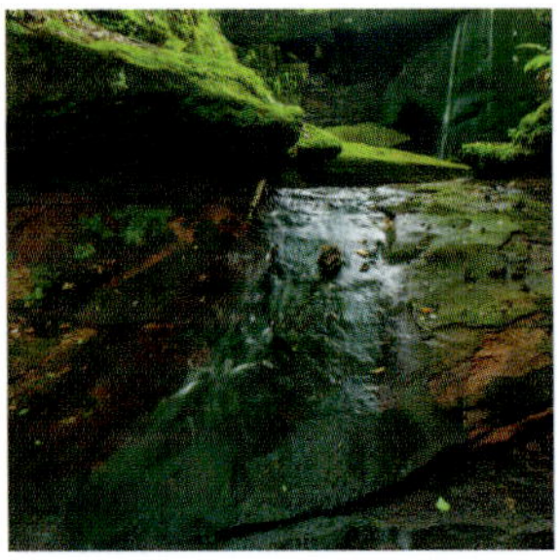

Must See:	5	GPS:	N47 08.878 W88 27.742
Height:	13 feet		
Time:	20-30 minutes		

Driving Information

Signs:	None
Road:	Main
Access:	Somewhat Easy
4WD:	N/A

Hiking Information

Path:	Unimproved Footpath
Length:	.16 miles
Elev. Change:	Steep gorge
GPS:	Recommended
Danger:	Elevated
WP Boots:	Required

Work your way up and down the ravine to travel just 250 feet up the gorge to this next waterfall.

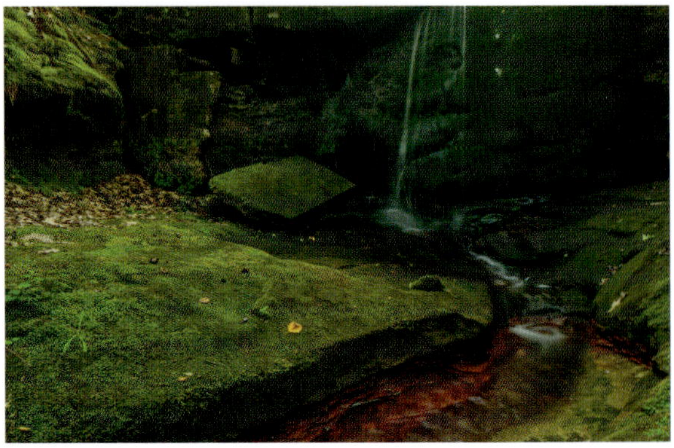

Slippery rocks and a steep climb down into the gorge are more easily mastered by using a rope attached to a tree part way down the ravine. Make sure it is in good condition before using. Concrete and steel incorporated into a small dam show the evidence of man's work here in years past.

I'd love to see this creek with a good amount of water flowing!

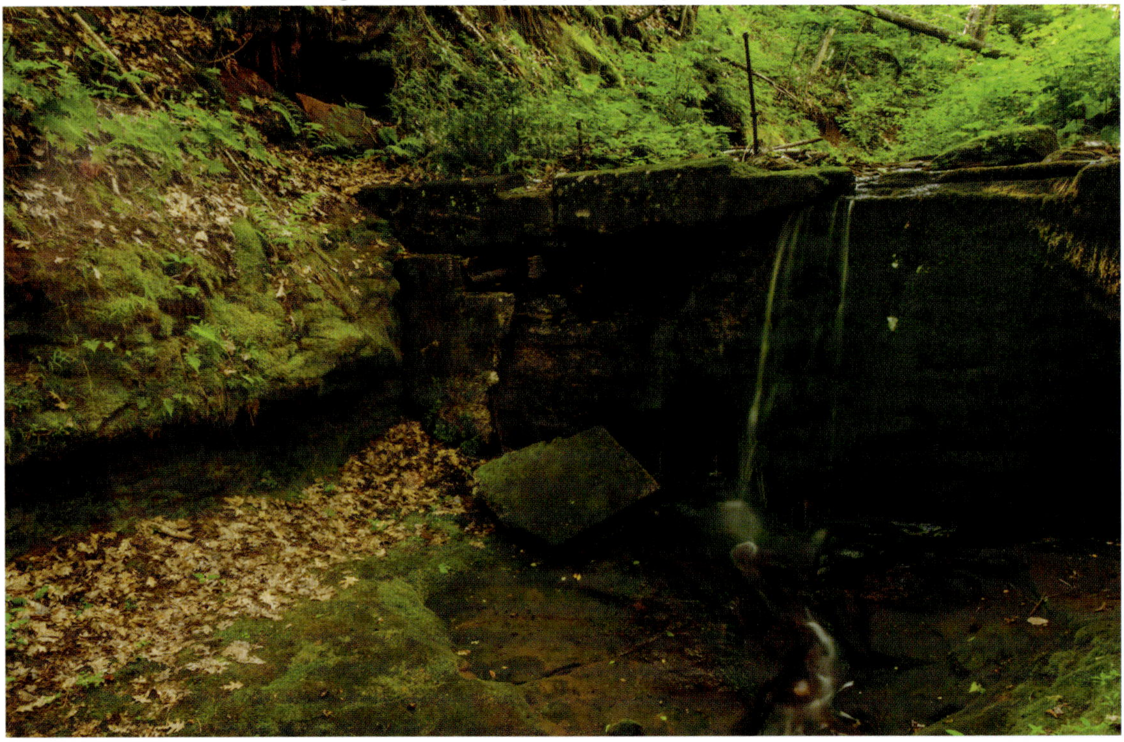

QUINCY FALLS #2 (QUINCY CREEK)

Private

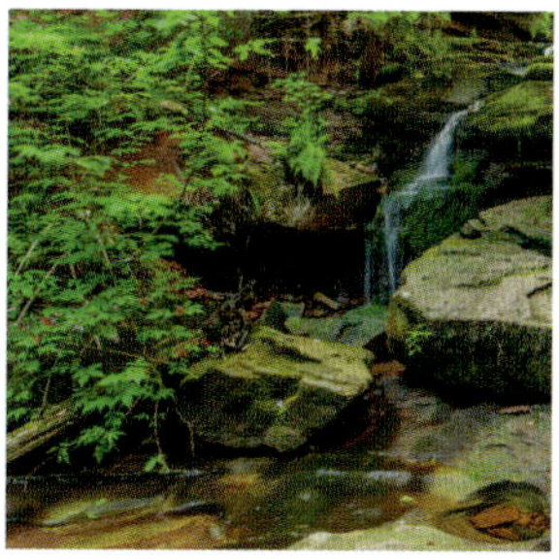

Must See:	5	GPS:	N47 09.036 W88 27.972
Height:	10 feet		
Time:	40-60 minutes		

Driving Information

Signs:	None
Road:	Main
Access:	Somewhat Easy
4WD:	N/A

Hiking Information

Path:	Unimproved Footpath
Length:	.46 miles
Elev. Change:	Steep gorge
GPS:	Recommended
Danger:	Elevated
WP Boots:	Required

It is .28 miles between #3 and #2 falls. Following the faint footpath at the top of the gorge is certainly the easiest way to travel between the falls.

The small creek cascades over terraced mossy rocks down to a quiet shallow pool where minnows play.

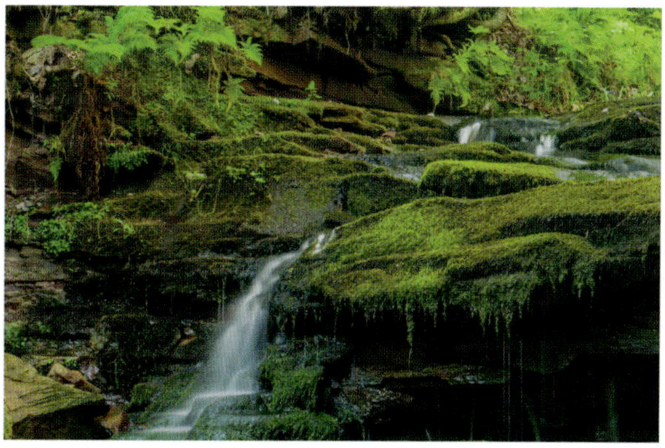

Small "potholes" are found here - similar to those found at the Kettles in Porcupine Mountains

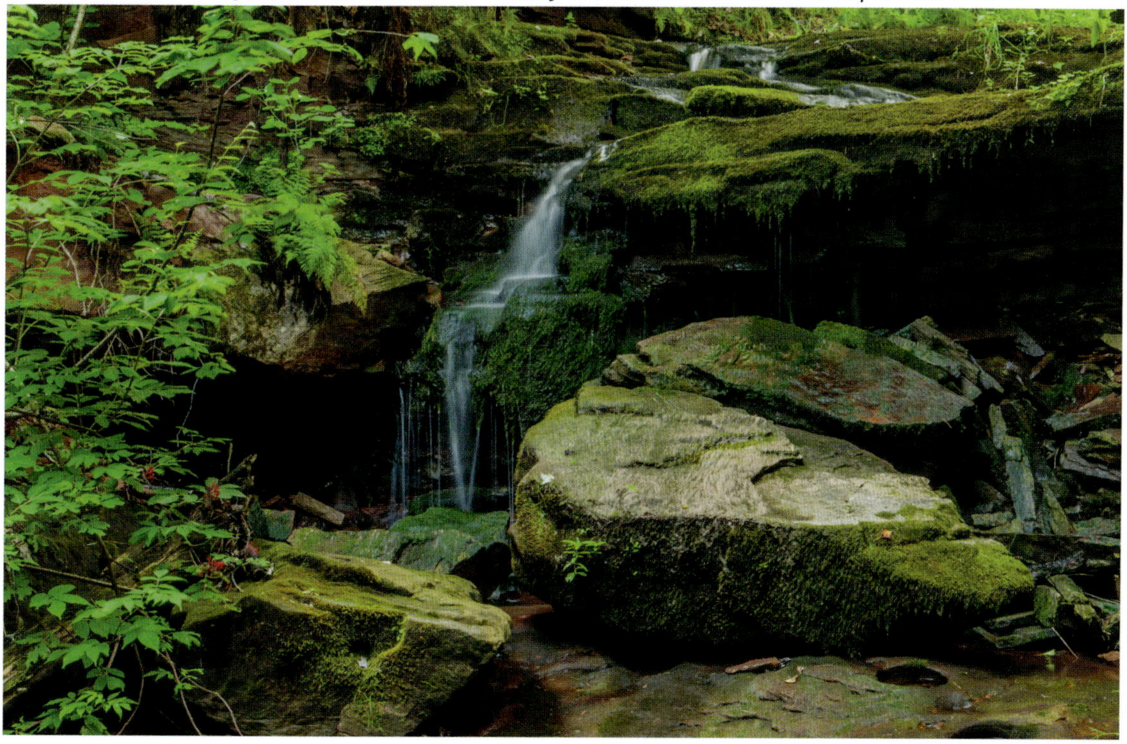

QUINCY FALLS #1 (QUINCY CREEK)

Private

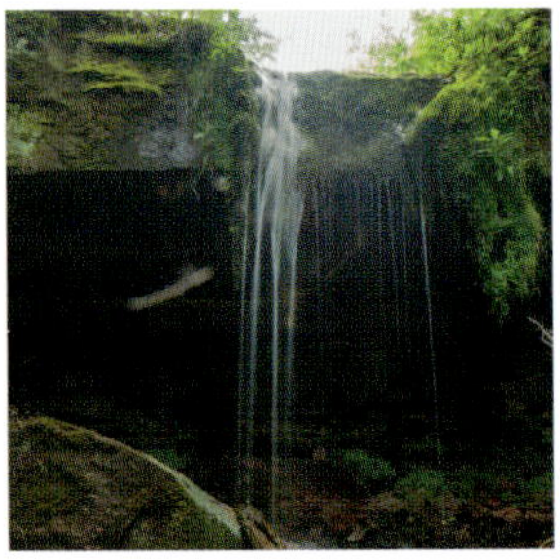

Must See:	6	GPS:	N47 09.077 W88 27.977
Height:	15 feet		
Time:	45-75 minutes	**Hiking Information**	
		Path:	Unimproved Footpath
Driving Information		Length:	.49 miles
Signs:	None	Elev. Change:	Steep gorge
Road:	Main	GPS:	Recommended
Access:	Somewhat Easy	Danger:	Elevated
4WD:	N/A	WP Boots:	Required

It's only 80 yards upstream from #2 to get to #1. The top two waterfalls are grouped together, as are the lower two waterfalls on Quincy Creek.

A curtain drop over a massive rock face greets you as the creek enters this rugged gorge. A tangled mass of boulders and tree trunks clog this top portion of the gorge.

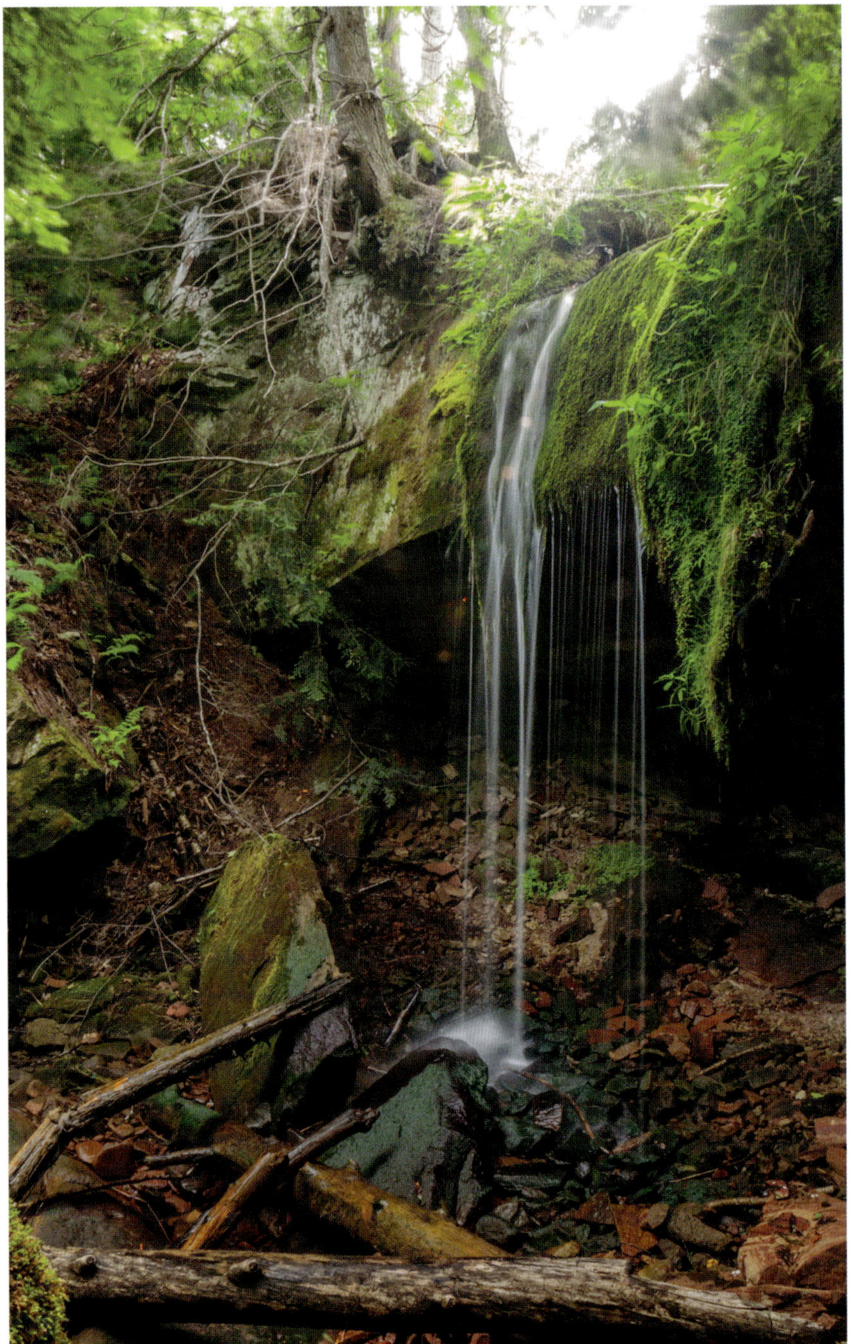

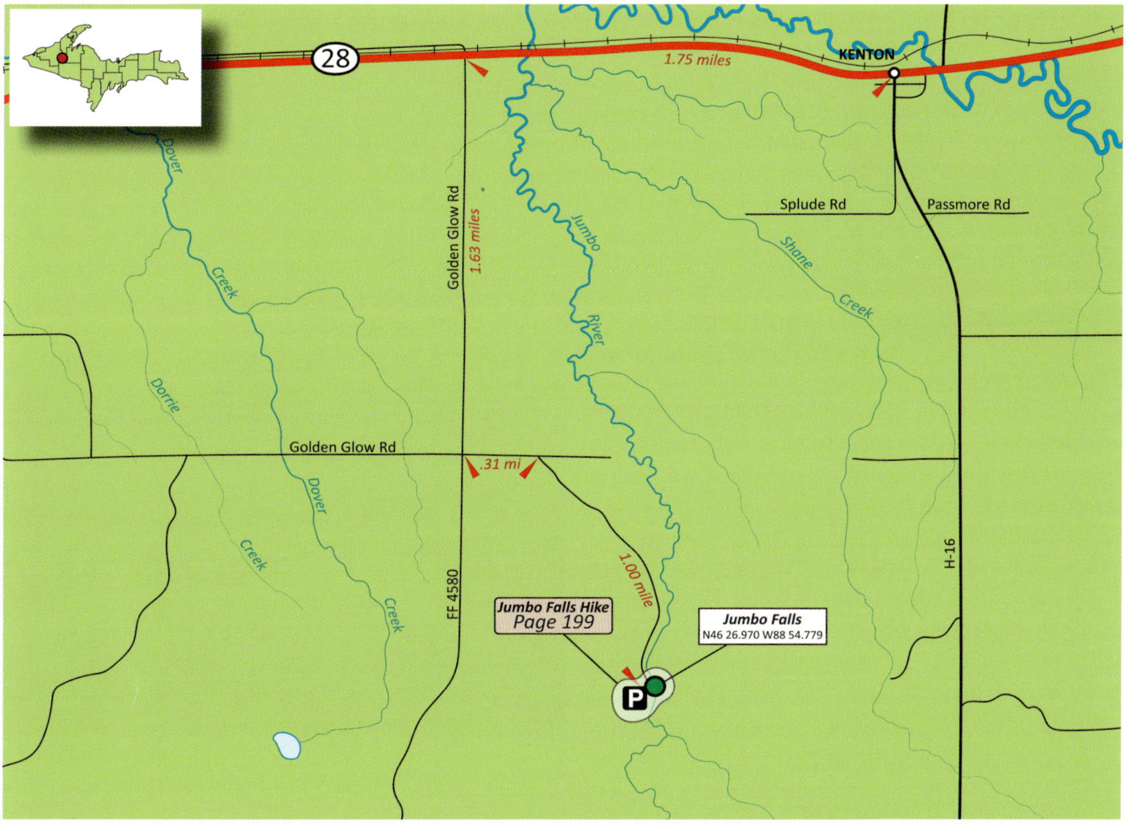

Jumbo Falls Hike

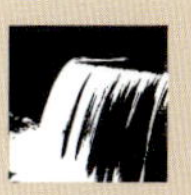

Jumbo Falls: A short, but nicely presented cascading waterfall greets you after a short hike through a mature section of forest. Beautiful wildflowers grow along the edges of the waterfall, adding a splash of color.

Directions: Travel 1.75 miles west on M-28 from Kenton. Turn left (south) on Golden Glow Road (the next road west of Jumbo River). After 1.63 miles follow the road to the left (east). In .31 miles veer to the right (southeast). In 1.2 miles park near the obvious trailhead to the falls. Hike 100 yards on a semi-improved trail to Jumbo Falls.

JUMBO FALLS (JUMBO RIVER)

Private

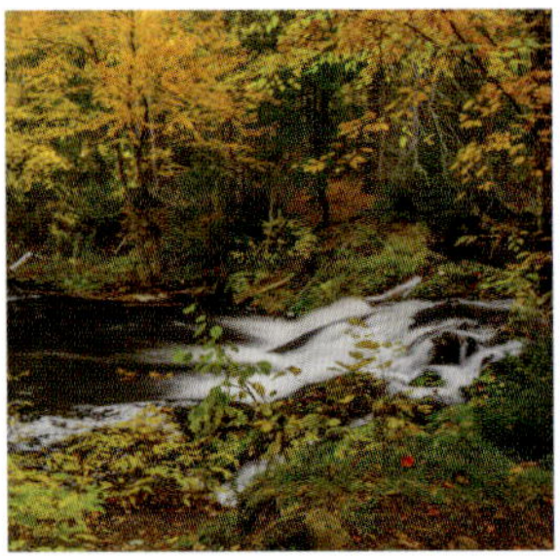

Must See:	8
Height:	6 feet
Time:	10-20 minutes

Driving Information

Signs:	None
Road:	Dirt
Access:	Somewhat Easy
4WD:	N/A

GPS:	N46 26.970 W88 54.779

Hiking Information

Path:	Semi-improved Footpath
Length:	100 yards
Elev. Change:	Slight
GPS:	N/A
Danger:	Slight
WP Boots:	N/A

This rates as a "kid-friendly" waterfall since it is a short hike down the well-travelled path that is normally not too muddy, and the river isn't especially deep and there are no major stumbling spots along the way.

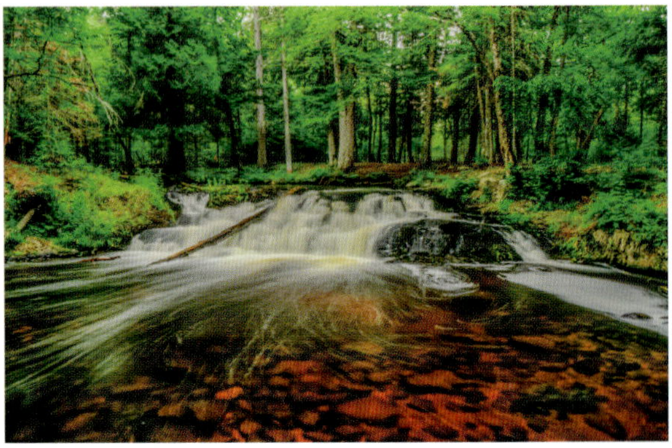

The Jumbo River, a little over 3 miles downstream from the Duppy Falls in Iron County, runs quietly through a beautiful forest. The minimally banked river turns a bend and cascades down 6 feet to a shallow, widened spill pool. A lovely viewing area is several dozen yards downstream as the river narrows below the pool.

Beware! The dirt road to the falls is not plowed in the winter.

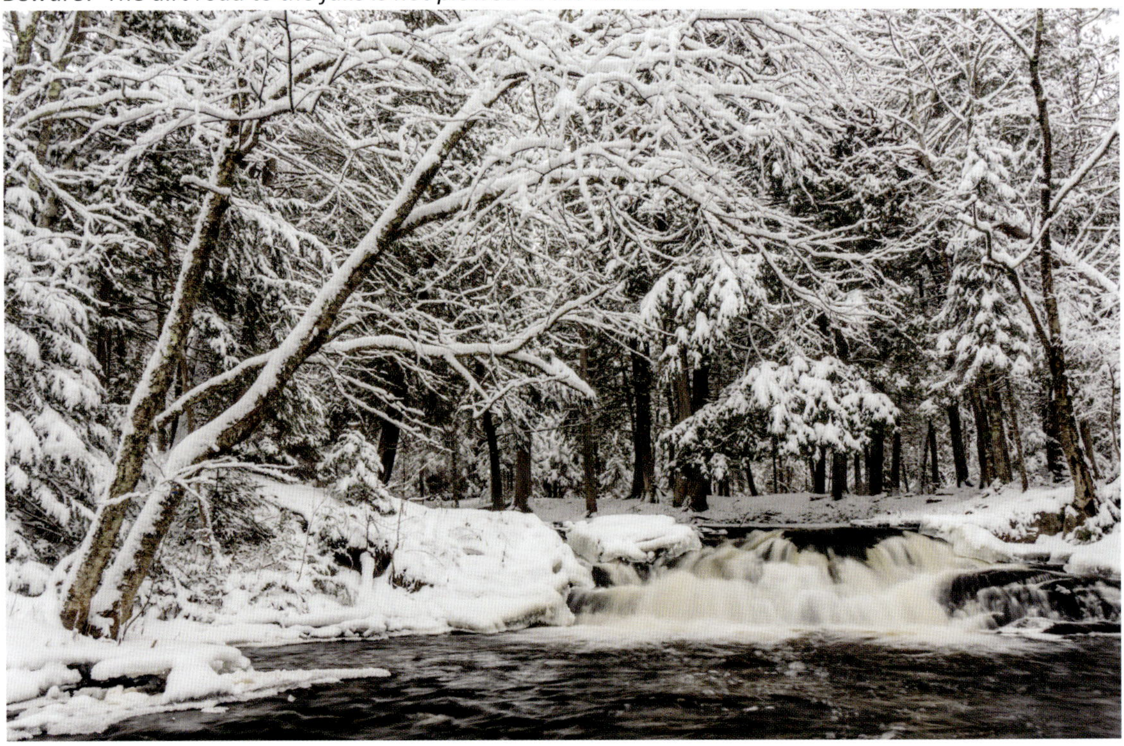

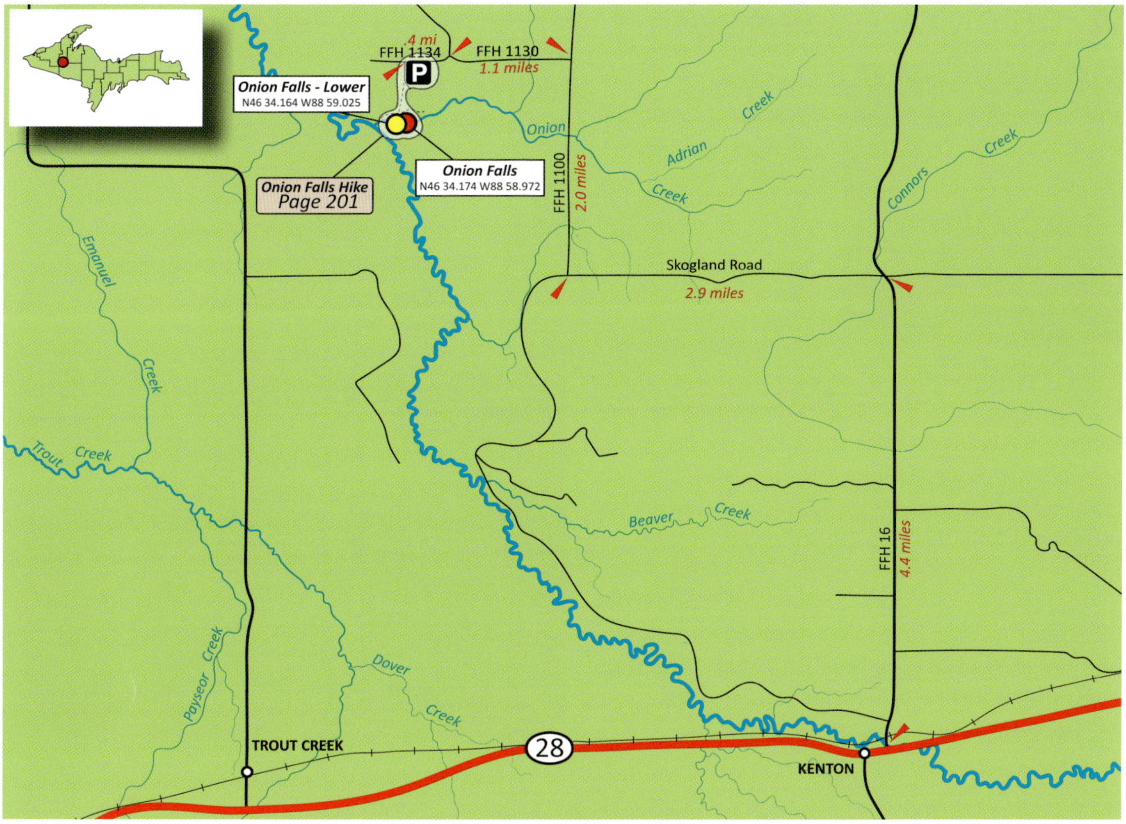

Onion Falls Hike

The small drops on Onion Creek are probably best suited for extreme waterfall enthusiasts. They are fairly remote, situated in a relatively steep gorge with unstable walls, and the waterfalls rate quite low. This being said, if you're up for an adventure, you might want to check this one out!

Directions: Turn north in Kenton onto FFH 16 off of M-28. Follow it north for 4.4 miles. Turn left (west) on Skogland Road. In 2.9 miles turn right (north) onto FF 1100. Follow it north for 2 miles to FF 1130. Turn left (west). In 1.1 miles veer left onto FF 1134 (it's a bit rough). Drive .4 miles. Park on the side of the road (only ATVs are allowed beyond this point). Hike south down FF 1134A for .2 miles. Turn right onto a good ATV trail. Go about .4 miles to a "T". Turn left. In about 100 yards turn right. Hike down the trail to a sharp bend. Leave the 2-track and climb down the steep bank to the falls.

Along the hike

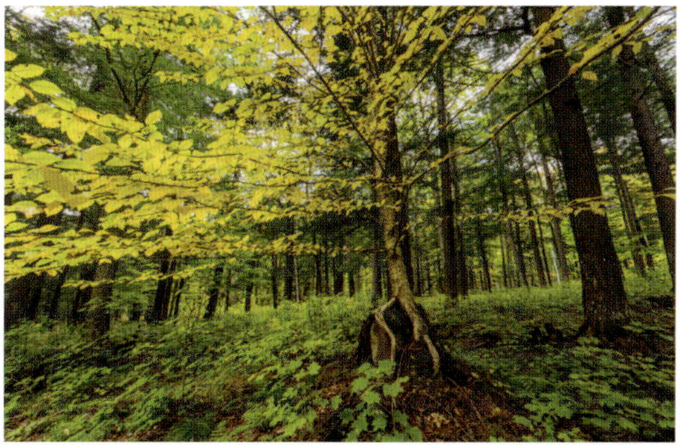

The steep ATV trail near the waterfall

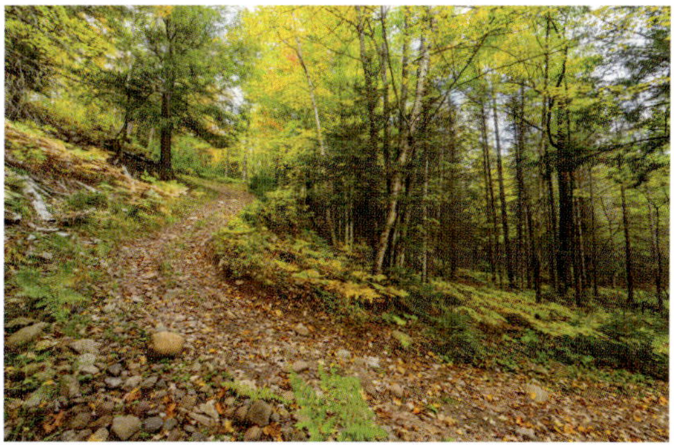

ONION FALLS (ONION CREEK)

Private

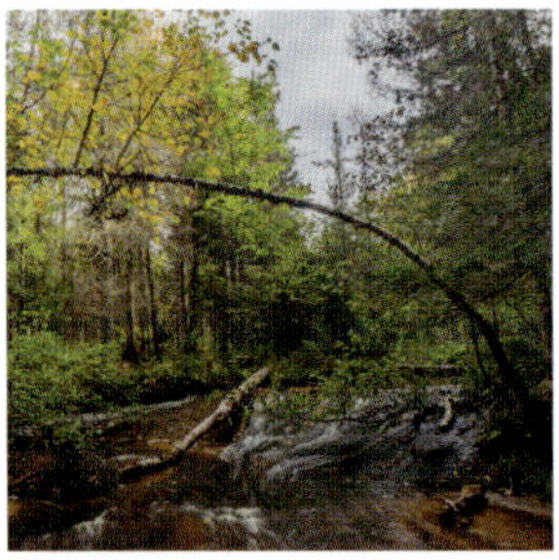

Must See:	3	GPS:	N46 34.174 W88 58.972
Height:	3 feet		
Time:	50-75 minutes		

Driving Information	
Signs:	None
Road:	Dirt
Access:	Difficult
4WD:	Helpful

Hiking Information	
Path:	ATV Trail Then None
Length:	.65 miles
Elev. Change:	Moderate
GPS:	Recommended
Danger:	Elevated
WP Boots:	Required

Onion Creek meanders through the base of a 25 foot deep ravine. The creek has cut down through layers of sandstone over the years, exposing the soft brown stone. Along the banks, flat shards have fallen as erosion continues to loosen the old bedrock. The 20 foot wide creek runs just inches deep most of the year. The waterfall is a 10 foot long slide, located in the center of a sharp "S" curve. Cedar and birch dominate the banks with an old white pine towering above the thick forest. The hike through the ancient forest may be more appealing than the waterfall!

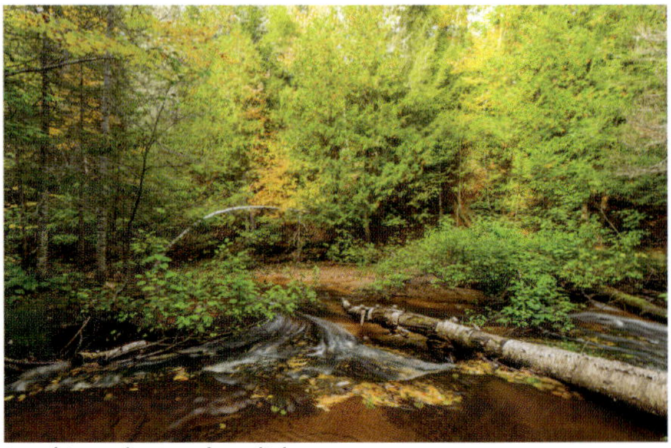

Looking down the slide

A large section of the ravine wall recently collapsed between Onion Falls and the Lower Falls

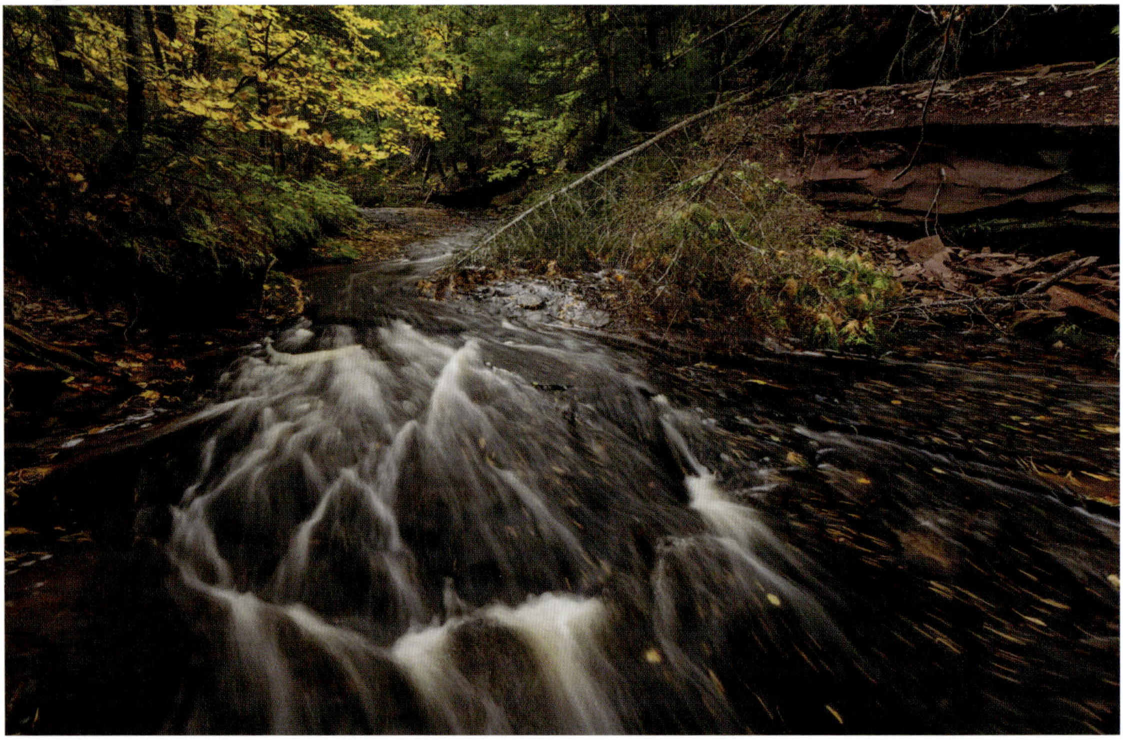

ONION FALLS - LOWER (ONION CREEK)

Private

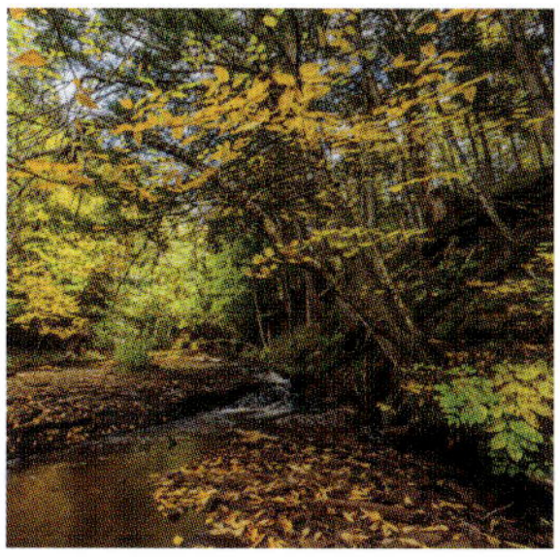

Must See:	4
Height:	2 feet
Time:	65-90 minutes

Driving Information

Signs:	None
Road:	Dirt
Access:	Difficult
4WD:	Helpful

GPS:	N46 34.164 W88 59.025

Hiking Information

Path:	ATV Trail Then None
Length:	.78 miles
Elev. Change:	Moderate
GPS:	Recommended
Danger:	Elevated
WP Boots:	Required

Follow the creek bed about 80 yards downstream. The ravine walls are quite steep and run right down to the creek bed, so walking through the water is the easiest route.

A rock shelf extends across the creek at a sharp angle. The creek divides and runs over both ends. As the water level rises, it flows over more and more length of the short waterfall. The sandstone bank on the far side is getting severely undercut. Large trees are now suspended over mostly air!

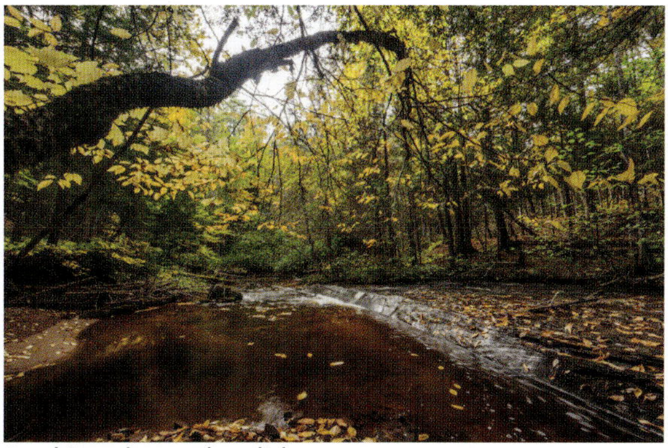

Looking down the slide

The steeply angled drop, although short, is quite interesting!

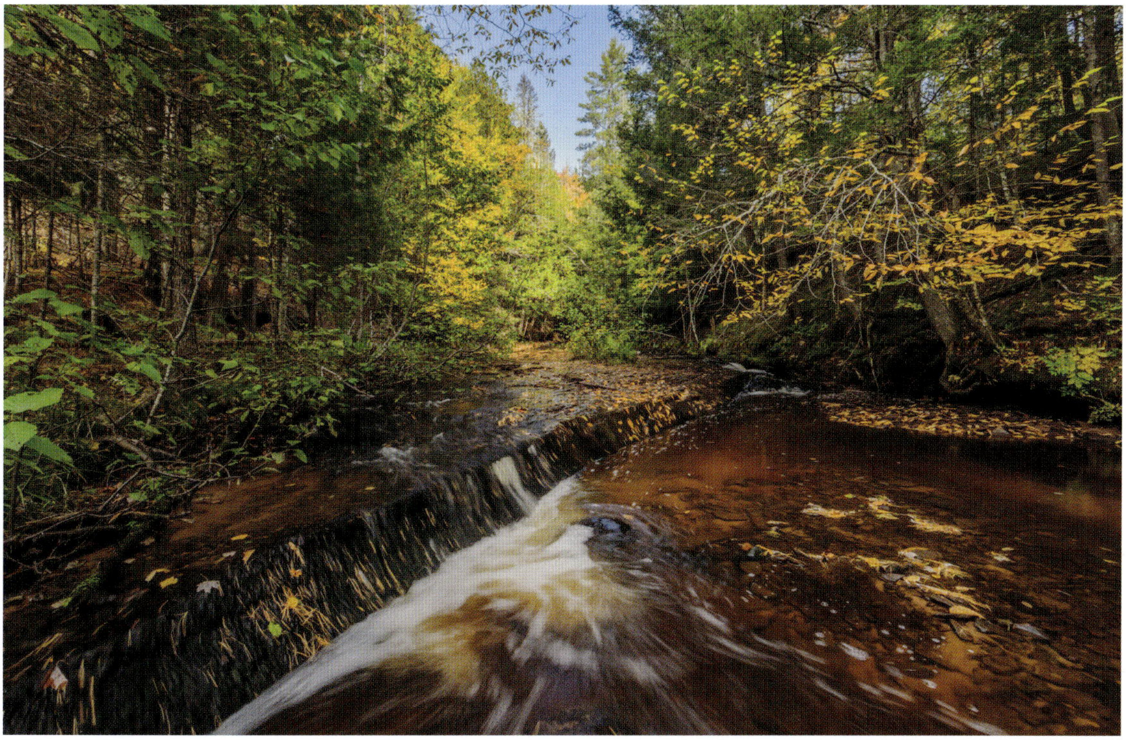

Otter Falls Area

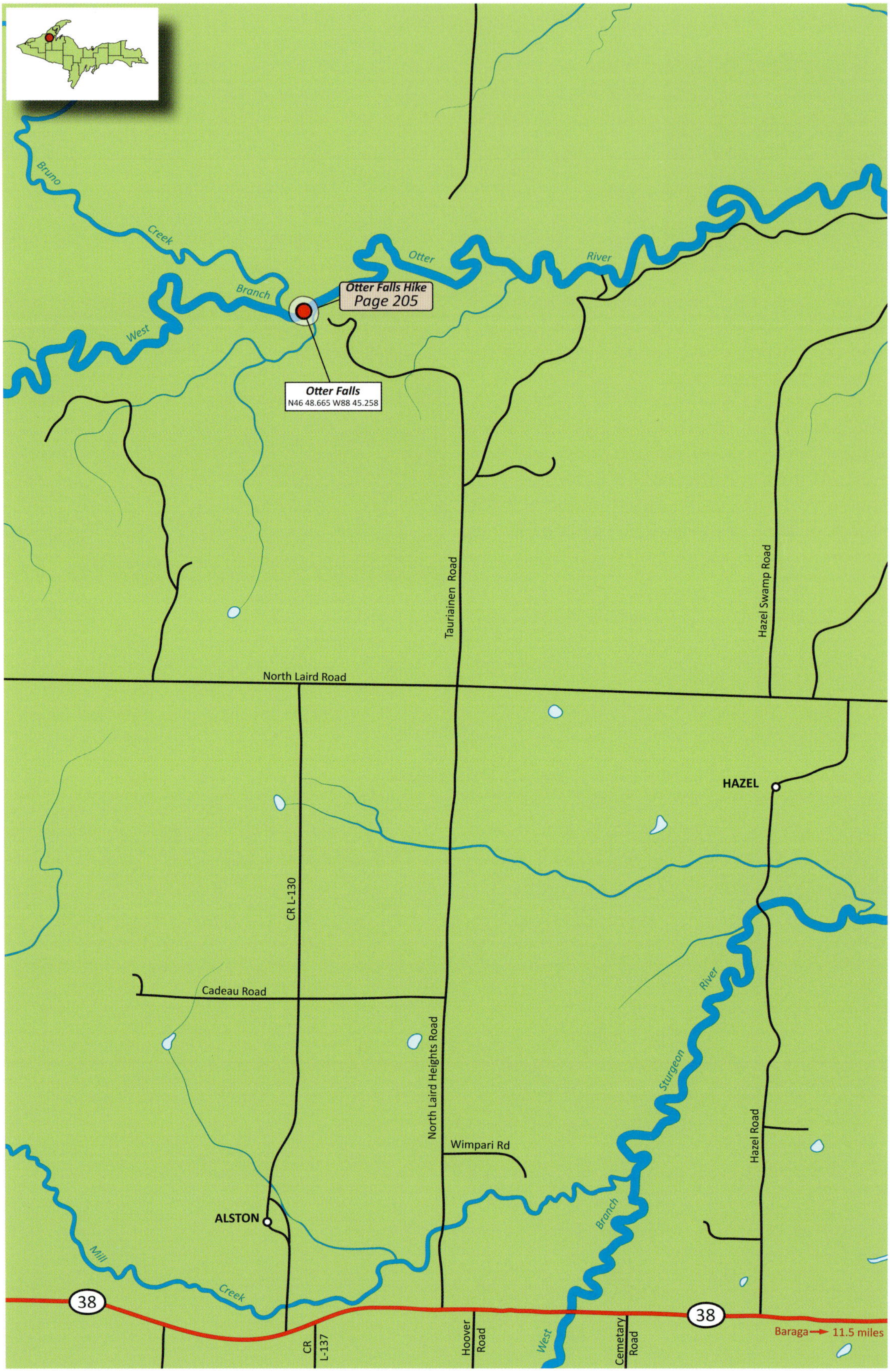

Otter Falls Hike

Otter Falls: The waterfall is on private land. Do not trespass. A nice cabin is right above the falls. Rounded rocks making up the falls account for the river's smooth undulating drop.

Directions: Some 2.5 miles east of Nisula off of M-38, turn north on N Laird Heights Road. In 2 miles the road becomes Taurianinen Road. In less than a mile the road becomes a private drive. It winds around until it ends at a cabin on the West Branch of the Otter River. This is a private residence. Trespassing prohibited.

OTTER FALLS (OTTER RIVER - WEST BRANCH)

Private

Must See:	3	GPS:	N46 48.665 W88 45.258
Height:	3 feet		
Time:	N/A	Hiking Information	
		Path:	Private Dirt Road
Driving Information		Length:	N/A
Signs:	None	Elev. Change:	Slight
Road:	Dirt	GPS:	N/A
Access:	N/A	Danger:	Slight
4WD:	N/A	WP Boots:	N/A

The falls are on private land. Do not trespass.

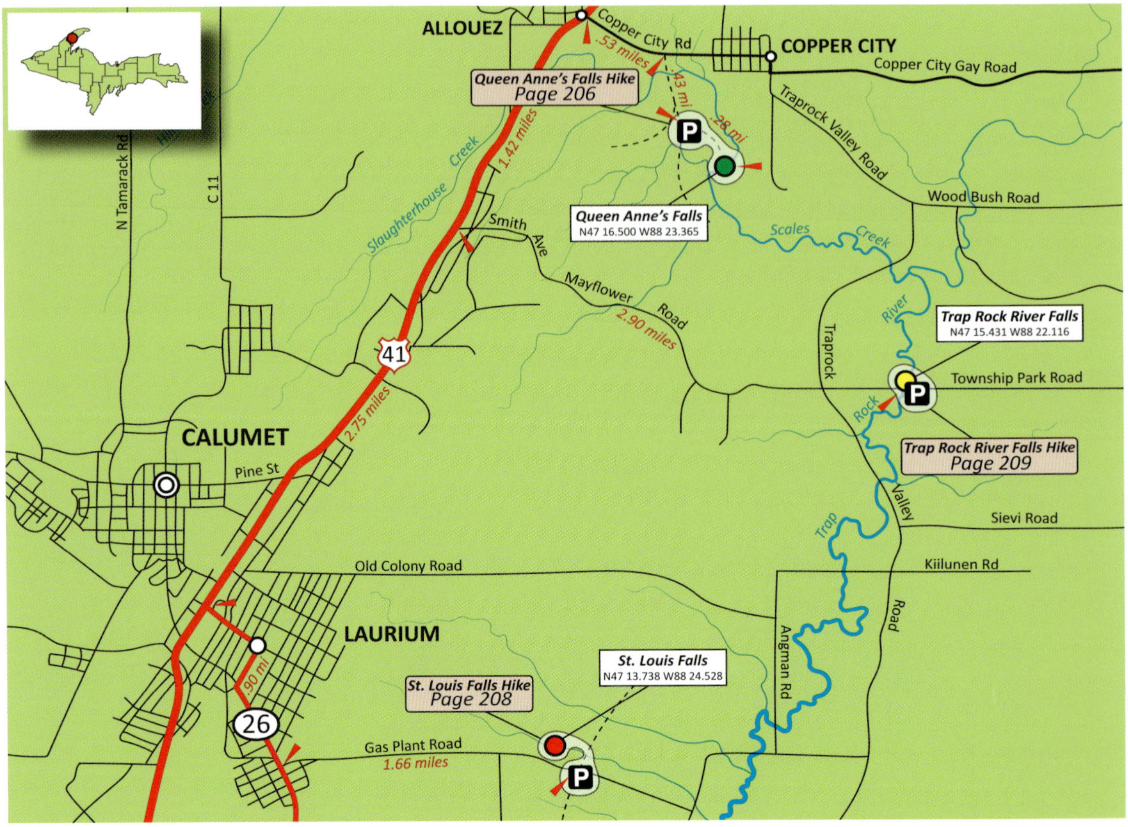

Queen Anne's Falls Hike

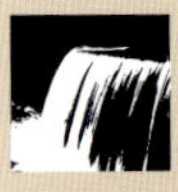

Queen Anne's Falls: The tall, narrow , zig-zag shaped waterfall is channelled down into a gorge through rough, exposed basalt bedrock. A popular spill pool awaits at the bottom of the falls before the creek continues on its way through the boulder strewn creek bed downstream. There is a dangerous climb down to the base of the falls. There is about 50 feet of elevation change. After leaving the ATV turnaround, the trail rapidly descends down a clay footpath. It can be very slippery - especially after a rain. After reaching the river at the top of the waterfall the trail mostly dissapears. Scramble down the rocky side of the waterfall to the base.

Several smaller cascades greet you at the top of the main drop as you first approach the creek. They're not large, but they are nice! Numerous small drops can be found for the next several hundred yards upstream.

Directions: On US-41 in Allouez, turn southeast onto Copper City Road. In less than .53 miles, turn right (south) onto a dirt road at N47 17.012 W88 23.688 (if you pass the bar on the right, you've gone too far). Drive .23 miles. Stay left and drive another .19 miles. Park on the left at the base of a steep 2-track. Hike up the 2-track 150 feet. Turn slight right @N47 16.654 W88 23.533. Turn right @ N47 16.646 W88 23.494. Turn right @ N47 16.621 W88 23.439. The narrow 2-track ends @ N47 16.528 W88 23.357. A well-worn footpath begins at the circle turnaround. (There is not much room to turn around. A very small vehicle is required, preferably a 4-wheeler.) Hike down the footpath. Slippery clay eventually gives way to steep rock at the waterfall. (The total hike length from vehicle to waterfall is .28 miles.)

QUEEN ANNE'S FALLS (SLAUGHTERHOUSE CREEK)

Private

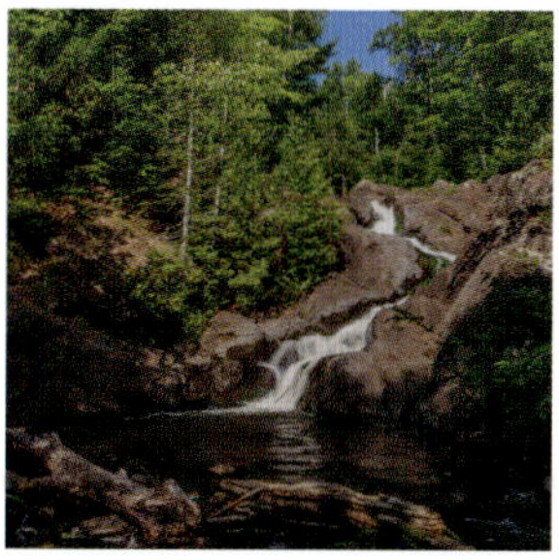

Must See:	7	GPS:	N47 16.500 W88 23.365
Height:	30 feet		
Time:	20-40 minutes	**Hiking Information**	
		Path:	Footpath
Driving Information		Length:	.28 miles
Signs:	None	Elev. Change:	Moderate
Road:	Dirt	GPS:	Helpful
Access:	Difficult	Danger:	Elevated
4WD:	Recommended	WP Boots:	Recommended

The dirt road off of Copper City Road is very sandy in places and getting stuck is a real possibility. Be very careful when trying to turn around or park. I very nearly buried my 4WD truck a couple of times out here. The shot to the right shows the top of the waterfall. Follow the creek upstream to view more small drops like this one.

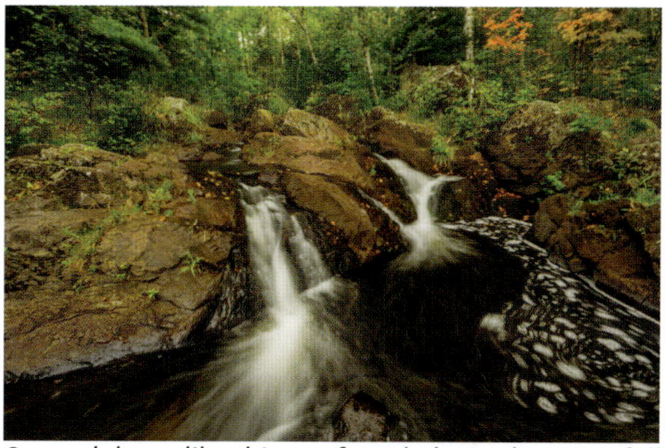

Several drops like this are found above the waterfall

The look from the far side of the creek

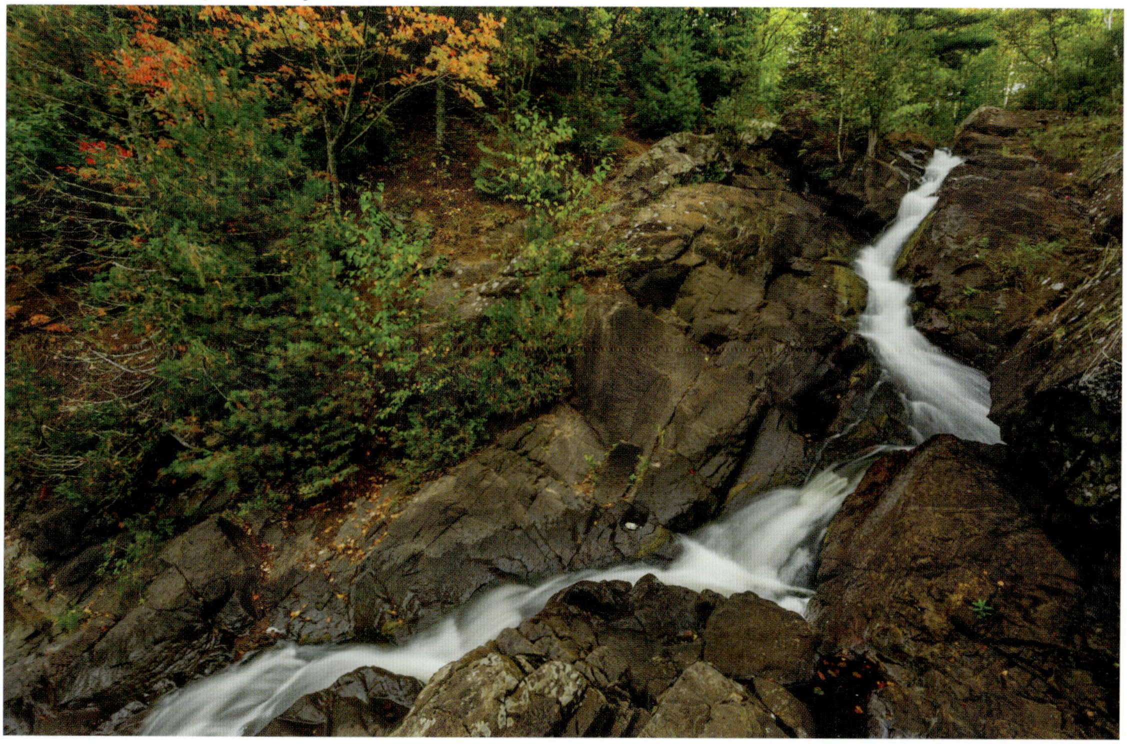

St. Louis Falls Hike

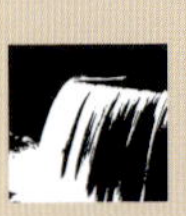

St. Louis Falls: Named after nearby "St. Louis Hill" or "Louis Hill", the small unnamed creek runs down through a steep and deep ravine with a fair amount of undergrowth. The base of the falls is tangled with boulders, fallen trees and undergrowth. The creek runs under these. A mossy face is visible above the lower tangle, revealing rivulets of water running down. Another exposed drop of 8 feet appears above the next mass of undergrowth. I ran into some stinging nettles here. Continuing up the ravine, the next drop runs down a carpet of moss-covered angled masses of rock.

Directions: From Laurium, turn southeast on M-26. It makes a couple of jogs as it winds through the village streets. After .9 miles turn left (northeast) onto Gas Plant Road. It quickly turns to the east. Follow it for 1.66 miles. Park on the side of the road. A small trail (old railroad grade) runs into the woods to the north. It bridges the ravine and then follows the creek back to the west/northwest. Follow it to get close to the GPS location. Pick a safe route to the bottom of the gorge, then hike upstream to the falls.

ST. LOUIS FALLS (UNNAMED CREEK)

Private

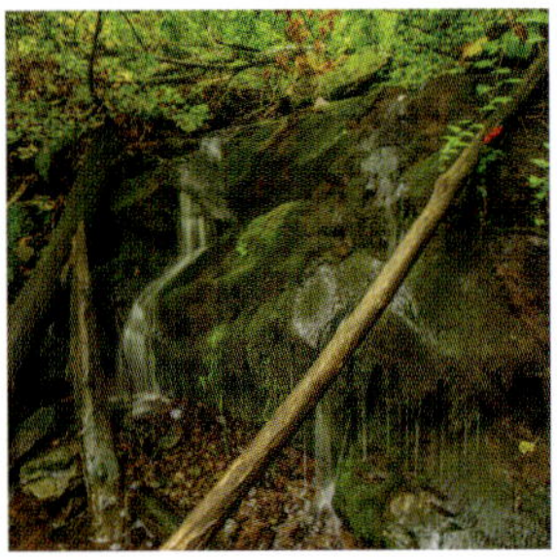

Must See:	2
Height:	20 feet
Time:	30-45 minutes

Driving Information

Signs:	None
Road:	Dirt
Access:	Somewhat Difficult
4WD:	N/A

GPS: N47 13.738 W88 24.528

Hiking Information

Path:	Trail Then None
Length:	.33 miles
Elev. Change:	Major
GPS:	Recommended
Danger:	Elevated
WP Boots:	Recommended

Much of the creek runs below the undergrowth and rocks that have fallen to the base of the ravine. The creek doesn't flow with enough force to self-clean the creek bed. It would be interesting to see what the waterfall looks like in the spring when snow melt swells the creek and the undergrowth hasn't greened up yet.

The undergrowth dominates the entire ravine, including the creek bed.

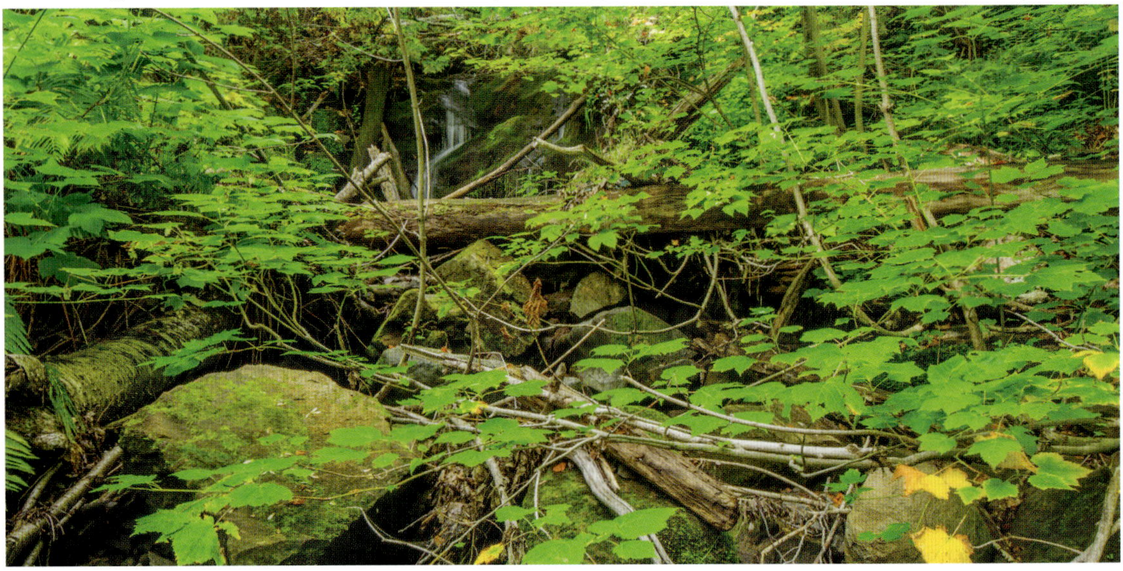

Trap Rock River Falls Hike

Trap Rock River Falls: A stone dam spans the river with a fish ladder built up the middle. Broken pieces of basalt line the riverbed for 20 yards downstream.

Directions: Take US-41 into Wolverine, just 2.75 miles north of M-26 in Calumet. Turn right (east) onto Smith Avenue. Various intersecting roads meet up at strange angles for the first .5 miles. Ignore these. Stay on the winding street. It soon becomes Mayflower Road. From US-41, the total distance to the falls is 2.9 miles. Park on the side of the road where it crosses Trap Rock River.

TRAP ROCK RIVER FALLS (TRAP ROCK RIVER)

Private

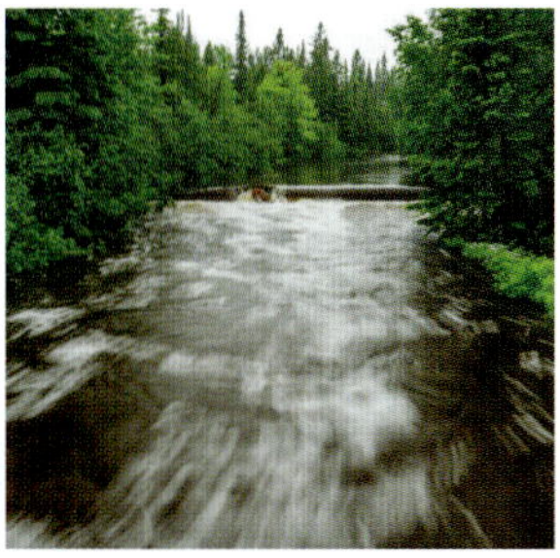

Must See:	4
Height:	2 feet
Time:	5-10 minutes

Driving Information

Signs:	None
Road:	Secondary
Access:	Somewhat Easy
4WD:	N/A

GPS: N47 15.429 W88 22.155

Hiking Information

Path:	N/A
Length:	N/A
Elev. Change:	N/A
GPS:	N/A
Danger:	N/A
WP Boots:	N/A

View from the vehicle while crossing the bridge on this quiet road. It wanting to view closer, hike the short distance along the east side of the river back to the dam.

In high water, the dam is barely discernible as the river overwhelms it - as seen above.

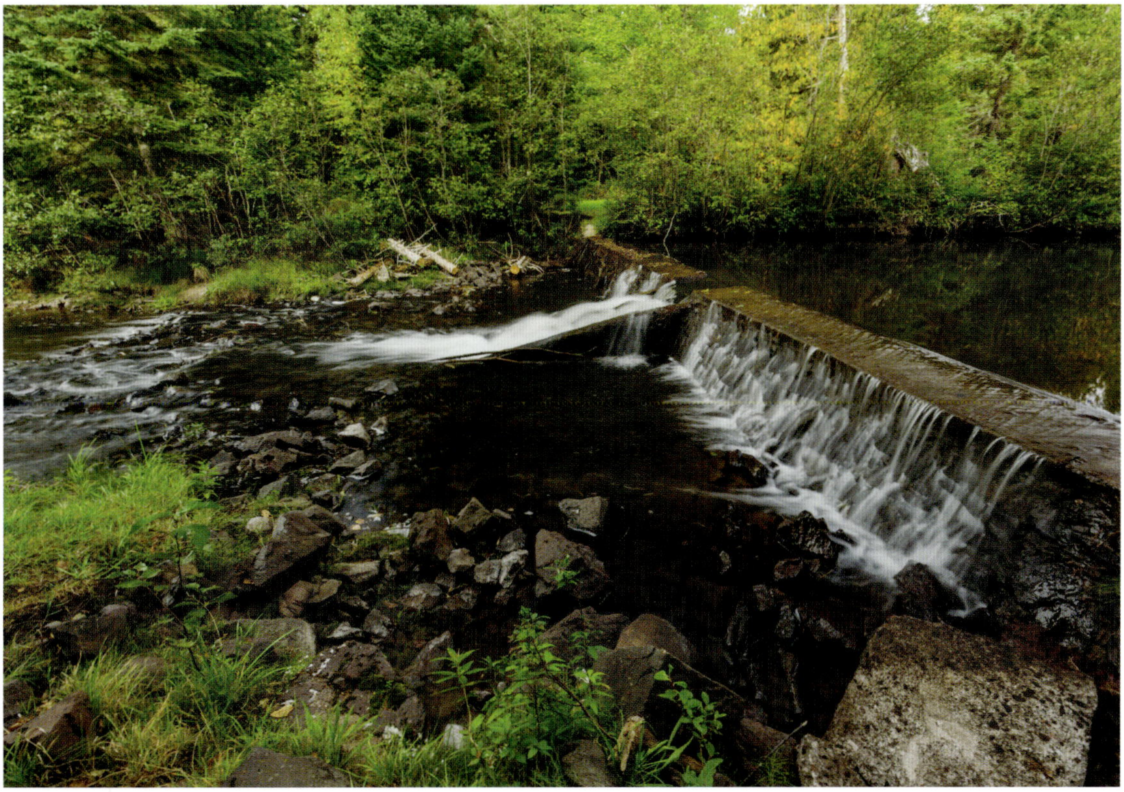

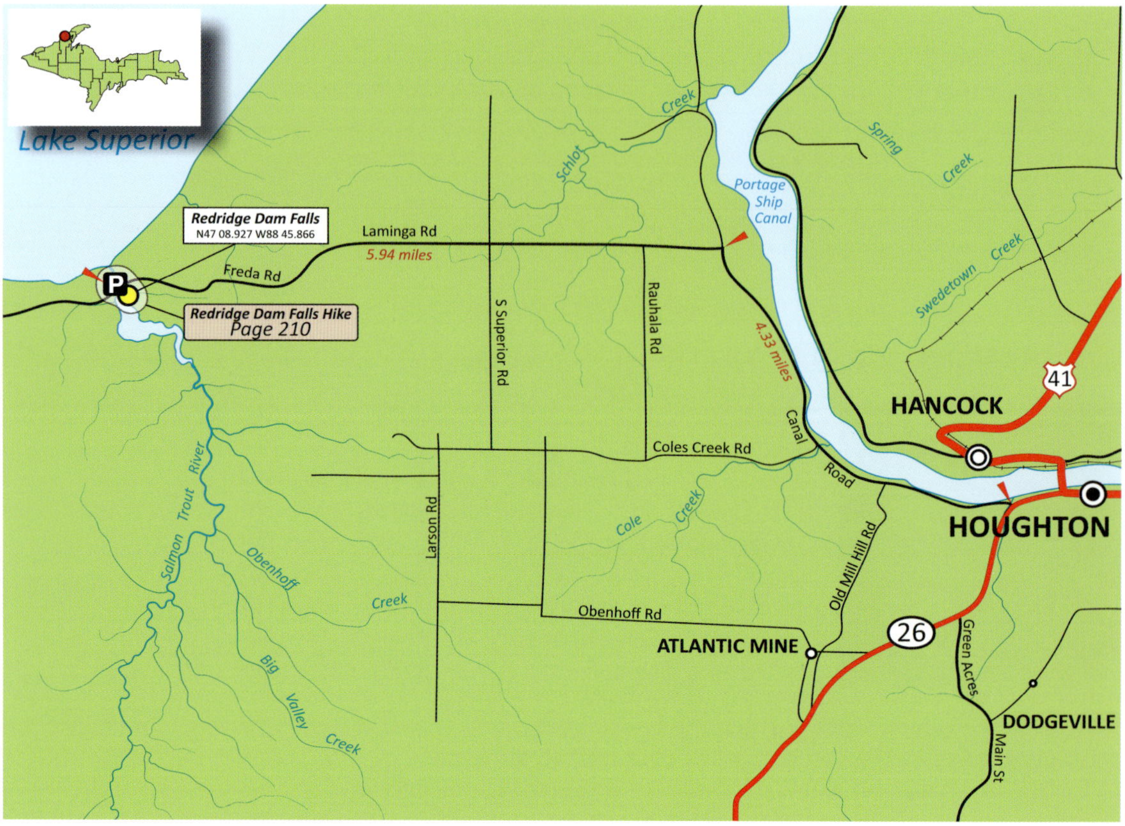

Redridge Dam Falls Hike

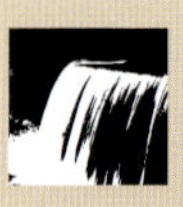

Redridge Dam Falls: A Crumbling wooden dam is back filled with mine tailings. Water filters down through the tailings and rotting wooden structure, then pours out through the base of the dam.

Directions: In Hougton, take Memorial Road (M-26) west from US-41. In .4 miles as the road bends toward the south, turn right (west) on Houghton Canal Road. Follow it along Portage River for 4.33 miles. Turn left (west) onto Liminga Road. Stay on it for 5.94 miles until entering the small village of Redridge. A parking area is near a historical marker. Park here and hike in past the steel dam to the wooden dam falls. Alternately, drive on a sandy trail directly to the dam. A 4WD is recommended.

REDRIDGE DAM FALLS (SALMON TROUT RIVER)

Private

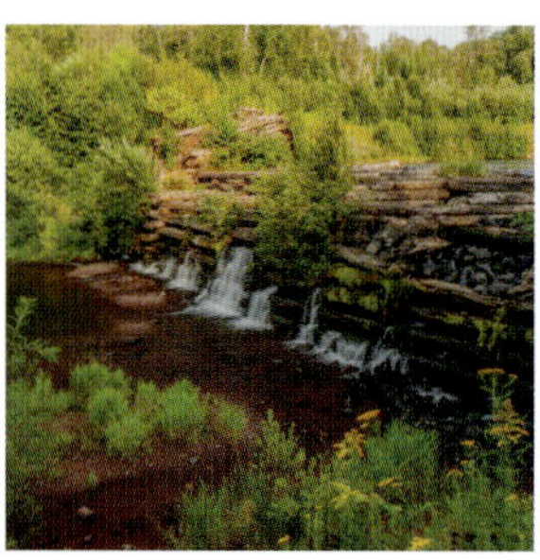

Must See:	6	GPS:	N47 08.927 W88 45.866
Height:	12 feet		
Time:	10-20 minutes	Hiking Information	
		Path:	Dirt Road
Driving Information		Length:	250 yards
Signs:	None	Elev. Change:	Minimal
Road:	Secondary	GPS:	N/A
Access:	Somewhat Easy	Danger:	Slight
4WD:	N/A	WP Boots:	N/A

A large steel dam, one of only two remaining in the United States, built in 1905 is situated just down river from the wooden dam that was previously built in 1894 by the Atlantic Mining Company. The top 13 feet of the wooden dam was removed in 2004 to reduce the possibility of a catastrophic failure of the wooden dam that might in turn damage the steel dam and result in dangerous flooding.

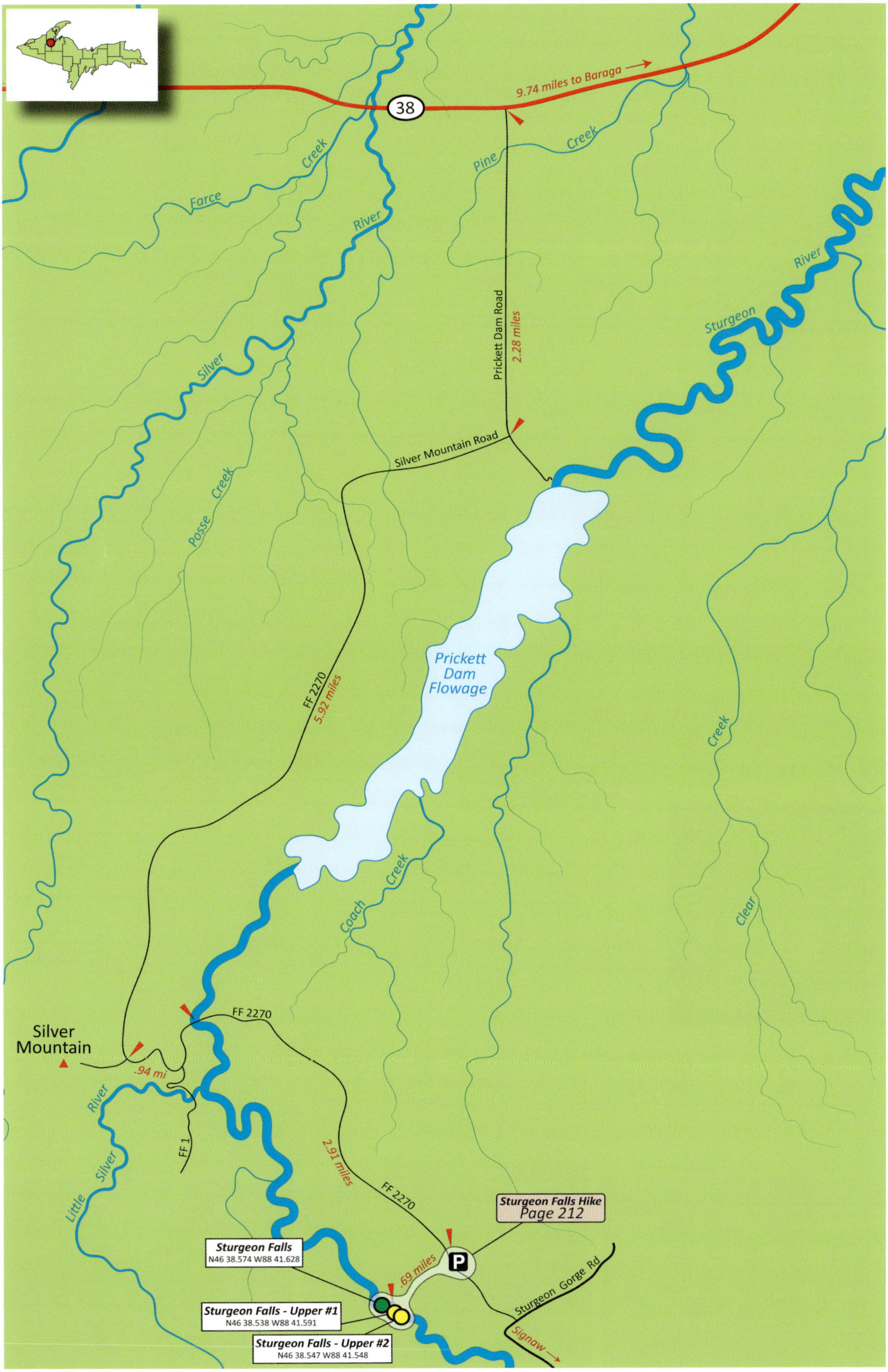
38
9.74 miles to Baraga
Pine
Creek
Farce
Creek
River
Silver
River
Sturgeon
Prickett Dam Road
2.28 miles
Silver Mountain Road
Posse
Creek
Prickett
Dam
Flowage
FF 2270
5.92 miles
Creek
Clear
Coach
Creek
FF 2270
Silver
Mountain
.94 mi
River
Silver
Little
FF 1
2.91 miles
FF 2270
Sturgeon Falls Hike
Page 212
Sturgeon Falls
N46 38.574 W88 41.628
.69 miles
Sturgeon Gorge Rd
Sturgeon Falls - Upper #1
N46 38.538 W88 41.591
Sturgeon Falls - Upper #2
N46 38.547 W88 41.548
Signaw

Sturgeon Falls Hike

This is a popular back country hike, but since it is quite a distance from major population centers, it is seldom crowded. Make sure that you are in good physical shape before attempting this hike. The narrow footpath is plainly visible, but the hike back out of the Sturgeon River Gorge is strenuous.

Sturgeon Falls: The switch-backing hike down into the deepest gorge in Michigan is rewarded with wonderful sights: overlooking an expanse of hardwoods, hiking through a mature forest with its sights and smells, and at last - the majestic Sturgeon Falls. Mist swirls through the air downstream from the pounding of thousands of gallons of water struggling to race over the falls on its way to Portage Lake.

Sturgeon Falls - Upper #1: From the rocky outcropping that rises above Sturgeon Falls one can look down on Sturgeon Falls and also see both of the Upper Falls off to the left. To better view the upper drops, climb down the large rocks to the riverbed. Situated between Sturgeon Falls and Upper #2 is this interesting drop (Upper #1). A large boulder sits centered in the falls, swirling water falling around either side.

Sturgeon Falls - Upper #2: As the river approaches the waterfall, it widens to 150 feet and then drops in a nearly straight line. Almost immediately afterward, the river narrows down to just 10 feet wide before tumbling over Upper #1 falls.

Directions: In Baraga, turn west onto M-38 off us US-41. Follow M-38 for 9.7 miles to Prickett Dam Road. Turn left (south) on Prickett Dam Road. In 2.3 miles turn right onto Silver Mountain Road @ N46 43.804 W88 40.562. After 5.9 miles stay left @ N46 40.075 W88 43.891 for another 3.8 miles to the trailhead parking area on the left. Park. Hike in on the obvious trail back across FF 2270, through a flat stretch of forest, then along the top of the gorge until the trail plunges down into the gorge and switchbacks back and forth to get to the bottom where it then flattens out again until getting close to the river. The trail meets the river at the top of Sturgeon Falls.

STURGEON FALLS (STURGEON RIVER)

Private

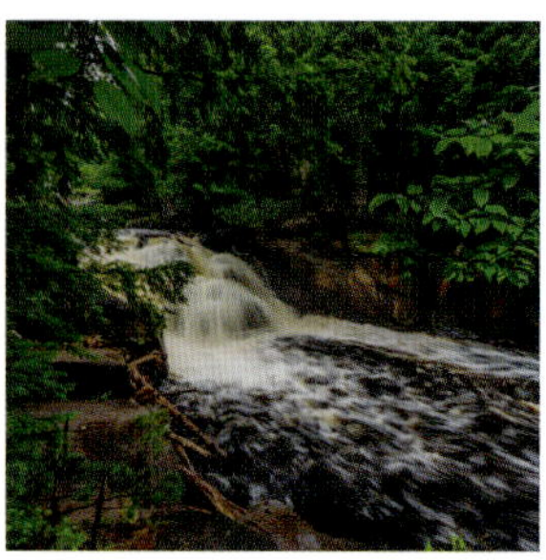

Must See:	10	GPS:	N46 38.574 W88 41.628
Height:	30 feet		
Time:	1-2 hours	Hiking Information	
		Path:	Semi-improved Footpath
Driving Information		Length:	.69 miles
Signs:	None	Elev. Change:	Major
Road:	Gravel	GPS:	Recommended
Access:	Difficult	Danger:	Moderate
4WD:	N/A	WP Boots:	N/A

Rugged and bold. This remote waterfall, located at the bottom of the deepest gorge in Michigan, shows off its power with a spray that can drift hundreds of feet downstream. Massive boulders, angular and black, make up the face of the waterfall. Twenty foot cliffs, topped with cedar trees, rise higher still on either side of the falls. Rough hewn boulders litter the river downstream. A sandy, flat beach below the falls shows traces of old campfires and tent sites.

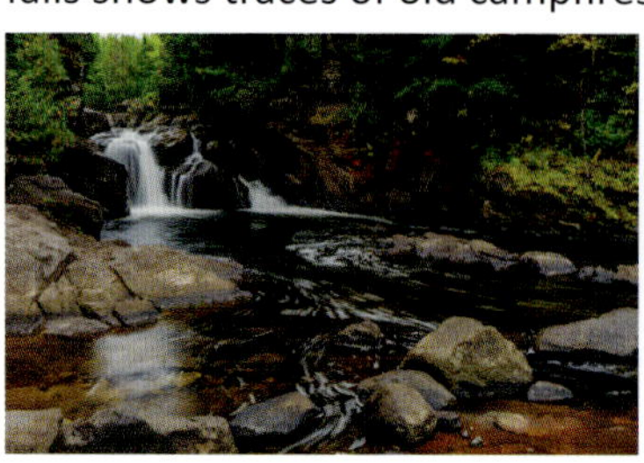
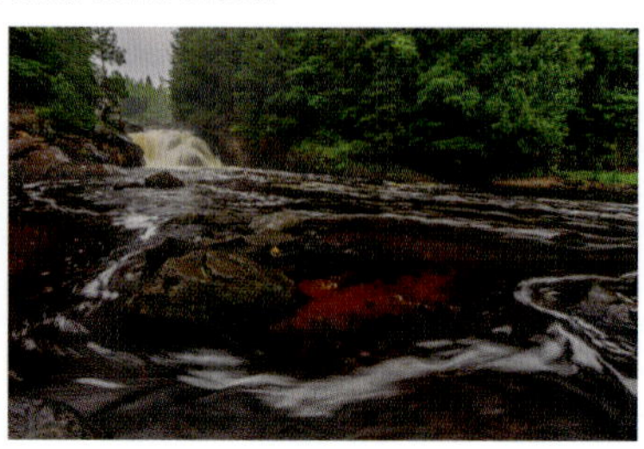
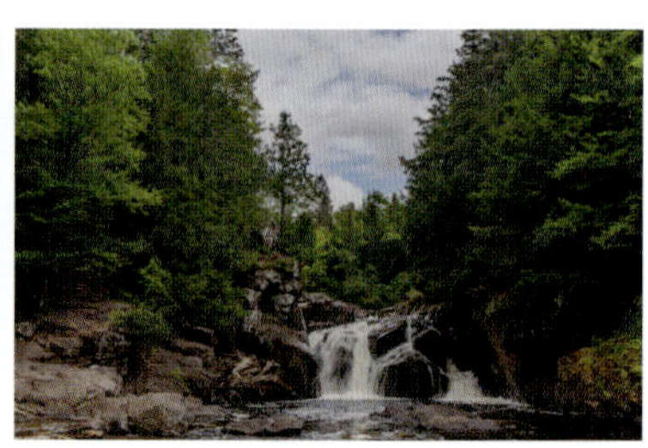

STURGEON FALLS - UPPER #1 (STURGEON RIVER)

Private

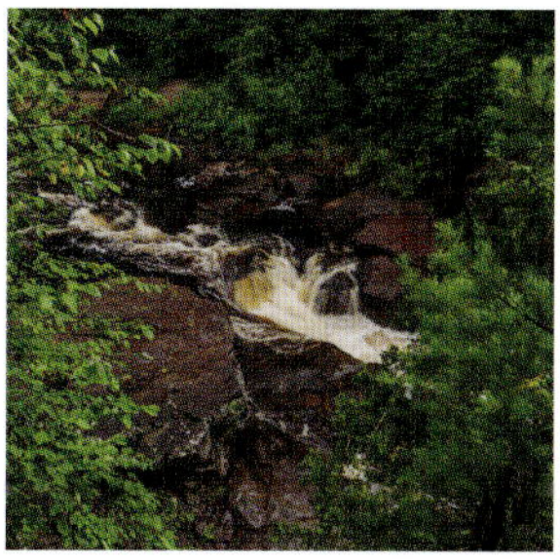

Must See:	6	GPS:	N46 38.538 W88 41.591
Height:	5 feet		
Time:	1-2 hours	Hiking Information	
		Path:	Semi-improved Footpath
Driving Information		Length:	.69 miles
Signs:	None	Elev. Change:	Major
Road:	Gravel	GPS:	Recommended
Access:	Difficult	Danger:	Moderate
4WD:	N/A	WP Boots:	N/A

It's amazing to think that just a hundred feet upstream from here the river is over 100 feet wide! It is channeled down to just a matter of several feet as the river prepares to plunge over Sturgeon Falls in another hundred feet. This narrowing of the river is what gives Sturgeon Falls the explosive power that it is known for (when the river is running high).

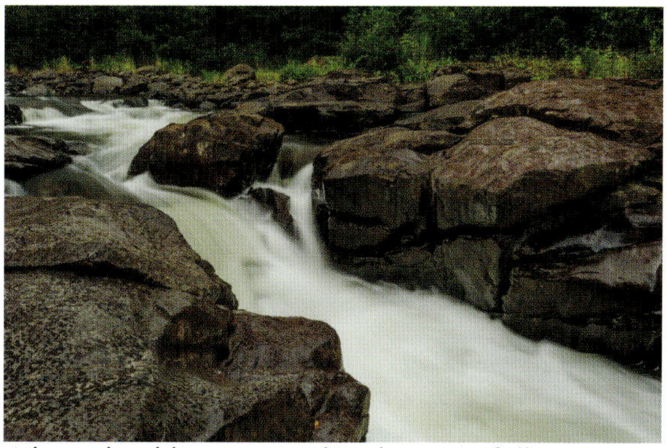

A large boulder, centered in the waterfall

Looking upstream from the top of Sturgeon Falls - Upper #1 appears almost immediately

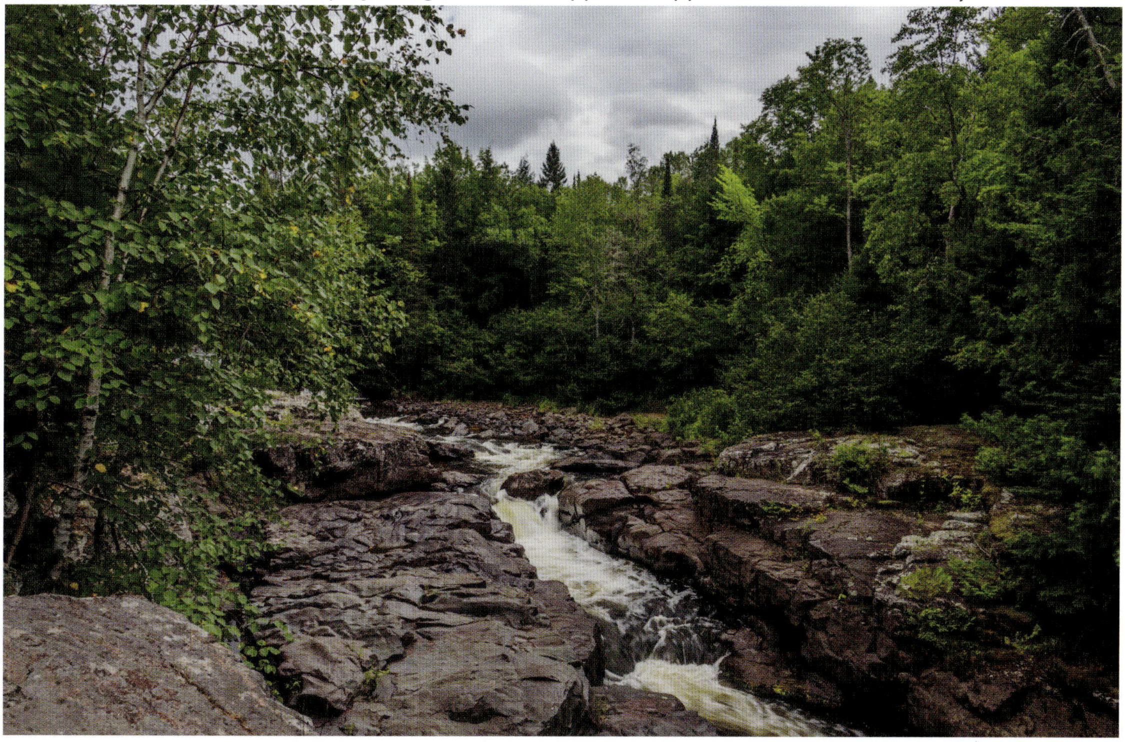

STURGEON FALLS - UPPER #2 (STURGEON RIVER)

Private

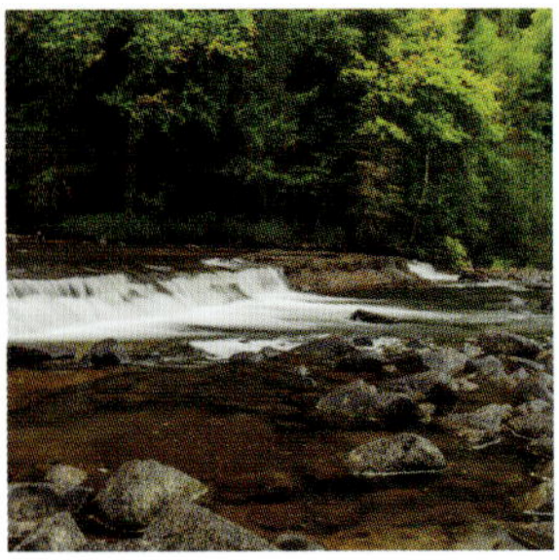

Must See:	6	GPS:	N46 38.547 W88 41.548
Height:	3 feet		
Time:	1-2 hours	Hiking Information	
		Path:	Semi-improved Footpath
Driving Information		Length:	.69 miles
Signs:	None	Elev. Change:	Major
Road:	Gravel	GPS:	Recommended
Access:	Difficult	Danger:	Moderate
4WD:	N/A	WP Boots:	N/A

The three drops on the Sturgeon Falls Hike are listed starting furthest down river, as the popular Sturgeon Falls begs to be viewed first! After being visually sated, it is nice to explore the calmer waters up above the raging fall.

It's amazing to see the long, straight, short ridge drop. It's such a contrast to the narrow, slot drop just downstream.

Be careful getting down to the riverbed from the high bank up above Sturgeon Falls. The steep bank requires agility, good footholds, and preferably non-slippery conditions.

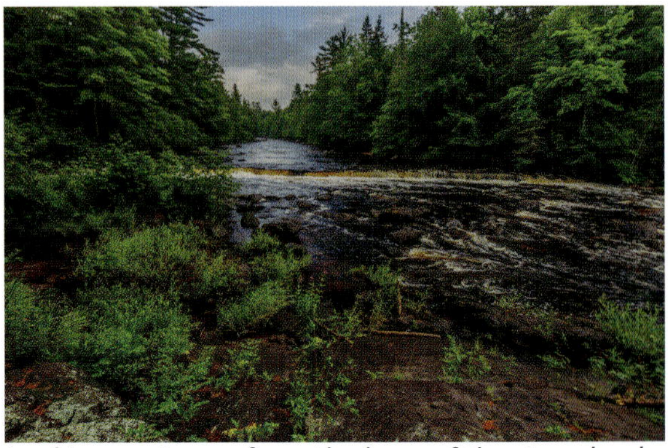

Looking upstream from the base of the steep bank

What a straight line. It's a short drop, but so long and interesting!

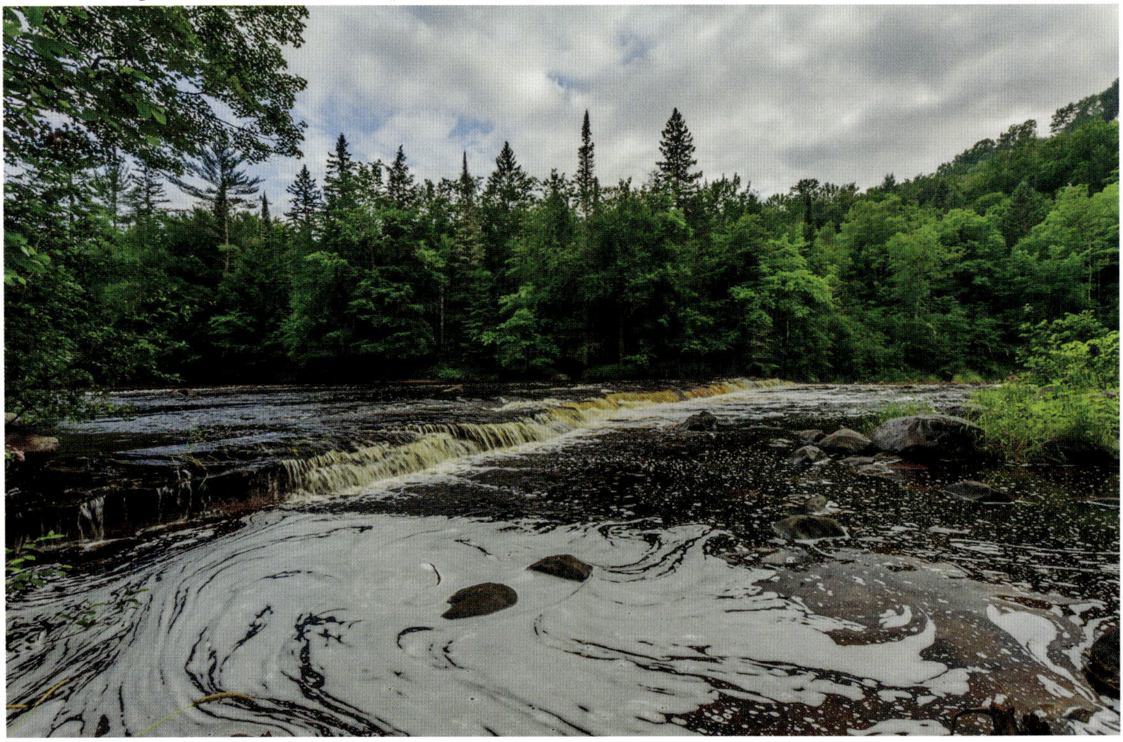

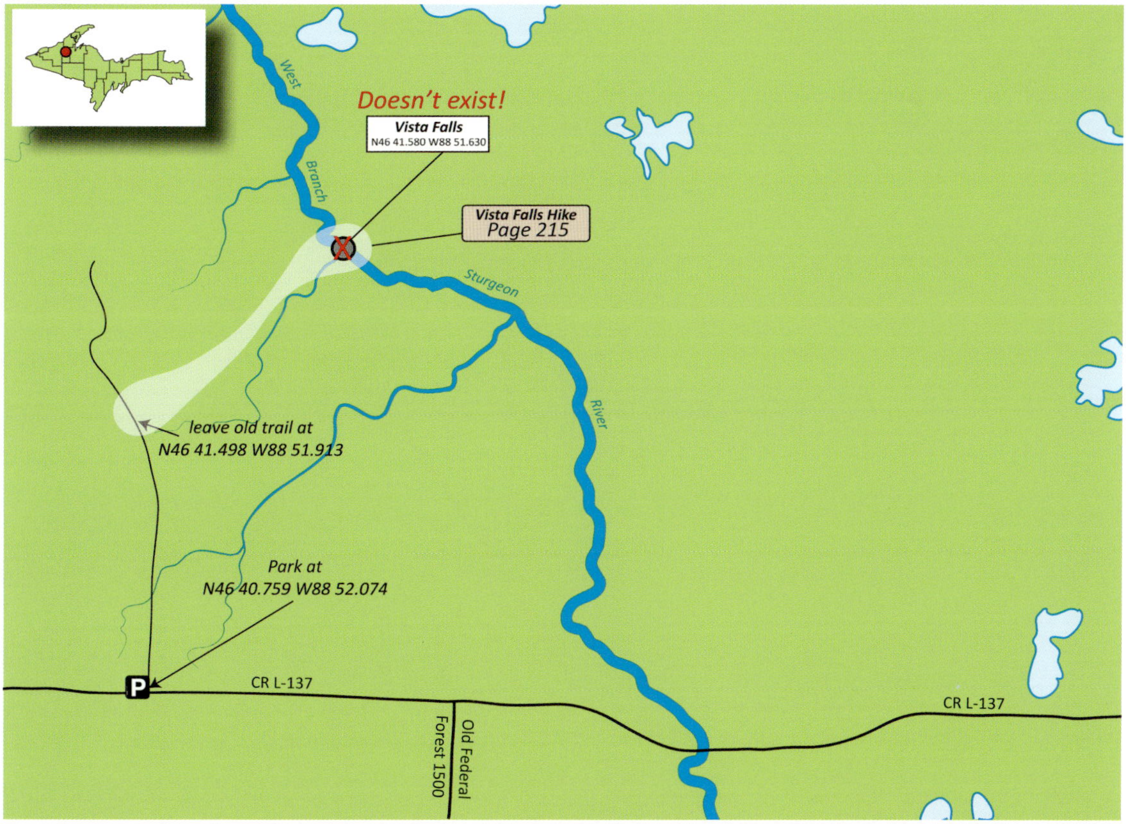

Vista Falls Hike

Every indication is that Vista Falls either never existed or is a minor stretch of rapids. I have searched four times for the waterfall, coming in from various angles and yet each time coming up dry. I have never spoken to anyone who has seen this waterfall.

Directions: Turn south onto S Laird Road off of M-38 near Alston. In 5.9 miles the road bends to the right (west). Continue for 5.1 miles. An old 2-track heads to the north. Park at the entrance since it has been blocked off. This area is part of the Ottawa National Forest and this is no longer an approved trail to drive on. Hike in on the overgrown trails as far as makes sense, then cut cross country to the river (and the nonexistent falls!).

VISTA FALLS (STURGEON RIVER - WEST BRANCH)

Private

Must See:	N/A	GPS:	N46 41.580 W88 51.630 (not verified)
Height:	N/A		
Time:	N/A	**Hiking Information**	
		Path:	2-Track Then None
Driving Information		Length:	1.2 miles
Signs:	None	Elev. Change:	Moderate
Road:	Good Gravel	GPS:	Required
Access:	Difficult	Danger:	Moderate
4WD:	N/A	WP Boots:	Required

Don't waste your time with this "waterfall". With a name like "Vista Falls", you'd think it would be an amazing one. But even though I have seen it listed on a number of atlases, waterfall lists, and area maps, it doesn't exist. Bummer...

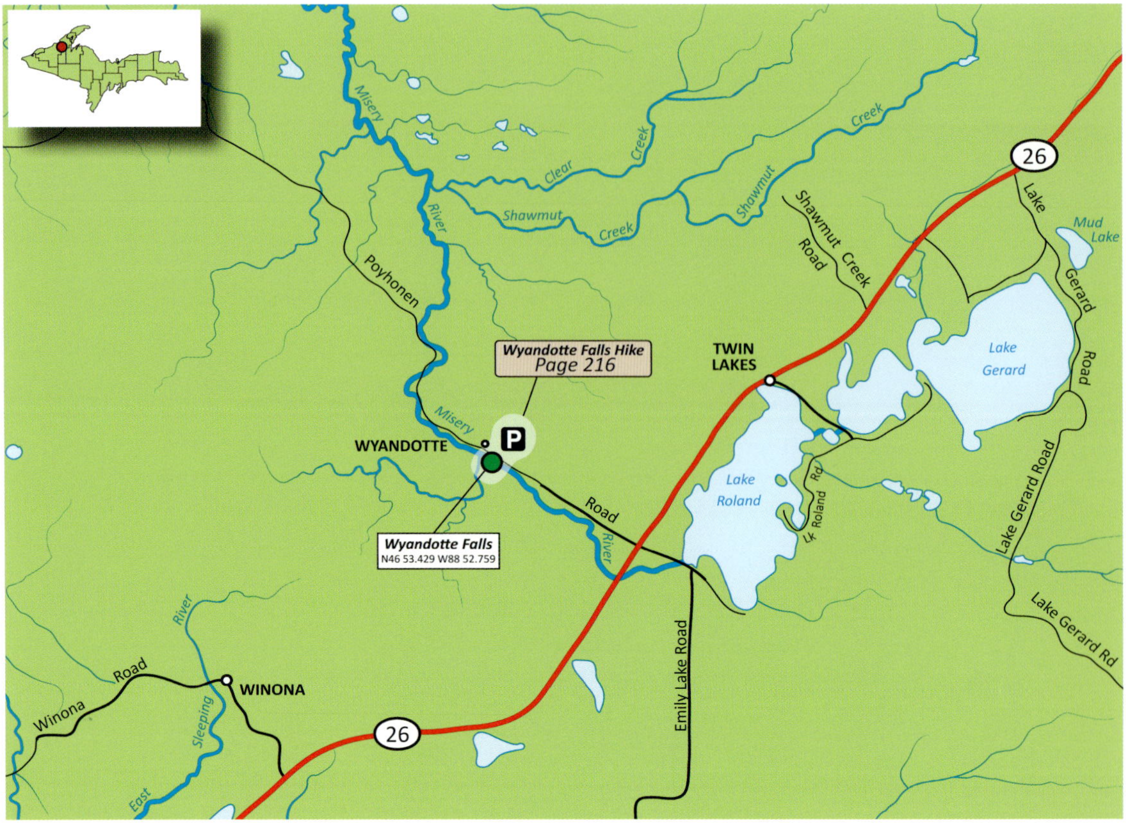

Wyandotte Falls Hike

The falls are on the Misery River. It is thought that early traders living along the river suffered from starvation, giving it the name "Misery River". Lake Roland empties via Misery River, and during summer months when the lake level is low the river can dry up completely. During spring snow melt, the river can rage. So the waterfall has a wide range of looks over the course of a year.

Wyandotte Falls: Angled mossy bedrock slabs separate the upper river with its little pools from the rock strewn continuation of the river below the falls. Slippery clay is found along the side and base of the falls.

Directions: Take M-26 to Lake Roland. Turn west/northwest onto Poynonen Road, traveling past Wyandotte Hills Golf Course. The blacktop deteriorates into a dirt road just past the golf course. Several hundred yards later is a parking area and an old wooden sign "promoting" the falls. Park. Hike a 160 yards through the forest on an obviously travelled footpath. The trail drops down several times as it gets close to the falls. Be careful. There is a lot of clay in this area, and the ground is extremely slippery when wet.

WYANDOTTE FALLS (MISERY RIVER)

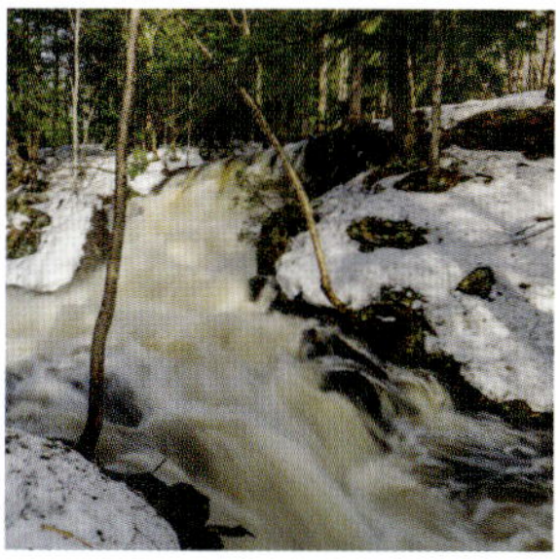

Must See:	7	GPS:	N46 53.429 W88 52.759
Height:	13 feet		
Time:	5-15 minutes		

Driving Information		Hiking Information	
Signs:	Wooden	Path:	Unimproved Footpath
Road:	Dirt	Length:	150 yards
Access:	Somewhat Difficult	Elev. Change:	Moderate
4WD:	Helpful	GPS:	N/A
		Danger:	Minor
		WP Boots:	Helpful

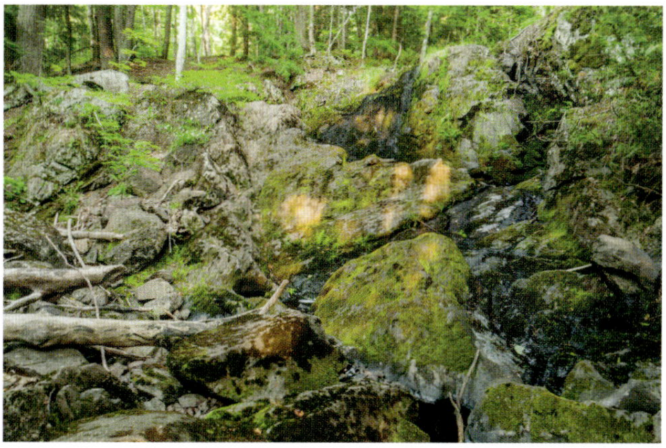

This can be a great, wonderfully flowing river. Or it can dry up to a trickle. Make sure you come after a good rain or during spring melt. The waterfall is split by a narrow outcropping with most of the water pouring over the near side. The cascade plunges into a narrow crevasse, turns to the far side, rushes out of a mere 2 foot wide gap in the ridge wall where it cascades while it widens back out, falling 4 feet and running around a number of fractured bedrock chunks lying in the shallow spill pool. The river turns and continues to cascade down a number of small drops over the next 30 feet or so.

Follow the river upstream for 100 yards to see more small drops.

Wildly different looks between these winter, summer, and autumn pictures!

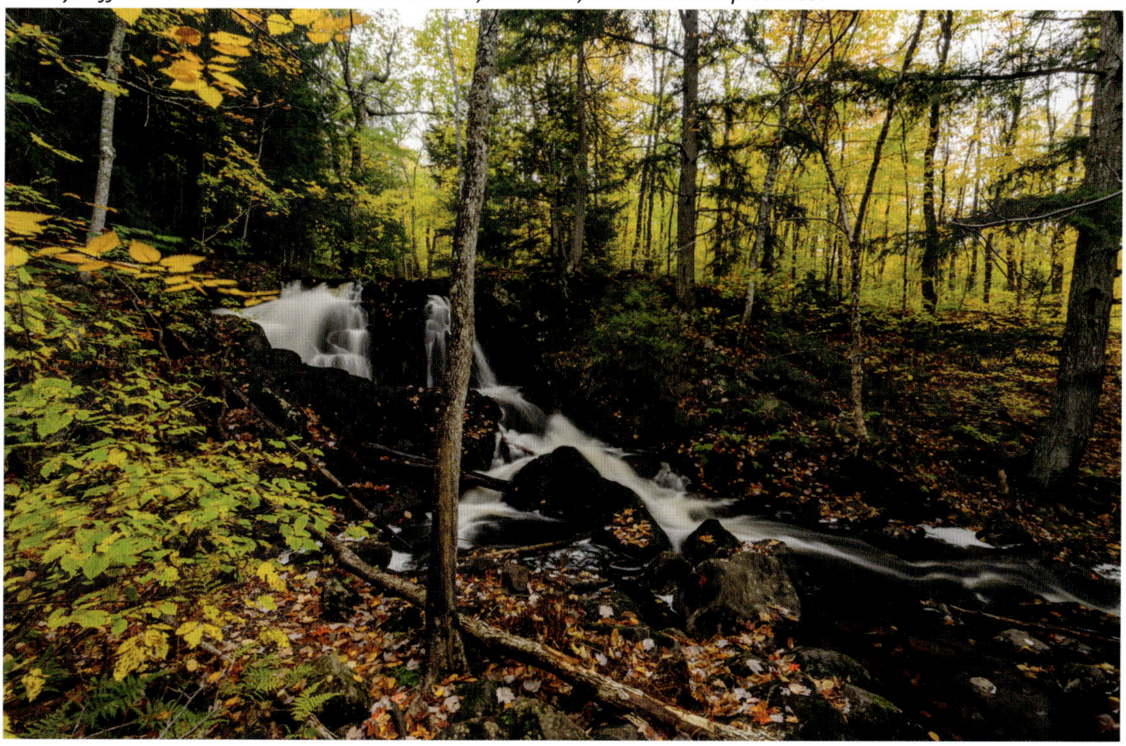

CHAPTER 3
IRON COUNTY

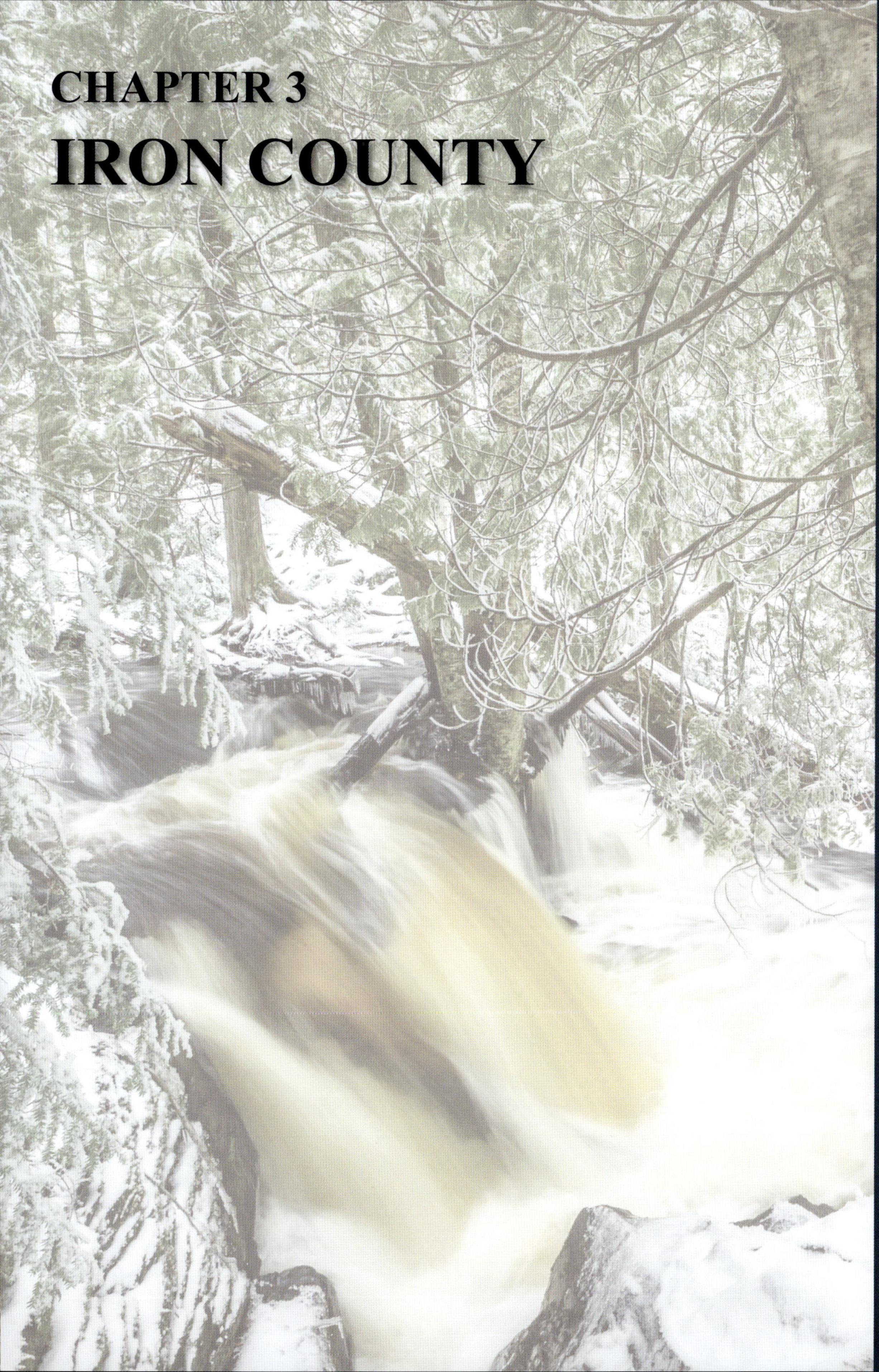

IRON COUNTY CONTENTS

IRON COUNTY MAP 222

CHIPMUNK FALLS AREA 224
CHIPMUNK FALLS HIKE 224
CHIPMUNK FALLS (NET RIVER) 224

CRYSTAL FALLS AREA 225
CHICAGON FALLS HIKE 225
CHICAGON FALLS (CHICAGON CREEK) 226
CRYSTAL FALLS DAM HIKE 227
CRYSTAL FALLS DAM (PAINT RIVER) 227
HEMLOCK FALLS DAM HIKE 228
HEMLOCK FALLS DAM (MICHIGAMME RIVER) 228
MARGESON FALLS HIKE 229
MARGESON FALLS (MARGESON CREEK) 229

DUPPY FALLS AREA 230
DUPPY FALLS HIKE 230
DUPPY FALLS (JUMBO RIVER) 231
DUPPY FALLS - MIDDLE (JUMBO RIVER) 232
DUPPY FALLS - UPPER (JUMBO RIVER) 233

HORSERACE RAPIDS AREA 234
HORSERACE RAPIDS HIKE 234
HORSERACE RAPIDS (PAINT RIVER) 234

MAPS
HIKES
WATERFALLS

TABLE OF CONTENT KEY

IRON COUNTY FACTS

Founded:	1885
Size:	1,211 square miles
Population (2010):	11,817
County Seat:	Crystal Falls

Iron County was carved out of Marquette County in 1885. The name comes from iron ore that was found in abundance in the early days of the county. Early on, in a daring move, the temporary county seat was moved from Iron River to Crystal Falls. Although there were a couple of attempts at getting it moved back to Iron River, the seat has stayed in Crystal Falls ever since. The magnificent county courthouse, built in 1890, is now in the National Register of Historic Places.

An elusive Upper Peninsula Moose

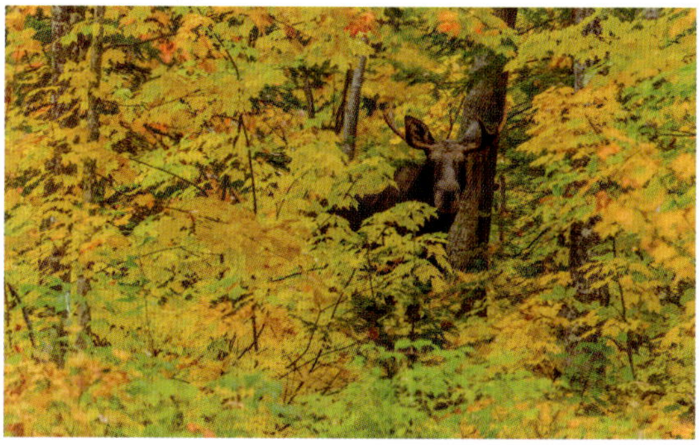

By far, the majority of Michigan's moose population is located on Isle Royale. Although the number has varied greatly over the years, there are typically between 500 and 1,000 in the remote National Park. On the "mainland" of Michigan, the bulk of the moose are found in the western end of the Upper Peninsula. Baraga, Marquette and Iron Counties account for the over 400 moose found there. There are also around 100 moose in the eastern side of the U.P., mostly in the Tahquamenon Falls area, with Newberry officially designated as the "Moose Capital of Michigan". These magnificent animals are large, and yet rarely seen. They tend to stay in marshy areas, although they may travel great distances during mating season. They are surprising quiet for their size and their long legs help them move very quickly when needed.

Sometimes the most difficult situations at the time make for the best stories later! Although there aren't a large number of waterfalls in Iron County, I've made memories at several of them. I look back with fondness at my adventures at Duppy Falls. During one of my early attempts at finding the waterfall I had wandered about .5 miles the wrong way. In the subsequent cross country trail-less hike up and down steep hills rain began to fall. Fortunately, I did find the waterfall on this hike. Even though by the time I got there the rain had stopped, I was soaked. In fact, it had rained so hard that it penetrated my pack, and my field notebook was soaked along one side. I had to take notes using just a portion of each page, and I hoped that my previous notes wouldn't be smeared too greatly so that I would be able to read them later on.

Another hike took me through an area with no trail. This was early summer and the thick undergrowth was well above waist-high. Numerous bumble bees swirled about my head as I carefully pushed my way through the tall, flowered stalks.

On a trip to Chicagon Falls, I had just got back to my vehicle at dusk when a black bear darted across the 2-track in front of me.

There are many adventures to be had. Go make some! Enjoy them for what they are, and the memories that they provide.

Iron County Map

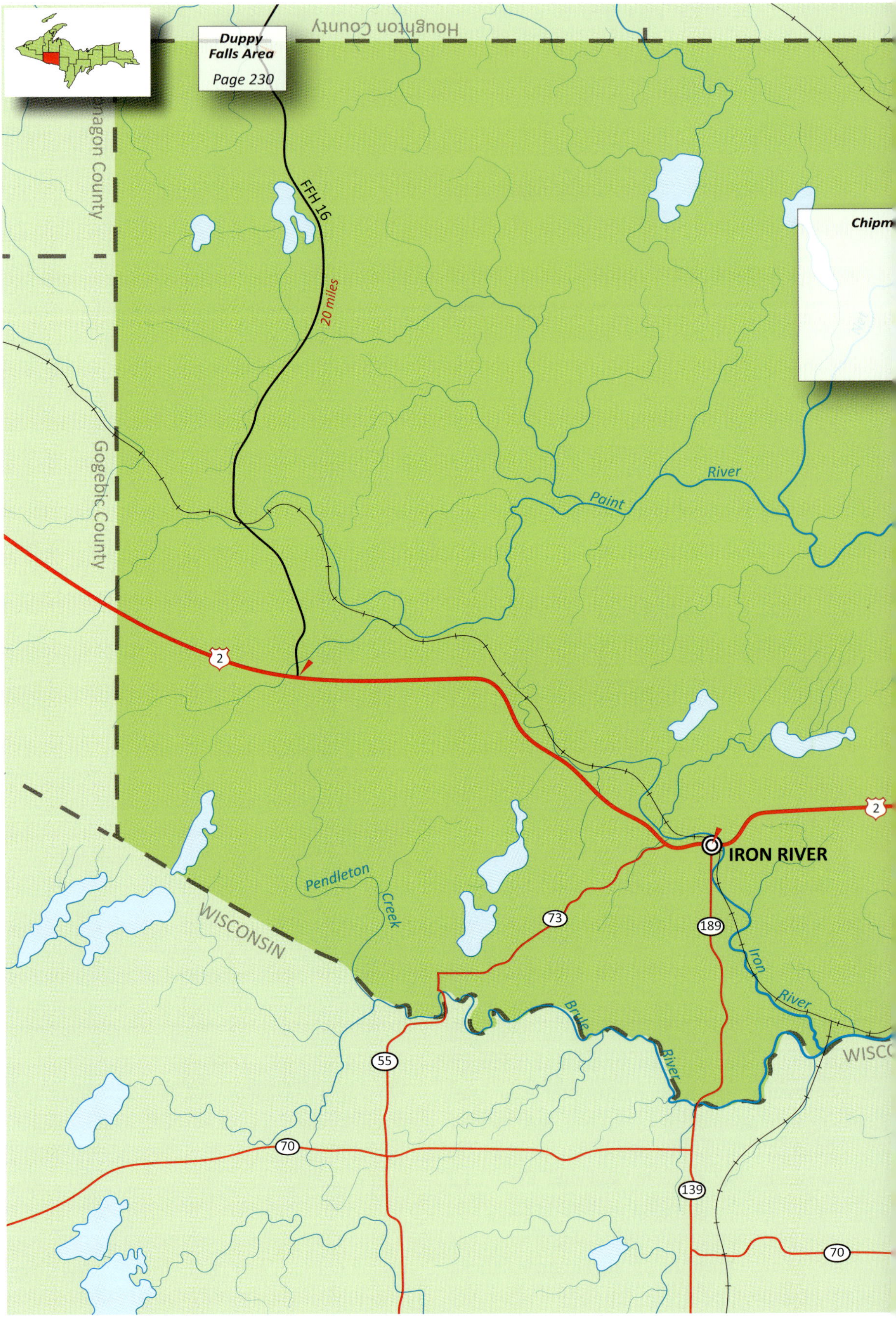

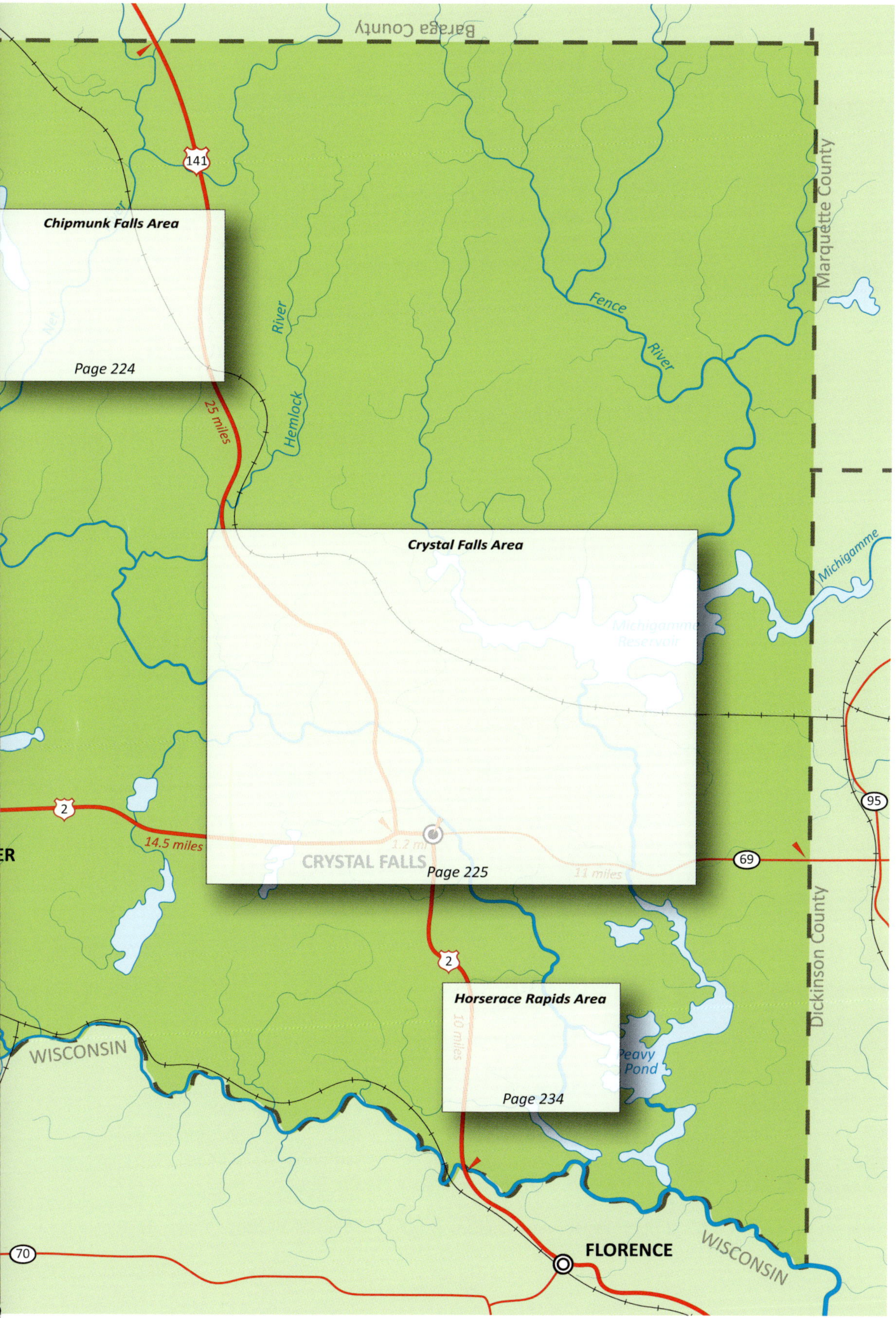
Baraga County
Marquette County
Dickinson County
Chipmunk Falls Area
Page 224
Crystal Falls Area
Page 225
Horserace Rapids Area
Page 234
Fence River
Hemlock River
Michigamme
Michigamme Reservoir
141
25 miles
2
14.5 miles
1.2 mi
CRYSTAL FALLS
11 miles
69
95
10 miles
Peavy Pond
WISCONSIN
WISCONSIN
70
FLORENCE
ER

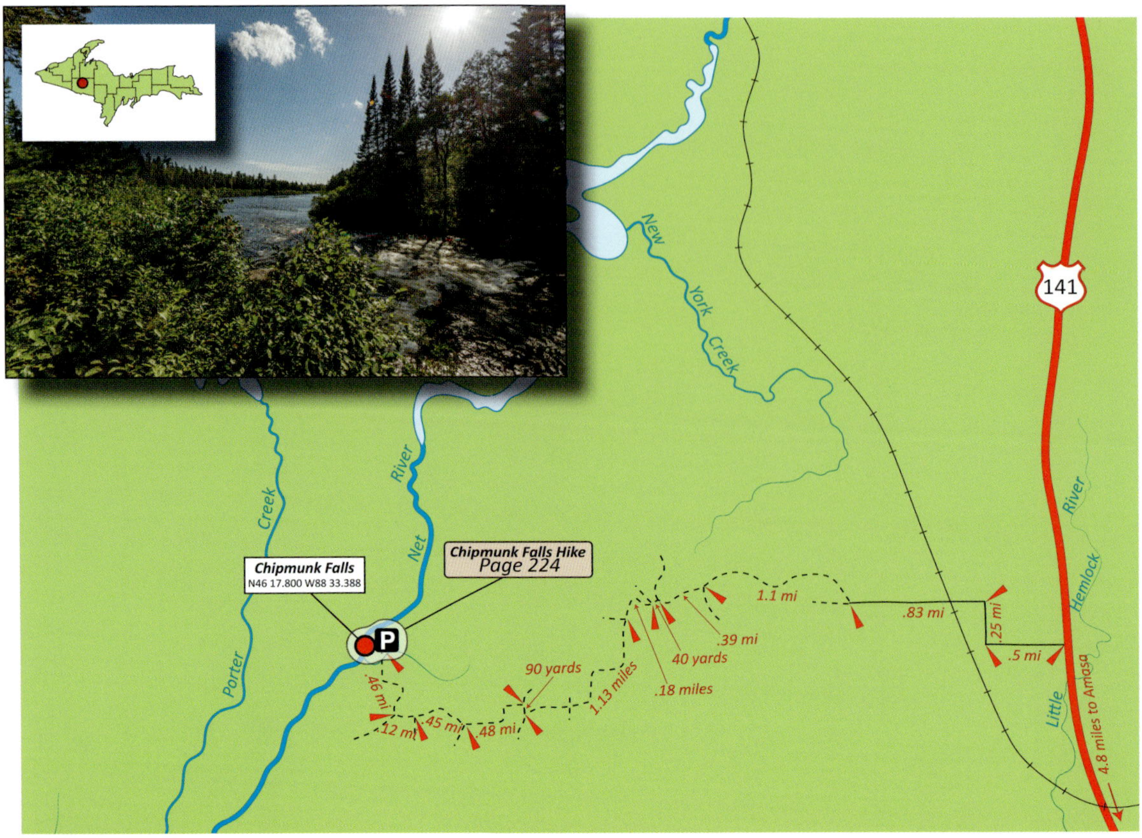

Chipmunk Falls Hike

Chipmunk Falls is on private property. Do not enter without permission. A remote, but often occupied cabin is at the trailhead to the falls.

Directions: From Amasa, drive north on US-141 for 4.8 miles. Turn left. In .5 miles turn right. Turn left in .25 miles. After .83 miles the nice straight roads end. Veer right onto a 2-track for 1.1 miles. Stay right for .39 miles. Stay left and in just 40 yards stay left again. In another .18 miles stay to the left also. Continue on the winding trail for 1.13 miles. Turn right at the "T". In 90 yards turn left. In .48 miles stay to the right for another .45 miles. Again, stay to the right for .12 miles. Then turn right and in .46 miles park at the cabin. (Make sure you have permission before coming out here!) Hike down the footpath along the river for 150 yards to the falls.

CHIPMUNK FALLS (NET RIVER)

Private

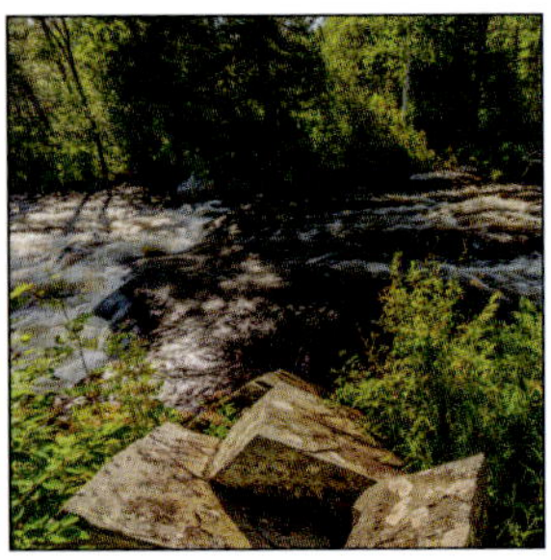

Must See:	2	GPS:	N46 17.800 W88 33.388
Height:	3 feet		
Time:	5-10 minutes	Hiking Information	
		Path:	Footpath
Driving Information		Length:	150 yards
Signs:	None	Elev. Change:	Slight
Road:	2-track	GPS:	Recommended
Access:	Very Difficult	Danger:	Slight
4WD:	Recommended	WP Boots:	N/A

Squared off blocks offer a platform to view the small falls. Three small drops make up the falls, a pinched down neck in the river.

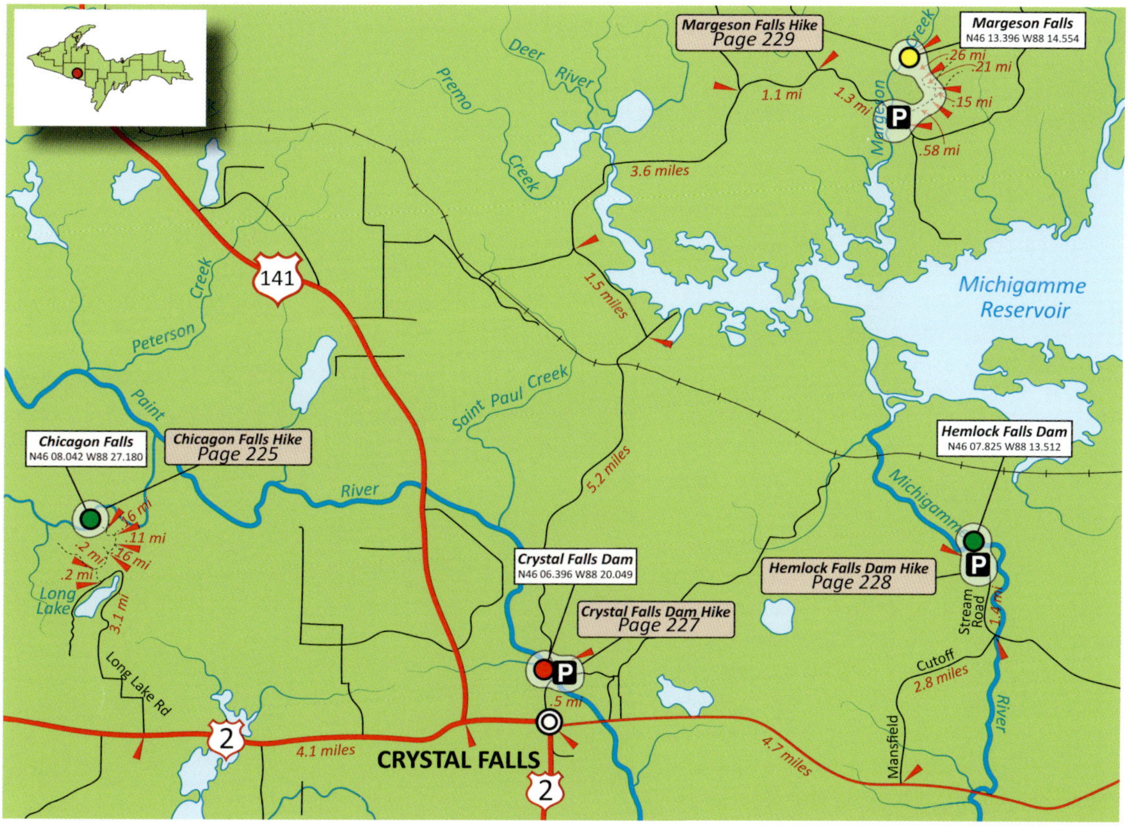

Chicagon Falls Hike

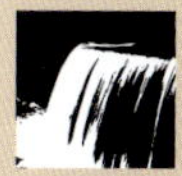

Chicagon Falls: Throughout a stand of cedar trees next to the waterfall are massive squarish boulders lying strewn about. Even the riverbed is full of boulders. This is one of the settings that seems to take on an unearthly quality. The trail to the falls deteriorates as you go. Park before getting into a portion of the trail that you are concerned about. Hike from there.

Directions: From Crystal Falls, take US-2 west about 4.5 miles to Long Lake Road. Turn right (north). Follow the winding road for 3.1 mile around to the north side of Long Lake. Turn right (northwest) on the unmarked 2-track. In .2 miles turn right (northeast). Stay to the right (northeast) in another .2 miles and drive .16 miles. Turn left (north) and drive .11 miles (this stretch is very bumpy, but most cars can probably make it). Turn left (northwest) for .16 miles (this is a VERY steep grade - a 4WD is required). Turn left (northwest) and drive to the end of the 2-track (a VERY high clearance vehicle is needed here - this is worse than the last segment). Park in the small parking area and hike 100 yards down the obvious footpath to the falls.

CHICAGON FALLS (CHICAGON CREEK)

Private

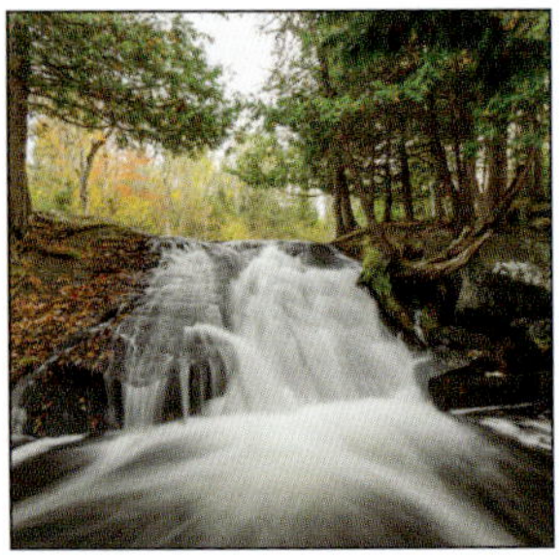

Must See:	7	GPS:	N46 08.042 W88 27.180
Height:	20 feet		
Time:	15-30 minutes	**Hiking Information**	
		Path:	Footpath
Driving Information		Length:	100 yards
Signs:	Small Hand Painted	Elev. Change:	Moderate
Road:	2-track	GPS:	Helpful
Access:	Difficult	Danger:	Moderate
4WD:	Recommended	WP Boots:	Recommended

A dilapidated footbridge may still cross the creek at the top of the falls, but don't count on it. Either cross at the base of the falls from rock to rock or wade across with a good pair of waterproof boots.

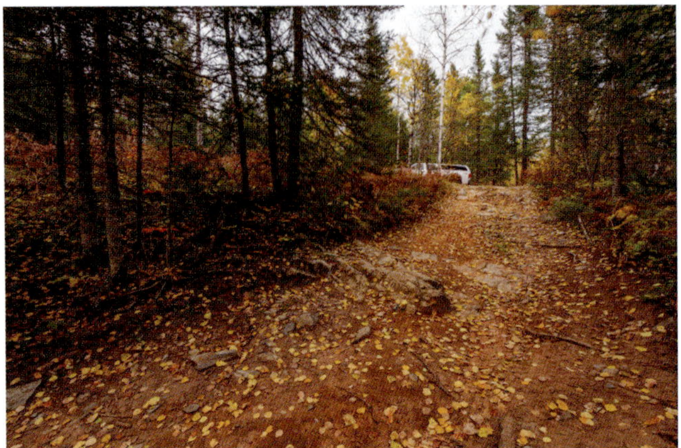

The steep 2-track - last portion of the drive

Large, chiselled blocks of bedrock run along both sides of the waterfall. The fractured rocks tilt down toward the creek below the falls. They resemble a peeled orange, with sections being pulled outwards, splaying open. Cedars grow in clusters among the fragments. These trees tend to fall into the creek, sometimes blocking the view of the waterfall.

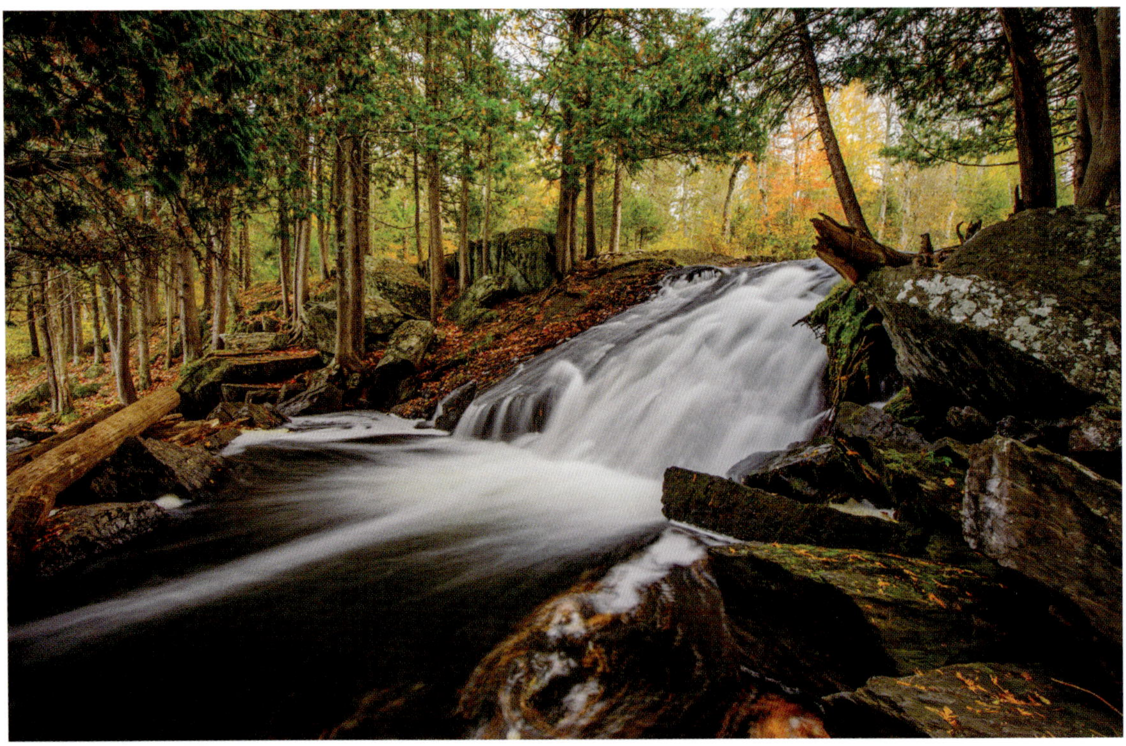

Crystal Falls Dam Hike

Crystal Falls Dam: Jagged peaks of bedrock leave much to imagine as the river is almost completely diverted through the hydro-electric plant that was built in 1891. Just blocks from downtown, the dam is built atop the original falls. When there is excess water, the falls become a raging river. Rusty streaks reveal the presence of trace amounts of iron in the bedrock.

This is one of the oldest (if not the oldest) active hydro-electric plants in operation in the Upper Peninsula. It is even listed in the National Register of Historic Places.

Directions: US-2 runs north/south through Crystal Falls. At the northern end of the city, the road turns to the west. Just one block west of the bend is N 6th Street. Turn north on N 6th Street. In .4 miles veer right onto Fairbanks Road. Cross the Paint River and turn left onto Rock Crusher Road. A small rustic roadside park is found immediately on the left near the base of the dam.

CRYSTAL FALLS DAM (PAINT RIVER)

Private

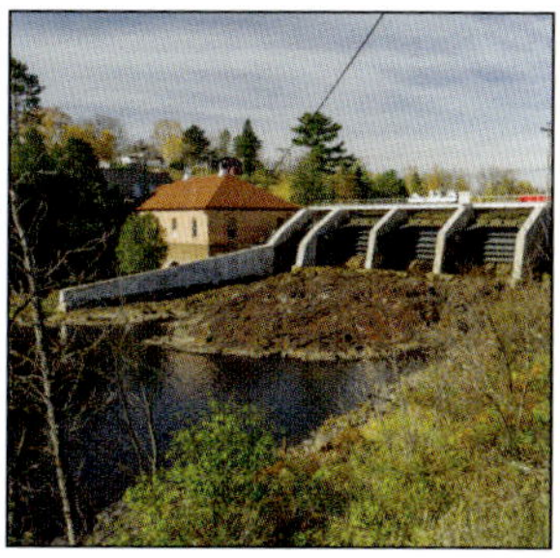

Must See:	2	GPS:	N46 06.396 W88 20.049
Height:	15 feet		
Time:	5-10 minutes	Hiking Information	
		Path:	N/A
Driving Information		Length:	N/A
Signs:	None	Elev. Change:	N/A
Road:	Secondary	GPS:	N/A
Access:	Somewhat Difficult	Danger:	N/A
4WD:	N/A	WP Boots:	N/A

A picnic table is located next to the small parking area. A nearby sign gives directions to a nearby restroom facility.

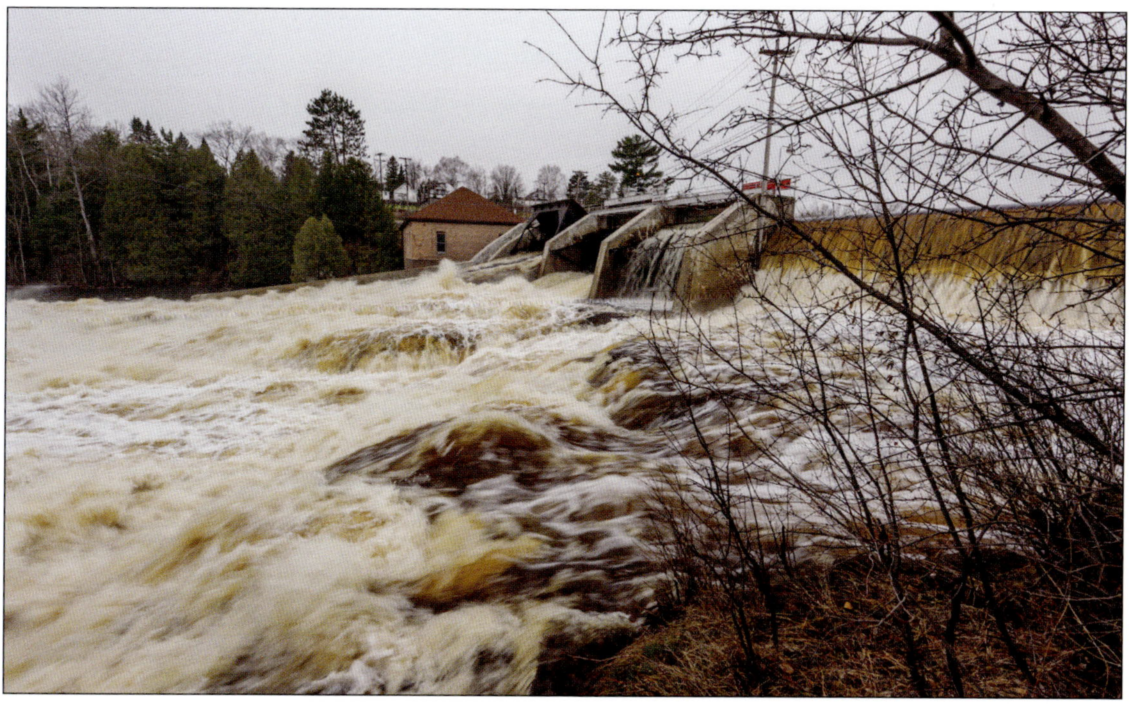

Hemlock Falls Dam Hike

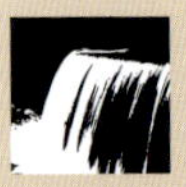

Hemlock Falls Dam: If the overflow at this hydro-electric plant is typical, this is a must see waterfall! The overflow gushes over what looks like a huge, rounded metal tube in sheets of white radiance. Towards the end of the "tube" are a couple of smaller "tubes", breaking up the visual monotony, and I suppose giving fish a ladder to climb. On the extreme left end, the river cascades in a torrent over natural bedrock. Once to the bottom of the man-made area, the falls continue in a frothing fight down a rocky ravine, below the access bridge, and finally into dissipate into the calm waters downstream.

Directions: From downtown Crystal Falls, head east on M-69 off of US-2. In 4.8 miles turn left (north) on Mansfield Cutoff. Veer right after 1.5 miles to stay on Mansfield Cutoff. In 1.4 miles turn left (northwest) just before Michigamme River on Stream Road (this is at Mansfield Dam). Follow it 1.3 miles to the end of the road. There are two parking areas. The road divides just before the dam. To the right the road heads down to the bottom of the falls. There is a pit toilet there. The road to the left leads to the bridge over the falls.

HEMLOCK FALLS DAM (MICHIGAMME RIVER)

Private

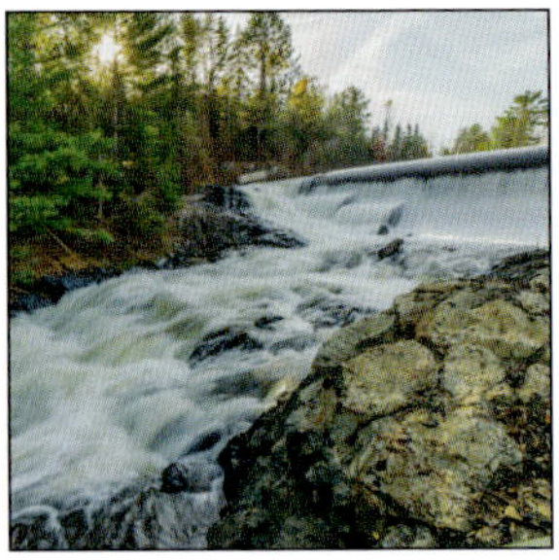

Must See:	7
Height:	25 feet
Time:	10-30 minutes

Driving Information

Signs:	None
Road:	Secondary
Access:	Somewhat Easy
4WD:	N/A

GPS:	N46 07.825 W88 13.512

Hiking Information

Path:	Footpath
Length:	100 yards
Elev. Change:	Slight to Moderate
GPS:	N/A
Danger:	Slight to Moderate
WP Boots:	N/A

View the base of the falls from the first parking area on the right. Vault toilets are here, and are used primarily by those fishing this popular area below the dam. The road to the left winds up to the dam just below the dam itself where the "fish ladder" and main portion of the rocky waterfall are located.

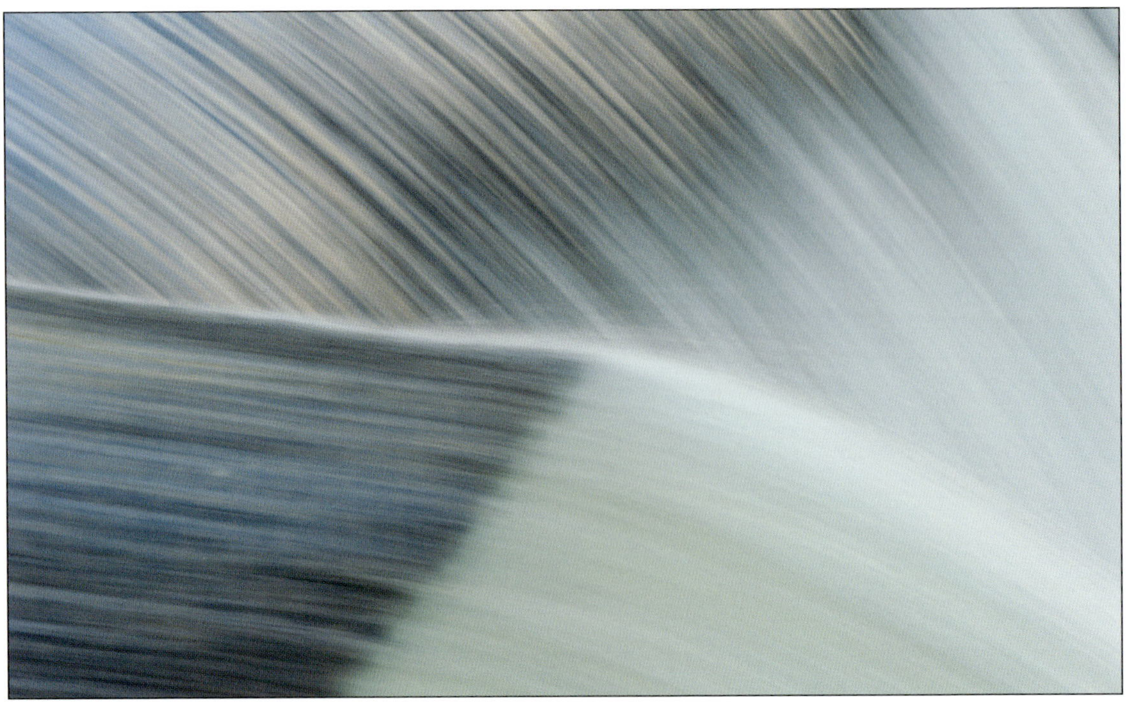

Margeson Falls Hike

I have heard that this is a wonderful waterfall in spring. However, the hike to it is without a trail and through difficult terrain with dense undergrowth and swampy conditions subtracting from its desirability.

Directions: In downtown Crystal Falls turn north onto N 6th Street for .4 miles. Turn right on Fair Banks Road. In .1 miles turn left onto Rock Crusher Road. After 5.2 miles turn left. In 1.5 miles keep right. Angle right after 3.6 miles. Turn right in 1.1 miles. In another 1.3 miles the road crosses Margeson Creek. Park. There are two 2-tracks here. Both have cables across them. Neither say, "No trespassing". The 2-track to the left ends shortly at a hunting cabin. The waterfall can't be hiked to "point-to-point". There is too much lowland in the way. Hike in a good sized arc down the 2-track on the right to avoid it. Be respectful. This may be on private land. Obey all NO TRESPASSING signs.

MARGESON FALLS (MARGESON CREEK)

Private

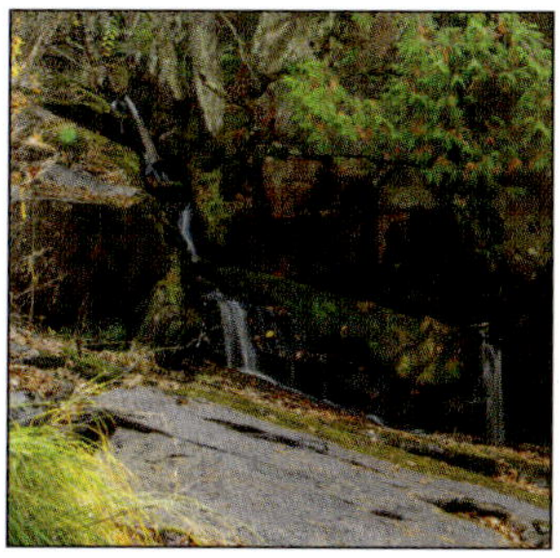

Must See:	4	GPS:	N46 13.396 W88 14.554
Height:	12 feet		
Time:	1.5 to 2 hours	Hiking Information	
		Path:	None
Driving Information		Length:	1 mile
Signs:	None	Elev. Change:	Moderate
Road:	Dirt	GPS:	Required
Access:	Difficult	Danger:	Elevated
4WD:	Helpful	WP Boots:	Required

After a 1 mile hike through ferns, poplars, small cedars (all the while attempting to skirt the wetlands), a canyon appears. The creek looks nothing like it does back where the bridge crosses it! Dropping down through a narrow slit in the canyon, most of the waterfall is hidden from view until it plunges off of an angled section of rock. It free falls for a couple of feet then slides down a lower angled section before finally entering the quiet, black waters at the base of a 50 foot mound of bedrock that makes up the far side of the canyon. Evergreens top the canyon, with hardwoods scattered here and there.

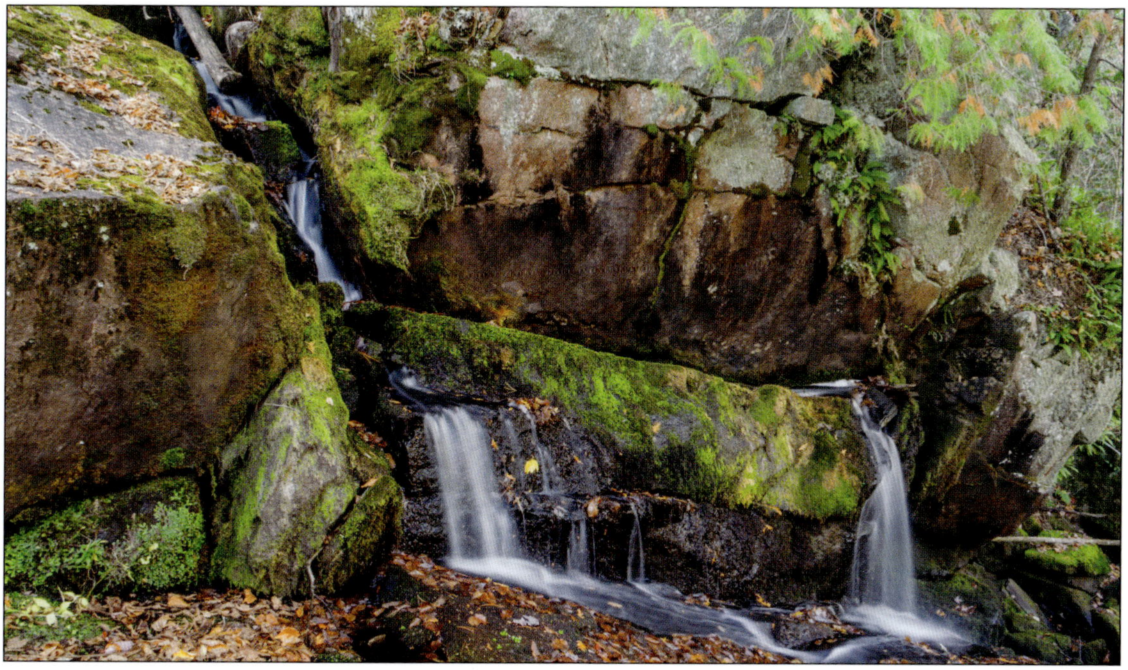

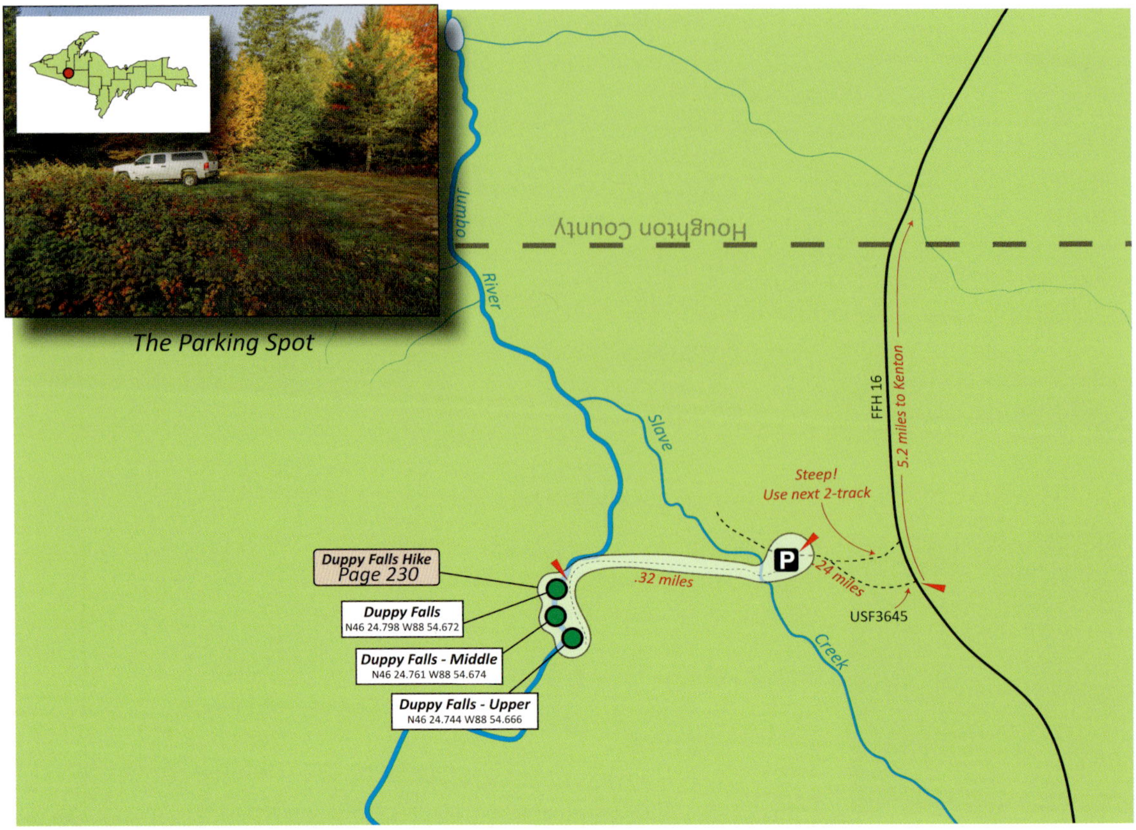

Duppy Falls Hike

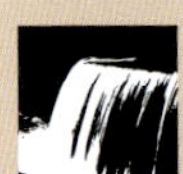

Duppy Falls: The main cascade is split in half. Most of the water runs to the left side. A secondary drop is just below the spill pool.

Duppy Falls - Middle: The middle waterfall is a triple cascade that pours over black rocks. The first two drops are lined up while the final fall is around a small bend in the river.

Duppy Falls - Upper: The last of the Duppy Falls along the hike is the furthest up river. An easily identifiable trail leads all the way from the parking area to here and beyond, although it does diminish somewhat after the first drop.

Directions: Turn south onto FFH 16 at the light in Kenton off of M-28. In 5.3 miles, just after entering Iron County, turn right (west) onto USF3645 @N46 24.813 W88 54.116 (2-track). Drive .22 miles to a clearing @ N46 24.863 W88 54.380 (on the left at the base of a steep part of the 2-track just before it turns hard to the right and enters the forest). Park. A well traveled footpath heads into the trees left of the 2-track. Follow it to a small creek (Slave Creek). Cross on the small wooden foot bridge. The trail heads westerly until it joins up with Jumbo River. The trail then turns to the southwest and continues along the east side of Jumbo River to the falls. This stretch of the hike is relatively flat. But after approaching Duppy Falls #1 from below the waterfall, the trail climbs up the rocky hillside (this section can be quite slippery and more difficult to navigate) to the upper two waterfalls.

DUPPY FALLS (JUMBO RIVER)

Private

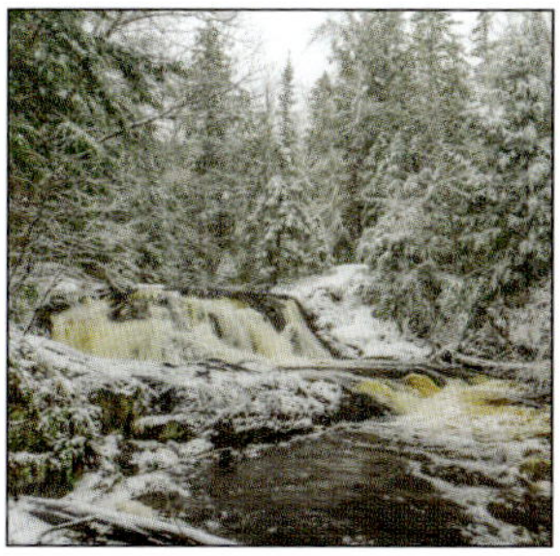

Must See:	8	GPS:	N46 24.798 W88 54.672
Height:	12 feet		
Time:	30-45 minutes	Hiking Information	
		Path:	Footpath
Driving Information		Length:	.32 miles
Signs:	None	Elev. Change:	Slight
Road:	2-track	GPS:	Helpful
Access:	Somewhat Difficult	Danger:	Moderate
4WD:	Helpful	WP Boots:	Recommended

I had the hardest time finding these three waterfalls for some reason. I tried in vain four times over three years. Twice I dragged my kids through miles of forest, over rolling and sometimes steep hillsides, breaking through dead pine branches and thick undergrowth. We would either end up in beaver flooded sections of Slave Creek, fighting through chest high wild flowers covered with bumble bees, or come in on a wrong 2-track, only to be heading to the wrong GPS coordinates. I finally got good information from the owner of Hoppy's Bar in Kenton. I'm glad I didn't give up! These are great waterfalls! I'm sure that you'll love them as well.

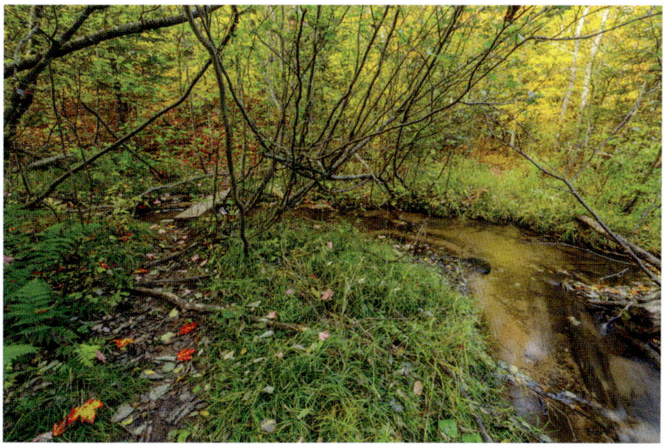

The bridge over Slave Creek

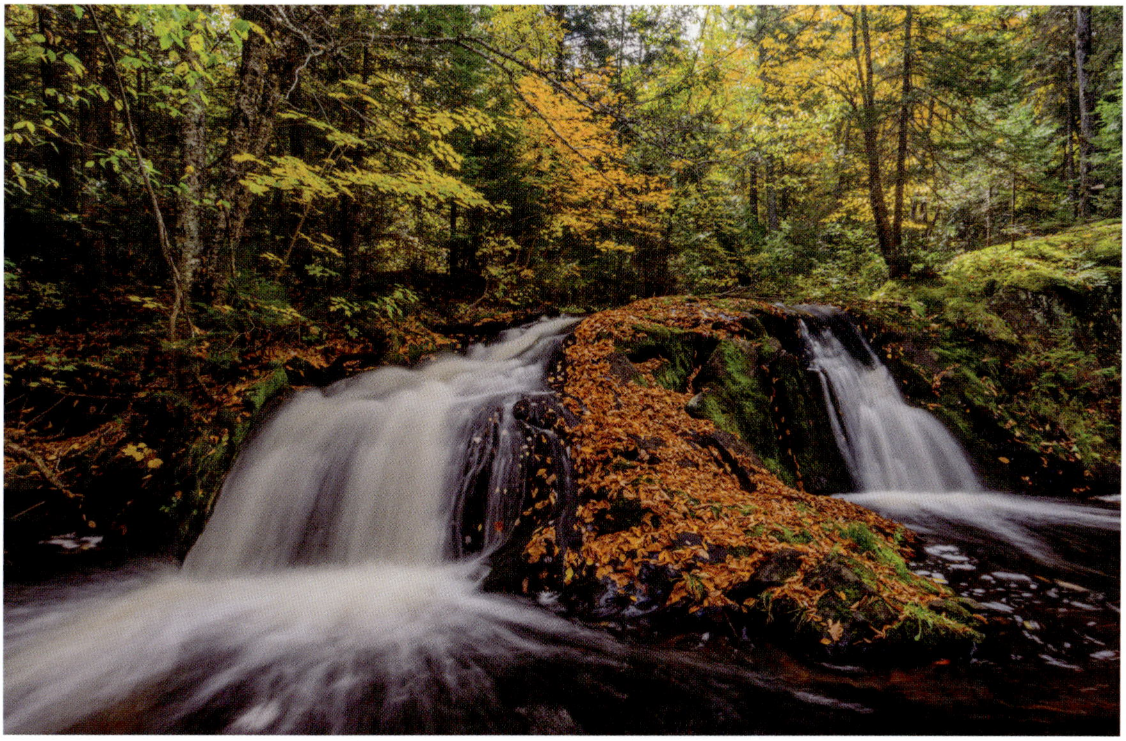

DUPPY FALLS - MIDDLE (JUMBO RIVER)

Private

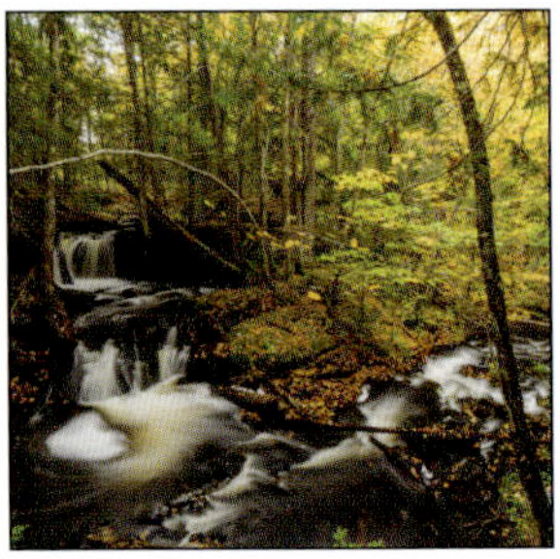

Must See:	7	GPS:	N46 24.761 W88 54.674
Height:	14 feet		
Time:	40-60 minutes	Hiking Information	
		Path:	Footpath
Driving Information		Length:	.36 miles
Signs:	None	Elev. Change:	Moderate
Road:	2-track	GPS:	Helpful
Access:	Somewhat Difficult	Danger:	Moderate
4WD:	Helpful	WP Boots:	Recommended

The trail between Duppy Falls and here climbs up some steep rocks. These can be quite slippery when wet or icy. Be careful!

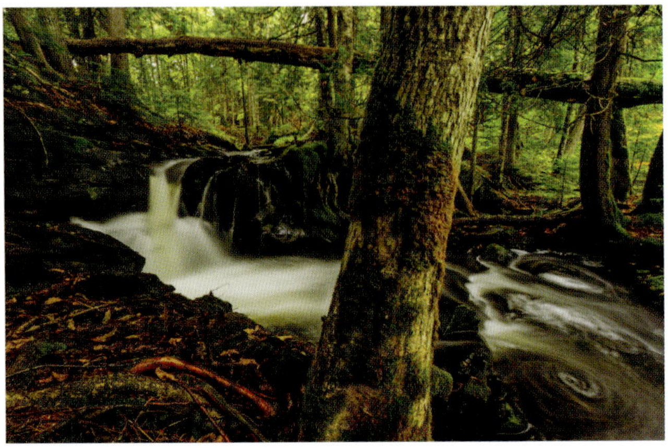

Halfway up the "Duppy Series" is this lovely triple drop. It starts with a 5 foot plunge into a heavily shaded shallow pool. Moss covered gnarled roots cling to the rock face next to this drop. Twenty feet later the river drops again, this time sliding down another 5 feet into a slightly deeper pool, churning before turning and cascading down a final 4 feet.

It can be very beautiful with snow! But the rocky trail can be treacherous in the winter. Be careful!

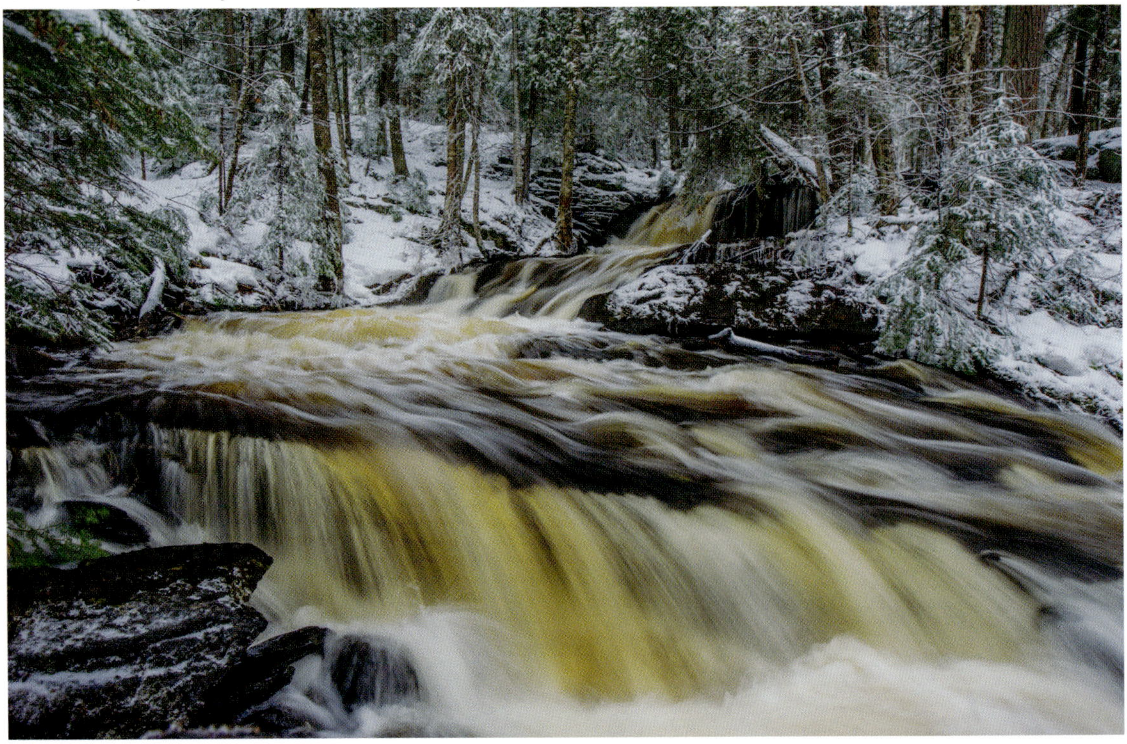

DUPPY FALLS - UPPER (JUMBO RIVER)

Private

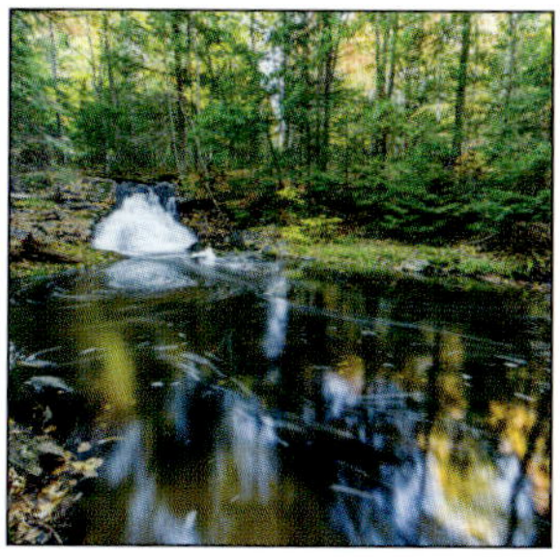

Must See:	7	GPS:	N46 24.744 W88 54.666
Height:	8 feet		
Time:	45-60 minutes	**Hiking Information**	
		Path:	Footpath
Driving Information		Length:	.40 miles
Signs:	None	Elev. Change:	Moderate
Road:	2-track	GPS:	Helpful
Access:	Somewhat Difficult	Danger:	Moderate
4WD:	Helpful	WP Boots:	Recommended

Climb up to the top of the Middle Falls. The viewing area below the Upper Falls will quickly come into sight.

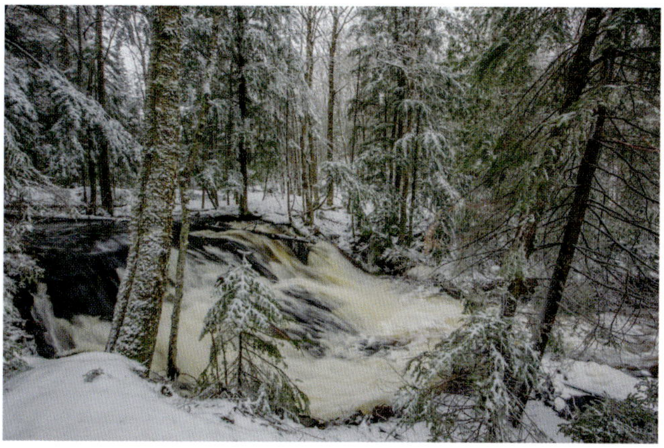

Slightly terraced black slate makes up the face of this cascading/sliding waterfall. In high water, the river runs from side to side. At the base of the waterfall, the river checks down to just 4 feet. It then enters a large, circular pool. The exit is like the entrance, only 4 feet wide. Cedars and yellow birch surround the waterfall and pool, golden leaves in abundance in the surrounding forest during October hikes.

There is a small slate quarry just 20 feet from the waterfall. More areas of rock removal from days gone by can be seen further downstream along the trail.

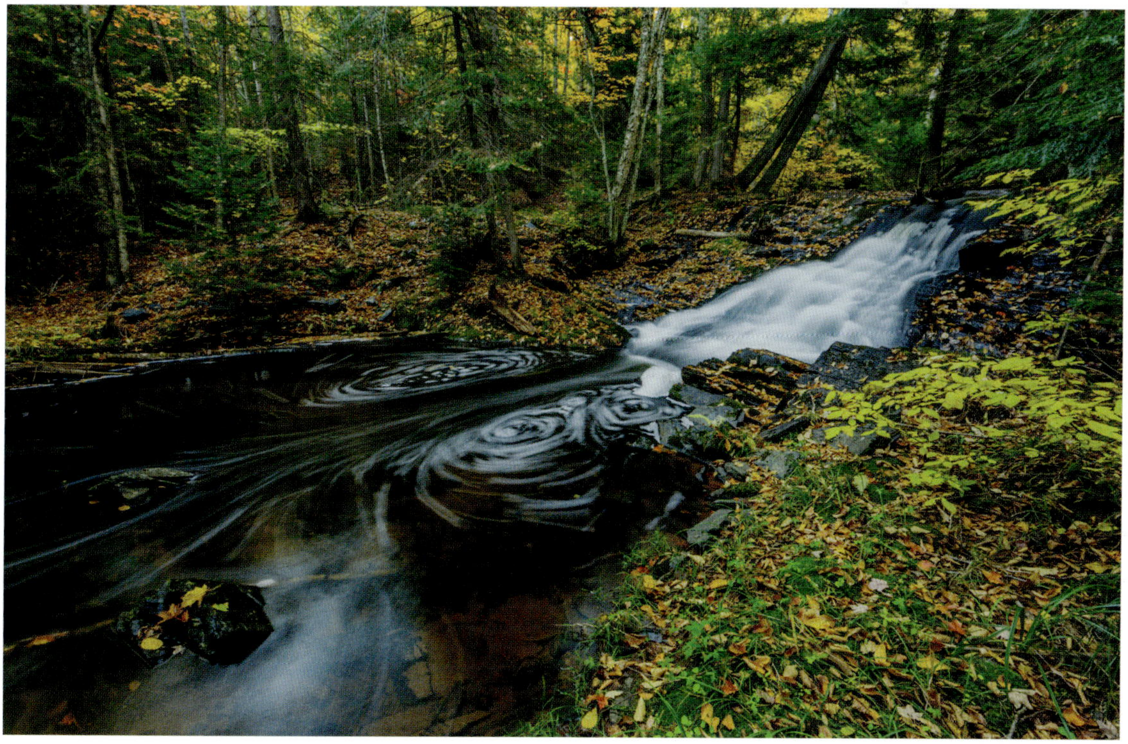

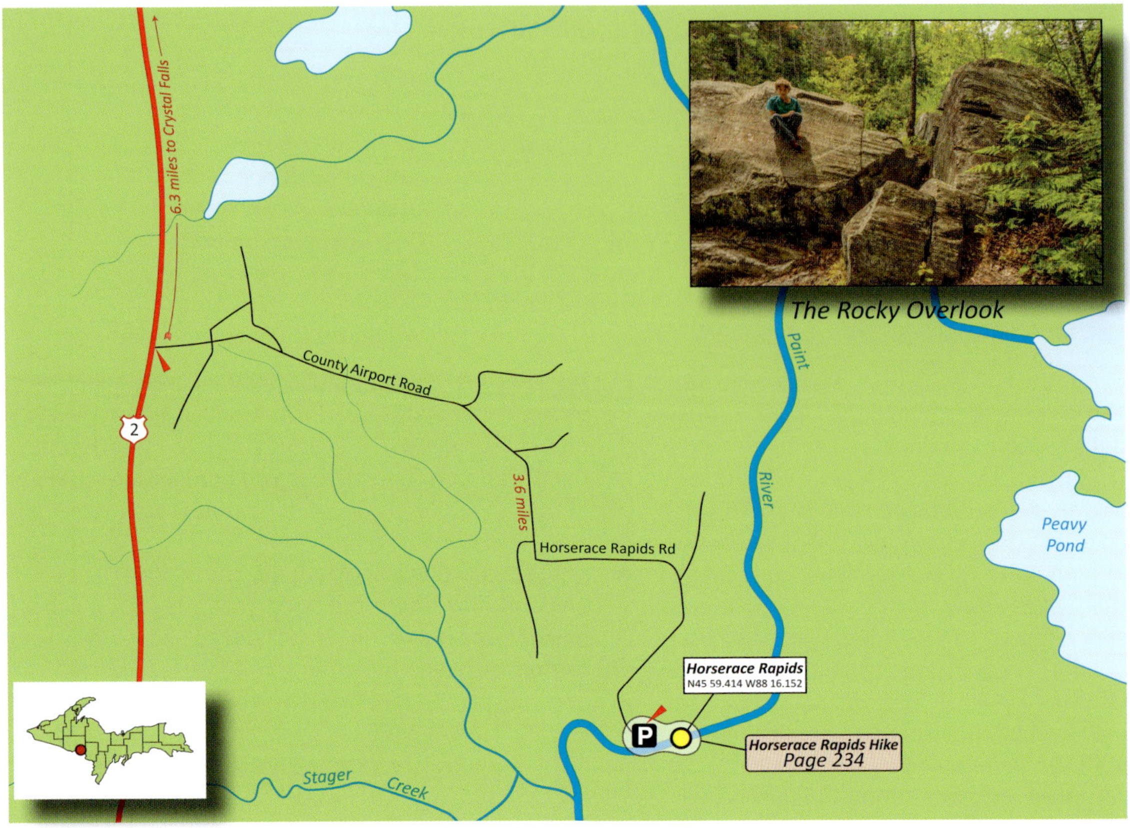

Horserace Rapids Hike

Horserace Rapids: Although not an official waterfall, this aggressive set of rapids is locally quite popular, with signage and a designated park assigned to it.

Directions: Head south from Crystal Falls on US-2 for about 6 miles. Turn left (east) at the signs for "Horserace Rapids" and the airport. The road is gravel, but should be navigable by most vehicles. Stay to the right at every intersection. After 3.6 miles the road ends at the parking lot. Hike .25 miles to the rocky overlook of the rapids.

HORSERACE RAPIDS (PAINT RIVER)

Private

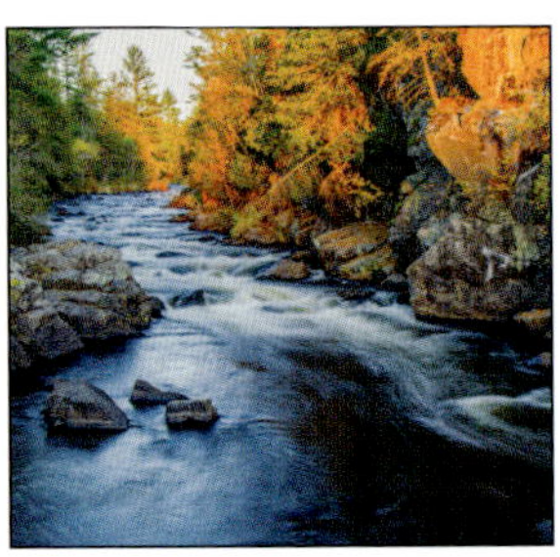

Must See:	5	GPS:	N45 59.414 W88 16.152
Height:	10 feet		
Time:	15-30 minutes	Hiking Information	
		Path:	Improved Footpath
Driving Information		Length:	.25 miles
Signs:	Metal Road Sign	Elev. Change:	Moderate
Road:	Gravel	GPS:	Helpful
Access:	Somewhat Easy	Danger:	Moderate
4WD:	N/A	WP Boots:	N/A

The river runs through a canyon with a 40 foot high rock wall on the far side. A short trail heading downhill from a parking lot with a pit toilet ends at an outcropping of jumbled basalt rocks overlooking the rapids. Smaller ripples occur down river from the viewing area, but the main feature is perfectly situated upstream. On the far side of the river a massive face of vertical, flat basalt show off its profile. Pine trees grow straight and tall from thin soil coverings. The near side isn't so rugged, but it still has numerous rock outcroppings and boulders strewn about.

CHAPTER 4
KEWEENAW COUNTY

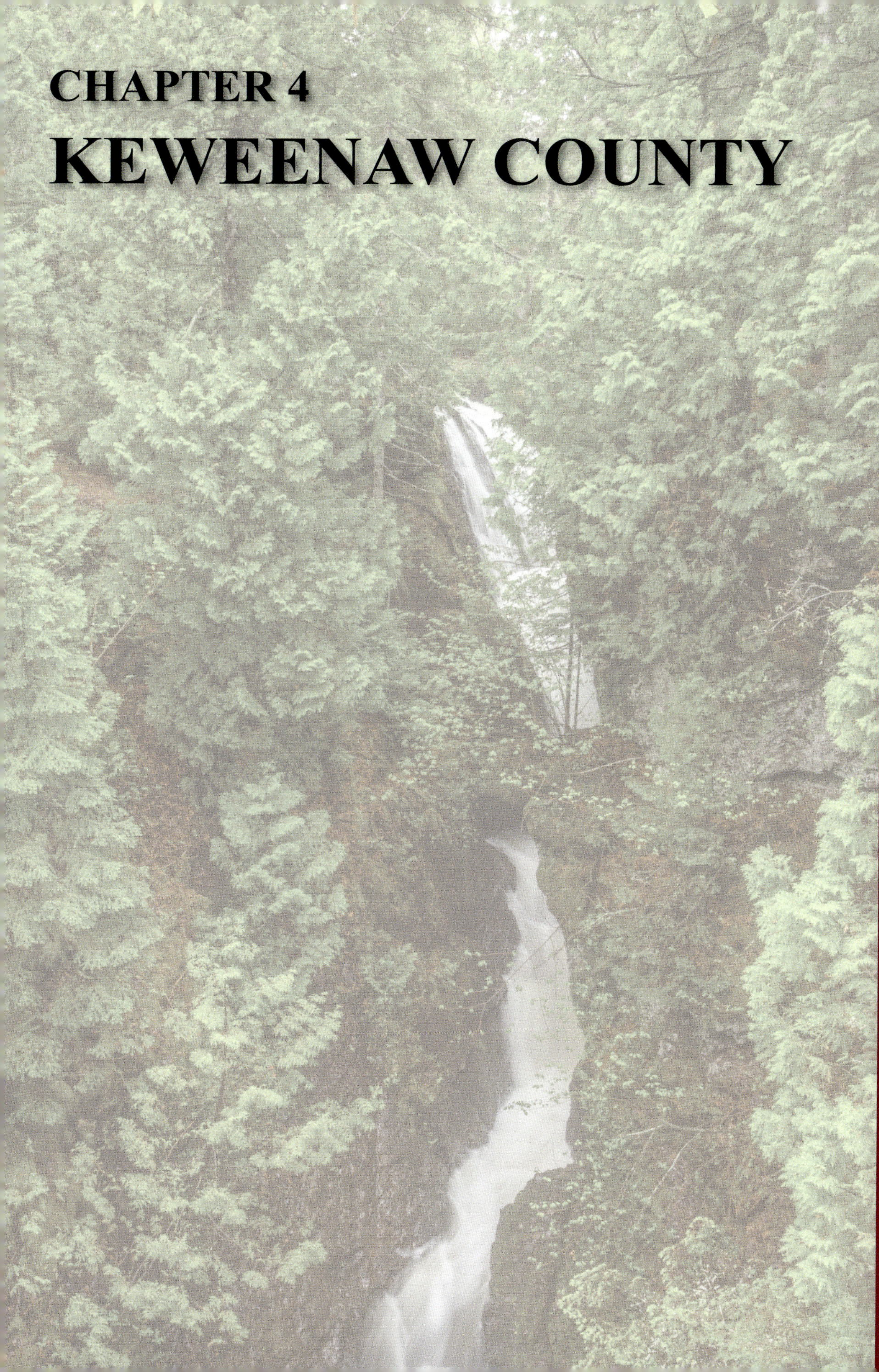

KEWEENAW COUNTY CONTENTS

KEWEENAW COUNTY MAP **240**

EAGLE RIVER AREA **242**

COPPER FALLS HIKE 242
COPPER FALLS (OWL CREEK) 242
EAGLE RIVER CASCADES HIKE 243
EAGLE RIVER CASCADES (EAGLE RIVER) 243
EAGLE RIVER FALLS HIKE 244
EAGLE RIVER FALLS (EAGLE RIVER) 244
EAGLE RIVER SLIDE HIKE 245
EAGLE RIVER SLIDE - UPPER (EAGLE RIVER) 245
EAGLE RIVER SLIDE - LOWER (EAGLE RIVER) 246
FENNERS FALLS HIKE 247
FENNERS FALLS (EAGLE RIVER) 247
JACOBS FALLS HIKE 248
JACOBS FALLS (JACOBS CREEK) 248
JACOBS FALLS #2 (JACOBS CREEK) 249
JACOBS FALLS #3 (JACOBS CREEK) 250
JACOBS FALLS #4 (JACOBS CREEK) 251
JACOBS FALLS #5 (JACOBS CREEK) 252
SILVER CREEK FALLS HIKE 253
SILVER CREEK FALLS (SILVER CREEK) 253
SILVER CREEK FALLS - UPPER #1 (SILVER CREEK) 254
SILVER CREEK FALLS - UPPER #2 (SILVER CREEK) 255
TEN FOOT FALLS HIKE 256
TEN FOOT FALLS (EAGLE RIVER) 256

GRATIOT RIVER AREA **257**

GRATIOT LOWER FALLS HIKE 257
GRATIOT FALLS - LOWER #3 (GRATIOT RIVER) 258
GRATIOT FALLS - LOWER #2 (GRATIOT RIVER) 259
GRATIOT FALLS - LOWER #1 (GRATIOT RIVER) 260
GRATIOT UPPER FALLS HIKE 261
GRATIOT FALLS - UPPER (GRATIOT RIVER) 261

HAVEN FALLS AREA **262**

EISTER FALLS HIKE 262
EISTER FALLS - LOWER (EISTER CREEK) 263
EISTER FALLS - MIDDLE #1 (EISTER CREEK) 264
EISTER FALLS - MIDDLE #2 (EISTER CREEK) 265
EISTER FALLS - UPPER (EISTER CREEK) 266
HAVEN FALLS HIKE 267
HAVEN FALLS (HAVEN CREEK) 267

MANGANESE FALLS AREA **268**

FANNY HOOE FALLS HIKE 268
FANNY HOOE FALLS (FANNY HOOE CREEK) 268
MANGANESE FALLS HIKE 269
MANGANESE FALLS (MANGANESE CREEK) 269

MAPS........
HIKES........
WATERFALLS........

TABLE OF CONTENT KEY

MONTREAL FALLS AREA **270**

MONTREAL FALLS HIKE 270

MONTREAL FALLS - LOWER (MONTREAL RIVER) 271

MONTREAL FALLS - MIDDLE (MONTREAL RIVER) 272

MONTREAL FALLS - UPPER (MONTREAL RIVER) 273

SILVER RIVER FALLS AREA **274**

SILVER RIVER FALLS HIKE 274

SILVER RIVER FALLS (SILVER RIVER) 274

SILVER RIVER FALLS - LOWER (SILVER RIVER) 276

SISKIWIT FALLS AREA **277**

LITTLE SISKIWIT FALLS HIKE 277

LITTLE SISKIWIT FALLS (LITTLE SISKIWIT RIVER) 277

SISKIWIT FALLS HIKE 278

SISKIWIT FALLS (SISKIWIT RIVER) 278

TOBACCO FALLS AREA **279**

TOBACCO FALLS HIKE 279

TOBACCO FALLS - LOWER (TOBACCO RIVER) 279

TOBACCO FALLS - UPPER (TOBACCO RIVER) 280

MAPS........
HIKES........
WATERFALLS........

TABLE OF CONTENT KEY

KEWEENAW COUNTY FACTS

Founded:	1861
Size:	5,966 square miles
Population (2010):	2,156
County Seat:	Eagle River

Keweenaw County, the largest county in Michigan at 5,966 square miles, has only 540 square miles of land, which makes it the lowest land to water ratio county in the United States!

The county is divided into two separate land masses. The tip of the Keweenaw Peninsula is the easiest of the two to access. Although Portage Lake cuts the top half of the peninsula off by water, the Portage Lake Lift Bridge connects these areas. Isle Royale, the other half of the county, however, is over forty miles out into Lake Superior, accessible only by boat or plane. It's one of the most remote National Parks in the United States, with around 15,000 visitors annually. The chain of over 400 islands is a cold water paradise!

Keweenaw County is home to Estivant Pines, a nature preserve with what is considered to be the last stand of virgin white pine in the Upper Peninsula. This is one of the many fine properties preserved by the Michigan Nature Association.

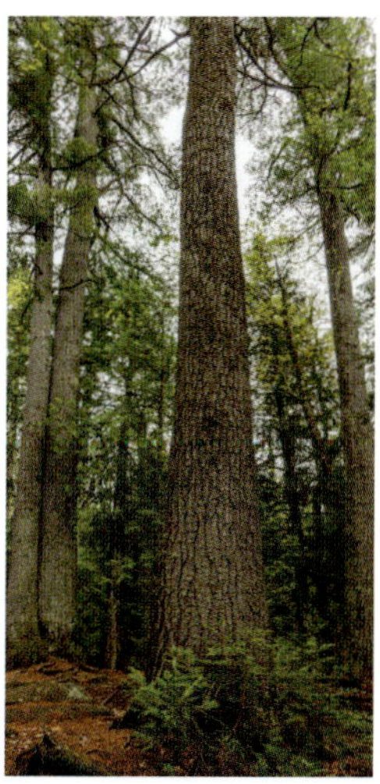

Fort Wilkins, just east of Copper Harbor, was built and garrisoned in 1844 to ensure safe passage of copper from the recently built copper mines as well as maintaining civil relationships with the indigenous Americans in the area. Just two years later, the soldiers were sent south to help in the Mexican-American War. Since there had been no trouble at the fort up to that time the fort remained vacant until shortly after the Civil War when soldiers with time left on their enlistments were sent to the cold northern fort to fulfill their service. The only fighting they did was with the elements in the winter and hordes of biting insects in the summer.

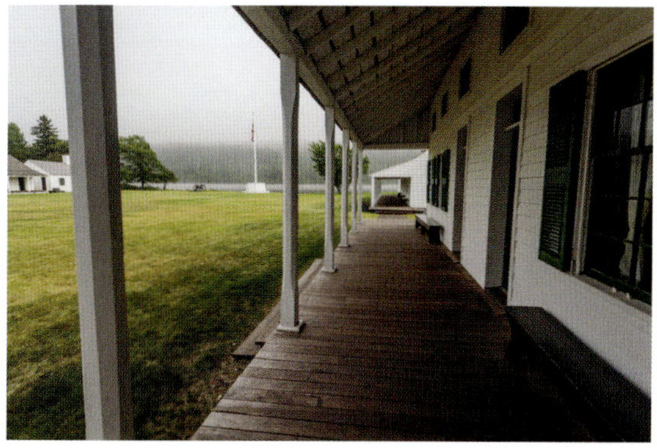

The northern end of US-41 lies just east of Copper Harbor, past Fort Wilkins. The road heads south, passing through eight states, ending in Miami, Florida 1,990 miles after its beginning toward the tip of the Keweenaw Peninsula.

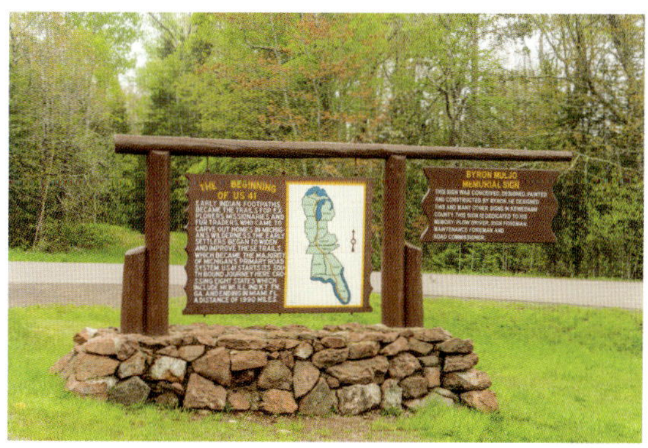

Keweenaw County Map

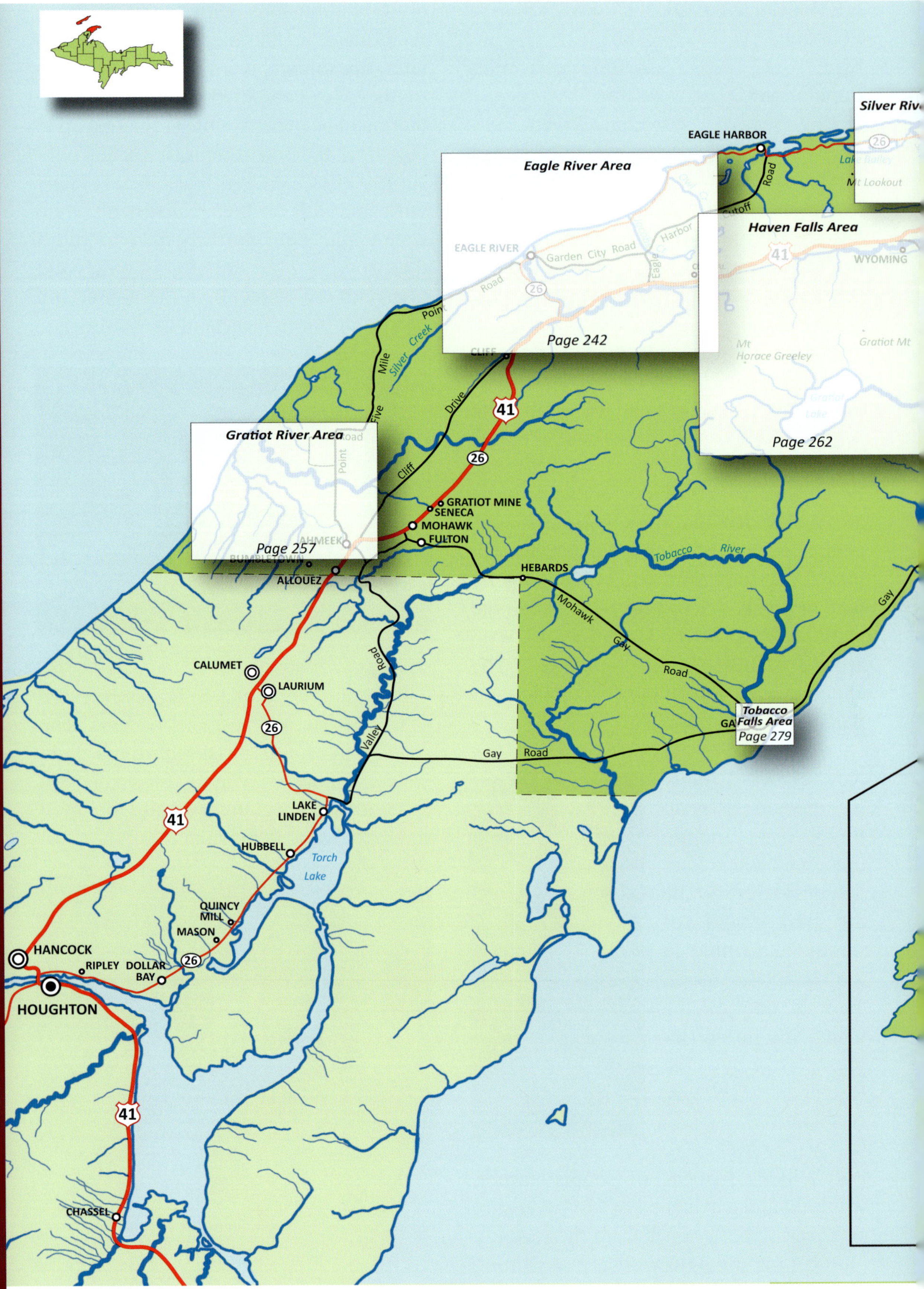

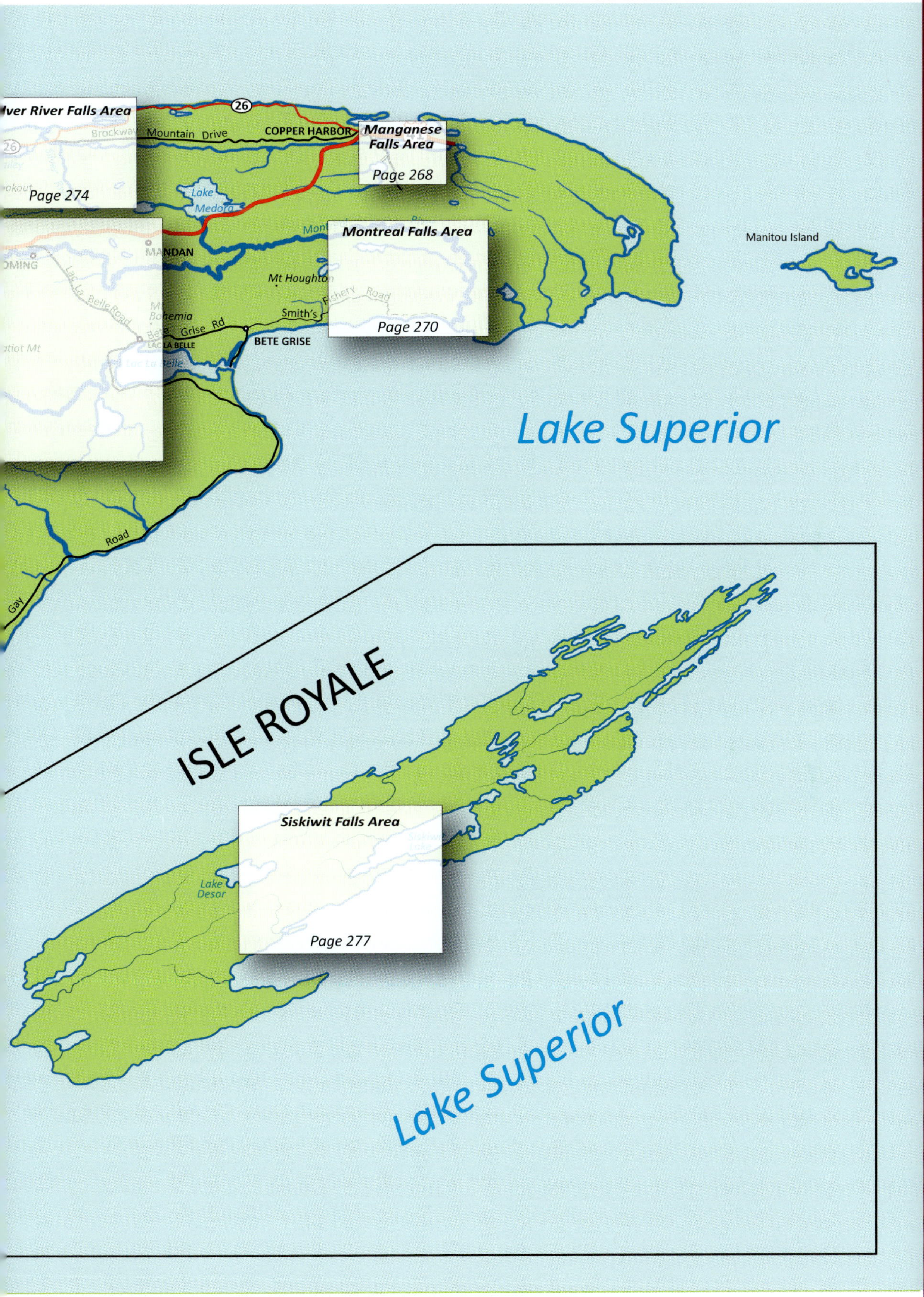
Manganese Falls Area
Page 268
Page 274
Montreal Falls Area
Page 270
Mountain Drive
COPPER HARBOR
Lake Medora
Mt Houghton
Smith's
BETE GRISE
Bete Grise Rd
Manitou Island
Lake Superior
Road
Gay
ISLE ROYALE
Siskiwit Falls Area
Page 277
Lake Desor
Lake Superior

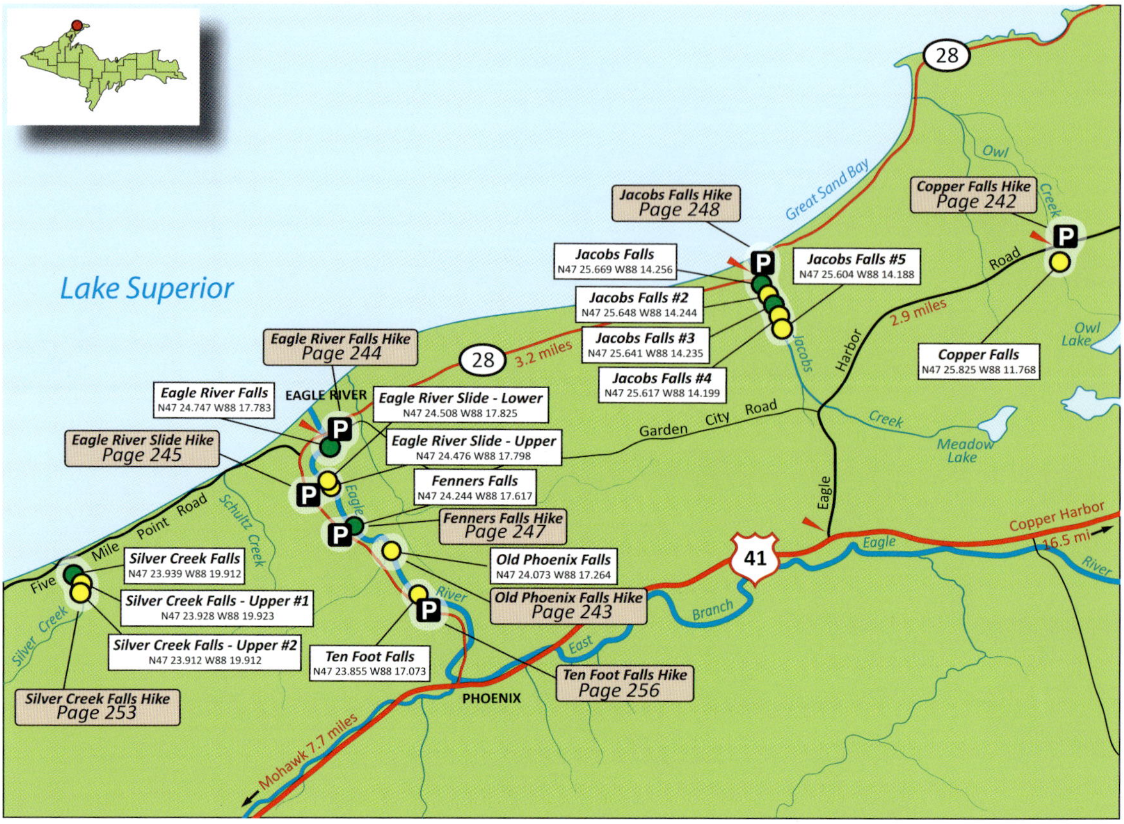

Copper Falls Hike

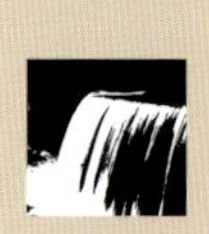

The narrow creek often has no more than a trickle of water flowing in it. The Must See rating of "2" would be likely much higher after a good rain or during spring melt.

Directions: Turn south onto Eagle Harbor Cutoff Road from M-26 in Eagle Harbor. In 2.9 miles park near the bridge over Owl Creek. Hike down to the creek bed and follow it upstream 130 yards to the waterfall.

COPPER FALLS (OWL CREEK)

Private

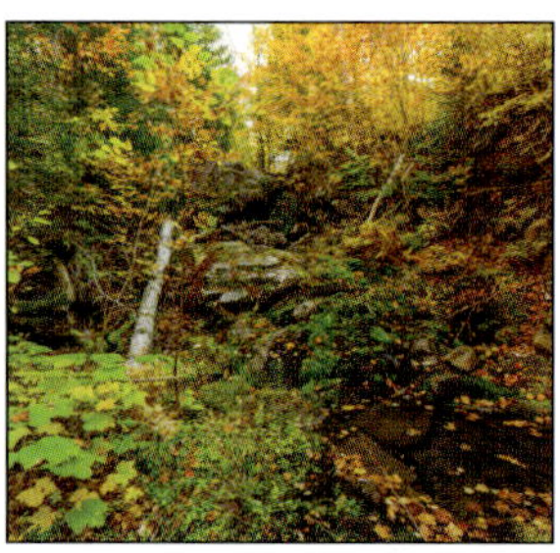

Must See:	4	GPS:	N47 25.825 W88 11.768
Height:	15 feet		
Time:	25-25 minutes	Hiking Information	
		Path:	None
Driving Information		Length:	130 yards
Signs:	None	Elev. Change:	Moderate
Road:	Secondary	GPS:	Helpful
Access:	Somewhat Easy	Danger:	Moderate
4WD:	N/A	WP Boots:	Helpful

A "V" shaped slot in the bedrock funnels the creek to the center of the waterway. It then cascades down a moss covered mass, overflowing a boulder filled spill pool to cascade down the second half of the waterfall. The creek then runs through a 20 foot deep gorge with fairly steep walls. Trees grow thick up the wall and in the forest beyond.

Old Phoenix Falls Hike

This was once a popular swimming hole, but due to poor waterfall etiquette it is now off limits to the public.

Directions: This waterfall is on private property and is not available to the public. Abuse of the property has made the owners restrict its usage. It's a good reminder to be respectful of land owners and always be courteous, clean and quiet when on other's property.

OLD PHOENIX FALLS (EAGLE RIVER)

Private

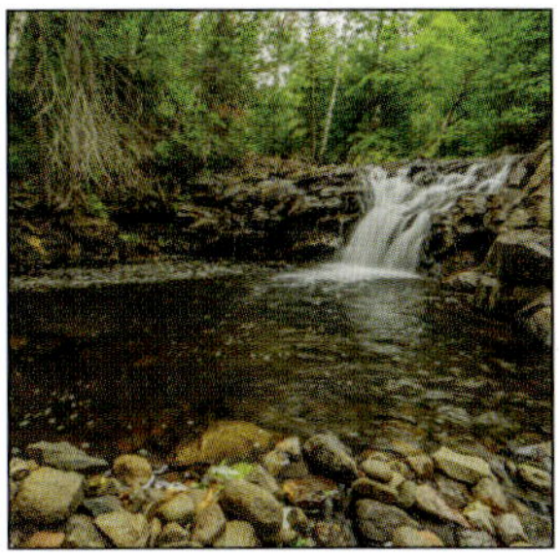

Must See:	6	GPS:	N47 24.073 W88 17.264
Height:	10 feet		
Time:	10-30 minutes	Hiking Information	
		Path:	Unimproved Footpath
Driving Information		Length:	50 yards
Signs:	None	Elev. Change:	Moderate
Road:	Main	GPS:	N/A
Access:	Easy	Danger:	Slight
4WD:	N/A	WP Boots:	N/A

The waterfall is in a horseshoe shaped cavity on the far side of the river. Wavy fractured basalt cascades the falls into a beautiful swimming hole. Cedars can be seen everywhere. This waterfall gets it name from the Old Phoenix Mine that was located nearby.

This waterfall is on private property and not accessible to the public.

What a contrast! The low water conditions perfectly defines the waterfall, while the torrent below shows off the river's magnificence during a major runoff.

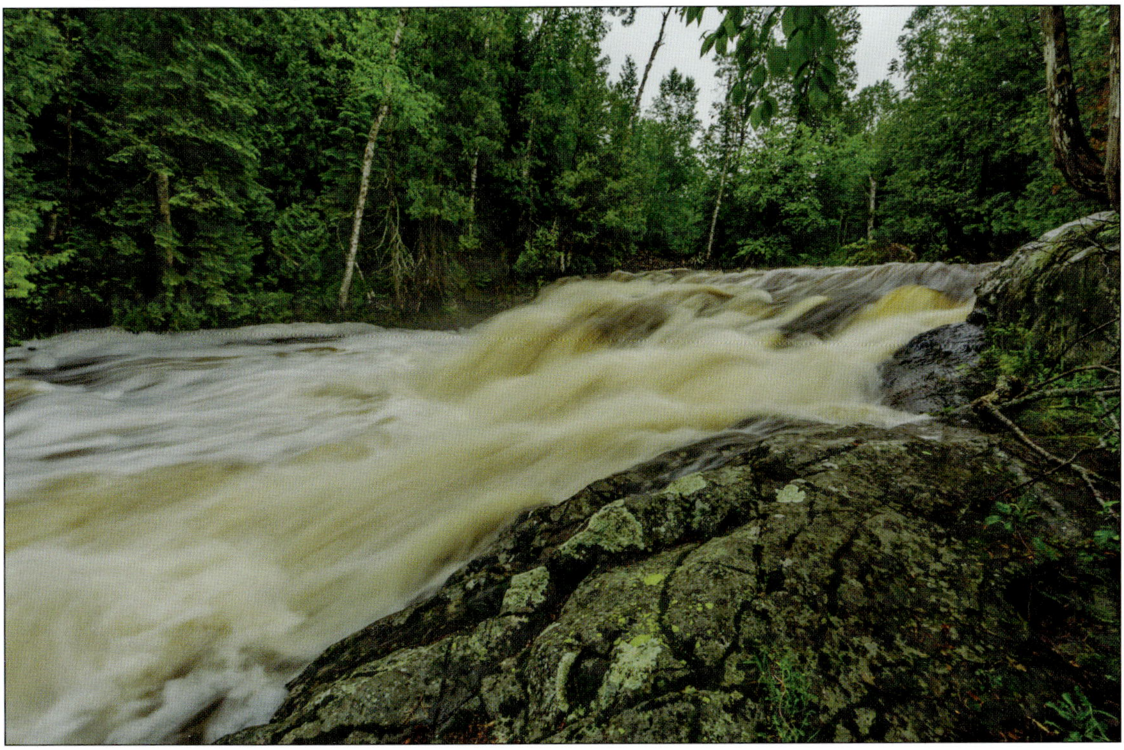

Eagle River Falls Hike

Eagle River Falls: The falls are extremely easy to find as they can be seen upon entering Eagle River on M-26. The original bridge that was built in 1915 is now a pedestrian bridge from which to view the falls. An old dam that spans the top of the falls was built to power the Lake Superior Safety Fuse Factory that was established in 1862. The plant that made safety fuses used in the mining industry burned to the ground in 1957. The bulging dam built 150 years ago diverts the river to the right side of the riverbed until the river rises to levels typically associated with spring melt and runoff.

Directions: The falls are in "downtown" Eagle River and can be seen from M-26 while driving over the Eagle River. Park in the good sized parking area just east of the river. Walk along the pedestrian bridge for a perfect viewing opportunity.

EAGLE RIVER FALLS (EAGLE RIVER)

Private

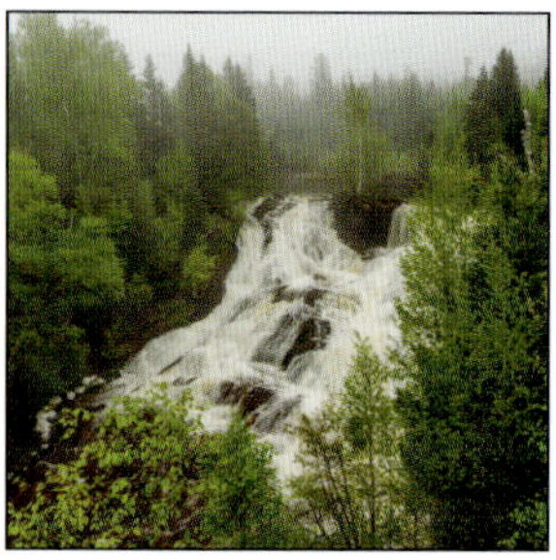

Must See:	8
Height:	60 feet
Time:	5-15 minutes

Driving Information

Signs:	None
Road:	Main
Access:	Very Easy
4WD:	N/A

GPS:	N47 24.747 W88 17.783

Hiking Information

Path:	N/A
Length:	100 feet
Elev. Change:	Slight
GPS:	N/A
Danger:	Slight
WP Boots:	N/A

This waterfalls is the largest in the Keweenaw in terms of width times height. When the river is running high with spring melt or after some intense rains the waterfall is amazing!

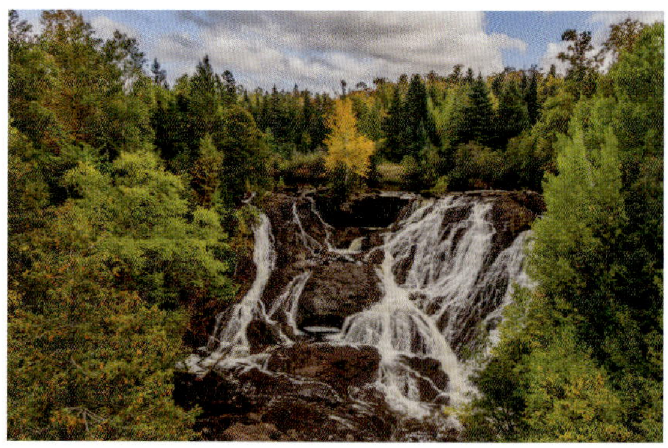

Note the difference between high and low water

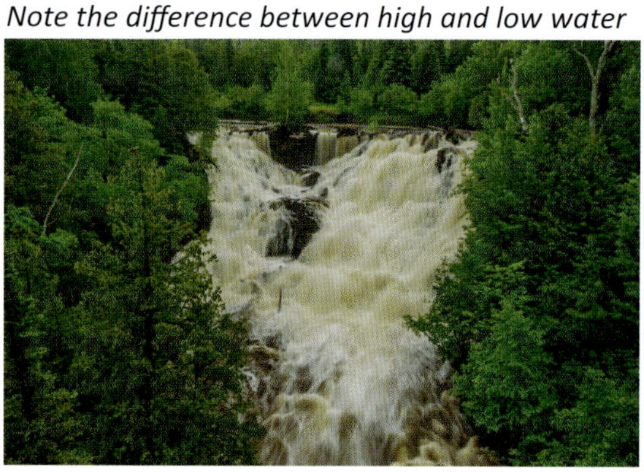

The old dam is still partially in place

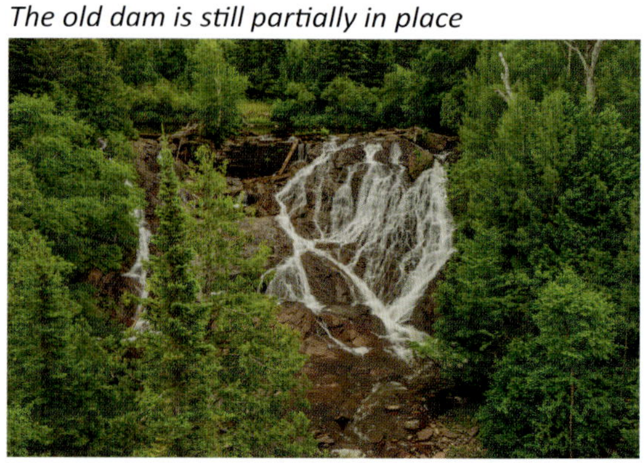

Eagle River Slide Hike

Eagle River Slide - Upper: These falls are not easy to find as there is no definite trail to them. In addition, undergrowth and downed trees can be difficult to navigate.

Eagle River Slide - Lower: The lower falls slide over basalt bedrock just down river from the Upper Slide.

Directions: From the bridge over the Eagle River follow M-26 .4 miles south. Park safely off the side of the road. Hike cross country to the river and the falls. Note: There is no trail. A GPS is required!

EAGLE RIVER SLIDE - UPPER (EAGLE RIVER)

Private

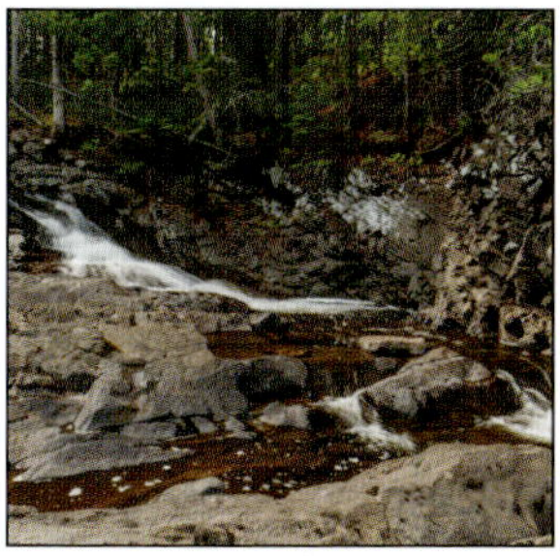

Must See:	4	GPS:	N47 24.476 W88 17.798
Height:	7 feet		
Time:	30-60 minutes	Hiking Information	
		Path:	None
Driving Information		Length:	.13 miles
Signs:	None	Elev. Change:	Minor
Road:	Main	GPS:	Required
Access:	Somewhat Difficult	Danger:	Moderate
4WD:	N/A	WP Boots:	Recommended

The fall slides over rugged bedrock to a quiet pool. The lower slide is 250 feet further down river. Of all the waterfalls on Eagle River, the Fenners Falls are the hardest to get to and the least interesting - perhaps explaining why there isn't a trail leading to them. I'm sure that during high water periods they would look much better (see the difference in Eagle River Falls just a page back).

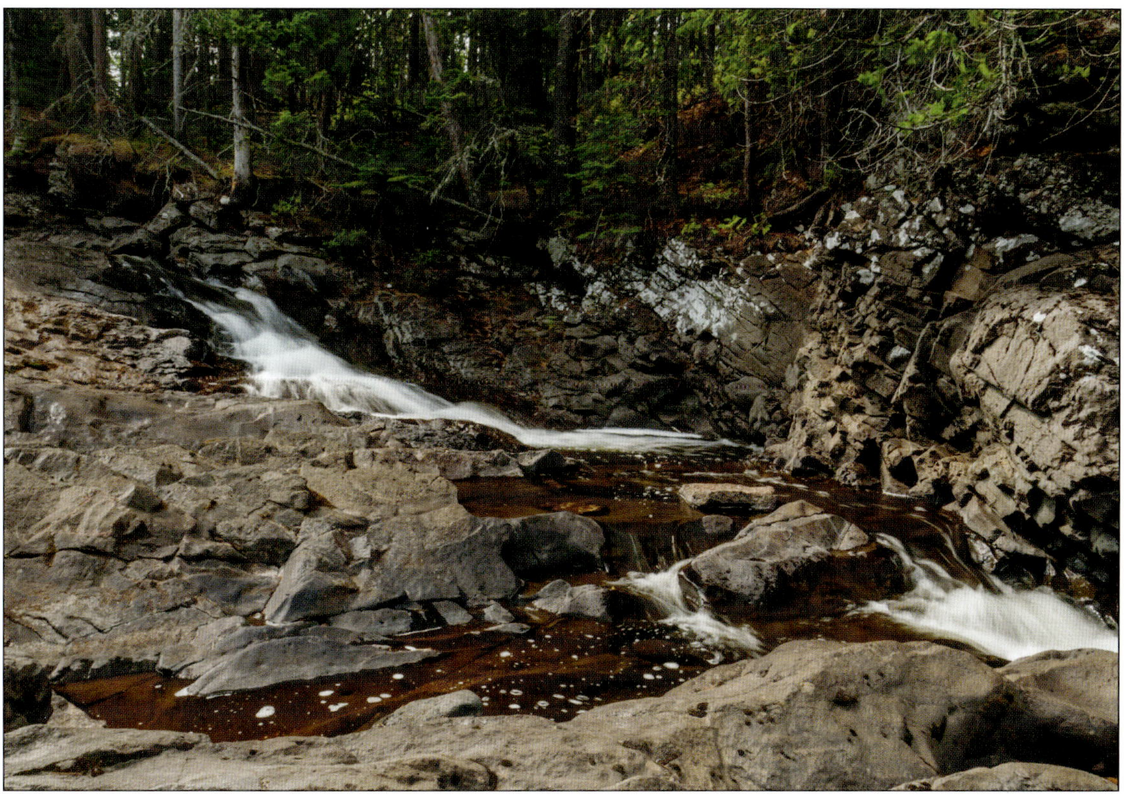

EAGLE RIVER SLIDE - LOWER (EAGLE RIVER)

Private

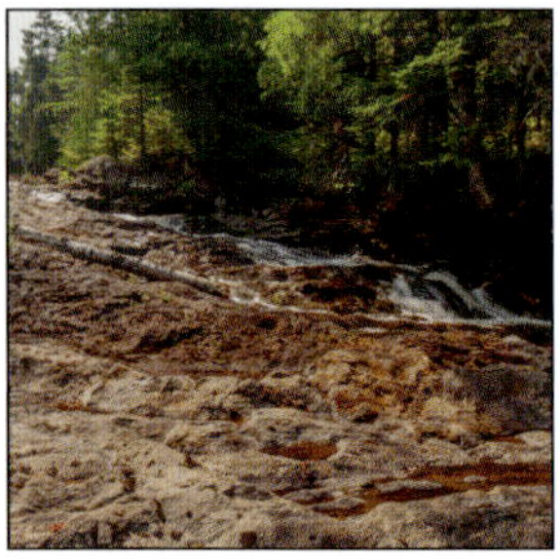

Must See:	4	GPS:	N47 24.508 W88 17.825
Height:	10 feet		
Time:	30-60 minutes	Hiking Information	
		Path:	None
Driving Information		Length:	.13 miles
Signs:	None	Elev. Change:	Minor
Road:	Main	GPS:	Required
Access:	Somewhat Difficult	Danger:	Moderate
4WD:	N/A	WP Boots:	Recommended

Follow the river downstream just 250 feet from the Upper Slide. Often, it is easiest to walk right down the river.

Crumbling basalt walls line the sides of the rough riverbed. Rugged forest stands between the river and M-26. Fortunately it is only about an 1/8 mile hike to the river.

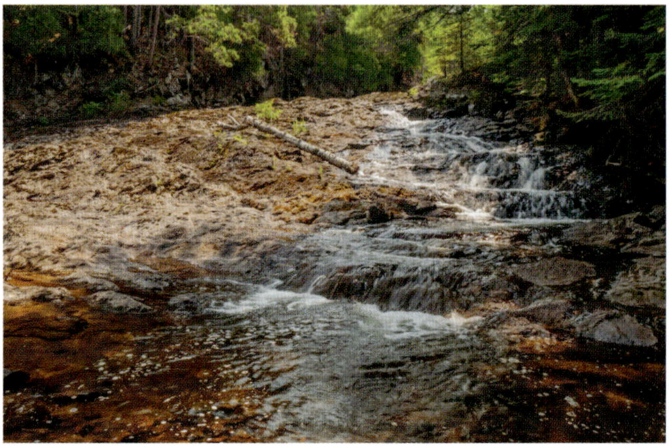

There is no trail. Thick undergrowth and downed trees dominate the woods between here and the road.

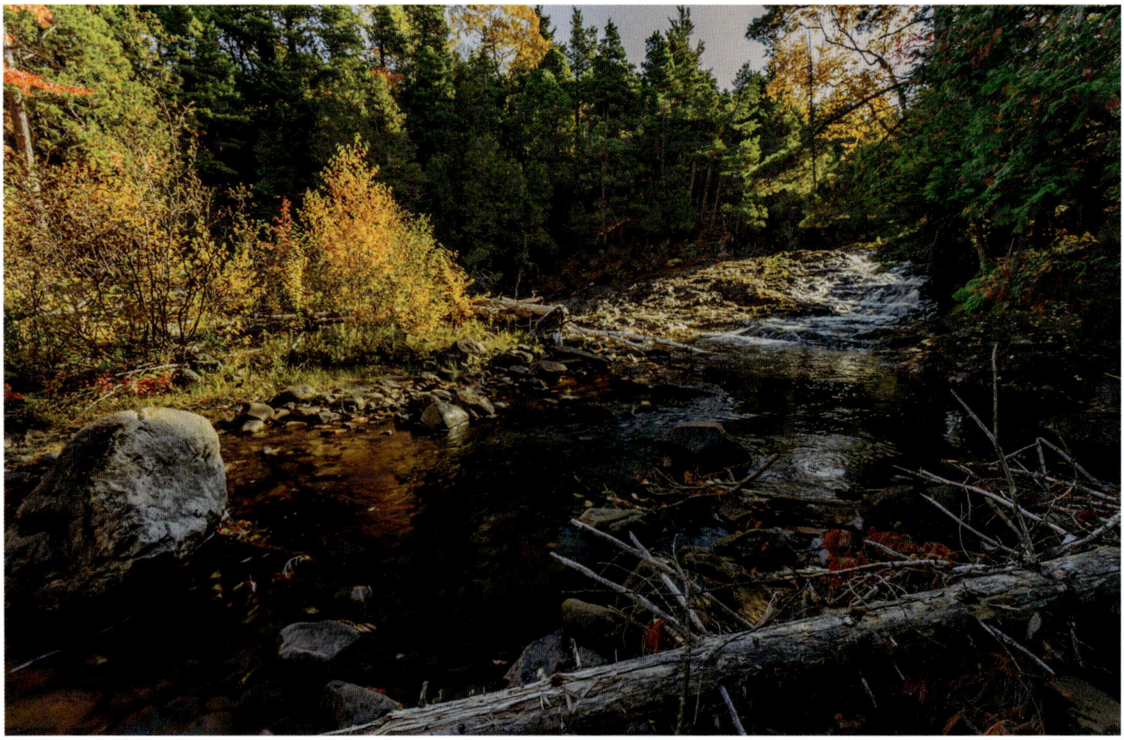

Fenners Falls Hike

The most dangerous of the hikes on the Eagle River ends at an amazing double drop waterfall. If you can manage the steep climb down into the gorge you will enjoy the sight that awaits you!

Directions: Drive south on M-26 from Eagle River Falls for .8 miles. Park safely off of the road (there is a narrow shoulder in this area - find an acceptable place to park). The trailhead to the falls is across from a driveway at N47 24.195 W88 17.629. A short, white post marks the beginning of the faint trail. Hike 80 yards to the top of the gorge. Follow the top of the gorge downstream for about 50 yards. The top of the gorge narrows to a point. Follow the end of the point down, paralleling the river. When you feel it's safe, head down the still steep bank to the river. It's not easy. Make sure you are up to the task. Follow the river back upstream to the falls. Waterproof boots are highly recommended, as you may need to walk partly in the river on the way back to the waterfall.

FENNERS FALLS (EAGLE RIVER)

Private

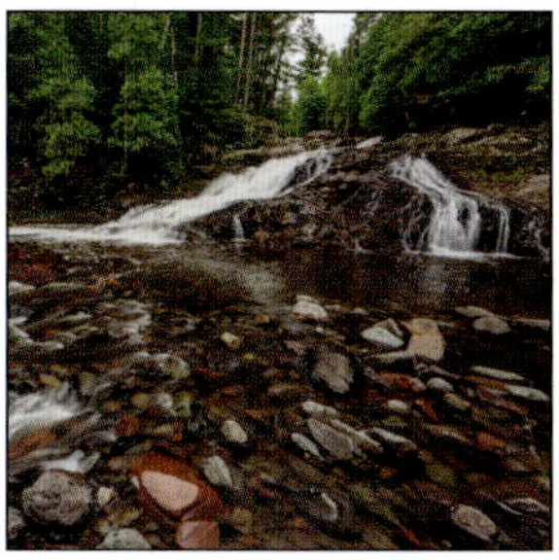

Must See:	8	GPS:	N47 24.244 W88 17.617
Height:	25 feet		
Time:	45-90 minutes	Hiking Information	
		Path:	Faint
Driving Information		Length:	150 yards
Signs:	None	Elev. Change:	Major
Road:	Main	GPS:	Helpful
Access:	Somewhat Difficult	Danger:	Elevated
4WD:	N/A	WP Boots:	Recommended

The Eagle River narrows to 10 feet wide and passes through a perfectly square, short canyon. A rope dangles from a cedar bough above, proof of playful activity in the pool above the falls. The river bursts over the edges of the pool, cascading down to another pool below. Another rope is suspended above this deep pool. From the upper canyon spill pool the river cascades down a jagged mass of slippery black rock. An elongated pool waits at the bottom. From the center of the pool, the river quietly exits, swirling around the rounded rocks that are so familiar in this river.

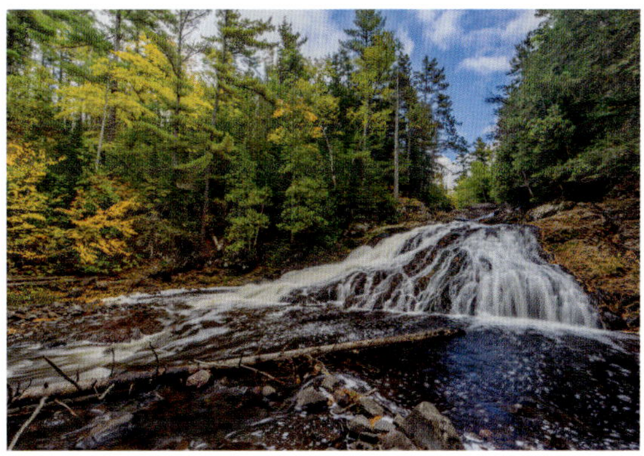

The river is choked with rocks below the falls

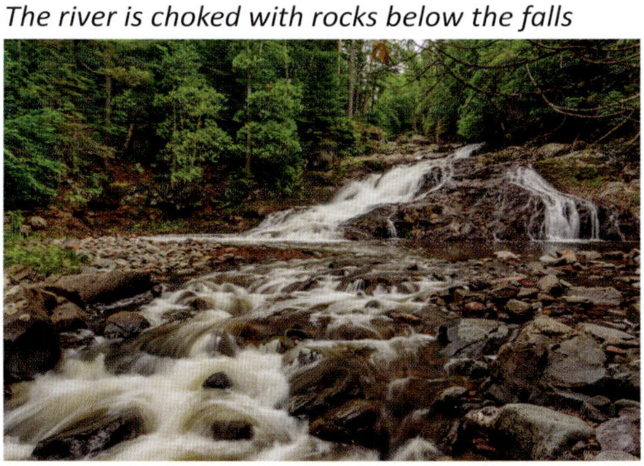

The look down from the top of the canyon

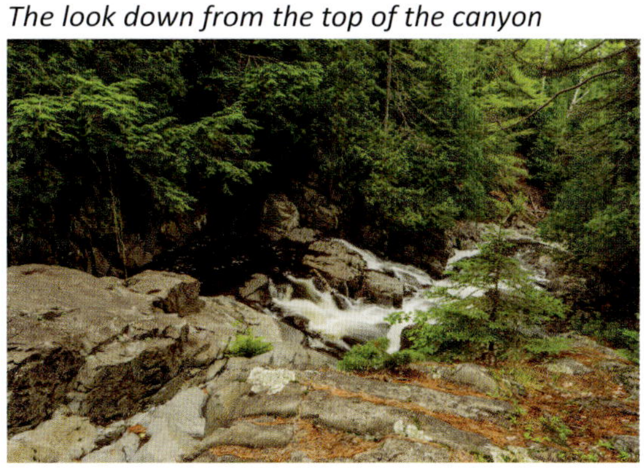

Jacobs Falls Hike

Jacobs Falls: This popular roadside waterfall attracts many tourists driving along the twisting road between Eagle River and Copper Harbor. A steep, unimproved footpath climbs quickly up the hillside following the creek upstream. Above Jacobs Falls are several more waterfalls. My favorite is a delightful cascade that spills into a 6 foot deep pool. It is tucked into a steep walled portion of the ravine that Jacobs Creek has cut into the fast descending hillside. In less than a mile, Jacobs Creek descends 400 feet!

Directions: Head northeast out of Eagle River (toward Copper Harbor) on M-26. In 3 miles a small parking area is on the right nearly at the base of the falls. Hike up the side of the falls to the upper falls.

JACOBS FALLS (JACOBS CREEK)

Private

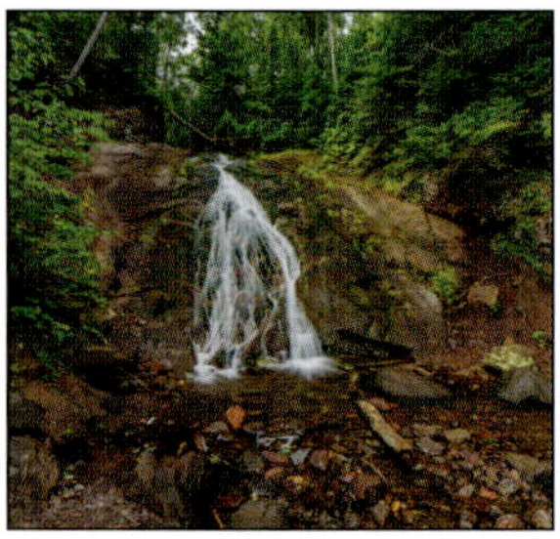

Must See:	7	GPS:	N47 25.669 W88 14.256
Height:	20 feet		
Time:	5-10 minutes	Hiking Information	
		Path:	N/A
Driving Information		Length:	N/A
Signs:	Roadside	Elev. Change:	N/A
Road:	Main	GPS:	N/A
Access:	Very Easy	Danger:	N/A
4WD:	N/A	WP Boots:	N/A

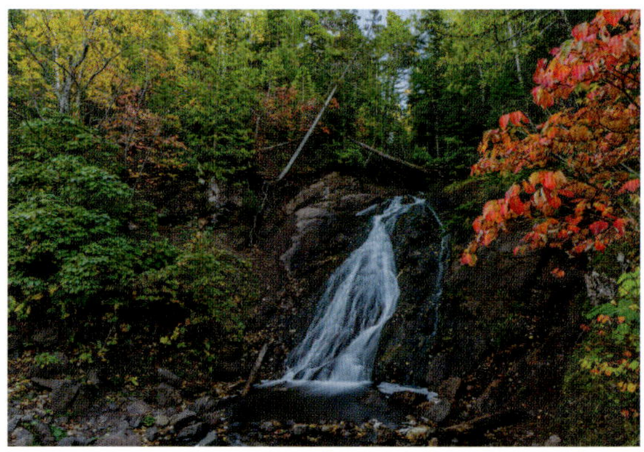

The waterfall presents itself nicely as it slides down toward the road along the steep rocky waterway. The creek then passes beneath M-26 on its way to Lake Superior.

The Jampot, a gift store just 100 yards up the road from Jacobs Falls, is well known for their sweet treats and preserves. It's run by the monks from the nearby monastery. For more information, check out www.societystjohn.com.

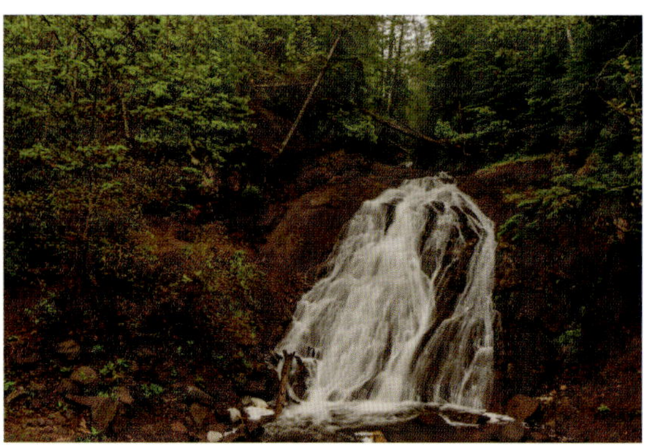

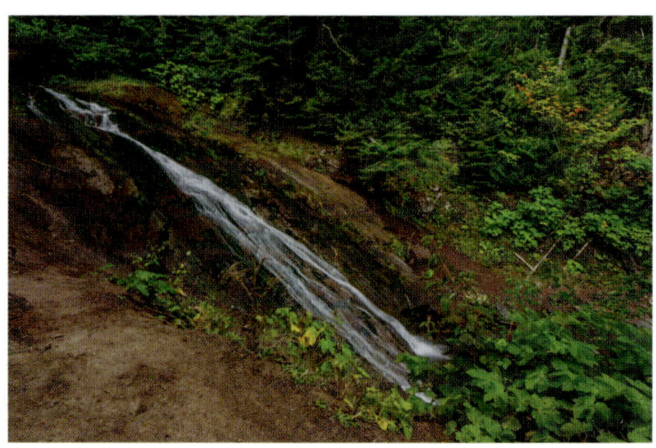

JACOBS FALLS #2 (JACOBS CREEK)

Private

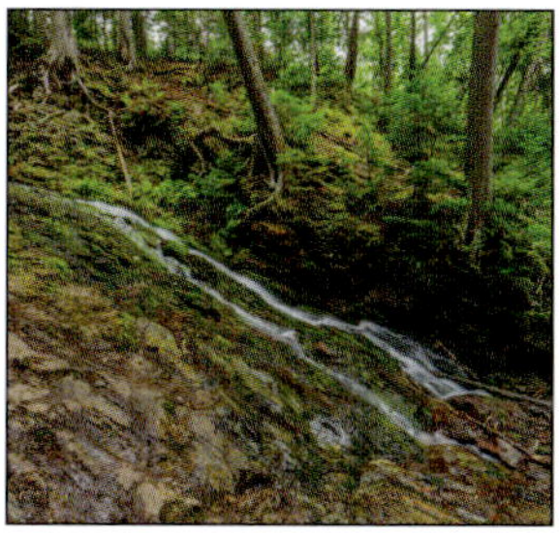

Must See:	6	GPS:	N47 25.648 W88 14.244
Height:	14 feet		
Time:	10-15 minutes	Hiking Information	
		Path:	Steep Rock
Driving Information		Length:	70 yards
Signs:	Roadside	Elev. Change:	Moderate
Road:	Main	GPS:	N/A
Access:	Very Easy	Danger:	Elevated
4WD:	N/A	WP Boots:	Recommended

The falls tumble over a moss encrusted slide. A severely fractured wall on the left, rising 30 feet high is topped with soaring evergreens. It makes one feel very small indeed. Scramble up the riverbed to see the falls. Be careful, though. It is quite slippery, especially if wet. The steep rocky side of Jacobs Falls makes the climb up here challenging. It's definitely not a place for young children.

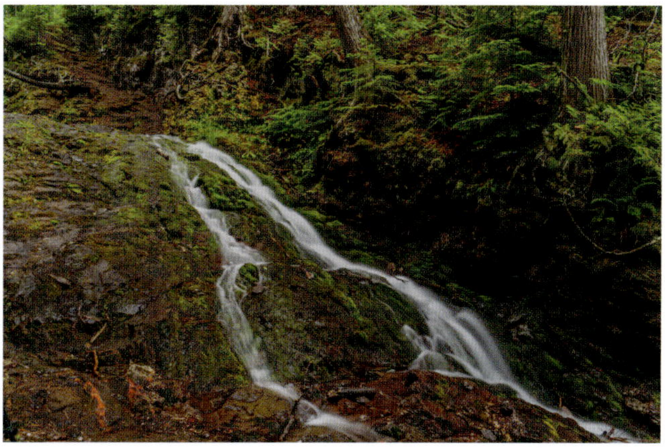

Looking back downstream the road can be seen in the distance through the slit created by the waterway. The easiest climb from below is directly up the creek bed. But even that is not "easy"!

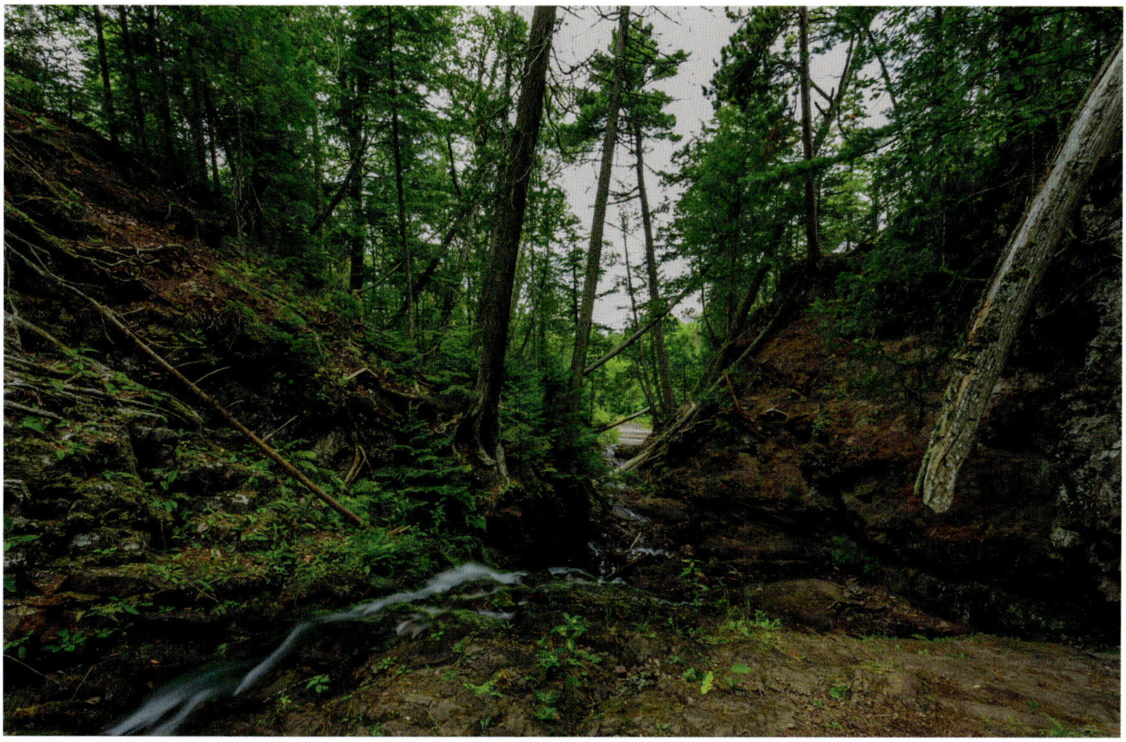

JACOBS FALLS #3 (JACOBS CREEK)

Private

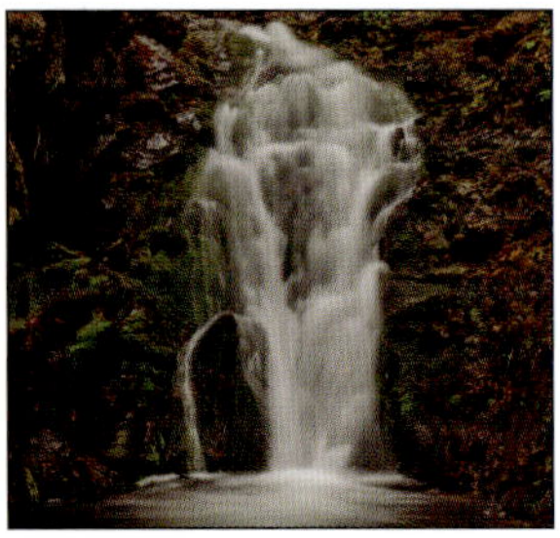

Must See:	7	GPS:	N47 25.641 W88 14.235
Height:	8 feet		
Time:	20-30 minutes	Hiking Information	
		Path:	Steep Rock
Driving Information		Length:	100 yards
Signs:	Roadside	Elev. Change:	Moderate
Road:	Main	GPS:	N/A
Access:	Very Easy	Danger:	Elevated
4WD:	N/A	WP Boots:	Recommended

Continue up the creek bed another 50 feet. The drops seem to keep coming as soon as you get up above the waterfall you're currently at!

A tree, bent over by rock erosion or weight struggles to once again find its way back up to the light. In so doing, it is bowed over the ravine above the waterfall for a very unique visual treat. The steep rocky side of Jacobs Falls makes the climb up here challenging.

A suspended tree trunk hangs awkwardly over the edge of the ravine. It appears that the rock face here was blasted away many years ago. Tell-tale blastholes can be seen in the creek bed, reminders of the hard rock mining that took place in the Keweenaw 150 years ago.

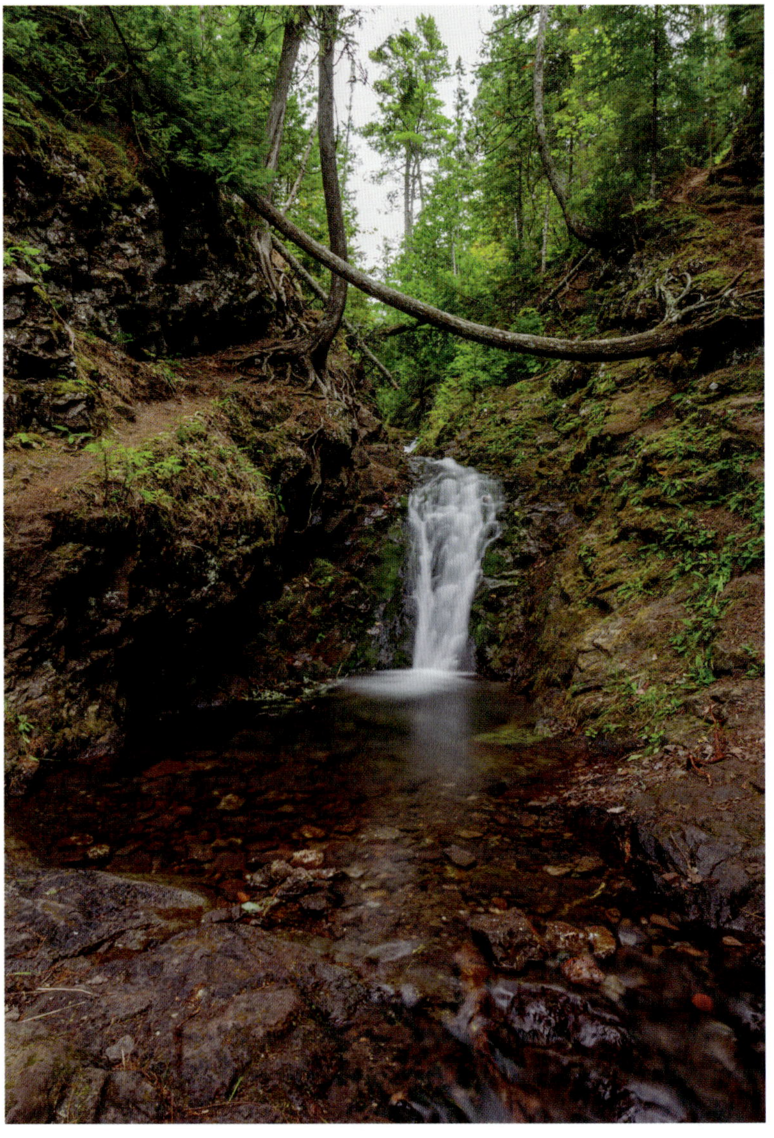

JACOBS FALLS #4 (JACOBS CREEK)

Private

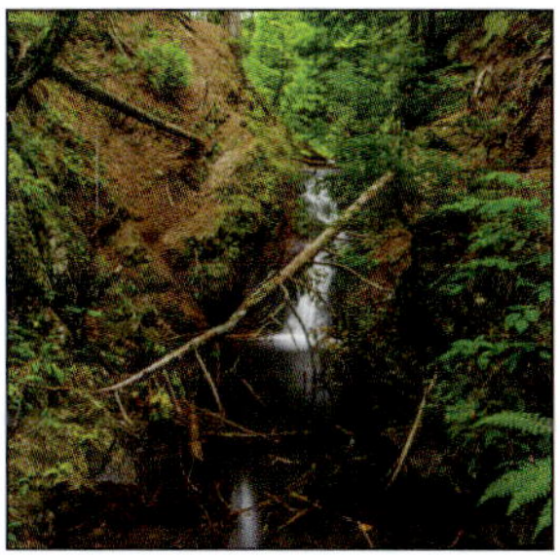

Must See:	6	GPS:	N47 25.617 W88 14.199
Height:	8 feet		
Time:	30-45 minutes	Hiking Information	
		Path:	Steep Rock
Driving Information		Length:	.10 miles
Signs:	Roadside	Elev. Change:	Moderate
Road:	Main	GPS:	N/A
Access:	Very Easy	Danger:	Elevated
4WD:	N/A	WP Boots:	Recommended

Climb up the steep slanted "path" on the right side of the #3 falls. Follow the trail along the top, climbing back down to the creek just before reaching the #4 falls. The waterfall slides down a narrow chute into an elongated spill pool trough where it calms down before running down another slighter slide below an overhanging wall.

See the "trails" on either side of the creek. They are narrow footpaths. This is typical of the scrambling that must be done on the climbs along Jacobs Creek. Make sure you are up for navigating this type of terrain before attempting to reach the upper falls.

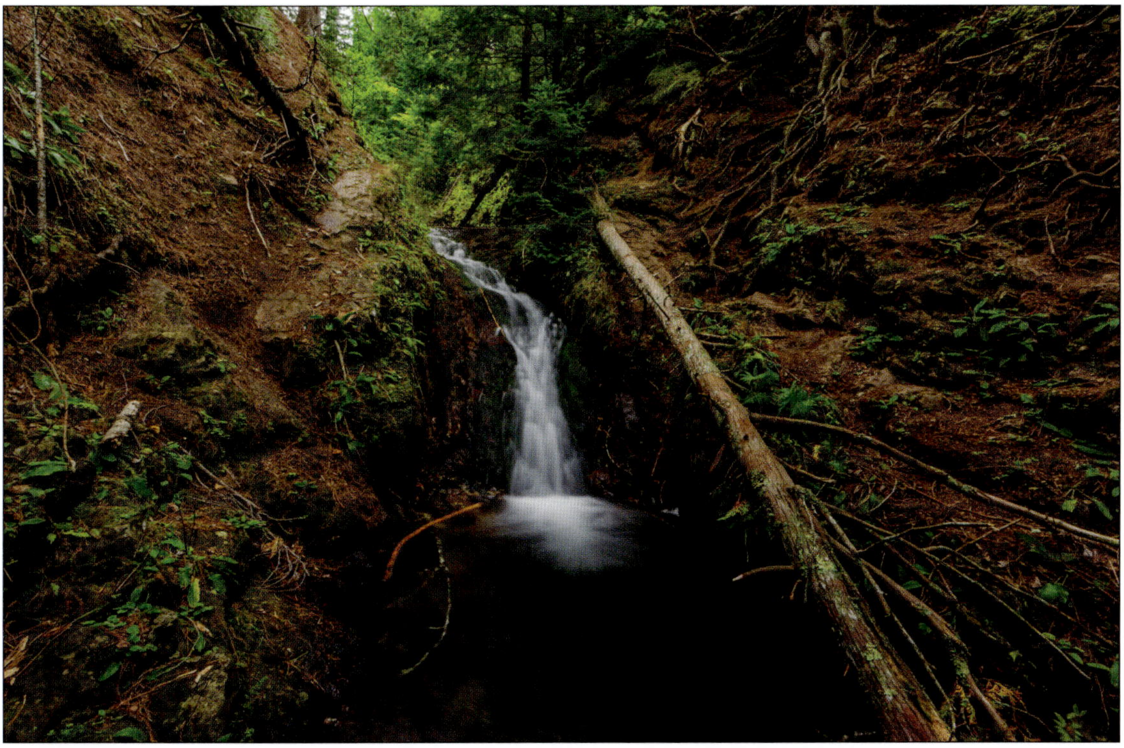

JACOBS FALLS #5 (JACOBS CREEK)

Private

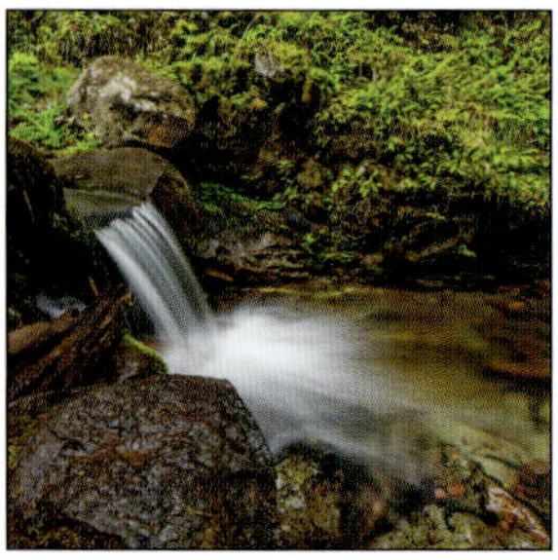

Must See:	5	GPS:	N47 25.604 W88 14.188
Height:	2 feet		
Time:	40-60 minutes	Hiking Information	
		Path:	Steep Rock
Driving Information		Length:	.13 miles
Signs:	Roadside	Elev. Change:	Moderate
Road:	Main	GPS:	N/A
Access:	Very Easy	Danger:	Elevated
4WD:	N/A	WP Boots:	Recommended

Who says small can't be cute? Climb up to the top of #4 to see this small free spill drop. At this point you have climbed up and out of the severely dropping section of the creek. Above this waterfall the creek is rock filled and the side walls descending into the ravine slope more gently. There are several more similar drops upstream from here, but most of those are created by fallen tree trunks damming the creek.

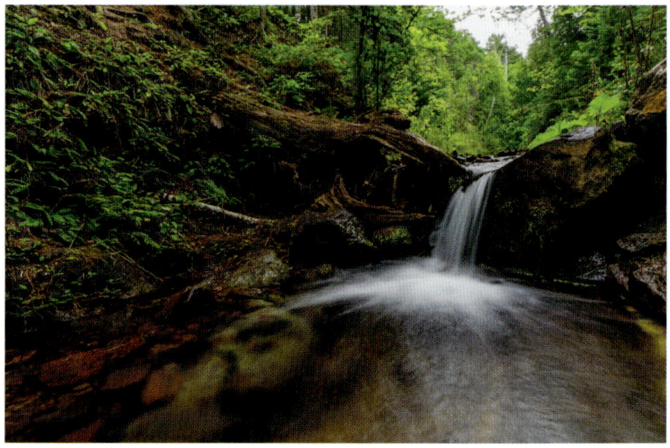

What secrets await the adventurous spirit? The commonly listed "Jacobs Falls" only describe the falls seen from the road. The vast majority of tourists never see the upper section of falls!

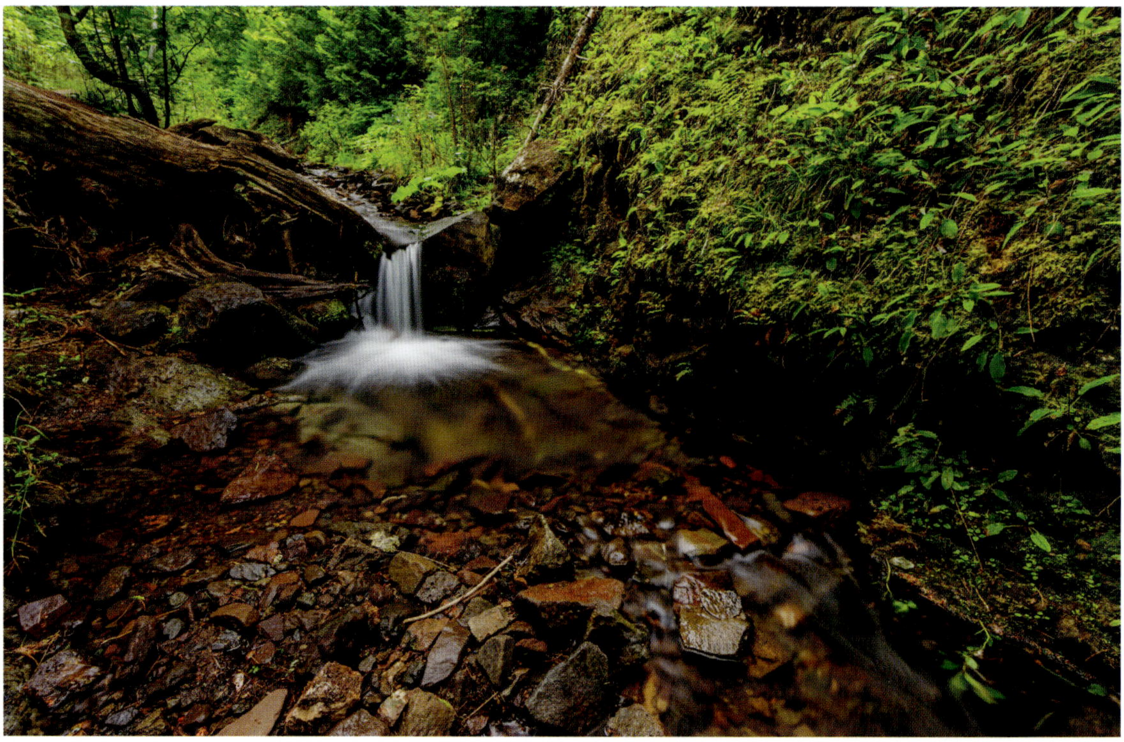

Silver Creek Falls Hike

These waterfalls on Silver Creek tumble over conglomerate as the creek cuts down through the quickly descending terrain near Lake Superior.

Directions: These waterfalls are on private property and are marked, "NO TRESPASSING". DO NOT ENTER.

SILVER CREEK FALLS (SILVER CREEK)

Private

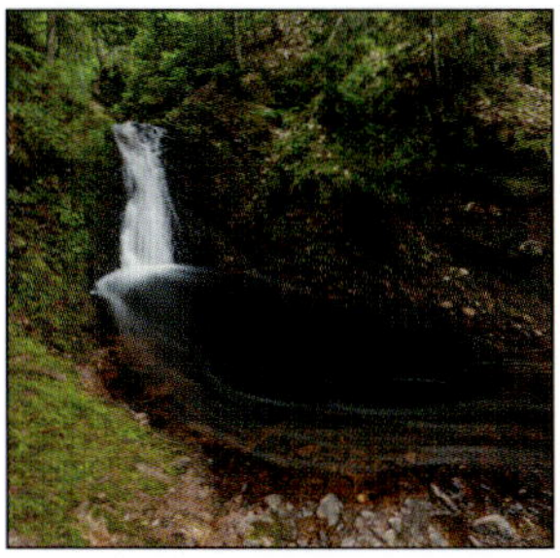

Must See:	8
Height:	15 feet
Time:	N/A

Driving Information

Signs:	None
Road:	Secondary
Access:	Fairly Easy
4WD:	N/A

GPS:	N47 23.939 W88 19.912

Hiking Information

Path:	Unimproved Footpath
Length:	150 yards
Elev. Change:	Moderate
GPS:	Recommended
Danger:	Moderate
WP Boots:	Recommended

A 10 foot slide down a conglomerate face leads to a deep spill pool (looks to be 5 to 6 feet deep). When the creek exits the spill pool it drops another 2 feet and shortly thereafter tumbles a final 3 feet. The creek then glides (typically just inches deep) between the sides of a steep and narrow ravine toward Lake Superior.

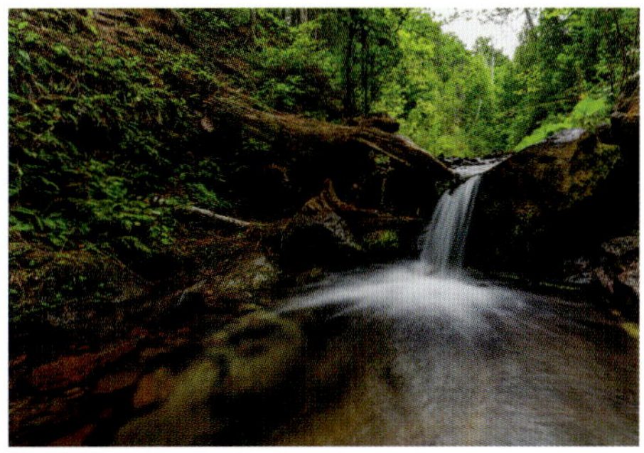

Recently, the access to this set of waterfalls has been restricted. There are "NO TRESPASSING" signs posted now. Be respectful of property owners. Do not enter posted property.

The main drop and the two lower drops can be seen in this shot

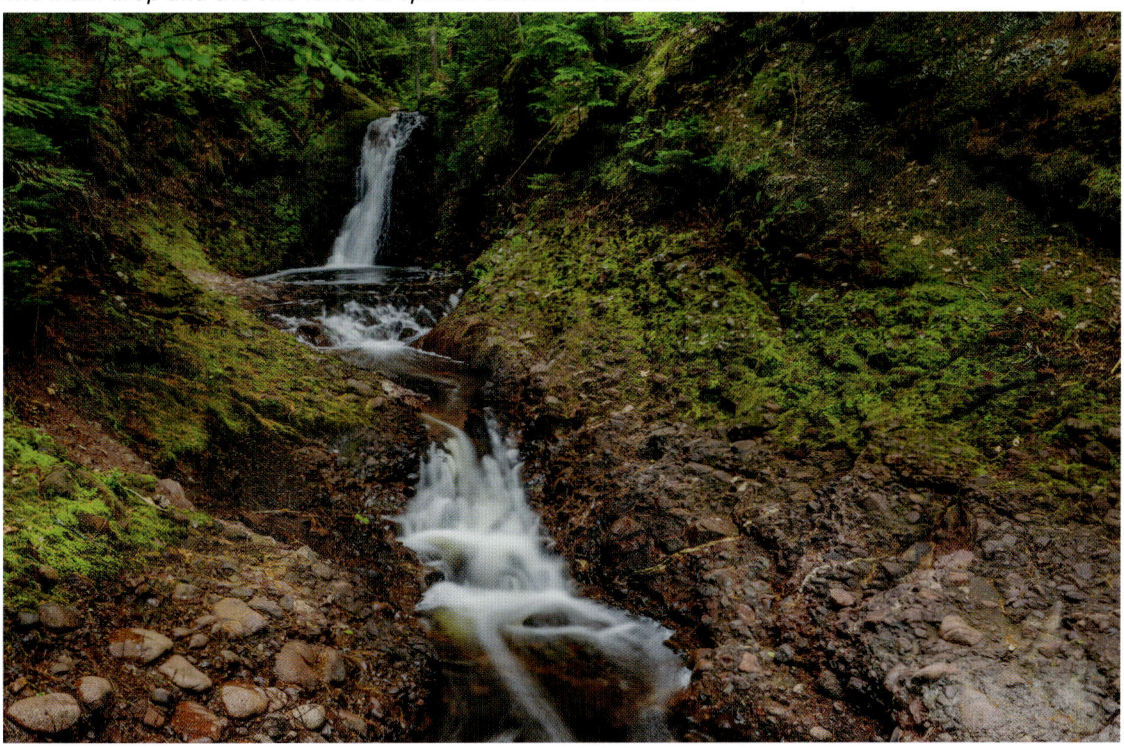

SILVER CREEK FALLS - UPPER #1 (SILVER CREEK)

Private

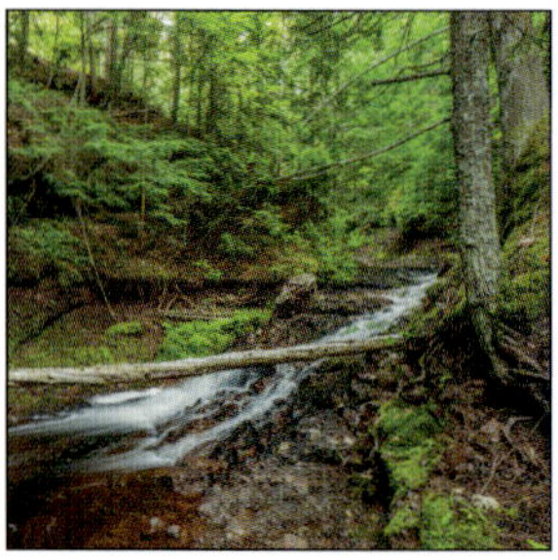

Must See:	5	GPS:	N47 23.928 W88 19.923
Height:	5 feet		
Time:	N/A	Hiking Information	
		Path:	Unimproved Footpath
Driving Information		Length:	175 yards
Signs:	None	Elev. Change:	Moderate
Road:	Secondary	GPS:	Recommended
Access:	Fairly Easy	Danger:	Moderate
4WD:	N/A	WP Boots:	Recommended

Just above the top of Silver Creek Falls, this 5 foot drop cascades/slides over a mass of conglomerate beneath a massive 40 foot high wall of conglomerate. It is hard to scramble down to the creek bed.

Recently, the access to this set of waterfalls has been restricted. There are "NO TRESPASSING" signs posted now. Be respectful of property owners. Do not enter posted property.

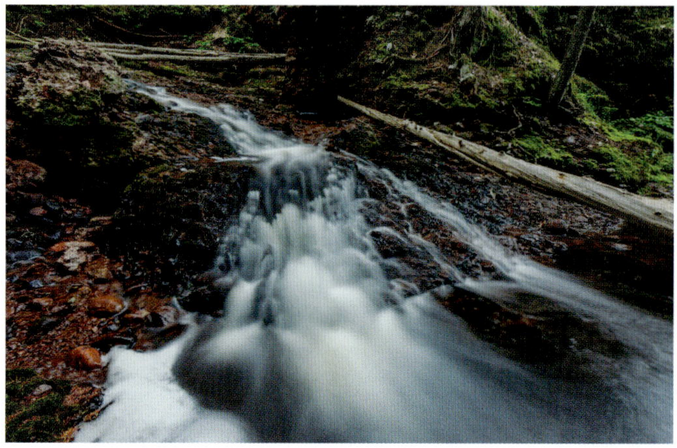

Looking along the slide to the drop into the ravine. The top of Silver Creek Falls is in the distance.

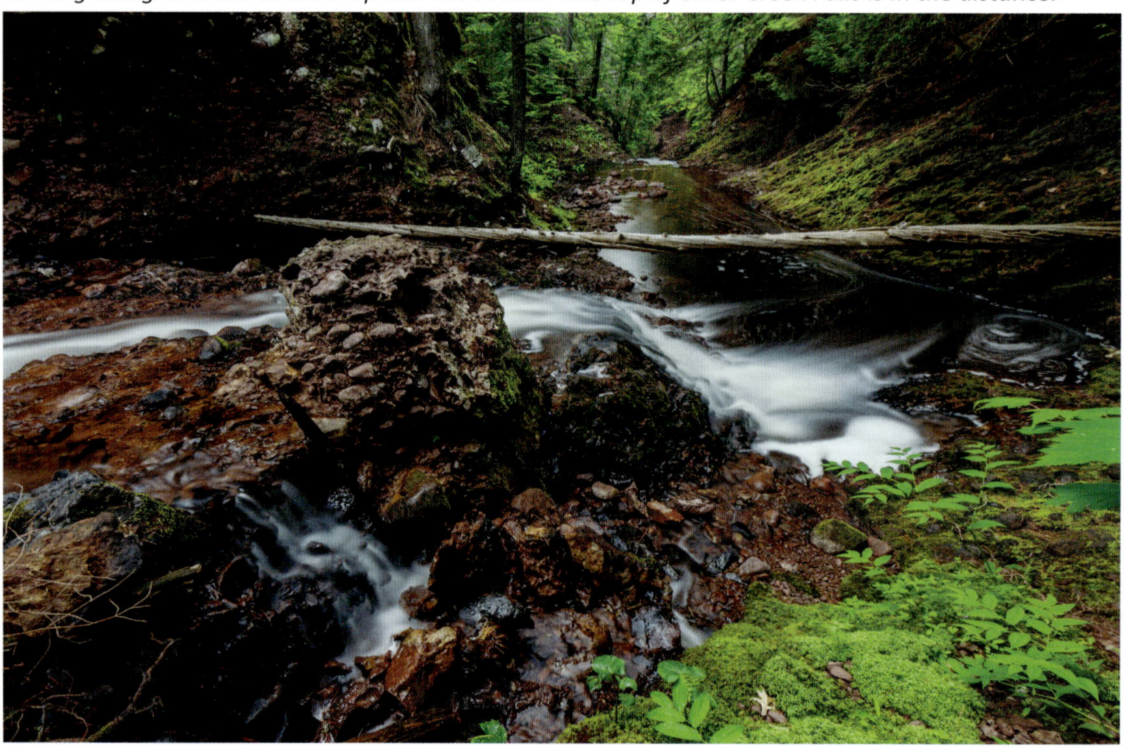

SILVER CREEK FALLS - UPPER #2 (SILVER CREEK)

Private

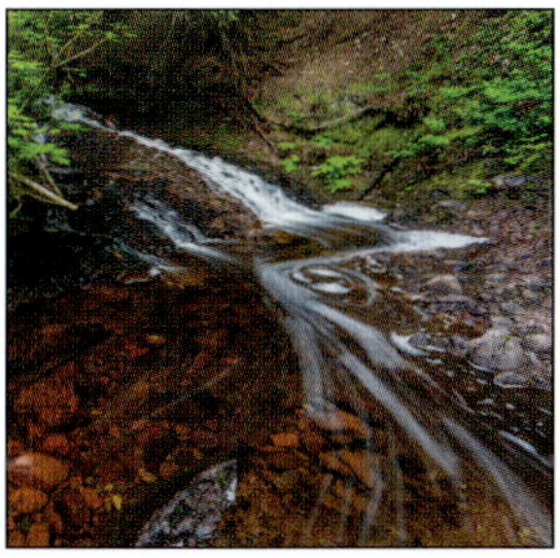

Must See:	6	GPS:	N47 23.912 W88 19.912
Height:	12 feet		
Time:	N/A	Hiking Information	
		Path:	Unimproved Footpath
Driving Information		Length:	200 yards
Signs:	None	Elev. Change:	Moderate
Road:	Secondary	GPS:	Recommended
Access:	Fairly Easy	Danger:	Moderate
4WD:	N/A	WP Boots:	Recommended

Hike 25 yards upstream from Upper #1. The creek fans out and rushes down a cobbled slide of conglomerate. It immediately turns hard to the right for 15 yards before turning again to the right to start its ride down over Upper #1.

Recently, the access to this set of waterfalls has been restricted. There are "NO TRESPASSING" signs posted now. Be respectful of property owners. Do not enter posted property.

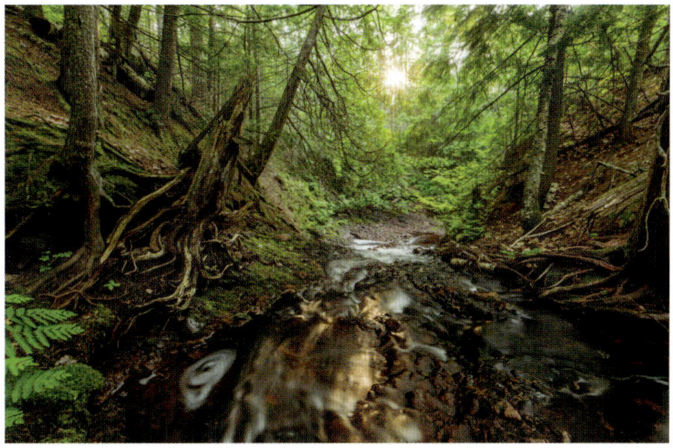

The look down the waterfall and the sharp turn at the base

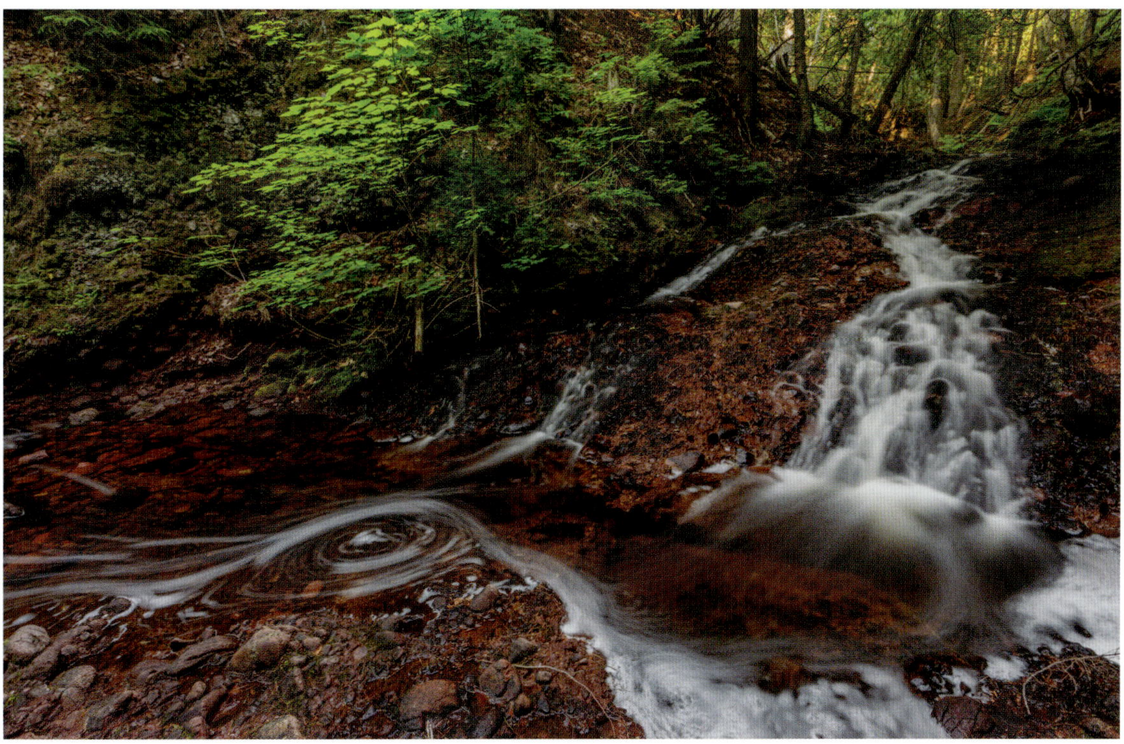

Ten Foot Falls Hike

Ten Foot Falls: As long as the river is calm this is a great place to take the family for a cool dip and picnic beneath the trees. When the river is raging, it is a force to be reckoned with.

Directions: Head north on M-26 off of US-41 in Phoenix. In .8 miles there is a dirt parking area on the right. Park and walk down the short trail to the falls.

TEN FOOT FALLS (EAGLE RIVER)

Private

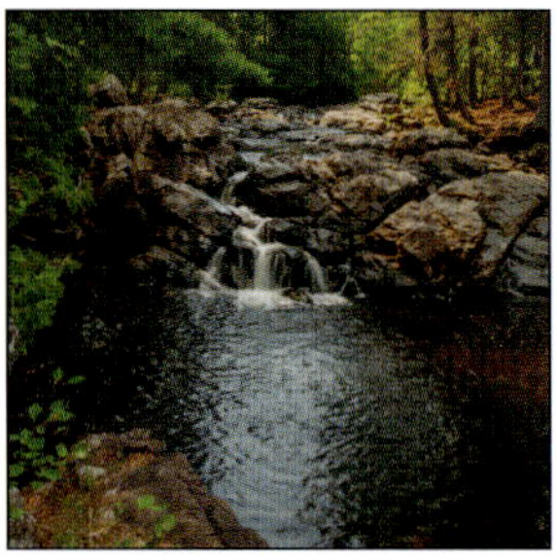

Must See:	6	GPS:	N47 23.855 W88 17.073
Height:	8 feet		
Time:	10-30 minutes	Hiking Information	
		Path:	Unimproved Footpath
Driving Information		Length:	25 yards
Signs:	None	Elev. Change:	Minor
Road:	Main	GPS:	N/A
Access:	Easy	Danger:	Slight
4WD:	N/A	WP Boots:	N/A

The original basalt bedrock has eroded and fractured over the years into what looks like an artistic assortment of closely placed boulders over which the river cascades to a popular swimming hole just yards off of M-26.

The relatively flat and open space at the top of the falls can be seen in the shot to the right.

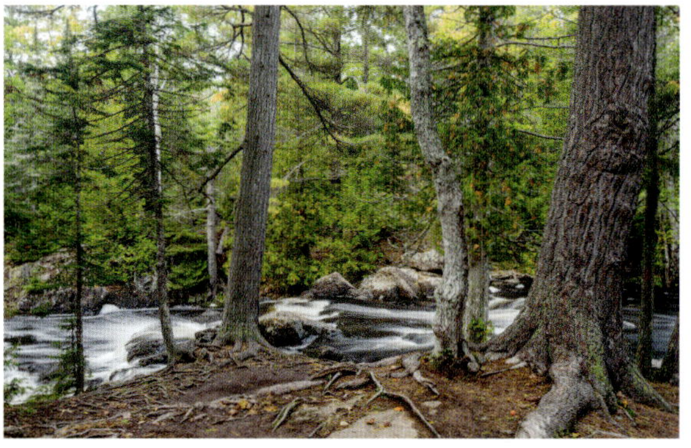

This is the first of the waterfalls on the Eagle River between US-41 and the city of Eagle River. The last waterfall on the river is the much better known Eagle River Falls.

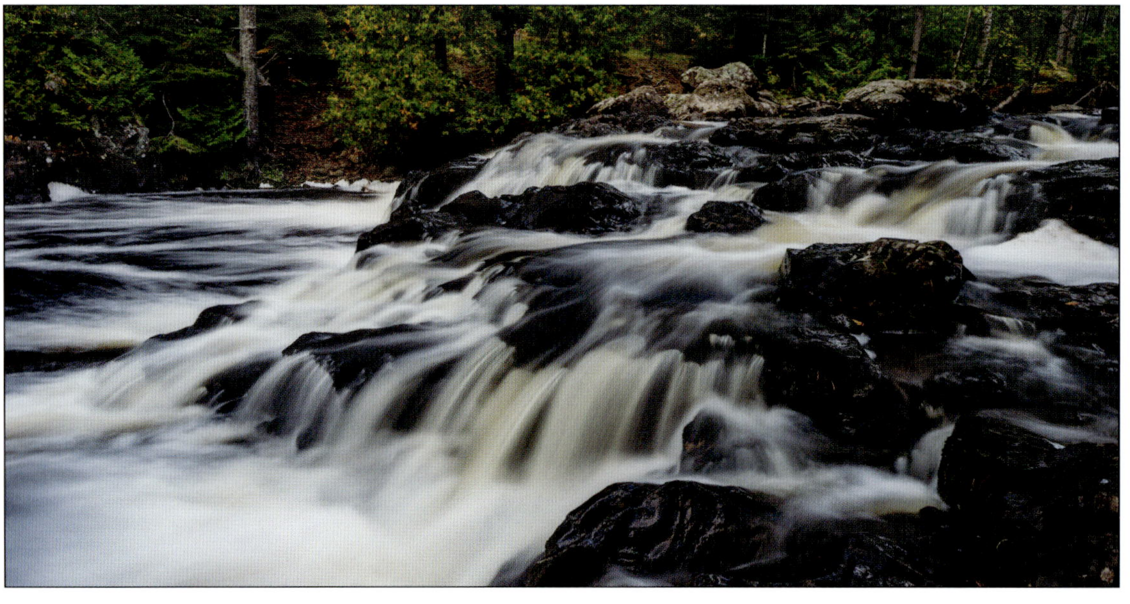

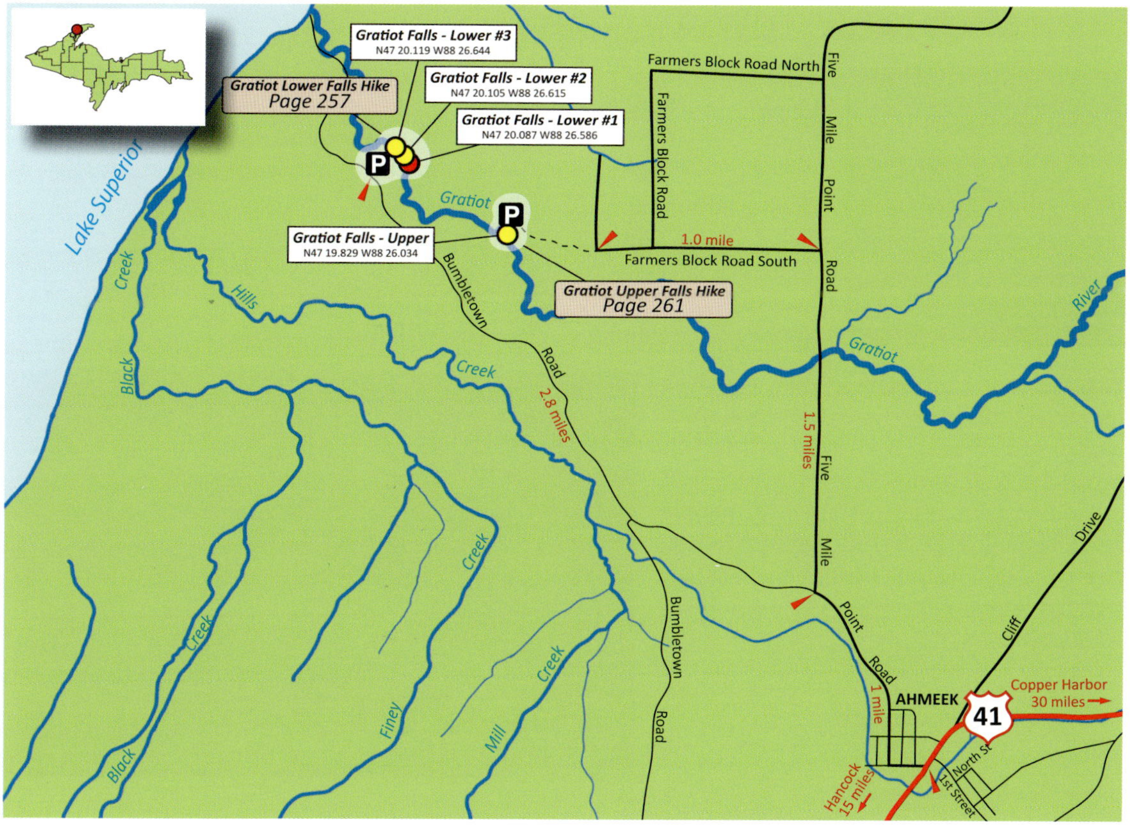

Gratiot Lower Falls Hike

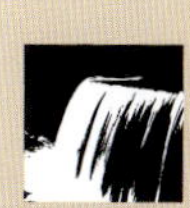

Gratiot Falls - Lower #3: The 4-wheeler trail ends abruptly at this, the lowest and most impressive of the lower falls.

Gratiot Falls - Lower #2: Highly fragmented basalt in the falls sends numerous cascades tumbling down the 4 foot falls. The river widens to 30 feet at the falls then narrows to 4 feet just below.

Gratiot Falls - Lower #1: The first of the three drops of the Lower Falls, this 2 foot small cascade is funneled to the center of the river by outcroppings on either side. A squarish black block of basalt sits centered just above the falls.

Directions: In Ahmeek, turn west onto Five Mile Point Road. It jogs a bit in Ahmeek. In 1 mile turn left at the sign for a park. The road is dirt. Follow it for 2.8 miles through dusty, cleared land, areas of scrubby pine, and finally into a forest. At a 2-track at N47 19.964 W88 26.729 turn right (east). In 600 feet park at a small parking area on the left at N47 20.038 W88 26.716. A 4-wheeler trail continues on from here. Hike 600 feet down to the #3 falls. Follow the river upstream to view the #2 and #1 falls.

For an additional adventure, continue northwesterly on the dirt road that parallels Gratiot River for another mile to arrive at the end of the road. The dog-friendly, no fee park found here is a hidden gem. The beautiful Lake Superior shoreline provides for spectacular sunset viewing. Fishermen can often be seen trying their luck near the mouth of Gratiot River.

GRATIOT FALLS - LOWER #3 (GRATIOT RIVER)

Private

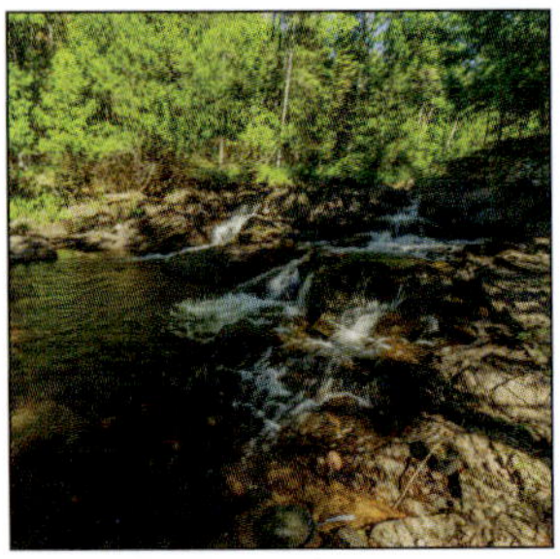

Must See:	6	GPS:	N47 20.119 W88 26.644
Height:	5 feet		
Time:	10-30 minutes		

Driving Information		Hiking Information	
		Path:	4-Wheeler Trail
Signs:	None	Length:	200 yards
Road:	Dirt	Elev. Change:	Minor
Access:	Difficult	GPS:	Helpful
4WD:	Helpful	Danger:	Slight
		WP Boots:	N/A

The capstone of the Lower Falls, the third and final drop is divided in half by a small wedge of bedrock. Both sides of the falls drop nicely, showing good character and are nicely presented. A smooth, pebble filled viewing area acts as a great viewing or picnic area. A stone fire ring and obvious signs of camping show this to be a popular local attraction.

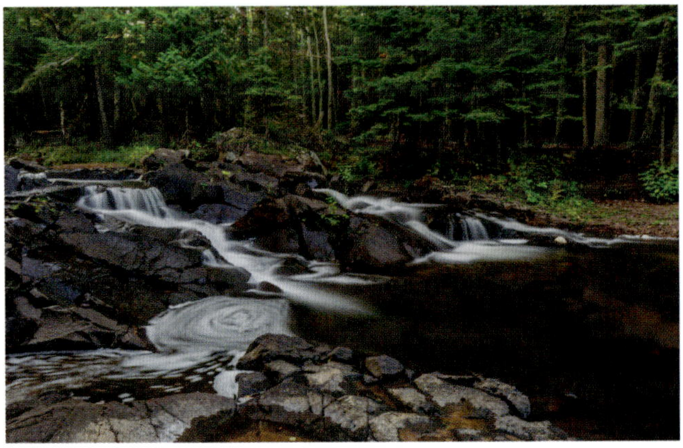

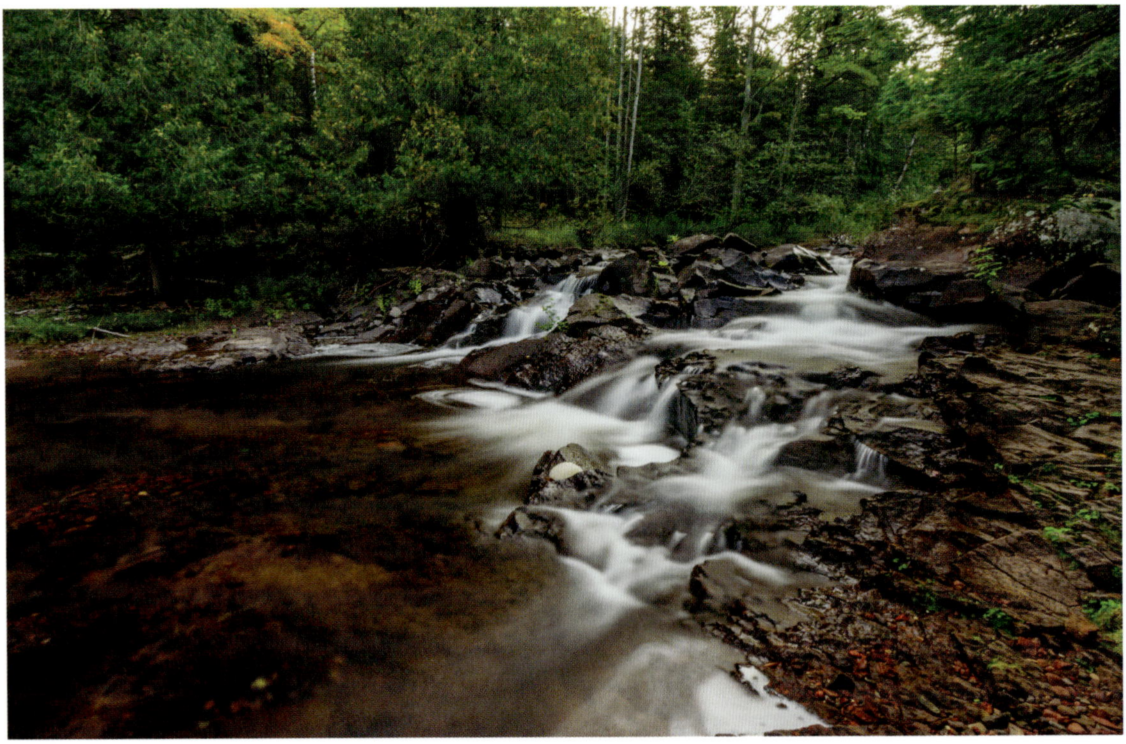

GRATIOT FALLS - LOWER #2 (GRATIOT RIVER)

Private

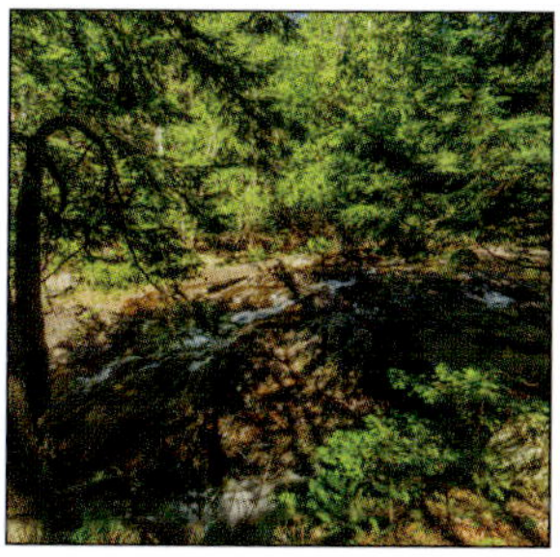

Must See:	5	GPS:	N47 20.105 W88 26.615
Height:	4 feet		
Time:	20-40 minutes		

Driving Information		Hiking Information	
		Path:	4-Wheeler Trail - None
		Length:	250 yards
Signs:	None	Elev. Change:	Minor
Road:	Dirt	GPS:	Helpful
Access:	Difficult	Danger:	Slight
4WD:	Helpful	WP Boots:	N/A

Follow the riverbank 50 yards from #3 upstream to #2. There is no steep ravine along this section of the river which makes this an easy set of falls to view and hike along.

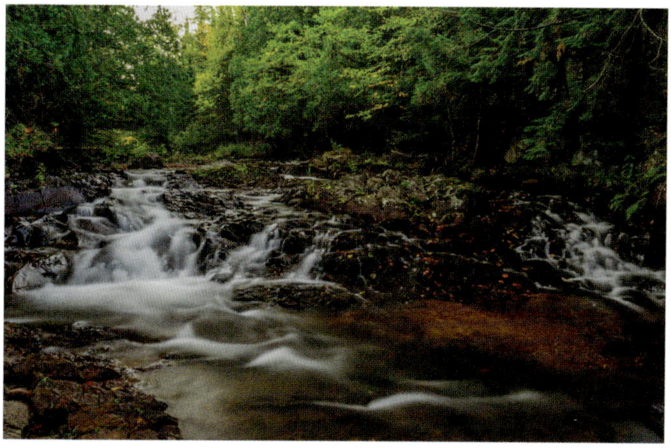

Note the low banks. This is somewhat unusual for waterfall prone rivers. This helps make it kid-friendly.

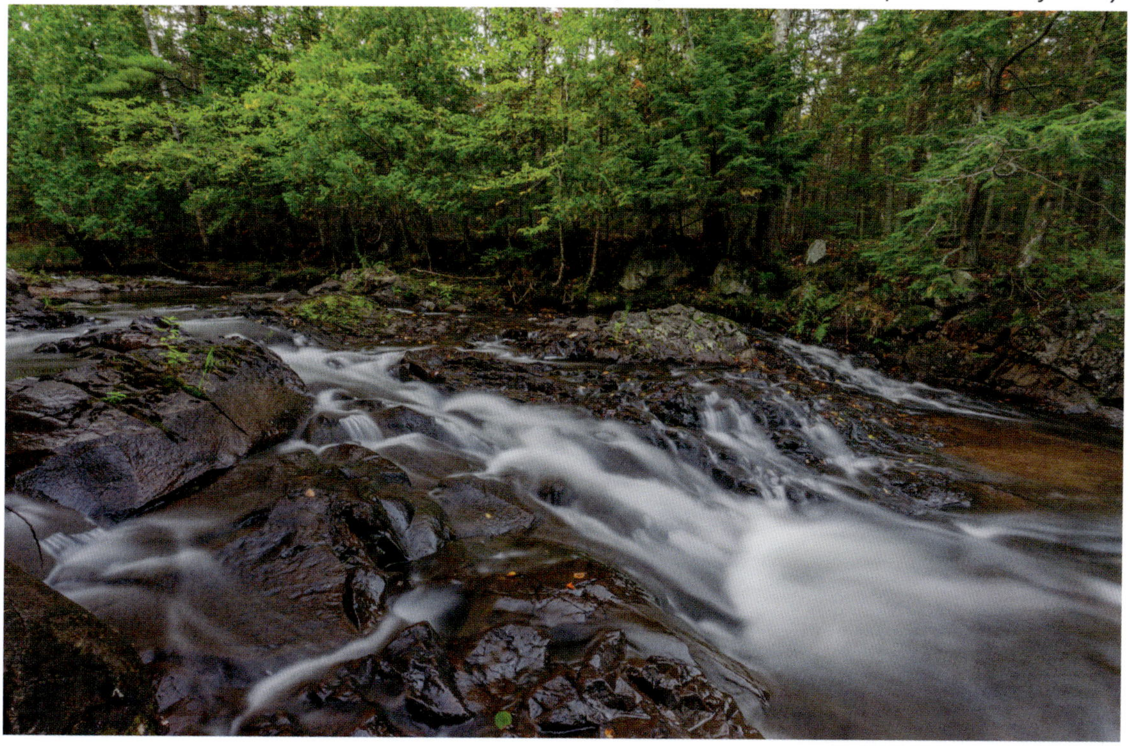

KEWEENAW COUNTY

Gratiot Falls - Lower #2

GRATIOT FALLS - LOWER #1 (GRATIOT RIVER)

Private

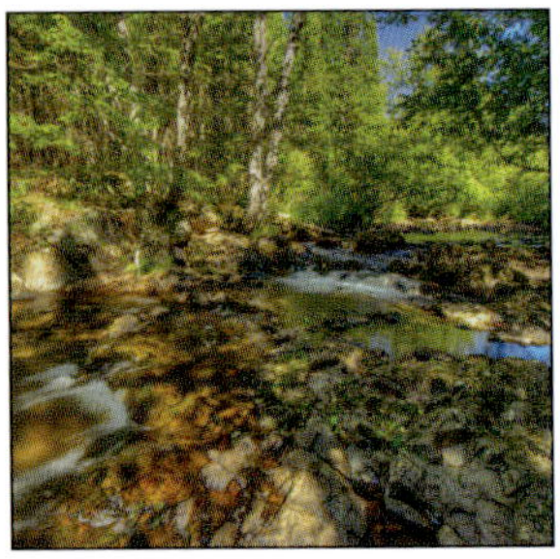

Must See:	3	GPS:	N47 20.087 W88 26.586
Height:	2 feet		
Time:	25-45 minutes		
Driving Information		**Hiking Information**	
		Path:	4-Wheeler Trail - None
		Length:	350 yards
Signs:	None	Elev. Change:	Minor
Road:	Dirt	GPS:	Helpful
Access:	Difficult	Danger:	Slight
4WD:	Helpful	WP Boots:	N/A

Large, loose chunks of bedrock have somehow ended up scattered over the riverbed. Up river from here the river flattens out and become much more tame. This is a much loved river for fishing, with many faint trails heading down to the river from the road between here and the river's mouth.

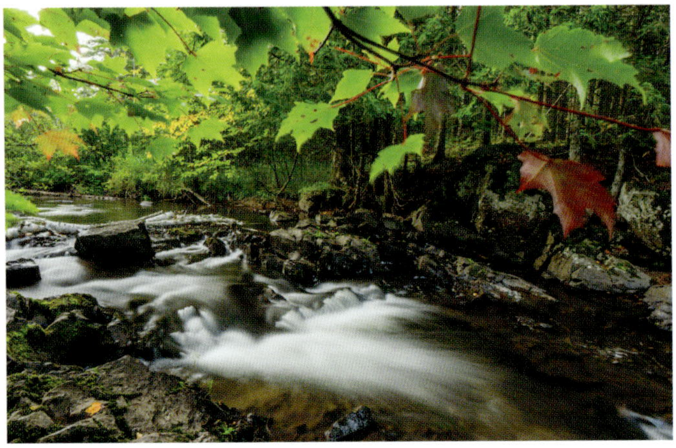

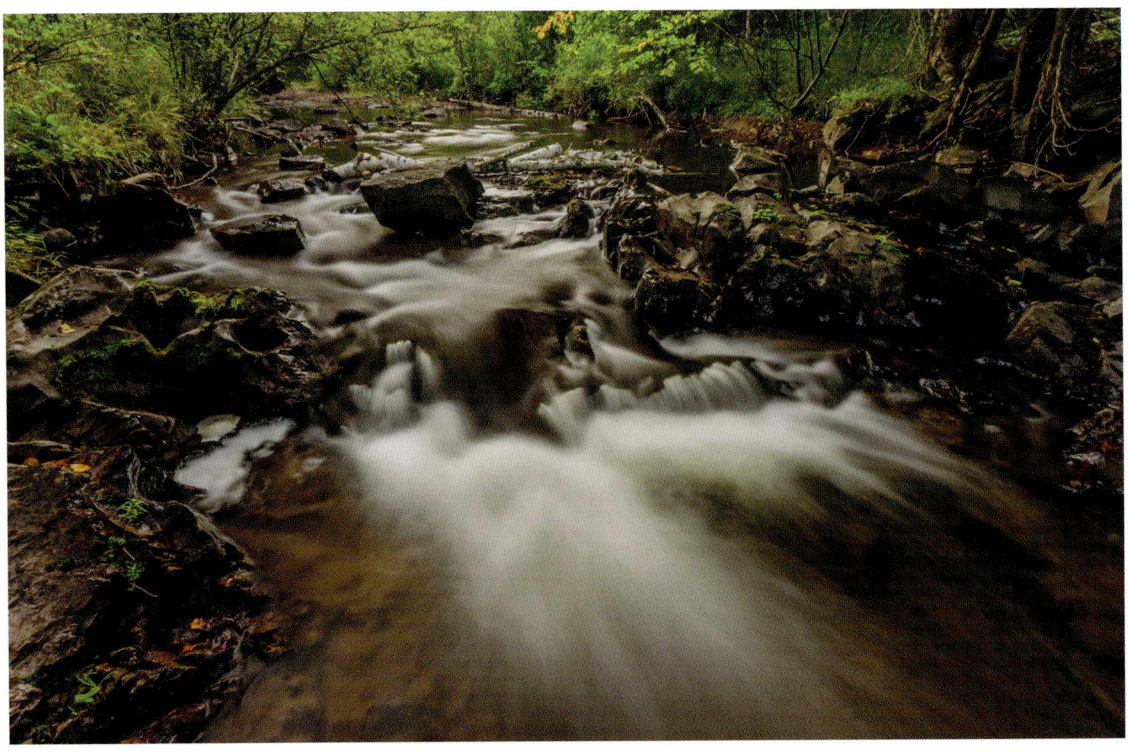

Gratiot Upper Falls Hike

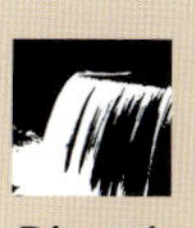

Gratiot Falls - Upper: Although not a spectacular waterfall, it is in a nicely wooded section of Michigan. And walking on a riverbed of conglomerate is a unique experience.

Directions: In Ahmeek, turn west onto Five Mile Point Road. It jogs a bit getting through Ahmeek. Follow it north for 2.5 miles to Farmers Block Road S. Turn left (west) and follow it until the road turns to the right. Continue straight on a 2-track (a 4WD is recommended for this last portion of the drive). The narrow and rough trail ends in a small clearing. There was a port-a-jon there when I was last there. Park. Hike down the obvious footpath a short way to the falls. Climb down to the river at the end of the hike.

GRATIOT FALLS - UPPER (GRATIOT RIVER)

Private

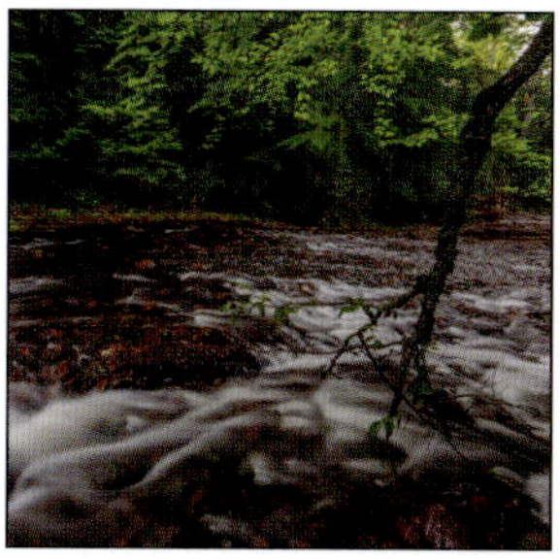

Must See:	5	GPS:	N47 19.829 W88 26.034
Height:	30 feet		
Time:	15-30 minutes	Hiking Information	
		Path:	Unimproved Footpath
Driving Information		Length:	150 yards
Signs:	None	Elev. Change:	Moderate
Road:	2-track	GPS:	N/A
Access:	Difficult	Danger:	Moderate
4WD:	Recommended	WP Boots:	N/A

The river slowly drops over conglomerate bedrock in a very lazy fashion. The river sweeps around a rise on the far side of the river in a large arc with the river hugging the inside of the bend and working its way out as the water level rises. Follow the river upstream for .15 miles to continue to see more slides like this.

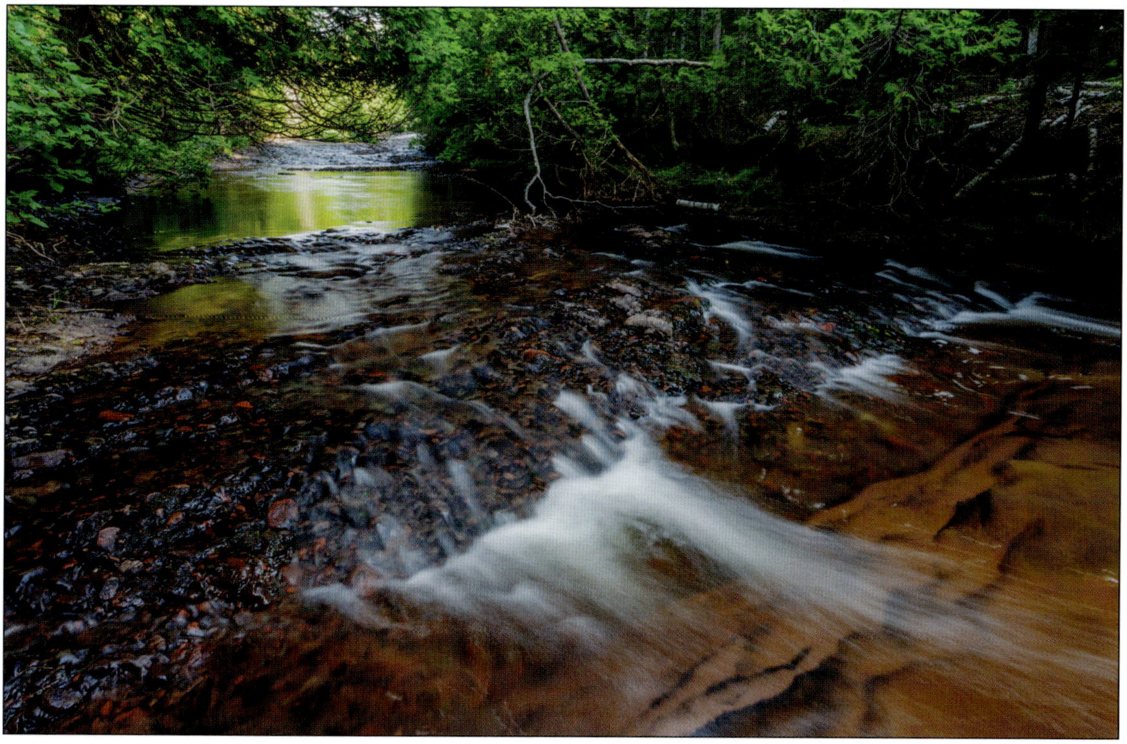

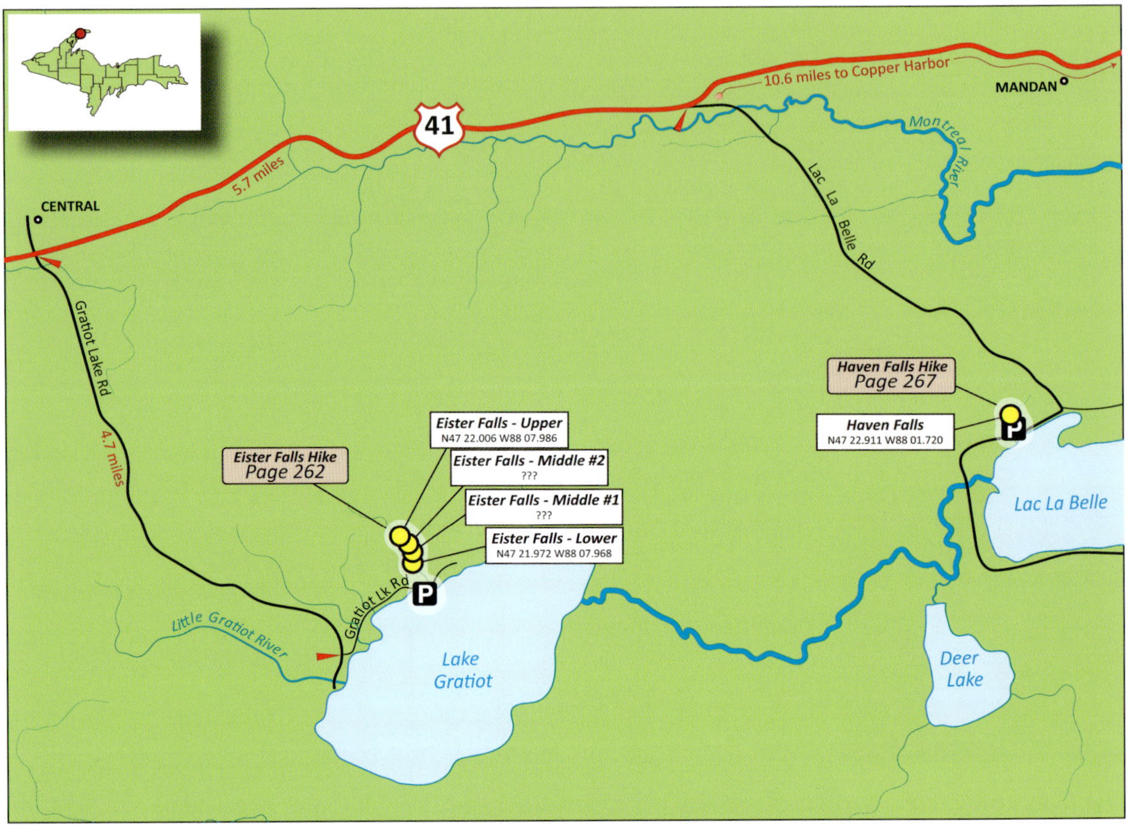

Eister Falls Hike

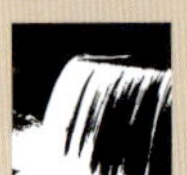

Eister Falls: Eister Creek runs down through a steep rocky ravine for a distance. There is an overlook spur trail that allows for viewing the upper section of the ravine. This area has a rapidly sliding waterfall with a steep overhanging gorge wall as a backdrop. The ravine winds down toward Gratiot Lake with the rapidly descending creek tumbling and sliding along with it. The conclusion of the fast stretch ends with the lower falls dropping into a shallow spill pool.

There is a pit toilet available for use when parking at the boat launch.

Directions: Turn south off of US-41 onto Gratiot Lake Road. In 4.7 miles, just before arriving at Lake Gratiot, turn left. Drive to the Gratiot Lake Boat Launch on the right. Park. Hike across the road to the trailhead. There will be a sign there from the Michigan Nature Association (MNA). Follow the trail as it heads into the forest and starts climbing up to the overlook, 400 feet above Gratiot Lake. About .2 miles into the hike the trail splits with the trail to the right ending shortly at the top of the ravine far above Eister Creek. Carefully climb down the steep embankment. Follow the creek back upstream to the lower falls. Continue to follow the creek up the ravine to Eister Falls which can also be seen from the MNA trail (further up from the first spur that I described). Continuing up the creek a short distance the terrain will flatten out a bit. Climb out of the now shallow ravine to the left (west). Hike to the west/southwest until finding the MNA trail. Follow it to the right (north and west) to continue to the Gratiot Lake Overlook or take the trail to the left (south) to head back to the Eister Falls Overlook and the trailhead.

EISTER FALLS - LOWER (EISTER CREEK)

Private

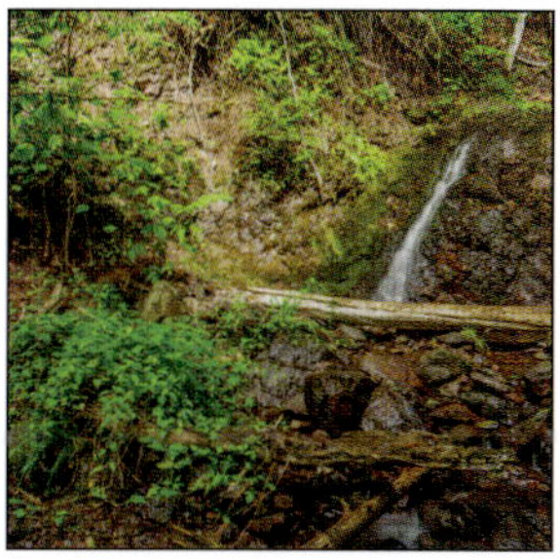

Must See:	6	GPS:	N47 21.972 W88 07.968
Height:	30 feet		
Time:	30-45 minutes	Hiking Information	
		Path:	Partway
Driving Information		Length:	.18 miles
Signs:	Small MNA Sign	Elev. Change:	Elevated
Road:	Secondary	GPS:	Recommended
Access:	Fairly Easy	Danger:	Elevated
4WD:	N/A	WP Boots:	Recommended

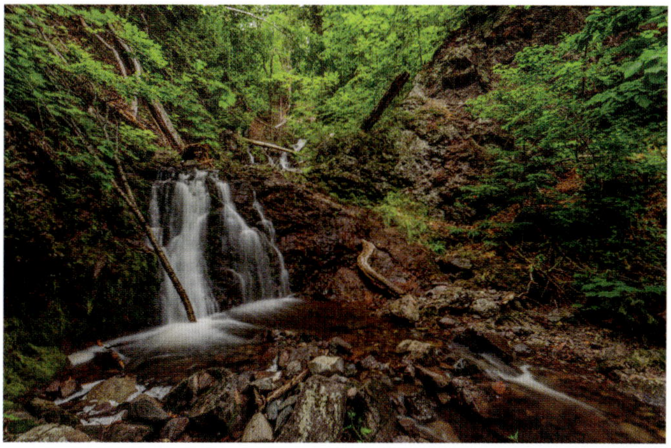

The Michigan Nature Association (MNA) overlook trail leads up from East Gratiot Lake Road. It will climb up into the bluffs overlooking Gratiot Lake. A side spur trail that is unmarked suddenly appears on the right. Follow it to the edge of the ravine that drops down to Eister Creek. Pick your way carefully down the steep and deep wall. Once at the creek, head upstream. The lower falls will be seen soon.

The waterfall needs a good flow to display itself nicely. A 20 foot cascade down the narrow creek widens out halfway down into several rivulets. The creek flows flat for 10 yards then pours over a 10 foot wide face for a final drop of 10 feet into a small spill pool. Downstream, the creek continues a good pace, winding its way to Lake Gratiot through tangled, overhanging undergrowth.

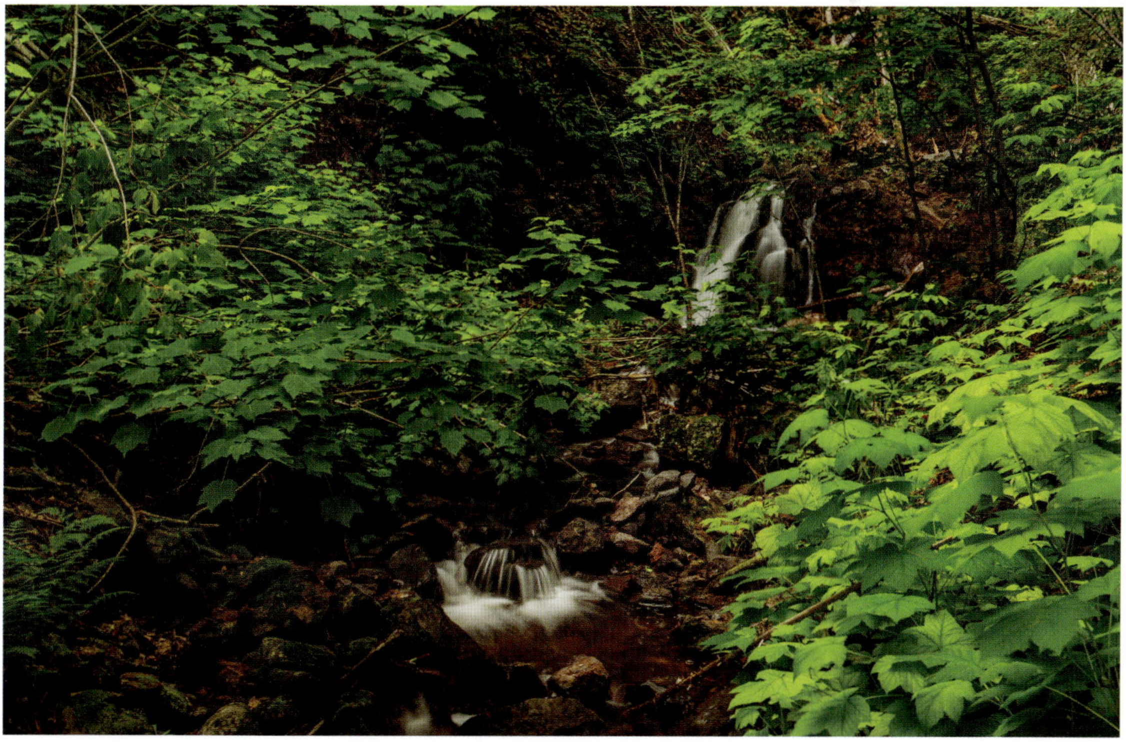

EISTER FALLS - MIDDLE #1 (EISTER CREEK)

Private

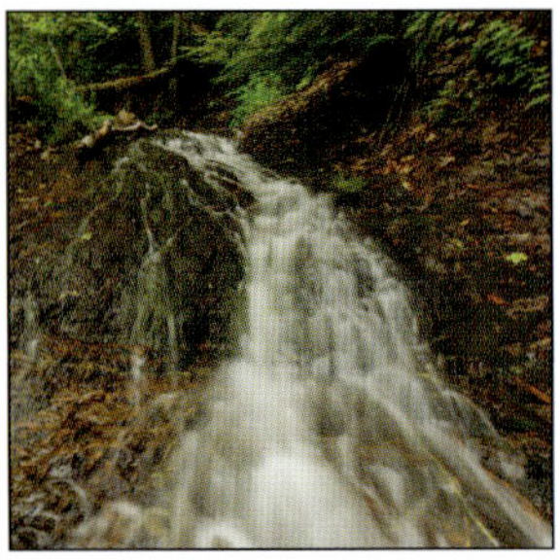

Must See:	5	GPS:	???
Height:	20 feet		
Time:	40-60 minutes	**Hiking Information**	
		Path:	Partway
Driving Information		Length:	.20 miles
Signs:	Small MNA Sign	Elev. Change:	Elevated
Road:	Secondary	GPS:	Recommended
Access:	Fairly Easy	Danger:	Elevated
4WD:	N/A	WP Boots:	Recommended

Climb up the riverbed alongside the Lower Falls. Just yards above the Lower Falls is this 20 foot slide over rippled and slippery bedrock.

Remember that this creek runs through a steep, narrow gorge. When the creek is rushing with a good deal of water it may not be possible to safely climb up it. The walls are so steep that climbing along it is not practical. It may be possible to hike along the top of the ravine but I don't know what the view might be from up there.

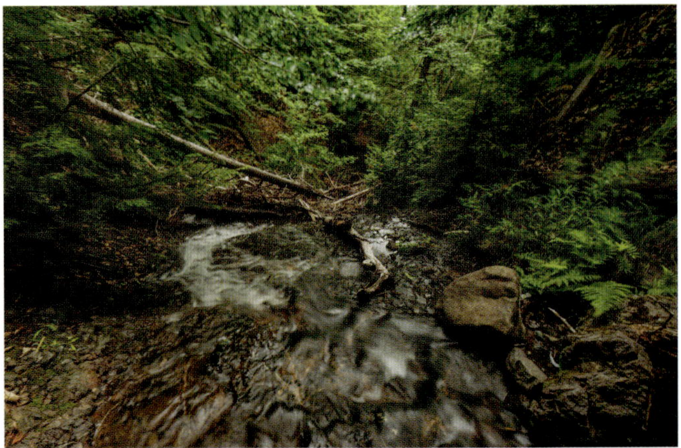

Looking down the slide at the collection of debris at the base.

The gorge was so steep and narrow that my GPS unit wouldn't work here, so I don't have the GPS coordinates for this waterfall.

Note the wet bedrock. This must be climbed up to get to the waterfalls upstream. Be careful.

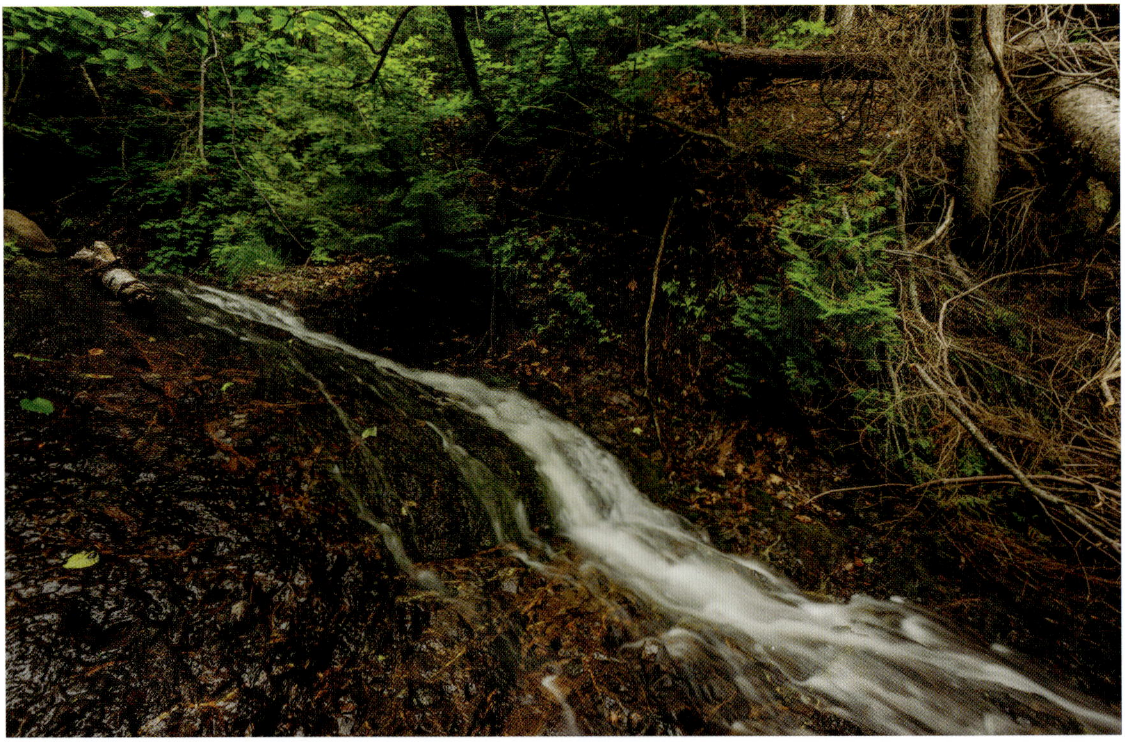

EISTER FALLS - MIDDLE #2 (EISTER CREEK)

Private

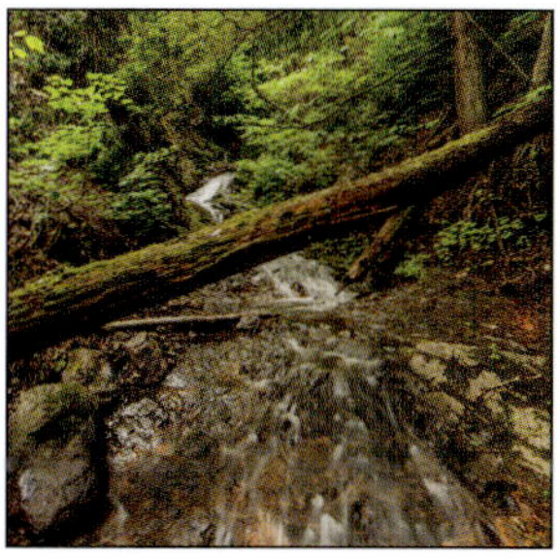

Must See:	5	GPS:	???
Height:	20 feet		
Time:	50-70 minutes	Hiking Information	
		Path:	Partway
Driving Information		Length:	.23 miles
Signs:	Small MNA Sign	Elev. Change:	Elevated
Road:	Secondary	GPS:	Recommended
Access:	Fairly Easy	Danger:	Elevated
4WD:	N/A	WP Boots:	Recommended

Climb up the steep and slippery water covered bedrock creek bed a couple dozen yards. Be careful. It can be dangerous. This is a rugged part of Michigan.

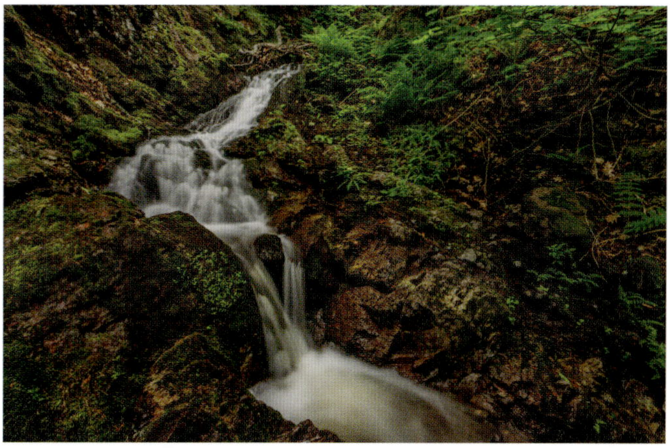

The 20 foot high slide arcs down through the steep sided gorge, moss hanging thick on the hard basalt. Red and green veins mark the healed portions of the ancient stone. Ferns and thimbleberries grow along the banks, while maples compete with cedar trees for sunlight in the dimly lit gorge.

The gorge was so steep and narrow that my GPS unit wouldn't work here, so I don't have the GPS coordinates for this waterfall.

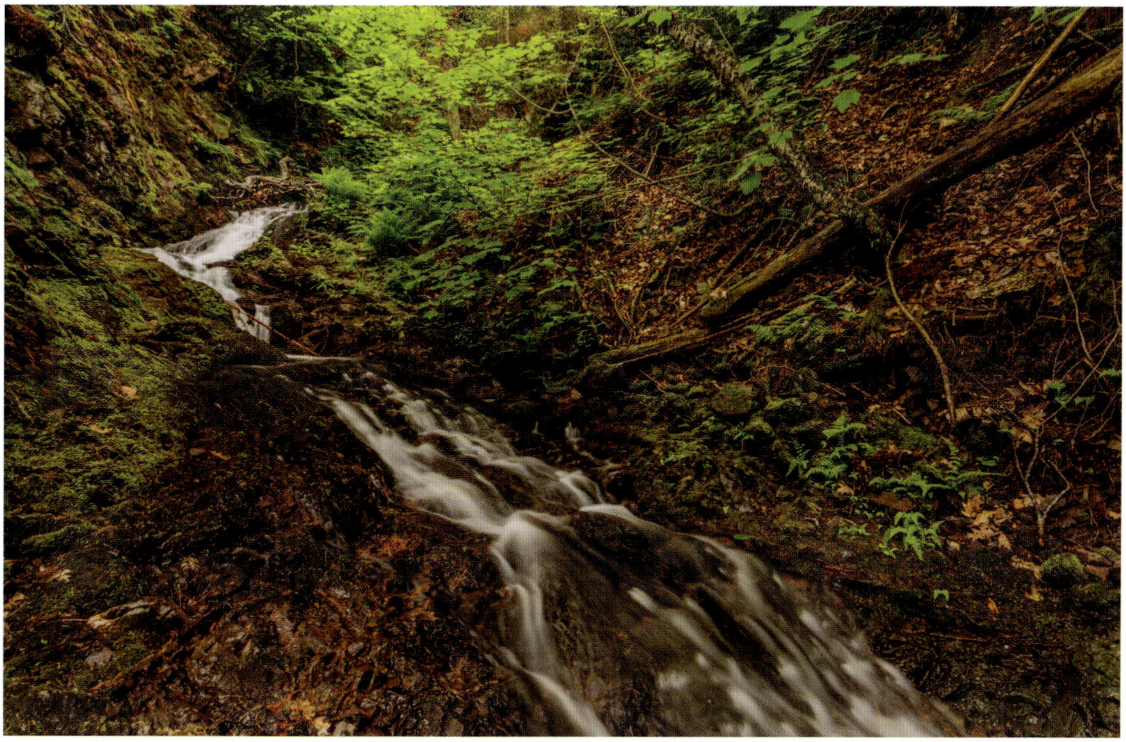

KEWEENAW COUNTY

EISTER FALLS - UPPER (EISTER CREEK)

Private

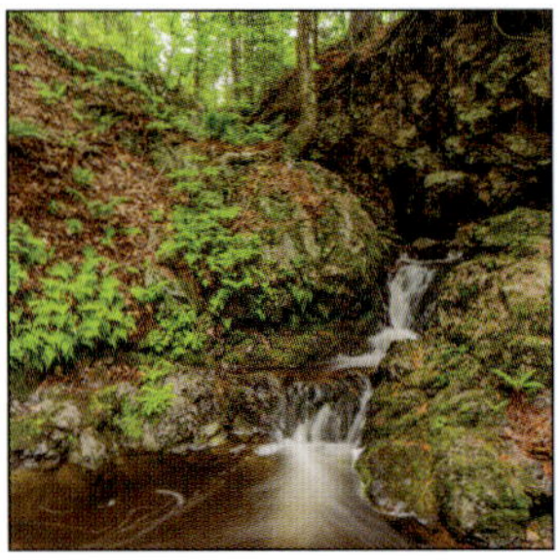

Must See:	5	GPS:	N47 22.006 W88 07.986
Height:	7 feet		
Time:	30-80 minutes	**Hiking Information**	
		Path:	Footpath or Partway
Driving Information		Length:	.25 miles
Signs:	Small MNA sign	Elev. Change:	Moderate or Elevated
Road:	Secondary	GPS:	N/A or Recommended
Access:	Fairly Easy	Danger:	Slight or Elevated
4WD:	N/A	WP Boots:	N/A or Recommended

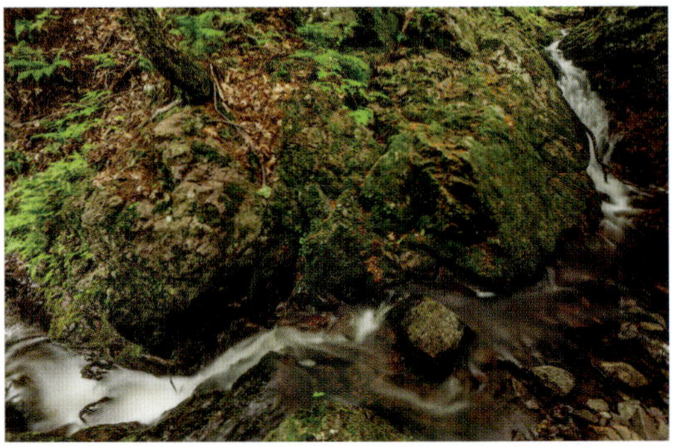

The "dual" Hiking Information above is based on either staying on the footpath and viewing the waterfall from afar or climbing down into the ravine at the lower falls and hiking up the creek bed through the Eister Falls series.

The Easy Way: From the overlook trail a sign stating "Falls" points the way to a short side trail heading east and ending at the top of the ravine overlooking the falls far below. From here the lower portion of this drop can be seen.

The Difficult Way: Eister Creek runs through a winding ravine. I recommend climbing down into the ravine either below the lower falls or above this waterfall. The ravine is steeper and deeper by the lower falls but it's easier to climb up the creek bed than to start at the top and work down the slippery rock to the bottom. Eister Falls - Upper is up at the top of the rocky trough. The slide runs through a narrow channel with moss covered angled rock on the left and fractured bedrock arching overhead on the right with a cedar tree hanging precariously directly above the spill pool. It looks like it could drop its tons of lumber straight down at any time.

This shot is from the MNA trail, "The Easy Way" - the other shots are from "The Difficult Way"

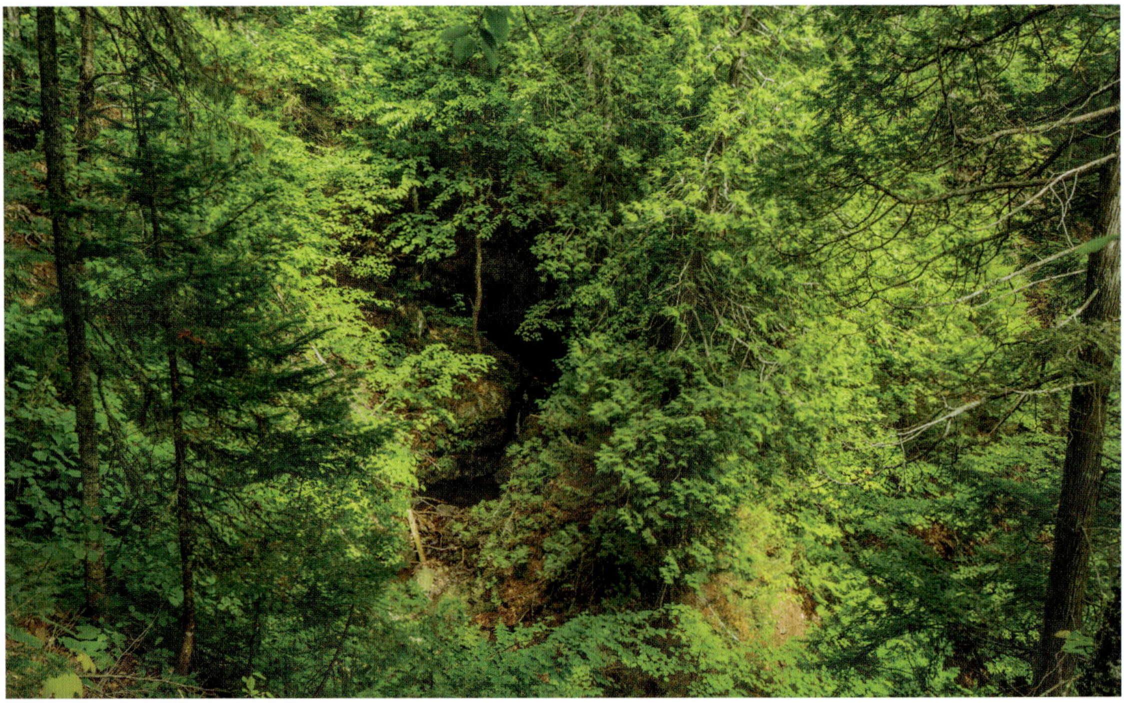

Eister Falls - Upper

Haven Falls Hike

Haven Falls: Haven Falls is another of the "view from the vehicle" waterfalls. Easy to drive to, easy to find, and easy to view; this is a great family stopping spot.

Directions: From US-41, turn south onto Lac La Belle Road. 4.3 miles later, turn right (southwest) at the sharp bend just beyond where Bete Gris Road veers off to the left. In .47 miles turn right (north) into the roadside park. The waterfall will be visible from the road.

HAVEN FALLS (HAVEN CREEK)

Private

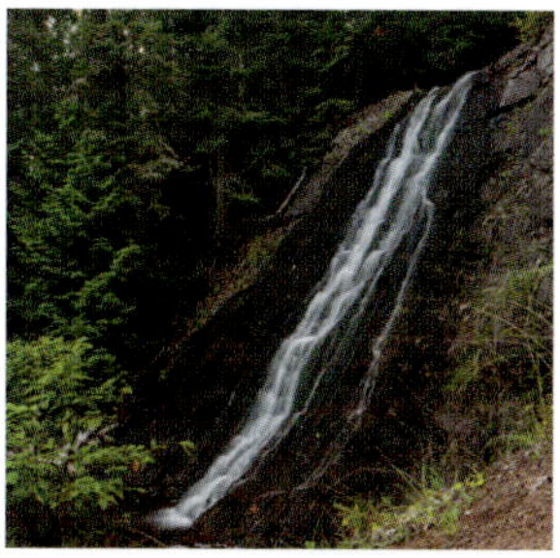

Must See:	6	GPS:	N47 22.911 W88 01.720
Height:	20 feet		
Time:	5-15 minutes	Hiking Information	
		Path:	N/A
Driving Information		Length:	N/A
Signs:	Clearly Marked	Elev. Change:	N/A
Road:	Main	GPS:	N/A
Access:	Very Easy	Danger:	N/A
4WD:	N/A	WP Boots:	N/A

This is a great family park with pit toilets, picnic tables and charcoal grills. The falls can be viewed from the vehicle, making this a great spot to check out for those wanting an easily accessed waterfall. Climb to the top of the falls up the clay bank for a small drop at the top that can't be seen from below. The bedrock tilts at the top of the falls between highly eroded banks, then suddenly tips to nearly vertical, ending in a very small spill pool. The creek then runs down another small stretch of rock before it meanders through Haven Park, passes beneath the road and ends up flowing into Lac La Belle.

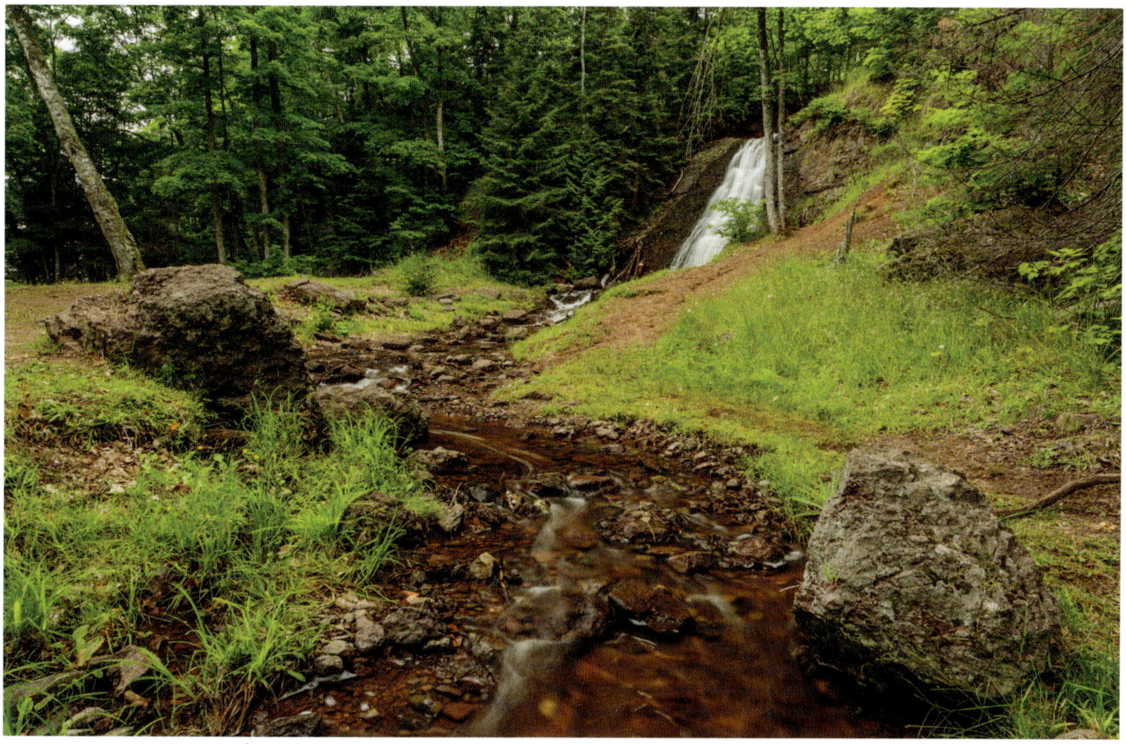

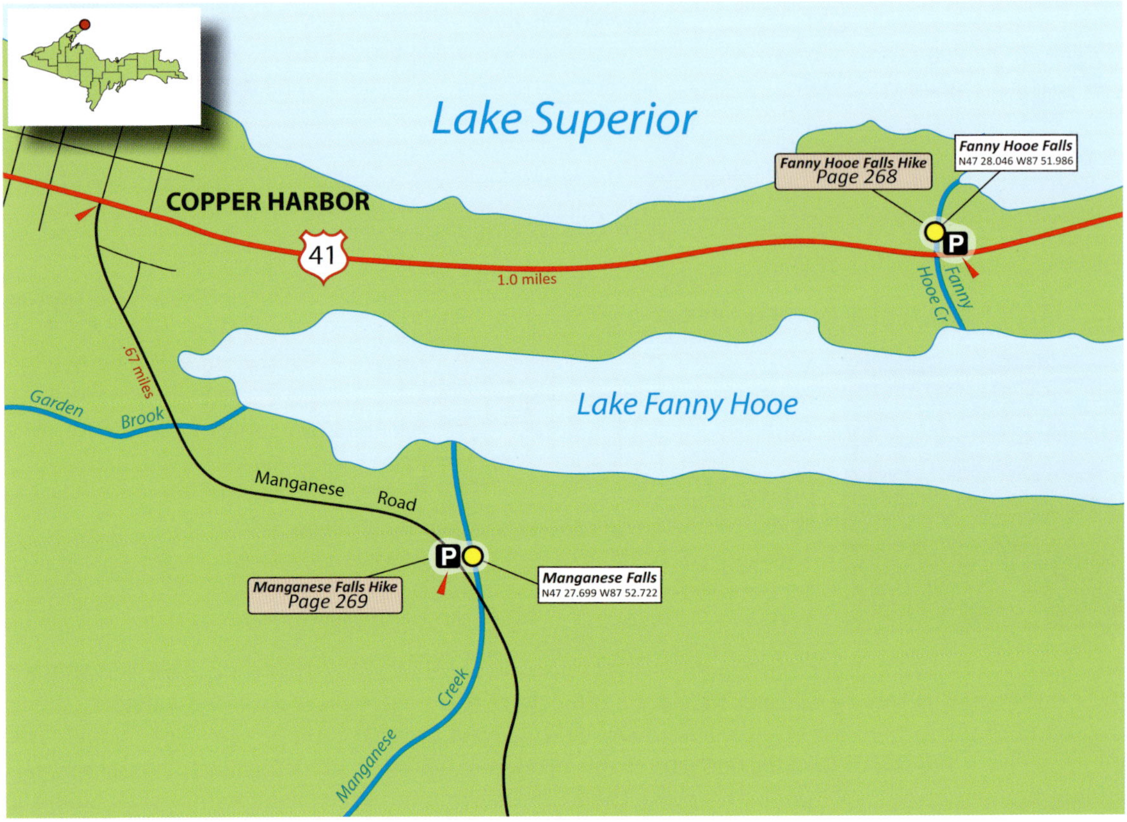

Fanny Hooe Falls Hike

Fanny Hooe Creek runs the short distance from Lake Fanny Hooe into Lake Superior, passing through Fort Wilkins State Park, under US-41, alongside the parking area for viewing Copper Harbor Lighthouse from across the bay, and into Lake Superior. It's in this short stretch that Fanny Hooe Falls occurs.

Directions: Follow US-41 through Copper Harbor to the east. Signage for Fort Wilkins State Park will be seen on the right. Immediately after crossing the bridge over Fanny Hooe Creek, turn left (north) into the parking lot for viewing the lighthouse. The waterfall is easily seen just yards into the woods next to the parking area.

FANNY HOOE FALLS (FANNY HOOE CREEK)

Private

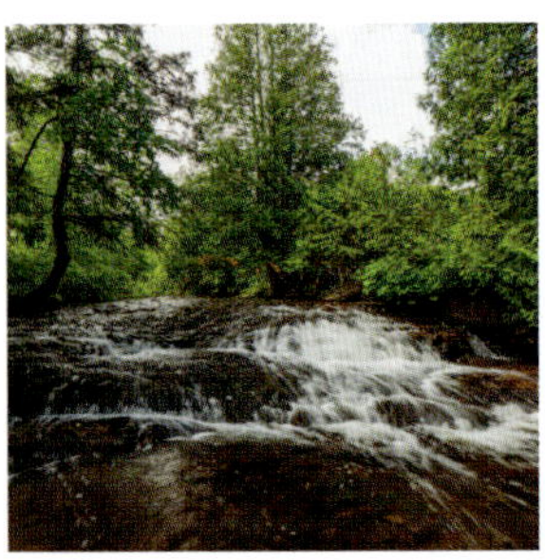

Must See:	5	GPS:	N47 28.046 W87 51.986
Height:	4 feet		
Time:	5-10 minutes	Hiking Information	
		Path:	N/A
Driving Information		Length:	50 feet
Signs:	None	Elev. Change:	Slight
Road:	Main	GPS:	N/A
Access:	Very Easy	Danger:	Slight
4WD:	N/A	WP Boots:	N/A

The creek cascades over cobbled bedrock just 100 yards before entering Lake Superior. There is a short, but steep bank on either side of the creek.

Manganese Falls Hike

Manganese Falls: This unique waterfall drops a long ways over several precipices at various angles into a narrow gorge. It is difficult to view due to the extremely narrow and steep gorge.

Directions: Turn south off of US-41 onto Manganese Road. In .7 of a mile, there will be a sign on the left for the falls. Park on the right, cross the road and follow the short path to the falls overlook.

MANGANESE FALLS (MANGANESE CREEK)

Private

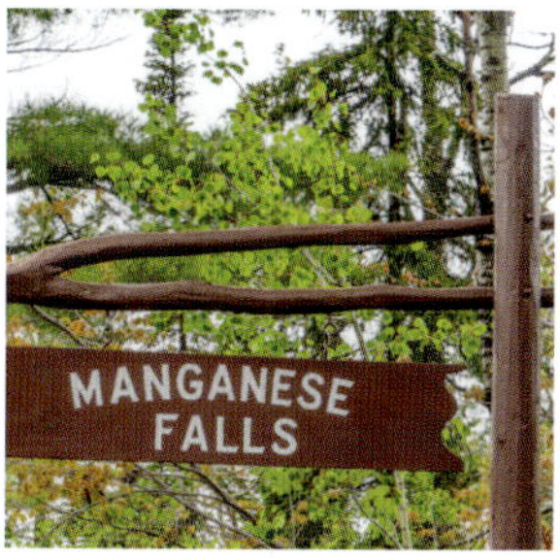

Must See:	6	GPS:	N47 27.699 W87 52.722
Height:	30 feet		
Time:	5-30 minutes	**Hiking Information**	
		Path:	Footpath/None
Driving Information		Length:	50 feet/100 yards
Signs:	Wooden	Elev. Change:	Slight/Moderate
Road:	Secondary	GPS:	N/A
Access:	Somewhat easy	Danger:	Slight/Moderate
4WD:	N/A	WP Boots:	None/Required

The split hiking information is for "The Viewing Deck" and "Base of the Falls". To get to the base of the falls, drive back toward Copper Harbor from the falls. Immediately on the right (east) will be a dirt road. Follow it down a good sized hill. At the bottom is a bridge. Park here. Wade up the creek, over an old, short dam, and to the base of the falls. Even from here, there is not much to see. The way that the rock is split, much of the falling water is hidden from any vantage point.

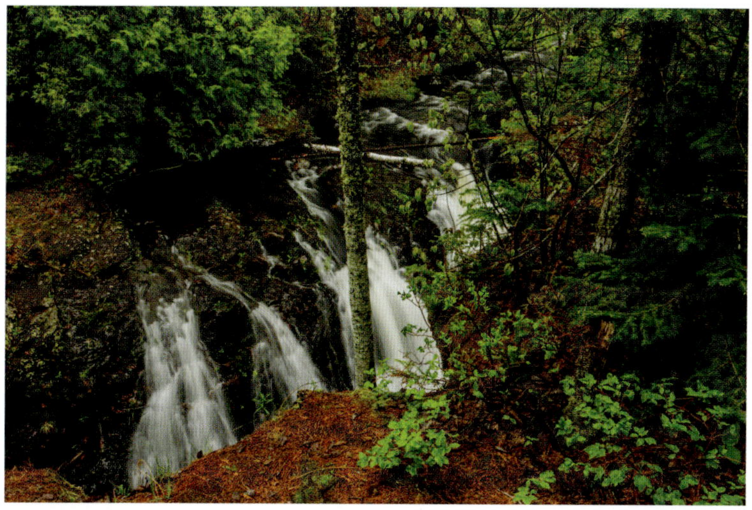

Looking down at the top of the waterfall as the creek tumbles into the narrow gorge about 75 feet upstream from the viewing deck

I took this shot from the "official overlook"

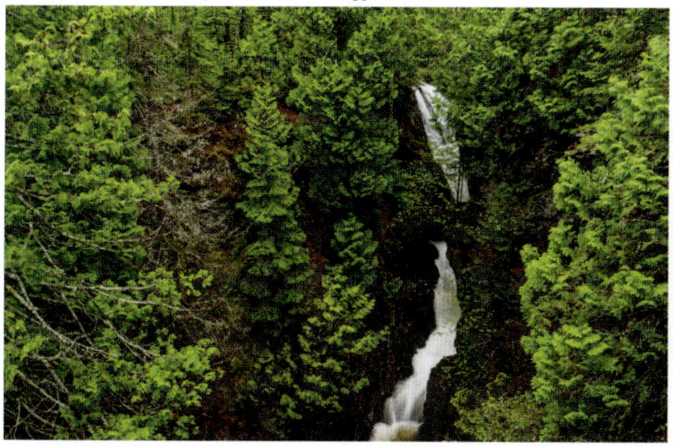

This is down at the base of the winding drops

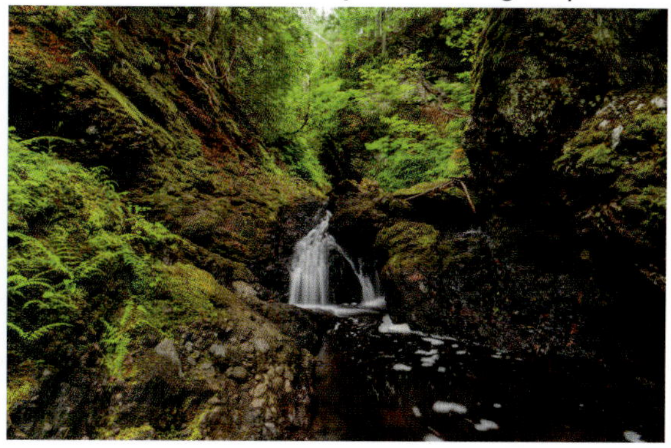

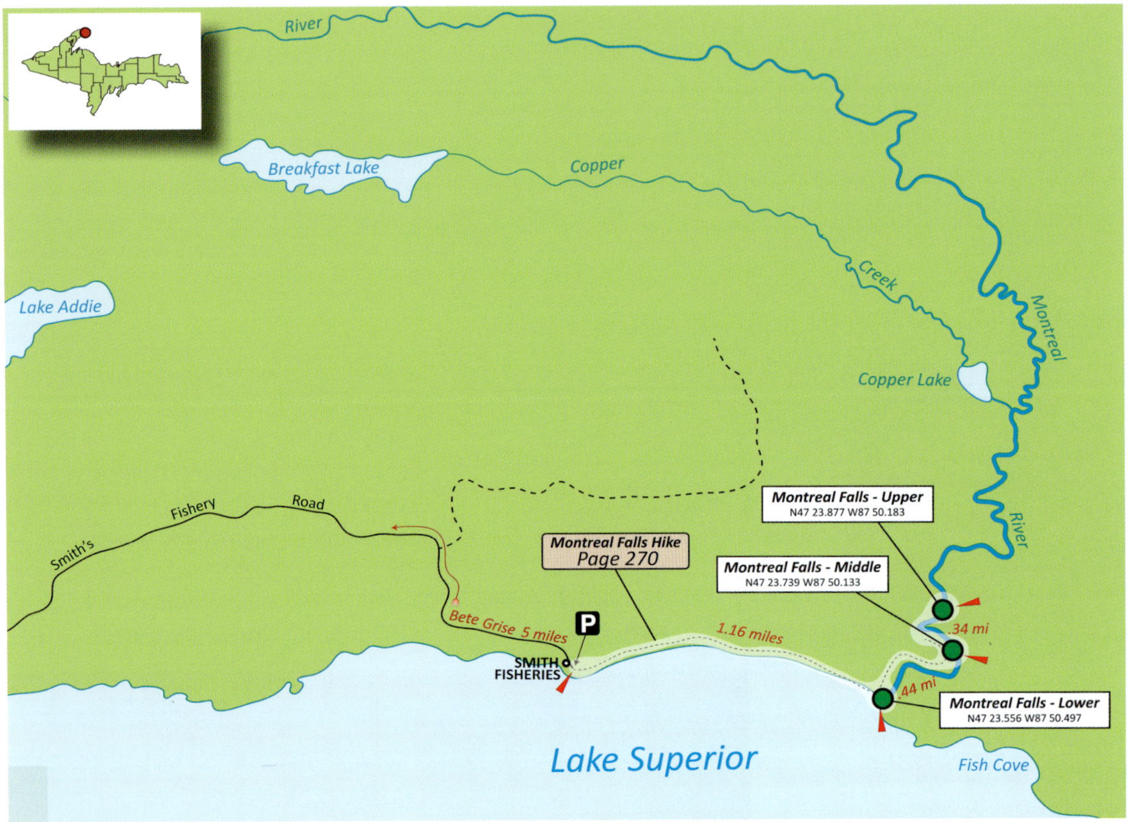

Montreal Falls Hike

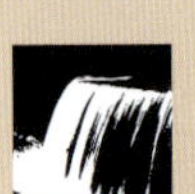

Prepare for a wilderness walk. These falls are at the end of the Keweenaw Peninsula. There is nothing past here but water - until ending up in Canada! The trail through rugged forest is not well maintained. Fallen trees often block the trail, forcing short, alternate routes. The trail skirts the edge of Lake Superior, but not at beach level. The lake is sometimes 10-15 feet below the ground level and a couple of times the trail comes to the very edge of the drop-off. All of these facts contribute to the sense of adventure and ruggedness that this hike embodies. Don't come to these waterfalls if you are looking for a short trip. Allow 3 to 4 hours at least. There is a great picnic spot at the lower falls, as the trail widens out at the beach, just as the waterfall also meets Lake Superior.

Directions: In Bete Grise, there will be a sign for the Smith Fishery. Please note that this is a private road. Be respectful. Follow that dirt road for the next 3 miles, keeping to the right. The road has been recently improved for logging operations. Just after the Smith Fisheries the road is blocked. There is room for 4 or 5 vehicles to park here. A 2-track continues to the east paralleling Lake Superior. Hike down the road. After about 1/2 mile, the 2-track ends, and a footpath enters the forest, still running parallel with Lake Superior. There are times that the path becomes very hard to follow. Just remember to keep Lake Superior to the right and don't wander too far inland. After a total of 1.16 miles of hiking, the lower falls come into view. Follow the river upstream for another .44 miles to see the middle falls. In another .34 miles are the upper falls. The trail to the upper falls is faint and sometimes nonexistent. Once again, follow the river and don't wander far from it, in order to keep from getting lost.

MONTREAL FALLS - LOWER (MONTREAL RIVER)

Private

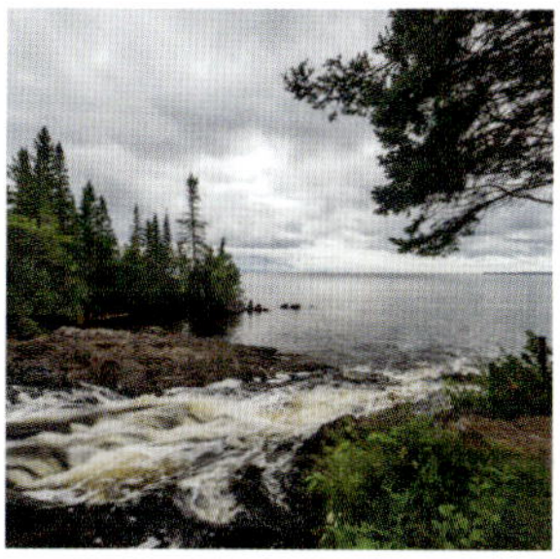

Must See:	7	GPS:	N47 23.556 W87 50.497
Height:	25 feet		
Time:	1.5-2 hours		
Driving Information		**Hiking Information**	
		Path:	Narrow footpath
		Length:	1.16 miles
Signs:	None	Elev. Change:	Slight
Road:	Gravel Road	GPS:	Helpful
Access:	Difficult	Danger:	Moderate
4WD:	Helpful	WP Boots:	Helpful

The waterfall drops directly into Lake Superior along side a small beach. This makes for a nice camping location or picnic area.

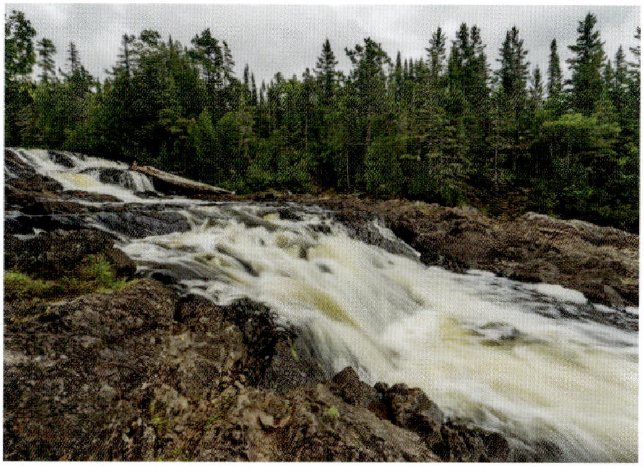

Rugged basalt forms the 40 foot wide riverbed. The river cascades down this rough blackened rock, forming various rivulets as the water level changes. A 25 foot long cascade that drops about 5 feet starts the waterfall about 50 yards above an 8 foot descent that is followed by 30 feet of relative calm. The river then narrows to 15 feet and rushes down another 5 feet before a final 2 foot cascade that falls directly into Lake Superior.

Looking out over Lake Superior from the trail

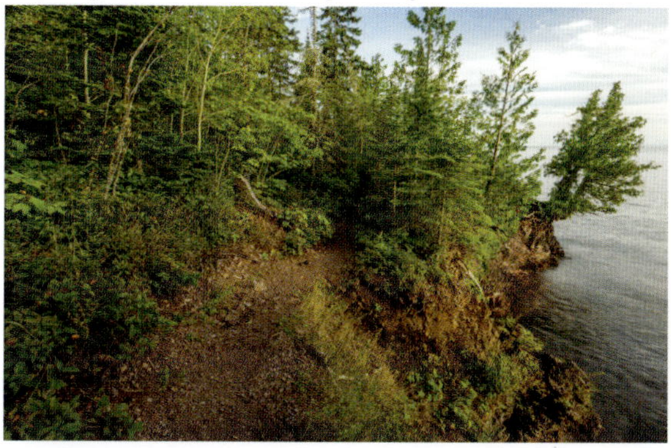

The scene heading back from the waterfall

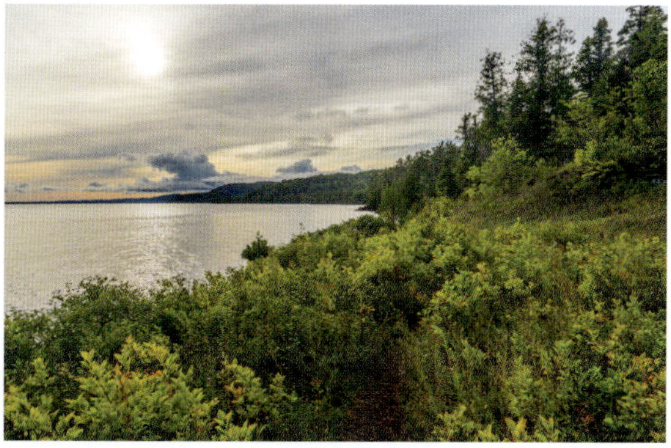

Thimbleberries line a portion of the trail

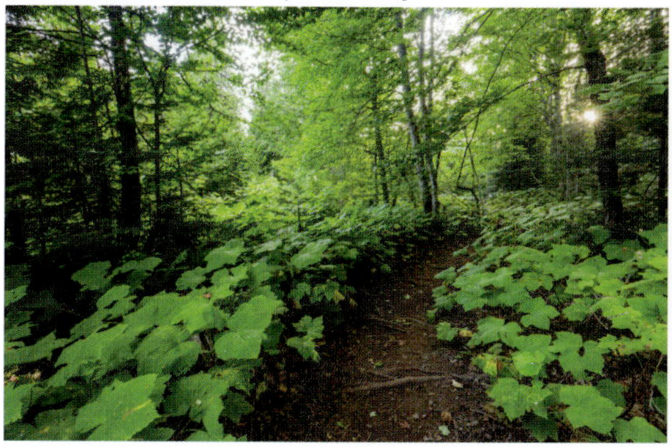

Looking down from the top of the waterfall

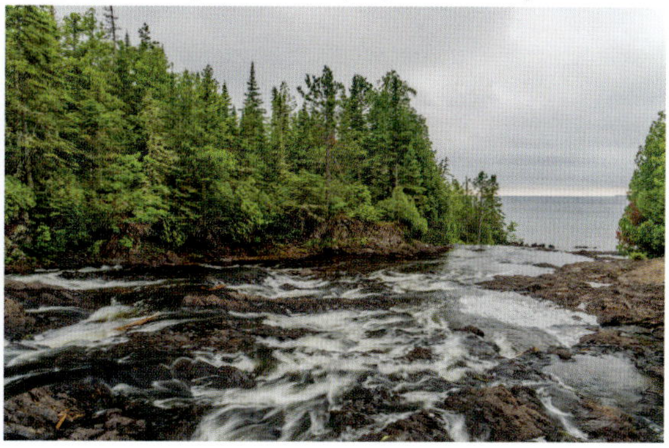

MONTREAL FALLS - MIDDLE (MONTREAL RIVER)

Private

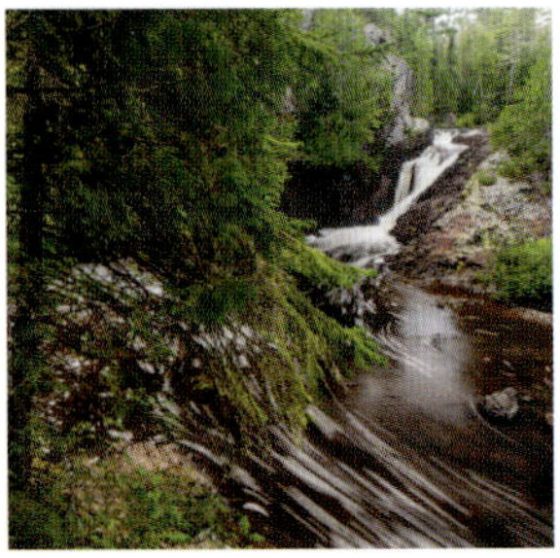

Must See:	8	GPS:	N47 23.739 W87 50.133
Height:	20 feet		
Time:	2-3 hours	Hiking Information	
		Path:	Rough Path
Driving Information		Length:	1.6 miles
Signs:	None	Elev. Change:	Moderate
Road:	Gravel Road	GPS:	Helpful
Access:	Difficult	Danger:	Moderate
4WD:	Helpful	WP Boots:	Helpful

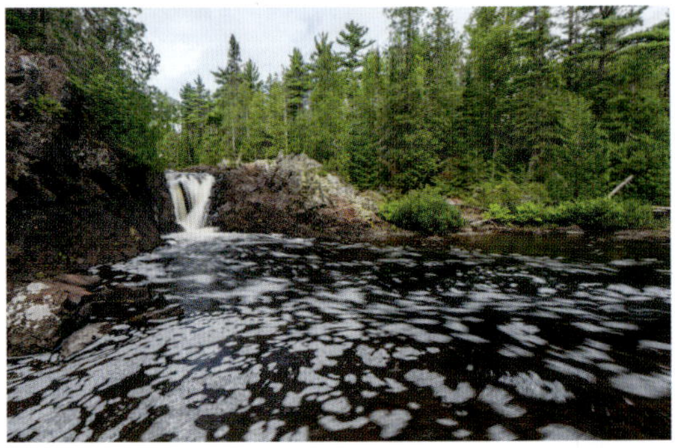

Follow the faint footpath upstream .44 miles from the Lower Falls. It wanders over, under, and around trees and undergrowth before ending up at this wonderful waterfall!

A 25 foot tall reddish-brown-black mass stands next to the waterfall on the near side. The river is dramatically narrower up here than it is downstream from the waterfall. At the top of the waterfall the river is 8 feet wide, narrowing at the base of the waterfall to just 3 feet, as the jagged basalt on the far side encroaches on the waterfall, pushing it back onto itself. A "V" shaped spill pool widens back out suddenly, filling a small cove lined with rough bedrock that's perfect for viewing the waterfall. The river turns and narrows again over a short rapids and then cascades down a 2 foot drop around a corner.

My son, Andrew, sets up for a shot on a lovely overcast July evening

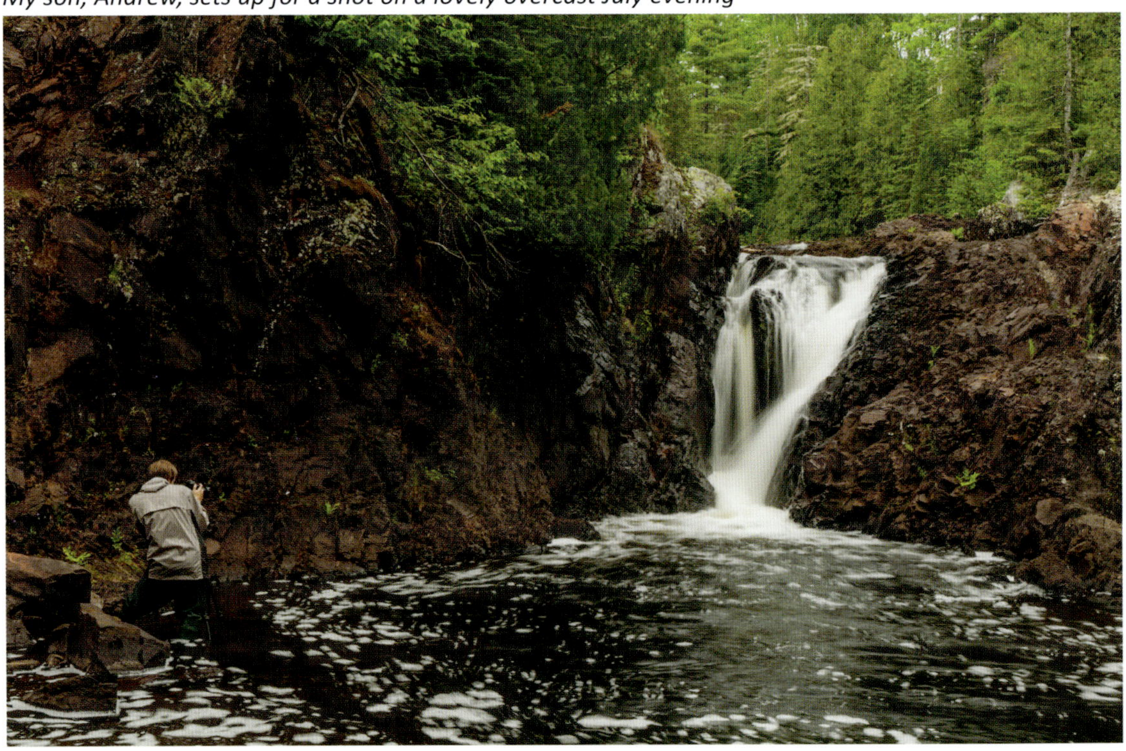

MONTREAL FALLS - UPPER (MONTREAL RIVER)

Private

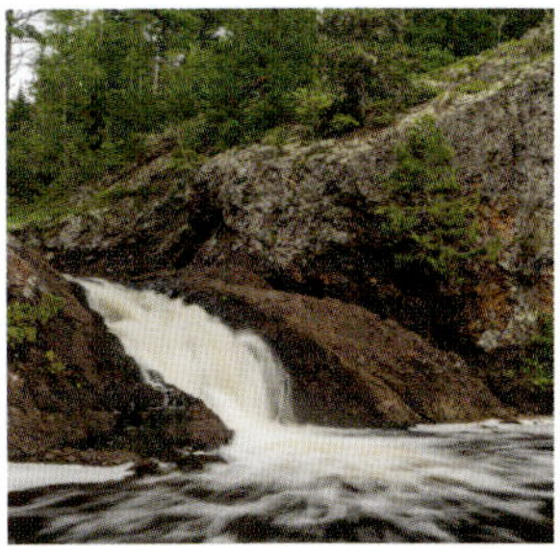

Must See:	7	GPS:	N47 23.877 W87 50.183
Height:	13 feet		
Time:	2.5-4 hours	Hiking Information	
		Path:	Rough Path/None
Driving Information		Length:	1.94 miles
Signs:	None	Elev. Change:	Elevated
Road:	Gravel Road	GPS:	Recommended
Access:	Difficult	Danger:	Elevated
4WD:	Helpful	WP Boots:	Helpful

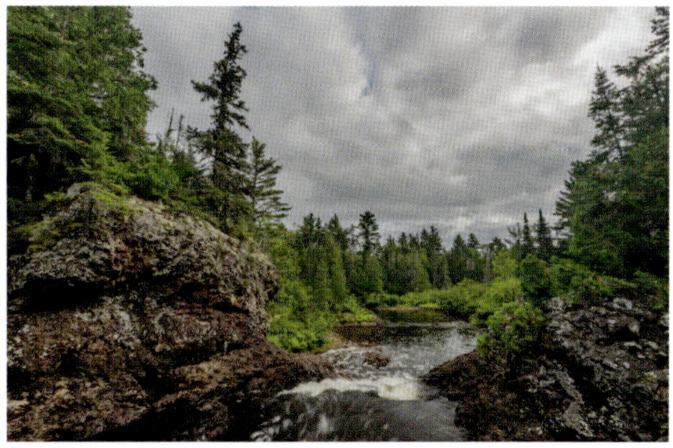

The dwindling trail between the Middle and Upper Falls must be taken into account when deciding to hike out to this furthest of the Montreal River Falls. Also, the waterfall is difficult to observe from the base.

A large spill pool widens out immediately below the waterfall with dense undergrowth running down to the water's edge. If you can pick your way along the base of the large bluff that stands up next to the waterfall, you'll see a smaller bluff that forms the actual edge of the waterfall. It's steep, but there are some stair-like hand holds that can be used to get to the top and observe the waterfall from above. The river, placid before the waterfall, suddenly drops 1.5 feet just after it enters a steep, rocky ravine. The bluffs rise on both sides with the river squeezed in between. Fifty yards after the initial drop, a second 1.5 foot drop occurs where the river has been channeled down to just two feet across (in most river conditions). In another 25 yards the river exits the gorge with a frothy 2, cascading down the crumbly conglomerate face in dramatic fashion.

It's a tough bust through a ton of thick undergrowth to get to this vantage spot. But I love it!

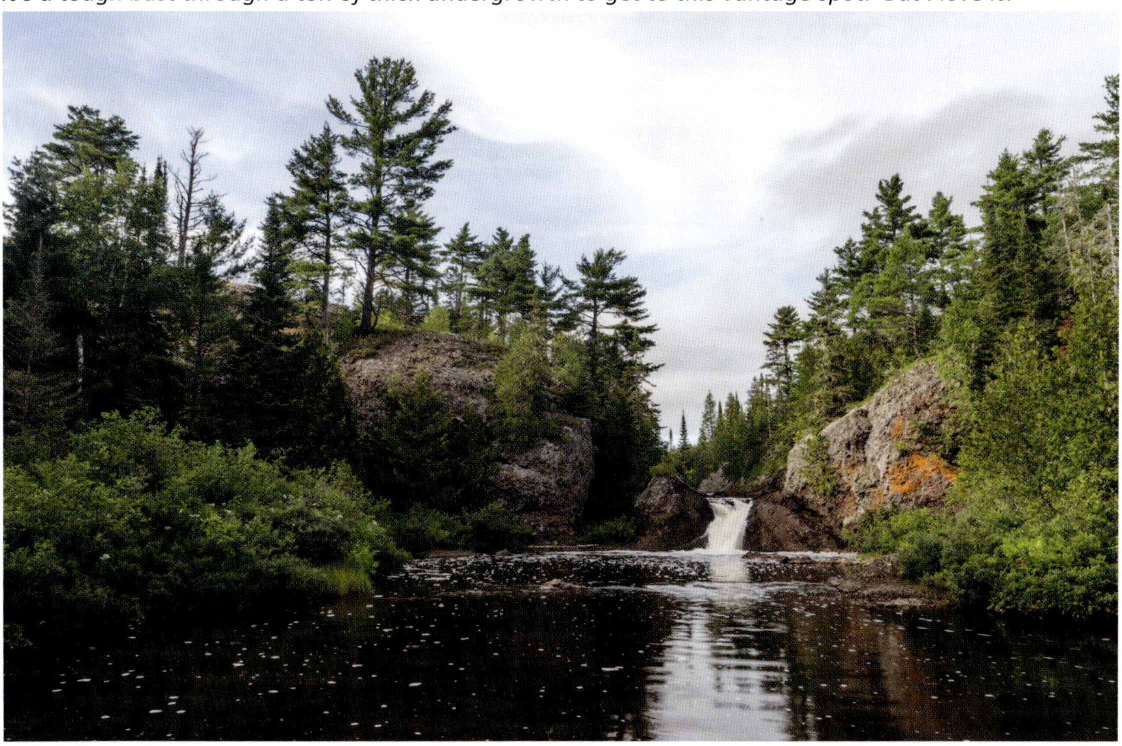

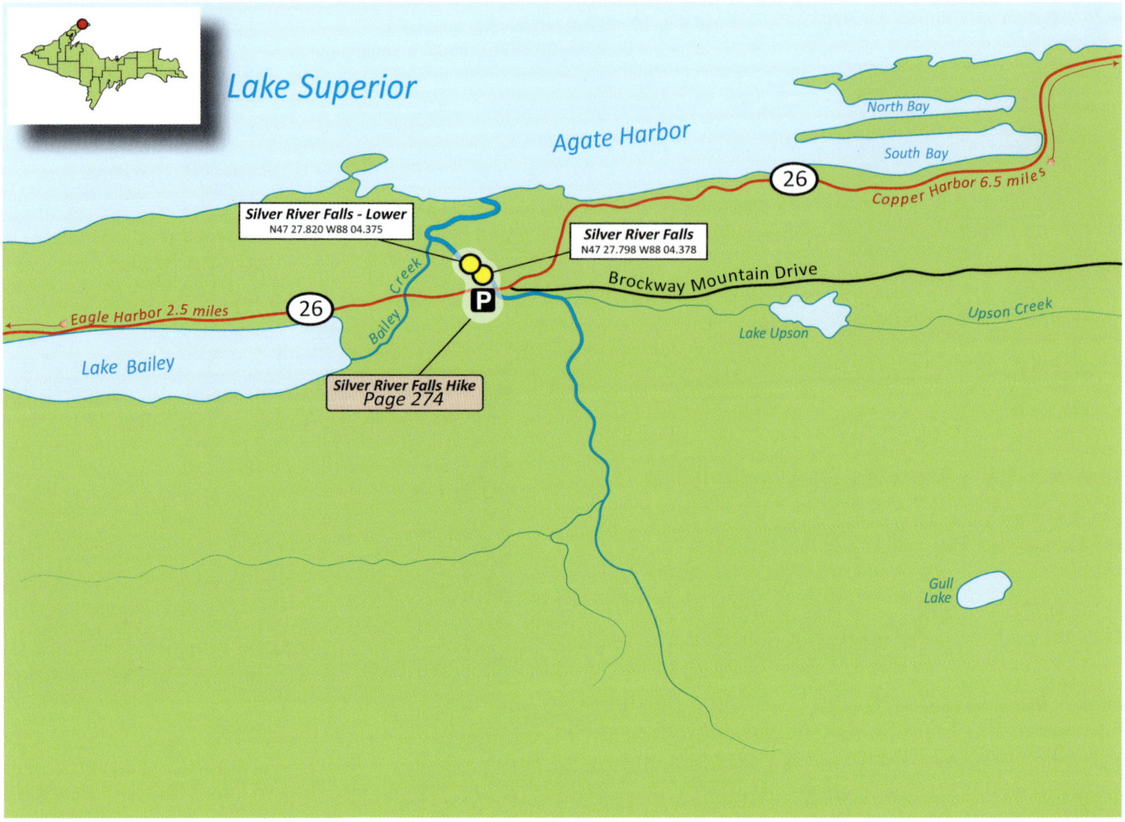

Silver River Falls Hike

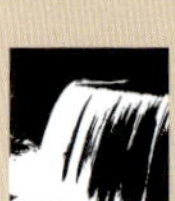

Silver River Falls: A rough cascading drop flows just below the bridge. Continue downstream along an easy to follow footpath on the west side of the river to the lower drop. They both present themselves nicely, if not dramatically.

Directions: On M-26, 12.5 miles east of Eagle River and 9.5 miles west of Copper Harbor is an obvious pull-off by the Silver River Bridge. Park and hike downstream 100 feet from the bridge on a well travelled footpath to view Silver River Falls as the river emerges from beneath the road. Continue downstream around the bend in the river to view the lower falls.

SILVER RIVER FALLS (SILVER RIVER)

Private

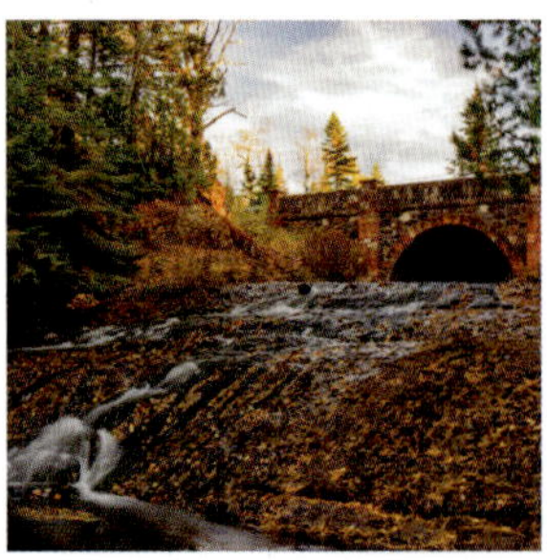

Must See:	6	GPS:	N47 27.798 W88 04.378
Height:	15 feet		
Time:	10-20 minutes	Hiking Information	
		Path:	Footpath
Driving Information		Length:	100 feet
Signs:	Clearly Marked	Elev. Change:	Minor
Road:	Main	GPS:	N/A
Access:	Very Easy	Danger:	Slight
4WD:	N/A	WP Boots:	N/A

Climb down the west side of the river to view the falls. The riverbed and tilted bedrock walls bordering the river are composed of conglomerate. The bridge, which sits just above the main sloped drop is made of precisely cut stone. After the 1st drop of 7 feet, the river continues to descend down at a gentle angle over the next 30 yards. A variety of shrubs and evergreens blanket both sides of the river.

A good look at the character of this easy to access waterfall

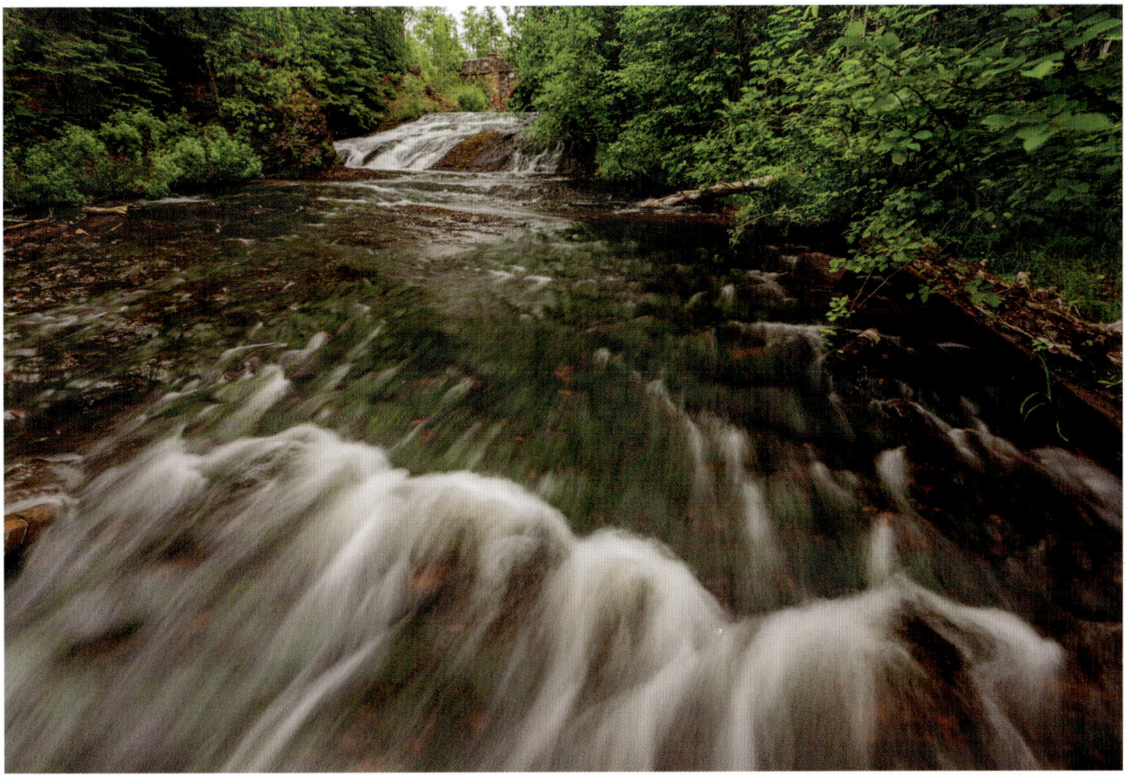

The look of the slide from the footpath that follows the river

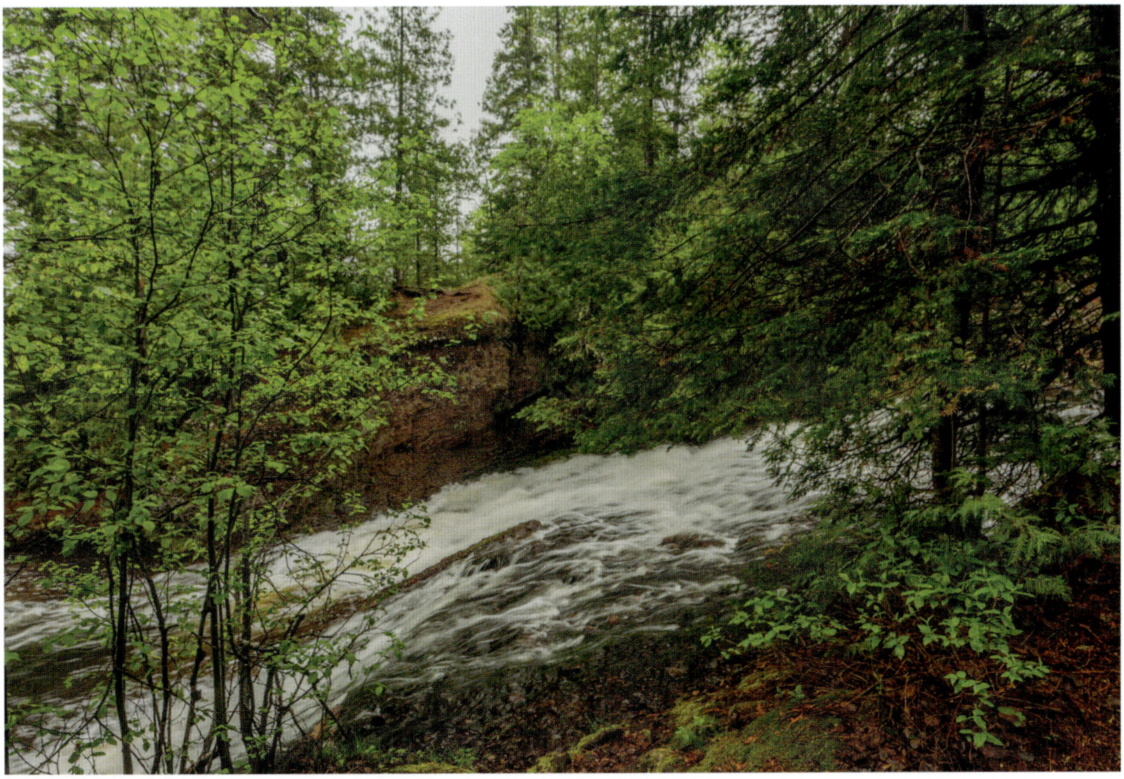

SILVER RIVER FALLS - LOWER (SILVER RIVER)

Private

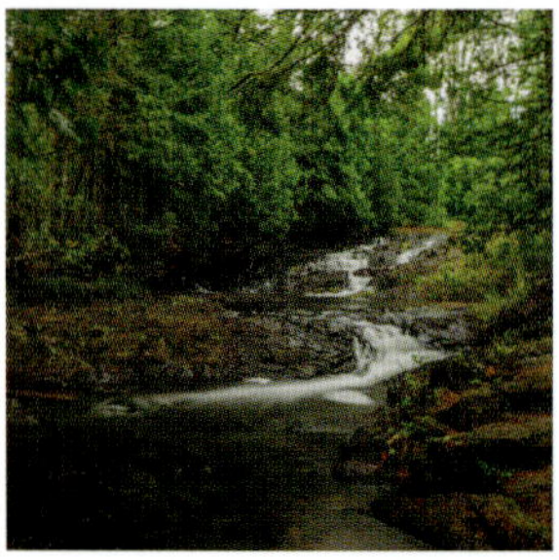

Must See:	5	GPS:	N47 27.820 W88 04.375
Height:	8 feet		
Time:	10-20 minutes	Hiking Information	
		Path:	Footpath
Driving Information		Length:	75 yards
Signs:	Clearly Marked	Elev. Change:	Minor
Road:	Main	GPS:	N/A
Access:	Very Easy	Danger:	Slight
4WD:	N/A	WP Boots:	N/A

Hike around the bend in the river from the "main" falls to view what is really a continuation of the stair stepped drops. Below the lower section of the falls the river calms down and meanders through the forest before dumping into Lake Superior.

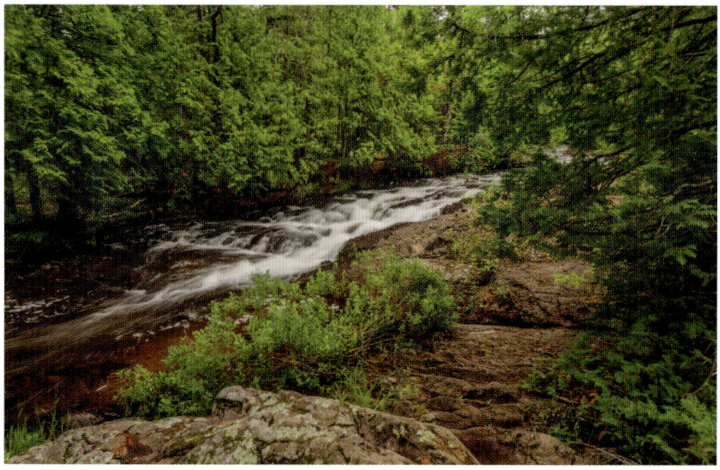

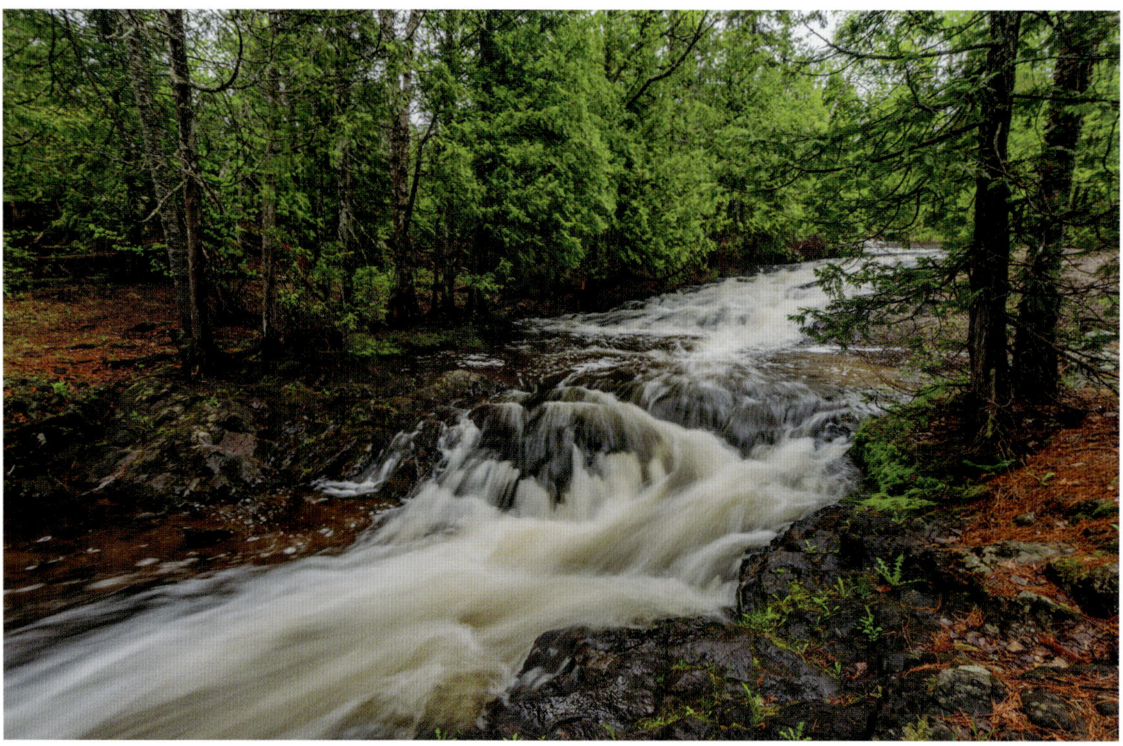

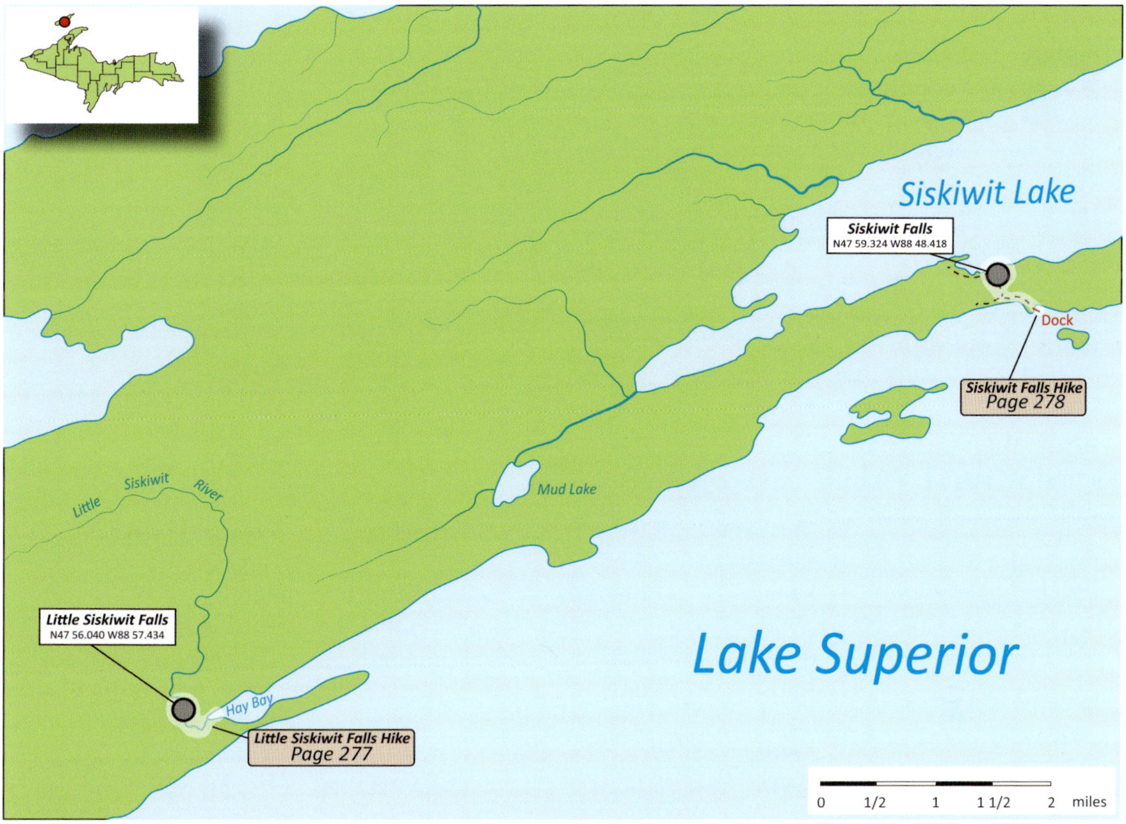

Little Siskiwit Falls Hike

I've been told by a ranger at Isle Royale National Park that this is a nice little waterfall in the back country. For more information about ferry service to the island check with the Isle Royale National Park Headquarters in Houghton (ferry service from Houghton) at (906) 482-0984 or the Isle Royale Line in Copper Harbor (ferry service from Copper Harbor) at (906) 289-4437.

Directions: Get to Isle Royale. This is accomplished either by flight or boat. Hire a boat to Hay Bay. It's then recommended to canoe or kayak up to the head of the bay. Hike upstream about 1/3 mile to the falls.

LITTLE SISKIWIT FALLS (LITTLE SISKIWIT RIVER)

Private

Must See:	?	GPS:	N47 56.040 W88 57.434
Height:	? feet		
Time:	? minutes	Hiking Information	
		Path:	None
Driving Information		Length:	1/3 mile (not verified)
Signs:	None	Elev. Change:	Moderate (not verified)
Road:	None - By Water	GPS:	Recommended
Access:	Very Difficult	Danger:	Not Known
4WD:	N/A	WP Boots:	Not Known

I'm told that this waterfall contains several drops over a rocky section in the north to south stretch of the river about 1/3 mile upstream from the mouth of the Little Siskiwit River as it empties into the southwest end of Hay Bay. Allegedly this waterfall is "better" than the easier to access Siskiwit Falls.

Siskiwit Falls Hike

Siskiwit Lake spills out over a low point about halfway down the rock wall that makes up the southeast border of the lake. As Siskiwit River leaves the lake it runs down quickly over rough basalt. There are several small drops in this minor waterfall. For more information about ferry service to the island check with the Isle Royale National Park Headquarters in Houghton (ferry service from Houghton) at (906) 482-0984 or the Isle Royale Line in Copper Harbor (ferry service from Copper Harbor) at (906) 289-4437.

Directions: Get to Isle Royale. This is accomplished either by flight or boat. Hire a boat to Malone Bay. Follow the footpath westerly about a 1/4 mile, generally following the shoreline. Take a trail north 1/3 mile to Siskiwit Lake and the waterfall.

SISKIWIT FALLS (SISKIWIT RIVER)

Private

Must See:	?	GPS:	N47 59.324 W88 48.418
Height:	? feet		
Time:	? minutes	Hiking Information	
		Path:	Footpath
Driving Information		Length:	.55 mile (not verified)
Signs:	None	Elev. Change:	Minor (not verified)
Road:	None - By Water	GPS:	Recommended
Access:	Very Difficult	Danger:	Not Known
4WD:	N/A	WP Boots:	Not Known

I've not been to this waterfall yet. I have seen pictures of it, however. My guess is that I'd rate it as a "Must See: 4". The oversized rapids exit the lake with several actual drops (maybe 6-12 inches high) haphazardly placed on either side of the shallow river.

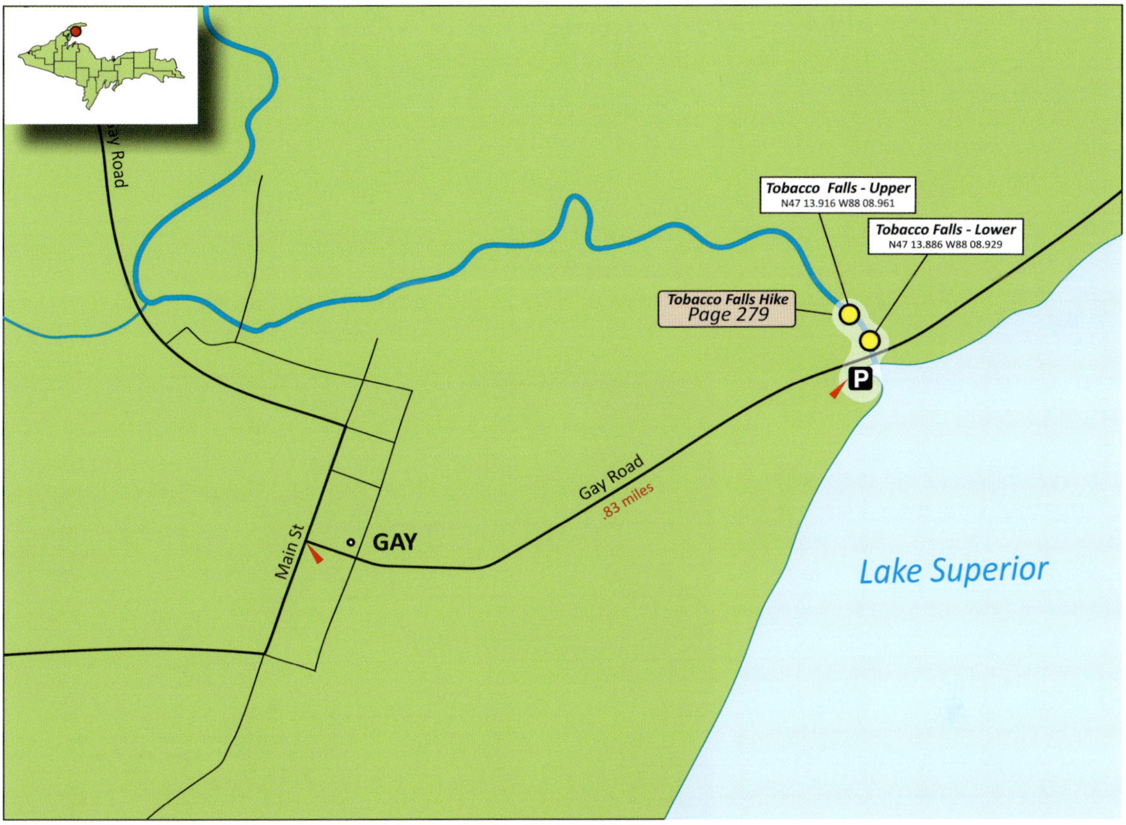

Tobacco Falls Hike

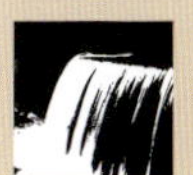

Water fills the riverbed from side to side. Undergrowth lines the sides of the river. Either wade up the normally shallow river or be prepared to contend with uneven terrain and flora between the lower and upper falls.

Directions: From Hancock, take M-23 to the east. Follow it to Lake Linden. Turn right (east) on 9th Street one block before M-26 turns to the left. Follow 9th Street for .6 miles. Turn left (northeast) onto Traprock Valley Road (S-641). In 1.4 miles turn right (east) onto Gay Road. It will take you into Gay in about 10.5 miles. Stay on Gay Road which runs along Lake Superior to the northeast. In .8 miles there is a small campground on the right (southeast) side of the road just before Tobacco River. Park in the day use area and hike along the river upstream. The lower waterfall is easily seen from the bridge and the upper drop is only about 75 yards up river from there.

TOBACCO FALLS - LOWER (TOBACCO RIVER)

Private

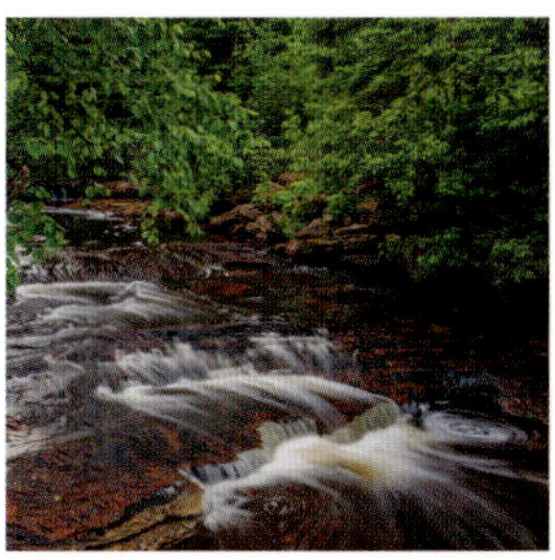

Must See:	4	GPS:	N47 13.886 W88 08.929
Height:	5 feet		
Time:	10-20 minutes	Hiking Information	
		Path:	Well Worn Path
Driving Information		Length:	50 yards
Signs:	None	Elev. Change:	Slight
Road:	Secondary	GPS:	N/A
Access:	Easy	Danger:	Slight
4WD:	N/A	WP Boots:	Helpful

Several small drops cascade the river over red rock slabs. A wavy ledge of black and red sandstone creates a vertical drop of 1 foot, then a second, larger cascading drop of 4 feet just upstream from the bridge.

TOBACCO FALLS - UPPER (TOBACCO RIVER)

Private

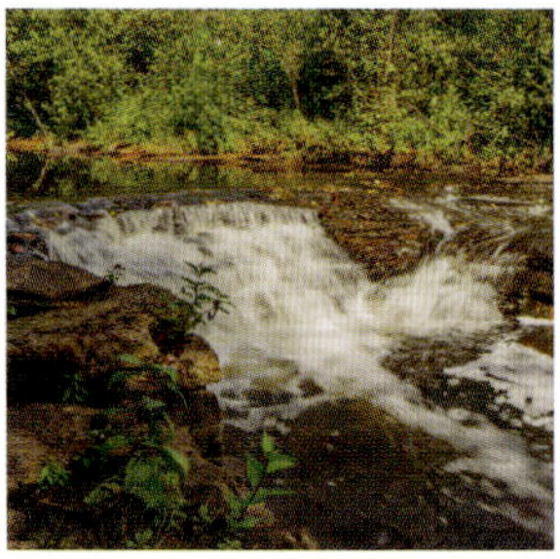

Must See:	5	GPS:	N47 13.916 W88 08.961
Height:	3 feet		
Time:	15-30 minutes	**Hiking Information**	
		Path:	Well Worn Path
Driving Information		Length:	150 yards
Signs:	None	Elev. Change:	Slight
Road:	Secondary	GPS:	N/A
Access:	Easy	Danger:	Slight
4WD:	N/A	WP Boots:	Helpful

Hike up alongside the river for about 75 yards.

The river gathers itself to the center of the bed and then falls over a horseshoe shaped stair stepping cascade just 200 feet up river from the lower falls.

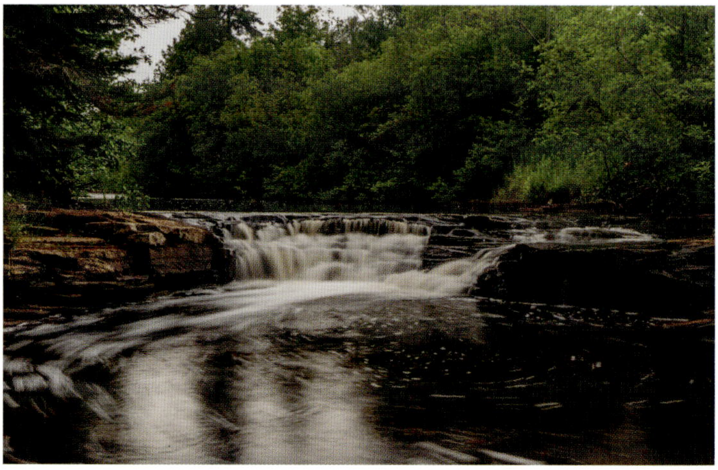

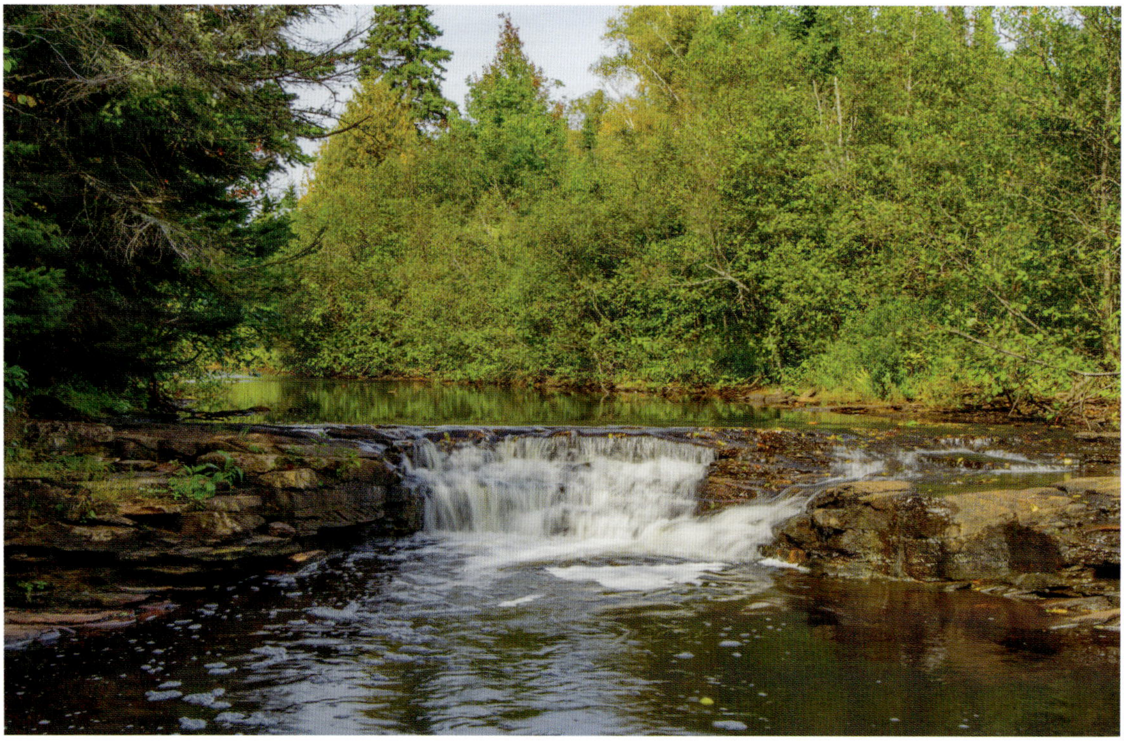

Would you care to seek out more amazing waterfalls in this great state? Then you'll want to check out the rest of the Waterfalls of Michigan Guidebook Series! These should be available at a store near you. If not, request them!

To order online, go to *www.mifalls.com*. That's where you'll also be able to browse through Phil's line of calendars, postcards, and other fine products, stocked in great retail locations around the state of Michigan.

Do you see an image you'd love to hang in your house or office space? The pictures in this book, and many more, are available as archival quality prints, ready to be framed. They can also be purchased, ready to be hung, as canvas wrapped or aluminum prints. Once again, head to *www.mifalls.com* for more information.

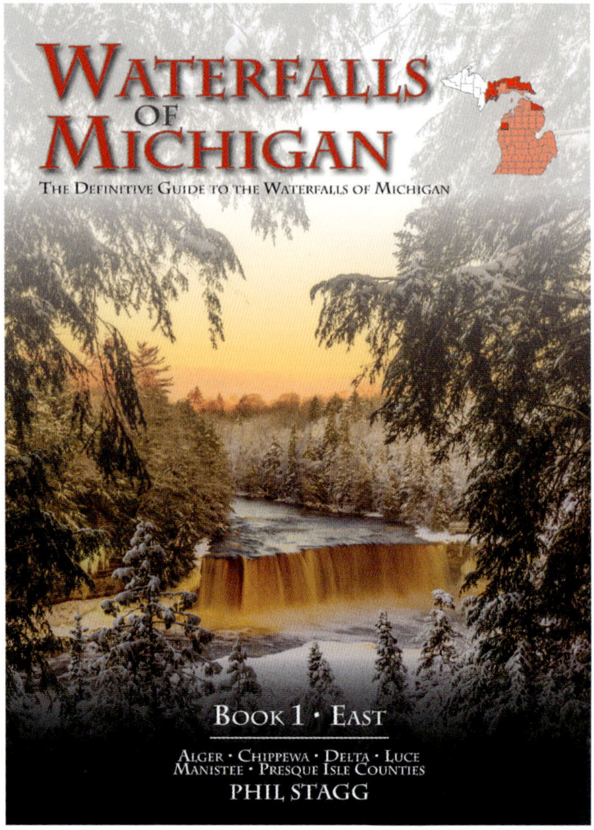

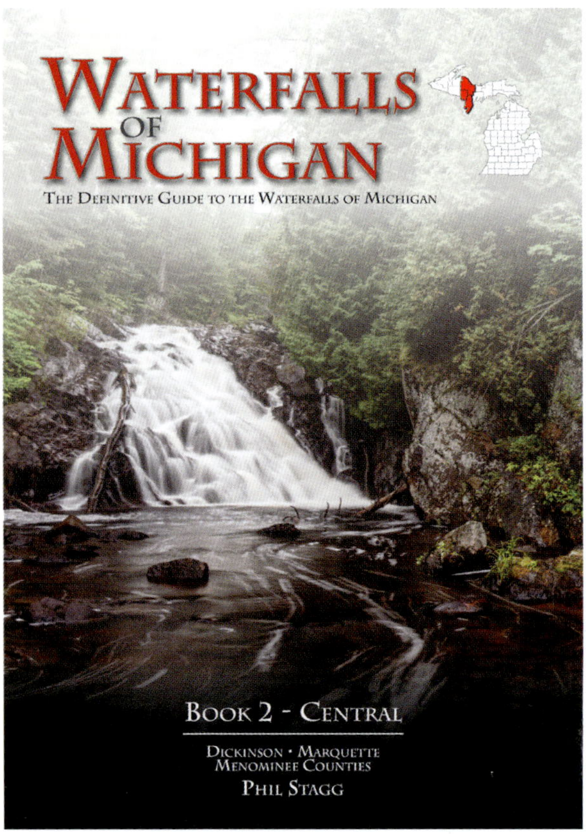

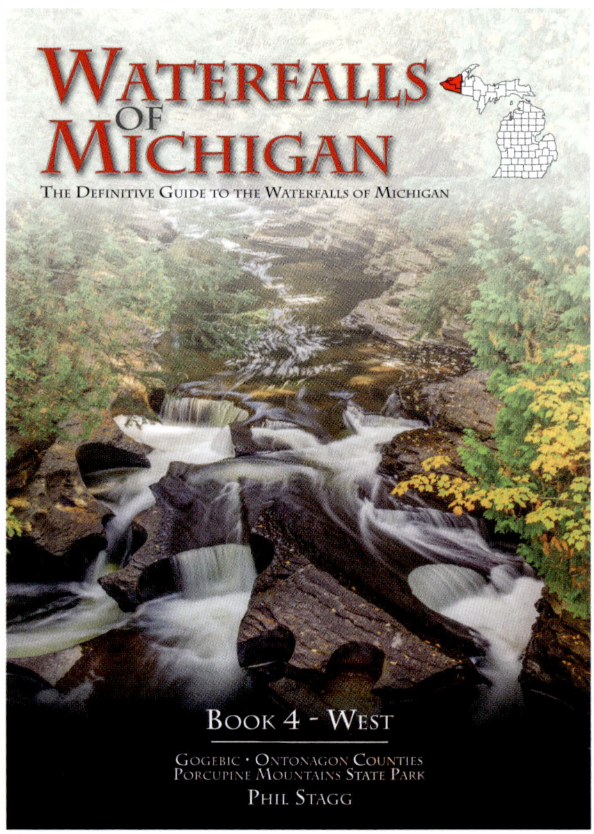

Index

ABUTMENT FALLS (SILVER RIVER) 87
ARROWHEAD FALLS (SLATE RIVER) 139
BABY STAIRCASE (SLATE RIVER) 140
BARAGA FALLS (SILVER RIVER) 119
BARAGA FALLS - UPPER (SILVER RIVER) 118
BARE HOLE FALLS (FALLS RIVER) 32
BIG ERICK'S FALLS (HURON RIVER) 53
BIG ERICK'S FALLS #2 (HURON RIVER) 54
BIG ERICK'S FALLS #3 (HURON RIVER) 55
BIG FALLS (HURON RIVER - EAST BRANCH) 56
BIG HOLE FALLS (FALLS RIVER) 37
BLACK BEAR CASCADES (SLATE RIVER) 157
BLACK BEAR FALLS (SLATE RIVER) 156
BLACK CASCADES (SLATE RIVER) 162
BLACK SLATE FALLS (SLATE RIVER) 135
BLACK SLATE FALLS - MIDDLE (SLATE RIVER) 136
BLACK SLATE FALLS - UPPER (SLATE RIVER) 137
CANYON FALLS (STURGEON RIVER) 11
CANYON FALLS - LOWER (STURGEON RIVER) 14
CANYON FALLS - MIDDLE (STURGEON RIVER) 13
CANYON FALLS - UPPER (STURGEON RIVER) 10
CASCADING FALLS (FALLS RIVER) 31
CHICAGON FALLS (CHICAGON CREEK) 226
CHIPMUNK FALLS (NET RIVER) 224
CHUTE FALLS (FALLS RIVER) 40
COPPER FALLS (OWL CREEK) 242
CRYSTAL FALLS DAM (PAINT RIVER) 227
DAM HOLE FALLS (FALLS RIVER) 33
DAULTS FALLS (DAULTS CREEK) 28
DAULTS FALLS - UPPER (DAULTS CREEK) 29
DEAD MAN'S FALLS (SILVER RIVER) 108
DOUGLASS HOUGHTON FALLS (HAMMELL CREEK) 187
DUPPY FALLS (JUMBO RIVER) 231
DUPPY FALLS - MIDDLE (JUMBO RIVER) 232
DUPPY FALLS - UPPER (JUMBO RIVER) 233
EAGLE RIVER FALLS (EAGLE RIVER) 244
EAGLE RIVER SLIDE - LOWER (EAGLE RIVER) 246
EAGLE RIVER SLIDE - UPPER (EAGLE RIVER) 245
EAST BRANCH FALLS (HURON RIVER - EAST BRANCH) 58
EAST BRANCH FALLS #2 (HURON RIVER - EAST BRANCH) 59
EAST BRANCH FALLS #3 (HURON RIVER - EAST BRANCH) 60
EAST BRANCH FALLS #4 (HURON RIVER - EAST BRANCH) 61
EAST BRANCH FALLS #5 (HURON RIVER - EAST BRANCH) 62
EAST BRANCH FALLS #6 (HURON RIVER - EAST BRANCH) 63
EAST BRANCH FALLS #7 (HURON RIVER - EAST BRANCH) 64
ECSTASY CASCADES (SLATE RIVER) 148
ECSTASY FALLS - LOWER (SLATE RIVER) 149
ECSTASY FALLS (SLATE RIVER) 150
ECSTASY FALLS - UPPER (SLATE RIVER) 151
EISTER FALLS - LOWER (EISTER CREEK) 263
EISTER FALLS - MIDDLE #1 (EISTER CREEK) 264
EISTER FALLS - MIDDLE #2 (EISTER CREEK) 265
EISTER FALLS - UPPER (EISTER CREEK) 266
ERICK'S CASCADES (HURON RIVER - WEST BRANCH) 66
ERICK'S FALLS (HURON RIVER - WEST BRANCH) 65
FALLS RIVER RAPIDS (FALLS RIVER) 38
FANNY HOOE FALLS (FANNY HOOE CREEK) 268
FELTMAN FALLS (SLATE RIVER) 146
FENNERS FALLS (EAGLE RIVER) 247
GOMANCHE FALLS (GOMANCHE CREEK) 97

GOMANCHE FALLS - UPPER (GOMANCHE CREEK) 98
GRAND STAIRCASE (SLATE RIVER) 138
GRATIOT FALLS - LOWER #1 (GRATIOT RIVER) 260
GRATIOT FALLS - LOWER #2 (GRATIOT RIVER) 259
GRATIOT FALLS - LOWER #3 (GRATIOT RIVER) 258
GRATIOT FALLS - UPPER (GRATIOT RIVER) 261
HARLEY FALLS #1 (HARLEY CREEK) 120
HARLEY FALLS #2 (HARLEY CREEK) 121
HARLEY FALLS #3 (HARLEY CREEK) 122
HARLEY FALLS #4 (HARLEY CREEK) 123
HARLEY FALLS #5 (HARLEY CREEK) 124
HARLEY FALLS #6 (HARLEY CREEK) 125
HARLEY FALLS #7 (HARLEY CREEK) 126
HARLEY FALLS #8 (HARLEY CREEK) 127
HARLEY FALLS #9 (HARLEY CREEK) 128
HARLEY FALLS #10 (HARLEY CREEK) 129
HARLEY FALLS #11 (HARLEY CREEK) 130
HAVEN FALLS (HAVEN CREEK) 267
HAYPRESS DAM FALLS (PESHEKEE RIVER) 48
HEMLOCK FALLS DAM (MICHIGAMME RIVER) 228
HERMAN CASCADES (SILVER RIVER) 115
HERMAN FALLS (SILVER RIVER) 117
HERMAN FALLS - UPPER (SILVER RIVER) 116
HOBBIT RUN (SLATE RIVER) 158
HOGGER FALLS (WEST BRANCH - STURGEON RIVER) 185
HORSERACE RAPIDS (PAINT RIVER) 234
HUNGARIAN DAM (DOVER CREEK) 193
HUNGARIAN DAM OVERFLOW (DOVER CREEK) 192
HUNGARIAN GORGE FALLS (UNNAMED CREEK) 188
HUNGARIAN LOWER FALLS (DOVER CREEK) 189
HUNGARIAN MIDDLE FALLS (DOVER CREEK) 190
HUNGARIAN TINY FALLS (DOVER CREEK) 191
HUNGARIAN UPPER FALLS (DOVER CREEK) 194
HURON GORGE CASCADES (HURON RIVER - EAST BRANCH) 67
JACOBS FALLS (JACOBS CREEK) 248
JACOBS FALLS #2 (JACOBS CREEK) 249
JACOBS FALLS #3 (JACOBS CREEK) 250
JACOBS FALLS #4 (JACOBS CREEK) 251
JACOBS FALLS #5 (JACOBS CREEK) 252
JUMBO FALLS (JUMBO RIVER) 200
KUCKUK'S FALLS (SLATE RIVER) 153
LETHERBY CASCADES (HURON RIVER - WEST BRANCH) 70
LETHERBY FALLS (HURON RIVER - WEST BRANCH) 69
LETHERBY FALLS - LOWER (HURON RIVER - WEST BRANCH) 71
LETHERBY FALLS - MIDDLE (HURON RIVER - WEST BRANCH) 72
LETHERBY FALLS - UPPER (HURON RIVER - WEST BRANCH) 73
LITTLE SISKIWIT FALLS (LITTLE SISKIWIT RIVER) 277
MANGANESE FALLS (MANGANESE CREEK) 269
MARDALE FALLS (FALLS RIVER) 41
MARGESON FALLS (MARGESON CREEK) 229
MITTEN HOLE FALLS (FALLS RIVER) 36
MONTREAL FALLS - LOWER (MONTREAL RIVER) 271
MONTREAL FALLS - MIDDLE (MONTREAL RIVER) 272
MONTREAL FALLS - UPPER (MONTREAL RIVER) 273
NELLIGAN CREEK FALLS (NELLIGAN CREEK) 49
NELLIGAN CREEK FALLS - LOWER #1 (NELLIGAN CREEK) 50
NELLIGAN CREEK FALLS - LOWER #2 (NELLIGAN CREEK) 51
OGEMAW FALLS (OGEMAW CREEK) 15
OGEMAW FALLS - LOWER (OGEMAW CREEK) 17
OGEMAW SLIDE (OGEMAW CREEK) 16

OLD PHOENIX FALLS (EAGLE RIVER) ... 243
ONION FALLS (ONION CREEK) ... 202
ONION FALLS - LOWER (ONION CREEK) ... 203
OTTER FALLS (OTTER RIVER - WEST BRANCH) ... 205
PAGE CREEK FALLS (PAGE CREEK) ... 103
PEA CAN FALLS - LOWER CASCADE (PEA CAN CREEK) ... 78
PEA CAN FALLS - LOWER SLIDE (PEA CAN CREEK) ... 80
PEA CAN FALLS - UPPER CASCADE (PEA CAN CREEK) ... 76
PEA CAN FALLS - UPPER SLIDE (PEA CAN CREEK) ... 77
PEA CAN RUN (PEA CAN CREEK) ... 79
PLUMBAGO FALLS (PLUMBAGO CREEK) ... 18
PLUMBAGO FALLS - LOWER (PLUMBAGO CREEK) ... 19
POWER DAM FALLS (FALLS RIVER) ... 45
POWER DAM FALLS - UPPER (FALLS RIVER) ... 46
POWER HOUSE FALLS (FALLS RIVER) ... 43
QUARRY FALLS (SLATE RIVER) ... 159
QUARTZITE FALLS (SLATE RIVER) ... 134
QUEEN ANNE'S FALLS (SLAUGHTERHOUSE CREEK) ... 207
QUINCY FALLS #1 (QUINCY CREEK) ... 198
QUINCY FALLS #2 (QUINCY CREEK) ... 197
QUINCY FALLS #3 (QUINCY CREEK) ... 196
QUINCY FALLS #4 (QUINCY CREEK) ... 195
RAVINE RIVER FALLS (RAVINE RIVER) ... 141
RAVINE RIVER FALLS - LOWER #1 (RAVINE RIVER) ... 142
RAVINE RIVER FALLS - LOWER #2 (RAVINE RIVER) ... 143
RAVINE RIVER FALLS - LOWER #3 (RAVINE RIVER) ... 144
RAVINE RIVER ROAD CASCADES (UNNAMED TRIBUTARY) ... 75
RAVINE RIVER ROAD FALLS (UNNAMED TRIBUTARY) ... 74
REDRIDGE DAM FALLS (SALMON TROUT RIVER) ... 210
SAARINEN FALLS (FALLS RIVER) ... 42
SECRET HOLE FALLS (FALLS RIVER) ... 39
SILVER CANYON FALLS (SILVER RIVER) ... 89
SILVER CREEK FALLS (SILVER CREEK) ... 253
SILVER CREEK FALLS - UPPER #1 (SILVER CREEK) ... 254
SILVER CREEK FALLS - UPPER #2 (SILVER CREEK) ... 255
SILVER FALLS - LOWER (SILVER RIVER) ... 90
SILVER FALLS - MIDDLE #1 (SILVER RIVER) ... 102
SILVER FALLS - MIDDLE #2 (SILVER RIVER) ... 105
SILVER FALLS - MIDDLE #3 (SILVER RIVER) ... 101
SILVER FALLS - MIDDLE #4 (SILVER RIVER) ... 100
SILVER FALLS - MIDDLE #5 (SILVER RIVER) ... 99
SILVER FALLS - MIDDLE #6 (SILVER RIVER) ... 96
SILVER FALLS - MIDDLE #7 (SILVER RIVER) ... 95
SILVER FALLS - MIDDLE #8 (SILVER RIVER) ... 94
SILVER FALLS - MIDDLE #9 (SILVER RIVER) ... 93
SILVER FALLS - MIDDLE #10 (SILVER RIVER) ... 92
SILVER FALLS - UPPER (SILVER RIVER) ... 131
SILVER GORGE FALLS (SILVER RIVER) ... 106
SILVER GORGE FALLS - UPPER (SILVER RIVER) ... 107
SILVER RAPIDS (SILVER RIVER) ... 88
SILVER RIVER FALLS (SILVER RIVER) ... 274
SILVER RIVER FALLS - LOWER (SILVER RIVER) ... 276
SISKIWIT FALLS (SISKIWIT RIVER) ... 278
SLATE BLOCK FALLS (SLATE RIVER) ... 160
SLATE CORNER FALLS (SLATE RIVER) ... 147
SLATE FLUME FALLS (SLATE RIVER) ... 161
SLATE RIVER FALLS (SLATE RIVER) ... 145
SLATE SLIDE (SLATE RIVER) ... 152
ST. LOUIS FALLS (UNNAMED CREEK) ... 208
STURGEON FALLS (STURGEON RIVER) ... 212

STURGEON FALLS - UPPER #1 (STURGEON RIVER) 213
STURGEON FALLS - UPPER #2 (STURGEON RIVER) 214
STURGEON FALLS - WB #1 (WEST BRANCH - STURGEON RIVER) 180
STURGEON FALLS - WB #2 (WEST BRANCH - STURGEON RIVER) 181
STURGEON FALLS - WB #3 (WEST BRANCH - STURGEON RIVER) 182
STURGEON FALLS - WB #4 (WEST BRANCH - STURGEON RIVER) 183
STURGEON FALLS - WB #5 (WEST BRANCH - STURGEON RIVER) 184
SUCKER HOLE (FALLS RIVER) 34
TAYLOR CREEK CANYON FALLS #1 (TAYLOR CREEK) 20
TAYLOR CREEK CANYON FALLS #2 (TAYLOR CREEK) 21
TAYLOR CREEK CANYON FALLS #3 (TAYLOR CREEK) 22
TAYLOR CREEK CANYON FALLS #4 (TAYLOR CREEK) 23
TAYLOR CREEK CANYON FALLS #5 (TAYLOR CREEK) 24
TAYLOR CREEK CANYON FALLS #6 (TAYLOR CREEK) 25
TAYLOR CREEK CANYON FALLS #7 (TAYLOR CREEK) 26
TEA CUP FALLS (UNNAMED CREEK) 81
TEN FOOT FALLS (EAGLE RIVER) 256
THE GRADE CASCADES (UNNAMED TRIBUTARY) 164
THE GRADE FALLS (UNNAMED TRIBUTARY) 163
THIMBLEBERRY CASCADES (SILVER RIVER) 111
THIMBLEBERRY FALLS (SILVER RIVER) 110
THIMBLEBERRY FALLS - LOWER (SILVER RIVER) 109
TIBBETS FALLS (STURGEON RIVER) 167
TIOGA FALLS (TIOGA RIVER) 168
TIOGA FALLS - UPPER (TIOGA RIVER) 169
TIOGA PARK FALLS (TIOGA RIVER) 170
TIOGA PARK RAPIDS (TIOGA RIVER) 171
TOBACCO FALLS - LOWER (TOBACCO RIVER) 279
TOBACCO FALLS - UPPER (TOBACCO RIVER) 280
TRACEY'S FALLS (HURON RIVER - WEST BRANCH) 68
TRAP ROCK RIVER FALLS (TRAP ROCK RIVER) 209
VICTORY FALLS (SLATE RIVER) 165
VISTA FALLS (STURGEON RIVER - WEST BRANCH) 215
WEST BRANCH FALLS (HURON RIVER - WEST BRANCH) 84
WEST BRANCH FALLS - LOWER (HURON RIVER - WEST BRANCH) 82
WEST BRANCH FALLS - UPPER (HURON RIVER - WEST BRANCH) 85
WEST BRANCH LEDGE (HURON RIVER - WEST BRANCH) 83
WYANDOTTE FALLS (MISERY RIVER) 217